The 1981 Compton Yearbook

A summary and interpretation of the events of 1980 to supplement Compton's Encyclopedia

F. E. Compton Company, a division of Encyclopædia Britannica, Inc.

CHICAGO · LONDON · TORONTO · GENEVA · SYDNEY · TOKYO · MANILA · SEOUL

Library of Congress Catalog Card Number: 58-26525
International Standard Book Number: 0-85229-382-8
International Standard Serial Number: 0069-8091
Copyright©1981 by Encyclopædia Britannica, Inc.

The 1981 Compton Yearbook

Editor in Chief, Yearbooks	James Ertel
Editor	Anita K. Wolff
Contributing Editors	David Calhoun, Charles Cegielski, Daphne Daume, Karen Jacobs Justin, Arthur Latham
Copy Director	J. Thomas Beatty
Deputy Director	Laurie A. Braun
Senior Copy Editors	Barbara Whitney Cleary, *supervisor;* Lawrence D. Kowalski, Julian Ronning
Copy Staff	Patricia Bauer, Anne E. Beadle, Elizabeth A. Blowers, Tibor Eszeki, Ellen Finkelstein, Claudette P. Gayle, Patrick M. Joyce, Kathleen Kuiper, Paul Mendelson, Rebecca A. Pope, Ellen C. Rutherford, Melinda Shepherd, Carol Smith, Anita A. Wayne
Copy Control	Mary C. Srodon, *supervisor;* Mayme R. Cussen
Art Director	Cynthia Peterson
Picture Editors	Holly Harrington, *senior picture editor;* LaBravia Jones, Kathy Nakamura
Design Supervisor	Ron Villani
Cartographers	Gerzilla Leszczynski, *supervisor;* William Karpa
Layout Artists	John L. Draves, Richard A. Roiniotis
Art Staff	Richard Batchelor, Kathryn Creech, Paul Rios, Lillian Simcox
Geography Editor	William A. Cleveland
Geography Research	Sujata Banerjee, *supervisor;* Sarah Gibbard Cook, Maura Edelman, David W. Foster, Kimberleigh S. Hemphill, Geo. Kenneth Leivers, Frank J. Yurco
Geography Correspondents	M. Faye Abernathy, Pamela G. Crumbley
Director Electronic Composition and Indexing	Robert H. Dehmer
Index Manager	Frances Latham
Supervisor	Rosa Casas
Senior Indexer	Helen Peterson
Editorial Typesetting Manager	Melvin Stagner
Typesetting Staff	Ronald Laugeman, *supervisor annual products;* Duangnetra Debhavalya, Judith Kobylecky, John Krom, Jr., Thomas Mulligan, Arnell Reed
Librarian	Terry Miller
Associate Librarian	Shantha Channabasappa
Administrative Secretary	Ines Baptist

Editorial Administration
Managing Editor, Encyclopædia Britannica, Inc.
Margaret Sutton

Director of Budgets and Control
Verne Pore

ENCYCLOPÆDIA BRITANNICA, INC.

Chairman of the Board	Robert P. Gwinn
President	Charles E. Swanson
Vice President, Editorial	Charles Van Doren

Contents

compton's pictured highlights and chronology

1980

JANUARY

2 The UN World Food Program announces that no more emergency food will be shipped to Cambodia during January because only a few hundred tons of the 30,-000 tons already ashore have been distributed to those in need; other international agencies plan to continue to send aid.

3 El Salvador's coalition government collapses when dozens of high-ranking officials resign their posts; the number includes 10 of the 11 Cabinet ministers and 2 civilians from the 5-man ruling junta.

4 U.S. Pres. Jimmy Carter announces that U.S. grain sales to the U.S.S.R. will be limited in 1980 to the eight million metric tons sanctioned by a 1976 trade agreement; because the Soviet Union initiated "an extremely serious threat to peace" by sending its military forces into Afghanistan on Dec. 27, 1979, Carter also cuts off shipments of high technology equipment, curtails Soviet fishing rights in the U.S. waters, postpones the opening of new consulates, and defers new economic and cultural exchanges.

6 In national elections held on January 3 and 6, Indira Gandhi's Congress (I) Party captures 350 of the 542 seats in the Lok Sabha, India's lower house of Parliament; the victory means that Gandhi will again assume the powers of prime minister.

7 The UN General Assembly elects Mexico to the Security Council seat reserved for a Latin-American nation, over Cuba and Colombia, neither of which could muster the two-thirds vote for inclusion.

9 Saudi Arabia publicly beheads 63 persons, all convicted by an Islamic court of murder in the November 1979 takeover of Islam's most sacred shrine, the Grand Mosque at Mecca.

Under terms of a new agreement reached by officials representing the U.S. and Turkey, two dozen military bases in Turkey will be made available to NATO forces.

11 In response to a growing economic crisis, Cuban Pres. Fidel Castro assumes personal control of the Ministries of Defense, Interior, Public Health, and Culture; he appoints trusted aides to head the Ministries of Industry, Economy, Communications, and Transportation.

13 The Soviet Union vetoes a proposed UN Security Council resolution, sponsored by the U.S., that calls for sanctions against Iran because it continues to hold U.S. hostages in Teheran.

14 The UN General Assembly overwhelmingly approves a resolution demanding "the immediate, unconditional and total withdrawal of the foreign troops" now in Afghanistan, by a vote of 104–18.

Ten black parties are officially registered to compete for the 80 seats reserved for blacks in the new national legislature of Zimbabwe.

18 Yukihisa Miyanaga, a retired army general, and two former subordinates are arrested in Tokyo on charges of spying for the U.S.S.R. and are accused of passing "highly sensitive military secrets" to Soviet agents while serving in the intelligence division of Japan's Self Defense Force.

22 Nobelist Andrey D. Sakharov, an internationally respected champion of human rights, is exiled with his wife to the Soviet city of Gorky and is stripped of all his Soviet honours.

23 President Carter, in his annual State of the Union address before a joint session of Congress, warns the Soviet Union: "An attempt by any outside force to gain control of the Persian Gulf region will be regarded as an assault on the vital interests of the United States of America. And such an assault will be repelled by any means necessary, including military force."

25 Iranian Finance Minister Abolhassan Bani-Sadr is elected first president of the Islamic Republic of Iran with 75% of the popular vote.

A military court in Seoul, South Korea, sentences 17 persons to prison for involvement in a demonstration that took place in the nation's capital on Nov. 24, 1979, in protest against the choice of Choi Kyu Hah to succeed the late Park Chung Hee as president.

29 U.S. and Canadian officials publicly acknowledge that six U.S. citizens (four men and two women) employed at the U.S. embassy in Teheran were spirited out of Iran on January 28, using Canadian diplomatic passports stamped with forged Iranian exit visas; the four Canadians who supplied the false documents represented the last members of the Canadian mission in Iran; they also departed with the Americans.

An emergency session of the Conference of Islamic States, convened in Islamabad, Pak., condemns "Soviet military aggression against the Afghan people" and demands that all troops be withdrawn immediately.

31 Thirty-nine Quiche Indians who invaded the Spanish embassy in Guatemala City lose their lives when fire sweeps through the building; the Spanish ambassador, who had been taken hostage by the Indians, is only slightly injured, but two former high-ranking Guatemalan officials reportedly die in the blaze; it is not known how the fire started.

Queen Juliana of The Netherlands, citing her age as the reason, unexpectedly announces that she will abdicate on her 71st birthday; her oldest daughter, 42-year-old Beatrix, will assume the throne April 30.

The New York Stock Exchange ends its busiest month in history: on the last day of the month 65.9 million shares are traded, bringing the monthly total to 1,160,-000,000 shares, 34% higher than the previous one-month total set in August 1978.

(Above) On January 25 Abolhassan Bani-Sadr was elected president of Iran. (Below left) On January 7 the Soviet delegate vetoed a UN Security Council resolution calling for the withdrawal of Soviet troops from Afghanistan. (Below right) Indira Gandhi was returned to power in the January 6 elections in India.

FEBRUARY

2 NBC news reports that for two years agents of the FBI have been gathering evidence of corruption against certain members of the U.S. Congress and local public officials; posing as Arab businessmen, FBI agents reportedly were able to obtain promises of special treatment from U.S. government officials in exchange for money; the ploy is code-named Abscam ("Abdul Enterprises Ltd.-scam").

4 In a report prepared for the Select Commission on Immigration and Refugee Policy of the U.S. Congress and the White House, the U.S. Census Bureau estimates that there are about six million illegal aliens living in the U.S. at any one time, and perhaps no more than 3.5 million, less than had been thought.

Libyans wreck and burn the French embassy in Tripoli and wreak havoc on the French consulate in Benghazi, apparently in reaction to French support of Tunisia.

5 About 50 armed members of the Popular League of February 28 take control of the Spanish embassy in San Salvador, taking hostages and demanding the release of 13 imprisoned comrades and a visit by the Organization of American States (OAS) to investigate violations of human rights.

8 A federal judge reveals another FBI investigation, code-named "Brilab" ("bribery-labour"); the governor-elect and lieutenant governor of Louisiana and the speaker of the Texas House of Representatives are accused of taking bribes in a kickback scheme.

9 The United Nations Industrial Development Organization ends a three-week conference in New Delhi, India, after voting 83–22 in favour of a resolution calling for the establishment of a huge fund to aid less developed nations; however, no concrete plan of action acceptable to industrialized nations is forthcoming.

10 James Grant, executive director of the UN Children's Fund (UNICEF), reports that food shipments have averted famine in Cambodia, at least for the next few months.

11 In an address before the National Assembly, Philippine Pres. Ferdinand Marcos admits that his party, the New Society Movement, engaged in fraud and terrorism to win the municipal elections held on January 30, but he accuses the opposition of using similar tactics.

14 China's armed forces are extensively reorganized in a shakeup that is part of an ongoing plan to modernize the nation's defense forces.

17 UN Secretary-General Kurt Waldheim names a five-man international commission to visit Iran to discuss its grievances; it is hoped that the visit will lead to the release of the U.S. hostages held in Teheran.

Indian Prime Minister Indira Gandhi dissolves nine state assemblies and places them under the control of the central government until new elections can be held in March.

According to reports emanating from northern Lebanon, at least 60 villagers in Qnat have been killed during a six-day artillery duel between Christian Falangists and Syrian troops.

18 The siege ends at the Spanish embassy in San Salvador after the government releases 11 imprisoned militants; ten people have been killed in antigovernment demonstrations in February in El Salvador.

Pierre Elliott Trudeau is in effect reelected prime minister of Canada when the Liberal Party that he heads wins 44% of the popular vote and 147 seats in the 282-seat House of Commons; Trudeau replaces Joe Clark, who assumed office on June 4, 1979.

Edward Babiuch becomes Poland's new premier when he replaces Piotr Jaroszewicz as chairman of the Council of Ministers.

19 The nine foreign ministers of the European Community issue a statement in Rome guaranteeing Afghanistan's neutrality if the U.S.S.R. agrees to withdraw its troops from that country.

Gen. Kriangsak Chamanand resigns as prime minister of Thailand during a special session of Parliament convened to discuss the nation's economic problems.

21 Shopkeepers, workers, and local government officials begin a general strike in Kabul, the capital of Afghanistan, to protest the presence of Soviet troops in that country; at least 300 civilians reportedly die in the violence that follows, and an unknown number of Soviet and Afghan troops lose their lives.

22 Soviet and Afghan troops are placed under a joint command, and martial law is imposed on Kabul.

25 The government of Prime Minister Henck Arron is toppled in Suriname by army sergeants in a predawn coup.

26 In simultaneous ceremonies in Cairo and Jerusalem, Egypt and Israel formally exchange ambassadors.

27 About 25 armed men and women, all members of the leftist M-19 Movement, seize control of the Dominican Republic embassy in Bogotá, Colombia, taking the U.S. ambassador and numerous other diplomats hostage.

29 South Korean Pres. Choi Kyu Hah grants amnesty to 687 political dissidents arrested for violating presidential decrees, hoping to effect national reconciliation; among those released are former president Yun Po Sun and longtime opposition leader Kim Dae Jung.

The 11th Central Committee of China's Communist Party approves the rehabilitation of Liu Shaoqi (Liu Shao-ch'i), who died in 1969 in political disgrace.

(Above) The Israeli embassy in Cairo opened in mid-February. (Below left) Pierre Elliott Trudeau was returned to power in Canada with the victory of his Liberal Party in the February 18 elections. (Below right) From this house in Washington, D.C., FBI agents conducted the "Abscam" investigation that ultimately led to the indictment of a number of federal and local officials on charges of corruption and bribery.

MARCH

1 All 15 members of the UN Security Council, including the U.S., approve a resolution calling on Israel to dismantle its settlements in the West Bank and the Gaza Strip, areas occupied by Israel after the 1967 war.

Tunisian Pres. Habib Bourguiba names Mohamed Mzali interim prime minister after Hedi Nouira, prime minister since 1970, suffers a stroke.

2 The Japanese government announces a plan to bolster the yen on world currency markets; on Oct. 31, 1979, the yen stood at a postwar high of 176.08 yen for one U.S. dollar, but on March 1, 1980, the rate had fallen to 249.80 yen per dollar.

3 The Parliament of Thailand names Gen. Prem Tinsulanonda prime minister.

4 Robert Mugabe, for six years the leader of the Zimbabwe African National Union (ZANU) guerrillas, is declared winner, with 62.9% of the popular vote, of the national election that is a prelude to the formal establishment of black rule in Zimbabwe.

5 Pakistani Foreign Minister Agha Shahi says that the U.S. offer of $400 million in aid is unacceptable: he says that the U.S. commitment to Pakistan's security is too weak and the "quantum of the aid package" is too small; the U.S. and Pakistan are also at odds over a nuclear facility being built near Islamabad.

11 The UN special commission of inquiry leaves Iran, having failed in its mission to mediate in the U.S. hostage crisis owing to conditions laid down by Ayatollah Ruhollah Khomeini.

Michael T. Somare, prime minister of Papua New Guinea, is removed from office by a parliamentary vote of no confidence and is replaced by Sir Julius Chan, leader of the opposition People's Progress Party.

12 The U.S. Immigration and Naturalization Service reports that more than 11,000 Iranian students, businessmen, visitors, and permanent residents have legally entered the U.S. since Iranian militants took U.S. diplomats hostage on Nov. 4, 1979; during the same period about 12,700 Iranians left the U.S.

13 A jury in Winamac, Ind., finds the Ford Motor Co. not guilty of reckless homicide in a case involving the deaths of three teenage girls who were killed in August 1978 when the Pinto subcompact in which they were riding burst into flames after it was struck from behind by a van; the girls' families contended that Ford knew of the Pinto's tendency to gas-tank fires.

14 The U.S.S.R. formally rejects a European Community proposal guaranteeing the neutrality of Afghanistan if Soviet troops are withdrawn.

15 Armed members of the Armed Forces of National Liberation (FALN), a Puerto Rican independence movement, invade the campaign headquarters of President Carter in Chicago and of George Bush in New York City; the masked terrorists bind and gag persons inside and spray slogans on the walls before departing.

17 President Carter signs into law the Refugee Act of 1980, which extends the definition of refugee to include persons from every part of the world and increases the number of refugees and immigrants allowed to enter the U.S. each year from 290,000 to 320,000.

19 According to Thai sources, rival factions of the National Liberation Movement of Cambodia engage in bloody fighting inside a refugee camp near the Thai border in which at least 46 persons are killed, many of them civilians.

Faced with a no confidence vote in Parliament, Italian Premier Francesco Cossiga resigns as head of a coalition government after announcing that Italy needs a stable government.

23 The deposed shah of Iran, Mohammad Reza Pahlavi, leaves Panama with his family and flies to Cairo, where he has been offered permanent asylum by Egyptian Pres. Anwar El-Sadat; though Iran was reportedly about to request the Panamanian government to extradite the shah, U.S. diplomats doubt that Panama would have honoured the petition.

24 Roman Catholic Archbishop Oscar Arnulfo Romero y Galdamez, one of El Salvador's most respected defenders of human rights and a champion of the poor, is shot and killed while saying Mass in a small chapel in San Salvador.

Westerners fleeing N'Djamena, the capital of Chad, estimate that more than 700 persons have been killed during several days of intense fighting between troops loyal to Pres. Goukouni Oueddei and those who support Hissen Habré.

26 Iran indefinitely postpones the second round of elections for its new 270-member Parliament, scheduled for April 4, after charges of fraud and irregularities are leveled against the first round of voting that took place on March 14.

27 After a week-long series of earthquakes and moderate emissions of smoke and ash, Mt. St. Helens erupts for the first time since 1857; a crater opens and volcanic ash is hurled some 4,500 m (14,500 ft) into the air and descends on a wide area of southwestern Washington and on parts of Oregon.

28 The Hungarian Socialist Workers' Party ends its 12th congress after hearing Janos Kadar, the party's first secretary, pledge continued loyalty to the U.S.S.R.

30 Bombs and sniper fire trigger a stampede in which about 30 persons are killed during the funeral services for Archbishop Romero in San Salvador.

(Above left) The Roman Catholic archbishop was assassinated as he said Mass in El Salvador on March 24. (Above right) Robert Mugabe was elected first prime minister of Zimbabwe on March 4. (Below) The Mexican ambassador served as a go-between in freeing the diplomats held in Bogotá since February.

APRIL

1 A 13-week strike against the state-owned British Steel Corp. ends when union leaders accept a 15.5% pay increase and other benefits.

A quarter of a million metalworkers in Brazil go on strike to enforce their demands for a 15% wage hike and a reduction in the workweek from 48 to 40 hours.

2 Many major U.S. banks increase their prime lending rate to an unprecedented 20%.

4 Police arrest 11 members of the Armed Forces of National Liberation (FALN), a terrorist organization advocating independence for Puerto Rico, in Evanston, Ill.; among them is Carlos Torres, the FBI's most wanted fugitive, who is the chief suspect in 11 bombings that have been attributed to the FALN since 1974.

6 Two members of the U.S. Congress report that the refugee problem in Somalia is even worse than that in Cambodia: according to one source, 1.3 million ethnic Somalis who have fled fighting in Ethiopia are living in 21 camps under squalid conditions.

7 The U.S. government formally severs diplomatic relations with Iran and orders all Iranian diplomats to leave the U.S. by midnight April 8; an additional 250 Iranian military trainees are told to depart the U.S. before midnight April 11.

Cuban Pres. Fidel Castro announces that the thousands of persons who are crowding into the embassies of Latin-American nations in Havana will be allowed to emigrate if other nations are willing to accept them.

The Japanese Diet (parliament) creates a committee on defense, the first such body since World War II, in a significant departure from past Japanese policy.

9 King Baudouin I of Belgium accepts the resignation of Prime Minister Wilfrid Martens after Martens fails for the second time to push through a constitutional change that would have established three administrative regions in the country based on linguistic differences: Wallonia, Flanders, and Brussels.

12 Liberian Pres. William R. Tolbert, Jr., and 27 others are slain in a coup led by 28-year-old Army Master Sergeant Samuel K. Doe.

13 Four small boats carrying 326 Haitian refugees arrive in Florida, the largest one-day total ever recorded; during March about 1,300 Haitians sailed to Florida to avoid harsh poverty and political oppression.

Equipment failure caused the aborting of a mission to rescue the 53 American hostages held in Iran. Eight servicemen lost their lives in the Iranian desert in an accident during withdrawal.

15 The Turkish government of Prime Minister Suleyman Demirel receives a promise of over $1 billion in aid from 16 nations of the Organization for Economic Cooperation and Development meeting in Paris.

18 After 90 years of white rule, Zimbabwe Rhodesia becomes the independent nation of Zimbabwe in a midnight ceremony presided over by Prince Charles of Great Britain; the Rev. Canaan Banana is sworn in as president and Robert Mugabe as prime minister.

A Taipei military court finds eight persons guilty of sedition for their part in a Dec. 10, 1979, demonstration that escalated into a riot.

19 Following talks with representatives of the National Iranian Oil Co., Japanese oil industry executives announce that they will not pay the $35-per-barrel price demanded by Iran but will rely instead on other oil-producing nations and will draw on their own reserves.

21 Abd-al Fattah Ismail resigns as chairman of the Presidential Council and secretary-general of the ruling Socialist Party of the People's Democratic Republic of Yemen (Aden; South Yemen) and is replaced by Prime Minister Ali Nasir Muhammad Husani.

25 Eight U.S. servicemen lose their lives in an aborted attempt to rescue the U.S. hostages held in Teheran by Iranian militants; a news release from the White House announces that: "The mission was terminated because of equipment failure. During the subsequent withdrawal, there was a collision between our aircraft on the ground at a remote desert location. There were no military hostilities but the President deeply regrets that eight American crewmen of the two aircraft were killed and others were injured in the accident. . . . The President accepts full responsibility for the decision to attempt the rescue."

Sweden's airports and Stockholm's subways are shut down as 14,000 workers go on strike and management locks out an additional 12,000 employees.

In the second such incident in April, a political opponent of Libyan leader Muammar al-Qaddafi is assassinated in London, actions apparently encouraged by the Libyan government.

27 Sixteen members of the M-19 Movement peacefully end their 61-day occupation of the Dominican Republic embassy in Bogotá, Colombia, by flying out of the country on a Cuban airliner with $2.5 million in ransom.

28 President Carter formally accepts the resignation of U.S. Secretary of State Cyrus Vance, who had asked to be relieved of his duties on April 21; Vance took the step because he vigorously opposed the use of military force to secure the release of the U.S. hostages.

30 Six Iranians from Khuzestan Province seize the Iranian embassy in London, then threaten to blow up the building and the hostages unless their demands are met: they insist that 91 persons allegedly held as political prisoners in Khuzestan be released and that the province be granted a measure of autonomy.

Thirteen members of the Liberian government were executed by firing squad after the takeover of the government on April 12; Pres. William Tolbert, Jr., was killed on the day of the coup.

SIPA PRESS / BLACK STAR

2 Pope John Paul II begins an 11-day tour of Africa that will include stops in Zaire, the Congo, Kenya, Ghana, Upper Volta, and the Ivory Coast.

4 President Tito of Yugoslavia dies in Ljubljana, where he has been hospitalized since January; Stevan Doronjski replaces Tito as chairman of the League of Communists, and Vice-Pres. Lazar Kolisevski becomes interim president of the State Presidency.

5 British commandos storm the Iranian embassy in London after terrorists inside kill one of their hostages; the embassy is retaken and 19 hostages are freed.

On a day that sees 3,500 Cuban emigrants arrive in Key West, Fla., President Carter says that the U.S. will welcome all such refugees with "an open heart and open arms."

8 Edmund Muskie is sworn in as U.S. secretary of state one day after being confirmed by the Senate.

11 About one-quarter of Sweden's workers, on strike since April 25, prepare to return to work after government-appointed mediators work out a wage settlement acceptable to both labour and management.

Tens of thousands of Brazilian metalworkers who have been on strike since April 1 return to work.

15 Cvijetin Mijatovic becomes president of the State Presidency of Yugoslavia, a post he will hold for one year.

16 The Japanese government falls when 69 members of Prime Minister Masayoshi Ohira's factious Liberal-Democratic Party abstain in a vote of no confidence.

U.S. Secretary of State Edmund Muskie holds a three-hour meeting with Soviet Foreign Minister Andrey Gromyko in Vienna; the private meeting is the first high-level contact between the two nations since the Soviet invasion of Afghanistan in December 1979.

17 Race riots erupt in Miami, Fla., hours after an all-white jury acquits four former Dade County policemen charged with murder in the fatal beating of Arthur McDuffie, a 33-year-old black insurance executive who died four days after being apprehended for a traffic violation in December 1979. During the rioting, which lasts three days, at least 14 persons are killed, more than 300 injured, and nearly 1,000 arrested; property damage is estimated at $100 million.

Virtually all of the nations bordering on the Mediterranean Sea sign, or are expected to sign, an antipollution pact sponsored by the United Nations Environment Program.

18 Mt. St. Helens in Washington State erupts with tremendous force, laying waste a huge area of the surrounding countryside and killing at least 34 people.

Total martial law is imposed on South Korea in the wake of growing antigovernment demonstrations in the capital and five other cities.

Fernando Belaúnde Terry, ousted from the presidency in an October 1968 military coup, is reelected president of Peru with 43% of the popular vote; Peru's current president, Gen. Francisco Morales Bermúdez, is expected to return the country to civilian rule on July 28 as promised.

20 Quebec voters turn out in large numbers to defeat a separatism referendum calling for association with but basic independence from the rest of Canada.

21 With an estimated 67,000 Cuban emigrants already in the U.S. (23,000 of whom are resettled), the Carter administration declares that the Cubans will be treated as applicants for asylum, not as refugees, and as such will have no automatic claim to government funds.

Antigovernment elements in Kwangju, South Korea, take control of the city to press their earlier demands that led to the imposition of martial law on May 18; the rebels seize military vehicles and thousands of rifles, then parade through the streets demanding the downfall of Gen. Chun Doo Hwan and the release of imprisoned dissident Kim Dae Jung.

22 The Conference of Islamic States ends a six-day meeting in Islamabad, Pak., after adopting a series of resolutions; one calls for negotiations to secure the "immediate, total and unconditional withdrawal of all Soviet troops" from Afghanistan, and another condemns the U.S. for its "recent military aggression" against Iran, *i.e.,* for its attempt to rescue the hostages held in Teheran.

24 Kim Jae Kyu, who assassinated South Korean Pres. Park Chung Hee while serving as head of the Korean Central Intelligence Agency, is hanged with four accomplices.

25 Ezer Weizman resigns his post as defense minister in the Cabinet of Israeli Prime Minister Menachem Begin.

27 South Korean troops retake the city of Kwangju by force from antigovernment militants; 170 persons die in the disturbances, including 144 civilians, according to the Martial Law Command.

28 Iran's new Parliament convenes for the first time even though 29 seats still remain vacant in the 270-seat legislature.

29 Vernon E. Jordan, Jr., black civil rights leader and president of the National Urban League, is critically wounded by gunfire in Fort Wayne, Ind.

31 In local elections in India, Prime Minister Indira Gandhi's Congress (I) Party wins control of eight of the nine state assemblies she dissolved on February 17.

(Above) Mt. St. Helens in Washington State, a quiescent volcano, began to stir early in the year and on May 18 erupted mightily, sending ash and debris over an area of 150 square miles. (Below left) Marshal Tito, who had served as president of Yugoslavia since 1953, died on May 4 after a long illness; he was one of the few remaining postwar political giants. (Below right) On May 17 Miami, Florida, erupted into rioting in the black Liberty City area in angry reaction to the acquittal of four former policemen charged with beating a black man to death; 14 persons were killed in the rioting.

JUNE

1 About 300 Cuban refugees, frustrated by what they consider unjustified delays in being released from the Ft. Chaffee, Ark., relocation centre, make two attempts to escape but are driven back by soldiers and police; about 40 persons are injured, and four buildings are burned to the ground.

Premier Hua Guofeng (Hua Kuo-feng), the first Chinese head of government ever to visit neighbouring Japan, returns to Beijing (Peking) after a series of meetings with Japanese Prime Minister Masayoshi Ohira.

2 Two West Bank Arab mayors, both staunch supporters of the Palestine Liberation Organization, are severely maimed by bombs that destroy their cars.

British Prime Minister Margaret Thatcher approves a proposal, worked out by the foreign ministers of the European Community, that would reduce Britain's 1980 budget contribution to a more equitable $865 million from an estimated $2.5 billion.

7 President Carter orders the U.S. Department of Justice to expel any refugee who has committed "serious crimes" in Cuba and to prosecute or deport those found responsible for the rioting at Ft. Chaffee on June 1; federal officials have already determined that about 700 Cubans are either guilty of past serious crimes or are mentally deficient, and of that number some 450 are "hardened criminals." More than 100,000 Cubans have arrived in the U.S. since the influx began in April.

Lebanese Prime Minister Selim al-Hoss, unable to control violent clashes among Lebanon's military factions, resigns together with his Cabinet.

8 Tribals in India's Tripura State massacre at least 378 immigrants from Bangladesh in the village of Mandai in an episode of the sporadic violence that is part of a continuing struggle by inhabitants of northeastern India to maintain their ethnic identity.

10 Ayatollah Khomeini warns fellow Iranians that internal political strife is driving the country toward chaos.

12 Japanese Prime Minister Masayoshi Ohira dies unexpectedly of a heart attack in a Tokyo hospital, ten days before national elections for both houses of the Diet (parliament); Masayoshi Ito, chief Cabinet secretary, automatically becomes acting prime minister.

13 The nine member nations of the European Economic Community issue a declaration on the Middle East at the end of a two-day conference in Venice, generally supporting the goals of the Palestinians.

Western news media report they have learned from unofficial Soviet sources that more than 250,000 auto workers in the U.S.S.R. staged separate two-day walkouts in early May; the strikes occurred at two of the nation's largest auto factories and involved more Soviet workers than any other strike in modern times.

The British Foreign Office orders Musa Kusa, the head of the Libyan diplomatic mission in London, to leave the country for publicly approving the planned assassinations of two more Libyans living in England (two Libyans were killed in April).

18 South Korea's Martial Law Command announces that former prime minister Kim Jong Pil and eight other officials, all accused of corruption, have agreed to donate their personal fortunes to the state and to leave politics in exchange for immunity from prosecution.

20 The Carter administration grants a six-month reprieve to all Haitian and Cuban boat people awaiting settlement of their legal status as potential immigrants; the Haitians claim to be seeking political asylum from conditions in their country.

22 The Liberal-Democratic Party is returned to power in Japan with solid majorities in both houses of the Diet.

23 The leaders of Canada, France, Italy, Great Britain, Japan, the United States, and West Germany end their two-day economic summit in Venice; all view inflation as their "immediate top priority" and pledge to reduce their dependence on imported oil.

24 The International Monetary Fund, which monitors economic performance in 140 countries, issues a report entitled *World Economic Outlook;* according to the report, there will be a sharp drop in the growth of world trade, increased inflation, a worldwide slowdown in production, and a worsening of the U.S. recession; less developed countries will be the most adversely affected by the economic downturn.

26 French Pres. Valéry Giscard d'Estaing announces the successful testing of a prototype neutron bomb that could go into production within a few years.

29 Early returns indicate that former Bolivian president Hernán Siles Zuazo has defeated other presidential candidates in the Bolivian election but has failed to win the 50% of the popular vote needed to obtain the presidency; the newly elected Congress will have to choose a president after it convenes on August 4.

30 Pope John Paul II begins a 12-day visit to Brazil, the first ever by a pope to that country, which has the world's largest Roman Catholic population.

The U.S. Supreme Court, in a 5–4 decision, overrules two federal district court judges who have held that Medicaid funds must be used to pay for abortions sought by poor women; in effect, the court is upholding the provisions of the Hyde Amendment, which prohibits the use of Medicaid funds for abortions except in pregnancies that result from rape or incest, or those that endanger the life of the woman. The court did not deny the constitutional right to abortions but merely ruled that the federal and state governments had no constitutional obligation to pay for the procedures.

(Above) Boatloads of Haitian refugees made the perilous crossing to the U.S. despite an uncertain future. (Below left) Japanese Prime Minister Masayoshi Ohira died in Tokyo on June 12, ten days before scheduled elections. (Below right) Pope John Paul II visited the slums of Brazil during his 12-day trip.

2 The British government releases a plan that will restore a degree of home rule to Northern Ireland, which, because of prolonged sectarian violence, has been ruled directly from London since March 1972.

4 The South African diplomatic mission in Salisbury is closed down by Robert Mugabe, prime minister of Zimbabwe, who charges that the mission is involved in the recruiting of 5,000 troops to be used to "destabilize" black African governments.

The Organization of African Unity ends its 17th annual summit conference in Freetown, Sierra Leone, on a note of discord over the disposition of the former Spanish Sahara, claimed by Morocco and the Polisario Front independence movement.

5 The U.S. begins airlifting arms to Bangkok to enhance the military capability of Thai forces stationed along the Cambodian border; the U.S. decision is a reaction to late-June incursions into Thailand by Vietnamese troops who control Cambodia.

8 In two days of intense fighting in and around Beirut, Christian militia of the Falangist Party of Lebanon decisively defeat the militia of the National Liberal Party, a rival Christian organization.

A bipartisan group of 68 U.S. senators sends a letter to President Carter saying they will not approve the sale of special F-15 jet-fighter equipment to Saudi Arabia because Saudi planes would then have an offensive capability that could be used against Israel.

9 South Korea's Special Committee for National Security Measures announces that 232 high-ranking government officials have resigned under pressure or been dismissed from their posts in a "purification drive" that is to affect thousands of bureaucrats.

10 The Iranian government announces that it has foiled a military coup reportedly involving armoured division and air force officers; more than 300 persons are arrested; former prime minister Shahpur Bakhtiar is accused of masterminding the plot from his exile in Paris.

11 Richard I. Queen, a 28-year-old U.S. vice-consul and one of the 53 hostages held by Iran, is unexpectedly released because of a serious but undiagnosed ailment that is later shown to be multiple sclerosis.

14 President Carter's brother, Billy, registers with the U.S. Department-of Justice as an agent of the Libyan government; he has been charged with violating the Foreign Agents Registration Act because he has not reported services performed for Libya since 1978.

17 Zenko Suzuki is elected prime minister of Japan by a decisive margin in both houses of the Diet (parliament).

18 Army Gen. Luis García Meza Tejada leads a military coup to prevent the Bolivian Congress from electing leftist Hernán Siles Zuazo president on August 4; García Meza, backed by the Navy and Air Force, disbands Congress and declares Bolivia a military zone.

The National Assembly of Botswana elects Vice-Pres. Quett Masire to the presidency to succeed Sir Seretse Khama, president since independence in 1966, who died July 13.

The Jamaican National Security Council places sections of Kingston under curfew in an attempt to curb night violence by armed gangs; during the month of July alone about 70 persons have been killed.

19 The Summer Olympic Games open in Moscow after months of heated controversy following the U.S. call for a boycott of the Games to protest the Soviet invasion of Afghanistan in December 1979; of the 65 nations that are not participating, more than half support the U.S. stand.

21 U.S. men between the ages of 19 and 20 begin to sign up for a possible future military draft.

24 The American Petroleum Institute reports that the U.S. imported 14% less crude oil during the first half of 1980 than it did during the first half of 1979; the decline is attributed to conservation, higher prices, and the economic recession.

The U.S. Senate sets up a special panel to investigate Billy Carter's involvement with the Libyan government.

26 Iranian Pres. Abolhassan Bani-Sadr selects Mostafa Mir-Salim as the first prime minister of the Iranian Islamic Republic; the nomination, a compromise, is rejected by the Majles (parliament), which is dominated by the Islamic Republican Party.

27 The deposed shah of Iran, Mohammad Reza Pahlavi, dies in an Egyptian military hospital in Cairo.

Nearly 200 pro-Ayatollah Khomeini Iranian demonstrators are arrested in Washington, D.C., after clashing with Iranian counterdemonstrators, U.S. citizens, and the police.

28 The presidential inauguration of Fernando Belaúnde Terry ends 12 years of military rule in Peru.

In a widely criticized action, the Israeli Knesset (parliament) passes a law formally making all of Jerusalem the nation's capital; the new law formalizes a claim that was first made in 1967 when Israeli troops occupied Arab East Jerusalem as a result of war.

31 Eight of 11 suspected Puerto Rican terrorists arrested in Illinois on April 4 are convicted in Chicago of conspiracy to commit armed robbery and of illegal possession of firearms; all are thought to be members of the Armed Forces of National Liberation (FALN), a terrorist group seeking independence for Puerto Rico.

(Above) The Summer Olympics opened in Moscow on July 19, minus the athletes of 65 boycotting nations. (Below left) U.S. hostage Richard Queen was released by his Iranian captors on July 11 for medical reasons. (Below right) On July 21, U.S. men began to sign up with the Selective Service.

AUGUST

2 A bomb planted in a waiting room at the central train station in Bologna, Italy, kills 76 persons outright and injures about 200 others; investigators believe neofascist terrorists are responsible.

5 U.S. government officials reveal that Pres. Jimmy Carter has endorsed a new military strategy to be used in the event of a nuclear war with the Soviet Union: in place of all-out retaliation against Soviet cities and industrial centres, the U.S. would concentrate on the country's ability to wage war by attacking its military installations and command posts.

The Belgian parliament votes 156–19 to grant limited autonomy to the country's two principal linguistic regions, Dutch-speaking Flanders and French-speaking Wallonia; a decision on the Brussels area is postponed because of its special problems.

6 Edgar Z. Tekere, secretary-general of the ruling Zimbabwe African National Union Patriotic Front party and a member of Prime Minister Robert Mugabe's Cabinet, is arrested and charged, with six accomplices, with the murder of a white farmer on August 4.

11 The Iranian parliament approves the selection of Mohammad Ali Raja'i as prime minister in secret balloting.

The Central Committee of the Chinese Communist Party publishes a directive calling for the removal of most public portraits, statues, slogans, and poems of the late Mao Zedong (Mao Tse-tung); the committee defends its action on the grounds that "inappropriate commemoration" of Mao "fosters the incorrect view that history is created by individuals."

13 Johan Ferrier, president of the small South American republic of Suriname since it gained independence from The Netherlands in 1975, is overthrown in a military coup and replaced by Prime Minister Hendrick R. Chin A Sen.

14 Labour unrest in Poland reaches crisis proportions after 17,000 workers go on strike and seize the Lenin shipyard in Gdansk.

20 The U.S. reveals that it has developed an airplane that can avoid detection by radar. The so-called stealth aircraft is reportedly coated with a special material that diffuses radar waves and is so shaped that the conventional sharp corners of a plane, which make the craft vulnerable to radar detection, have been substantially modified.

The UN Security Council approves a resolution urging all nations to disregard Israel's declaration that the

Polish shipyard workers at Gdansk, led by Lech Walesa, successfully struck for improved working conditions and for the right to form their own unions. They received nationwide support.

entire city is its undivided capital; the U.S., which abstained in the voting because the resolution was "flawed," maintains that the status of Jerusalem is a matter to be negotiated, not decided by a single nation.

21 A Soviet nuclear submarine catches fire and surfaces in international waters some 160 km (100 mi) east of Okinawa; the Soviets, apparently unwilling to risk the possible disclosure of military secrets, will accept no aid from the British or Japanese crews in the area.

The U.S. and Somalia sign an agreement that bolsters Somalia's defense capabilities and facilitates U.S. military access to the Indian Ocean and the Persian Gulf; Somalia will receive $25 million in military aid in 1981 and additional aid later.

22 Billy Carter, the president's brother, concludes two days of testimony before a Senate subcommittee investigating his dealings with Libya; the panel is severely critical of Carter for accepting a $200,000 loan from a government that has "engaged in terrorism and assassination."

24 Fifteen top Polish officials, including Council of Ministers Chairman Edward Babiuch, are ousted in a shake-up linked to the government's inability to suppress the strike of Polish workers begun August 14 that is spreading across the country, affecting nearly 150,000 workers.

25 The newly created African nation of Zimbabwe is admitted to the United Nations as the 153rd member.

27 South Korea's National Conference for Unification elects Chun Doo Hwan president; the 48-year-old former army general, who immediately assumes the full powers of his office, replaces South Korea's fourth president, Choi Kyu Hah, who resigned on August 16 to establish "the precedent of peaceful transfer of power."

The French government uses navy tugboats armed with water cannons and tear gas to prevent striking fishermen from blockading the country's largest oil tanker terminal at Fos in southern France.

29 Seventy-two leaders of eight different political groups in the Philippines announce the signing of a document called Covenant for Freedom, calling for an end to exploitation and injustice and for the establishment of "a new order based on social justice"; the signatories pledge to end martial law and restore democracy.

31 Rep. Michael O. Myers of Pennsylvania and three co-defendants become the first persons convicted of bribery and conspiracy in the case code-named Abscam. Videotapes introduced by government prosecutors showed Myers accepting $50,000 in cash from an undercover agent in exchange for a promise to introduce special immigration legislation that would permit certain "Arab sheiks" to reside in the U.S.

The last of the demands of striking Polish workers, government recognition of the right to strike and form independent trade unions, is granted; the nationwide strike has been a triumph for the workers.

(Below left) Wreaths mark the site of a terrorist bomb blast that killed 76 people in Bologna, Italy. (Below right) Billy Carter testified before a Senate subcommittee on his dealings with Libya.

LAFORET—GAMMA/LIAISON

© 1980 DENNIS BRACK—BLACK STAR

SEPTEMBER

1 After secret negotiations between Libyan and Syrian representatives, Libyan leader Col. Muammar al-Qaddafi publicly proposes the merger of the two nations so they can oppose Israel more effectively.

4 The head of Saudi Arabia's national oil company confirms that his country has completed the takeover, begun in 1973, of the Arabian American Oil Co. (Aramco) with the payment of $1.5 billion to four U.S. oil companies.

6 Edward Gierek, secretary of the Polish Communist Party, is replaced by Stanislaw Kania; Kania, whose previous responsibilities included supervision of various security forces and relations with the Roman Catholic Church, was believed to have counseled moderation during the recent confrontation between the government and Poland's striking workers.

7 China's National People's Congress, which has been in session since August 30, approves a number of changes in the nation's leadership that are meant to serve as guidelines for years to come: as expected, Premier Hua Guofeng's (Hua Kuo-feng's) resignation is accepted, and Zhao Ziyang (Chao Tzu-yang) is named in his place. Deng Xiaoping (Teng Hsiao-p'ing) and six other elderly vice-premiers also resign to make room for three younger men. However, Deng and Hua remain chairman and vice-chairman, respectively, of the Chinese Communist Party.

11 By a margin of more than two to one, Chilean voters indicate their approval of a new constitution that will permit Gen. Augusto Pinochet Ugarte to retain the presidency until 1989.

12 Ayatollah Ruhollah Khomeini announces four conditions that the U.S. will have to meet to secure the release of 52 of its citizens held hostage since Nov. 4, 1979: the U.S. is to cancel all claims against Iran, turn over to Iran all property of the late shah, release Iran's frozen assets, and promise not to interfere politically or militarily in Iran.

Gen. Kenan Evren, chief of staff of Turkey's armed forces, leads a bloodless coup and takes over control of the government from Prime Minister Suleyman Demirel; Parliament is dissolved and the constitution suspended.

The April 6 Liberation Movement, an anti-Marcos group, is responsible for a series of bombings in the Manila area; one person is killed and 60 are injured.

17 Anastasio Somoza Debayle, president of Nicaragua for 23 years before he was forced to flee the country in July 1979, is assassinated in Asunción, Paraguay.

Kim Dae Jung, former leader of the opposition New Democratic Party, is sentenced to hang after being found guilty of sedition by a military court in Seoul, South Korea.

18 The Cuban government, having issued a stern warning the previous day to potential hijackers, arrests two Cubans the moment they land in Havana aboard a Delta Air Lines jet they hijacked in South Carolina and returns them to the U.S., where they face charges of air piracy. Since August 10 there have been 11 other successful hijackings by Cuban refugees seeking to return to their native land.

19 A fuel explosion at an underground Titan 2 nuclear missile silo near Damascus, Ark., kills one person and injures 21 others; the blast hurls the Titan's nuclear warhead about 225 m (750 ft), but initial reports indicate there were no radiation leaks and no significant damage to the ten-megaton warhead; the warhead's detonator is later safely disarmed.

20 The National Security Council of Turkey chooses Adm. Bulent Ulusa prime minister.

22 Fighting between Iran and Iraq reaches new intensity when Iraqi aircraft attack ten Iranian airfields and an oil refinery at Kermanshah; the conflict has escalated into major warfare, with naval, air, and ground troops engaged and Iraqi troops on Iranian soil.

24 A national federation of Poland's new independent labour unions is registered under the name Solidarity in a Warsaw court.

26 A bomb explosion at the entrance to the site of Munich's Oktoberfest kills 12 persons and injures more than 200 others; police speculate that a member of an outlaw rightist organization known as the Defense Sports Group had planted the bomb shortly before he was killed when the explosive detonated prematurely.

Unidentified gunmen in Paris machine-gun a Jewish synagogue, school, day-care centre, and a memorial to Jews who were deported during World War II; the attacks are the latest in a series of anti-Semitic outbursts in France seen as tied to rising neofascist sentiment.

28 The UN Security Council unanimously approves a resolution calling on Iran and Iraq to submit their border dispute to mediation and to refrain immediately from further use of force. All other nations are urged "to exercise the utmost restraint and to refrain from any action which may lead to a further escalation and widening of the conflict."

30 The U.S. government sends four air force radar command planes to Saudi Arabia to help the country better protect its eastern oil fields from possible Iranian attacks; at the same time, the U.S. affirms its neutrality in the Iran-Iraq conflict and declares that the planes are solely for defense purposes.

The U.S. government ends its 1980 fiscal year with a budget deficit of $58,960,000,000, the second highest deficit in U.S. history and more than twice as large as the deficit of the previous year.

(Top) The fighting between Iran and Iraq threatened the world oil supply; the oil refineries at Abadan, Iran, were heavily damaged. (Left) The government of Turkey was overthrown in a bloodless coup on August 12 led by the armed forces chief of staff. (Above) On August 17 Anastasio Somoza, who fled Nicaragua in 1979 after his overthrow by the Sandinista guerrillas, was assassinated by ambush in Asunción, Paraguay, where he had sought asylum.

OCTOBER

5 West Germany's ruling coalition of Social Democrats and Free Democrats increases its majority in the Bundestag (lower house of Parliament) from a modest 10 seats to a substantial 45; the victory guarantees Helmut Schmidt four more years as federal chancellor.

10 El Asnam, a city of 125,000 in northern Algeria, is hit by two devastating earthquakes hours apart that reduce most of its buildings to rubble and kill more than 4,000 people.

13 The UN General Assembly votes 74–35, with 32 abstentions, against a resolution that would have ousted the UN representative of the Pol Pot regime that ruled Cambodia before it was taken over by Vietnamese troops.

15 A tentative settlement is reported between the Fiat auto manufacturing company and striking workers at its plants in Turin, Italy; the strike shut down the plant for more than a month.

16 The Sri Lanka Parliament votes 139–18 to expel former prime minister Sirimavo Bandaranaike from Parliament and to revoke her civil rights for seven years; a special commission found Bandaranaike guilty of abusing power while serving as head of government.

China detonates a nuclear device in the atmosphere for the first time since December 1978; the blast occurred at the Lop Nor test site in northwestern China.

17 During a week-long visit of French Pres. Valéry Giscard d'Estaing to China, it is announced that China will purchase two 900-Mw nuclear reactors from France at a cost of about $950 million each.

18 Australian Prime Minister Malcolm Fraser is returned to power for a second time when a coalition of his Liberal Party and the National Country Party retains their majority in the lower house of Parliament.

19 A convention of the American Society of Travel Agents is called off in Manila when 20 persons are injured by a bomb that explodes shortly after Philippine Pres. Ferdinand Marcos addressed the delegates; the April 6 Liberation Movement claims responsibility for this and a series of earlier attacks.

20 NATO's Defense Planning Committee unanimously approves Greece's return to the alliance's integrated military organization; Greece withdrew its troops from NATO in 1974 after NATO member Turkey sent combat forces into Cyprus and took control of the northern section of the island.

21 In an address before a plenary session of the Communist Party Central Committee, Soviet Pres. Leonid Brezhnev explains that two consecutive poor grain harvests due to bad weather and lack of farm equipment have created food shortages of serious dimensions; major cities have inadequate supplies of meat and milk.

22 South Korean voters overwhelmingly approve a referendum sanctioning fundamental changes in the constitution: the new charter limits the president to one seven-year term, allows for the establishment of political groups, guarantees human rights, reinstates habeas corpus, and outlaws the torture of prisoners; in addition the president no longer has the right to appoint one-third of the National Assembly.

Lebanese Pres. Elias Sarkis appoints former minister of justice Shafiq al-Wazzan prime minister to replace Selim al-Hoss, who has been acting as caretaker since his resignation on June 7.

23 Aleksey N. Kosygin, chairman of the Council of Ministers (premier), resigns as head of the Soviet government; the 76-year-old leader is replaced by his first deputy, 75-year-old Nikolay A. Tikhonov, a Ukrainian industrial planner.

Some 60,000 members of the Screen Actors Guild and the American Federation of Television and Radio Artists end their 94-day strike—the longest in the industry's history—by accepting a new contract that guarantees them a share in revenues derived from original programs that were made for pay television or video discs and video cassettes.

25 According to reports, El Salvador has launched a major offensive against guerrillas operating in the mountainous northern provinces of the country to stave off a major insurrection; its troops are supported by heavy artillery, helicopter gunships, tanks, and armoured cars.

27 The Cuban government pardons and releases 30 U.S. prisoners in what is generally regarded as a gesture of goodwill by Cuban Pres. Fidel Castro; 5 of the 30 were arrested when their plane landed in Miami, Fla., as four faced charges of plane hijacking and one of violating his parole.

28 Democratic candidate Pres. Jimmy Carter meets Republican candidate Ronald Reagan in a nationally televised 90-minute debate.

Saudi Arabia severs diplomatic relations with Libya following a series of speeches by Libyan Leader Muammar al-Qaddafi criticizing Saudi Arabia's acceptance of four radar planes from the U.S.

29 A bomb explosion inside the main Beijing (Peking) railway terminal kills 9 persons and injures 81 others; police suspect that the unknown person who carried the bomb into the station died when the bomb exploded, possibly prematurely.

30 Jamaican Prime Minister Michael Manley, leader of the People's National Party, is defeated by Edward Seaga of the Jamaica Labour Party; Manley's defeat is seen as an emphatic repudiation of his socialist policies and the special ties he had fostered with Cuba.

(Above) Pres. Jimmy Carter and Republican candidate Ronald Reagan faced each other in a televised debate on October 28. (Below) On October 10 the city of El Asnam, Algeria, was struck by two powerful earthquakes four hours apart; much of the city was reduced to rubble.

NOVEMBER

2 The Iranian Majlis (parliament) approves conditions for the release of 52 U.S. hostages as outlined by Ayatollah Ruhollah Khomeini on September 12.

4 Iraqi Pres. Saddam Hussein warns Iran that Iraq may broaden its claims if its call for a cease–fire and peace talks falls on deaf ears; the two countries signed a border agreement in 1975, but Iraq is now demanding sovereignty over the vital Shatt al-Arab waterway, three small islands, and a section of land along the Iraqi-Iranian border. Iran vows to continue fighting so long as Iraqi soldiers occupy Iranian territory.

Ronald Reagan, a conservative Republican and former governor of California, soundly defeats incumbent Democratic Pres. Jimmy Carter in the presidential elections. The margin of Reagan's victory is unexpected; he receives more than 43.2 million votes, while Carter gets a bit more than 34.9 million, and John Anderson, a Republican running as an independent, receives about 5,580,000 votes. The Reagan victory also gives Republicans control of the U.S. Senate for the first time since 1956.

6 Representatives of 23 Islamic states conclude a three-day meeting in Ankara, Turkey, a conference convened mainly to strengthen economic bonds among Islamic nations; the delegates approve a ten-point program calling for greater cooperation in such areas as science, technology, industry, agriculture, communications, health, and finance.

7 Tanzanian Pres. Julius Nyerere names a new Cabinet following his reelection to a fourth five-year term on October 26; Cleopa David Msuya is named prime minister, and Ahmed Salim Salim foreign minister.

8 Members of Israel's Labour Party create an uproar when they announce their support for a Jordanian-Palestinian state to extend beyond Jordan into the West Bank and include the Gaza Strip; Palestinians would constitute a majority in the proposed state.

Sadegh Ghotbzadeh, former Iranian foreign minister, is arrested on orders issued by the Teheran public prosecutor; Ghotbzadeh has charged that the state broadcasting system, which he once headed, is falling under the control of Islamic fundamentalists who have no legitimate authority to determine the content of its broadcasts.

10 Warren Christopher, U.S. deputy secretary of state, arrives in Algeria carrying the U.S. response to Iran's conditions for the release of the 52 U.S. hostages.

The Polish Supreme Court averts a nationwide strike by ruling that the charter of the labour union federation Solidarity need not acknowledge the "leading role" of the Polish Communist Party and of socialism in Polish society.

Michael Foot, a member of Great Britain's Parliament

for 30 years, is elected by his Labour Party colleagues to lead their party, the post having been vacated in October by former prime minister James Callaghan.

The U.S. International Trade Commission rules that there is not sufficient justification for placing restrictions on automobile and light-truck imports into the U.S., despite the serious financial problems plaguing U.S. automobile manufacturers.

12 The U.S. unmanned spacecraft Voyager 1 comes within 125,000 km (77,000 mi) of the planet Saturn; among other discoveries, the Voyager 1 flight reveals that Saturn has far more rings than anyone had suspected, some of which are eccentric. The three new moons of Saturn that Voyager photographs increase the known number to 15.

14 Lech Walesa, head of Solidarity, Poland's independent federation of trade unions, meets with Communist Party leader Stanislaw Kania; the two men reportedly discuss the role of Solidarity in solving the serious economic and political problems plaguing the nation.

Luis de Almeida Cabral, president of the small African nation of Guinea-Bissau, is ousted from power by Premier João Bernardo Vieira.

15 Pope John Paul II arrives in Cologne, West Germany, to begin a five-day religious pilgrimage aimed at strengthening the Roman Catholic Church and improving relations with Protestant churches; it was the first papal visit to Germany since 1782.

20 The long-awaited trial of Jiang Qing (Chiang Ch'ing), leader of the gang of four and widow of the late Chinese Communist Party chairman Mao Zedong (Mao Tse-tung), and nine of her associates gets under way in Beijing (Peking); the four major crimes listed in the indictments are: framing and persecuting party and state leaders and plotting to overthrow the political power of the dictatorship of the proletariat; persecuting and suppressing large numbers of cadres and ordinary people; plotting to assassinate Chairman Mao and stage an armed counter revolutionary coup d'etat; and planning an armed rebellion in Shanghai.

23 An earthquake measuring 6.9 on the Richter scale wreaks immense damage in dozens of cities, towns, and villages in southern Italy; the hardest hit provinces are Naples, Salerno, Potenza, and Avellino, where more than 3,000 persons are reported killed.

25 The government of Sangoulé Lamizana, president of Upper Volta, one of the world's poorest nations, is overthrown in a military coup led by Col. Saye Zerbo.

28 Haitian police begin to round up about 200 persons whose criticism of the government has been labeled Communist-inspired agitation; it is the largest roundup of the government's critics since Jean-Claude Duvalier assumed power in 1971.

(Above) Separate raging fires caused widespread destruction in southern California in November, engulfing hundreds of houses. (Below left) On November 4 Ronald Reagan was elected 40th president of the United States. (Below right) The Voyager 1 unmanned spacecraft flew by Saturn on November 12.

DECEMBER

2 Pres. Jimmy Carter, speaking through his press secretary, sternly warns the U.S.S.R. that relations between the two countries will be seriously affected by a Soviet invasion of Poland.

4 UNESCO issues a report on the extent of illiteracy around the world: one-third of the world's population can neither read nor write; in Africa, two-thirds of the people are uneducated, and in non-Soviet Asia about one-half of the population.

Portuguese Premier Francisco Sá Carneiro is killed in a plane crash near Lisbon.

5 Members of the Warsaw Pact convene in Moscow to discuss the serious problems faced by Poland and to decide what position the Pact should take to meet the crisis facing one of its members; the Soviet Union and its six Eastern European allies express confidence that Poland will be able to overcome its difficulties without damaging its socialist system of government.

6 Voters in Taiwan go to the polls to select members of the Legislative Yuan and for the National Assembly; the ruling Kuomintang's candidates capture 57 of the 70 contested seats in the legislature, giving it more than 92% of the body's 360 seats and 63 of the 76 contested seats in the National Assembly.

7 Gen. António Ramalho Eanes is reelected president of Portugal; the election has been strongly affected by the death of Premier Francisco Sá Carneiro.

8 Edgar Z. Tekere, head of Zimbabwe's manpower, planning, and development ministry, is freed by a Salisbury court even though he has been found guilty of murdering a white farmer in early August; the decision to set Tekere and one of his aides free is based on a 1975 law that protects government officials from criminal charges resulting from antiterrorist activities.

Ex-Beatle John Lennon is shot and killed outside his apartment building in New York City; his death signals for many the end of an era in popular culture that began in the early 1960s.

10 Mounting tension between Jordan and Syria begins to abate when both countries agree to begin withdrawing troops from the border separating their two countries, where they began to mass in late November.

A federal grand jury in Chicago indicts 11 persons on charges of terrorism connected with more than a score of bombings that have taken place in the Chicago area beginning in June 1975; the indicted are suspected of being members of the FALN, a Puerto Rican organization seeking to gain independence for their country through violent means.

12 Members of the Red Brigades, a terrorist organization responsible for numerous acts of violence throughout Italy, kidnap Giovanni D'Urso, a director general in the ministry of justice responsible for the disposition and care of terrorists.

After a two-day meeting presided over by Stefan Cardinal Wyszynski, Poland's Roman Catholic bishops caution dissidents that extremism could destroy "the freedom and statehood of the fatherland"; fear persists that the Soviet Union might invade Poland if continued unrest is perceived as a threat to Poland's Communist government.

13 Uganda's state electoral commission announces that the Uganda People's Congress has won a majority of seats in the parliamentary elections and that, as a consequence, Milton Obote will become president of Uganda for the second time.

16 Libyan troops, at the request of Goukouni Oueddei, president of Chad, use heavy artillery and aircraft to drive troops loyal to Premier Hissen Habré out of the nation's capital; after fleeing to Cameroon, Habré signs, "with reservations," a cease-fire agreement worked out by the Organization of African Unity.

18 Aleksey N. Kosygin, chairman of the Soviet Union's Council of Ministers for 16 years, dies in Moscow.

Carlos Romero Barceló, the incumbent governor of Puerto Rico, is officially declared the winner of an exceedingly close gubernatorial election six weeks after the election was held.

19 Most large U.S. banks raise their prime interest rate to an all-time high of 21.5%, the interest they charge on loans to preferred corporate customers.

25 Iraqi Pres. Saddam Hussein announces that Iraqi forces moved into Iran's Kurdistan Province the previous week; the multipronged offensive extended the war to almost the entire border area of the two countries.

26 Abdelkarim Gheraieb, the Algerian ambassador to Iran, announces that he has visited all 52 U.S. hostages in Teheran and found "the conditions of their present existence satisfactory."

27 Some 5,000 Afghans mark the first anniversary of the Soviet invasion of their country by attacking the Soviet and Afghan embassies in Teheran, Iran.

28 Mexico announces that it is about to give formal notice to the U.S. that it will terminate all existing fishing agreements between the two countries; the decision follows several years of unsuccessful negotiations to determine each country's fishing rights.

31 The U.S. Census Bureau publishes statistics on the 1980 population survey, which is required by law every ten years: the total population of the country is put at 226,504,825—an 11.4% increase over the 1970 figure. Overall, the Northeast and Midwest have lost population to the South and West.

(Above) People around the world mourned the death of former Beatle John Lennon, senselessly murdered in New York City on December 8. (Below) The trial of the "gang of four" moved onward in China; among the accused was Jiang Qing (Chiang Ch'ing), widow of Mao Zedong (Mao Tse-tung).

女皇梦

EVENTS OF THE YEAR

1980

Advertising for designer blue jeans from several makers was attacked for using young models in what many felt were overtly erotic poses. Some ads aired on national television were pulled when stations received complaints from viewers who thought the ads were tasteless and exploitative.

PETER SCHAAF—TIME INC.

ADVERTISING

A new opportunity for U.S. advertising opened up in June 1980 when the Federal Communications Commission (FCC) took a first step toward deregulating radio stations. By diluting the clear-channel spectrum currently held by 25 AM radio stations, the FCC paved the way for creation of more than 100 new nighttime AM stations. The FCC limited the reach of the 25 stations by protecting them from interference only within a radius of 750 mi from their transmitters. This allowed for the additional stations, each with a ten-mile broadcast radius. At the same time, the FCC eliminated broadcaster guidelines dictating the amount of nonentertainment programming and the number of commercial minutes per hour.

Each year the magazine *Advertising Age* names the 100 largest national advertisers of the previous year. In 1979 the top five included Procter & Gamble, General Foods, Sears, Roebuck, General Motors, and Philip Morris. The 100 leading advertisers increased their advertising spending in 1979 to $11.7 billion, a 13.6% increase over 1978. Together, they accounted for more than half the total advertising expenditures in newspapers, magazines, network and spot television, farm publications, network and spot radio, and outdoor. The U.S. government was in the number 28 position, spending more than $140 million, a 14% increase over 1978.

In October 1980 a federal appeals court upheld a finding of the Federal Trade Commission (FTC) that the American Medical Association (AMA) could not interfere with physicians' attempts to advertise. Physicians would now be allowed to advertise their fees and services, but the court did agree that the AMA could issue ethical guidelines for its members concerning false and deceptive advertising.

The U.S. Treasury Department removed some advertising and merchandising restrictions on the alcoholic beverage industry that had been in existence since the 1930s. The changes would permit distillers to spend more for in-store signs and product displays and for reimbursement of retailers for handling coupons. No limit was placed on the number of indoor signs provided they had no value other than as advertising. Under the new rules, a distiller could place up to $100 worth of promotional displays per brand with a retailer at any one time. The Treasury Department was also considering proposals for comparative advertising in this industry.

Sex as a dominant theme in marketing returned to television with a series of controversial ads for designer jeans (the most controversial featured preteen or teenaged models). The message presented was that the buyer could achieve status and attract the opposite sex by wearing tight jeans emblazoned with a designer's name. Newcomers in this industry were spending as much as 15% of their sales revenue on advertising, compared with 2% for the largest U.S. jeans manufacturer, Levi Strauss. A study by the Television Bureau of Advertising indicated that in the first six months of 1980 the 15 leading television advertisers of ready-to-wear apparel spent $28.7 million on TV commercials, an increase of 160% over 1979. Designer jeans companies spent about $15.5 million during this period, compared with $1.9 million in 1979.

The U.S. boycott of the Olympic Games in Moscow cost NBC $100 million, approximately 85% of which was covered by insurance from Lloyds of London. By the time the boycott was announced, NBC had already paid for thousands of souvenirs, including T-shirts, duffel bags, and warm-up suits inscribed "NBC Moscow 1980," and had paid the Soviet Union most of the $87 million for production facilities and services and television rights. NBC also had to come up with 152 hours of programming to fill the time alloted for the Games.

The U.S. Department of Justice filed suit in July against the National Association of Broadcasters' television code, charging that it unfairly controls

A decoy device to protect civilian airliners against attack made its first appearance at London's Heathrow Airport in 1980. The device, mounted in each of the engine pylons, emits a flare of intense heat to deflect a surface-to-air missile from striking the plane. The devices are shown fitted on an El Al Boeing 707.

LONDON DAILY EXPRESS/PICTORIAL PARADE

the marketplace by restricting the amount of advertising time available to manufacturers and retailers.

An all-sports radio network inaugurated in late 1980 gave charter advertisers exclusive rights for their product categories. Commercials were slotted into sportscasts that went on the air every half hour, all-night talk shows, and two-and-one-half-minute tapes of memorable moments in sports. A cooperative newspaper buying service introduced in 1980 gave advertisers an opportunity to place one order for co-op ads in 62 of the top 100 metropolitan markets. The service handled insertion orders to the newspapers, shipped the advertising materials, accepted the billings, audited the claims, and paid the papers. Advertisements placed by manufacturers included the names of local dealers or retailers where the product could be purchased.

A weekly 60-minute talk show devoted exclusively to advertisements began to appear on 350 cable television systems in September, with an audience of three million homes. The show was co-sponsored by 40 advertisers at $3,500 per ten-minute slot. Each show was devoted to the products of five advertisers, and viewers were given an opportunity to place immediate orders by calling a toll-free telephone number. Advertisers used the program to sample viewer reaction to new products or new concepts.

AEROSPACE

At a time when Europe and the U.S. were experiencing major recessions their aerospace industries weathered the storm, and record sales were almost commonplace. The airlines, on the other hand, caught between competition that forced them to lower fares and steeply rising inflation and fuel costs, ran into great difficulties, and few made a profit.

Trade figures continued to emphasize the importance of aerospace in the industrialized and the less developed countries, both as a source of revenue and as a catalyst for developing nonaeronautical technology. In 1979 Boeing Co., with orders for 479 new aircraft, headed *Fortune* magazine's list of the top 50 exporting U.S. firms, and McDonnell Douglas Corp., Lockheed Corp., and Northrop Corp. were also among the first 11. Signs were that this preeminence would be repeated in 1980.

The supersonic Concorde remained the most prestigious commercial aircraft, although its star was increasingly eclipsed by problems with noise, route shortages, and crippling fuel costs. Braniff, which had begun a service using the Concorde between London and Paris and Dallas-Fort Worth, Texas, shelved the arrangement because of high fuel costs. British Airways in a major economy drive also dropped one of its Concorde services, that to Singapore. Meanwhile, the U.S. government increased funding of an advanced supersonic transport in order to keep open U.S. options for a 1990s design.

Sales of wide-body jets—the Boeing 747, Lockheed L-1011 TriStar, and Airbus Industrie A300—continued to be strong, though passenger resistance to the McDonnell Douglas DC-10 was clearly marked. This was due to three major DC-10 disasters in 1979. Decisions by Singapore Airlines and Thai Airlines to sell their DC-10s because they were unsuitable for their routes cast further doubts on the aircraft's credibility.

Sales of new-generation airliners to replace the aging Boeing 707s and Douglas DC-8s proceeded slowly, the 200/210-seat Boeing 767 vying with the identically sized Airbus Industrie A310. U.S. operators bought the 767 and European ones the A310. Meanwhile, sales of the smaller, 170-seat Boeing 757 remained static, encouraging McDonnell Douglas to relaunch yet again its Advanced Technology Medium Range 170-seat product, this time as the slightly more definitive DC-XX 180-seater. By November 1980 there were only four 757 customers —Eastern Airlines, British Airways, and two newcomers, Aloha and Transbrasil; Delta Air Lines was reportedly also negotiating an order for approximately 50 of the planes.

But if the manufacturing industry thrived, the airlines did not. The revenues carefully hoarded since the 1974 fuel crisis to buy the new equipment that would put them on a faster road to recovery vanished as the airlines sought desperately to keep themselves in the black. Virtually all airlines found themselves in this situation, and predictions voiced at the annual meeting of the International Air Transport Association in October were gloomy. Some observers attributed airline misfortunes to the 1978 U.S. Airline Deregulation Act, but a number of the larger operators put the blame on inflation and, more importantly, their skyrocketing fuel bills. During the year the British government emerged as a proponent of free trade, as evinced by its approval of no fewer than four operators to service the London–Hong Kong route. It was also sympathetic toward the gathering tide of criticism against the mostly nationalized European trunk airlines for their alleged gross overcharging, and there was talk of bringing some cases to the European Court of Justice for possible prosecution for violation of European Economic Community (EEC) rules.

Deregulation did severely curtail airline services between many smaller terminals in the U.S., and the burden of providing such service fell largely to the so-called third-level airlines. The growing importance of this segment of the industry emerged at the annual National Business Aircraft Association meeting at Kansas City; it became evident there that while U.S. industry was providing a fine range of aircraft seating up to 15 people, it had nothing to offer the sudden large and growing market for commuter planes carrying between 15 and 20 passengers. This sector was currently being supplied by Canada, Brazil, and the U.K.

The Hanover (West Germany) Air Show in May provided an opportunity to show off ideas for the proposed British-West German-French European Combat Aircraft (ECA). The ECA would replace the British and French Jaguars and the West German Phantoms. But this project was likely to remain stalled while governments thrashed out costs; the West Germans made no secret of their dissatisfaction with the alarming increases in costs for the British-West German-Italian Tornado multirole combat aircraft since it was launched in 1970. In the U.S. discussion about a new manned bomber was gaining momentum as the threat from the U.S.S.R.'s new aircraft fleets became more clearly defined. The new U.S. plane might turn out to be the so-called stealth bomber, the existence of which was leaked to the press during the year, apparently to show that the Carter administration had the interests of the defense community at heart. (*See also* Defense.)

AFGHANISTAN

The Soviet military intervention launched in December 1979 to contain the insurgency and stabilize the Marxist revolutionary government of Pres. Babrak Karmal failed to achieve its purpose, and problems, both political and economic, multiplied during the following months. As the Soviet Union increased the strength of its force from an initial 30,000–40,000 men to an estimated 85,000 by October 1980, resentment against the Soviet military occupation rose both within and outside Afghanistan. All estimates indicated that hatred of the Soviet Union among the 15 million Afghans was near total, and the insurgency, which was originally confined to mountainous areas of the northeast and a few provinces bordering Pakistan, was spreading throughout the country. Externally, except for the Soviet bloc and some pro-Soviet members of the nonaligned movement, no nation was prepared to condone the continued Soviet military presence.

Anti-Soviet feeling among the Afghans rose to a high pitch in February, when a general strike and violent demonstrations were staged against the Soviet presence in Kabul and other major towns. The mass uprising was quelled after Afghan armed forces and Communist militia inflicted heavy casualties on the demonstrators. As cases of Soviet soldiers disappearing began to increase, the Soviet troops assumed more and more direct control of the security situation from the Afghan Army. The riots were repeated at the end of April, this time staged by students from Kabul University and other educational institutions. The April demonstrations, which took place during the anniversary celebrations of the Saur (April) Revolution launched by former president Nur Mohammad Taraki on April 27, 1978, resulted in the brutal killings of more than 50 students.

Afghan rebels display a Soviet helicopter captured through a ruse by an officer who deserted from the Army to join the rebel cause. The rebels welcomed deserters, many of whom brought with them valuable equipment.
ALAIN DEJEAN—SYGMA

The Soviet Union announced a token withdrawal of one of its divisions in June, but this failed to placate the Afghans. Except for a small percentage consisting of ruling People's Democratic Party cadres, bureaucrats, and intellectuals, no section of the population would accept the government's thesis: that all the country's ills either were caused by saboteurs and agents from Pakistan and the U.S. or resulted from the tyrannical measures adopted by the short-lived regime of Karmal's predecessor, former president Hafizullah Amin. During a visit to Moscow October 16–17, Karmal was welcomed by Soviet Pres. Leonid Brezhnev. Their subsequent discussion and joint signature of a document in the Kremlin was seen as a formal acknowledgment of the Afghan government's puppet status.

The Karmal government also had to contend with large-scale desertions from the Afghan armed forces. From an estimated 80,000 at the time of the Soviet intervention, the Afghan Army's strength was down to 30,000 by June. The government launched an all-out recruiting drive and announced a series of measures to attract young people to the Army, but the result was poor.

As rebel activities increased, travel outside Kabul became unsafe. The night curfew imposed on Kabul and other major towns soon after the Soviet forces moved in was becoming a permanent fixture. Except for the long supply line to the Soviet border in the north, the highways out of Kabul remained closed to traffic for weeks on end as rebel snipers held up convoys. The Soviets unleashed a series of offensives against the insurgents in the provinces of Paktia, Konarha, Ghazni, Herat, Qandahar, and Badakhshan in the months following the February riots. But while the Soviet sweeps managed to clear targeted valleys and mountain ranges of insurgents, the rebels returned soon after the operations were ended. A stalemate situation emerged, with the Soviets bottled up in the large towns while the in-

Chinese Foreign Minister Huang Hua visited a camp in Pakistan for refugees fleeing the fighting in Afghanistan.
BOCCON-GIBOD—SIPA PRESS/BLACK STAR

surgents roamed at will in the countryside.

The Soviet forces, using tanks, MiG jet fighters, and Mi-24 helicopter gunships, were said to have razed a number of villages. Villagers fleeing to Pakistan complained about the use of napalm bombs by the Soviet forces, but this could not be confirmed. The exodus of Afghan refugees to Pakistan continued without interruption. Outside estimates placed the number seeking shelter in Pakistan by September at over 900,000.

Attempts to bring about a peaceful solution of the Afghan crisis and Soviet withdrawal from the country were made by the Islamic Conference in Islamabad, Pak., in May, and by various nonaligned nations, especially India, which had taken a moderate stand on the issue. No headway could be made, however. Pakistan refused to have any direct talks with the Karmal regime, since this would involve recognition of the Soviet-backed government. Karmal insisted that all subversive activities against his country must stop before any international discussion on the crisis could be held. The Soviet Union announced that there would be no further withdrawals of Soviet forces until peace was restored.

AFRICAN AFFAIRS

The Organization of African Unity (OAU) held its 17th annual summit in July in Freetown, Sierra Leone, whose president, Siaka Stevens, became organization chairman for 1980–81. Zimbabwe was admitted as its 50th member state. The conflicts in the Western Sahara, Chad, South West Africa/Namibia, and South Africa dominated the debates. A majority of OAU members favoured accepting Western Sahara as an independent country, but a final decision to recognize the Saharan Arab Democratic Republic was delayed pending a final mediation effort to reach an agreement with Morocco, which remained committed to its policy of incorporating the former Spanish Sahara into its king-

Conditions in Uganda reached a crisis point in 1980: communications and supply lines were totally disorganized, and starvation was widespread.

WILLIAM CAMPBELL—SYGMA

dom. The OAU also decided on one final mediation attempt to halt the civil war in Chad before admitting defeat and handing the problem over to the UN for international action. An ultimatum given to Western powers declared that unless they succeeded in persuading South Africa to implement the UN plan for Namibia's independence, the UN Security Council would be asked to impose economic sanctions against the Pretoria regime. Proposals for tougher sanctions against South Africa over its policy of racial separation were adopted, including the idea of an international oil embargo and a total boycott of all air flights to and from that country.

Southern Africa

The achievement of an independent Zimbabwe under a Patriotic Front government in April left South Africa as the only independent country still under white minority rule. The new regime of Robert Mugabe suspended diplomatic relations with South Africa while accepting the need for continued economic links. However, a new initiative was launched to reduce the economic dependence on South Africa of its border nations. For this purpose a new regional organization, the Southern African Development Coordination Conference, was formed comprising Botswana, Angola, Mozambique, Lesotho, Zimbabwe, Zambia, Tanzania, Malawi, and Swaziland.

The level of violence in South Africa rose with the increasing success of the African National Congress in infiltrating its guerrilla fighters into the urban areas to attack strategic targets. The Namibian liberation movement, the South West Africa People's Organization, also kept up its pressures on South Africa from its bases in Angola. South Africa took strong countermeasures, launching major military attacks across its own borders into Angola and Zambia.

The Horn of Africa

International attention focused more sharply on the Red Sea and northern Indian Ocean region following the Soviet Union's military intervention in Afghanistan and the worsening crisis in the Persian Gulf area. The NATO powers, especially the U.S., embarked on a new policy of strengthening the Western military presence in the region. In June the U.S. acquired naval and air facilities in Kenya, and in August it signed an agreement with Somalia for the use of that nation's naval facilities at Berbera. Simultaneously, facilities were acquired in Egypt for the installation of Rapid Deployment Forces, and the U.S. Congress authorized a substantial expenditure to develop an air base on the Indian Ocean island of Diego Garcia.

These developments produced strong reactions from a number of African countries. The OAU unanimously supported Mauritius's claim for the return to it of Diego Garcia. Meanwhile, fighting in Ethiopia continued, especially in Eritrea, the Ogad-

ALAIN NOGUES—SYGMA

The Organization of African Unity held its 17th annual summit meeting in Sierra Leone in July. Zimbabwe was admitted as the 50th member state.

en, Tigre, and Bale. Soviet efforts to mediate in the conflict between the Eritrean liberation movements and Ethiopia remained unsuccessful. Lieut. Col. Haile Mengistu Mariam's regime in Ethiopia charged that Somalia's Army was again involved in the fighting in the Ogaden and threatened to attack its neighbour unless Somali intervention was stopped.

Coups and Inter-African Affairs

A dozen or so coups against established regimes were attempted during the year, but only five were successful. In January head of state Mohamed Mahmoud Ould Louly was deposed in Mauritania and replaced by Premier Mohamed Khouna Ould Haidalla. Liberia's Pres. William R. Tolbert, Jr., was assassinated in April by noncommissioned officers and privates, led by Master Sergeant Samuel Doe, who established a new military regime under the People's Redemption Council. In May Pres. Godfrey L. Binaisa of Uganda was overthrown by a six-man military commission, which established an interim government pending arrangements to hold multiparty elections in December. The fourth successful coup was in Guinea-Bissau, where Pres. Luis Cabral was overthrown in November. Also in November Pres. Sangoulé Lamizana was ousted by the military in Upper Volta.

Libya was involved in a number of interventions that caused its leader, Col. Muammar al-Qaddafi, to be regarded as a major troublemaker in the continent. In January he was involved in the attack on Gafsa, Tunisia, by opponents of Pres. Habib Bourguiba of Tunisia; in June he was accused by Pres. Léopold Sédar Senghor of Senegal of being in-

volved in a coup attempt there and in October of a similar attempt against the president of The Gambia, Sir Dawda Jawara. The Gambia and Senegal both broke off diplomatic relations with Libya. Border tensions between Egypt and Libya became sharper in June when Qaddafi called on the Egyptian Army to overthrow Pres. Anwar El-Sadat. Both Mali and Niger complained of Libyan interference in their internal affairs. However, the most blatant Libyan action was taken in Chad, where its forces occupied the capital in December in support of the regime of Pres. Goukouni Oueddei. Libya's proposed union with Syria was viewed with considerable skepticism in Africa in view of the previous failure of similar moves at union with Egypt, Tunisia, and Sudan.

Even before the November coup Guinea-Bissau's relations with neighbouring Guinea deteriorated seriously over a dispute about the limits of their offshore waters, which was related to possibilities of an oil discovery. Disagreements persisted between Kenya and Sudan, on one side, and Tanzania on the other, over the role of Pres. Julius Nyerere in Uganda.

Political Systems

The trend toward a greater liberalization of government noted in recent years continued during 1980. The outstanding achievement was the success of the multiparty elections in Zimbabwe that ended 15 years of an embittering civil war. For the first time since the revolution in Zanzibar in 1964 the islanders were given an opportunity in January of electing their government. Zanzibaris also participated in the elections in Tanzania in October, where popular discontent was effectively demonstrated by the defeat of about half the former national assemblymen, although President Nyerere himself was reelected. The Ivory Coast relaxed the tight control of its ruling party by allowing villagers to nominate their own candidates for Parliament instead of having to vote for party appointees. Botswana effected a harmonious transition after the death in July of its charismatic president, Sir Seretse Khama, who was replaced by the former vice-president, Quett Masire.

Notwithstanding its economic and security problems, Uganda held a tightly contested election in December in which former president Milton Obote emerged as victor. The turbulent political democracy of the continent's most populous state, Nigeria, made significant progress during the first year after the Army's withdrawal from the government; and though the restoration of civilian rule in Ghana was not without its problems, Pres. Hilla Limann's regime weathered the attacks made by his political opponents.

External Relations

Although international involvement in the continent's affairs showed little sign of declining, the impact of external forces was less sharp than in recent years. Cuba, especially, appeared to favour reducing its military presence on the continent, now estimated at perhaps 30,000 troops, mostly in Angola and Ethiopia. The Soviet Union, though still heavily engaged in Ethiopia, did not significantly increase its African role. East Germany remained the most active of the Eastern European countries in Africa, particularly in providing military assistance. Through exchanges of high-level visits China continued to maintain an active presence.

Only three African countries (Angola, Ethiopia, and Mozambique) voted against the UN General Assembly resolution condemning the Soviet intervention in Afghanistan. Although 24 African countries accepted invitations to participate in the Olympic Games in Moscow, 17 boycotted them. Twenty-five African nations were represented at the Franco-African summit conference held in Nice in May; most supported President Senghor's initiative to launch a Commonwealth á la Française, modeled on the Commonwealth of Nations. Pope John Paul II visited Congo, Zaire, Kenya, Ghana, Upper Volta, and Ivory Coast.

Social and Economic Conditions

With the exception of Africa's half-dozen oil-producing states the continent was doubly hit by the international economic crisis—first by the higher costs of oil imports and second by the higher costs of importing capital goods and food from the developed nations. The latest round of oil price increases meant, for example, that Ghana would have to use 65% of its total foreign exchange earnings to pay for its oil imports alone, while Tanzania would

have to devote 60% similarly. Consequently, few African countries could service their foreign debts. A UN Food and Agriculture Organization report showed that 29 less developed countries, mostly African, were suffering from acute food shortages in 1980, as compared with 16 in 1979. Nearly half the world's refugee population of four million was to be found in Africa, which meant that roughly one out of every 200 Africans was a displaced person.

(*See also* articles on the various countries.)

AGRICULTURE

World food supplies tightened in 1980 as world food output failed to recover from the decline experienced in 1979, largely because of poor grain harvests in both the United States and the Soviet Union. Although the buildup in world cereal stocks in earlier years made it possible to cover the production shortfalls of the last two years, these stocks were drawn down to unusually low levels. The situation that made world food security and market stability heavily dependent upon harvests around the world in 1981. The suspension of U.S. grain sales to the Soviet Union early in 1980 placed food and agricultural policy in the political arena.

Total agricultural and food production in the world (excluding China) failed to increase in 1980 for the second year in a row, according to preliminary indexes prepared by the Economics, Statistics, and Cooperatives Service of the U.S. Department of Agriculture (USDA). Farm output fell about 2.5% in the developed countries, as a nearly 6.5% reduc-

Corn from the record 1979 harvest is poured into railway cars for shipment; some was to go to China as part of a grain deal announced by Pres. Jimmy Carter in October 1980.
UPI

The severe and prolonged drought that hit many parts of the United States in 1980 dried up cornfields in Kansas, destroying thousands of acres of young corn.
UPI

tion in U.S. production because of drought—together with smaller output in Japan and Oceania—failed to completely offset substantial gains in Canada and Western Europe. Agricultural production climbed about 2.4% in the less developed countries, but it hardly rose at all in the centrally planned economies (U.S.S.R. and Eastern Europe) because of smaller Eastern European production. Chinese agricultural production (not covered by the USDA indexes) also appeared to have remained unchanged in 1980.

Measured on a per capita basis world food production fell more than 1.5%, with the developed countries declining more than 2% and the centrally planned nations close to 1.5%. Rapid population growth cut the growth in per capita food production in the less developed countries to less than 0.5%, with both East Asia and Africa registering losses. Per capita production of food in Africa remained about 15% below the level of a decade earlier.

The United Nations Food and Agriculture Organization (FAO) in mid-October 1980 listed 29 countries in Asia, Africa, and Latin America that were affected by abnormal food shortages as a result of poor crops, the effects of strife, or difficult economic situations. The year was notable for the recovery in Bangladesh that caused that nation to be dropped from the list and also for the substantial improvement in the critical conditions in Cambodia, where a major international relief operation was undertaken in the face of continuing military and political conflict. The worsening food situation in parts of Africa resulted in the calling of a special conference by the FAO director general in November, at which time donor countries substantially increased their pledges for African food aid.

Major Commodities

World grain production was expected to decline for the second year in a row in 1980–81. Although total harvested area was expected to be about 1.5% above the 712.6 million ha of 1979–80, yields were forecast to fall an equal percentage from 1.96 metric tons per hectare (1 ha=2.5 ac). A sharply reduced U.S. corn crop and another disappointing Soviet grain harvest were primarily responsible for the decline in output. World grain stocks were expected to decline by the end of 1980–81 to the lowest level—measured as a percentage of grain utilization—recorded during the past two decades. Grain prices were on the rise, and low stock levels strongly indicated that world food security in 1981–82 would depend upon successful harvests in 1981.

The United States responded on January 4 to the Soviet Union's invasion of Afghanistan with a limited suspension of grain sales to the U.S.S.R. This had as a principal economic objective the creation of difficulties for the Soviet livestock and dairy sectors. Also banned were other animal feeds, such as soybean, and meat, poultry, dairy products, and some animal fats that could be used to supplement Soviet production. Other measures that were intended to have a direct effect on Soviet food and agriculture included the prohibition of sales of phosphate—used to manufacture fertilizer—and restrictions on Soviet fishing in U.S. waters.

The suspension was not applied to the not-yet-shipped balance of the eight million tons of wheat and coarse grains that the U.S. was committed to supply under a five-year agreement between the two countries. The ban did apply to sales beyond the eight million tons that had not yet been shipped. The USDA estimated that the suspension affected 13 million tons of U.S. corn, 4 million tons of wheat, and about 1.3 million tons of soybeans and soybean meal, as well as some other commodities.

Australia, Canada, and the European Economic Community (EEC) agreed to restrain sales to the Soviet Union so that they would not replace U.S. shipments, but Argentina refused and concluded a five-year agreement to supply the U.S.S.R. with four million tons of corn and sorghum and 500,000 tons of soybeans annually beginning in 1981.

Although world output of oilseeds was expected to fall about 8.2% in 1980–81 from the 174.9 million tons produced in 1979–80, world supplies of soybean and other protein meals and vegetable oils were expected to be little changed from 1979–80 because of a substantial drawdown of stocks of oilseeds for crushing in 1980–81. A 17.3 million-ton decline in U.S. oilseed production from the 72.8 million harvested in 1979–80 was largely responsible for the fall in production; U.S. soybean area and yields were both reduced by the severe drought.

Although world meat production was leveling off in the last half of 1980, total output was expected to exceed the 1979 level of 138 million tons by 1%, according to FAO estimates. Beef and veal production had been declining for three years, but increases in pork and poultry offset the reduction.

A midsummer heatwave in the southern U.S. caused the worst drought in Texas in 50 years; millions of cattle and poultry died from heat and thirst.

OWEN FRANKEN—SYGMA

Production of beef and veal in the major importing regions (U.S., Canada, EEC, and Japan) was expected barely to exceed the 18.1 million tons (carcass weight) in 1979 because all but Canada recorded very small increases, according to the USDA. But output in the major exporting countries (Australia, New Zealand, Central America, Mexico, Argentina, and Uruguay)—except for Mexico—was forecast to be down about 7.2% from the 7.2 million tons in 1979. Cattle herds in 1980 were expanding, and most were expected to be larger at the beginning of 1981 than they had been a year earlier.

Pork output was expected to increase strongly throughout the world in 1980. Production in the major importing regions was likely to exceed the 18.2 million tons in 1979 by about 4.6%. Rapid increases in pork supplies together with dampened consumer demand weakened pork prices in some countries, leading to a cutback in the breeding of pigs that was expected to reduce pork output in major producing regions in 1981.

The expansion of world poultry production in 1980 was likely to continue in 1981. Although poultry producers faced similar conditions to those met by pork producers, strong import demand from the Middle East and the U.S.S.R. buoyed prices, and an expansion of poultry-producing capacity was under way in the Middle East.

Production of fluid milk in 36 major producing countries was expected to increase about 1.1% in 1980 over that in 1979. Most of the increase resulted from improved yields per animal, although output fell in the U.S.S.R. because of poor feed supplies. Butter production in the major producing countries was expected to be unchanged in 1980 at 6.1 million tons, while consumption would decline 2.9% from 5.8 million in 1979; stocks were forecast to increase nearly 8% above the 784,000 tons in 1979. The U.S. accounted for almost all the increase in stocks as the result of a nearly 12% increase in output. Soviet production was expected to decline 5% from 1.4 million tons in 1979.

Output of cheese in the major producing countries was forecast to reach nine million tons in 1980, 2.9% above that in 1979, as cheese producers continued to maintain their large share of milk use relative to other products. Consumption of cheese in 1980 increased about 2.1% to 8.6 million tons and seemed likely to rise again in 1981 as consumers responded to rising prices for red meat.

Although world production of centrifugal sugar was expected to recover in 1980–81 from the sharply reduced level of 1979–80, consumption was likely to remain at about that year's 90 million-ton level. With consumption exceeding production, stocks were expected to be drawn down for the second year in a row to about 21 million tons by the end of 1980–81, the lowest since 1973–74.

World coffee production was forecast to about equal that in 1979–80, while exportable production (harvested production less domestic consumption in

UPI

U.S. Ambassador to China Leonard Woodcock (left) and Chinese Minister of Foreign Trade Li Qiang signed a grain agreement in October under which the U.S. agreed to sell six million to eight million metric tons of grain each year from 1981 to 1984.

producing countries) was expected to fall about 400,000 bags (60 kg each) to 60.2 million bags. Stocks in producing countries were expected to result in only an 8% reduction in world stocks from the 24.6 million bags at the end of 1979–80.

World cocoa consumption in 1980–81 was expected to be less than output for the fourth year in a row, resulting in both a further buildup in stocks and a softening of prices. Increased production in Brazil and Malaysia was expected to slightly more than offset less favourable growing conditions in Africa and result in another record crop in 1980–81. Cocoa bean grindings were expected to increase about 2% in 1980–81 to about 1,480,000 tons.

World tea production was forecast to increase about 2.5% in 1980. Exports of tea were expected to exceed the 795,700 tons shipped in 1979 by about 3.3%. The largest gains were expected to be made by China, India, and Kenya, while substantial reductions were forecast for Bangladesh and Sri Lanka. India is the largest tea exporter (24% of the 1980 world total), followed by Sri Lanka (23%), China (13%), and Kenya (11%). Imports were likely to be up in the U.K. and the U.S. World tea prices had remained relatively stable since 1978, reflecting a well-balanced supply-demand situation.

World cotton production was forecast to decline about 3% below 1979–80 output because of a 23% reduction in the U.S. harvest caused by severe drought. Production was expected to rise about 3% outside the U.S., where the area planted to cotton was 2% higher.

(*See also* Flowers and Gardens; Food; Textiles.)

ALBANIA

Albania and Yugoslavia concluded a five-year trade agreement, which was drafted by the Albanian minister of foreign trade, Nedin Hoxha, on his visit to Belgrade in July 1980. It was the first time in

30 years that an Albanian minister had been the guest of the Yugoslav government. For some years relations between the two countries had been improving, apart from accusations of oppression of the Albanian minority in Yugoslavia, and the new agreement gave evidence of their wish to extend economic cooperation. It was hoped that trade between them would increase from a current $70 million to $110 million in 1981.

Speaking in Tirana on Nov. 18, 1979, Hoxha had proclaimed that Albania had no wish to restore diplomatic relations with the U.S.S.R. and the U.S. but would resume them with the U.K. if the British government shipped back the estimated £15 million of Albanian gold it held (according to British sources the gold amounted to £8 million).

On April 26, 1980, Mehmet Shehu was relieved of his duties as minister of defense and was succeeded by Kadri Hazbiu, minister of the interior. The latter post was then entrusted to Fecor Shehu.

ALGERIA

At the end of April 1980, in Kabylie (the mountain region east of Algiers where most Berbers live), riots occurred after riot police were sent in to end a general strike in Tizi-Ouzou. The incidents began when a lecture on ancient Kabyle poetry was banned in March, and they spread to Algiers, Oran, Batna, and Setif. They mirrored the frustration of Algeria's Berber minority of some three million to four million, arising from decisions by the National Liberation Front (FLN) Central Committee in January and May to make Arabic the sole official language. The Berbers feared that this would lead to the demise of their culture. The government made minor concessions, but not on the central issue. Pres. Chadli Bendjedid used the riots to secure his power base within the FLN and the government after the FLN's June congress. Severe criticism of party organization had been voiced after the Kabylie incidents, and the president was given complete powers to reshape it.

At its end-of-December 1979–Jan. 1, 1980, meeting the FLN decided to curtail dependence on foreign aid in order to reduce Algeria's foreign debt, currently $19 billion. Oil and gas exports were also to be reduced to conserve stocks, while oil prices were increased until by June the price for crude oil stood at $40 per barrel, including a $3 exploration surcharge. The government also intended to create parity between gas and oil prices.

The 1980–84 five-year plan, announced in June after a two-year delay, still favoured industry, which was to receive 38.6% of total investment. Agriculture, despite its current crisis—with 40% of arable land uncultivated—received only 6% of the $104 billion available. Education, housing, and health received increased investment.

The struggle in the western Sahara against Morocco by the Popular Front for the Liberation of Saguia el Hamra and Río de Oro (Polisario Front) continued to receive wholehearted Algerian support. Algeria also maintained links with Libya; new commercial agreements were signed at the fourth summit meeting between the two countries. The Libyan link created embarrassment when, in late January, the Tunisian town of Gafsa was attacked by Libyan-backed guerrillas, who entered the country from Algerian territory. The crisis subsided only when President Bendjedid visited Tunis in March.

In discussions within the Organization of Petroleum Exporting Countries, Algeria wanted to link oil prices to third world inflation rather than to the lower rate in the developed world. Algeria improved relations with France, signing agreements in late September over immigrant repatriation and social security matters.

At year's end Algeria acted as go-between in negotiations over the release of the U.S. hostages held in Iran. Ahmed Ben Bella, Algeria's first president, was freed in October after 15 years' detention.

ANGOLA

A large Soviet military mission visited Luanda in January 1980 and, coincidentally, the ruling party, the Popular Movement for the Liberation of Angola (MPLA), undertook a purge of all elements disagreeing with the Marxist party line. Pres. José Eduardo dos Santos also pledged total support for the independence struggles of the peoples of Zimbabwe, Namibia, and South Africa.

Backed by large quantities of Soviet military aid and encouraged by the improved efficiency of its troops—resulting from training by Soviet and Cuban military advisers—the government had launched a vigorous operation against Jonas

The town of El Asnam, Algeria, was almost totally leveled by an earthquake that struck on October 10, leaving an estimated 4,000 persons dead and thousands more injured.
UPI

South African troops
raided a SWAPO
headquarters in
southern Angola in full
force in June.
UPI

Savimbi's National Union for the Total Independence of Angola (UNITA) at the end of 1979. By April 1980 severe losses had been inflicted on the guerrillas. UNITA suffered another blow when Zaire's Pres. Mobutu Sese Seko, in a gesture of friendship to the Angolan government, refused the use of bases in Zaire to Savimbi's forces. Savimbi's hopes were further undermined when South Africa, disappointed by his lack of success, reduced the level of its assistance. UNITA's disruptive activities continued in 1980, but on a greatly reduced scale.

On August 10 UNITA saboteurs damaged oil storage tanks in the port of Lobito at the Atlantic end of the Benguela Railway. This raid, UNITA claimed, was carried out as a reprisal for the executions, earlier in the month, of 16 of its members found guilty of waging a bombing campaign in Luanda. A fortnight later, however, nine more rebels were executed after having been found guilty of similar bomb outrages. The government also claimed that as a result of its military successes large numbers of Savimbi's supporters, emaciated from lack of food and weak from disease, were returning to the settled areas and creating a serious problem for the local authorities.

With guerrilla activity reduced, the government was able to concentrate its attention on the enormous task of economic reconstruction. Increasing oil revenue gave hope that capital might become available to revive the country's industries and agriculture. At the same time, foreign investors were beginning to be tempted by the foreign investment law of June 1979, which allowed repatriation of profits, and by the growing political stability.

In April Angola was represented at an economic summit conference in Lusaka, Zambia, where leaders of several central and southern African states met to map plans for reducing their economic dependence on South Africa. One important aspect of this campaign was the need to provide an adequate, independent system of transport and communications. With this end in view, it was agreed to set up a southern African regional transport and communications commission.

In an attempt to improve efficiency, the president reorganized his Cabinet in July. Col. Pedro Maria Tonha was appointed minister of defense, and a Ministry of State Security was created with Kundi Paihama, formerly minister of the interior, as its head. There were also changes in the portfolios of health, labour, and social security, and Augusto Teixeira de Matos was appointed deputy minister of finance in charge of the budget.

South Africa continued to harass bases occupied by forces of the South West Africa People's Organization (SWAPO) inside Angola. Late in June a strong force of South African troops established a temporary base across the Angolan border from Namibia. This was followed by another raid in July, in which a number of Angolan troops and SWAPO guerrillas were killed.

ANIMALS AND WILDLIFE

Civil disorder in Uganda brought on a massive slaughter of wildlife in that country for such valuable items as ivory and rhino horn but also because its people were starving. In reports to the World Wildlife Fund in 1980, researchers said that poaching there had reached an unprecedented level. Of Uganda's three national parks, Kabalega, Rwenzori, and Kidepo, Kabalega was hardest hit. Its 19 rare northern white rhinos were gone, and the animal was now believed extinct in Uganda. Karl Van Orsdol, a wildlife scientist working in Rwenzori National Park since 1977, estimated that 14,000 of the 46,500 large mammals in the park had been killed, including Ugandan kob, buffalo, hippo, topi, elephant, and lion—a 30% loss in three and one-half months. Kidepo, located in fairly remote country, had escaped serious damage.

The problems began in the spring of 1979, with the fall of the Amin government. Retreating Amin troops slaughtered wildlife and looted park equipment, leaving park authorities with virtually no defense against gangs of poachers who moved in with sophisticated automatic weapons. In Rwenzori four park officials were killed. Other reports said that Tanzanian occupation troops killed large numbers of animals with machine guns, selling the meat to Ugandan civilians. The new Ugandan government announced a five-year ban on hunting in August, but the underequipped park authorities were having difficulty enforcing the ban. Conservation organizations, including the World Wildlife Fund, the New York Zoological Society, the Frankfurt Zoological Society, the Fauna Preservation Society, and the African Wildlife Leadership Foundation, set up a fund to rehabilitate the parks.

In recent years elephant populations of Africa have suffered drastic declines caused by poaching and habitat destruction. A three-year survey sponsored by the International Union for Conservation of Nature and Natural Resources reported that some 1,343,340 elephants were left on the continent, down from an estimated five million only five years earlier. The ivory trade accounted for from 50,000 to 150,000 elephants per year. While many restrictions had been placed on ivory trade, funding for enforcement had not kept up with the rising price of ivory. According to Ian Parker, in *The Ivory Trade Report*, a pair of elephant tusks could bring the poacher between $370 and $444, the equivalent of 8 to 17 months' wages.

Also suffering from overhunting was the African rhino. Rhino horns, actually dense masses of hair compacted into solid keratin, were thought to have magical and aphrodisiac powers in some cultures, and commanded a high price in the Orient. In addition, dagger handles carved from rhino horn were prized in the Middle East, and a growing number of men from the oil-rich states could now afford the expensive ($6,000) status symbol. Demand for the horn drove the three species of Asian rhino—Sumatran, Javan, and Great Indian—to the endangered level, and poachers turned to the African rhino to meet the continuing demand.

African rhino populations were down as much as 90% from just a few years earlier. Between 10,000 and 20,000 black rhinos and about 3,500 white rhinos remained alive in Africa, but at present levels of trade they would be gone within ten years.

Feral Burros

On May 19 Assistant Secretary of the Interior Robert Herbst ordered the removal of an estimated 350 feral burros from Grand Canyon National Park. (The number of animals later proved to be

BRUCE MCCLELLAN—WIDE WORLD

A cowboy with a burro across his saddle watches as another of the surplus animals is airlifted out of the Grand Canyon area to await adoption through a Fund for Animals program.

much greater.) Park officials said that the animals' trails and grazing habits were seriously damaging the park's ecology. The feral (once-domesticated animals gone wild) burros are descended from animals brought into the area by prospectors at the turn of the century. The National Park Service agreed to grant a 60-day trial period to allow the public to attempt to capture the burros alive. Burros that remained in the park after the trial would be shot if necessary.

The Fund for Animals, a New York-based group opposing the removal, arranged an effort to save the burros by airlifting them out of the canyon. Captured burros were available for adoption to people who agreed to allow Fund representatives to inspect the burros' living conditions to prevent mistreatment of the animals. The airlift began July 27; the first burros rescued were taken to homes in Colorado and to the Fund's ranch in Texas. By the year's end the Fund had brought 500 burros out of the park, and private individuals had rescued more. The organization planned to resume the effort in late autumn and, after a month's break, to continue in 1981. National Park Service spokesmen said that the government had no plans to begin shooting the burros as long as the live removal program was effective. They also noted that the government had tried airlifting the burros in the mid-1970s but found the $1,400-per-burro effort too expensive.

Panda Population Declines

Chinese scientists revealed in 1980 that the giant panda population had declined sharply in recent years owing to a genetic quirk of the bamboo plants upon which the panda's diet is based. The plants bloom en masse once about every 100 years and then die, leaving only seeds, which take several years to ripen to the point where they can provide nourishment for the pandas. Data on the panda population were difficult to gather because their habitat was mostly inaccessible mountain terrain, but researchers estimated that at least 140, and possibly many more, had died of starvation. No one knows how the pandas survived earlier periods when the bamboo died, but some scientists speculated that since they had a much wider range to forage in, the loss of the bamboo may not have had such serious consequences.

Dolphins Killed in Japan

The small Japanese island of Iki, 1,200 mi southwest of Tokyo, became the centre of an international uproar in 1980 when fishermen there killed at least 1,000 dolphins between February 28 and March 4. The fishermen blamed the dolphins for declining harvests of fish and insisted that the action was necessary to protect their livelihood. Witnesses on Goto Island, 110 mi southwest of Iki, said that fishermen there killed an additional 1,200 dolphins in shallow bays February 29. Two hundred carcasses were distributed to residents of nearby towns for food.

Because of its large population and small amount of arable land, Japan was heavily dependent on fish protein. That overharvesting and pollution had destroyed many of Japan's coastal fisheries was perhaps the reason the dolphins had moved into Iki's fishing grounds. Iki was once one of Japan's richest fisheries, but by the mid-1970s harvests had declined so much that fishermen began to methodically trap and kill the dolphins. In 1978, intending to arouse government awareness of their need for help, they announced their intention in a press conference. Their act unleashed a worldwide storm of protest. Nevertheless, the fishermen continued to kill the sea mammals, 1,368 in 1978 and 1,600 in 1979.

Dexter Cate, of Hilo, Hawaii, was arrested by the Japanese after he freed part of a group of dolphins that the fishermen had trapped in a nearby bay February 29. A field agent of the Fund for Animals, Cate was held in a Japanese prison for three

Dolphins killed by Japanese fishermen from Iki Island are hauled from the water to be processed into fertilizer. At least 1,000 of the animals were killed despite an international protest; local fishermen claimed that the dolphins were eating scarce fish needed for human food and that they had tried unsuccessfully to drive them away from fishing grounds.

HIDEYUKI—GAMMA/LIAISON

months, found guilty of "forcibly obstructing business," released on probation, and deported.

IWC Moves to Protect Orcas

Killer whales were added to the list of protected species at the 32nd annual meeting of the International Whaling Commission held in Brighton, England, in July. The action was taken to protect the small cetaceans in the light of reports that the Soviets took more than 900 of them in Antarctic "factory ships" in the 1979–80 season.

A move to end commercial whaling was blocked at the meeting. Only 13 of the commission's 24 member nations supported the indefinite moratorium, which required a three-fourths majority to pass. Canada and South Africa joined whaling nations Japan, the Soviet Union, South Korea, Iceland, Peru, Spain, and Chile. Two other whaling countries, Norway and Brazil, abstained. The same countries also blocked a Swedish proposal to begin the moratorium in two years, giving the whaling countries time to phase out the industry.

The IWC reduced the annual quota on whale kills to 14,553 for 1981, down 9.2% from 1980's 15,883. The pro-whaling coalition, led by Japan, also stopped a ban on killing sperm whales, but the commission sharply reduced the legal sperm whale kill from 1,350 to 890.

Arguing that a ban on hunting the critically endangered bowhead whale was unfair to Eskimo natives, who have been hunting bowheads in relatively small numbers for thousands of years, the United States asked the IWC not to reduce the bowhead whale quota from 1980's 18. The commission set a three-year quota of 65 struck, 45 landed, with no more than 17 landed in any single year. The U.S. position generated heated controversy, as conservationists pointed out that the bowhead herd in the Bering Sea was seriously threatened, numbering less than 2,500, down from an estimated 15,000 only a few years earlier.

The antiwhaling nations lost an attempt to win a total ban on the use of the "cold harpoon," a weapon that killed whales by allowing them to slowly bleed to death. Whalers would be permitted to use the cold harpoon only when hunting the plentiful minke whale. Cold harpoons were to be totally banned in the 1981–82 season.

Condor Recovery Program Begins

A planned 35-year program aimed at preventing the imminent extinction of the California condor, North America's largest land bird, got under way in 1980. Only 20 to 30 of the birds remained alive, in and around the Sespe Condor Sanctuary in Los Padres National Forest, northwest of Los Angeles. Early in the year field biologists located a nesting pair and observed a chick hatch—the first ever documented. Later they located a second chick. In the autumn they planned to live trap the birds, mark and sex them, take blood and tissue samples to determine their pesticide load, and to install radio transmitters on some birds. Eventually, scientists hoped to live trap several condors, breed them in captivity, and return their offspring to the wild. Devised after four years of study, the plan involved trying radical recovery techniques, which the researchers would first test on Andean condors in Peru. The plan's opponents, notably the environmental group Friends of the Earth, said that it was unnecessary and could hasten the condors' extinction. They suggested that alternative measures, such as cleaning up pesticides in the birds' habitat, expanding its protected range, and placing harsh restrictions on its use by humans, would make captive breeding unnecessary.

The worst fears of project opponents seemed to be confirmed June 30, when one of the chicks died while it was being examined in its nest by a field worker. The 13-lb nestling was flown to the San Diego Zoo for an autopsy, which showed that it had died of heart failure and shock. All permits for the project were immediately revoked. Supporters of the program announced that they would seek new permits, pointing out that the other chick was handled without mishap.

Government Action

On September 29 Pres. Jimmy Carter signed a bill establishing a matching-grant program to assist states in improving management of nongame fish and wildlife species. Nongame fish and wildlife are those species not hunted for sport, food, or fur. The law provided $5 million in each of fiscal years 1982 through 1985 to states that developed nongame fish and wildlife conservation plans following a complete inventory and assessment of wildlife resources. The legislation also ordered a Fish and Wildlife Service study of ways to finance the program besides through appropriations, such as the excise taxes that were funding the Dingell-Johnson and Pittman-Robertson conservation programs.

The U.S. House of Representatives cleared a bill increasing the penalties for illegal trade in fish and wildlife July 28. The legislation would combine the current Lacey and Black Bass acts into a single comprehensive law controlling interstate and foreign commerce in fish and wildlife. Current laws were not considered a deterrent to a multimillion-dollar black market that was a factor in driving rare species to extinction.

The Senate once again prohibited the use of funds appropriated for the Interior Department to enforce nontoxic-shot regulations on federal wildlife refuges in states that disagreed with those rules. The regulations were originally set by the Fish and Wildlife Service in an effort to reduce lead poisoning losses among migratory waterfowl. Two million to three million birds per year were dying after ingesting spent lead-shot pellets as they sought seeds and grit in shallow feeding areas.

(*See also* Environment; Zoos.)

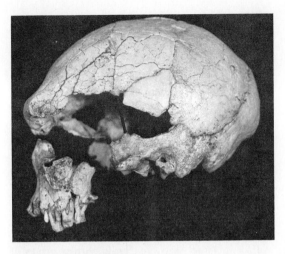

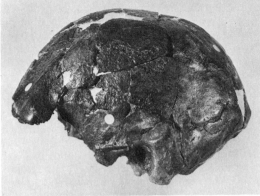

PHOTOS, COURTESY, PROFESSOR M. H. DAY, ST. THOMAS'S HOSPITAL MEDICAL SCHOOL, LONDON

Two skulls found in East Africa were judged by anthropologists to be representative of two types of early man: a skull from Tanzania (left) could be a link between Homo sapiens *and* Homo erectus, *while a skull from Ethiopia about 10,000 years older was thought to be an early form of* Homo erectus.

ANTHROPOLOGY

In 1976 a fossil early human skull was recovered from the Ngaloba beds at Laetoli in northern Tanzania. This skull, first reported in 1980, served to focus attention on the problem of the first appearance of *Homo sapiens.* The Ngaloba skull is that of a male who lived at the very end of the Middle Pleistocene period, about 120,000 years ago. It is particularly interesting because it shows a mixture of characteristics linking it both to the earlier *Homo erectus* phase of human evolution and to modern *Homo sapiens.* The long, low contour of this skull and its large browridge, heavy face, angled occipital region, and exceptionally thick bone are all characteristics found in *Homo erectus.* However, the general expansion of the braincase, particularly in the parietal region, is a characteristic of *Homo sapiens.*

Fully modern populations of *Homo sapiens* are known from Europe, Africa, and Asia from the period beginning about 40,000 years ago. Modern human populations may also have been present in North America at this time.

One of the major unanswered questions in anthropology is the course of evolution that led to the appearance of fully modern *Homo sapiens* from *Homo erectus* ancestors. *Homo erectus* first appears in Africa and Java in the Early Pleistocene period, prior to 1.5 million years ago, and is known throughout the early part of the Middle Pleistocene from these areas as well as from China and Europe. These *Homo erectus* fossils have considerably smaller brain sizes than do later representatives of this species. The Ngaloba skull is consistent with this trend and suggests that at least some of the features characterizing these modern populations result from the continued expansion of the brain.

However, there are a number of factors that argue against the appearance of modern *Homo sapiens* merely as the result of a gradual increase in brain size in the *Homo erectus* ancestors. Other African early human skulls have been found that are of the same general age as Ngaloba but are diverse in form.

Understanding of the emergence of *Homo sapiens* from *Homo erectus* ancestors is complicated not only by the diversity of skeletal material from Africa but also by the diversity of later Middle and Late Pleistocene fossil material from other areas of the world. In Europe the Steinheim skull from Germany (about 250,000 years old) and the Swanscomb skull from England (also about 250,000 years old) show many modern features, while the Arago material from Spain is strongly reminiscent of older populations. In Java the Solo population of 11 skulls, which may be early Upper Pleistocene in age, are very like *Homo erectus* in form.

A particular problem facing anthropologists is the position of Neanderthal man in human evolution. Neanderthal man is a type of early human being who lived from about 90,000 years ago to about 40,000 years ago. It has the same robusticity of skull form as the earlier African hominids, but it also has unique features of the face and postcranial skeleton. These have led many anthropologists to consider it as representing an extinct race of human beings that occupied Europe during the early advances of the last glacial period.

The idea that there were at least two very distinct racial types of human beings in this period is confirmed by the presence of much more gracile and modern skulls from the Near Eastern area, in particular the Jebel Qafzeh and Skhul remains from Israel. Most anthropologists believe that these Near Eastern fossils represent the parent population of modern Europeans. However, Europe and the Near East comprise a relatively restricted area of the world. Understanding of recent human evolution is marred by an unfortunate absence of fossils recording the appearance of *Homo sapiens* in other areas.

Late in 1979 an extremely interesting skull was reported from Cossack in Western Australia. This is a skull of a male who may have lived as recently as 6,500 years ago. It is important because, at this late date, it shows features that are very different from contemporaneous populations elsewhere in the world. The skull is long, the forehead slopes sharply backward, the face is large with the jaw-bones jutting beyond the upper face, the supraorbital margins are well developed, and the bone making up the skull is very thick. In form, this skull is similar to other robust craniums from southeastern Australia. At the same time, other skulls found in southeastern Australia are more lightly built and range in age from 26,000 years ago at Lake Mungo to 13,000 years ago at Keilor to 6,000 years ago at Green Gully. These two groups of fossils clearly show that there was greater variation in human skull form in Australia at this time than there is between any of the modern races of human beings.

It has been suggested that these two different Australian populations may have entered Australia via two different migration routes as early as 40,000 years ago: a gracile group via Indochina, Borneo, and New Guinea, and a robust group via Timor. If this idea proves correct, it points to the conclusion that, prior to about 40,000 years ago, there was greater variation among human populations throughout the world than there is today. Besides the distinction between Neanderthal man and the more modern Near Eastern populations, there is the distinction between the robust southern Asian parent population and the more gracile northern Asian parent population of the second Australian group. (*See also* Archaeology.)

ARCHAEOLOGY

Archaeologists with field programs in southwestern Asia understandably had a nervous year in 1980. Essentially, nothing could be done in Iran, and there were rumours that the remains of one important and well-known site, dated far earlier than the beginnings of Islam, were being bulldozed away. In the autumn the Iran-Iraq war made excavations impossible in Iraq as well, nor were conditions for fieldwork propitious in Lebanon and Syria.

As usual, there were caprices. Earlier in the year, the Iraqi antiquity authorities had demanded the return of all excavated antiquities, whether or not these had come from bona fide excavations and thus had been legally "divided" between the government's antiquity service and the excavators. When war came, bombs fell near the Baghdad museum. Workmen near Cairo, doing restoration on the Sphinx, overzealously began dismantling the beast's left front paw and were hurriedly made to desist. During the past few years, there had been much publicity and a movie (*In Search of Noah's Ark*) purporting that wood found on Mt. Ararat, in Turkey, came from the remains of the biblical Ark. By 1980 specimens of the wood had been assayed by the carbon-14 method in five different and highly reputable laboratories; the age determinations, far

too late for Noah, clustered about AD 600 to 800, with only one earlier, at AD 270.

There was news that Chinese archaeologists had resumed work at the cave where Peking man was found in the 1920s. New age determinations of *c.* 460,000 BP (before present), stone tools, and a new skull were reported. The useful new journal *Early Man News* indicated much activity by Soviet prehistorians on such well-known paleolithic sites as Kostenki and Borshevo, as well as on sites in the Ukraine and about the Caucasus.

In Egypt the remains of a very ruined (evidently purposely) pyramid of the son of the pharaoh Khufu was under excavation. The son, Djedefre, reigned only briefly and came to an unknown end. It was hoped that his remains might be encountered. A Tel-Aviv University excavation at Tell Aphek in Israel recovered an important group of cuneiform letters. In Jerusalem, Hebrew University archaeologists believed they might have encountered the palace-fortress of King David or King Solomon.

Investigations on sites of Greco-Roman age and contact included the underwater ruins of palaces claimed to be those of Cleopatra and Mark Antony in Alexandria Harbour, Egypt. At Quseir al-Qadim, a small Egyptian port on the Red Sea, Roman and early Islamic remains with important implications for the history of trade were uncovered. Another port, Caesarea in northern Israel, was being studied by means of submersible vacuum cleaners and scuba divers. In Cyprus new architectural clearances were made on the sanctuary of Apollo Hylates near the ancient city of Kourion. The international salvage effort at Carthage, in Tunisia, was in its final stages. As a comment on the vast reach of Roman influence, at least in attenuated form, potsherds of roulette decorated pottery—well identified as *c.* AD 1 to 200 Romano-Indian from finds on the Madras coast—were found in northwest Java.

In Greece itself the work of the various foreign institutes proceeded, and a Royal Ontario Museum excavation at a port town in southern Crete continued. In Rome there was increased concern over the destructive effect on the monuments of air pollution and the September 1979 earthquake tremors. Within Rome an ingenious example of archaeological investigation was going forward. Using earth drillings and test pits in a variety of central city building basements, Edmund Buchner (president of the German Archaeological Institute) was well advanced in the recovery and plotting of the grid pattern of the emperor Augustus's great sundial; originally, the peak of a transported Egyptian obelisk had cast the critical shadow on the grid in a city square. New excavations at Herculaneum hinted that many residents did die during the Vesuvius eruption that also buried Pompeii. The Pompeii ruins were reported seriously damaged by the November earthquake.

An elaborate radar system developed for use in space exploration revealed on Earth an intricate network of irrigation canals in the forests of Guatemala and Belize. The canals were believed to be 1,000 years old. The lower photo is an older radar image, while the top photo, with the more advanced radar, shows the canals clearly.

PHOTOS, UPI

Early Man News contained Thurstan Shaw's fine summary of Late Stone Age finds in West Africa. From China came word that a new type of characteristic pottery found in southeast coastal China—a black or red, shell- or fingernail-impressed ware—had been identified for the time range of about 6,000 years ago. The key collection was made on the island of Quemoy. Australian investigators established that New Guinea became inhabited by 50,000 years ago and that both wet and dry systems of horticulture were already in use by 9,000 years ago. Some of the smaller Melanesian islands were not inhabited until later, but by 3,000 years ago exotic materials had already reached islands as much as 3,000 km (1,850 mi) away.

Western Hemisphere

In South Dakota a 4.5-m (15-ft)-deep mass grave, containing 500 bodies and dating to between AD 900 and 1400, was exposed during a severe inbank erosion of the Missouri River and excavated by Thomas Emerson of the University of South Dakota Archaeological Laboratory. Knife cuts on the skulls suggested that scalping was practiced in precolonial times. Interruptions in the growth rings on bones indicated both malnutrition and the likelihood of drought conditions in this late prehistoric period. The predominance of male skeletons suggests that the massacre was selective; women and girls were probably taken as captives. This picture of drought and intergroup conflict was quite different from the pre-contact perfection previously assumed by some scholars.

An 18-m (60-ft)-deep gorge near the Mexican border in California, exposed by Tropical Storm Kathleen in 1976, made possible a find that rekindled the debate over the antiquity of man in the New World. The more conservative and accepted position had been that fluted points dating to c.

12,000 BP are the earliest traces of human activity in the hemisphere. Morlin Childers and Herbert Munsell of the Imperial Valley College Museum, Imperial, Calif., found what appear to be human-made stone tools in a location and geological context suggesting a date between 50,000 and 100,000 BP, although the antiquity of the find had yet to be tested by laboratory methods.

Perhaps the most exciting archaeological revelation in Mesoamerica was provided by advanced remote-sensing technology. Until recently, many scholars had agreed that the ancient Maya lived in their jungle environment by the intensive use of shifting, slash-and-burn agriculture. From radar pictures taken in a 1978 aerial radar survey by the Jet Propulsion Laboratory of Pasadena, Calif., Richard Adams of Cambridge University and T. Patrick Culbert were able to detect an extensive network of canals and field systems under the forest near the Pasión River in Guatemala. When checked on the ground, these faint radar images were documented as 3-m (10-ft)-wide and 0.6-m (2-ft)-deep ditches from which the rich sediments were scooped to raised agricultural plots, much like those in the surviving Aztec floating garden in Mexico City. This clearly suggests that Maya civilization was dependent on intensive irrigation agriculture and that many of the so-called Maya "temples" may have been administrative buildings necessary to oversee the construction and maintenance of the elaborate canal system.

Excavations by Terrence Greider of the University of Texas in the little-known Andean Valley of Pallasca, 800 km (500 mi) north and 160 km (100 mi) inland from the coastal capital of Lima, revealed what may be the earliest and largest temple complex yet known in Peru. The La Calgada site contains the remains of two large preceramic temples and a cluster of dwellings dated by carbon-14

The remains of a massive structure in Turkey, which archaeologists called the earliest known monumental building, were determined to date from about 7500 BC.
COURTESY, UNIVERSITY OF CHICAGO

to between 1800 and 2400 BC. The inhabitants practiced agriculture and lived in thatched structures with stone foundations. This site also produced what may be the earliest multicoloured dyed textiles yet identified in South America.

(*See also* Anthropology.)

ARCHITECTURE

The need to conserve energy remained a major topic of concern for architects in 1980. The U.S. Department of Energy proposed a set of standards that posed increasingly complex problems for architects and engineers. Pres. Jimmy Carter's administration submitted a proposal to Congress for tax incentives to encourage the use of passive solar heating and cooling in both houses and nonresidential buildings. Under the proposals builders of suitable buildings would qualify for a tax credit.

Careful consideration was given to energy conservation in the design by Davis, Brody and Associates of the new biochemistry laboratory for Princeton University. It has four distinct elevations, each responding to a different environmental factor. Large areas of glass were used on the east and west walls, where maximum daylight was required. On the south wall, where the intensity of the sun was greatest, the glazed areas were small, and the north facade was nearly blank.

In the quest for designs that made economical use of energy, common sense and good design practice remained foremost. Many design features, such as atriums, courts, skylights, sun-control devices, and window patterns were inspired by energy considerations.

Public and Commercial Buildings

In New York City plans were finally agreed upon, after years of controversy, for the new Expo-

sition and Convention Center designed by I. M. Pei & Partners in association with Lewis, Turner Partnership. The design appeared to be a series of rectangular and cubic forms made of reflective glass on a steel space frame. Contrasting areas of opaque and translucent glass varied the exteriors. The structure would offer the largest exhibition space ever contained within a single building. Designs showed a 500,000-sq-ft exhibition hall adjacent to a skylighted central hall defined by a dramatic 130-ft-high interior space. Pei described his design as inspired by the Grand Palais in Paris, a vast 19th-century exhibition hall of steel and glass.

Architects Marvin DeWinter Associates chose a right isosceles triangle as the shape for the Gerald R. Ford Presidential Museum in Grand Rapids, Mich. The two-story building, which borders the Grand River, was scheduled for completion in the winter of 1980–81 with formal dedication planned for July 4, 1981. The main design feature was on the long side of the triangular building, where a 300-ft-long mirrored glass wall recessed under an overhang faced the river. The two other sides of the building were of thick concrete, intended partly to insulate the museum from noise generated by a nearby freeway.

The geometric theme of the Merck, Sharp & Dohme headquarters at West Point, Pa., was a series of three three-story square elements set at 45° angles and connected at diagonally opposed corners. Designed by Marcel Breuer Associates of New York, it provided 117,000 sq ft of accommodation. Completion was expected to be in mid-1981.

Right angles and diagonals, the square, and the triangle are central to the "field theory" of architect Walter Netsch of Skidmore, Owings & Merrill. This strict geometric formula was the rationale behind his design for the Miami University Art Museum in Oxford, Ohio. Based on a series of geometric forms in increasing volumes, with emphatic use of diagonals, it combined the square and the triangle to develop a series of exhibition galleries in proportionate sizes, the smaller ones for display of prints and drawings and the bigger for such larger-scale works as sculpture.

Simple rectangular forms predominated in the design of the highly praised shopping centre for Milton Keynes in England, which opened in 1980. The centre, designed by architects of the Milton Keynes Development Corp., won two major awards, the European Steel Award and a 1980 Royal Institute of British Architects (RIBA) prize. The pyramidal elevation of the main front was reminiscent both of classical design and of Art Deco. Reflective and clear glass were widely used, and the arcades let in daylight, in contrast to many pedestrian shopping malls of the last decade. The simple and clearly organized forms were praised as combining the best of functional design with the excitement and variety of technological gloss.

The Atheneum, New Harmony, Ind., by Richard Meier & Partners was also an exercise in geometric organization, this time in the well-known Neo-Modernist genre, of which Meier was a leading exponent. The building, which houses a visitors' orientation centre, owes much to the International Style of the 1920s and 1930s with its contrast of solid volumes and open spaces, flat white surfaces, lack of ornament, and shiplike staircases and railings. The steel frame is clad in white porcelain panels. The facade is defined by a projecting triangular volume at one end and the open space of staircases balancing this at the opposite end. Though the plan itself is almost a square, the main facade incorporates both a curve and an angle. It is a superb example of geometry as a generator of form.

Restoration and Renovation

"Recycling" of historic buildings continued to provide interesting results. One of the most highly praised of such projects in 1980 was the restoration by architects of the Greater London Council's Historic Buildings Division of the Central Market in London's Covent Garden. The original market building, in a Greek Revival idiom, was built about 1830 to designs by Charles Fowler. The building was vacated when the market moved south of the River Thames in 1974. It was restored to house a variety of stalls, restaurants, shops, pubs, and boutiques on two levels. An undoubted architectural success, the project was to be studied to determine whether it would be equally successful in economic terms. If it was, a similar development might come to fruition for Billingsgate Market, London's wholesale fish market soon to vacate its historic site, where Chrysalis Associates and Ove Arup were commissioned to design a commercial project.

Jung/Brannen Associates converted part of the old Boston Chamber of Commerce building into ar-

COURTESY, I. M. PEI & PARTNERS, NEW YORK

The skyline of Singapore is now dominated by the 52-story Oversea-Chinese Banking Corp. building by I. M. Pei & Partners.

chitects' offices. The original granite structure, incorporating a dramatic rotunda 75 ft in diameter, dates from 1890–92 and was designed by Shepley, Rutan & Coolidge. The new offices made use of white surfaces with oak trimming, blending them successfully with the historic original.

Awards

In an effort to improve the quality of federal architecture in the U.S., Sen. Daniel Moynihan (Dem., N.Y.) presented a bill to Congress proposing that a post of federal "supervising architect" be created. The federal government employed such an

COURTESY, RICHARD MEIER & PARTNERS; PHOTO, EZRA STOLLER © 1979 ESTO

The Atheneum in New Harmony, Indiana, designed by Richard Meier & Partners, houses a visitors' orientation centre for the town. The exterior of the building is clad in white porcelain panels.

architect until 1939, attached to the Department of the Treasury, to oversee standards. The bill also suggested the adoption of a "Statement of Principles of Architectural Excellence for Public Buildings." Among the proposals was a requirement for design competitions for major projects. Reac-

tions to the proposals were initially favourable.

The American Institute of Architects presented its annual awards in June. Among the winners were the Rouse Co. for its restoration of the historic Faneuil Hall Market Place in Boston; Cyril M. Harris, architectural acoustician, teacher, and lex-

A winner of two major awards was this shopping centre in Milton Keynes, England. The centre won the European Steel Award and a Royal Institute of British Architects prize.
BUILDING

COURTESY, JUNG/BRANNEN ASSOCIATES INC.; PHOTO, © PETER VANDERWARKER

Imaginative use of existing structures continued to capture the creativity of city architects. Jung/Brannen Associates Inc. converted part of the 1890 Chamber of Commerce building in Boston into architects' offices featuring white surfaces with oak trimming.

icographer; *Progressive Architecture* magazine for its annual design awards program; M. Paul Friedberg, landscape architect and urban designer; and Lady Bird Johnson, for her efforts to promote national beautification and natural preservation.

The 1980 Pritzker Architectural Prize was awarded to Luis Barragán, a Mexican landscape architect whose most famous work was the 1940s design of El Pedregal, a residential complex in Mexico City set among gardens carved out of volcanic terrain. His designs were praised for their romantic evocation of Mexico's past and future.

The RIBA Gold Medal for 1980 was awarded to James Stirling. His early major works included the pioneering "brutalist" University of Leicester Engineering Building, the History Faculty Library for the University of Cambridge, and the Olivetti Training School, Haslemere.

(*See also* Engineering Projects; Landmarks and Monuments.)

ARCTIC AND ANTARCTIC

According to the Atlantic Richfield Co. (ARCO) at the end of June 1980, the third anniversary of the

trans-Alaska pipeline, more than 1,260,000,000 bbl of oil had been transported from the Prudhoe Bay oil fields. Other statistics showed that the oil had been loaded onto 1,670 tankers at the Valdez, Alaska, terminal for shipment to markets and that the production rate of 1.5 million bbl per day comprised 17% of the total U.S. domestic oil production. Earlier in 1980 the Alaska Oil and Gas Conservation Commission reported that proven oil reserves in the Prudhoe Bay field amounted to 8,400,000,000 bbl as of January 1. The same report also indicated that the total value of Alaskan oil and gas production in 1979 was $5,585,129,000, a 200% increase over 1978.

In a significant step forward for the construction of a natural gas pipeline, the Canadian government in July granted approval to Foothills Pipe Lines (Yukon) Ltd. to proceed with construction of about 2,400 km (1,500 mi), or 30% of the total project, which was designed to move gas from Prudhoe Bay in Alaska through Canada to the United States.

In July the first sale of natural gas from the Canadian Arctic Islands, worth more than $4 billion during the life of the project, was announced by

The Soviet Union initiated an air route from Moscow to the Antarctic to facilitate travel for scientists. The runway is composed of compressed snow.

the Arctic Pilot Project, a consortium led by Petro-Canada. The sales agreements, scheduled to begin in 1983, called for Arctic Islands gas to be shipped by tankers to eastern Canada, which would free gas in western Canada for export to the U.S.

Greenland Eskimos, claiming that the $1.5 billion project would destroy the environment and the sources of their traditional fishing and sealing economy, objected to the initial shipping routes proposed. Their opposition forced Petro-Canada to move the tanker routes away from the Greenland coast toward the centre of the 480-km (300-mi)-wide Davis Strait.

In March it was announced that the world's most northerly weather station was in operation at Malloch Dome on Ellef Ringnes Island in the Canadian Arctic Islands. The unmanned station, using a satellite communication system, was established to gather meteorological data to assist in the design and operation of a liquefied natural gas port facility at Ellef Ringnes Island.

In May *Canada Weekly* reported the biggest natural gas discovery to date in the Canadian Arctic Islands, just south of King Christian Island. A gas flow of 2.3 million hl (8.2 million cu ft) per day was reported from a drilling operation that was conducted from an ice platform in about 240 m (800 ft) of water.

Eskimos

"Nunavut," an Eskimo word meaning "Our Land," was the name of a proposed new province covering most of the area above the tree line in Canada. The approximately 17,000 Eskimos living there made specific proposals regarding political and administrative changes that would eventually result in full provincial status for the area. The idea appeared to gain momentum during the year among the Eskimos, who were demanding greater local control over all social, economic, and land-use activities. The Canadian government was reluctant to approve the plan, however, because of the oil, gas, and other resource developments taking place in the region that might conflict with the traditional Eskimo way of life.

Arctic natives from Greenland, Canada, and Alaska met in Godthab, Greenland, late in June at the second Inuit Circumpolar Conference to develop and promote a comprehensive policy. The conference considered a charter to establish a permanent organization and addressed itself to the Arctic aspects of such matters as culture, development, education, and health.

Antarctica

During 1979–80 the 13 Antarctic Treaty nations plus West and East Germany completed an agreement for the conservation and management of Antarctica's living marine resources. Initialed in Canberra, Australia, in May and signed in September, the agreement applies to the entire ecosystem —all the living resources—south of the Antarctic Convergence. It would enter into force following ratification by 8 of the 15 nations. A permanent commission would be established in Hobart, Tasmania, to monitor compliance.

The major U.S. effort in Antarctica was concentrated in the Ellsworth Mountains. Although initially delayed by bad weather and search efforts for the Air New Zealand DC-10 that crashed in 1979, the two-year scientific program was completed in one season. Fossil plants and fauna 500 million years old were discovered; they had been deposited when Antarctica was located only 5° from the Equator. Shallow ice cores were drilled at the Soviet Union's Vostok Station, and a hot-water drill was used to make 37 holes at Dome C for seismic measurements of the ice cover. Marine geology surveys in and near the Ross Sea revealed several submarine canyons, the largest of which was 1,000 m (3,280 ft) deep and 100 km (60 mi) long. An undersea mountain chain 24 km (15 mi) long was discovered off Cape Adare.

ARGENTINA

The military junta headed by Pres. Jorge Rafael Videla in October 1980 nominated Gen. Roberto Viola as military president to assume office in March 1981 for a three-year term. The question of the reinstatement of a civilian government remained unclear. The minister of the interior, Gen. Albano Harguindeguy, suggested that the nation could be returned to civilian rule in 1984 if it succeeded in its antileftist campaign. Two basic conditions had been established by the armed forces for the restoration of a civilian government. The first one, published in a document at the end of 1979, was the institutionalization of the armed forces' participation in government. The second was made clear by General Viola in April 1980 and established that there should be "no revision of what had happened during the fight against terrorism," or, in the blunter words of the minister of the interior, "no victorious army was ever asked to explain its behaviour during a war."

Yet the government continued to face pressure both locally and abroad to explain the disappearance of thousands of people in recent years. International organization reports concluded that the "disappeared" people must be presumed dead. The U.S. government report on human rights, published on February 5, indicated that after 1976 the security forces embarked on a widespread countercampaign of violence against elements of society considered subversive and that there was evidence of torture, arbitrary arrest, invasion of homes, and suspension of political freedom by those forces. This report agreed in general terms with that produced by the Inter-American Commission on Human Rights, which visited the country in September 1979. The report of this commission, which had been established by the Organization of American States, was published in Argentina on April 18, 1980. The government of Argentina answered it publicly by stating that it was neither objective nor

Gen. Roberto Viola (right) was nominated as military president of Argentina, to take office in 1981, succeeding the junta headed by Pres. Jorge Rafael Videla (left).

balanced. A mission of the New York City Bar Association that visited Argentina in 1979 reported the number of disappearances as 10,000, and Amnesty International increased that figure to 15,000–20,000.

The government response to the international reports was not aimed at clarifying the situation of those who were missing but at explaining the necessity of all actions committed in pursuit of victory during the "war." But on August 14 there was a public demonstration organized by the Madres de Plaza de Mayo (Mothers of the Plaza de Mayo), a group including relatives of those who had disappeared. The 1980 Nobel Peace Prize, awarded to Adolfo Pérez Esquivel (*see* Nobel Prizes), an Argentine sculptor and leader of a Christian peace movement in Latin America, was accepted by Pérez in the name of disappeared persons.

On the external front the government refused on January 10 to participate in imposing the grain embargo against the Soviet Union organized by the U.S. In consequence the U.S.S.R. became an important commercial partner for Argentina in 1980, as a purchaser of beef and grains. Unlike the West, the Soviet Union adopted a low profile on the human rights situation in Argentina.

Relations with the U.S. were not good during 1980. After the Argentine rejection of the grain embargo against the Soviet Union, there were some signs of improvement when a mission headed by U.S. Deputy Secretary of Commerce Luther Hodges, Jr., visited the country, and the Export-Import Bank announced preliminary loan commitments for the Yacyreta hydroelectric project. However, an announced visit by the U.S. assistant secretary of state for inter-American affairs, William Bowdler, in late July was canceled following

Argentina's recognition of the military junta in Bolivia. Suggestions that its government was involved in the Bolivian coup were rejected by Argentina, but President Videla made it explicit that his sympathies lay with the new Bolivian government, and a $50 million credit was to be granted to that country.

ART AND ART EXHIBITIONS

For several years it had been said that the days of large, lavish loan exhibitions of works of art were past, but some major shows of the "old" order were mounted in 1980, notwithstanding the ever increasing costs of transportation and insurance coupled with the problems posed by economic recession. "The Avant-Garde in Russia, 1910–1930: New Perspectives" was an example of this genre. Shown at the Los Angeles County Museum of Art, it was the first major exhibition ever devoted to this subject in a museum in the U.S. The huge exhibition of more than 450 works by 40 artists covered all aspects of art and the decorative arts, including many distinctive and individual areas, culminating in Suprematism (which reached its definitive form in the paintings of K. Malevich) and Constructivism. All the exhibits were drawn from non-Communist sources, essential since material of this kind was now considered anti-Soviet. The art of this period in Russia represented one of the great art movements of the 20th century and was an art of ideas and form. Works by El Lissitzky and V. Tatlin were among those shown. The exhibition was due to travel from Los Angeles to the Hirshhorn Museum and Sculpture Garden, Washington, D.C.

"Post-Impressionism—Cross-Currents in European Painting" was another vast and varied exhibition with something to interest all visitors from the hedonistic to the academic. Mounted at the Royal Academy of Art in London in the winter and moved, with some changes, to the National Gallery of Art, Washington, D.C., in May 1980, it afforded an opportunity to study the complex interrelationships that existed in the fine arts in France, Germany, Britain, The Netherlands, Belgium, Italy, and Scandinavia from about 1880. The subtitle was a more accurate reflection of the scope of the show, since the Postimpressionists themselves represented only a small sector of the artists on display. The show was really a comprehensive survey of European modern art of the period 1880 to 1905. High points included an entire wall of Gauguins, some splendid works by Van Gogh, and the Pointillists, including Seurat. In most rooms the artists were grouped by nationality rather than style. Multiple visits would have been required for the visitor wishing to absorb fully all the visual material in this enormous show.

Also ambitious in scope and size was the Arts Council of Great Britain's exhibition devoted to the 1930s, mounted in late autumn of 1979. "British Art and Design Before the War" was an attempt to place visual arts, architecture, and design into a social and historical context that included material relating to science and engineering, press photographs of society events, and items referring to various leftist organizations. This was arguably less successful than the display of objects themselves, which included items inspired by the Arts and Crafts Movement, Jazz Style, International Style, and Avant Garde Modern Movement furniture and textiles. The display of textiles, always difficult to show, was particularly imaginative; here they were hung vertically, falling in folds as if they were curtains.

"Hommage à Monet" at the Grand Palais, Paris, from February to May 1980 was another "modern movement" retrospective and brought together the artist's best works from all periods of his life. Examples came from as far afield as the U.S. and the U.S.S.R. The selection was careful and thus not too overwhelming. An important retrospective devoted to the work of Eugène Viollet-le-Duc, the 19th-century French "Gothic Revival" architect, restorer, painter, and theorist, was seen at the Grand Palais from February to May. At the same time, the École des Beaux-Arts held a smaller show chronicling the artist's visit to Italy. The exhibition, organized to mark the centenary of his death in 1879, reassessed his importance and influence.

The Grand Palais was the venue for a show of Picasso's works, later to be housed in the new Musée Picasso, scheduled to open in 1981. This legacy, which had taken some six years to sort out, included paintings, sketches, sculpture, and prints that the artist had retained for his own collection throughout his life. The show was seen from October 1979 to January 1980.

Many of these works were shown at the Walker Art Center, Minneapolis, Minn., before going on to become part of the immense "Pablo Picasso: A Retrospective," which opened at the Museum of Modern Art in New York City in May. Filling all of MOMA's gallery space, the Picasso show included almost 1,000 items, illustrating the many media in which Picasso had worked and ranging from his early conventional paintings through many periods and styles to works done in old age. The cumulative impact on the viewer was overwhelming, confirming the artist's unique and seminal position in 20th-century art. The exhibition had been assembled by William Rubin, director of MOMA's department of painting and sculpture, and Dominique Bozo, future curator of the Musée Picasso. It would probably never be duplicated, since many of the works, finally freed from the legal entanglements surrounding Picasso's estate, were destined for permanent disposition elsewhere. "Guernica," the huge antiwar mural housed at MOMA for many years, was to go to Spain in accordance with the artist's wishes.

Twentieth-century art was also the theme of "Abstraction: Towards a New Art—Painting 1910–

A massive retrospective of the works of Pablo Picasso was mounted by the Museum of Modern Art in New York City in the summer. Almost 1,000 works of Picasso were assembled for the show, representing the artist's prodigious output over 75 years of active work.

20" at the Tate Gallery, London, in the spring. Its professed aim was to explain abstract art by elucidating the problem of abstraction itself. Although the approach was a scholarly one, the works were allowed to speak for themselves, and it was clear how, as artists freed their perception from the visible world, many varied forms of abstraction emerged, such as Cubism, De Stijl, Suprematism, Vorticism, and Futurism. Emphasis was on three major figures of the decade: Malevich, Mondrian, and Kandinsky. Key items were lent from collections in Munich, West Germany, Paris, The Netherlands, and New York City.

Another important 20th-century art movement was Surrealism, and the work of its most famous exponent, Salvador Dali, was shown at the Tate Gallery in 1980 in what was said to be the first major exhibition of the artist's work in Britain. The exhibition had been seen previously at the Centre National d'Art et de Culture Georges Pompidou (the Beaubourg) in Paris. Describing Dali's art in *Apollo*, James Burr wrote: "His greatest achievement is to give reality and substance to the elusive nightmare horror of subconscious fantasies that molest us in dreams."

A series of exhibitions was mounted in Florence, Italy, by the Council of Europe as its 16th Exhibition of Art, Science, and Culture. The subject of this ambitious series was "Florence and the Tuscany of the Medici in Sixteenth-Century Europe." A section entitled "The Primacy of Drawing" presented a wide survey of examples of the draftsman's art, including works by Michelangelo, Leonardo da Vinci, Pontormo, Bronzino, and Cellini. Another fascinating section, "The Medici as Collectors," was exhibited in the Palazzo Vecchio. In the church of Santo Stefano al Ponte, "Religious Life in Florence in the Sixteenth Century," arranged by the archbishop of Florence, took as its theme Florentine religion after Savanarola. "Power and Space" dealt with fortifications, building, and urbanism, while "The Princely Stage" was devoted to theatres of the court. Other exhibitions included "The Rebirth of Science" and "Astrology, Magic, and Alchemy." Though the group of exhibitions centred on Florence, complementary regional exhibitions were shown throughout Tuscany.

A show at the Pierpont Morgan Library in New York City from December 1979 to March 1980, "William and Mary and Their House," was an exhibition of trophies from the Dutch Royal Collections from the time of William the Silent to Queen

"*Treasures from the Bronze Age of China*" *toured U.S. cities in 1980. Featured in the show were a huge bronze cauldron from 1030 BC (above) and six life-size terra-cotta figures of soldiers and two of their horses, part of an incredible 7,000-man army found buried in Shaanxi Province near the Yellow River.*

COURTESY, THE METROPOLITAN MUSEUM OF ART; PHOTOS, SETH JOEL

Juliana but focusing on King William and Queen Mary of England. The highlights of the show were opulent items of silver furniture. The bicentenary of the death in 1779 of the most famous actor of 18th-century England, David Garrick, was celebrated in an exhibition at the British Library in London, opened in 1979. The show illustrated Garrick's career as an actor and manager with costumes, mezzotints, engravings, and other items. The centrepiece was a marble sculpture of Garrick by Louis-François Roubilliac.

"The Art of Hollywood," sponsored by a television company and exhibited at the Victoria and Albert Museum, London, from October 1979 to January 1980, featured many early designs for pictures, some from the beginning of the 20th century. Enjoyable and flamboyant, it was entered through an "Alhambra" foyer and included a model of an early "picture palace," complete with cardboard silhouettes of an audience in cloches and boaters.

"The Vikings," at the British Museum from February to July and later shown at the Metropolitan Museum of Art in New York City, included objects illustrating every aspect of the Viking world. Items showing clothing, jewelry, trade, coinage, and the emergence of Christianity were included, many lent from Scandinavian museums. They ranged from gilt bronze jewelry of great delicacy and finesse to impressive examples of monumental sculpture.

In the U.S., as always, American themes were popular for major exhibitions. "American Light:

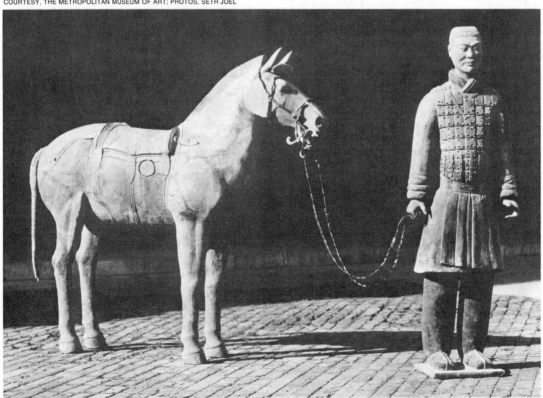

A replica of the Viking ship "Odin's Raven" rested in the forecourt of the British Museum in London for the five-month Viking Era exhibition, which later moved to the Metropolitan Museum of Art in New York City. The show was the most comprehensive ever attempted on the subject.

The Luminist Movement (1850–1870)," mounted by the National Gallery of Art, Washington, D.C., included a vast selection of American landscape paintings including works by Frederic E. Church and John F. Kensett. In all, there were 250 paintings, 40 drawings, and 24 photographs, most of them by relatively unknown artists. A retrospective exhibition of the American painter Edward Hopper, at the Whitney Museum in New York City, included little-known early works in the "French" style as well as the characteristic Realist paintings of the artist's later years. "A Man of Genius—The Art of Washington Allston" celebrated the 200th anniversary of the birth of this important 19th-century American artist, who spent the years from 1811 to 1818 in England. Organized by the Museum of Fine Arts, Boston, it later traveled to the Pennsylvania Academy of Fine Arts in Philadelphia.

"In Praise of America: 1650–1830" was the title of an exhibition at the National Gallery of Art in Washington, devoted entirely to American decorative art. It was the first such exhibition the gallery had held and was on view in the East Wing from February to July. Eighty pieces were chosen to illustrate the best in American design during the first 200 years of the country's history. Each piece in the show was displayed as a separate "rarity,"

and no attempt was made to create ensembles.

The work of Andrew Wyeth (b. 1917), celebrated for his images of American country life painstakingly observed and exquisitely executed, was shown at the Royal Academy, London, in the first major exhibition of Wyeth's work to be seen in Europe. A large one-man show devoted to his work had been mounted in New York City in 1967 at the Whitney Museum. The 60 tempera, watercolour, and dry brush paintings on display afforded English gallerygoers an opportunity to assess the artist's merits in an international context.

The Yale Center for British Art held the first large showing in the U.S. of works by the English Camden Town Group, including paintings by H. Gilman and Spencer Gore. The work of this early 20th-century group of painters was little known in the U.S. Also at Yale, the University Art Gallery showed a collection of American paintings and decorative objects from the Francis P. Garvan collection. The collection included about 10,000 pieces of silver, furniture, pewter, ceramics, textiles, glass, paintings, prints, and sculpture.

A number of shows devoted to sculpture were worthy of note. "The Romantics to Rodin: French Nineteenth-Century Sculpture from North American Collections" was organized for the Los Angeles

County Museum of Art and traveled to the Minneapolis Institute of Arts. Many pieces dusted off for the show had previously languished in museum cellars and storerooms. Works by Auguste Clessinger, Gustave Doré, and J.-P. Dantan were especially notable. "Twentieth-Century Sculptors and Their Drawings: Selections from the Hirshhorn Museum and Sculpture Garden," an interesting show organized as a circulating exhibition by the Smithsonian Institution Traveling Exhibition Service, included works by Barbara Hepworth, Archipenko, and Matisse.

The first comprehensive exhibition to be devoted to the work of the 18th-century French artist Jean-Honoré Fragonard since 1921 was staged in Japan at the National Museum of Western Art, Tokyo, and later at the Municipal Museum, Kyoto. The 90 oils and 73 drawings, assembled and cataloged by English art historian Denys Sutton, allowed a fresh assessment of this major artist. Over 200,000 visitors saw the show, and those unable to visit Japan could console themselves with the excellent catalog, in which every oil was illustrated in colour.

An exhibition devoted to 71 drawings by Ingres was shown at the Victoria and Albert Museum. Most of the drawings were on loan from the Musée Ingres, Montauban, France. Included were portraits, landscapes, and studies for history paintings. The finest works were undoubtedly the 20 portrait drawings, which ranged over a 70-year period and included a study of the artist's father done as a boy, as well as two of his mother, one in middle age and one showing her in old age. Organized by the Arts Council of Great Britain, the exhibition was small in scale but broad in scope.

An exhibition devoted to the work of the English artist Stanley Spencer at the Royal Academy, London, comprised 260 paintings and drawings and 16 murals, removed for the first time since their installation at the Oratory of All Souls, Burghclere, Hampshire. Portraits and landscapes predominated. An exhibition of work by the artist William Nicholson organized by the Arts Council emphasized his skill at sensitive landscape rendition and fine portraiture. The show traveled to Cambridge, Stoke on Trent, Bristol, and Bradford.

The Tate Gallery showed 99 paintings and 53 drawings, many from collections abroad, by the 18th-century English artist Thomas Gainsborough. The fine portraits and landscapes were a visual delight. "Turner in Yorkshire" was a loan exhibition shown at the York City Art Gallery and organized in conjunction with the York Festival.

ASTRONOMY

Probably the most spectacular visual excitement in astronomy during 1980 resulted from the continuing unmanned exploration of the planets. While earlier satellites concentrated on studies of Venus and Mars, the recent Pioneer 11 (renamed Pioneer Saturn) and the Voyager 1 and 2 satellites vastly improved views and knowledge of Saturn and Jupiter, revealing novel features of their moons, magnetic fields, and ring systems.

The numbers of discovered moons belonging to these two planetary titans had been increasing steadily throughout the past decade. Pioneer 11 discovered a 13th or possibly 14th moon of Saturn; Voyager 1 raised the number to 15. Even more startling, it appeared that two of the moons shared a single orbit. The latter observation was made by ground-based observers at the Pic du Midi Observatory in France.

Pioneer 11 and Voyager 1 each returned hundreds of photographs of Saturn. Along with the three new moons, they revealed a huge encircling cloud of neutral hydrogen gas and a complex system of major and minor rings, two of which appear to be interwoven in a braided pattern and one of which consists of icy boulders averaging about 1 m (3 ft) in diameter. Also provided was the first direct measurement of the planet's magnetic field, which has a strength about 20% that of the Earth's equatorial magnetic field.

When Voyagers 1 and 2 raced past Jupiter in 1979, they revealed the presence of a 14th moon. Later, Stephen P. Synnott of the Jet Propulsion Laboratory in Pasadena, Calif., discovered a 15th moon while studying photographs from the two probes in order to determine the orbit of the 14th. A mere 80 km (50 mi) across, the new moon actually appeared to lie within the newly discovered ring system of Jupiter. Designated 1979J2, it was the second to be found by examining Voyager photographs.

While spacecraft directly studied Jupiter and Saturn, it would be many years (or decades) before man reached directly to the outermost planet in the solar system, Pluto. Nevertheless, scientists at Palomar Mountain Observatory in California, using the 5-m (200-in) telescope and employing the new technique of speckle interferometry, were able to make a reliable determination of the size of Pluto. They found it to be 3,600 km (2,230 mi) in diameter. By combining this measurement with the mass determination made using the 1979 discovery of Charon, the lone moon of Pluto, the scientists found the planet's density to be nearly ten times less than that of the Earth.

Though it is rare for man to go out in the solar system, it is even more rare for the solar system to come to us. Nonetheless, Luis W. Alvarez of the University of California at Berkeley suggested that about 65 million years ago, at the end of the Cretaceous Period, an Apollo asteroid smashed into the Earth's atmosphere and was subsequently responsible for the termination of many life forms on Earth, including the dinosaurs. The theory was based on the discovery of large concentrations of the rare earth element iridium in rocks from the Gubbio Valley in Italy and from regions around Copenhagen in Denmark. The 25-fold increase in the trace

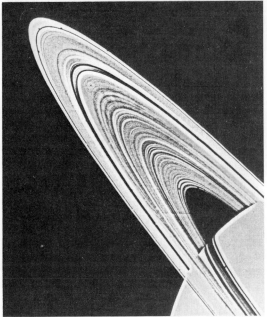
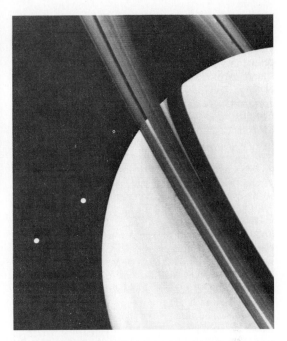

Even at a distance of five million miles the rings of Saturn are breathtaking in their beauty. Voyager 1 sent back to Earth a stunning array of photographs of the planet in the fall, including clear documentation of three new moons, bringing the total to 15. Two of the known moons, Dione and Tethys, were photographed from a distance of eight million miles on November 3.

element corresponds precisely with the Cretaceous-Tertiary boundary. This element, while rarely found on the surface of the Earth, is abundant in extraterrestrial (meteoritic) material. The hypothesized meteorite impact would have produced an explosion equivalent to 100 million megatons, polluting the atmosphere with dust for the succeeding decade and drastically changing the conditions for life on Earth. Alvarez and his group concluded that the impact of an asteroid of only 10 km (6 mi) in diameter, about the size of the moons of Mars, would suffice to explain the excess of iridium and absence of dinosaurs.

Finally, what could well turn out to be the most important discovery in the solar system during the year was the first reliable report of the variability of the solar luminosity. Using detectors aboard the Solar Maximum Mission satellite, scientists detected a variation in the total solar energy output by about 0.1% over a period of several months. Though corresponding to a change of only about 10 K (compared with a solar temperature of about 5,700 K), the existence of such a change over such a short time implied the possibility of even larger, long-term changes in solar luminosity, which could have profound influence on the Earth's weather.

Supernovas and Neutron Stars

Supernovas are thought to represent the explosive death of stars. Though theory suggests that such stellar violence should give rise to an expanding shell and a dense, rapidly rotating neutron star at its centre, only two such supernova-neutron star associations had been found by 1980: the famous Crab Nebula, remnant of a supernova that occurred in AD 1054, and the Vela Supernova, which occurred about 10,000 years ago. In 1980 G. Garmire and L. Tuohy (California Institute of Technology) reported a third such association in the southern supernova remnant RCW 103 by observing a soft (low-temperature) X-ray source within it. According to the X-ray photographs made by the orbiting Einstein X-ray Observatory, other supernova remnants, including those left behind by supernovas occurring in our galaxy during the past 2,000 years, left behind no obvious hot neutron stars at their centres. This led astronomers to conclude either that such objects cool much faster than they had previously believed or that supernovas only rarely make neutron stars.

In a remarkable piece of astrophysical and geophysical collaboration, the record of some of those supernovas in the Antarctic ice sheet was reported by Robert T. Rood and Craig L. Sarazin (University of Virginia) and Edward J. Zeller (University of Kansas) and Bruce C. Parker (Virginia Polytechnic Institute). In analyzing the atmospheric nitrates deposited in ice over the past 800 years, they found only a few unusually high concentrations. These coincided with the dates of the supernovas observed by Tycho Brahe in 1572 and by Johannes Kepler in 1604. The authors predicted that a deeper ice core should lead to the record of the great supernovas of 1006 and 1054.

Perhaps the most exciting discovery of the year in this field was the identification of the origin of the spectacular burst of gamma rays detected by both Soviet and U.S. satellites on March 5, 1979. It was found to have arisen from a supernova remnant, N49, in the Large Magellenic Cloud, the nearby companion galaxy to the Milky Way. At its great distance the source had to have had a brief luminosity of 100 billion suns, brighter than the entire energy output for the Milky Way galaxy. While the precise origin of the gamma rays was unclear, an association with a neutron star in the relatively young (10,000 years old) supernova remnant seemed the most likely explanation.

Cosmology

The most distant objects known are the quasars, strong sources of radio, optical, and X-ray radiation, mainly lying at the very edge of the visible universe. There are perhaps a few hundred well-studied quasars spread throughout the entire sky, so that it was a great surprise in 1979 when two quasars were found to lie a mere six arc seconds from one another. Despite the similarity in their optical spectra, the two objects were considered by many astronomers to be distinct entities that chance had brought together. In 1980, however, a group at the California Institute of Technology working with the optical telescopes of the Mount Wilson and Palomar observatories were able to obtain detailed spectra of the individual objects. Meanwhile, Alan Stockton of the University of Hawaii was able to get clear photographs of the two quasars. After image processing it became clear that the system consisted of a single quasar with an elliptical galaxy lying nearly in the line of sight between the Earth and the quasar. The intervening galaxy acted as a lens, in fact, a gravitational lens, bending light to form two images of the single quasar.

The likelihood of finding such a fortuituous alignment is not great, and so astronomers began arguing that it was not surprising that just one such system had ever been found. Then in June 1980 a group headed by Ray Weymann of the University of Arizona reported the discovery of a second gravitational lensing system involving not two, but three distinct quasar images. Though the presumed foreground spiral galaxy had not been detected by the end of the year, the discovery of this second example added further strength to the gravitational lens interpretation of these sets of multiple quasar images and lent additional weight to the validity of Einstein's general theory of relativity, which predicts these effects by analogy with the gravitational bending of light by the Sun.

A radio astronomy group from Bonn (West Germany) University headed by W. Reich reported what appeared to be the largest object in the universe. Assuming its red shift correctly indicates the distance to this particular quasar, called 3C345, the object is 78 million light-years in diameter.

(*See also* Space Exploration.)

A dramatic image-enhanced photo released in August shows a bleak and windswept landscape on the surface of Mars. The photo was taken by the Viking Lander 1 spacecraft.
UPI

AUSTRALIA

Although public opinion polls put the issue of taxation at the top of the list of voters' priorities in the election year of 1980, both political parties ignored the taxation question and preferred to concentrate their energies elsewhere. The Australian Labor Party (ALP) claimed that it was necessary above all else to stimulate the economy, while the Liberal-National Country Party government based its electoral strategy upon the deteriorating international situation, of which the crisis in Iran and the Soviet invasion of Afghanistan were the main features. In connection with this outlook, defense expenditure in the August budget was boosted by 17.7% to A$3,541,000,000. Prime Minister Malcolm Fraser described the new strategic situation after the Soviet move into Afghanistan as being the most serious threat to world peace since World War II. Fraser wholeheartedly supported U.S. Pres. Jimmy Carter's line on Afghanistan, and Australian primary producers were prevented from replacing with Australian grain the grain lost to the U.S.S.R. as a result of the U.S. embargo.

The government also tried to mobilize domestic opinion against the U.S.S.R. by preventing Soviet cruise ships from visiting Australian ports, stopping Soviet scientific vessels from berthing, rejecting the Soviet airline Aeroflot's advances regarding the opening of direct flights between Australia and the U.S.S.R., and withdrawing official support for bilateral cultural activities. However, the Australian Olympic Committee turned down Fraser's boycott request, and Australian athletes attended the Games.

In the period leading up to the federal elections on October 18, Fraser made the management of the economy a leading theme of his campaign. William Hayden, for the ALP, promised income tax cuts in a package of measures to benefit the average family. The election saw Fraser's government returned to office with a reduced majority. In the House of Representatives the Liberal Party won 54 (67 in 1977) seats and the National Country Party (NPC) 20 (19), giving their coalition 74 (86), as against the ALP's 51 (38). In the Senate the Liberals secured 28 (30) seats, the NPC 3 (5), the ALP 27 (26), and the Australian Democrats, led by Don Chipp, 5 (2); there was one independent. The government thus lost control of the Senate.

Foreign Affairs

In July Foreign Minister Andrew Peacock was reported to have threatened to resign over the Australian government's recognition of the Pol Pot government in Cambodia. Peacock disagreed with Prime Minister Fraser and in a bitter dispute offered to resign when Fraser refused to withdraw recognition of the Pol Pot regime, which was diverting relief supplies intended for needy women and children to its own troops. Fraser took the position that the Australian government ought not to do anything that might imply approval of the Vietnamese intervention against Pol Pot in Cambodia.

Australia faced diplomatic problems over Indonesia and the New Hebrides. In Indonesia Radio Australia's representative was asked to leave because the Indonesian government believed that the overseas service of Radio Australia had been persistently broadcasting news items unfavourable to the Indonesian government. The separatist movement, which disrupted normal life in the Anglo-French condominium of the New Hebrides on the eve of its independence as the republic of Vanuatu, was also a problem for Australia. Australia viewed with deep concern the breakdown of law and order on the island of Espíritu Santo. When, on May 28, supporters of a secessionist group caused extensive damage to government offices in Santo town and obstructed the police, the Australian government called upon the British and French authorities to

Prime Minister Malcolm Fraser jubilantly acknowledges his party's victory in the October elections.
UPI

BRISBANE COURIER MAIL

In 1980 the Australian Council of Trade Unions threw their support with Aborigines protesting a number of mining and oil-drilling operations; the labour support threatened to shut down development sites.

ensure the maintenance of law and order and the protection of Australian citizens in the New Hebrides. Independence was granted as scheduled, and troops from Papua New Guinea reoccupied Espíritu Santo.

The Economy

Unemployment, strikes, the 35-hour week, the role of the Conciliation and Arbitration Commission, and inflation were the chief economic issues in 1980. By June, the end of the financial year, Commonwealth Employment Service figures showed 427,429 Australians unemployed; the general picture was that of continuing deterioration. The Amalgamated Metal Workers Union demanded an unprecedented 35-hour workweek for its members, and an 11-week strike by wool storemen held up A$500 million in exports.

Higher gasoline prices pushed Australia's inflation rate to 10.7% for 1979–80, the highest in almost three years. In the second quarter of 1980 higher fuel and transport costs contributed to a cost-of-living rise of 2.8%, the largest increase for a corresponding period since 1975.

A serious dispute took place between the government and the miners over the government's determination to tax subsidized housing. In the central Queensland coal-mining town of Blackwater the federal treasurer, John Howard, was met by a violent demonstration. The miners remained adamant that they would not end their six-week-old strike, which by August had cost the major mining companies A$150 million in lost revenue and had deprived the Queensland government of A$8 million a week in lost royalties. The strike was finally settled by a compromise agreement in September.

The Western Australian government also faced a revolt against its plans to drill for oil on sacred Aboriginal sites at Noonkanbah. The Australian Council of Trade Unions formed a picket line in an attempt to prevent a convoy of trucks from reaching the Noonkanbah area, but the line was broken and the demonstrators were ousted. The government took steps to tighten safeguards on the movement of uranium after it was discovered that a worker had stolen two tons of uranium oxide from the Mary Kathleen Uranium Mine near Mount Isa, Queensland.

Federal Treasurer Howard delivered the 1980–81 budget in August. The budget was based on a continued deflationary strategy, and Howard expected it would result in the first domestic surplus since 1973–74. Apart from the big boost to defense expenditure already referred to, there was no change from the tone of earlier years, as the government continued to stress the need to help the private sector to expand. In his budget speech Howard strongly defended the oil import parity pricing policy, insisting that by making Australians pay world market prices for a scarce resource, Australia's capacity to withstand world energy problems had been improved.

AUSTRIA

Federal Pres. Rudolf Kirchschläger was confirmed in office for a second six-year term in Austria's May 1980 presidential election. In the province of Vorarlberg a citizens' initiative seeking greater autonomy for the province within the Austrian federal structure was approved by more than 60% of the voters in a June 15 provincial referendum.

A 1978 referendum had narrowly rejected the bringing into operation of the Zwentendorf nuclear power station (Austria's first), but the nuclear issue continued to arouse controversy. In November a "popular initiative" calling for Zwentendorf's admission to service secured some 422,000 votes, opening the way to eventual repeal of the antinuclear legislation passed in 1978.

Vienna's new 2,100-bed general hospital, under construction since 1960, was at the centre of a financial and political scandal during 1980. Investigations revealing serious deficiencies in design and construction, spiraling costs, and evidence of extensive bribery led to a number of arrests. Allegations of bribes being paid into party funds and of the involvement of the vice-chancellor and finance minister, Hannes Androsch, led Chancellor Bruno Kreisky to take drastic action. He made his continuance as chancellor conditional upon his party's acceptance of a ten-point code of ethics imposing greater controls over politicians' business interests. Androsch, seemingly the main target of Kreisky's demands, agreed to closer supervision of his ministry; on December 11 he resigned (effective Jan. 31, 1981) to direct the Creditanstalt Bank.

Kreisky continued his personal diplomacy aimed at furthering a peaceful settlement of the Middle East conflict. In February he had talks with Palestine Liberation Organization (PLO) leader Yasir Arafat in Riyadh, Saudi Arabia, and in March the PLO was accorded de facto diplomatic recognition when Ghasi Hussain became its accredited representative in Austria. Differences between Iran and Iraq had repercussions in Austria in July when, following a bomb explosion believed to have been meant for the Iranian embassy in Vienna, two Iraqi diplomats were expelled. The Austrian ambassador to Colombia was among a number of diplomats seized as hostages by left-wing guerrillas at the embassy of the Dominican Republic in Bogotá in February, but he was released after being held for nine days.

In August the government vetoed the export by Steyr-Daimler-Puch AG of 200 tanks, worth some 2 billion schillings, to Chile. The decision, made following strong public opposition to the deal and a refusal by railway union members to handle transportation of the tanks, was based on humanitarian grounds.

During 1980 the Austrian economy remained one of the most stable in Europe, with a growth rate of 3–4% and an inflation rate around 6%.

AUTOMOBILES

Chrysler Corp. in 1980 once again was the focus of attention in the automobile industry. The huge losses experienced in 1979 that compelled the firm to seek $1.5 billion in government loan guarantees in order to survive continued to mount, and by year's end it appeared that further help would be needed to keep the company afloat. But unlike 1979, when Chrysler alone was ailing, it soon became obvious that its domestic competition in the U.S. was far from healthy either.

In the first six months of 1980 the four U.S. automakers, General Motors Corp., Ford Motor Co., Chrysler, and American Motors Corp., posted a combined loss of $1.9 billion, the first time in industry history that losses topped the $1 billion mark. By the third quarter of the year the red ink had spread, and combined losses topped the $3.5 billion mark. In the third quarter Ford reported a $595

In the first high-level contact between the United States and the Soviet Union since the Soviet invasion of Afghanistan, U.S. Secretary of State Edmund Muskie (centre right) met with Soviet Foreign Minister Andrey Gromyko (centre left) in Vienna in May. The occasion was a celebration of the 25th anniversary of Austria's liberation from Allied occupation after World War II.

ALAIN MINGAM-UDO
SCHREIBER–GAMMA/LIAISON

million loss, highest ever for any three-month period in auto industry history. For the first nine months it lost a record $1,230,000,000.

A combination of factors affected the auto industry. Among them were the switch by consumers to more fuel-efficient but less profitable small cars, high interest rates that hindered both the dealers who had to finance the purchase of cars for inventory and consumers trying to obtain loans, and the huge multibillion-dollar expense associated with bringing the new, smaller cars to market.

In the 1980 model year, which ran from Oct. 1, 1979, to Sept. 30, 1980, U.S. domestic auto sales fell 22.4% to 6,787,846 from 8,758,064 in the 1979 model year. GM sales declined 17.4% to 4,228,231 from 5,119,078 the previous year; Ford sales fell 34.1% to 1,556,771 from 2,363,117; and Chrysler was down 34.2% to 649,043 from 986,649. For the first time since 1962 Chrysler sales dropped below the 900,000 mark.

American Motors sales rose 11.9% to 163,502 from 146,078 a year earlier, the first year-to-year sales gain for AMC since 1974. Volkswagen sales of its subcompact Rabbit, built in Pennsylvania, rose 32.9% to 190,299 from 143,144.

Though its sales were down sharply, GM experienced a sharp rise in market share during the 1980 model year. Its share of domestic sales rose to 62.3% from 58.4% in 1979; Ford fell to 22.9% from 27%; and Chrysler's share declined to 9.6% from 11.3%. AMC's market share rose to 2.4% from 1.7%, and Volkswagen increased to 2.8% from 1.6%.

Sales in the U.S. by domestic automakers faltered, but manufacturers from other nations had a field day. Sales rose so rapidly that both the United Auto Workers and Ford petitioned the International Trade Commission to set restrictions on the number of foreign cars that could be sold in the U.S.

A decade earlier imported automobiles were accounting for sales of about 1.2 million annually, or one out of every ten cars sold in the U.S. By 1980 this figure had risen to more than two million, or one out of every four cars sold in the U.S. Nearly 80% of these foreign-made cars carried a Japanese nameplate.

Other than imports, one often-cited reason for sales problems was price. In the fall of 1978 when the 1979 models were introduced, the average base price of a U.S.-made car was $5,666. In the fall of 1979 when the 1980 models were brought out, the average base had risen to $6,731. In the fall of 1980 as the 1981 models were introduced, the average base price had skyrocketed to $7,856. Industry leaders adopted a trend in the 1980 model year of boosting prices every three months to keep up with inflation. As 1981 got under way, they said that they would continue that practice.

For the 1981 model year the government's Environmental Protection Agency required each automaker to obtain an average of 22 mi per gal (mpg) from its fleet of cars, up from an average of 20 mpg in the 1980 model year. In releasing its annual mileage ratings on cars, the EPA announced that the mileage champion was a Volkswagen Rabbit model powered by a four-cylinder diesel engine. It was rated at 42 mpg in city driving. The highest rated gasoline-powered car was a new mini model from Toyota, called Starlet, which averaged 39 mpg in the city. The Chevrolet Chevette, Ford Escort, and Mercury Lynx all were rated at 30 mpg for city driving, and the Dodge Omni and Plymouth Horizon came in at 28 mpg.

The most talked-about new cars were the so-called K-body compacts from Chrysler. These were the cars the automaker said would turn the corporation around and the reason it needed federal loan guarantees. These cars, the Dodge Aries and Ply-

Chrysler's "K-cars" were the company's offerings for the market for well-designed, fuel-efficient smaller automobiles, a market that had been dominated by Japanese and European imports.

COURTESY, CHRYSLER CORPORATION; PHOTO, KENYON AND ECKHARDT ADVERTISING

Paul Tippett, president of American Motors, shows off the Renault 18i, the newest offering in the two companies' partnership. The car was the U.S. version of a front-wheel-drive sedan that had been successful in Europe.

UPI

mouth Reliant, replaced the Dodge Aspen and Plymouth Volare. Built on 99.6-in wheelbases, the K-cars were offered in two-door, four-door, and wagon models, the only front-wheel-drive compact wagons on the market. Their fuel economy of 25 mpg topped the EPA list for midsize cars.

The first day the K-cars went on sale, October 2, sales totaled 5,011 units, a Chrysler record. Chrysler also brought out a new Imperial luxury two-door sedan, resurrecting a name last used in 1975. The $18,311 luxury model featured a "bustle back" rear end similar to that on the 1980 Cadillac.

At Ford the emphasis was on cars that would compete against the imports. The firm brought out the Ford Escort and Mercury Lynx, successors to the Ford Pinto and Mercury Bobcat. Both were built on 94.2-in wheelbases, were 165 in long overall, and featured front-wheel drive. They were offered in two-door hatchback and four-door wagon versions. Ford said that it would introduce sporty two-passenger versions of each car later in the model year, the Escort EXP and Lynx LN-7.

The big news from GM was reserved for mid-1981, when it would bring out its own subcompact, front-wheel-drive competitors to the imports, dubbed the J-cars. The Escort-size models would be available in two-door coupé, hatchback, four-door sedan, and wagon models.

At American Motors new for 1981 were the subcompact Eagle SX/4 and Kammback models. The firm also made the 2.5-litre four-cylinder engine it purchases from GM standard in all Eagle models. That move gave both the compact and subcompact Eagles 22-mpg city fuel economy ratings, a considerable improvement over the 16-mpg fuel economy rating on the compact 1980 Eagle, which had a 258-cu in, six-cylinder engine as standard. AMC also began marketing the Renault 18i subcompact luxury sedan, a high-mileage (24 mpg city) subcompact.

In addition to cars, men made news in 1980.

Henry Ford II, who had been slowly relinquishing his duties as head of Ford Motor Co., stepped down as chairman on March 13. Philip Caldwell, vice-chairman and president, was named to succeed him, the first time a non-Ford family member would run the company. In a somewhat surprising move Donald Petersen, who had headed Ford's overseas operations, was named president. William Bourke, head of North American Automotive Operations, had been expected to be named to that post. Bourke resigned from Ford.

At General Motors Roger Smith, an executive vice-president, was named to succeed Thomas Murphy as chairman when Murphy retired on Dec. 31, 1980. F. James McDonald, another executive vice-president, was named to succeed E. M. "Pete" Estes as GM president when Estes retired on Jan. 31, 1981.

Honda confirmed that it would begin building a new Accord model in Marysville, Ohio, starting in 1982 for the 1983 model year. The company said that it was running out of production capacity in Japan and was forced to enter the market in the U.S. with an assembly plant. Nissan (Datsun) said that it would build a plant near Nashville, Tenn., to produce Datsun pickup trucks beginning in late 1983. Volkswagen, which already had an assembly plant in Westmoreland, Pa., announced that a second plant would be built in Sterling Heights, Mich., and probably would be producing trucks in late 1982.

Renault increased its equity interest in American Motors in 1980. In 1978 Renault purchased 4.7% of AMC's common stock for $150 million. In October 1980 it reached an agreement with AMC to invest an additional $200 million in return for a 49.9% stock interest in AMC within two years. Under terms of the agreement Renault could purchase more than a 50% interest by exercising certain stock warrants.

Among other major developments during 1980,

37

Ford was ruled innocent of reckless homicide charges in a Winamac, Ind., trial involving the deaths of three teenage girls who died when their subcompact Ford Pinto was struck in the rear and the Pinto's gas tank exploded. (*See* Consumer Affairs Special Report.)

AUTO RACING

The 1980 Formula One season opened at Buenos Aires with the Argentine Grand Prix, the winner being Alan Jones, from Nelson Piquet of Brazil in a Brabham and Keke Rosberg (Fin.) in a new Fittapaldi. Jones's best lap was 194.527 kph. At São Paulo, Brazil, also in January, René Arnoux (France) gained his first grand prix victory in a turbocharged Renault over the Interlagos course. Arnoux made fastest lap, at 192.421 kph. Elio De Angelis (Italy) was second for Lotus, and third place went to Jones. The teams moved to Kyalami for the South African Grand Prix a month later, and there Renault was unassailable with Arnoux finishing first after achieving a fastest lap at 201.96 kph. It was a great French occasion, with Jacques Laffite's (France) Ligier second and Didier Pironi's (France) Ligier third.

At Long Beach, Calif., Piquet took the U.S. West Grand Prix, with fastest lap at 146.601 kph, Italian Riccardo Patrese's Arrows finishing second and Brazilian Emerson Fittipaldi's Fittipaldi third. The European racing began at Zolder with the Belgian Grand Prix in May, won by Pironi, although Laffite (Ligier) made best lap time at 189.703 kph. Jones finished second and Carlos Reutemann of Argentina, in a Williams, third. The Monaco race was a victory for Reutemann's Williams, which also had the fastest lap, 136.393 kph, under damp conditions. Second place went to Laffite and third to Piquet.

Owing to a jurisdictional dispute, the Spanish Grand Prix at Jarama was disallowed in the rankings. So Jones had a hollow victory (and made best lap, at 157.994 kph) over Jochen Mass (West Germany) in an Arrows and De Angelis in a Lotus. The French Grand Prix, run over the Paul Ricard circuit, was won by Jones, who set a lap record of 206.171 kph, from the Ligiers of Pironi and Laffite.

In the British Grand Prix at Brands Hatch, Jones gained another victory for the Williams team, but only after Pironi had set a new lap record of 209.239 kph for Ligier. Piquet in a Brabham placed second, ahead of Reutemann. There were many changes of fortune at Hockenheim during the German Grand Prix, the winner being Laffite's Ligier from Reutemann's Williams. Jones was third.

In the Austrian Grand Prix at Zeltweg, Jabouille in the yellow turbocharged Renault beat Jones for first place. Finishing third was Reutemann. Arnoux set a new lap record in the other Renault, at 231.197 kph. In the Dutch Grand Prix at Zandvoort, Piquet won in a close finish with Arnoux, and Laffite placed third.

UPI

Driver Johnny Rutherford (left) and master car builder Jim Hall pose with their trophy after winning the Indianapolis 500 race in May.

At Imola for the Italian Grand Prix, Piquet was troubled by a sticking throttle in the Ford engine of his Brabham, and Jones had braking problems. Piquet eventually won, thereby gaining a one-point championship lead over Jones. The latter, however, left no doubt about the championship at the Canadian Grand Prix, but it was a dramatic moment when his Williams brushed with Piquet's Parmalet-Brabham at the rush away from the starting grid. The race was restarted, with Piquet now using his spare car, but the engine failed while it was in the lead, two laps from the finish, and all Jones had to do was drive carefully to win the race and clinch the world championship. Reutemann finished second, ahead of Pironi, who had the fastest lap at 185.90 kph.

Jones was to demonstrate that he was unquestionably a great champion at the last race of the season, the U.S. East Grand Prix, in which he set a new lap record of 208.115 kph for the Watkins Glen, N.Y., circuit. Again his teammate Reutemann followed him home. As in Canada, Pironi's Ligier-Gitanes placed third.

Johnny Rutherford won the Indianapolis 500 rather handily with an average speed of 230.008 kph (142.862 mph). He also won the pole position at 309.532 kph (192.256 mph). His margin of victory over second-place Tom Sneva was 29.58 sec as only 4 of the starting 33 finished the full 200 laps around the 2½-mi course. Bobby Unser won the other two Triple Crown events, at Pocono in Pennsylvania and at Ontario, Calif.

In other United States Auto Club (USAC) championships, Rich Vogler won the sprint car title easily from Steve Chassey but fought veteran Mel Kenyon to the final race in the midget division before taking that title, too. The USAC/SCCA (Sports Car Club of America) Mini-Indianapolis champ was Peter Kuhn, while Gary Bettenhausen was the dirt-car king, and Joe Ruttman won the stock-car title.

The National Association for Stock Car Auto Racing (NASCAR) weathered the economic storm somewhat better than USAC, thanks to a season-long race for the Winston Cup crown, eventually won by Dale Earnhardt at the Ontario 500.

This was the final year of "big" stock cars for NASCAR. For 1981 wheelbases would be downsized five inches to 110.

BANGLADESH

In 1980 Pres. Ziaur Rahman, who completed five years in office in November, made several trips abroad seeking external assistance to prop up his country's sagging economy. The tours produced no tangible results, although Zia was promised help by government leaders in Washington, London, Paris, and Tokyo if specific projects could be drawn up. In May the Bangladesh Aid Consortium, meeting in Paris, decided to allocate $1.3 billion in assistance for the fiscal year 1980–81. Of the total, $700 million was for project assistance, $350 million was in commodity aid, and the rest was in food aid.

The second five-year plan, launched in July, provided for a development outlay of 255,970,000,000 taka, three-quarters of which was earmarked for the public sector, and sought a growth rate of 7.2%, compared with the current 4.9%. Despite World Bank aid totaling $1,274,000,000 since 1972, mainly for agricultural development, output of food grains and of jute, the major foreign exchange earner, failed to improve. The nation had barely

Pres. Jimmy Carter received Pres. Ziaur Rahman of Bangladesh at the White House when he visited the U.S. in August.

UPI

recovered from the drought of 1978–79 when floods over vast areas took a heavy toll in lives and damaged crops. The shortfall in food grains was estimated at three million metric tons. By the end of August nearly half the country's 144,000 sq km had been flooded; about 20 million people in 14 of the 21 districts were said to have been directly affected, and approximately 5 million were homeless. The jute industry was also hard hit by lower prices and lack of demand in the international market, forcing the government to abolish the minimum support price to the farmer.

In April President Zia dropped eight of his ministers, including five of Cabinet rank. Earlier, in January, Zia had sacked Deputy Prime Minister Moudud Ahmed and the minister for jute, Nur Mohammed Khan.

Mounting economic problems led to a wave of strikes and agitation in various parts of the country, the most serious being a stoppage by about 500,000 lower-grade government employees demanding higher wages. Zia accused the pro-Moscow Communist Party of Bangladesh of fomenting trouble and arrested its top leaders. Reports of an attempted coup in June, when Zia was visiting London, were quickly denied by the government.

An insurgency problem developed in the Chittagong Hill Tracts area, where Chakma Buddhists attacked the police and armed forces in an effort to block government plans for large-scale resettlement of Muslims in the Hill Tracts region. The Shanti Bahini guerrilla force of the Chakam tribals was officially blamed for the ambush killing of 100 soldiers and policemen in the first half of the year.

Zia's visit to Beijing (Peking) in July produced two agreements: for the opening of an air link between the two capitals and for a Chinese development loan of $44 million. Relations with India were slightly strained, however, as many issues evaded solution. The irritants included the sharing of the Ganges waters and the demarcation of maritime and land boundaries, complicated by the emergence of new islands in the Bay of Bengal which both sides were claiming.

BASEBALL

On October 21 in Philadelphia, the Phillies defeated the Kansas City Royals 4–1 to win the 77th World Series, four games to two, and atone for years of frustration and disappointment. Philadelphia third baseman Mike Schmidt's two-run single in the third inning of the sixth game was the key hit in the Phillies' Series-winning victory before an ecstatic home crowd of 65,838. Schmidt batted .381 for the Series, knocked in seven runs, and was named most valuable player.

The favoured Royals jumped to a 4–0 lead in the first game of the Series on October 14 at Philadelphia, but the Phillies rallied to win 7–6. Likewise, one night later, the Royals were ahead 4–2 entering the bottom half of the eighth inning. But the Phillies roughed up Kansas City's best relief pitcher, Dan Quisenberry, to win 6–4.

When the Series moved to Kansas City on October 17, the Royals came to life. They won the third game 4–3 in ten innings and then rode Willie Aikens's third and fourth home runs of the Series to a 5–3 triumph October 18. But in the pivotal fifth game the Phillies staged another of their comebacks, scoring two runs in the ninth inning for a 4–3 conquest on October 19. To ensure that victory, Tug McGraw, Philadelphia's leading relief pitcher, had to survive a bases-loaded situation in the Kansas City ninth inning.

Two evenings later veteran Philadelphia left-hander Steve Carlton hurled seven strong innings to achieve his second win of the Series, with help from McGraw, and the city was immersed in a loving celebration of its baseball team, culminated by a parade that was viewed by more than a million citizens. The Series was the first ever won by the Phillies in their 97 years as a team.

Play-offs

Many observers deemed the World Series anti-climactic because of the dramatic nature of the play-offs that determined the league pennant winners. The Phillies had to endure a grueling best-of-five series with the Houston Astros before claiming their first National League title since 1950. On October 7 in Philadelphia the Phillies beat the Astros 3–1, but the Astros triumphed 7–4 in 10 innings the next night and then 1–0 in 11 innings at Houston on October 10. But the redoubtable Phillies tied the play-offs at two victories each by winning 5–3 in ten innings on October 11 and then rebounded from a

5–2 deficit the next night to prevail 8–7 in ten innings for the pennant. The Phillies had won East Division championships in 1976, 1977, and 1978 but each time had failed to win the pennant.

Similarly, the Royals had been West Division champions in the American League for 1976, 1977, and 1978, only to lose the pennant each time to the New York Yankees. But in 1980 the Royals exacted a measure of revenge by sweeping the Yankees in three games during the American League play-offs. The Royals, an expansion team formed in 1968, thus achieved their first pennant.

Regular Season

While the Royals coasted to their division crown, the Yankees, Phillies, and Astros all laboured through arduous races. The Astros led the National League West by three games with three games to go in 1980. They lost all three of those contests by one run to the Los Angeles Dodgers, who tied Houston for first place after the regular schedule of 162 games was completed. That forced a divisional play-off in Los Angeles on October 6, and the Astros arose to defeat the Dodgers 7–1 for their first division crown.

The Phillies, who were 6 games out of first place with 55 to go, enjoyed a splendid closing month of the season to win the National League East by one game. They were tied with the Montreal Expos entering the final three-game series of the regular schedule at Montreal. The Phillies won the first match 2–1 and then clinched the division title on October 4 with a 6–4 triumph.

The Yankees accumulated a seemingly insurmountable lead during the first half of the season,

Mike Schmidt of the Phillies was the hero of the World Series when Philadelphia defeated the Kansas City Royals four games to two to win its first World Series. Schmidt's two-run single (left) proved to be the winning hit of the final game.
WIDE WORLD

but then the defending American League champion Baltimore Orioles made a charge. However, the Yankees stood firm and won the division by three games over the Orioles, who were runners-up despite a sparkling 100–62 record.

The Royals never were challenged. Despite a lukewarm spell in the closing stages of the season, they finished 14 games ahead of surprising Oakland. Brett, however, kept matters interesting by chasing the coveted .400 batting mark. He stayed close to it for much of the summer and several times passed it but eventually fell back and finished with a still-exemplary .390 average, the best in baseball since Ted Williams of the Boston Red Sox hit .406 in 1941. Bill Buckner, a first baseman for the Chicago Cubs, won the National League batting title with .324, while Schmidt led the league with 48 home runs and 121 runs batted in. Carlton paced the league in wins with 24 (he lost 9) and strikeouts with 286, while Chicago's Bruce Sutter once again topped relief pitchers with 28 saves.

Brett was not the only Kansas City player to excel offensively. Teammate Willie Wilson, a disappointment in the World Series, had 230 hits and became only the second switch-hitter in history to get 100 hits from either side of the plate. Cecil Cooper of the Milwaukee Brewers led the American League in runs batted in with 122, while teammate Ben Oglivie tied Reggie Jackson of the Yankees for the home-run leadership with 41. Baltimore's Steve Stone (25–7), New York's Tommy John (22–9), and Oakland's Mike Norris (22–9) were the top starting pitchers, while Quisenberry and the Yankees' Rich Gossage each totaled 33 saves in relief. Oakland's Rickey Henderson stole 100 bases, breaking the American League record of the legendary Ty Cobb.

The midsummer All-Star Game in Los Angeles had a familiar result. The National League defeated the American League 4–2 for its 9th consecutive victory and 17th in the last 18 contests.

Little League

Teams from Taiwan again won two Little League World Series championships in 1980. In the original series for 11- and 12-year-olds, played at Williamsport, Pa., the victory was the fourth straight and ninth overall for Taiwan.

The Far East team from the town of Hua Lian defeated Tampa, Fla., 4–3 in the final game of the double-elimination series. Back-to-back homers in the third gave Taiwan a 4–1 lead. Tampa added runs in the fourth and sixth innings of the six-inning game but could not catch up.

Taiwan reached the finals by defeating Willemstad, Curaçao, the Latin-American entry, 6–0 and trampling Trail, B.C., representing Canada, by a 23–0 score. Tampa wiped out Pawtucket, R.I., 20–3 and Kirkland, Wash., 16–0. In the other first-round games, Trail defeated the European entry of Madrid, Spain, 9–8, and Kirkland beat Des Moines, Iowa, 15–0. In the consolation game, Kirkland won over Trail by a 2–1 score.

A Taiwanese team also won the Senior League title for players aged 13 to 15. Taiwan defeated Kaneohe, Hawaii, 12–4 in the final game of the series at Gary, Ind. It was Taiwan's ninth straight Senior series title.

Buena Park, Calif., won the Big League series for ages 16 to 18 at Fort Lauderdale, Fla. In the cham-

The Taiwan Little League team trampled the Canadian entry 23–0 in a semifinal game of the Little League World Series held in Williamsport, Pennsylvania, in August. Taiwan took the final title for the ninth time.
WIDE WORLD

WIDE WORLD

Kansas City Royals third baseman George Brett was chosen as the American League's most valuable player for the year.

pionship game, the Californians squeezed by an Orlando, Fla., team by a score of 3–2. The Taiwanese team did not reach the Big League series in 1980.

Two Little League Softball series for girls were played at Kalamazoo, Mich. Glendale, Calif., won the Little League Softball title for 11- and 12-year-olds by its 9–4 defeat of Seymour, Conn. Naples, Fla., took the Senior Softball title for ages 13–15 when it nosed out Tallmadge, Ohio, 5–3 in the championship game.

BASKETBALL

If Earvin Johnson was "Magic" in college basketball, he bordered on the miraculous as a professional. The eager rookie's mile-wide grin and remarkable ability delighted fans and filled arenas throughout the United States during the 1979–80 season, adding up to the National Basketball Association's most successful year since the New York Knicks packed Madison Square Garden in the early 1970s. Dropping out of Michigan State University after leading the Spartans to the 1979 National Collegiate Athletic Association (NCAA) championship, Johnson completed a rare double by sparking the Los Angeles Lakers to the 1980–81 NBA crown.

"New Faces of 1980" was a hit show from coast to coast; forward Larry Bird also made a sensational NBA debut for the Boston Celtics, outpolling Johnson for rookie of the year honours. Bird, of Indiana State, and Johnson had first collided in the 1979 collegiate final, with Johnson's team winning though Bird was named college player of the year.

Bird did not get a chance to even the score with Johnson in an NBA final play-off confrontation. The Philadelphia 76ers beat the Celtics in the Eastern Conference showdown before losing to the Lakers in a lively six-game championship round. The perfect Hollywood finish should have taken place on the Lakers' home court in suburban Inglewood, Calif., but Johnson, who was voted the series' most valuable player, wrote his own script. With 7-ft 2-in centre Kareem Abdul-Jabbar (voted NBA most valuable player) out of action after severely spraining an ankle, the 20-year-old rookie took personal charge of the final game, played in Philadelphia. The 6-ft 8-in Johnson played forward and centre as well as guard, scoring 42 points and demoralizing the 76ers with all-around brilliance.

Overlooked in the Magic show was the demise of the defending champion Seattle SuperSonics in a welter of controversy and conflict. As it had been for every NBA champion since the 1968–69 season, the strain of repeating was too much for the Sonics, who began unraveling late in the season. The bickering rose to a crescendo while they were being eliminated by the Lakers in the Western Conference finals. In the meantime the 76ers were ousting Boston in the East to reach the finals. But despite spectacular contributions from Julius ("Dr. J") Erving and backboard-shattering Darryl Dawkins, the 76ers were no match for Los Angeles.

At its meeting in February the NBA admitted Dallas, bringing league membership to 23 teams. Orderly expansion would have called for two new franchises, providing a balanced circuit of two six-team divisions in the Eastern and Western conferences, but no other city was willing to meet the $12 million price tag.

The move did force long-overdue realignment, however, Dallas forming a Texas trio (with Houston and San Antonio) in the Midwest Division along with Kansas City, Denver, and Utah. Chicago and Milwaukee shifted to the Central Division, making the Mississippi River the dividing line between East and West and providing a sense of geographic reality overlooked by the football and baseball major leagues.

In women's professional competition Pearl Moore led the New York Stars to the Women's Basketball League title. The Stars defeated the Iowa Cornets three games to one in the championship series.

College Competition

It seemed anticlimactic when Louisville struggled past UCLA 59–54 to win the 1980 NCAA Tournament

The NCAA championship finals pitted UCLA against Louisville; led by Darrell Griffith's 23 points, Louisville was victorious.
WIDE WORLD

at Indianapolis, ending the Bruins' bid for their 11th basketball championship. This was the first time that UCLA had lost an NCAA final, but there was ample consolation. Rebounding from a shaky 1979–80 start under new coach Larry Brown, the Bruins came together with a rush at tournament time.

The target of strong criticism earlier, Brown suddenly found himself being compared to the retired coach John Wooden, who had produced many national champions for UCLA. Brown explained that his underclassmen-laden team needed experience, and they got it by knocking pretourney favourite DePaul out of the running in a second-round upset.

But nothing could stem the Louisville tide, powered by brilliant 6-ft 4-in guard Darrell Griffith. The Cardinals capped a 33–3 campaign by erasing a late deficit to beat UCLA behind Griffith's 23 points. Two Big Ten teams, Purdue and Iowa, also made the prestigious final four but had to settle for the third-place game, won by Purdue 75–58.

As further proof of the Big Ten's growing basketball dominance, Minnesota and Illinois reached the semifinals of the National Invitation Tournament. Minnesota won that contest, but Virginia's awesome 7-ft 4-in freshman centre, Ralph Sampson, piled up 15 points and the same number of rebounds to beat the Gophers 58–55 in the NIT final. Sampson then surprised the sports world by turning

down a multimillion-dollar offer from the Boston Celtics to stay in school. Illinois defeated Nevada-Las Vegas to take the third-place NIT trophy.

Louisville's Griffith, centre Joe Barry Carroll of Purdue, and forward Mark Aguirre of DePaul were the standout college performers, earning unanimous selection to All-America teams. Votes for the other two first-team berths were widely scattered.

An unprecedented triple triumph was achieved by tiny North Park College of Chicago in NCAA Division III competition. Behind slender 6-ft 10-in centre Michael Harper, the Vikings swept to their third straight national championship, outscoring Upsala (N.J.) College 83–76 in the final.

In women's competition Old Dominion of Virginia coasted to its second AIAW (Association of Intercollegiate Athletics for Women) crown in a row, brushing aside Tennessee 68–53 despite 26 turnovers. Inge Nissen scored 20 points to win the tournament's most valuable player honours. Her Old Dominion teammate Nancy Lieberman, was supreme in the backcourt, cementing her position as the nation's best collegiate woman guard.

Olympic Games

Twelve men's and six women's teams competed in the Olympic Games at Moscow, but because of the U.S.-led boycott, they did not truly represent the strength of world basketball. The final round in

SARA KRULWICH—THE NEW YORK TIMES

The Los Angeles Lakers defeated the Philadelphia 76ers for the 1980–81 NBA crown.

men's play pitted Yugoslavia against Italy; Yugoslavia, undefeated, won 86–77. The remaining finalists, in order of finish, were the Soviet Union, Spain, Brazil, and Cuba.

In the women's competition, the Soviet Union retained the championship easily. Bulgaria was second, followed by Yugoslavia and Hungary. (*See also* Olympic Games.)

BELGIUM

Belgium's 150th anniversary celebrations in 1980 were marked by a major, albeit not yet decisive, step toward the long-promised regionalization. After two aborted attempts, Parliament approved two bills (made law on August 8 and 9, respectively) reorganizing the country's structure on the basis of three regions: Flanders, Wallonia, and Brussels. A solution for the Brussels region, where the French- and Dutch-speaking communities live side by side, was left pending.

Disagreement among the Social Christians, the Socialists, and the Front Démocratique des Francophones (FDF; Brussels federalists) had arisen over the second and third phases of the proposed reform of the state structure, and the FDF's insistence on equal status for the Brussels region led to the resignation of the FDF ministers from the government early in the year. This forced Prime Minister Wilfried Martens to bring the Liberals into the coalition in order to obtain the two-thirds majority in Parliament required for constitutional change. After a slight reshuffle of the Cabinet on January 23, the Martens government (his second) carried on with its former program. However, Flemish Social Christian senators demanded that technical guarantees be granted to Flemish members of the future Brussels regional council. Despite an appeal by the prime minister before the vote, several Social Christian senators remained adamant. Lacking a two-thirds majority, Martens's government resigned on April 9.

Martens was then invited by King Baudouin to form a new Cabinet. The Socialists accepted the presence of the Liberals in order to obtain the two-thirds majority. The third Martens government of May 18 thus brought together the three traditional parties. The Liberal (PRL and PVV) proposals providing for tax reductions for married couples and drastic cuts in public expenditure were accepted.

Internal strife plagued Belgium; Flemish demonstrators clashed with police at Voeren (Fourons) in March.

UPI

With the Liberals in the majority, the two main bills dealing with the state reform passed after protracted debates. Tension between the communities persisted in two communes with special facilities for the minority language group. Violence erupted repeatedly at Voeren (Fourons), and in Comines (Komen) a request for a Flemish school was ignored by local authorities, forcing the government to step in.

Despite growing unemployment and warnings by employers that a 38-hour week would further jeopardize the competitive position of Belgian industries, the trade unions held to their demands, refusing to countenance any infringement of social benefits.

With a BFr 82 billion deficit in current spending in 1980, the government planned a BFr 90 billion deficit for 1981. A 2% levy on contributions by civil servants toward a pension fund was proposed, but the government rescinded the measure in the face of strong trade union opposition.

Disagreement over measures to finance the social security system led to the fall of Marten's third government on October 4. His fourth, composed of Social Christians and Socialists, took office October 22.

BIOLOGY

Experiments involving the engineering of primitive life remained a focus of attention in 1980, but the kind of attention varied according to the recency of the experiment. The primordial one, conducted by nature, originated life on Earth, and a major task of paleobiologists has been to trace as far into the past as possible the sequence and timing of life's beginnings. In June a team of U.S. and Australian investigators headed by J. William Schopf of the University of California at Los Angeles announced its discovery of what it felt to be convincing evidence of structurally preserved microfossils in Australian rock dated at 3,500,000,000 years. The structures take the form of filaments that were interpreted to be chains of bacterial cells. Microfossils resembling blue-green algae (cyanobacteria) and dated at 3,400,000,000 years had been recovered in 1977 from sediments in Africa, but evidence that they had once been living organisms was not conclusive. Prior to the Australian find, the oldest microfossils of organisms for which there was generally undisputed evidence were dated at 2,300,-000,000 years.

Contemporary engineering experiments, conducted by scientists in several countries and primarily centred on genetic manipulation of bacterial life, were receiving increased attention from legal and business sectors as, in the words of one molecular biologist, "suddenly our discoveries are worth money." On June 16 the U.S. Supreme Court ruled five to four in favour of Ananda Chakrabarty, a microbiologist who since 1972 had sought to patent a bacterium that he had endowed with additional genetic material to improve its ability to degrade oil slicks. The ruling, which made laboratory-developed microorganisms patentable, was expected to clear the way for the U.S. Patent Office to begin processing the more than 100 outstanding applications that had been filed by genetic engineering firms, pharmaceutical companies, and other organizations to protect their investments.

The court's decision was narrow in the sense that it addressed only the statutory question of whether in formulating the current patent laws the U.S. Congress had intended in any way to exclude inventions that are alive. In so doing it interpreted the laboratory-contrived microorganism as a "manufacture" and not a "hitherto unknown natural phenomenon," but it did not attempt to distinguish between the living and the nonliving or to make judgments on the potential dangers of creating new life forms. Observers favourable to the decision felt that it had given deserved recognition to the rapidly advancing field of biotechnology but were undecided about its practical importance, particularly in what way the decision would affect rulings on patent applications that were seeking to protect for their discoverers some of the basic techniques of recombinant DNA technology, or gene splicing. Critics of the ruling pointed out that the ability to patent life forms might inhibit the free flow of scientific information by encouraging secrecy. Another fear was that patenting, and thereby profit seeking, would increase the use of engineered life forms throughout the world and the consequent risk of environmental mishap. (*See* Special Report.)

Among reports published in 1980 that dealt with ancient animal life appeared one of an unusual finding by University of California scientists headed by E. M. Prager. Using immunological techniques,

Fossil remains found in rocks in northwestern Australia were thought to be the oldest biological cells ever found on Earth; the bacterialike creatures may have existed 3,500,000,000 years ago in the Archaeozoic Era.
WIDE WORLD

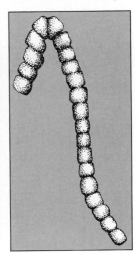

they succeeded in detecting a common protein, serum albumin, in muscle sampled from a mammoth frozen perhaps as long as 40,000 years and accidentally discovered in 1977. Furthermore, even though the mammoth albumin had undergone postmortem changes, it was shown to be quite similar to that of living Indian and African elephants. Previous attempts to study proteins from the remains of extinct animals had been unsuccessful.

Yet another study in evolutionary zoology provided the first evidence of the ability of carnivorous dinosaurs to swim. More than 40 footprints were found in the fossilized mud of an ancient Connecticut lake bottom. From their size and shape W. P. Coombs, Jr., of Western New England College, Springfield, Mass., argued that the tracks were probably made by indigenous species of large carnivorous dinosaurs as they floated in the water and pushed themselves along with their toes.

A new method of dating ancient life was described by M. Ikeya and T. Miki of Yamaguchi University in Japan. They used electron spin resonance (ESR) spectroscopy, a technique that detects the presence of unpaired electrons in a substance by its behaviour in a magnetic field. The ESR signal of interest results from radiation-induced changes in the crystalline structure of fossil bones and provides

a measure of the total dose of natural radiation received. The investigators called this age-dependent dose the "archaeological dose." They found a good correspondence between the ages of samples determined from ESR spectroscopy and from established methods.

In 1978 E. S. Savage-Rumbaugh and co-workers of the Yerkes Regional Primate Research Center in Georgia described the first observation of symbolic communication between two nonhuman primates (chimpanzees). Two years later another study, conducted by Robert Epstein, Robert P. Lanza, and B. F. Skinner of Harvard University, extended this result to the pigeon. After two birds were taught to recognize letter and word symbols, one pigeon was given the opportunity to use the symbols to communicate information about hidden colours to another pigeon in order for both to obtain food. Furthermore, the two pigeons had a prolonged and natural "conversation" without any urging from the experimenters. These results, although suggesting that even some nonprimate animals are able to communicate symbolically with one another, also support behavioural interpretations of such activity, which explain these apparent exchanges of information in terms of simple concepts of reinforced learning.

Unusual footprints (above) found in fossilized mud in an ancient lake bottom in Connecticut were interpreted as evidence of swimming by large carnivorous dinosaurs such as Megalosaurus (left), which inhabited the region about 180 million years ago.

(TOP) WALTER P. COOMBS; (BOTTOM) ADAPTED FROM "SWIMMING ABILITY OF CARNIVOROUS DINOSAURS," W. P. COOMBS, SCIENCE, VOL. 207, NO. 4436, PP. 1198–99, MARCH 14, 1980; ART BY MATTHEW HYMAN

1 meter

Special Report:
The Business of New Life

by Nicholas Wade

On June 16, 1980, the U.S. Supreme Court ruled that "a live human-made micro-organism is patentable subject matter"; in other words, that bacteria and similar organisms may be patented if they have been altered in the laboratory by processes of genetic manipulation. This long-awaited decision marked the commercial debut of genetic engineering, a technology likely to become increasingly visible throughout the decade. Some observers consider that genetic engineering will become the characteristic new technology of the 1980s just as microelectronics was of the 1970s.

The ruling of the Supreme Court concerns a patent application filed in 1972 by General Electric Co. for a form of *Pseudomonas* bacterium, which had been genetically engineered to improve its ability to digest oil slicks. The inventor, Ananda Chakrabarty, later of the University of Illinois, used well-established techniques of bacterial genetics to introduce additional genes into the organism.

Medical Applications of Gene Splicing

In 1973 a new and unprecedentedly powerful method for manipulating DNA, the genetic material of all life, was discovered by Stanley Cohen of Stanford University and Herbert Boyer of the University of California at San Francisco. Called recombinant DNA technology, or gene splicing, the technique makes it possible to cut out precisely defined segments of DNA from one organism and splice them into the genome, or gene set, of another. Though developed as a tool of pure research, which its inventors at first did not even think to patent, gene splicing was soon recognized as possessing an extraordinary potential wealth of practical applications. In theory it is a general way of tailoring the properties of living organisms in almost any desired manner. The first commercial applications of gene splicing, however, have been much more specific. They consist broadly of genetically programming bacteria to manufacture human protein products of medical importance.

The three products on which greatest headway has been made are insulin, interferon, and growth hormone. Insulin traditionally has been extracted from pig and cattle glands, but that source of supply will not always be enough. In addition, because animal insulin differs slightly from the human variety, it may have undesirable side effects in the diabetic patient. In the gene-splicing approach the DNA sequences for the two separate protein chains of human insulin are first obtained by chemical synthesis in the laboratory. Each synthetic DNA molecule is then inserted into its own carrier, a natural ring-shaped DNA molecule known as a plasmid, and each plasmid is introduced into a separate bacterium. Each bacterium, with its new gene, is allowed to divide repeatedly into a colony of identical daughter cells known as a clone, and the cloned bacteria are then stimulated to produce the protein product of the inserted gene. Finally, the two protein chains are united chemically to produce the intact insulin molecule. The gene-splicing method of making human insulin was developed commercially by Genentech, Inc., of San Francisco for the pharmaceutical company Eli Lilly. Clinical trials of the insulin began in London in July 1980, the first step toward obtaining approval of the drug by the U.S. Food and Drug Administration.

Genentech also developed a gene-splicing method for producing human interferon, the body's natural antiviral substance, which is also believed—though not yet proved—to be of possible use against cancer. Although the method is similar to that for insulin, only one gene is involved, and because the gene for interferon is as yet too large a piece of DNA to be synthesized in the laboratory, it has been obtained by ingenious techniques from cells that naturally produce copious amounts of interferon.

A third project near commercial realization in 1980 was the bacterial production of human growth hormone, needed for treating dwarfism. The substance at present is obtained from cadavers since animal varieties do not work in humans. Other products that have been made by gene-spliced bacteria include somatostatin, a brain hormone that controls the pituitary gland's release of growth hormone, and thymosin alpha-1, a hormone from the thymus gland that is believed to stimulate the immune response.

It would probably be 1981 at the earliest before the first gene-spliced product reached the general market. The first such product to be sold in any market was a scientific specialty item, DNA ligase, an enzyme used by researchers and marketed in 1975 by New England BioLabs of Beverly, Mass.

Financial Interest

The new technology was taken up by the business world slowly at first, but recently with gathering momentum. As is often the case with radical innovations, it has been small companies that have pioneered the first applications. Genentech, the most successful of the new enterprises, was founded in 1976 by Robert Swanson, a 28-year-old investment banker with a bachelor's degree in chemistry, and by Boyer. Genentech's main rivals include Cetus, a microbiology company founded in California in 1972 that quickly added gene splicing to its repertoire; Biogen, a Geneva-based venture with both U.S. and European scientists on its board of directors; and Genex, located in Maryland.

In an effort to raise private capital, the officers and backers of these four small companies have vigorously spread word in industrial and financial circles about the potential of gene splicing. They seem to have succeeded beyond their expectations. By September 1979 the four small companies had a total paper value of more than $225 million, and by May 1980 the total value had more than doubled to $500 million. U.S. investors include such large oil companies as Standard Oil of California and Standard Oil of Indiana, which together with National Distillers own most of Cetus. Lubrizol Corp. holds some 25% of Genentech, and Koppers Co. is a major backer of Genex. The four companies at present operate mostly under contract to produce particular products. For example, Genentech, under contract to Hoffmann-La Roche, is engaged in a race to produce interferon with the rival partnership of Biogen and the drug firm Schering-Plough.

Genentech recently took the step of offering a share of its equity to the public. So eager were investors to buy its stock that the offering, on October 14, was a historic occasion on Wall Street. Within 20 minutes of trading, the shares, initially $35 each, shot to $89 and closed the day at $71.25. The closing valuation gave Genentech a theoretical worth of $529 million, almost a tenth the value of Du Pont, even though Genentech did not have a single product on the market.

The lead of the four small companies in trying to develop commercial applications of gene splicing has been followed at a more sedate pace by the large pharmaceutical houses and chemical corporations, several of which have begun setting up in-house research teams in genetic engineering. Basic research knowledge, however, is still the limiting factor in applying the technique, and the advantage presently rests with the small companies, which by establishing attractive managerial and stock ownership roles have formed special relationships with leading academic scientists. Nevertheless, as gene splicing eventually becomes a commoner art, advantage may pass to those with large marketing resources, such as the drug companies, or with special expertise in fermentation technology, such as the Japanese. On the other hand, Genentech, like Xerox or IBM before it, may grow with and dominate the industry it is pioneering.

The Commercial Future

Less spectacular than the production of medically important proteins but of considerable commercial significance will be the use of recombinant DNA to improve or vary all processes in which microorganisms are used. These range from brewing and cheese-making to manufacture of antibiotics and the biological synthesis of ethanol for use in gasohol. Another application that may come to fruition in the near future is the genetic modification of plants. Plants are susceptible to such genetic manipulation because a whole plant can be propagated from a single cell, a characteristic that allows plants to be cloned like bacteria. When more is known about the genetic mechanisms of plants, it should be possible to introduce genes that confer such desirable properties as disease resistance and high yield.

The increasingly evident power of the new technique inevitably raises questions of how and in what form it could become directly applicable to human beings. It is possible to envisage treatments for such genetic diseases as sickle-cell anemia, caused by an error in the gene for hemoglobin. Patients might be able to have all the blood-forming cells in their bone marrow replaced by new cells into which the correct version of the hemoglobin gene had been inserted.

Such a procedure, if and when it becomes possible, would benefit only the afflicted individuals and not their children, since the reproductive cells would not be affected. To make a permanent, inheritable genetic change it would be necessary to intervene directly in the human reproductive process, perhaps using gene-splicing techniques in combination with newly developed procedures for test-tube conception. With increased knowledge it may become technically possible to repair genetic defects, eliminate unwanted characteristics, and eventually even to improve any desired human quality that is under genetic control. Whether such intervention will prove ethically acceptable, however, is a matter for which even the most advanced technology alone has no answer.

BOATING

Dean Chenoweth of Tallahassee, Fla., was the outstanding driver of the unlimited-class hydroplane racing season. Survivor of a 200-mph crash in October 1979, he returned to competition in June and won the first five races of the 1980 season, including his third American Power Boat Association (APBA) Gold Cup on July 6 in Madison, Ind. Before losing to Bill Muncey in "Atlas Van Lines" at the Columbia Cup on July 27 in Tri-Cities, Wash., Chenoweth and the Rolls-Royce Griffon-powered "Miss Budweiser" had won a record 20 consecutive competition heats.

The 1980 offshore season saw Bill Elswick of Fort Lauderdale, Fla., sweep the major awards in his 39-ft-deep vee "Long Shot." Elswick won the Bacardi Trophy race on May 10 at Miami, Fla., the Benihana Grand Prix on July 16 at Point Pleasant, N.J., and the Le Club International on October 4 at Fort Lauderdale to earn his first APBA national championship. Elswick's victories in the Benihana and the historic Cowes–Torquay race off the coast of England also gave him the Harmsworth Trophy, recently returned to international competition.

Catamaran or tunnel hulls won three races. Defending national champion Betty Cook of Newport Beach, Calif., won the inaugural event at New Orleans, La., in "Kaama." Joel Halpern of Tarrytown, N.Y., won the Spirit of Detroit regatta, and Michel Meynard of Concord, Mass., won the Guy Lombardo Classic off Long Island.

Sailing

Boats from Australia, the U.K., Sweden, and France challenged the U.S. titleholders for possession of the America's Cup in August–September 1980. An elimination series selected the challenger for this cup, which the U.S. had never lost. In Dennis Conner the U.S. found a dedicated young sailor whose attention to detail could not be faulted. He built up his team on the West Coast using two 12-m boats and finally choosing "Freedom," in which he easily won the U.S. selection series. In the challengers' series the British team in "Lionheart" threw away any chance it might have had of winning by sacking skipper John Oakeley at the last minute and changing mast and sails. "Lionheart" showed only flashes of speed and was defeated by the French yacht in the capable hands of Bruno Troublé. In the other pairing the Australians beat Pelle Petterson's Swedish challenge, the Swedish yacht "Sverige" never quite having sufficient boat speed. Against the French the Australians, under Jim Hardy for the third time, had the boat speed, and an easy victory looked likely, but Bruno's team went down fighting.

The British in one of their last-minute changes had produced a new mast with a flexible top section; the Australians saw it, thought the idea was right, and quickly produced a copy. They used it in their final-round challenge against the U.S.'s "Free-

dom." It may have given them almost equal boat speed with "Freedom" and perhaps a little more in light winds. The Australians won one race, but Dennis Conner, master of match-race starting techniques, proved too good, and "Freedom" retained the cup for the U.S. 4–1.

In sailing competition at the 1980 Olympic Games the six gold medals were shared by five nations, Brazil winning in both the 470 and Tornado classes. Valentin Mankin piloted a Soviet boat to victory in the Star class, while Esko Rechardt of Finland triumphed in the Finn races. Boats from Denmark and Spain won the Soling and Flying Dutchman classes, respectively. (*See also* Olympic Games.)

The U.S. entry "Freedom" successfully defended the 24th America's Cup challenge in 1980 under the command of skipper Dennis Conner.
WIDE WORLD

BOLIVIA

In July 1980 yet another military coup aborted the democratic process in Bolivia. On January 13 Congress had resolved that general and presidential elections would be held at midyear. Lydia Gueiler Tejada was confirmed in her post as interim president and was to govern with the support of the centre-right Movimiento Nacionalista Revolucionario (MNR), led by Víctor Paz Estenssoro, until a new president could be elected. During the early part of the year a steep rise in prices as a result of the 19% devaluation of the peso in November 1979 led to a series of strikes. Although freezes were in effect for rents and the most important basic foods, and the urban minimum wage was increased to 3,500 pesos a month plus a compensatory lump-sum payment to lower-paid workers, the central labour union organization claimed that much higher wages were needed and called a series of crippling strikes in the banking, transport, and agricultural sectors.

Despite violence from the right, elections were held as planned on June 29. With 90% of the votes cast, Hernán Siles Zuazo of the left-wing Unidad Democrática y Popular (UDP) led, followed by Paz Estenssoro. The presidential election was to be decided by a joint session of Congress on August 4, as no candidate had obtained half of the overall poll. However, the newly appointed army commander, Maj. Gen. Luis García Meza Tejada, led a coup on July 17, deposing interim president Gueiler and setting aside the election result. A military junta took over the government and arrested and reportedly tortured leaders of the political parties and labour unions. At the same time, all university teachers and magistrates were dismissed, and a state of siege was declared. The U.S. cut off all economic and military assistance and recalled its ambassador, while Bolivia's Andean Group partners (Colombia, Ecuador, Peru, and Venezuela) protested against the annulment of the elections; Ecuador broke off diplomatic relations. The U.K. canceled its $40 million mining assistance program (the largest British aid scheme in the area), and West Germany and Belgium reduced their aid. Meanwhile, Argentina, Brazil, Uruguay, Paraguay, Chile, Taiwan, Israel, and South Africa recognized the regime. There were reports that Argentine advisers had assisted in planning and executing the coup. The U.S. Department of State alleged that some of Bolivia's new rulers were connected with the nation's flourishing traffic in cocaine, which further damaged the regime's credibility.

Economic performance in 1980 declined from its low 1979 level. Petroleum production fell by 8% to less than 30,000 bbl a day, necessitating higher imports of crude oil from Argentina. The eventual supply of Bolivian natural gas to Uruguay and Chile was discussed.

BOWLING

In December 1979 a total of 321 bowlers from 30 nations competed in the ninth world bowling championships of the Fédération Internationale des Quilleurs (FIQ) at Manila, Philippines. For the first time the Philippines became top nation in the championships with four first-place gold medals and one second-place silver. Especially notable was Lita de la Rosa of the Philippines. She had already won the Bowling World Cup, recognized as the most important annual singles event, in Bogotá, Colombia, in 1978. Now in Manila she also won the gold medal in individual masters all-events. No individual had ever won both titles before. In addition she won the singles, teamed up with Bong Coo (Phil.) to win the doubles, and, with Bong Coo and Nellie Castillo (Phil.), finished second in the trios event.

In the men's world championships Gerry Bugden (England) became the reigning king, beating Philippe Dubois (France), the winner of the 1979 World Cup, in the masters all-events, with a score of 379–372 in the two-game grand final. In the opening matches Bugden defeated Finland's 19-year-old

Tanks prowled the streets of La Paz after a coup staged by the Army in July. Maj. Gen. Luis García Meza Tejada became the new Bolivian chief of state.

MICHEL PHILIPPOT–SYGMA

Mikko Kaartinen 195–192 and then Malaysia's J. B. Koo 201–181 to earn his shot at the top-seeded Dubois. In the five-man event Australia won its first world title, rolling 5,892 to leave Great Britain in second place (5,793). Another nation won its first world title in the three-man event as Malaysia scored 3,582 to edge out the U.S. (3,564). A second gold medal was won for Australia by its doubles partners, Eric Thompson and Ronald Powell, who totaled 2,460. The runner-up was a pair from South Korea, who won their nation's first bowling medals; the U.S. pair finished third. The men's singles was won by Ollie Ongtawco (Phil.) with 1,278; Rogelio Felice of Venezuela finished second at 1,265, and Michio Matsubara of Japan placed third.

In the women's world championships Lita de la Rosa won the six-game singles (1,220); in the final masters all-events matches she first defeated Yvonne Nilsson of Sweden 224–200, and then in the grand final, over two games, she beat Daniela Gruber of West Germany 416–331. The U.S. won the gold medals in the five-woman and three-woman events, with scores of 5,667 and 3,419, respectively. The runners-up were West Germany (5,577) and the Philippines (3,331). The women's doubles was won by Bong Coo and Lita de la Rosa, with a total score of 2,348. Second place was won by Finland.

United States

The American Bowling Congress tournament has been dominated by U.S. bowlers throughout its 77-year history, but this reign almost was interrupted in the 1980 meet at Louisville, Ky. Mats Karlsson of Stockholm took the lead in the Regular Division all-events standings on the sixth day of the tournament with a nine-game total of 2,073, and his score remained the best until the next to last day of the 80-day spectacle. Then Steve Fehr from Cincinnati, Ohio, totaled 2,076 to win the all-events honour.

Other ABC Regular Division winners included: team, Stroh's Beer, Detroit, 3,115; singles, Mike Eaton, Grand Rapids, Mich., 782; doubles, Ron Thacker and Bob Bures, Cleveland, Ohio, 1,378.

In the Women's International Bowling Congress (WIBC) tournament in Seattle, Wash., the biggest surprise occurred in Division I singles, where Cheri Mason of Lansing, Ill., bowled the highest series of her life, 651, to win the championship. The best previous score that the 24-year-old Mason had rolled was 457. Other Division I champions included: team, Walker's Body Shop, Aurora, Ill., 2,703; doubles, Katherine Alexander and Marie Fouche, Los Angeles, 1,176; all-events, Verida Morris, Del City, Okla., 1,711. The professional Open Division winners were: team, All Japan, Tokyo, 3,014; singles, Betty Morris, Stockton, Calif., 674; doubles, Carole Lee, Hempstead, N.Y., and Dawn Raddatz, East Northport, N.Y., 1,247; all-events, Cheryl Robinson, Van Nuys, Calif., 1,848. Donna Adamek of Duarte, Calif., won the WIBC Queens tournament

Lita de la Rosa of the Philippines won first place in singles at the world bowling championships, held in Manila, with 1,220 pins in six games.

for the second successive year, defeating Cheryl Robinson 213–165 in the title game.

For the first time in many years there was no dominant figure among the male professionals. Mark Roth, the Professional Bowlers Association (PBA) bowler of the year in 1977–78–79, did not win a PBA tournament until October, although many strong performances had placed him second in the late season prize standings with $93,000. Wayne Webb of Rehoboth, Mass., led with $98,000.

Neil Burton, little known younger brother of long-time professional star Nelson Burton, Jr., won the ABC Masters tournament. In a one-game semifinal match Neil defeated his brother 205–191, and in the title game he defeated Roth 204–192 to take the $25,000 first prize.

BOXING

Undefeated Larry Holmes (U.S.) successfully defended the World Boxing Council (WBC) championship four times in 1980, stopping Lorenzo Zanon (Italy) in six rounds, Leroy Jones (U.S.) in eight, Scott LeDoux (U.S.) in seven, and Muhammad Ali (U.S.) in ten. Ali, 38, came out of retirement in an attempt to become champion for the fourth time, facing Holmes in Las Vegas, Nev. He could not recapture the brilliant form of the past, and Angelo Dundee, his trainer, retired him at the end of the tenth round.

WORLD BOXING CHAMPIONS
As of Dec. 31, 1980

Division	Boxer
Heavyweight	Larry Holmes, U.S.
	Mike Weaver, U.S.*
Cruiserweight	Carlos de León (Puerto Rico)
Light Heavyweight	Matthew Saad Muhammad, U.S.
	Eddie Mustafa Muhammad, U.S.*
Middleweight	Marvin Hagler, U.S.
Junior Middleweight	Maurice Hope, England
	Ayub Kalule, Uganda*
Welterweight	Sugar Ray Leonard, U.S.
	Thomas Hearns, U.S.*
Junior Welterweight	Saoul Mamby, U.S.
	Aaron Pryor, U.S.*
Lightweight	Jim Watt, Scotland
	Hilmer Kenty, U.S.*
Junior Lightweight	Rafael ("Bazooka") Limón, Mexico
	Yasutsune Uehara, Japan*
Featherweight	Salvador Sánchez, Mexico
	Eusebio Pedroza, Panama*
Junior Featherweight	Wilfredo Gómez, Puerto Rico
	Sergio Palma, Argentina*
Bantamweight	Lupe Pintor, Mexico
	Jeff Chandler, U.S.*
Super Flyweight	Rafael Orono, Venezuela
Flyweight	Shoji Oguma, Japan
	Peter Mathelbula, South Africa*
Junior Flyweight	Hilario Zapata, Panama
	Yoko Gushiken, Japan*

*Recognized as champion by the World Boxing Association.

The World Boxing Association (WBA) heavyweight championship changed hands when Mike Weaver (U.S.) knocked out John Tate (U.S.) in the 15th round. Weaver retained the crown by stopping Gerrie Coetzee (South Africa) in 13 rounds.

The WBC introduced a new weight division, cruiserweight, with a maximum weight of 182 lb (82.6 kg). Marvin Camel (U.S.) became the first WBC cruiserweight champion, outpointing Mate Parlov (Yugos.), but he later lost to Carlos ("Sugar") de León (Puerto Rico). Among the light-heavyweights, Matthew Saad Muhammad (U.S.) remained WBC champion, stopping John Conteh (England), Louis Pergaud (Cameroon), and Alvaro ("Yaqui") Lopez (U.S.). Eddie Gregory (U.S.) won the WBA title, defeating Marvin Johnson. Gregory later changed his name to Eddie Mustafa Muhammad and retained the championship by beating Jerry Martin (U.S.).

The middleweights remained the only division with one undisputed champion accepted by both the WBC and WBA. The title changed hands twice. Alan Minter (England) won it from Italian-born Vito Antuofermo (U.S.) and then stopped Antuofermo in a return bout. But he later lost the title to Marvin Hagler (U.S.) in three rounds. Maurice Hope (England) successfully defended his WBC junior middleweight title against Carlos Herrera (Arg.).

The welterweight division provided good contests. Sugar Ray Leonard (U.S.), a former Olympic champion, won the WBC championship, stopping Wilfredo Benítez (Puerto Rico) in the 15th round. Leonard successfully defended his title by knocking out Dave Green (England) in four rounds. Then in a hard-fought battle Roberto Durán (Panama), former lightweight champion, captured the title by outpointing Leonard. But in November Leonard regained his crown. Durán suddenly withdrew from the fight in the eighth round, claiming that he was suffering from stomach cramps. José Pipino Cuevas (Mexico) lost the WBA championship to Thomas Hearns (U.S.), who successfully defended the title against Luis Primera (Venezuela). Saoul Mamby

Former heavyweight champion Muhammad Ali (right), in a listless performance, was defeated by World Boxing Council heavyweight champion Larry Holmes in a bout in Las Vegas, Nevada, in October.
UPI

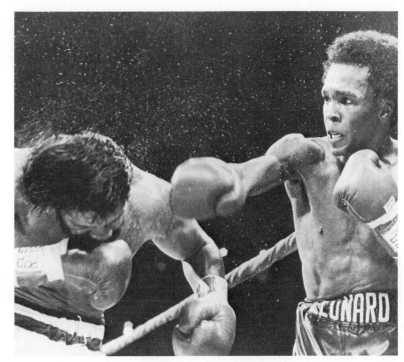

Sugar Ray Leonard pounded Roberto Durán during the sixth round of their welterweight championship bout in New Orleans in November. Durán, who had taken the title from Sugar Ray in June, was forced to stop fighting owing to stomach cramps; Leonard regained the championship.
UPI

(U.S.) took the WBC light-welterweight title from Sang Hyun Kim (South Korea). Aaron Pryor (U.S.) won the WBA crown, knocking out Antonio Cervantes (Colombia).

Jim Watt (Scotland) retained the WBC lightweight title by defeating Charlie Nash (Northern Ireland), Howard Davis (U.S.), and Sean O'Grady (U.S.). The WBA lightweight crown changed hands when Hilmer Kenty (U.S.) stopped Ernesto España (Venezuela). Kenty successfully defended the title by defeating Yong Oh Ho (South Korea). Alexis Argüello (Nicaragua) retained the WBC junior lightweight title with wins against Bobby Chacon (U.S.), Ruben Castillo (U.S.), and Rolando Navarette (Philippines) but gave up the championship to move up into the lightweight division. Rafael ("Bazooka") Limón (Mexico) later took the title. Yasutsune Uehara (Japan) won the WBA title from Sam Serrano (Puerto Rico) and successfully defended it against Leonal Hernández (Venezuela).

Eusebio Pedroza (Panama) retained the WBA featherweight championship, beating Shig ("Spider") Nemoto (Japan), Johnny Aba (Papua New Guinea), Kim So Wong (South Korea), and Rocky Lockridge (U.S.). But Salvador Sánchez (Mexico) became the new WBC champion, stopping Danny López (U.S.) in López's tenth defense. Wilfredo Gómez (Puerto Rico) recorded his 11th consecutive WBC junior featherweight title win by defeating Ruben Valdez (Colombia). Gómez also beat Nick Perez (U.S.) and Derrick Holmes (U.S.). Sergio Palma (Argentina) became new WBA champion when he beat Leo Randolph (U.S.). Lupe Pintor (Mexico) retained the WBC bantamweight title by

defeating Alberto Sandoval (U.S.), drawing with Eijiro Murata (Japan), and knocking out Johnny Owen (Wales) in 12 rounds. Tragically, Owen never regained consciousness and died 45 days after the fight. Pintor later defeated Alberto Davila (U.S.). Jeff Chandler (U.S.) beat Julian Solis (Puerto Rico) to become the new WBA champion.

Rafael Orono (Venezuela) became the first champion of the new WBC super flyweight division. Shoji Oguma (Japan) became new WBC flyweight champion, defeating Park Chang Hee (South Korea). Kim Tae Shik (South Korea) won the WBA crown from Luis Ibarra (Panama) but later lost it to Peter Mathelbula (South Africa).

In Europe John L. Gardner (England) won the heavyweight title vacated by Lorenzo Zanon (Italy), stopping Rudi Gauwe (Belgium); he later defeated Zanon. Kevin Finnegan (England) won the middleweight title from Gratien Tonna (France), retained it in a draw with Georg Steinherr (West Germany), but lost it to Matteo Salvemini (Italy), who in turn lost it to Tony Sibson (England). Marijan Benes (Yugos.) retained his junior middleweight title. Giuseppe Martinese (Italy) won the vacant junior welterweight title, beating Clinton McKenzie (England). Charlie Nash surrendered the lightweight crown to challenge Watt for the WBC title. Francisco León (Spain) became the new champion. Carlos Hernández (Spain) won the junior lightweight title from Rodolfo Sánchez (Spain) and successfully defended it against Salvatore Liscapade and Aristide Pizzo (both of Italy). Roberto Castañón (Spain) retained the featherweight crown, beating four challengers.

EDGAR MOURA—GAMMA/LIAISON

Striking metalworkers rallied daily in São Paulo in support of their cause; more than 160,000 workers were idled.

BRAZIL

In October 1979 Pres. João Baptista de Oliveira Figueiredo sent a bill to Congress providing for the reform of Brazil's system of political parties, including the extinction of the two existing parties and establishment of new ones. The bill was bitterly criticized by many, and more than 500 amendments were introduced in Congress. Eventually, on Nov. 22, 1979, the new Party Reform Bill was passed, and it was signed by the president a few days later. Political leaders were to have eight months to organize their parties under detailed regulations published by the Superior Electoral Tribunal in February 1980. Five new political groupings were eventually formed: the Social Democratic Party (PDS), backing the government; the Brazilian Democratic Movement Party (PMDB), liberal, mostly composed of members from the old opposition party; the Popular Party (PP), mildly conservative; the Brazilian Labour Party (PTB), with elements from the old Labour Party; and the Party of the Workers (PT), which had more independent labour tendencies.

In his message to Congress in March 1980, Figueiredo declared himself willing to discuss all political problems with opposition leaders, includ-

ing the postponing of the municipal elections scheduled for Nov. 15, 1980. On September 5 Congress, over the protests of opposition party members, voted to postpone the elections for two years, extending the terms of about 44,000 municipal officeholders until 1982.

The Economy

Since the inception of his administration, President Figueiredo had insisted that the struggle against inflation was the most important problem facing the nation. Unexpected increases in the price of imported oil, the paralyzing effect of the labour strikes, the drought in the northeastern states, the frosts that destroyed the crops of many coffee plantations during mid-1979, and above all the financing of Brazil's huge foreign debt of $55 billion had brought the country to a precarious situation economically. In a speech delivered to the National Council of Economic Development, President Figueiredo declared that the country would have to adopt a "war economy" to deal with the situation. By August 1979 the annual inflation rate was estimated at 58%.

In August 1979 Antônio Delfim Netto, an experienced economist who had served in important capacities during previous administrations, was appointed minister of planning, with broad powers to carry into effect stringent economic policies adopted by the administration. These included the control of prices. On Dec. 7, 1979, the president announced a new set of economic measures, including cutting many government subsidies to private industry and some to agriculture, reducing un-

Thousands of miners with pick and shovel joined the gold rush at Serra Pelada near Maraba in the Brazilian Amazon region to exploit the newly discovered goldfields there.

WARREN HOGE—THE NEW YORK TIMES

necessary government regulation of the private sector, and devaluing the exchange rate of the cruzeiro by 30%. It was expected that the new measures would result in a temporary increase in the inflation rate, but that they also would help to increase exports and decrease imports. At the end of 1979 inflation was running at the rate of 77.2%.

Because the rising cost of imported oil contributed the most to inflation, the administration took steps to cut down such imports by promoting the use of alcohol distilled from sugarcane, cassava, and other tropical plants as an automotive fuel. By 1981 about 18% of Brazil's new automobiles were to be built with engines adapted to burning pure alcohol.

BULGARIA

During 1980 preparations for the launching of a Soviet-Bulgarian spacecraft named Bulgaria 1300 neared completion. The launching into Earth orbit was planned for 1981, when Bulgaria would celebrate 1,300 years of statehood. (In 681 the first Bulgar state, founded south of the Danube by Khan Asparukh, was officially recognized by the Byzantine emperor Constantine IV.)

On June 3–7, 1980, a Bulgarian delegation led by the Communist Party first secretary and head of state, Todor Zhivkov, paid an official visit to Romania. Among the various agreements signed by Zhivkov and Romanian Pres. Nicolae Ceausescu, probably the most important was the protocol on diversion of the Danube River as the first stage of building the Turnu Magurele-Nikopol hydroelectric complex. The diversion was necessary because of the difference in height between the Bulgarian and Romanian banks of the Danube at the selected site. Preliminary agreements concerning the project had been signed by representatives of the two nations in Sofia in 1972 and 1977.

Zhivkov visited Soviet Pres. Leonid Brezhnev on Aug. 7, 1980. A joint communiqué stated that the meeting took place in "an atmosphere of cordiality and was marked by complete identity of views on all the questions discussed."

Legislation was enacted in March to allow joint enterprises to be set up in Bulgaria by Bulgarian and foreign firms. Previously, such enterprises had been permissible only in third countries.

BURMA

Attempts in 1980 by such neighbours as Thailand and Singapore to persuade Burma to join the Association of Southeast Asian Nations (ASEAN) were not successful, as Pres. U Ne Win preferred to maintain his completely neutral policy. Singapore's Deputy Prime Minister Sinnathamby Rajaratnam and Thai Prime Minister Prem Tinsulanond held talks in Rangoon seeking the support of Burmese leaders against what they called the "growing belligerency and expansionism" of Vietnam. While sympathizing with the plight of Cambodia, Ne Win believed that ASEAN was developing into an anti-Communist bastion and to join it would compromise Burma's independent foreign policy.

After the 1979 anticorruption drive among members of the ruling Burma Socialist Program Party (BSPP) Central Committee, Ne Win introduced improved retirement benefits for elected representatives. He held the view that BSPP officials would be less corruptible if their future was assured.

Except for Japan, which continued to provide assistance in agriculture and oil exploration, aid from advanced countries was slow in coming. One bright aspect of the economy was a slight surplus of 50,000 metric tons in rice output, achieved by better utilization of the $34 million aid provided by the International Development Association.

The amnesty offered in late May to former Burmese leaders who had fled abroad was accepted by U Nu, former prime minister, who left central India for Rangoon in July to be a Buddhist monk. The campaign against insurgent groups was assisted when both Indian and Chinese authorities tightened border security and denied sanctuary to Burmese rebels during the year.

BUSINESS AND INDUSTRY

The year 1980 was the year the long-expected recession hit the United States. The slide began in January, according to the National Bureau of Economic Research, the Cambridge, Mass., study group that is the arbiter of economic cycles. Then the economy plunged 9% in the second quarter, nearly equaling the sharpest drop in gross national product (GNP) since World War II.

Yet the 1980 recession appeared to rank among the shortest and most narrowly based downturns on record. Nearly 40% of the rise in unemployment to 7.8% in May was concentrated in three states—Michigan, Ohio, and Pennsylvania—which accounted for only 12% of the nation's jobs. And by October the Department of Commerce's index of leading economic indicators had risen for four months running.

It was a three-pronged recession, undercutting the auto and steel industries in the Midwestern industrial states and attacking the housing industry nationwide. Housing construction saw the worst slump since World War II, pressured by mortgage rates that never dropped below 12% even at the depth of the recession.

Meanwhile, the oil industry continued increasing profits at a prodigious rate almost equal to 1979 as higher energy costs fueled the recession. But oil imports for the first nine months of the year fell a startling 17% below year-earlier levels owing to conservation, some coal conversion, and the general recession. The soft market actually forced gasoline prices down from peaks of around $1.30 per gallon to about $1.20 a gallon during the fall, and some major oil companies reported profit declines during the third quarter.

Detroiters, hard hit by the recession in auto sales that many blamed on unfair foreign competition, lined up to take a whack at a Toyota for $1; the proceeds of the stunt went to Chrysler.

The shift to fuel-efficient foreign cars and a generally slow market due to high auto-loan rates and cautious consumer spending spelled the worst news for Detroit in decades. In October, General Motors Corp. reported the largest quarterly loss of any U.S. company in history—$567 million in the third quarter—only to be bested the next day by Ford Motor Co.'s report of a $595 million third-quarter loss.

Recession notwithstanding, the conclusion was inescapable to many that troubles in autos and steel were as much a result of shortsightedness in those industries as they were due to the general downturn. Detroit had too long delayed the introduction of cars combining quality and comfort with fuel efficiency, choosing instead to rely on the high profit margin of bigger cars and allowing foreign automakers to capture nearly one-third of the U.S. market. Steel's preponderance of outmoded plants and technology had contributed significantly to its difficulties.

In light of these conditions, and the fact that Detroit alone projected spending billions over the coming years to meet foreign competition, government policymakers became obsessed with capital investments, productivity improvements, and a new vogue word during the year, "reindustrialization." The consensus was that U.S. companies had failed to invest in the new production equipment and technology that could improve a lagging rate of productivity gains and maintain their edge over foreign competitors not only abroad but also in the domestic market.

More rapid depreciation write-offs (a mechanism to allow companies to report lower taxable earnings and reinvest the tax savings) were seen as one route out of the bind. Unfortunately, Congress by October had failed to agree on any one of a variety of new depreciation policies. But growing bipartisan concern over the plight of American industry made business tax cuts in 1981 a virtual certainty, despite the effect that they might have on the government deficit or inflation.

And it was clear that inflation had not been tamed by year-end. After a moderate rate of increase over two months, the consumer price index in September leaped at an annual rate of 12.7% to a level two and a half times 1967 prices. The prime rate, used by banks to fix loan rates for their best customers, followed a dizzying climb to a record 20% in April with an equally sharp drop to 11% by July, but then it began to rise again, hitting 14% in October and surpassing the April record in December with a new high of 21½%.

The prime is influenced in part by the funds rates set by the Federal Reserve Board for member banks. The Fed stood between a rock and a hard place at the close of 1980, moving to keep the money supply down and thus ease inflationary pressures, but in doing so forcing up the cost of money over the short term and setting the stage for a burst in interest rates and possibly an economic relapse.

The stock market placed an interpretation on the events of 1980 that pleasantly surprised even the most optimistic analysts. The plunge in interest rates in the spring freed billions of dollars that had been safely harboured in money-market funds collecting 15% or more from investments in bonds and bank certificates of deposit. The market also apparently felt the high interest rates had been a straitjacket on industry, and when the rates fell the Dow Jones industrial average soared from a low of about

759.13 in April to 1,000.17 on November 20 before slipping back to close the year at 963.99.

Steel

A sharp decline in steel demand began in mid-March, and throughout most of the year the steel industry suffered from slow sales of domestic automakers, foreign competition, slack demand for consumer appliances using steel, and the general recession. The only bright spots were in commercial construction and oil and gas pipeline sales.

Shipments at U.S. Steel, the largest U.S. producer, ran at the slowest pace since 1961 for the first nine months of 1980, and in June the company laid off 25,000 workers. The giant steelmaker operated at 51% of capacity during the third quarter, a capacity drastically cut in 1979 by the permanent closing of all or parts of 15 inefficient plants in the austerity moves that led to the massive losses of the fourth quarter of 1979.

Steel executives—and the past year had seen new men placed in charge of all three of the country's largest steel companies—continued to complain that a large share of the steelyard blues came from foreign dumping, costly environmental controls, and unrealistic depreciation rules. The year saw the general acceptance of the "bubble" approach to pollution controls, allowing the company to select the buildings to target to best reduce overall emissions on a site rather than having to meet rigid standards for each building.

Washington also bowed to pressure to control alleged dumping when U.S. Steel filed suit against seven European steelmakers charging they were selling in the U.S. market below their actual costs. The company dropped its suit in return for a program that included trigger prices for foreign steel. If imports fell below certain prices, the government promised to investigate for dumping and, if necessary, impose duties to keep up the foreign prices while the investigations were in progress. Washing-

ton also promised faster implementation of depreciation guidelines and a case-by-case review of environmental restrictions that the companies claimed led to major cleanup investments with no return in productivity.

Energy

The oil companies were the star performers in the soaring stock market of 1980 as world oil prices increased and controls on domestic prices gradually fell away. The industry reported an average profit increase of 91% in the first quarter of 1980 compared with a year earlier and a 32% boost in the second quarter despite the 9% drop in GNP in that period, the imposition of the windfall profits tax in March, and overall corporate profits down 18% from the year-earlier period.

With all domestic controls on oil slated to disappear by October 1981, the industry remained in good shape despite third-quarter earnings declines reported by a few of the big producers, including Gulf Oil, Conoco, Amerada Hess, and Marathon. *Business Week* estimated that 40% of all U.S. manufacturing profits would be garnered by the oil industry in 1980, an infusion of capital to that sector and a drain on other industries that many observers found very disturbing. Drilling budgets increased during the year, especially in domestic exploration, but in many cases not enough to absorb all the new revenue. Nonenergy investments such as those by Exxon in office equipment and Mobil in real estate promised to become more common.

Coal, while it returned to vogue among some adventuresome homeowners and profited from gradual switchovers by oil-burning utility plants, remained far from fulfilling its energy promise in 1980. Possibly coal's best prospects lay within the realm of synthetic fuels—oil and gases produced from coal, oil shale, and organic materials. Synfuels received a big boost from legislation to create in 1981 the U.S. Synthetic Fuels Corporation., a gov-

"Lee Iacocca sent us!"
OLIPHANT © 1980 WASHINGTON
STAR/UNIVERSAL PRESS SYNDICATE

STEVE ILKO—THE NEW YORK TIMES

U.S. Steel won court permission to close down its two plants in Youngstown, Ohio, which the company said could not be operated profitably. The court did not give the company permission to dismantle the plants, and there was hope that they could be upgraded and reopened.

ernment entity with a first-year budget of $20 billion from the windfall profits tax. The number of synfuel plants in planning or under construction, expecting investment or loans from the synfuel corporation or other government backing, expanded sharply in 1980. The strongest investment interest focused on coal gasification and fuel production from oil shale, though even optimistic projections did not envision more than 500,000 bbl a day of synfuels production by 1987—less than one-tenth of current U.S. imports of oil.

The nuclear industry remained logy during the year, suffering the aftereffects of the Three Mile Island accident in 1979. No new plants were announced, and some utility companies began selling off their shares in plants under construction that had been stalled by increasing consumer and government scrutiny. Yet at the same time, a study commission looking at the Three Mile Island case gave the technology a vote of confidence and blamed the failure there on poor training methods for plant personnel. With the incoming Republican administration believed to be friendly toward nuclear power, it was possible that absent another failure like Three Mile Island the industry might begin to recover.

Airlines

The oil industry's gain was the airline companies' loss in 1980. Losses totaling nearly $500 million industry-wide were a stunning reversal from the early days of deregulation in 1979, when the companies found no difficulty in passing on higher fuel costs. Discounts on coast-to-coast fares as low as $99 for one-way tickets and underpricing on other major routes led to what one airline executive called "competitive madness" in which no one stood to earn any money. The red ink was symbolized by Pan American's sale of the landmark Pan Am building in Manhattan for $400 million to raise needed capital and offset losses. When the major carriers moved to drop routes where their larger planes flew unprofitably, this retrenchment opened the door for small regional carriers such as USAir and Air Florida, which turned handsome profits during the year.

On April 2 Pres. Jimmy Carter signed the windfall profits tax bill, which he called "the keystone of our national energy policy." The oil profit tax was expected to raise at least $227.3 billion in ten years; the money could finance a tax cut for citizens.

TERESA ZABALA – THE NEW YORK TIMES

It was not clear whether the experience of the airline industry held any lessons for the trucking industry, which entered the throes of deregulation in 1980. In the first phase, truckers were allowed to move rates 10% up or down from levels of the previous year. Toward year-end, experience was too limited to read an outcome.

Autos

Chrysler had drawn down $800 million of its $1.5 billion in federal loan guarantees by late August. Chairman Lee A. Iacocca optimistically bet New York City Mayor Edward Koch that Chrysler would pay back its federally guaranteed loans before Koch's city paid back its loans.

But that day would not be soon in either case. The four major automakers lost a total of more than $1.5 billion during the second quarter, when sales dropped 42% from the same period in 1979. In all, Iacocca projected the U.S. auto industry would lose as much as $8 billion by year-end.

Detroit's efforts during the year aimed at delivering the sort of cars that the public appeared to be buying from European and Japanese automakers before high interest rates put a damper on the whole market. General Motors introduced the successful, fuel-efficient X-cars, front-wheel driven to maximize passenger space, late in 1979. Chrysler was a little late with its competitors, the K-cars, which appeared in the summer of 1980. Ford appeared to be a step ahead with its smaller "world cars," even more fuel-efficient but less roomy.

Detroit was not backing away from its intermediate cars, however, mindful that for most of the year Chevy Caprice and Oldsmobile 88 outsold every foreign model except Toyota Corolla.

But Chevy Citation and Chevette sold better, an indication of the way to go. What surprised many

observers were the price tags Detroit set on such products. Prices on General Motors cars were up an average of 4.4% during the first week of the 1981 model year, with the largest hikes falling on the most popular models. Chrysler boosted new car prices twice before the models went on sale. At the same time, the automakers squeezed dealer profit margins, despite the fact that over 900 of the country's 28,000 dealers had closed up shop in 1980. The higher prices—an average of $9,700 for a GM car—meant a calculated risk to bring in the kind of cash Detroit needed to retool and reengineer for cars to meet foreign competition and to produce the automobiles consumers wanted.

CAMBODIA

In 1980, a year after Hanoi-backed guerrillas headed by Heng Samrin overturned Cambodia's first Communist regime led by Pol Pot, events in the country remained centred around the legitimacy of the government. The ousted Pol Pot won another recognition vote at the UN in October, helped by an unprecedented lobbying campaign by the non-Communist countries of Southeast Asia, which resolutely opposed Vietnam's invasion of Cambodia in 1978–79.

In August Khieu Samphan of the fallen Pol Pot regime invited foreign journalists to a jungle hideout and announced a change in his group's political line: survival, not socialism, was to be the new goal. He admitted serious errors in the past. Said Ieng Sary: "People are still a bit afraid of us, but we tell them we are nationalists before we are Communists."

The change of tune did not seem to satisfy the Association of Southeast Asian Nations (ASEAN), which was spearheading the campaign to keep Heng Samrin at bay. Unofficially, some ASEAN

Although food and other relief supplies poured into Cambodia following a worldwide appeal for help, distribution of food and especially of seed grain for planting was a source of controversy throughout the year; severe breakdown of transportation facilities and political wrangling complicated the problem.

SIPA PRESS / BLACK STAR

members started looking for a "third force," tainted neither by the Pol Pot atrocities nor by Hanoi's patronage. By September there was open campaigning for the Khmer People's National Liberation Front (KPNLF) led by former Cambodian premier Son Sann, considered by some as a viable non-Communist resistance movement. Rapidly gaining influence in the crowded Cambodian refugee camps on the Thai side of the frontier, the KPNLF turned down strong suggestions from Thailand and China that it coordinate its anti-Vietnamese work with that of the Pol Pot forces. Subsequently, there were suggestions that Cambodia's charismatic former head of state, Prince Norodom Sihanouk, be persuaded to join up with the KPNLF. But Front sources indicated that the prince would be welcome only as a figurehead.

All internal developments in Cambodia remained overshadowed by the fighting, though it was confined to the eastern and northeastern border areas. There were reports of widespread famine conditions despite the arrival of massive international aid. At one point, the UN's World Food Program was shipping 32,000 tons of food each month, with an additional 16,000 tons a month for the refugees in Thailand. The Phnom Penh regime said the aid material was used to prop up Pol Pot's group and to attract famine-threatened Cambodian peasants to the Thai border, where large numbers were armed and sent back to their country to destabilize the government. Some international relief officials lent credence to such allegations.

CANADA

Pierre Elliott Trudeau triumphantly returned as prime minister of Canada early in 1980, after having been out of office for nine months. Beginning his 12th year in power and heartened by the resounding defeat of separatism in the Quebec referendum of

May 20, the 60-year-old Trudeau dramatically introduced a new plan to resolve the long-standing dispute between the federal government and the provinces over a procedure for amending Canada's constitution and to entrench a charter of basic human rights in the document. In asserting a unilateral federal role in revising the constitution, Trudeau aroused the angry opposition of a majority of the provinces. His initiative represented the culmination of his public career, the purpose for which he had entered Canadian political life.

The Liberals returned to power following a short and often inept Progressive Conservative administration under Joseph ("Joe") Clark, an Alberta MP who had led the party since 1976. After 16 years in opposition, the minority Conservative government moved slowly. It waited almost six months before calling Parliament, spending the interim in reorganizing the federal administration. It also clung to election promises even when the country clearly did not favour the measures.

In the course of the election campaign, Clark had promised to move the Canadian embassy in Israel from Tel Aviv to Jerusalem. This action had to be abandoned, as did a plan to "privatize" the state-owned oil company, Petro-Canada. The government failed to introduce a promised $2 billion cut in personal taxes or to bring down rising interest rates. Its downfall, in December 1979, came on its first budget, which contained a proposal to impose an 18-cents-a-gallon tax on gasoline and to allow Canadian oil prices to move upward toward the world price. The opposition parties combined to defeat the budget, forcing Clark to call a general election for February 18.

During the campaign it became apparent that the Clark government had lost the confidence of the electorate. The 40-year-old prime minister was perceived as well meaning but lacking in authority. His victory the previous May had benefited from a large protest vote against Trudeau and the Liberals, but he had not managed to turn that sentiment into positive support for his new government. In the media he suffered in comparison with the experienced Trudeau. The latter had been persuaded by his party to lead it through another election even though he had announced his wish to resign as leader just before the budget defeat.

The voting on February 18 revealed a modest Liberal gain in the Atlantic provinces, a virtual sweep of Quebec, where the formerly significant Social Credit movement was wiped out, and a 20-seat gain in the vital central province of Ontario. The Conservatives held two-thirds of the seats in the west, but these were not sufficient to give them more than 103 members in the 282-seat House of Commons. Four Conservative Cabinet ministers went down to defeat. The Liberals won 147 seats, a solid majority, and the third party, the socialist New Democrats (NPD), collected 32 seats in Ontario and the west. The Liberals won 44% of the popular vote, while the Conservatives, at 33%, fell 3% below their 1979 showing.

Trudeau returned to power on March 3, ending the Clark government's 272 days in office. It was Trudeau's fourth electoral victory, putting him in an unchallenged position in national politics. He chose two of his closest colleagues for key positions in his Cabinet: Allan MacEachen as minister of finance and deputy prime minister and Marc Lalonde as minister of energy. Seventeen former ministers were included, 5 were dropped, and 14 new ones were named. The lack of Liberal members from western Canada obliged Trudeau to appoint three senators to the Cabinet to represent the region. For the first time in Canada's history, a woman, Jeanne Sauvé, was named speaker of the House of Commons.

Trudeau's strength was enhanced by the results of the referendum on Quebec's independence on May 20. The goal of Premier René Lévesque and his Parti Québécois government ever since their advent to office in 1976, the independence option was termed "sovereignty-association." The concept envisaged Quebec enacting its own laws, collecting taxes from its people, and establishing relations with foreign countries. Simultaneously, it would form an economic union with the rest of Canada based on a common currency. In the referendum the Lévesque government did not ask directly for approval of the new status but sought authority to negotiate it with the rest of Canada. A second referendum was promised before the decisive step to separation was taken.

After a bitterly fought campaign in which Trudeau, federal ministers, and provincial premiers took part, the Quebec electorate rejected the plan. The "No" forces won 59.6% of the popular vote with 2,172,000 votes. Even among French-speaking residents, a small majority voted "No" to separation. The rejection was a deep disappointment to Lévesque, who vowed, however, to accept its consequences by continuing to work within the federal system. A provincial election would be required in 1981, and the PQ seemed intent on securing a new mandate through having provided good government rather than because it advocated Quebec's independence.

The process of creating a "renewed federalism" began immediately after May 20. Trudeau called the ten provincial premiers to meet him in Ottawa on June 9 and presented them with a list of priority items for constitutional reform. These ranged from a charter of human rights, including minority language protection, to broad powers affecting the economy and institutional changes such as a reconstructed Supreme Court. Expanded to 12 subjects, the list was discussed in a series of federal-provincial meetings, some among officials, others among

Former Canadian prime minister Pierre Elliott Trudeau was called out of his newly announced retirement to lead the Liberal Party to victory in elections held in February.

EVANS—GAMMA/LIAISON

ministers, over the summer. These led up to a summit conference of first ministers in Ottawa, September 8–13.

By this time it was apparent that wide differences existed between Ottawa and the provinces over what should be done to reform the constitution. Quebec's concerns over cultural and linguistic identity were supplemented by the Western provinces' demand for control over natural resources and by Newfoundland's claim that it possessed jurisdiction over offshore Atlantic resources. The long-standing quarrel between Ottawa and Alberta over energy pricing and revenue sharing, which had not been resolved despite personal negotiations between Trudeau and Alberta Premier Peter Lougheed, introduced further strains into the discussions. Thus the first ministers moved from a consideration of what might have pleased Quebec to a discussion of the claims of all the provinces.

After four days of fruitless argument, the premiers presented a list of demands representing each other's final positions. It did not include the entrenched charter of rights or the provisions for the free movement of labour, capital, and goods that Trudeau desired to strengthen Canada as an economic union. He and the federal ministers rejected the provincial consensus, and the conference dissolved in recriminations and forebodings.

As Parliament prepared to resume after the summer recess, Trudeau took a dramatic step. On October 2 he announced to the nation that he would ask the Commons and Senate to approve a resolution requesting the British Parliament to transfer the authority to amend Canada's constitution to Canada. Although a sovereign state, Canada had never possessed the power to amend its own constitution, an anomaly resulting from the inability of the provinces and the federal government to agree on an amending formula. Thus in the past the British Parliament has legally approved changes in the constitution on the request of the Parliament of Canada. Trudeau proposed to correct this situation by making the constitution a Canadian act (patriation). At the same time, he declared his desire to entrench in the act "a package for the people"—a charter of human rights and freedoms binding on the provinces as well as the federal government.

When Parliament met on October 6, Trudeau introduced his constitutional changes. The Conservatives immediately opposed them as a unilateral measure that violated the federal principle, while the NDP gave them qualified support. At a meeting of the provinces in Toronto on October 14, five provinces ranging from British Columbia to Newfoundland announced they would take the constitutional changes to court. This would be done by preparing a reference question that would be submitted to one of the provincial appeal courts. Trudeau pressed on with his plan to send his resolution to a joint Commons-Senate committee, hoping to have it endorsed so that the new Canadian constitution could be proclaimed on the country's next national day, July 1, 1981. It was a bold stroke on the success of which Trudeau's place in Canada's history would be based. (*See* Special Report.)

The Economy

The economy faltered in 1980, showing a decline of 1.7% in real gross national product for the first half of the year. The GNP in current dollars was expected to reach $281.4 billion for the year, an inflation-swollen figure that masked the slowest growth rate in a quarter of a century. The recession turned on weaknesses in consumer demand and such negative forces as high interest rates and a decline in sales to the United States. Inflation, at a rate of

Former Cabinet minister Jeanne Sauvé was escorted to the rostrum by former prime minister Joe Clark (left) and Prime Minister Pierre Trudeau in April when she became the first woman to be chosen speaker of the Canadian House of Commons.
WIDE WORLD

Banners on neighbouring houses in Quebec state the two sides of the issue in the referendum held in May to decide whether Quebecers would choose independence from the rest of Canada; the separatists lost the vote by a 3–2 margin.

JEAN-PIERRE LAFFONT—SYGMA

10.7% in August, was somewhat higher than in 1979, while unemployment, running at a seasonally adjusted rate of 7.4% in September, remained about the same as in 1979.

On March 10 the Bank of Canada announced the move to a floating bank rate, to be set in relation to the interest yield at the weekly auction of 91-day federal government treasury bills. After climbing to over 16% in April, the rate began to decline, standing at 13.9% in late November. The Canadian dollar fluctuated between 84 and 87 cents (U.S.) during the year.

Economic planning in 1980 was hindered by the continuing inability of the federal government to work out an acceptable oil-pricing agreement with Alberta, the chief producing province. The Clark administration was close to achieving such an agreement when it fell, having accepted Alberta's contention that Canadian oil prices must be allowed to rise slowly to near world levels. The Trudeau government refused to follow this policy, believing that domestic prices should be based on production and replacement costs in Canada. At stake also were the division of revenues from oil and gas and the federal government's imperative need to recover a larger share to support its subsidy for higher-cost imported oil needed in eastern Canada.

With over 8,000 jobs at risk, the Canadian provincial governments extended aid to the hard-pressed Chrysler Corp. on May 10. Ottawa agreed to provide $200 million in loan guarantees to Chrysler Canada, while Ontario gave the company $10 million toward financing a research centre at Windsor to test aluminum and plastic parts for automobiles. In return, the Canadian subsidiary of Chrysler promised that it would maintain employment levels in Canada at 9% of Chrysler's labour force in the U.S.

Foreign Affairs

Canada's disapproval of the Soviet intervention in Afghanistan was strongly shown in 1980. Ottawa agreed to hold wheat sales to the Soviet Union to the traditional level of slightly more than three million metric tons. Lifting of the commitment was announced on July 24 following conversations between Trudeau and U.S. Pres. Jimmy Carter at the Venice (Italy) economic summit meeting. Canada dropped out of the embargo in November but said it would not try to replace U.S. grain being withheld. A Canadian boycott of the Olympic Games in Moscow, first announced by the Clark administration, was confirmed by the Trudeau government on April 22.

Canadian actions against Iran were more symbolic than real, since Canadian-Iranian trade was negligible. Nevertheless, on May 22 imports and exports and banking deals were cut off to protest the taking of U.S. hostages at the U.S. embassy in Teheran on Nov. 4, 1979. A more spectacular act was the Canadian initiative in hiding six U.S. diplomats in the Iranian capital for almost three months and then removing them to safety through the use of false Canadian passports. Canada's ambassador to Iran, Kenneth Taylor, the architect of the Canadian rescue operation, was honoured by the U.S. Congress and given the Order of Canada.

Strains occurred between the two North American nations in 1980. Canada complained of the failure of the U.S. Senate to approve the 1979 treaty setting quotas for fish stocks in shared Atlantic coastal waters. The agreement also referred the disputed maritime boundary across the Gulf of Maine to international arbitration. The Senate balked at the treaty, feeling it was too generous to Canadian fishermen. Canada refused to accept amendments, as did the Carter administration.

Canada

THE CANADIAN CABINET

Members of the Canadian Cabinet in order of precedence:

Prime Minister .. Right Hon. Pierre Elliott Trudeau
Deputy Prime Minister and Minister
   of Finance ...... Hon. Allan Joseph MacEachen
Minister of Transport .... Hon. Jean-Luc Pepin
Minister of Justice, Attorney
   General, and Minister of State
   for Social Development ..... Hon. Jean Chrétien
Minister of Indian Affairs and
   Northern Development .. Hon. John Carr Munro
Minister of State for Economic
   Development ...... Hon. Horace Andrew Olson
Minister of Industry, Trade,
   and Commerce .... Hon. Herbert Eser Gray
Minister of
   Agriculture .... Hon. Eugene Francis Whelan
Minister of Consumer and
   Corporate Affairs and
   Postmaster General .... Hon. André Ouellet
Minister of Veterans
   Affairs .... Hon. Daniel MacDonald
Minister of Energy, Mines,
   and Resources .... Hon. Marc Lalonde
Leader of the Government
   in the Senate .... Hon. Raymond Joseph Perrault
Minister of Fisheries
   and Oceans .... Hon. Roméo LeBlanc
Minister of State for Science
   and Technology and Minister
   of the Environment .... Hon. John Roberts
Minister of National Health
   and Welfare .... Hon. Monique Bégin
Minister of Supply
   and Services .... Hon. Jean-Jacques Blais
Secretary of State and Minister
   of Communications .... Hon. Francis Fox
Minister of National
   Defence .... Hon. Gilles Lamontagne
Minister of Regional Economic
   Expansion .... Hon. Pierre DeBané
Minister of State (Canadian
   Wheat Board) .... Hon. Hazen Robert Argue
Minister of Labour and
   Minister of State (Sports) ... Hon. Gerald Regan
Secretary of State for
   External Affairs .... Hon. Mark MacGuigan
Solicitor General ..... Hon. Robert Phillip Kaplan
Minister of State
   (Multiculturalism) .. Hon. James Sydney Fleming
Minister of National
   Revenue .... Hon. William Rompkey
Minister of State (Finance) ... Hon. Pierre Bussières
Minister of State
   (Small Business) .... Hon. Charles Lapointe
Minister of State (Trade) ... Hon. Edward Lumley
President of the Privy
   Council and Leader of the
   Government in the House
   of Commons .... Hon. Yvon Pinard
President of the Treasury
   Board .... Hon. Donald Johnston
Minister of Employment and
   Immigration .... Hon. Lloyd Axworthy
Minister of Public Works .... Hon. Paul Cosgrove
Minister of State (Mines) .... Hon. Judy Erola

Acid rain was another Canadian concern, especially after President Carter introduced an energy bill into Congress requiring 50 power plants in the eastern U.S. to use coal instead of oil for fuel. A memorandum of intent was signed on August 5, providing for work groups to begin a study of air quality and for more vigorous enforcement of current antipollution standards.

President Carter's failure to visit Canada during his first term, making him the first U.S. president in recent years not to do so, disappointed Canadians. The most positive note struck in the bilateral field involved Congress' action to clear away the last roadblocks to the Alaskan Highway natural gas pipeline across western Canada and Canada's decision, on July 17, to allow the southern arm of the line to be started ahead of the main project. To run 850 km (530 mi) and cost $1.6 billion, the "prebuild portion" would deliver Canadian gas to the U.S. market by 1981.

After three years of evaluation, the Trudeau government announced on April 10 that it would buy 137 F-18A Hornet fighter aircraft from the McDonnell Douglas Corp. for defense needs in North America and Western Europe. The contract amounted to $2.7 billion for the planes and another $2 billion for spare parts and missiles. Under the arrangement, some of the components would be built in Canada. Another U.S. aircraft, the long-range Aurora patrol plane (an updated U.S. Navy Orion) built by the Lockheed Corp., began to arrive in Canada in May under another large procurement program worked out in 1976.

A billboard at the Ambassador Bridge facing Canada from Detroit expresses the gratitude of Americans for Canada's help in the escape of six U.S. diplomats from Iran in January.
WIDE WORLD

Special Report: Canada's Constitutional Dilemma

by Peter Ward

Disagreement over the future shape of Canada kindled a blaze of discord in 1980, pitting eight of the nation's ten provinces against the federal government and constituting a threat to Canadian union almost as dangerous as the rise of the separatist movement in Quebec. Only Ontario, Canada's most populous province, and New Brunswick backed Prime Minister Pierre Elliott Trudeau in his effort finally to give Canada its own constitution. Trudeau was seeking to rewrite the rules of Canadian confederation unilaterally, and he accused the dissenting provinces of petty regionalism. The provinces, on the other hand, were clamouring against what they saw as a blatant federal power grab and an attempt to impose centralism on a nation with tremendous regional diversity.

The British North America Act

Canada does not have its own constitution. The British North America Act, passed by the British Parliament in 1867 to establish the Canadian confederation, apportioned powers between the federal and provincial governments and set up a governmental structure for Canada based on the British parliamentary model. The Canadian Parliament has a House of Commons and a Senate, equivalent to Britain's House of Lords, with a specific number of seats allocated to each province; the senators are appointed by the government in power. Each province also has a legislature, with powers specified in the BNA Act. Legal systems were also specified. For criminal matters, all of Canada is under British-style common law. In civil law, the British common law pertains in all the provinces except Quebec, which has a codified system in the French style. The BNA Act can be amended only by the British Parliament, which in practice has not done so except at Canada's request. Customarily, such requests were made only when Ottawa and all the provincial governments were in agreement.

Periodically in Canadian history, the federal and provincial governments have struggled to reach agreement on a formula for revoking the BNA Act, so that Canada could write its own constitution. The latest series of meetings on the constitution began in 1967, Canada's centennial year, under the impetus of the populist, nationalist movement coming to the fore in Quebec. Trudeau, who was then federal justice minister, won national political recognition during the 1967 talks. He gained the leadership of the Liberal Party largely on the strength of his performance at that conference.

As prime minister beginning in 1968, Trudeau continued the push for constitutional reform. In 1971 his hopes foundered when Quebec's government rejected an agreement reached by the premiers at Victoria, B.C. Trudeau made another try at achieving constitutional agreement in the mid–'70s, but that, too, failed. Defeated in the May 1979 election, Trudeau intended to retire but reversed his plans when Joe Clark's short-lived Conservative government fell unexpectedly in December. Following the Liberal victory in February 1980, Trudeau set out to win his constitutional goals on the strength of his parliamentary majority—acting unilaterally if necessary. This would involve Canada's Parliament asking Britain's to pass legislation "patriating" (giving Canada sole authority over) the Canadian constitution without first obtaining the approval of the provinces.

The constitution and the danger that Quebec might separate from Canada had always been Trudeau's major themes, and the perception that he could deal with the Quebec problem was one of his political strong points. His writings before he entered federal politics in 1965 played on the dual themes of necessary political reform for Quebec and Quebec's future place within Canada. He maintained that Quebec would be foolish to separate from Canada. By remaining within the confederation, it could have a share of the whole rich nation. Trudeau suggested that Quebec could wield at least half the influence in Canada.

The Trudeau theme was repeated by federalists throughout the spring of 1980, as Quebec prepared for a referendum in which René Lévesque's separatist government sought authority to negotiate independence. The vote was lost by the separatists, with almost 60% of those going to the polls opting to stay within Canada. In Trudeau's view, constitutional reform was now even more urgent, because the federalists had won the Quebec referendum at least in part on the basis of a promise of such reform, although it is likely that the federalists would have won in any case.

Quebec separatists claim that the French language and culture can be preserved only by building a wall of protection around the province, making it a Francophone island in predominantly English-speaking North America. Trudeau wants language rights for French-speaking Canadians enshrined in a Canadian constitution that would require all provinces to provide French services and education wherever numbers warrant. Such a document would give French-speaking Canadians economic and cultural mobility throughout Canada. The quid pro quo would be similar rights for English-speaking Canadians in Quebec, which has strict language laws limiting English-language education and the use of English in business.

Clash with the Provinces

Trudeau wants a made-in-Canada constitution with a charter of human rights, including language rights. It is an aim that gives rise to a cultural clash with many of the provinces. Trudeau is a lawyer of the Quebec bar, trained in codified law in the continental tradition. Codified law assigns specific rights to individuals, and in theory they have no others. In British common law, citizens have all rights except those specifically withdrawn by law.

The philosophical clash between Trudeau and most of the English-speaking provinces is thus based to some degree on the difference between the British tradition of an unwritten constitution and customary law developed through judicial precedents and the more structured French approach, which reduces all matters of law to a written constitution and written legal codes. Adding to the nervousness of the dissenting provinces is the fact that in Canada members of the judiciary, with a few minor exceptions, are appointed by the central government. With a written bill of rights, their powers would be enhanced.

The conflict is also pragmatic: a battle between the two central provinces of Ontario and Quebec, which seek to maintain their traditional domination of the Canadian confederation, and the smaller and less populous provinces, many of which are enjoying or anticipating economic booms based on energy resources. In the west, Alberta, Saskatchewan, and British Columbia all have oil or natural gas. On the eastern seaboard, Newfoundland, with significant offshore oil and gas discoveries, is eagerly awaiting an energy bonanza.

Under existing Canadian laws, jurisdiction over resources is a provincial matter. Revenue from oil and natural gas has meant billions to the three western provinces, enabling them to enjoy budgets that are nearly in balance or actually in surplus. Newfoundland, traditionally a poor province, is confident that energy resources will make balanced budgets possible within a few years. Meanwhile, the federal government has been sliding deeper into debt each year. The predicted federal deficit in fiscal 1980–81 was $14 billion. Trudeau's intention is to move into the resources field for revenue by taxing energy, thus switching the flow of several billion dollars from provincial to federal coffers.

Energy and the Constitution

None of the energy-producing provinces likes the current federal policy of holding the price of oil and natural gas in Canada below world prices, yet it

The premiers of the ten Canadian provinces met with Prime Minister Pierre Trudeau in Ottawa in September to debate the proposed changes to the Canadian constitution. The issues at stake were basic to the continued cohesion of the country.
CANADIAN PRESS

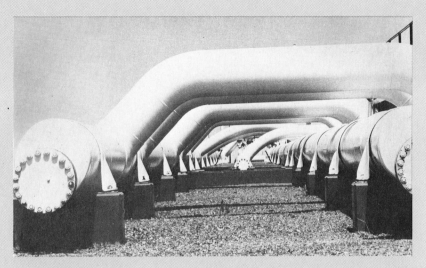

One problem that Canada must resolve is the tensions between the eastern population centres and the resource-rich western provinces. These natural gas lines tap the vast reserves in Alberta.

THE NEW YORK TIMES

was Clark's attempt to hike the price of gasoline that helped win the election for Trudeau in February 1980. Canadian domestic oil prices are roughly half the world price. Canada sells $4.5 billion in natural gas annually to the U.S. at double the price of natural gas in the domestic Canadian market. Lower energy prices benefit the industrial provinces of Ontario and Quebec but cost the energy-producing provinces billions in lost revenue. Canada imports 420,000 bbl of foreign crude oil daily at world prices for use in eastern Canada and subsidizes the cost from federal tax revenue to maintain a national fixed price. That subsidy could cost almost $3 billion in fiscal 1980–81.

The energy-producing provinces view this policy as being unfairly designed to aid industry in Ontario and Quebec. Trudeau's moves to take even more energy revenue away from the producing provinces are seen by those provinces as a centralist attempt to halt the rapid shift westward of Canada's economic centre of gravity. The centralist-dominated government, on the other hand, reasons that the rapid increase of energy prices worldwide bears no relation to production costs. In the eyes of Ontario and Quebec, increased provincial energy revenue is a windfall resulting from unnatural international conditions—the rise to power of the Organization of Petroleum Exporting Countries. Newfoundland is on the side of the energy-producing provinces because Trudeau refuses to concede to that province jurisdiction over offshore hydrocarbon discoveries.

Trudeau's position is made more difficult by the fact that, in the February 1980 election, the Liberals failed to elect a single member from the three western provinces with energy resources and elected only two members in Manitoba. His majority government is based on massive support from Ontario and Quebec. With 170 seats in the House of Commons out of a total of 282, those two provinces dominate Canada politically.

Trudeau's formula for replacing the British North America Act with a made-in-Canada consti-

tution was placed before the Canadian Parliament on Oct. 6, 1980. It made no mention of changes in the division of federal-provincial powers except for the introduction of a bill of rights, including language rights, and the creation of a system for amending the constitution. Language rights involve education, currently under provincial jurisdiction.

As for the amending procedure, for two years after patriation, the traditional unanimous agreement of all the provinces and the federal government would be required for any amendment. At the same time, unanimous agreement would be sought on a new amending formula, and Trudeau plans intensive constitutional meetings with the provinces during the two-year period. Lacking such agreement, a referendum would be held on any method approved by eight provinces (one of which would have to be Quebec) representing 80% of the population; an alternative method could also be offered by Ottawa. If no eight-province proposal was put forward, a modified Victoria formula would go into effect automatically. (The Victoria formula, so-called from the 1971 constitutional conference in Victoria, B.C., where it emerged, would require approval of any proposed amendment by a majority of provinces including Ontario, Quebec, two western provinces, and two Atlantic provinces.) This arrangement gives Ontario and Quebec, which between them contain slightly more than half of Canada's population, an effective veto. Both Alberta and British Columbia insist that they will not accept a veto by Ontario or Quebec unless they, too, hold veto power.

The stage is thus set in Canada for lengthy and bitter constitutional warfare, involving the courts, where federal unilateral moves are to be challenged, and the political arena, where feelings are so strong that the three wealthy western provinces may threaten separation. It may well be the stormiest period in Canadian history since the Riel Rebellion, which raged intermittently in western Canada for some 15 years a century ago.

CARIBBEAN STATES

Hurricane Allen struck the eastern Caribbean on August 4–7 with 200-mph winds; it was one of the worst Atlantic storms of the century. In St. Lucia 16 were killed; virtually all of the important banana crop was destroyed in St. Lucia and St. Vincent. In Haiti over 200 were killed, and one-fifth of the country's gross national product was lost. Thousands throughout the region were made homeless.

The Bahamas

In May the Bahamian government, which in matters of foreign policy continued to maintain a low profile, was faced with a major crisis following the sinking of a Bahamian coast guard vessel by Cuban military aircraft. The incident, in which four Bahamians were killed, occurred after the Bahamian vessel seized two Cuban fishing craft for illegally fishing in Bahamian waters. The Cuban government subsequently apologized and paid compensation.

The Bahamas continued to suffer from pressures created by an influx of illegal Haitian refugees. In May Prime Minister Lynden Pindling indicated that the 25,000 illegal immigrants were creating an impossible burden on finances and health services. By the latter part of the year the Bahamian government had begun to fly some of the illegal immigrants back to Haiti.

Barbados

At 7% Barbados's economic growth in 1979 was the highest in the region, though preliminary figures for 1980 indicated that this high level was unlikely to continue. Growth in tourist arrivals fell (up 6.9% in the winter of 1979–80, compared with 9% for 1978–79); increased consumer expenditure led to stricter credit controls; inflation (16% in 1979) grew; and energy prices increased. Even so, the island did not suffer as much from these problems as many of its neighbours.

Technical cooperation agreements with Trinidad were put into effect. Barbados continued to act as a catalyst for a joint coast guard and fisheries protection service embracing St. Lucia and St. Vincent.

Dominica

After months of mounting economic and administrative chaos under the interim government of Oliver Seraphine, Dominicans opted for stability on July 21, 1980, in the island's first general elections since independence in 1978. In choosing Dominica's broadly conservative Freedom Party by 17 seats to 4, the island's voters also provided the Caribbean's first female prime minister, Eugenia Charles.

During the year the existence of an agreement between the Seraphine government and the U.S.-based, Iranian-linked Inter-Continental Development Corp. was revealed. Under pressure from the U.S., implementation of the agreement was halted when it became known that the corporation had been allowed to issue Dominican passports.

Grenada

Throughout 1980 Grenada's People's Revolutionary Government (PRG) pursued three separate but related policies. Domestically, emphasis was placed on creating employment in agriculture and related industries and on improving education and public-sector management. The PRG sought close relations with its Caribbean neighbours, but overtures to Trinidad were rebuffed. Internationally, closer relations developed with Cuba, Eastern Europe, and Canada, but relations with the U.S. remained at a low ebb. In mid-June a bomb exploded beneath a platform on which virtually the entire government was sitting. The officials escaped, but two children and an adult were killed.

Guyana

In June 1980 Walter Rodney, one of the Caribbean's leading historians and a member of the opposition Working People's Alliance (WPA), died after a bomb blast. Throughout the year opposition groups alleged violent intimidation by government

Hundreds of Haitians took to the sea to escape the poverty and political repression of their homeland. More than 100, marooned on a small island in The Bahamas for longer than a month, were forcibly returned to Haiti in November.

MIAMI HERALD/BLACK STAR

Edward Seaga of the pro-Western Jamaica Labour Party defeated incumbent prime minister Michael Manley of the socialist People's National Party in the October elections.
UPI

supporters. Under the long-awaited new socialist constitution, Prime Minister Forbes Burnham on October 6 became executive president, with wide powers. Burnham was declared the winner in elections held December 15, with 76% of the vote.

Economically, the republic remained in a parlous state. In late 1979 the government had been unable to meet International Monetary Fund (IMF) terms for a three-year Guy$206 million credit, but by the end of 1980, under a more favourable arrangement, Guyana received a joint IMF-World Bank package of U.S. $133 million.

Haiti

Haitian Pres. Jean-Claude Duvalier's marriage to Michèle Bennett in May 1980 reduced the influence of the hard-liners surrounding his mother, Simone Duvalier. Several ministerial changes during the year were reportedly made to soften international criticism of the regime, which had grown following the arrival of 2,300 Haitian "boat people" in Florida in January–March. Considerable press freedom was permitted, and in September death sentences of four alleged saboteurs were commuted. In late November, however, there was a turnabout as journalists, human rights activists, and other opponents were arrested in a crackdown on dissent.

The economy made modest progress in 1979, with the growth rate of 2% (1978, 3.5%) resulting mainly from an increase in farm output and a strengthening of the external sector; however, the damage caused by Hurricane Allen was a severe blow to the economy.

Jamaica

Jamaicans decisively rejected the People's National Party (PNP) government led by Prime Minister Michael Manley at elections on Oct. 30, 1980. Winning by 51 seats to 9, the Jamaica Labour Party, led by Edward Seaga, pledged to restore the island's run-down economy by seeking assistance from the International Monetary Fund (IMF) and other Western aid donors and by creating a climate in which private enterprise could flourish.

Jamaicans rejected the PNP government because of a decline in their standard of living, a belief that the PNP government was associated with godlessness and Communism, a traditional desire to change government after two terms, and an ever increasing level of violence (at least 600 people were reported as murdered for political reasons during the first nine months of 1980).

In spite of new bauxite arrangements that would bring $1 billion in investment to Jamaica over four years, unemployment stood at 31.5%.

Saint Lucia

Early in 1980, after Deputy Prime Minister George Odlum had announced that Prime Minister Allan Louisy had gone back on his agreement to hand over the leadership of the ruling St. Lucia Labour Party after six months in office, an acrimonious public debate broke out. It centred mainly on Louisy's appointment on February 22 of Boswell Williams to succeed retiring Sir Allen Montgomery Lewis as acting governor-general. A Cabinet reshuffle in which Louisy emerged triumphant resolved differences. But, as a result, few of the government's election proposals were introduced. Yet the island remained economically buoyant until Hurricane Allen struck in August.

Saint Vincent and the Grenadines

Prime Minister Milton Cato's St. Vincent Labour Party government pursued a broadly conservative policy during 1980, the islands' first year of independence. The opposition remained in disarray. James Mitchell, leader of the New Democratic Party—who had lost his seat in the December 1979 general election—moderated his demands for seces-

Chemistry

sion of the Grenadines after being returned to Parliament in a by-election. The state of emergency proclaimed following an armed uprising on Union Island (one of the St. Vincent Grenadines) on Dec. 7, 1979, was lifted in May.

Suriname

On Feb. 25, 1980, a group of noncommissioned army officers overthrew the government headed by Prime Minister Henck Arron and set up a National Military Council (NMC). In March the NMC appointed Hendrick R. Chin A Sen prime minister. The immediate motive of the coup was a conflict between Arron and the military cadre over conditions of service, but the silent support of the majority of the population indicated that discontent with the Arron government was widespread. In May an attempted invasion by a mercenary force proceeding from neighbouring French Guiana was repulsed.

There was a further coup on August 13, led by one of the NMC's original leaders, Sgt. Maj. Daysi Bouterse. Two of the NMC's members were imprisoned; Pres. Johan Ferrier was dismissed; and Chin A Sen, who remained prime minister, was named president as well.

Trinidad and Tobago

With its vast reserves of oil and natural gas, Trinidad and Tobago remained the wealthiest Caribbean nation in 1980. In January Prime Minister Eric Williams announced a record TT$5 billion budget, of which a massive TT$2,168,000,000 was to be spent on capital projects. These included a vast high-technology complex at Point Lisas, which was to comprise an ultramodern iron and steel plant; liquefied natural gas, methanol, and fertilizer plants; an aluminum smelter; and a number of related industries. By the year's end all of the projects except the aluminum smelter were well under way. However, in spite of the large capital expenditures in the budget, many utilities such as water supply, electricity, and the telephone system remained in poor condition.

CHEMISTRY

Computers played a valuable role in the work of Frederick Sanger of the University of Cambridge in England, Walter Gilbert at Harvard University, and Paul Berg of Stanford University, who shared the 1980 Nobel Prize for Chemistry (*see* Nobel Prizes). Their studies on the sequences of the chemical units known as nucleotides, which make up the RNA and DNA present in the cells of living organisms, relied heavily on computerized analysis of experimental results. Only by knowing nucleotide sequences could DNA from one organism be combined with that of another, by means of gene splicing, to produce recombinant DNA. Microorganisms could thus be turned into tiny biochemical factories to synthesize gene products foreign to their nature. (*See* Biology Special Report.)

Perhaps the most exciting laboratory synthesis of the year was that of leukotriene C (1) by Elias J. Corey and his co-workers at Harvard in collaboration with Bengt I. Samuelsson and Sven Hammerstrom of the Karolinska Institutet in Stockholm. Leukotriene C, a biologically powerful natural product of the body, is well known for its role in the lungs during asthma attacks. Elucidation of its structure could lead to the design of drugs for treating asthmatic diseases. Other chemists added to the list laboratory-made antibiotics with the synthesis of (+)-thienamycin, lasalocid A, and a new group of drugs, known as penems, that are related to penicillins and cephalosporins. Other interesting syntheses included those of the anticancer compound streptonigrin, a complex compound nicknamed LICAM-C that proved extraordinarily successful in removing plutonium from living tissue, and enviroxime, an antiviral agent that might ultimately lead to a cure for the common cold.

Among structurally novel compounds produced during the year were structures dubbed spherands (2). Spherands are ligands, or coordinating molecules, which contain spherical cavities that can incorporate certain ions but reject others. Donald J. Cram and his team from the University of California at Los Angeles were tailoring spherands of different sizes to provide a means of improving separation techniques.

The study of chemical reactions, the properties of liquids, and the electronic structures of large molecules was being dominated increasingly by computers. In one instance, Robert Langridge and his collaborators at the University of California at San Francisco developed a computer program for illustrating in colour the shapes and structures of such complex molecules as proteins and DNA.

Lasers found their way into more chemistry laboratories, but interest in laser-induced photolysis declined because far fewer compounds than expected were found to give breakdown products that differed according to the kind of light—laser or conventional—used to initiate the reaction. James J. Turner and co-workers at the University of Nottingham, England, broke new ground with their photolysis studies of compounds in liquid xenon. Xenon had been used previously as an inert solid matrix near absolute zero (−273° C) for trapping chemical entities that would be unstable at normal temperatures. Turner's method provided a means for studying the kinetics of the decomposition and reaction of unstable molecules.

Work to emulate photosynthesis included attempts to generate hydrogen and oxygen from water using visible light and soluble catalysts. A ruthenium catalyst-based system developed by Michael Grätzel and his co-workers at the Federal Polytechnic Institute in Lausanne, Switz., showed much promise.

News was also made when Koji Nakanishi of Columbia University in New York City and Barry

UPI   UPI   WIDE WORLD

Their work in unraveling the secrets of DNA, the basic genetic material, won the Nobel Prize for Chemistry for (from left) Paul Berg of Stanford University, Frederick Sanger of Cambridge University in England, and Walter Gilbert of Harvard University. It was the second Nobel Prize for Sanger, whose first award came in 1958.

Honig of the University of Illinois, Urbana, provided a chemical model of how the human eye perceives colours. It had been known that a key molecule in the retina, 11-*cis*-retinal, which is bound to complex proteins called opsins, carries a light-absorbing group that constitutes the basis of colour recognition, but not how that group could be "tuned" to absorb more than one colour. The researchers offered evidence that minute differences in the positioning of electrical charges on the various opsins subtly affect the colour-absorption spectrum of retinal.

There were several notable studies of chemical reactions. Perhaps the study that generated the most comment was that of Ralph Dougherty of Florida State University, whose experiments to synthesize a compound called isophorone oxide in a spinning tube led him to conclude that gravity was affecting the yields of right- and left-handed products. He also suggested that prebiotic gravitational fields on Earth created the predominance of the left-handed amino acids found in plants and animals. Also interesting was a study by James P. Ferris and Robert Benson of Rensselaer Polytechnic Institute, Troy, N.Y., of the kinetics of photolysis of phosphine. One aim was to understand the nature of the Great Red Spot on Jupiter, thought to be due to the light-induced breakdown of phosphine in the upper atmosphere to red phosphorus.

CHESS

The Soviet chess championship went to a veteran grand master, Yefim Geller. The European junior championship was won by V. Chernin (U.S.S.R.), and the Soviet team won the European team championship at Skara, Sweden, without much difficulty. Though world champion Anatoly Karpov failed to win a single game in the event, he was awarded the Oscar Prize for his achievements over the whole

year. A knockout tournament held on BBC television was won, surprisingly, by the West German grand master Lothar Schmid, even though Viktor Korchnoi was competing.

The Candidates quarterfinal matches for the world championship were played in March 1980. Winners were Lev Polugaievsky (U.S.S.R.), Korch-

A new development in the chess world was the introduction of a hexagonal chessboard. The first European championship in the new game was held in London in August.

KEYSTONE

noi (Switz.), Lajos Portisch (Hung.), and Robert Hübner (West Germany). Later in the year Korchnoi beat Polugaievsky and Hübner beat Portisch in the semifinals. The two finalists in the women's Candidates matches were Nana Joseliani and Marta Litinskaya.

Britain won an Olympiad among the European Economic Community countries held in West Berlin. First prize in one of the strongest tournaments ever held in London, the Phillips and Drew Kings grand master tournament, was shared among Ulf Andersson (Sweden), Korchnoi, and Anthony Miles (England). The very young Garry Kasparov (U.S.S.R.) won first prize at an international tournament at Baku, U.S.S.R., in May and thereby gained the grand master title. In Yugoslavia Karpov scored an outstanding success at the very strong international tournament at Bugojno, and British grand master Michael Stean won first prize at Smederevska Palanka. The U.S. championship at Greenville, Pa., in June resulted in a triple tie among Browne, Larry Christiansen, and Larry Evans.

There was a tie for the British championship at Brighton between John Nunn and William Hartston. The U.S. Open at Atlanta, Ga., resulted in a tie between Florin Gheorghiu (Rom.) and the international master John Fedorowicz. The Rubinstein Memorial tournament, held at Polanica Zdroj, Poland, was won by the Soviet grand master Oleg Romanishin. Karpov repeated his previous year's success at Tilburg, where he won first prize in an immensely powerful tournament.

After some failures Danish master Bent Larsen won the Clarin grand master tournament at Buenos Aires, Arg., ahead of Karpov, who lost two games. The U.S.S.R. regained its world team championship in the Olympiad at Malta that ran from November 20 to December 6; Hungary was second and Yugoslavia third. A record 81 countries entered the event.

CHILE

On Sept. 11, 1980, the seventh anniversary of the military coup that overthrew Pres. Salvador Allende's government, Chile's new constitution was submitted to a national plebiscite. Pres. Augusto Pinochet received 67.5% of the votes cast, giving him an additional eight-year term of office and an option to serve a subsequent eight-year term after that, although he stated that he would not. The new constitution considerably extended previous plans for a return to constitutional government over a transition period of five years. There were objections regarding electoral procedures from leaders of opposition parties, especially the Christian Democrats. The Cabinet resigned in December to permit the president to reshuffle the government.

Important labour legislation passed during 1979 produced labour unrest in 1980. An unsuccessful strike by 10,000 mine and smelter workers January

WIDE WORLD

Soldiers guarded the polling places as Chileans cast their ballots in a nonbinding plebiscite to ratify a new constitution; the measure passed.

19–31 shut down the El Teniente copper mine, which was producing about one-third of Chile's copper; strikers rejected a 9% wage increase and protested against the new labour laws. The most notable features of the new labour code were that labour union affiliation and the payment of union dues was made voluntary; collective bargaining was allowed, although negotiations were restricted to the individual plant or company level; labour agreements had to be for a term of at least two years and were legally binding; and strikes were permitted but only if approved by secret ballot and only for a period of up to 60 days after which workers would be assumed to have dismissed themselves. The government intended that these measures should be used to hold wage increases in line with individual plant productivity and to reduce inflationary wage agreements. However, certain unions saw in this legislation a method of reducing the strength and influence of the unions and their political supporters.

Repression continued during 1980, although there were signs of political liberalization. In February the government implemented laws that would banish its opponents into internal exile for up to three months or place "disruptive elements" under house arrest. The state of emergency was extended on March 8 for a further six months, after the lifting of the state of siege. Nevertheless, unrest continued, and Lieut. Col. Roger Vergara Campos, director of Chile's army intelligence school, was assassinated in Santiago on July 15 by four men, who escaped. It was announced officially that 20 police detectives would be tried for kidnapping and torture. Because of the actions of his subordinates, Gen. Ernesto Baeza, head of the Criminal Investigation Department, resigned on August 11.

Main economic indicators implied that Chile had

made remarkable economic progress since 1973. In the period 1976–79 the gross domestic product (GDP) growth rate averaged 8%, reaching 8.5% in 1979, as compared with 1974, when the GDP fell by 12%. Inflation increased by 38.9% in 1979, with rates of 27% forecast for 1980; this compared with a rate of 600% in 1973. The balance of payments showed a surplus of $1,048,000,000, a marked reversal of the $112 million deficit of 1973.

These policies resulted in the return of foreign investors to Chile, although projects were mainly concentrated in the mining sector. Of the 346 projects that had been approved since 1974, 14 mining enterprises accounted for approximately 90% of total investment. Also, in line with the government's free market economic policies, many state-owned enterprises held by Corfo (the state development agency) had been sold by late 1980. In all, 400 companies had been returned to the private sector at a total purchase price of some $800 million. However, Chile's economic achievements were gained at some cost; real wages fell from 1972 levels, and there was marked unemployment, which lingered around the 14% mark in 1980.

CHINA

In 1980 the new pragmatic leadership of the Chinese Communist Party, under the guidance of Vice-Chairman Deng Xiaoping (Teng Hsiao-p'ing), consolidated its power, streamlining the party's ideology and structure and shaping domestic and foreign policies. Hua Guofeng (Hua Kuo-feng), the handpicked successor of Mao Zedong (Mao Tse-tung), remained chairman of the party but was replaced as premier by Zhao Ziyang (Chao Tzu-yang).

At the fifth plenum of the 11th party congress in February, Deng outlined China's major tasks for the 1980s as economic development and growth, opposition to Soviet hegemonism, and solving the problem of reunification of China and Taiwan. Unprecedentedly but realistically, he considered world peace and not world revolution as the main aim of Chinese Communist policy. Moreover, he emphasized that the number one priority was the program of Four Modernizations, and he would not allow the movement for human rights to interfere with the modernization drive. Deng proposed that the provision of art. 45 of the 1978 constitution granting Sida (Ssu Ta; literally, the "four bigs"), the four freedoms and rights (speaking out freely; airing views fully; holding great debates; and writing big-character posters), be deleted because these rights had "consistently been abused." The fifth plenum endorsed Deng's recommendation to propose deletion of art. 45 to the National People's Congress (NPC; the nominal legislature).

One of the most dramatic events of the fifth plenum was the complete rehabilitation of the late Liu Shaoqi (Liu Shao-ch'i), China's former president who had been purged in 1968. But glorification of Liu carried an implicit criticism of Mao's ideology and position, since he had been the man most responsible for Liu's downfall. Consequently, the fifth plenum's resolution on Liu's rehabilitation made the late defense minister Lin Biao (Lin Piao) and the "gang of four" (Mao's widow, Jiang Qing [Chiang Ch'ing], and three leaders of the Cultural Revolution) the scapegoats. It also asserted that Liu's restoration demonstrated "the party's determination to restore the true qualities of Mao Zedong Thought."

The 12-day session of the NPC, attended by 3,255 appointed delegates, was marked by a greater sense of openness and realism than in previous years. Various officials outlined China's new economic and financial policies, designed to make profit incentives and local accountability the driving forces behind economic growth. Vice-Premier Yao Yilin (Yao I-lin), the head of the State Planning Ministry, declared that free enterprise, factory autonomy, local decision making, and competition would be expanded. Peng Zhen (P'eng Chen), the former mayor of Beijing, introduced several new bills on taxes, marriage, and nationality and a constitutional amendment to outlaw wall posters; he stated that a graduated income tax would be imposed for the first time, but it would affect only about 20 Chinese and was aimed mainly at foreigners.

In a two-hour report to the NPC on September 7, Chairman Hua formally announced that, in accordance with the party's policy against officials holding high posts in both party and government, he would relinquish the premiership to Zhao. Seven aging vice-premiers, including Deng at 76, also resigned to make way for younger and technically qualified leaders. Head of state Marshal Ye Jianying (Yeh Chien-ying) had been widely expected to retire as well, and the postponement of his resigna-

China's new premier, Zhao Ziyang (right), succeeded Hua Guofeng, who relinquished the top post in September.
XINHA NEWS AGENCY / UPI

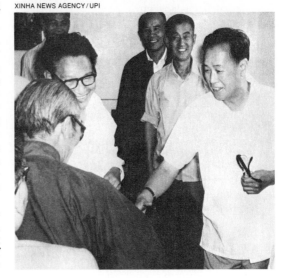

Former head of state Liu Shaoqi, who as an opponent of Mao Zedong (Mao Tse-tung) was purged in the Cultural Revolution, was posthumously "rehabilitated"; a memorial service was held on May 17.

tion was thought to reflect the Army's displeasure over its low priority in China's modernization program and over attacks on some of Mao's policies.

On Zhao's recommendation, the NPC appointed three vice-premiers, including Huang Hua, foreign minister since 1976. Congress closed the session by adopting a resolution on the revision of the constitution and four new laws, including the abolition of the right to put up "big character wall posters."

The trials of the gang of four, who had been under arrest for four years, and six followers of Lin Biao lasted from November 20 to December 29. The charges included persecuting officials, attempting to overthrow the state, and plotting to murder Mao. Jiang, who repeatedly disrupted the proceedings, claimed she had acted entirely at Mao's behest. A verdict was expected early in 1981.

The Economy

China's economy, founded on the Soviet model of public ownership of the means of production under centralized state control, was undergoing significant changes. The economic structure and management were being decentralized by giving more authority and responsibility to managers in agricultural communes and industrial plants. New material incentives and bonus systems were introduced. Rural markets selling peasants' homegrown products and the surplus produce of communes were revived. Individually owned shops closed during the Cultural Revolution were gradually being restored, and self-employed peddlers and craftsmen began to reappear.

The Statute of Joint Venture was promulgated in July, and subsequently the Commission for Foreign Investment was established to facilitate the formation of joint ventures with foreign concerns and the transfer of capital and technology from abroad. Negotiations between the Chinese authorities and various foreign governmental financial and industrial institutions, both public and private, resulted in agreements to undertake joint ventures involving billions of dollars. The effect on trade was apparent. China's total trade rose 28% in 1979 to $29,570,000,000, with imports exceeding exports by $2 billion. In the first half of 1980, however, exports rose 35% to $8.4 billion, while imports increased only 7.8%, to $8,270,000,000.

Official figures indicated that output in several key industries had risen over 1978 levels: steel production increased 8.5%, from 31,780,000 to 34,480,000 tons; coal rose 2.8%, from 618 million to 635 million tons; and electric power reached 282 billion kw-hr, a gain of 9.9%. Much larger gains, amounting to 25% or more, were made in light industries producing consumer items such as television sets, cameras, and wristwatches.

Foreign Affairs

In the spring China replaced Taiwan in the International Monetary Fund and the World Bank. Through 1980 relations between Beijing and Washington progressed rather smoothly, with exchanges of political, communications, economic, educational, and cultural missions as well as the significant July meeting of U.S. Pres. Jimmy Carter and Chairman Hua in Japan. On the other hand, the 30-year Sino-Soviet alliance expired on April 11 without any fanfare. Beijing joined Washington in denouncing the Soviet invasion of Afghanistan and indicated concern over any prospective Soviet moves against Pakistan and Iran.

About a week after the expiration of the Sino-Soviet treaty, a new Chinese ambassador, Yang Shouzheng (Yang Shou-cheng), arrived in Moscow, ending an 11-month hiatus. However, normalization talks with Moscow stalled in May over the issue of Soviet support of Vietnam's invasion of Cambodia. In early June, China and the Soviet Union signed a trade agreement, but the Soviet role in China's economy had declined sharply.

High-level talks on the border dispute between Beijing and Hanoi came to nothing because the Vietnamese refused to discuss their occupation of Cambodia. In March, Khieu Samphan, premier of the Khmer Rouge government deposed by the Vietnamese forces, made an official visit to Beijing to seek material and political assistance. Vietnamese strikes into Thailand in June in pursuit of Cambodian rebels brought sharp protests from China and the U.S. and a flow of U.S. arms to Thailand. Both China and the U.S. supported the Khmer Rouge regime's right to hold Cambodia's seat in the UN. (*See* Cambodia; Vietnam.)

Despite the ideological gulf between Washington and Beijing, their global interests in resisting Soviet expansionism seemed to coincide. On January 5, immediately after the Soviet invasion of Afghanistan, U.S. Secretary of Defense Harold Brown arrived in Beijing for an eight-day tour of important industrial and military establishments. On January 24 the U.S. Congress overwhelmingly approved a most-favoured-nation trade agreement with China. Returning Brown's visit, Geng Biao (Keng Piao), vice-premier for security and secretary-general of

the Military Affairs Commission of the Communist Party, arrived in the U.S. on May 25 for a two-week tour. In sum, the U.S. agreed to sell to China a variety of high-technology and military hardware. In March the U.S. and China signed an accord providing for U.S. government assistance in designing and building major hydroelectric and flood-control projects in China and in training Chinese engineers in the U.S. In June the U.S. Export-Import Bank for the first time extended government credit to China, amounting to nearly $70 million for construction of a steel mill near Shanghai. These aid projects led to a number of business deals with U.S. companies and encouraged Sino-U.S. joint ventures. U.S. trade with China had doubled, to over $2.3 billion, between 1978 and 1979.

In early September William J. Percy, U.S. undersecretary of defense for research and engineering, led a high-level Pentagon delegation on an official mission to China. In mid-September a high-level Chinese delegation led by Vice-Premier Bo Yibo (Po I-po) arrived in Washington for the first formal session of the Sino-American Joint Economic Committee. President Carter and Vice-Premier Bo signed four major agreements on September 17, governing civil aviation, shipping, consulates, and textile trade. Carter declared that normalization of relations between the two countries was "at last complete."

Hua visited Japan in late May; he was the first head of a Chinese government to visit Japan in some 2,000 years. In a joint communiqué issued on May 29, the leaders of the two countries expressed concern over conflicts and tensions in the Asia-Pacific and Middle East regions and affirmed the importance of continued expansion of trade and economic exchange and cooperation. Hua returned to Tokyo on July 8 to attend a memorial service for Prime Minister Masayoshi Ohira, who had died on June 12. President Carter also attended the service, and his special meeting with Hua afterward demonstrated Washington's desire to affirm and increase its friendship with the two leading Asian countries.

The long-awaited trial of the "gang of four" opened in Beijing (Peking) in November. Ten defendants were on trial, including Jiang Qing (right), widow of Mao Zedong, for various treasonous crimes including plotting the murder of Mao.

CHINE NOUVELLE/SYGMA

CITIES AND URBAN AFFAIRS

In the mid-1970s, advisers to Pres. Gerald R. Ford declared that the urban crisis was over in the U.S. The year 1980 proved them wrong. After many years of comparative calm in impoverished inner-city neighbourhoods, underlying tensions rooted in racial animosity and economic hardship erupted again, this time in Miami. A riot in the Florida city's black section, the Liberty City area, left a total of 18 persons dead, more than 300 injured, and hundreds of shops and homes looted and burned in a 100-block area. The disorders were ignited by the acquittal of four former Dade County policemen accused of the fatal beating of a black insurance executive. But analysts all agreed that despite major gains since the riots of the 1960s, things were still very hard indeed for those remaining in the worst ghettos, where unemployment among black youths still hovered around 40%. Moreover, the Miami events also highlighted another growing urban problem, the mounting tension between the black populace and a Hispanic minority that was rapidly swelling in many cities, competing for the same jobs and living space as the blacks.

The Miami episode was only the most vivid event in a year that left urban leaders uneasy and uncertain about the future. By year's end, a national election had swept in a new president, Ronald Reagan, a conservative Republican who had promised to slash federal spending on social programs and who was considered by many mayors to be insensitive to the needs of urban dwellers. The election also swept out many liberal senators and congressmen who could be counted on in years past to back the social programs that many mayors felt had helped reverse

The Boston public transit system, the Massachusetts Bay Transportation Authority, went broke in late 1980 when the state legislature failed to vote needed funds.

WIDE WORLD

the decline of major cities. It remained to be seen, of course, how the new president would treat the cities, but it was clear that Pres. Jimmy Carter's urban policies, which fared badly even in a heavily Democratic Congress, were largely dead. They seemed destined to be replaced by a policy that relied much more heavily on urban revival based on private initiatives. A lame-duck session of Congress did pass a renewal of the $4.6 billion general revenue-sharing program, after intense lobbying, which some cities had come to depend on to provide the most basic of services. But the fate of many other urban priorities, such as strengthening of the fair-housing laws, public works, and energy conservation aid, was left in doubt.

Already on the wane, big-city political power was expected to suffer even further as a result of the decennial census of the population taken in 1980. It was widely known that population had shifted dramatically in the 1970s toward the South and West and toward smaller cities and towns. But the preliminary figures issued by the Bureau of the Census still came as a shock to many big cities. New York City was said to have lost about one million persons, or about 14% of its 1970 population. Philadelphia was down by 18% and St. Louis by 31%. Other northern and industrial cities suffered similar losses. But mayors of the older cities were not ready to accept the numbers without a fight. The Census Bureau was hit by a dozen or more lawsuits charging that breakdowns in census procedures had caused a severe undercounting in large cities with heavy concentrations of the poor and of illegal aliens, thereby cheating those places of both political power and much-needed federal and state aid. While previous head counts had been plagued by such error, this one was much more bitterly contested because in the past decade Congress had based the allocation of dozens of aid programs on population counts—programs now worth about $50 billion a year to local governments.

In September Federal District Judge Horace Gilmore upheld the suit brought by Detroit, invalidating the 1980 census until the Census Bureau came forward with a means of artificially adjusting the count for those believed to have been missed. Meanwhile, another federal judge in New York ordered the bureau to turn over to the city its address lists so that the city's demographers could check to see if the census takers had missed any dwellings. The Census Bureau appealed both decisions. The bureau maintained that despite many problems the count was the most accurate in history. Whatever the outcome of the legal actions, which seemed headed to the Supreme Court, it was certain that there would be major losses in congressional power by the big cities in 1982, as well as shifts in the power balance within the states; the only question was how extensive the change would be.

Meanwhile, the tax revolt that began in California had spread to the East Coast. It was most

Tensions and outrage boiled over in Miami in May into bloody, destructive rioting after a jury freed four former Dade County policemen in the beating death of a black man; 18 people died, including several whites who were dragged from their cars in riot areas and beaten to death.

dramatic in Massachusetts, where an antiquated tax structure had caused growing public resentment. Over the warnings of local officials that services would be sharply cut, voters there overwhelmingly approved a referendum, nicknamed Proposition 2½, that promised to cut property taxes in the state, taxes that were among the highest in the country. It was meant to reduce and limit annual property levies to 2.5% of the "full and fair cash value" of the property. It was not immediately clear what the vote's ultimate impact would be on public services. But the most dramatic effects were likely to occur in the state's largest city, Boston, which was heavily dependent on an extremely high tax rate and burdened with a large poor population. The tax revolt was felt, though, even before the proposition had its effect, when the Massachusetts Bay Transportation Authority, which runs the buses and subways in the Boston area, ran out of money in November. Neither the state legislature nor the advisory board of local officials that oversees the system would appropriate more funds, and on November 18, the day of the season's first snowstorm, the system was ordered shut down. Over 250,000 commuters would have been stranded had not Gov. Edward J. King used emergency powers to take over the system and keep it running. The Massachusetts Supreme Court ruled November 28 that Governor King had acted without legal authority, however, and ordered the transit system to

shut down at midnight on December 5 unless the state legislature, meeting in special session, could pass a funding bill to allow the system to operate until the end of the year. The legislature missed the court's deadline, and the transit system was shut down for more than a day before a funding measure was finally passed.

School desegregation also continued to be a major urban issue. Court-ordered busing began in St. Louis and Pittsburgh, and busing was expanded in Cleveland, Indianapolis, Los Angeles, Seattle, and other cities. There was little of the overt public opposition of previous years, and the courts generally supported the claims of integrationists. But their aims were nevertheless being thwarted by bigger forces, the pressures of demography—a white birthrate that was falling faster than the black one, and a continuing exodus of white families to the suburbs. It all meant that there were fewer and fewer white children in the big cities with whom to achieve racial integration. The effort was further complicated by the growing influx of Hispanic children in the northern cities, throwing many a busing plan out of kilter. Moreover, Congress passed a bill that prevented the Justice Department from using any of its funds to press for busing as a remedy for school segregation; the bill was vetoed by President Carter. Civil rights advocates remained fearful, however, over what the new administration might mean for racial relations in the coming decade.

WIDE WORLD

Leftist guerrillas of the M-19 group were given asylum in Havana in April after they had held diplomats hostage in the Dominican Republic embassy in Bogotá, Colombia, for 61 days.

COLOMBIA

Colombia's midterm (*mitaca*) municipal and local elections were held in March 1980, the ruling Liberal Party gaining about 1.8 million of the votes and the Conservative Party 1.1 million. Although the elections passed without incident in spite of problems caused by the occupation of the Dominican Republic's embassy by guerrillas, 72% of the electorate abstained from voting, apparently indicating the electorate's dissatisfaction with political arrangements.

The two parties acted in unison to pass legislative and judicial reforms through Congress, effectively strengthening the political system. Against Colombia's background of continuing economic and political discontent, increasing violence, and the problems brought about by the illicit drug trade, there was no likelihood in 1980 that the state of siege imposed in 1976 or the security statute of September 1978 would be repealed.

On February 27 the Dominican Republic embassy in Bogotá was occupied by members of the left-wing M-19 guerrilla organization, marking the start of a two-month siege; 57 hostages were taken, including the ambassadors of Austria, Brazil, Costa Rica, Dominican Republic, Egypt, Guatemala, Haiti, Israel, Mexico, Switzerland, the U.S., Uruguay, and Venezuela. On April 27 the

siege was ended upon payment of a ransom thought to amount to some $2.5 million and an investigation of the human rights situation in Colombia by the Inter-American Human Rights Commission. The terrorists obtained asylum in Cuba. As part of the negotiations Pres. Julio Turbay Ayala appointed a team of lawyers to find a method of speeding up the trial of 219 of the M-19 guerrillas, against whom proceedings had begun at the end of 1979. On April 1 a report on Colombia was issued by Amnesty International, a human rights watchdog group. The report recommended that the state of siege that had been continuously enforced for the previous 30 years should be lifted and that the trial of civilians by military courts should cease, and it stated that there was evidence of cases of torture in Colombia.

It was expected that Colombia would become a member of the General Agreement on Tariffs and Trade (GATT) early in 1981. A protocol for Colombia's accession to GATT was signed in Geneva on April 17 but was not fully ratified by the Colombian Congress by year's end.

Colombia's economy performed well during 1979, with a gross domestic product growth rate of 5.5%; although a respectable increase by world standards, this did not compare favourably with 1978, when a rate of 8.8% was achieved. The main economic problem was inflation, which rose by 29.8%, as opposed to 17.8% during 1978. The external sector remained strong, with a balance of payments surplus of U.S. $1 billion and an increase in international reserves to $4 billion.

COMMUNICATIONS

New Earth satellite developments and fibre-optics applications were the leaders in communications technology in 1980. Meanwhile, the regulatory problems of the communications industry remained unsolved, and giant AT&T provided new services remarkably like data distribution and processing, further blurring the distinction between communications and computing.

Satellites

As more Earth satellites joined those already in space, legal questions about their orbits and frequency assignments continued to be debated. Much of this effort took place under the jurisdiction of the UN-sponsored World Administrative Radio Conference (WARC), which finished several months of discussion at the end of 1979. WARC is a general meeting occurring once every 20 years, although smaller, more specialized meetings are held in the interim. Its purpose is to divide up frequencies and satellite orbits to avoid electrical and physical interference. WARC left most questions of how to allocate old, still unassigned frequencies and new frequencies in the 14-gH range still unsettled. Also unsolved was the problem of the Western Hemisphere, which was fast running out of synchronous-

British satellite engineers, moving into the lucrative, high-demand field of communications satellites, work on a Maritime Communications Satellite to be used for worldwide communications for shipping at sea.
KEYSTONE

orbit parking spaces for satellites over North America.

Among satellites launched by the National Aeronautics and Space Administration in 1980, the Solar Maximum Mission Satellite (SMM) was designed to watch for the solar flares that would be peaking over the next few years. These bursts of electromagnetic noise can all but wipe out military and commercial communications, and early warning is vital to minimizing and compensating for outages. Theoretically, the satellite could be picked up by the space shuttle in 1982 or 1983 and refurbished for use, saving millions of dollars over the cost of launching a completely new satellite. However, the shuttle's timetable continued to slip. (*See* Space Exploration.) Communications satellites planned for launch by the shuttle were switched to the tried and true launch-rocket approach, among them the 14-gH digital technology satellite launched in November by Satellite Business Systems Corp. and geared to office and factory communications.

Fibre Optics

The application of fibre-optic technology to practical systems in 1980 was led by AT&T, which started development of a 983-km (611-mi) system to link Boston, New York, Philadelphia, and Washington by a laser-powered light-wave system. The largest system announced so far, it would ultimately connect 19 of Bell's electronic digital switches. The all-digital system would let Bell carry voice, video, and data signals. It was the strongest evidence yet of Bell's commitment to a future all-digital network making extensive use of fibre-optic technology.

Looking even further ahead, Bell tested equipment with an eye to laying a fibre-optic cable 6,500 km (4,000 mi) under the Atlantic to Europe. The system would be powered by laser diodes operating at a 1.3-micrometer wavelength. At this longer wavelength—0.8 micrometers had been used heretofore—cable attenuation is lower, and far fewer costly amplifiers would be needed as compared with electrical, coaxial cable systems. Each amplifier would have an operating laser and three standbys, giving the system a mean time between failures of eight years. The digital amplifiers could carry 4,032 conversations per fibre, compared with 200 for copper systems.

Information Systems

Computer-controlled communications services became more available, again spearheaded by AT&T. The Bell Telephone Co. of Pennsylvania offered a service delivering voice messages to other subscribers in the network, a form of electronic mail in which the sender specifies phone number, message, and delivery time. Some form of this service would also be offered by Bell's Advanced Communications Service, though software and organizational problems continued to plague it in 1980. Xerox Corp.'s XTEN, a system with similar goals but with microwave transmission for local distribution, was also troubled. Questions were raised about the size of the market and the amount of capital needed.

COMPUTERS

Computers became more commonplace in 1980—a familiar sight in banks, libraries, travel agencies, even pharmacies. As the cost per unit of computing power continued to drop (an average of 15% a year), spokesmen for data processing technology boasted that similar progress in the automobile in-

Computers that monitored and reported in dashboard readouts fuel consumption, speed, and engine function and gave warnings of malfunction of electrical equipment or low levels of necessary fluids turned up in late-model luxury cars.
FORD MOTOR CO.

dustry would have resulted in 1980 Rolls-Royces selling for $70 apiece. The remarkable decline in the price of computer hardware, making it possible for businesses of all sizes and even individuals to own a computer, remained primarily attributable to the chip, a sliver of silicon containing the computer's complicated integrated circuitry.

Surprisingly, then, one of the few serious problems facing the computer industry in 1980 concerned those very chips: demand simply far outstripped supply. The world market for semiconductor circuits reached $10 billion, and industry officials predicted that figure would more than double within five years as the chips continued to find new uses in a variety of consumer products and industrial processes.

A problem for U.S. manufacturers was a possible Japanese invasion of U.S. computer markets. The Japanese computer companies—benefiting from government-subsidized research and development —could offer customers a level of technology fully comparable to that of their U.S. counterparts. The crucial difference lay in software, the programmed instructions that tell the computer what to do. As the decade opened, U.S. companies were still enjoying a clear edge in computer software.

Without question the most aggressive U.S. company in fending off the Japanese invasion was IBM Corp. The giant U.S. computer maker, long dominant in the general-purpose (mainframe) portion of the industry, steadily increased its interest in minicomputers (a Japanese strength) and in creating a network of interrelated information devices (the "office of the future"). The increasing preference for distributed data processing, in which smaller computers and a multitude of terminals replace the single large central processor, forced IBM to reorient its approach to the market.

Other mainframe manufacturers discovered that the road to survival lay in software specialization. As a consequence Sperry Univac developed units specifically designed for governmental applications, while NCR concentrated on meeting the computer needs of retailers. Burroughs Corp., Honeywell Inc., and Control Data Corp. similarly sought out niches of the $10 billion mainframe market, and all participated in the 15–20% growth rate that segment of the computer market enjoyed.

The minicomputers, however, remained the fastest-growing segment of the computer hardware industry. Expected to grow at an annual rate of more than 30% a year through the 1980s, the minicomputer industry looked to Digital Equipment Corp. as its leader.

Applications

While predicting that the age of electronic equipment for automobiles was just starting, carmakers equipped 1980 vehicles with a variety of computer-related gear. The Lincoln Mark VI featured a dashboard with three microcomputers: a bar-chart fuel gauge, a digital speedometer, and a message centre. The message centre could spell out information about 36 mechanical conditions as well as provide a reading on how many miles remained to a particular destination. Cadillac's Seville and Eldorado models used a chip to determine fuel consumption, on both an average and instantaneous basis.

For 1981 General Motors planned to include a computerized emission-control system on every car, while Ford and Chrysler models would also be laden with chip-controlled devices. And it was thought that by 1983 the automakers might even provide talking computers to tell owners what was wrong with their malfunctioning cars.

Viewdata, a system in which ordinary television receivers are transformed into computer terminals via a telephone hookup between the sets and a large computerized information bank, was launched on a pilot basis in Canada. The system allowed 1,000 Canadian homes and offices to view on their TV screens a wide variety of information, including airline schedules, stock market listings, and news bulletins.

CONGRESS, U.S.

The 96th Congress completed action on Pres. Jimmy Carter's energy program in 1980. It took significant steps toward deregulation of banking, railroads, and trucking, doubled the size of the national park system, established a method of coping with environmental disasters, and stepped up the pace of military spending.

It failed to act on the SALT II disarmament treaty, welfare reform, national health insurance, and a revised criminal code. It took steps to reduce paperwork the federal government imposes on the public but failed to act on overall regulatory reform. It failed to take dramatic action on the economy.

The Budget

Congress took no final action on a tax cut. President Carter opposed such a cut in 1980, arguing that the first priority had to be control of inflation. In line with that stand, Congress and the president worked together to produce the first balanced budget resolution in the six-year-old congressional effort at budget reform. The balanced preliminary budget, however, was thrown out of kilter by recession in early summer.

The final budget, delayed until after the elections, included a deficit of $27.4 billion. House Budget Committee Chairman Robert N. Giaimo (Dem., Conn.) told the House that spending figures reflected across-the-board cuts that would have to be worked out in detail by the Reagan administration. He also said the projected federal revenue figure of $605 billion was low enough to allow a 1981 tax cut

of $30 billion to $35 billion. The budget anticipated a tax cut of $39 billion.

For the first time, Congress adopted a so-called reconciliation resolution, a further step in its budget reform. All committees were required to change spending resolutions to meet the limits set in the budget resolution. The reconciliation measure called for $4.6 billion in savings on programs already on the books and increased the revenue projections, thus cutting the deficit $8.2 billion below what it would have been otherwise.

Energy Legislation

The major piece of economic legislation of the session was the windfall profits tax on oil. It was the largest single tax ever levied on an American industry: the revenue for the federal government was estimated at $227.3 billion over ten years. This would recover part of an extra $1 trillion that oil companies were expected to make in that period as the result of a 1979 presidential order gradually decontrolling oil prices.

Most oil from wells in production before 1979 was taxed at 70% of the difference between selling price and an inflation-adjusted base price. There were special, lower rates for small amounts of output by producers who did not sell at retail, for stripper oil reclaimed from largely exhausted wells, for oil discovered after 1978, and for special oil resulting from special procedures that raise total well output. Alaskan oil except for the Sadlerochit reservoir on the North Slope was exempted, as was oil from land owned by Indians, state and local

The first two congressmen found guilty in the FBI's Abscam bribery setup were (left) John W. Jenrette (Dem., S.C.) and Michael Myers (Dem., Pa.); Myers was expelled from the House. Harrison A. Williams (right) of New Jersey was the only senator to be indicted in the case.

WIDE WORLD   WIDE WORLD   GEORGE TAMES–THE NEW YORK TIMES

Republican congressional leaders conferred after the November election, which changed the balance of power in Congress. Sen. Howard Baker (left foreground), who had been Senate minority leader, was later chosen Senate majority leader for the 97th Congress.
GEORGE TAMES – THE NEW YORK TIMES

governments, nonprofit medical and educational institutions, and churches that donated their proceeds to such institutions.

Congress rejected a presidential plea to put windfall tax receipts in a trust fund for mass transit, fuel assistance to the poor, and development of alternative energy sources. Instead, it channeled the money into the government's general fund, with a directive that 60% go for income tax relief, 25% for aid for fuel assistance to low-income families, and 15% for energy and transportation programs.

The bill also provided new or increased tax credits for solar, wind, geothermal, hydroelectric, and biomass projects and for synthetic and alcohol fuel investments. (Biomass projects involve use of organic waste, such as crop, timber, or animal waste, including sewage.) Credits were allowed for residential power or insulation projects. Grants of $3.1 billion to states were authorized to help poor families with rising fuel bills in the 1981 fiscal year.

A second major element of the nation's energy policy adopted in 1980 was a synthetic fuels bill. It created a Synthetic Fuels Corporation with authority to spend $20 billion to promote private production of substitutes for petroleum and natural gas made from coal, shale, tar sands, heavy oil, and hydrogen obtained from water. The law set a goal of producing 500,000 bbl a day of synthetic fuels by 1987 and two million a day by 1992. (Oil imports were about six million barrels a day in 1980.) In effect, the bill set a pattern for distributing part of the money generated by the windfall tax.

Lesser but still substantial authorizations were made for other undertakings: $1.2 billion to promote production of alcohol and other fuels from biomass; $250 million for urban waste projects; $2.5 billion for energy conservation; and $525 million

for solar energy, to be used for construction loan subsidies by a Solar Energy and Conservation Bank. President Carter's request for an energy mobilization board to cut red tape on energy projects was not adopted.

A standby gasoline-rationing plan, for use only in an emergency that involved a 20% shortfall of gasoline supply for 30 days, was set up when Congress failed to block presidential action. The plan, proposed by President Carter, would authorize ration coupons for motorists, based on their states' record of gasoline consumption. Coupons could be bought and sold openly. Congress retained a veto over putting the plan into effect.

Congress passed, over President Carter's veto, a measure killing an oil import fee the president had ordered. The fee would have been passed on to consumers as a surcharge of ten cents a gallon on gasoline. It was the first time since 1952 that a veto of a Democratic president had been overridden.

Other Economic Action

A major banking bill ordered the gradual phasing out of interest rate ceilings on consumer deposits over six years. The rate at the time of passage was 5¼% for commercial banks and 5½% for savings and loan institutions. A Depository Institutions Deregulatory Committee was given a target of a ¼% increase within 18 months and further ½% increases yearly in the third, fourth, fifth, and sixth years. The bill authorized financial institutions to begin or continue interest-bearing, check-type accounts using what were styled negotiable orders of withdrawal (NOW accounts). Savings and loan institutions were given the right to make new types of consumer loans and to increase the maximum amount covered by a single mortgage. Federal Reserve Board requirements on reserves were applied to all depository institutions.

Railroad rates were substantially deregulated. Carriers were allowed to fix rates anywhere below a stated percentage of variable, out-of-pocket hauling costs. Congress fixed the percentage at 160 at the start, rising to 170–180 by 1984. Until 1984 annual 6% increases were authorized within specified ceilings. Contracts setting special rates for special services were allowed under most conditions. Much of the railroads' immunity to antitrust laws, however, was revoked. Conrail was allocated $329 million in fiscal 1981, and $1.4 billion was made available to aid railroads in financial difficulties.

The trucking industry also was substantially deregulated. The new trucking law made it easier for new haulers to obtain permits and allowed increases or decreases of 10% a year in rates. Most antitrust exemptions relating to rates for single-line hauls would be ended by 1984; meanwhile, only firms directly involved would be allowed to participate in decisions by rate bureaus.

An Office of Information and Regulatory Affairs was ordered to pass on all federal requests for information from the public. The director of the office would have to make sure the information was needed, that it could not be obtained elsewhere, and that it would be collected effectively. The goal was a 25% reduction within three years in the amount of paperwork the federal government requires from citizens. It was estimated that the total cost of preparing information now required by the federal government was $100 million a year.

The Environment

A total of 104.3 million ac in Alaska—an area larger than all of California—was protected under an act that President Carter called one of the most important pieces of conservation legislation in the history of the nation. Included were 43.6 million ac for new national parks, 53.8 million for wildlife refuges, 3.4 million in national forests, 1.2 million for the wild and scenic rivers system, and 2.2 million for other types of conservation areas. The action doubled the size of the national park and wildlife refuge systems. (*See* Environment.)

A $1.6 billion fund to clean up toxic waste spills and chemical dumps was authorized. The money would be accumulated over five years, with 87.5% coming from new taxes on the chemical industry and 12.5% from general tax revenues. The federal government was authorized to file suits through the Environmental Protection Agency to cover cleanup costs. The bill did not cover oil spills, but Congress promised to tackle that problem in 1981.

U.S. companies were authorized to explore the ocean floors for minerals but not to begin commercial development before 1988. By then it was hoped that an international treaty on the subject would be in effect.

Defense and Foreign Affairs

For the first time since the war in Vietnam, Congress appropriated more for defense than the president had requested. A $52.8 billion weapons authorization bill was $5.9 billion above the president's request. The main military appropriations bill of $160.1 billion, passed later in the session, was another $5.6 billion above the request. Included in the bills besides a buildup of ships and combat planes were funds for the MX mobile missile system and for development of the experimental CX cargo plane and a new manned bomber. There was $3,150,000 allocated for construction of a plant to produce a new lethal weapon, binary nerve gas.

Congress voted bigger housing and food allow-

©1980 GAMBLE—NASHVILLE BANNER

Billy Carter testified before a Senate subcommittee in August on his involvement with the Libyan government. The panel found nothing illegal in his actions but thought that he showed poor judgment in dealing with a country that advocated terrorism and assassination as political tools.

JACK M. DOUTHITT–KEYSTONE

ances for military personnel, increased sea duty pay, voted an 11.7% military pay increase, and raised bonus pay for doctors, submariners, and enlisted specialists who extended overseas tours in some critical jobs. A revival of draft registration for 19- and 20-year-old men was approved. Actual resumption of the draft, however, would take further congressional action.

China was added to the nation's list of most favoured nations for trade purposes. Countries on the list were entitled to the lowest import tariff rate the United States imposed on a given commodity. A presidential order restricting grain shipments to the Soviet Union in retaliation for the invasion of Afghanistan was followed by plunging grain prices. To offset the loss to farmers, Congress raised crop loan rates and authorized a four million metric ton food reserve to take excess wheat off the market.

Significant Domestic Action

The revenue-sharing program for state and local governments was extended through fiscal 1983, but no provision was made for state grants for the first year of the extension. In the second and third years states were to be given a choice between general, unrestricted grants and categorical grants for specific purposes. The categorical grants would be reduced dollar for dollar for any unrestricted money a state accepted.

A money bill that contained a provision barring the Justice Department from taking actions that would lead to school busing for integration was vetoed by President Carter. There was no attempt to override, and the appropriations were included in a last-minute measure that was passed without the busing provision. It seemed likely that the issue would be revived in the 97th Congress. President-elect Ronald Reagan had said that he would sign legislation containing antibusing language.

The Department of Education was barred from using funds to prevent voluntary prayer or meditation in public schools. It also was prohibited from enforcing final regulations on bilingual education before June 1981.

Student aid for higher education was continued, but interest on Guaranteed Student Loans was increased from 7 to 9% and on National Direct Student Loans from 3 to 4%. Maximums for direct aid by basic opportunity grants were increased.

Members of Congress

Rep. Michael Myers (Dem., Pa.) was expelled from the House after being found guilty of bribery in the Abscam investigation. (*See* Law.) Rep. John W. Jenrette, Jr. (Dem., S.C.), also convicted, resigned while a House committee was considering a staff recommendation for expulsion. Rep. John M. Murphy (Dem., N.Y.) and Frank Thompson, Jr. (Dem., N.J.), also were found guilty in 1980, but there were no House proceedings because they had been defeated for reelection and there was no time for House action before they left office.

Earlier in the year, Rep. Charles C. Diggs, Jr. (Dem., Mich.), resigned after exhausting his appeals from a conviction for payroll padding. Diggs subsequently went to prison. Rep. Charles H. Wilson (Dem., Calif.) was censured for personal use of campaign funds and for accepting gifts from an individual with a direct interest in legislation before Congress. The action came a week after he was defeated in his state's primary election.

Adjournment marked the end of 26 years of Democratic control of the U.S. legislative process. The Democrats retained control of the House in the 97th Congress, 243–192, down from 273–159 in the 96th. A net gain of 12 seats put Republicans in control of the Senate 53–47, for the first time since 1954. This enabled the party to take over all Senate chairmanships and take over committee majorities.

(*See also* Elections; State Governments.)

Members of the Congress of the United States

1st Session, 97th Congress*

THE SENATE

President of the Senate: George Bush

State	Senator	Current Service Began	Current Term Expires
Ala.	Howell Heflin (D)	1979	1985
	Jeremiah Denton (R)	1981	1987
Alaska	Ted Stevens (R)	1968	1985
	Frank H. Murkowski (R)	1981	1987
Ariz.	Barry Goldwater (R)	1969	1987
	Dennis DeConcini (D)	1977	1983
Ark.	Dale Bumpers (D)	1975	1987
	David Pryor (D)	1979	1985
Calif.	Alan Cranston (D)	1969	1987
	S. I. Hayakawa (R)	1977	1983
Colo.	Gary W. Hart (D)	1975	1987
	William L. Armstrong (R)	1979	1985
Conn.	Lowell P. Weicker, Jr. (R)	1971	1983
	Christopher J. Dodd (D)	1981	1987
Del.	William V. Roth, Jr. (R)	1971	1983
	Joseph R. Biden, Jr. (D)	1973	1985
Fla.	Lawton Chiles (D)	1971	1983
	Paula Hawkins (R)	1981	1987
Ga.	Samuel A. Nunn (D)	1972	1985
	Mack Mattingly (R)	1981	1987
Hawaii	Daniel K. Inouye (D)	1963	1987
	Spark M. Matsunaga (D)	1977	1983
Idaho	James A. McClure (R)	1973	1985
	Steven D. Symms (R)	1981	1987
Ill.	Charles H. Percy (R)	1967	1985
	Alan J. Dixon (D)	1981	1987
Ind.	Richard G. Lugar (R)	1977	1983
	Dan Quayle (R)	1981	1987
Iowa	Roger W. Jepsen (R)	1979	1985
	Charles E. Grassley (R)	1981	1987
Kan.	Bob Dole (R)	1969	1987
	Nancy Landon Kassebaum (R)	1978	1985
Ky.	Walter (Dee) Huddleston (D)	1973	1985
	Wendell H. Ford (D)	1974	1987
La.	Russell B. Long (D)	1948	1987
	J. Bennett Johnston, Jr. (D)	1972	1985
Maine	William S. Cohen (R)	1979	1985
	George J. Mitchell (D)	1980	1983
Md.	Charles McC. Mathias, Jr. (R)	1969	1987
	Paul S. Sarbanes (D)	1977	1983
Mass.	Edward M. Kennedy (D)	1962	1983
	Paul E. Tsongas (D)	1979	1985
Mich.	Donald W. Riegle, Jr. (D)	1977	1983
	Carl Levin (D)	1979	1985
Minn.	David Durenberger (R)	1978	1983
	Rudy Boschwitz (R)	1979	1985
Miss.	John C. Stennis (D)	1947	1983
	Thad Cochran (R)	1978	1985
Mo.	Thomas F. Eagleton (D)	1968	1987
	John C. Danforth (R)	1977	1983
Mont.	John Melcher (D)	1977	1983
	Max Baucus (D)	1978	1985
Neb.	Edward Zorinsky (D)	1977	1983
	J. J. Exon (D)	1979	1985
Nev.	Howard W. Cannon (D)	1959	1983
	Paul Laxalt (R)	1974	1987
N.H.	Gordon J. Humphrey (R)	1979	1985
	Warren Rudman (R)	1980	1987
N.J.	Harrison A. Williams, Jr. (D)	1959	1983
	Bill Bradley (D)	1979	1985
N.M.	Pete V. Domenici (R)	1973	1985
	Harrison H. Schmitt (R)	1977	1983
N.Y.	Daniel P. Moynihan (D)	1977	1983
	Alfonse M. D'Amato (R)	1981	1987
N.C.	Jesse A. Helms (R)	1973	1985
	John P. East (R)	1981	1987
N.D.	Quentin N. Burdick (D)	1960	1983
	Mark Andrews (R)	1981	1987
Ohio	John H. Glenn, Jr. (D)	1974	1987
	Howard M. Metzenbaum (D)	1977	1983
Okla.	David L. Boren (D)	1979	1985
	Don Nickles (R)	1981	1987
Ore.	Mark O. Hatfield (R)	1967	1985
	Bob Packwood (R)	1969	1987
Pa.	H. John Heinz, III (R)	1977	1983
	Arlen Specter (R)	1981	1987
R.I.	Claiborne Pell (D)	1961	1985
	John H. Chafee (R)	1977	1983
S.C.	Strom Thurmond (R)	1956	1985
	Ernest F. Hollings (D)	1966	1987
S.D.	Larry Pressler (R)	1979	1985
	James Abdnor (R)	1981	1987
Tenn.	Howard H. Baker, Jr. (R)	1967	1985
	James R. Sasser (D)	1977	1983
Texas	John G. Tower (R)	1961	1985
	Lloyd M. Bentsen (D)	1971	1983
Utah	Jake Garn (R)	1974	1987
	Orrin G. Hatch (R)	1977	1983
Vt.	Robert T. Stafford (R)	1971	1983
	Patrick J. Leahy (D)	1975	1987
Va.	Harry F. Byrd, Jr.†	1965	1983
	John W. Warner (R)	1978	1985
Wash.	Henry M. Jackson (D)	1953	1983
	Slade Gorton (R)	1981	1987
W.Va.	Jennings Randolph (D)	1958	1985
	Robert C. Byrd (D)	1959	1983
Wis.	William Proxmire (D)	1957	1983
	Robert W. Kasten, Jr. (R)	1981	1987
Wyo.	Malcolm Wallop (R)	1977	1983
	Alan K. Simpson (R)	1979	1985

* Convened January 1981.
† No party designation (Independent).

THE HOUSE OF REPRESENTATIVES*

Speaker of the House: Thomas P. O'Neill, Jr.

Alabama
Jack Edwards, 1 (R)
William L. Dickinson, 2 (R)
Bill Nichols, 3 (D)
Tom Bevill, 4 (D)
Ronnie G. Flippo, 5 (D)
Albert Lee Smith, 6 (R)
Richard C. Shelby, 7 (D)

Alaska
Donald E. Young (R)

American Samoa
Fofo I. F. Sunia (D)†

Arizona
John J. Rhodes, 1 (R)
Morris K. Udall, 2 (D)
Bob Stump, 3 (D)
Eldon D. Rudd, 4 (R)

Arkansas
Bill Alexander, 1 (D)
Ed Bethune, 2 (R)
John P. Hammerschmidt,
   3 (R)
Beryl F. Anthony, 4 (D)

California
Eugene Chappie, 1 (R)
Don H. Clausen, 2 (R)
Robert T. Matsui, 3 (D)
Vic Fazio, 4 (D)
John L. Burton, 5 (D)
Phillip Burton, 6 (D)
George Miller, 7 (D)
Ronald V. Dellums, 8 (D)
Fortney H. (Pete) Stark, 9 (D)
Don Edwards, 10 (D)
Tom Lantos, 11 (D)
Paul N. (Pete) McCloskey,
   Jr., 12 (R)
Norman Y. Mineta, 13 (D)
Norman D. Shumway, 14 (R)
Tony Coelho, 15 (D)
Leon E. Panetta, 16 (D)
Charles (Chip) Pashayan,
   17 (R)
William Thomas, 18 (R)
Robert J. Lagomarsino, 19 (R)
Barry Goldwater, Jr., 20 (R)
Bobbi Fiedler, 21 (R)
Carlos J. Moorhead, 22 (R)
Anthony C. Beilenson, 23 (D)
Henry A. Waxman, 24 (D)
Edward R. Roybal, 25 (D)
John H. Rousselot, 26 (R)
Robert K. Dornan, 27 (R)
Julian C. Dixon, 28 (D)
Augustus F. Hawkins, 29 (D)
George E. Danielson, 30 (D)
Mervyn M. Dymally, 31 (D)
Glenn M. Anderson, 32 (D)
Wayne Grisham, 33 (R)
Daniel E. Lungren, 34 (R)
David Dreier, 35 (R)
George E. Brown, Jr., 36 (D)
Jerry Lewis, 37 (R)
Jerry M. Patterson, 38 (D)
William E. Dannemeyer,
   39 (R)
Robert E. Badham, 40 (R)

Bill Lowery, 41 (R)
Duncan L. Hunter, 42 (R)
Clair W. Burgener, 43 (R)

Colorado
Patricia Schroeder, 1 (D)
Timothy E. Wirth, 2 (D)
Ray Kogovsek, 3 (D)
Hank Brown, 4 (R)
Ken Kramer, 5 (R)

Connecticut
William R. Cotter, 1 (D)
Samuel Gejdenson, 2 (D)
Lawrence J. DeNardis, 3 (R)
Stewart B. McKinney, 4 (R)
William R. Ratchford, 5 (D)
A. Toby Moffett, 6 (D)

Delaware
Thomas B. Evans, Jr. (R)

District of Columbia
Walter E. Fauntroy (D)†

Florida
Earl D. Hutto, 1 (D)
Don Fuqua, 2 (D)
Charles E. Bennett, 3 (D)
Bill Chappell, Jr., 4 (D)
Bill McCollom, 5 (R)
C. W. (Bill) Young, 6 (R)
Sam M. Gibbons, 7 (D)
Andrew P. Ireland, 8 (D)
Bill Nelson, 9 (D)
L. A. (Skip) Bafalis, 10 (R)
Dan Mica, 11 (D)
Clay Shaw, 12 (R)
William Lehman, 13 (D)
Claude D. Pepper, 14 (D)
Dante B. Fascell, 15 (D)

Georgia
Bo Ginn, 1 (D)
Charles F. Hatcher, 2 (D)
Jack Brinkley, 3 (D)
Elliott H. Levitas, 4 (D)
Wyche Fowler, Jr., 5 (D)
Newt Gingrich, 6 (R)
Lawrence P. McDonald,
   7 (D)
Billy Lee Evans, 8 (D)
Ed Jenkins, 9 (D)
Doug Barnard, 10 (D)

Guam
Antonio Borja Won Pat (D)†

Hawaii
Cecil Heftel, 1 (D)
Daniel Akaka, 2 (D)

Idaho
Larry Craig, 1 (R)
George V. Hansen, 2 (R)

Illinois
Harold Washington, 1 (D)
Gus Savage, 2 (D)
Martin A. Russo, 3 (D)
Edward J. Derwinski, 4 (R)
John G. Fary, 5 (D)
Henry J. Hyde, 6 (R)
Cardiss Collins, 7 (D)
Dan Rostenkowski, 8 (D)

Sidney R. Yates, 9 (D)
John E. Porter, 10 (R)
Frank Annunzio, 11 (D)
Philip M. Crane, 12 (R)
Robert McClory, 13 (R)
John N. Erlenborn, 14 (R)
Tom Corcoran, 15 (R)
Lynn M. Martin, 16 (R)
George M. O'Brien, 17 (R)
Robert H. Michel, 18 (R)
Thomas F. Railsback, 19 (R)
Paul Findley, 20 (R)
Edward R. Madigan, 21 (R)
Daniel B. Crane, 22 (R)
Melvin Price, 23 (D)
Paul Simon, 24 (D)

Indiana
Adam Benjamin, Jr., 1 (D)
Floyd J. Fithian, 2 (D)
John P. Hiler, 3 (R)
Daniel R. Coats, 4 (R)
Elwood Hillis, 5 (R)
David W. Evans, 6 (D)
John T. Myers, 7 (R)
H. Joel Deckard, 8 (R)
Lee H. Hamilton, 9 (D)
Philip R. Sharp, 10 (D)
Andrew Jacobs, Jr., 11 (D)

Iowa
James A. S. Leach, 1 (R)
Tom Tauke, 2 (R)
Cooper Evans, 3 (R)
Neal Smith, 4 (D)
Tom Harkin, 5 (D)
Berkley Bedell, 6 (D)

Kansas
Pat Roberts, 1 (R)
Jim Jeffries, 2 (R)
Larry Winn, Jr., 3 (R)
Dan Glickman, 4 (D)
Robert Whittaker, 5 (R)

Kentucky
Carroll Hubbard, Jr., 1 (D)
William H. Natcher, 2 (D)
Romano L. Mazzoli, 3 (D)
M. G. (Gene) Snyder, 4 (R)
Harold Rogers, 5 (R)
Larry J. Hopkins, 6 (R)
Carl D. Perkins, 7 (D)

Louisiana
Bob Livingston, 1 (R)
Lindy Boggs, 2 (D)
W. J. (Billy) Tauzin, 3 (D)
Buddy Roemer, 4 (D)
Jerry Huckaby, 5 (D)
W. Henson Moore III, 6 (R)
John B. Breaux, 7 (D)
Gillis W. Long, 8 (D)

Maine
David F. Emery, 1 (R)
Olympia J. Snowe, 2 (R)

Maryland
Roy Dyson, 1 (D)
Clarence D. Long, 2 (D)
Barbara A. Mikulski, 3 (D)
Marjorie S. Holt, 4 (R)

Gladys N. Spellman, 5 (D)
Beverly Byron, 6 (D)
Parren J. Mitchell, 7 (D)
Michael D. Barnes, 8 (D)

Massachusetts
Silvio O. Conte, 1 (R)
Edward P. Boland, 2 (D)
Joseph D. Early, 3 (D)
Barney Frank, 4 (D)
James M. Shannon, 5 (D)
Nicholas Mavroules, 6 (D)
Edward J. Markey, 7 (D)
Thomas P. O'Neill, Jr., 8 (D)
John Joseph Moakley, 9 (D)
Margaret M. Heckler, 10 (R)
Brian J. Donnelly, 11 (D)
Gerry E. Studds, 12 (D)

Michigan
John Conyers, Jr., 1 (D)
Carl D. Pursell, 2 (R)
Howard Wolpe, 3 (D)
David A. Stockman, 4 (R)
Harold S. Sawyer, 5 (R)
Jim Dunn, 6 (R)
Dale E. Kildee, 7 (D)
Bob Traxler, 8 (D)
Guy Vander Jagt, 9 (R)
Donald J. Albosta, 10 (D)
Robert W. Davis, 11 (R)
David E. Bonior, 12 (D)
George W. Crockett, 13 (D)
Dennis M. Hertel, 14 (D)
William D. Ford, 15 (D)
John D. Dingell, 16 (D)
William M. Brodhead, 17 (D)
James J. Blanchard, 18 (D)
William S. Broomfield, 19 (R)

Minnesota
Arlen Erdahl, 1 (R)
Tom Hagedorn, 2 (R)
Bill Frenzel, 3 (R)
Bruce F. Vento, 4 (D)
Martin Olav Sabo, 5 (D)
Vin Weber, 6 (R)
Arlan Stangeland, 7 (R)
James L. Oberstar, 8 (D)

Mississippi
Jamie L. Whitten, 1 (D)
David R. Bowen, 2 (D)
G. V. (Sonny) Montgomery,
   3 (D)
Jon C. Hinson, 4 (R)
Trent Lott, 5 (R)

Missouri
William (Bill) Clay, 1 (D)
Robert A. Young, 2 (D)
Richard A. Gephardt, 3 (D)
Ike Skelton, 4 (D)
Richard Bolling, 5 (D)
E. Thomas Coleman, 6 (R)
Gene Taylor, 7 (D)
Wendell Bailey, 8 (R)
Harold L. Volkmer, 9 (D)
Bill Emerson, 10 (R)

Montana
Pat Williams, 1 (D)
Ron Marlenee, 2 (R)

Nebraska
Douglas K. Bereuter, 1 (R)
Hal Daub, 2 (R)
Virginia Smith, 3 (R)

Nevada
James Santini (D)

New Hampshire
Norman E. D'Amours, 1 (D)
Judd Gregg, 2 (R)

New Jersey
James J. Florio, 1 (D)
William J. Hughes, 2 (D)
James J. Howard, 3 (D)
Christopher H. Smith, 4 (R)
Millicent Fenwick, 5 (R)
Edwin B. Forsythe, 6 (R)
Marge Roukema, 7 (R)
Robert A. Roe, 8 (D)
Harold C. Hollenbeck, 9 (R)
Peter W. Rodino, Jr., 10 (D)
Joseph G. Minish, 11 (D)
Matthew J. Rinaldo, 12 (R)
James A. Courter, 13 (R)
Frank J. Guarini, 14 (D)
Bernard J. Dwyer, 15 (D)

New Mexico
Manuel Lujan, Jr., 1 (R)
Joe Skeen, 2 (R)

New York
William Carney, 1 (C-R)
Thomas J. Downey, 2 (D)
Gregory W. Carman, 3 (R)
Norman F. Lent, 4 (R)
Raymond J. McGrath, 5 (R)
John LeBoutillier, 6 (R)
Joseph P. Addabbo, 7 (D)
Benjamin S. Rosenthal, 8 (D)
Geraldine Ferraro, 9 (D)
Mario Biaggi, 10 (D)
James H. Scheuer, 11 (D)
Shirley Chisholm, 12 (D)
Stephen J. Solarz, 13 (D)
Frederick W. Richmond, 14 (D)
Leo C. Zeferetti, 15 (D)
Charles Schumer, 16 (D)
Guy V. Molinari, 17 (R)
S. William Green, 18 (R)
Charles B. Rangel, 19 (D)
Theodore S. Weiss, 20 (D)
Robert Garcia, 21 (D)
Jonathan B. Bingham, 22 (D)
Peter A. Peyser, 23 (D)
Richard L. Ottinger, 24 (D)
Hamilton Fish, Jr., 25 (R)
Benjamin A. Gilman, 26 (R)
Matthew F. McHugh, 27 (D)
Samuel S. Stratton, 28 (D)
Gerald B. Solomon, 29 (R)

David O'B. Martin, 30 (R)
Donald J. Mitchell, 31 (R)
George Wortley, 32 (R)
Gary A. Lee, 33 (R)
Frank Horton, 34 (R)
Barber B. Conable, Jr., 35 (R)
John J. LaFalce, 36 (D)
Henry J. Nowak, 37 (D)
Jack Kemp, 38 (R)
Stanley N. Lundine, 39 (D)

North Carolina
Walter B. Jones, 1 (D)
L. H. Fountain, 2 (D)
Charles Whitley, 3 (D)
Ike F. Andrews, 4 (D)
Stephen L. Neal, 5 (D)
Eugene Johnston, 6 (R)
Charles Rose III, 7 (D)
W. G. (Bill) Hefner, 8 (D)
James G. Martin, 9 (R)
James T. Broyhill, 10 (R)
William M. Hendon, 11 (R)

North Dakota
Byron Dorgan (D)

Ohio
Willis D. Gradison, Jr., 1 (R)
Thomas A. Luken, 2 (D)
Tony P. Hall, 3 (D)
Tennyson Guyer, 4 (R)
Delbert L. Latta, 5 (R)
Bob McEwen, 6 (R)
Clarence J. Brown, 7 (R)
Thomas N. Kindness, 8 (R)
Ed Weber, 9 (R)
Clarence E. Miller, 10 (R)
J. William Stanton, 11 (R)
Robert N. Shamansky, 12 (D)
Donald J. Pease, 13 (D)
John F. Seiberling, 14 (D)
Chalmers P. Wylie, 15 (R)
Ralph S. Regula, 16 (R)
John M. Ashbrook, 17 (R)
Douglas Applegate, 18 (D)
Lyle Williams, 19 (R)
Mary Rose Oakar, 20 (D)
Louis Stokes, 21 (D)
Dennis E. Eckart, 22 (D)
Ronald M. Mottl, 23 (D)

Oklahoma
James Rogers Jones, 1 (D)
Mike Synar, 2 (D)
Wes Watkins, 3 (D)
Dave McCurdy, 4 (D)
Mickey Edwards, 5 (R)
Glenn English, 6 (D)

Oregon
Les AuCoin, 1 (D)
Denny Smith, 2 (R)
Ron Wyden, 3 (D)
James Weaver, 4 (D)

Pennsylvania
Thomas M. Foglietta, 1 (I)
William H. Gray III, 2 (D)
Raymond F. Lederer, 3 (D)
Charles F. Dougherty, 4 (R)
Richard T. Schulze, 5 (R)
Gus Yatron, 6 (D)
Robert W. Edgar, 7 (D)
James K. Coyne, 8 (R)
E. G. (Bud) Shuster, 9 (R)
Joseph M. McDade, 10 (R)
James L. Nelligan, 11 (R)
John P. Murtha, 12 (D)
R. Lawrence Coughlin, 13 (R)
William J. Coyne, 14 (D)
Donald L. Ritter, 15 (R)
Robert S. Walker, 16 (R)
Allen E. Ertel, 17 (D)
Doug Walgren, 18 (D)
William F. Goodling, 19 (R)
Joseph M. Gaydos, 20 (D)
Don Bailey, 21 (D)
Austin J. Murphy, 22 (D)
William F. Clinger, Jr., 23 (R)
Marc L. Marks, 24 (R)
Eugene V. Atkinson, 25 (D)

Puerto Rico
Baltasar Corrada‡

Rhode Island
Fernand J. St. Germain, 1 (D)
Claudine Schneider, 2 (R)

South Carolina
Thomas F. Hartnett, 1 (R)
Floyd Spence, 2 (R)
Butler C. Derrick, Jr., 3 (D)
Carroll A. Campbell, Jr., 4 (R)
Kenneth L. Holland, 5 (D)
John L. Napier, 6 (R)

South Dakota
Tom Daschle, 1 (D)
Clint Roberts, 2 (R)

Tennessee
James H. Quillen, 1 (R)
John J. Duncan, 2 (R)
Marilyn Lloyd Bouquard, 3 (D)
Albert Gore, Jr., 4 (D)
Bill Boner, 5 (D)
Robin L. Beard, 6 (R)
Ed Jones, 7 (D)
Harold E. Ford, 8 (D)

Texas
Sam B. Hall, Jr., 1 (D)
Charles Wilson, 2 (D)
James M. Collins, 3 (R)
Ralph M. Hall, 4 (D)
Jim Mattox, 5 (D)
Phil Gramm, 6 (D)
Bill Archer, 7 (R)
Jack Fields, 8 (R)

Jack Brooks, 9 (D)
J. J. (Jake) Pickle, 10 (D)
J. Marvin Leath, 11 (D)
James C. Wright, Jr., 12 (D)
John Hightower, 13 (D)
William N. Patman, 14 (D)
E. (Kika) de la Garza, 15 (D)
Richard C. White, 16 (D)
Charles W. Stenholm, 17 (D)
Mickey Leland, 18 (D)
Kent Hance, 19 (D)
Henry B. Gonzalez, 20 (D)
Tom Loeffler, 21 (R)
Ron Paul, 22 (R)
Abraham Kazen, Jr., 23 (D)
Martin Frost, 24 (D)

Utah
James V. Hansen, 1 (R)
Dan Marriott, 2 (R)

Vermont
James M. Jeffords (R)

Virginia
Paul S. Trible, Jr., 1 (R)
G. William Whitehurst, 2 (R)
Thomas J. Bliley, 3 (R)
Robert W. Daniel, Jr., 4 (R)
W. C. (Dan) Daniel, 5 (D)
M. Caldwell Butler, 6 (R)
J. Kenneth Robinson, 7 (R)
Stan Parris, 8 (R)
William C. Wampler, 9 (R)
Frank R. Wolf, 10 (R)

Virgin Islands
Ron de Lugo (R)†

Washington
Joel Pritchard, 1 (R)
Allen Swift, 2 (D)
Don Bonker, 3 (D)
Sid Morrison, 4 (R)
Thomas S. Foley, 5 (D)
Norman D. Dicks, 6 (D)
Mike Lowry, 7 (D)

West Virginia
Robert H. Mollohan, 1 (D)
Cleve Benedict, 2 (R)
Mick Staton, 3 (R)
Nick Joe Rahall, 4 (D)

Wisconsin
Les Aspin, 1 (D)
Robert W. Kastenmeier, 2 (D)
Steven Gunderson, 3 (R)
Clement J. Zablocki, 4 (D)
Henry S. Reuss, 5 (D)
Thomas E. Petri, 6 (R)
David R. Obey, 7 (D)
Tobias A. Roth, 8 (R)
F. J. Sensenbrenner, 9 (R)

Wyoming
Richard Cheney (R)

* Numbers after names indicate congressional districts; where no number is given, congressman is elected at large.
† Nonvoting elected delegate.
‡ Nonvoting elected commissioner; member of New Progressive Party.

CONSUMER AFFAIRS

Consumers the world over continued to voice dissatisfaction with the quality and performance of products and services—often with good reason. For example, of the 62,000 formal complaints made to Australian government consumer agencies in 1979, it appeared that fully 95% justified attention and further action. Belgium's first free information centre for consumers, Test Achats, reported receiving requests for advice from more than 40,000 consumers in its first year. The French Union Féderale des Consommateurs (UFC) introduced a new advertisement column in its monthly magazine to evaluate the frequency and magnitude of complaints.

International Cooperation

A major concern of consumer groups and nongovernmental and international organizations continued to be infant formula. In May the World Health Assembly unanimously adopted a resolution on infant and child feeding, including a mandate to draft a marketing and advertising code for infant formulas and breast-milk substitutes. The World Health Organization/UNICEF saw the substitution of artificial feeding for breast-feeding as a major public health problem because of the hygienic and economic hazards it posed in poverty areas.

The president of the International Organization of Consumers Unions (IOCU) called the campaign on infant formula the first worldwide campaign by consumer groups. IOCU looked on the promotion of infant formula as but one of many examples of irresponsible market practices on the part of companies operating in less developed countries. Multinationals tended to observe lower standards of advertising and promotion in less developed countries than in advanced ones, and products developed for the needs of developed countries might well be inappropriate in less developed areas.

U.S. Issues

In the U.S. the Federal Trade Commission (FTC), in an August report, recommended the adoption of new trade rules for the consumer-finance industry. Under the proposed rules, creditors would be allowed to seize, after a default, only those household items bought under a defaulted credit contract. Also, a creditor would have to give the borrower credit for the fair retail market value of any item that was repossessed if the creditor attempted to collect money still owed by the borrower. Lenders would be prohibited from selling repossessed products at distress prices and then making the borrower pay the difference between the amount received and the amount still owed.

In May Pres. Jimmy Carter signed legislation needed to keep the FTC in operation. The bill included a provision allowing Congress to intervene, veto, and nullify regulations of the commission. It also limited the commission's power to investigate several industries, although it did not bar the FTC from regulating any industry other than agricultural cooperatives, trademarks, and the insurance and funeral industries. The new restrictions resulted from strong lobbying by business interest groups.

Procter & Gamble, the leading national advertiser in the U.S., agreed to spend a portion of its advertising budget, beginning in October 1980, on a campaign to discourage women from using its Rely tampons. The company voluntarily withdrew the product from retail shelves after a report issued by the Food and Drug Administration (FDA) linked tampon use with toxic-shock syndrome. (*See* Medicine.) The FTC reported that the Ford Motor Co. was placing advertisements in national magazines telling owners of its 1979 and 1980 models about major engine and transmission problems and informing them that Ford would pay for all or part of the repair cost after warranties expired.

The U.S. Supreme Court overturned a lower-court ruling that real estate firms and local realty boards were not in violation of the Sherman Act when they agreed on a fixed commission fee. The case resulted from a class-action suit brought in 1975 on behalf of all New Orleans, La., homeowners who had used brokers to sell property during the preceding four years. The real estate industry argued that the work of real estate brokers was local in nature and outside the reach of federal antitrust laws. However, the Supreme Court unanimously adopted a broad view of business activity and denied the industry's claim. This ruling would have a substantial effect on commission practices. A recent California law required all real estate listing agreements to include a notice informing the homeowner that brokers' fees are not fixed by law and are negotiable.

A bill was signed by President Carter in October deregulating the moving industry. Consumer groups and movers of household goods supported the legislation, which allowed more competition, reduced government paperwork, and permitted more rate freedom. Moving companies would no longer be required to give customers estimates of their charges, but if they made estimates, certain requirements had to be met. The customer would be allowed to delay payment for final charges exceeding 110% of the estimate; companies would be allowed to increase or decrease rates by 10% without Interstate Commerce Commission approval; and customers would be allowed to go to an arbitration board instead of the courts to settle disputes. Adding weight to a load to increase the price would become a federal crime. Movers were required to notify customers whenever the pickup or delivery date could not be met, and misleading advertising was prohibited.

The FDA entered into an agreement with pharmaceutical firms manufacturing common tranquilizers requiring these firms to inform physicians that antianxiety drugs should not be recommended to alleviate everyday stress.

Special Report: Where Does the Buck Stop?

by David C. Beckwith

For ten weeks in early 1980, a parade of ranking officials and engineers from the Ford Motor Co. marched in and out of the tiny county courthouse in Winamac, Ind. Their corporation was in the dock on three counts of reckless homicide, the first corporation so charged in U.S. history.

The case arose from the fiery deaths of three local teenage girls when the gas tank of their Ford Pinto exploded in a 1978 accident. After four days of deliberations, the jury on March 13 acquitted Ford of the charges, leaving the lesson to be drawn from the episode in sharp dispute. But the case was clearly a noteworthy, if tangential and tentative, step in a product liability revolution that has markedly altered the U.S. commercial landscape over the past two decades.

Who Bears Responsibility?

Prior to the recent developments, an accident victim could collect for his injuries only if he could prove the manufacturer was totally at fault. A factory worker maimed by a machine or the victim of a poorly tested drug often could rely only on personal insurance or workmen's compensation money. That led to serious inequities and finally prompted courts to redistribute the risks. Their rationale was aptly stated by the California Supreme Court in *Greenman* v. *Yuba Power Products*, the 1963 case considered the Lexington and Concord of the product liability revolution: "The costs of injuries resulting from defective products [should be] borne by the manufacturers that put such products on the market rather than by the injured persons who are powerless to protect themselves."

This raises fundamental, difficult questions about the rights of citizens in a free society to take responsibility for their actions. Should a drill press operator, paid by the amount he produces, be allowed to use a faster, more dangerous machine and then be compensated when he is injured? Should a consumer who buys a cheap tire be able to sue the manufacturer when it blows out and injury results? If the solutions had been hammered out in legislatures, with policy questions dispassionately considered, the changes might have been orderly and predictable. In the U.S., however, society's toughest problems are often decided in a courtroom—where each jury has leeway to determine the law in its case—and the answers are apt to be contradictory, confusing, and erratic.

Prior to a landmark 1916 case against the Buick Motor Co., the victim of a defective product could sue only the person who sold the product to him. Following that decision, however, courts nationwide made manufacturers responsible for their negligent conduct to all who might be foreseen as using their product. The courts also gradually developed a theory of "implied warranty of fitness," which required all parties in the distribution chain to act with due care.

The Liability Explosion

The Greenman case, over a cutting saw accident in a workshop, introduced a far more radical change. It clearly held that the maker of a defective product could be held liable under tort law, not merely for a breach of contract. The distinction is important. No longer does the obligation of a manufacturer depend in any way on his agreement, and no longer do the tricky escape clauses of sales law apply. The victim can also claim exemplary, or punitive, damages.

As it happened, at the very moment that the California decision was announced, experts were rewriting the *Restatement of Torts*, the legal fraternity's bible in that area. They quickly folded the Greenman ruling into their text, and within a few years, tort liability for purveyors of defective products was almost universally accepted.

The initial product liability cases in tort involved

Relatives of the persons killed sued Ford for reckless homicide due to the design of this car.
WIDE WORLD

defects in construction or breach of an express warranty—a pin in a candy bar, a shatterproof bottle that shattered—all relatively easy liability questions. But imaginative plaintiffs' lawyers quickly pushed the idea further, into the murkier areas of defect in design and duty to warn. If a man is crushed when he rolls his automobile, should the car manufacturer be held liable because he failed to design a stronger roof support? The common desk stapler has no shield mechanism and no warning; should an individual who staples his hand be allowed to sue? According to Victor Schwartz, a torts law expert, "True strict liability would mean that the injured plaintiff would win every time."

With courts around the country deciding such matters on a case-by-case basis, the incidence of huge judgments started to soar in the 1970s. In one well-publicized case, for example, an Oklahoma man bought commercial glue that plainly demanded cross ventilation and open windows during use. But there were no windows in his workroom, and a jury later awarded him $600,000 for burns he suffered when the glue fumes exploded. With that type of horror story as background, insurance carriers panicked and raised premiums by an average 300% in the mid-1970s. The country had muddled itself into a product liability crisis.

Task Force Findings

Although individual states set their own tort law, the nationwide situation prompted the federal government to set up a task force study group in 1976. The inquiry revealed that virtually all sides of the controversy had made exaggerated and misleading claims. Plaintiffs' lawyers, for example, had claimed that the occasional million-dollar judgments were not significant factors in the crisis, but the study found the tort judgments had spurred insurance companies into "panic pricing." Numerous insurance industry ads suggested that a million product liability claims were being filed annually; the study put the number at 60,000 to 70,000.

The report also questioned several underlying assumptions of the revolution. The Greenman decision noted that manufacturers were much better able to absorb increased costs and spread the risk through liability insurance than were individual accident victims. But some smaller companies could not afford increased premiums and stopped buying insurance. Thanks to group insurance and social security, an individual accident victim might well be covered for his losses while the producer company was not.

The task force eventually recommended that groups of manufacturers be allowed to band together to insure themselves, exempt from state insurance regulation. A risk retention bill, to be considered by Congress early in 1981, would permit just that. It also suggested a model state statute, which was gradually gaining acceptance at year's end.

The model act holds manufacturers liable for violations of their own promises: if a drug is advertised as non-habit-forming and a user becomes addicted, then the drug company must pay. It also holds manufacturers responsible for construction defects, errors in production that do not meet their own standards. These can be forecast statistically, covered by insurance, and included in the cost of the product. In the twilight area of design defects, the model act recommends a negligence standard: at the time of manufacture, did the company take care to ascertain all forseeable risks and the reasonable cost of reducing them? If so, the company is not negligent.

In the 1970s the federal government set up several agencies—the Consumer Product Safety Commission, the Occupational Safety and Health Administration, and the National Highway Transportation Safety Administration, among others—designed to protect workers and consumers through regulation. Unfortunately, there has been little progress in coordinating the regulations drawn up by the consumer protection agencies with product liability law as elaborated through the court system. For example, should a manufacturer be relieved of liability if his lawn mower meets the specifications of an appropriate agency but causes an accident anyway? The answer, even under the model code, is no.

An Expensive Road to Safety

Even before the criminal trial in Indiana, Ford had been hit with more than a dozen civil verdicts —including a record $125 million punitive damage award in California—for deaths and injuries that occurred when the Pinto's poorly protected gas tank ruptured in rear-end collisions. The Indiana prosecutors attempted to transform the company's cost-cutting decisions (a $6.65 part would have shielded the tank) into a criminal act. Ford faced only a $30,000 fine if convicted, but a guilty verdict would have weakened the company's position in pending civil actions dramatically. Ford executives were more than willing to spend over $1 million defending the Winamac case.

Ford also designed better-protected tanks into future cars. But even if the threat of civil suits prompts manufacturers and employers to promote safety, as the plaintiffs' lawyers suggest, it may be an overly expensive way to accomplish a worthy goal. Insurance industry statistics indicate that of every dollar paid to an accident victim, 38 cents goes to his attorney. An additional 42 cents is paid out by insurance companies to defend the case.

Schwartz, who headed the federal study, cautions that his group's suggested reforms may merely amount to pouring new wine into old bottles. "What we may really need," he says, "is a new compensation system—one that gets the money to the accident victims without these middlemen going to court."

MICHAEL PHILIPPOT—SYGMA

These Cuban refugees were among the first to arrive in San José, Costa Rica, part of the huge wave that emigrated when Cuban authorities removed restrictions in April.

COSTA RICA

Political problems disturbed Costa Rica's stability in 1980, especially with regard to labour relations. These largely stemmed from increases in the cost of living; although the minimum wage was increased by 10.8% in 1980, this did not compensate for inflation, officially stated as running at 9.6% but actually at 18.5% according to the labour unions. Labour disputes included the Standard Fruit banana workers' strike, which ended on Jan. 17, 1980.

Costa Rica offered asylum during the year to up to 300 Cuban refugees, and plane flights from Havana began on April 16. On July 25 Costa Rica guaranteed asylum to more than 200 peasants from El Salvador and flew them to San José.

Costa Rica's negotiations with the International Monetary Fund (IMF) resulted in a move taken to alleviate balance of payments problems, which stemmed from a slide in the value of coffee exports and an increase in the price of oil imports along with heavy debt service expenses. The IMF was to make available its Special Drawing Rights, but only on condition of cuts in public expenditure, increased taxation, and control of money supply growth. The gross domestic product rose 5.9% in 1979 but slowed during 1980 as a result of the end of the coffee boom and controlled public expenditure. In August Mexico and Venezuela guaranteed Costa Rica's oil supply under special financial arrangements.

CRIME AND LAW ENFORCEMENT

In a year marked by a resurgence of right-wing violence, Europe's bloodiest act of terrorism since World War II occurred on Aug. 2, 1980, when a massive bomb exploded at a railway station in Bologna, Italy, leaving a reported 76 persons dead and more than 160 injured. The atrocity was believed to have been perpetrated by a neofascist group. Only hours before, a judge in Bologna had indicted eight right-wing extremists for the 1974 bombing of a passenger train in which 12 persons were killed.

Right-wing extremists were also believed responsible for one of the worst terrorist attacks in West German history when, on September 26, a bomb exploded at closing time at Munich's crowded Oktoberfest, killing 12 and injuring more than 200. Among the dead was a young member of a neo-Nazi organization suspected of planting the high-explosive device. Neo-Nazis claimed responsibility for a series of attacks on Jewish targets in France during the year, culminating in a powerful bomb explosion outside a Paris synagogue on October 3, which killed four people and injured at least nine others. Following the explosion, members of all the major French political parties joined in a massive public demonstration in Paris held to denounce the growing wave of anti-Semitic violence in France.

Paris was also the site of attacks by assassins acting on behalf of various parties in the Middle East. Former Iranian prime minister Shahpur Bakhtiar narrowly escaped death in mid-July when his suburban Paris apartment was stormed by gunmen posing as reporters. Days later a gunman succeeded in killing former Syrian premier Salah al-Din Bitar, an opponent of Pres. Hafez al-Assad, at his Paris office. Several opponents of Libyan leader Col. Muammar al-Qaddafi were slain in separate incidents in London, Bonn, Rome, and elsewhere.

In Latin America, where politically motivated violence reached epidemic proportions, the outspoken archbishop of San Salvador, Oscar Arnulfo Romero, was mortally wounded in March by a lone gunman as he officiated at Mass. It was widely suspected that rightists in El Salvador had ordered the assassination in an attempt to foment chaos that could lead to a right-wing military takeover. In September the exiled former dictator of Nicaragua, Anastasio Somoza Debayle, and two companions were killed in an ambush in Asunción, Paraguay. A leftist Argentine guerrilla group, thought to be acting in association with Nicaraguan revolutionaries, was believed responsible.

Past acts of violence were recalled for North Americans during the year. In New York Cathlyn Wilkerson, once one of the most hunted fugitives in the U.S., surrendered to authorities in July. Wilkerson, a member of the radical Weatherman group, which was responsible for a series of bombings in

Mourners in New York City gathered at former Beatle John Lennon's apartment building after he was shot and killed on December 8.

ANDY LEVIN—BLACK STAR

the late 1960s, had been on the run for ten years. Another '60s figure, Abbie Hoffman of the Yippies (Youth International Party), also surrendered to authorities in New York. Hoffman had been underground since 1974. In December Bernadine Dohrn surrendered in Chicago, where she was wanted on charges stemming from the Weather Underground's "Days of Rage" disturbances in 1969.

In Canada Nigel Barry Hamer was charged in July with the kidnapping of British Trade Commissioner James Cross on Oct. 5, 1970, an act that marked the beginning of that country's most serious peacetime crisis. The Cross kidnapping, and that of Quebec Minister of Labour Pierre Laporte by members of Le Front de Libération du Québec, had prompted the Canadian government to invoke the War Measures Act, suspending the civil liberties of many Canadians. Laporte was murdered, but Cross had been released unharmed.

Murder and Other Violence

Blacks were victims of murderous attacks in a number of U.S. states, giving rise to fears that at least some of the crimes might be linked in a racially motivated conspiracy. In the most notorious incident, in May, Vernon Jordan, president of the National Urban League, was seriously wounded by a rifle bullet in the parking lot of a Fort Wayne, Ind., motel. The shooting appeared to have been carried out by a single expert marksman. A year-long series of racial sniper attacks claimed at least ten lives in five states. In August, for instance, two black youths were shot to death with a high-powered rifle as they jogged with two white women in Salt Lake City, Utah. In Buffalo, N.Y., six black males were killed during six weeks in September and October, two of them cab drivers whose hearts were cut out. In Atlanta, Ga., 11 black children were murdered over 16 months, and four others were reported missing. In late October John Paul Franklin, an admitted racist, was indicted in connection with the Salt Lake City sniper attacks.

A wave of airplane hijackings reminiscent of the late 1960s plagued U.S. airlines. In one week during August, six planes were diverted to Cuba, three of them in one day. In most cases the hijackers were recent refugees from Cuba who wished to return to their homeland. While U.S. authorities strengthened security procedures, the Cuban government announced that the hijackers faced "drastic penal measures" and possible extradition to the U.S.

A bizarre slaying occurred in New York City's Metropolitan Opera House in July. Helen Hagnes, a member of the orchestra's violin section, disappeared during a break in a performance by the Berlin Ballet and was found dead the next morning, having been stripped, bound, gagged, and thrown down an airshaft. Following an intensive police manhunt, Craig Crimmins, a stagehand, was charged in late August with murder and attempted rape. Crimmins reportedly was apprehended after a

WIDE WORLD

Top detectives from across the U.S. aided in the investigation of the abduction and slaying of 11 black children in Atlanta, Georgia.

ballerina under hypnosis supplied police with a description of the killer.

Joy Adamson, author of the best-selling book *Born Free*, was the victim of murder in a remote Kenyan game reserve in January. The death was at first attributed to mauling by a lion, but police investigation showed that she had been stabbed to death. An African herdsmen, Paul Wakwaro Ekai, a former employee of Adamson, was subsequently arrested and charged with her murder. On December 8 John Lennon, a member of the Beatles, was shot to death in New York City. Charged with the murder was Mark David Chapman.

In the newly independent African nation of Zimbabwe, Edgar Tekere, a prominent member of the ruling Zimbabwe African National Union, was the suspected ringleader of a band of men accused of murdering a white farmer in August. The court found that he and a bodyguard had committed the murder, but he was freed under a law, passed by the previous white minority regime, that protected ministers acting "in good faith" to suppress terrorism. In Saudi Arabia the largest mass execution in the country's history occurred in January when 63 persons were beheaded. Those executed were Muslim fundamentalists who had seized the Grand Mosque at Mecca late in 1979.

Nonviolent Crime

In February press leaks resulted in the premature disclosure of a controversial FBI undercover operation code-named Abscam (for Abdul-scam, named for the fake company Abdul Enterprises Ltd., used as a front for the operation). In the course of Abscam, FBI agents, posing as wealthy Arabs, tried to entice members of Congress and other public officials into taking bribes. (*See* Law.)

Following a lengthy and highly publicized trial, Bert Lance, former presidential adviser and director of the Office of Management and Budget, was acquitted in Atlanta on April 30 of nine counts of bank fraud. The jury remained deadlocked on three other counts of banking violations. Less fortunate was former Maryland governor Marvin Mandel, who lost his bid in the U.S. Supreme Court to avoid a four-year prison sentence; Mandel had been convicted of bribery and racketeering in 1977.

The question of a manufacturer's criminal responsibility for injuries produced by a defective product was raised in the Winamac, Ind., trial of the Ford Motor Co. on charges of reckless homicide. The charges, the first of their type ever brought against an automaker, arose from an accident in 1978 when the gas tank of a Ford Pinto exploded after the car was hit from the rear, killing three teenage girls. The prosecution alleged that design faults, known to Ford but not corrected, led to the girls' deaths. The giant automaker was acquitted and later paid the parents of the three girls a total of $22,500 in exchange for a promise not to proceed with civil suits against the company. (*See* Consumer Affairs Special Report.)

In the Soviet Union a "great caviar scam" was reportedly uncovered following months of investigation. The scam allegedly involved the diversion of tons of state-produced caviar to clandestine packing plants, where it was sealed in cans marked "smoked herring." Sold at herring prices to an unnamed Western European company, the caviar was repacked and resold for enormous profits, some of which were deposited in Swiss bank accounts for Soviet officials. While Soviet authorities refused to comment about the scandal, Western sources claimed that a number of senior bureaucrats, including a former minister of fisheries, were among the suspects.

The sinking of the oil tanker "Salem" off West Africa in January drew attention to maritime frauds. The "Salem," which had left Kuwait with a cargo of light crude oil bound for Italy, sank following a series of mysterious explosions. It was alleged that the cargo had been sold secretly in South Africa, after which the vessel was deliberately scuttled. Lloyd's of London, which was involved in the disputed multimillion-dollar insurance claim, estimated that more than 100 cargo ships had been intentionally sunk in 1979 alone.

The soaring price of oil sparked a dramatic increase in the theft of oil products in the U.S. and elsewhere. In Houston, Texas, for example, law enforcement agencies uncovered a $12 million-a-year oil theft ring. Seventeen suspects were arrested in July when the U.S. Coast Guard and other authorities surrounded two oil barges, anchored in the

UPI

A bomb placed by extortionists demanding $3 million exploded as technicians attempted to defuse it by remote control at Harvey's Resort Hotel, in Stateline, Nevada.

Houston Ship Channel, as they began the illegal transfer of their cargo. The boom in world prices of other commodities, especially gold and silver, also prompted a rash of crime. Police in the U.S. reported that burglars had begun to concentrate on silverware and gold jewelry. The "snatch and run" theft of gold chains from wearers' necks became commonplace; New York City transit authorities recorded nearly 2,000 such thefts on the city's subways during the first eight months of the year.

The theft of art works continued to increase. While the Paris-based international police organization Interpol said worldwide official figures were impossible to obtain, authorities did not dispute reports that more than 40,000 works of art changed hands illegally each year. In France alone, more than 8,000 works of art were stolen during 1979; less then 10% of them were recovered.

Law Enforcement

The FBI's *Uniform Crime Reports* recorded a 9% rise in serious crime in the U.S. during 1979, the largest increase since 1975; violent crimes rose 11% and property offenses almost 9%. These discouraging statistics came at a time when the U.S. Congress seemed likely to slash federal government spending on such criminal justice agencies as the Office of Justice Assistance, Research, and Statistics. The cut was prompted in large part by dissatisfaction over the agencies' ineffectiveness in solving the nation's crime problem.

A report released in May by the U.S. General Accounting Office (GAO) criticized the FBI's "quality over quantity" policy, first announced in 1975. That policy required concentration of FBI resources on high-level organized and white collar crime cases, while leaving most other cases to state and local enforcement agencies. According to the GAO, over two-thirds of the $30.3 million spent by the FBI to investigate property crimes in fiscal 1978 was devoted to nonquality cases, more than 90% of which did not lead to prosecution. Among "quality cases" that did result in prosecution was the FBI's Operation Unirac (for union racketeering). Beginning in 1975, this massive four-year effort involved hundreds of agents in a crackdown on labour racketeering in major U.S. ports. Among the 116 persons indicted as a result were 56 members or associates of the International Longshoremen's Association and 43 individuals associated with the management of shipping or other companies.

After more than two years of delay, two former senior FBI officials were convicted in November on charges that they had approved illegal break-ins, wiretaps, and mail openings in the early 1970s. In Canada a royal commission continued to investigate allegations of illegal break-ins, wiretaps, and other misconduct on the part of the Royal Canadian Mounted Police during the same period. A report was expected in early 1981.

In September the International Association of Chiefs of Police, a professional organization with a membership extending to more than 60 nations, resolved that police should "use deadly force in cases where an officer has reasonable belief to fear for his or another's life or safety and/or in the cases consistent with laws applying within their jurisdiction." The resolution did not meet with the approval of the U.S.-based National Organization of Black Law Enforcement Executives, which felt that police departments should sanction the use of deadly force only in "defense of life" situations. On average, at least one citizen a day was killed by police in the U.S., and while many of the fatalities were unavoidable, some provoked bitterness and violence, especially among minority groups. Rioting in May in Liberty City, a black suburb of Miami, Fla., followed the acquittal of four white former police officers on various charges stemming from the 1979 beating death of a black businessman.

(*See also* Prisons.)

CUBA

In major governmental changes announced on Jan. 11, 1980, 11 ministers were dismissed from office, and Pres. Fidel Castro himself took on the portfolios of defense, interior, public health, and culture. Managers of state enterprises were given more immediate powers for the imposition of work discipline, as well as greater freedom in hiring and firing. The first wage adjustment in 15 years was announced in March and became effective in July. To curtail black market activities, smallholders were permitted to sell their excess food in Havana. At the same time, licenses were issued to craftsmen wishing to set up their own businesses.

During the early months of 1980, increasing numbers of Cubans wanting to leave the country sought asylum in foreign embassies, particularly those of Peru and Venezuela. On April 1 a Cuban guard was accidentally killed when six Cubans forced their way into the Peruvian embassy. Three days later the Cuban guards were withdrawn from the embassy, and the government permitted all who so wished to apply to leave the country. An estimated 10,000 would-be emigrants, most of them motivated by a desire to escape Cuba's economic ills, crowded into the Peruvian embassy compound during the following days.

By April 16 the U.S., Canada, Argentina, Brazil, Costa Rica, Ecuador, Peru, Belgium, Spain, Sweden, and West Germany had offered to take varying numbers of refugees, and the first flights out of Cuba began. Without consulting Washington, Castro allowed Cuban expatriates in the U.S. to collect relatives from Cuba by boat, and on April 21 a seaborne exodus from the port of Mariel began. Despite measures to restrict the traffic imposed by U.S. Pres. Jimmy Carter on May 14, some 120,000 Cubans had entered the U.S. by the time Castro closed Mariel to U.S. boats on September 7. By then some refugees, dissatisfied with the treatment

Thousands of Cubans seeking political asylum and, ultimately, permission to emigrate crammed the compound of the Peruvian embassy in Havana in April.

EFE—SIPA PRESS/BLACK STAR

Thirty men freed from jail in Cuba were sent back to the U.S. on October 27; all were glad to be back, although some faced legal problems for criminal action in the U.S.
WIDE WORLD

they had received in the U.S., were hijacking airliners in an effort to return to Cuba. (*See* United States.)

Castro's removal of restrictions on emigration, especially for "undesirables," indicated a reaction to increased U.S. hostility following alleged Cuban involvement in the disorders in El Salvador. Tension eased in May, but Castro insisted that any negotiations with the U.S. should encompass lifting of the trade embargo, closing of the Guantánamo naval base, and cessation of U.S. reconnaissance overflights. In late October, Castro pardoned 33 Americans being held in Cuban jails, many of them hijackers. Thirty chose to return to the U.S., including five who faced federal criminal charges.

During a visit to Cuba in August, Pres. José López Portillo of Mexico backed Castro's demands on these three issues. Also affirmed during the meeting was support for the independence of Belize. On trade, Cuba would continue to sell sugar to Mexico (a first consignment of 400,000 metric tons was sold in 1980) but would not take advantage of low interest rates on Mexican and Venezuelan oil, since it preferred to buy oil from the U.S.S.R.

Cuba's approval of the Soviet invasion of Afghanistan jeopardized its chairmanship of the nonaligned movement. Opposition from nonaligned countries prompted Cuba in January to withdraw its candidacy for the vacant Latin-American seat on the UN Security Council and to support Mexico's successful candidacy.

The sinking of a Bahamian patrol vessel by Cuban MiG fighters on May 10 (for which Cuba subsequently paid compensation) aroused fears of a more aggressive Caribbean policy. Cuban involvement in the Caribbean and Central America continued to be one of the major obstacles to improved relations with the U.S. Aid was being given to Grenada, El Salvador, and Nicaragua (to the latter in the form of doctors and teachers). Cuba also continued to provide aid to 14 African countries. Estimates at the end of 1979 put the total personnel involved at 45,000, ranging from limited numbers of security advisers in some countries to 25,500 military and civilian personnel in Angola. Several thousand military instructors and civilian advisers were also reported to be in Yemen (Aden).

In May Cuba and the Soviet Union reached agreement in Moscow on cooperation in the construction of a nuclear research station in Cuba. On June 1, during a visit by Erich Honecker, the East German Communist Party leader and premier, a 25-year accord, including scientific and technical cooperation, was signed. Three new sugar mills were to be built in Cuba with the aid of a U.S. $20 million loan from the International Investment Bank of the Soviet-bloc Council for Mutual Economic Assistance (Comecon). However, to reduce its dependence on Comecon, Cuba signed a five-year agreement, to begin in 1981, to double its trade with Japan.

Economic growth, at around 3%, was lower in 1980 than in previous years. In July, when the 1981–85 five-year plan was announced, Castro declared that austerity would continue, since Cuba had been unable to raise the loans it needed on the international market. Cane rust and bad weather limited the sugar crop to 6.7 million metric tons (compared with 7,990,000 in 1979). However, with the price of sugar more than double 1979 levels, Cuba's export earnings increased. The tobacco crop, severely affected by blue mold, produced only 5,000 of the forecast 45,000 tons, and tobacco factories had to be closed.

CYPRUS

Life in Cyprus remained conditioned by the Turkish invasion and internal disruption of 1974, and 1980 saw a continuation of attempts to reunite the Greek and Turkish communities. Responsibility for that difficult task lay with the UN. Its peacekeeping force of almost 2,500 troops still patrolled the buffer zone across the island.

After a year of deadlock, UN special envoy Javier Pérez de Cuellar paid a surprise visit to the island in June in an effort to persuade both sides to return to the negotiating table. His attempt failed, but the new UN local representative, Hugo Gobbi of Argentina, subsequently succeeded, and weekly meetings began on September 16. Gobbi said progress toward an eventual settlement would be slow and cautioned against overoptimism.

Taking a keen interest in the problem was Libya. Col. Muammar al-Qaddafi offered to act as host to a summit in Tripoli to help work out a peace formula. The offer was made unnecessary when the talks commenced, but Libya's interest was maintained by its eagerness to construct a radio station in Cyprus to beam programs of a cultural, educational, and religious nature to the Arab world. Fearing that such a station would upset those moderate Arab states with which the island had considerable trade, the Cypriots decided against the idea, even though the Libyans were offering relatively vast sums of money. The start of the talks coincided with the military coup in Turkey, but it and Greece's agreement in October to rejoin NATO had no immediate effect on the situation.

Dominating economic life in both the Greek and Turkish sectors were the rising cost of oil products and the bleak world financial picture. Fuel prices soared and, particularly in the government-controlled south, there was a noticeable increase in the number of industrial stoppages as workers pressed for higher wages. The situation was made even worse by revelations during the summer that the massive cooperative movement, the source of employment for many Cypriots, was in dire financial straits. The government injected several million pounds to maintain the organization, and courts of inquiry were set up to investigate charges of mismanagement.

Politically, 1980 was marked by the split within the ruling Democratic Party. Alecos Michaelides, leader of the House of Representatives and acting vice-president of the republic, resigned in mid-October to set up his own party, the New Democratic Movement. Four other parliamentary deputies from Pres. Spyros Kyprianou's party also quit to join him. This had been preceded by a major Cabinet reshuffle on September 10, in which seven ministers were replaced by technocrats. The political turmoil made elections in the autumn appear certain, but technical difficulties with the electoral list made it necessary to postpone them until the spring of 1981.

CZECHOSLOVAKIA

The economy and its troubles dominated Czechoslovak concerns in 1980, to the virtual exclusion of other issues. The problem was much the same as before—stagnation. Both the planning mechanism and the capacity of the economy were weak in relation to expectations. Possibly the most revealing figures were those published at the beginning of 1980 about plan fulfillment for the previous year. The category used as the equivalent of gross national product per capita—net material product growth—had fallen to 2.7%, while the other key indicator, increase in real wages, registered a mere 0.6%.

In 1980 the Czechoslovak economy was suffering from chronic tensions: between cost and output, investment outlays and returns, export targets and capacity, agricultural output and food consumption, supply and demand in consumer goods. The solution adopted was, for all practical purposes, an austerity program under another name. Real wages would remain at the 1979 level, and any increase in the standard of living would come through higher social benefits. The broader economic strategy adopted by the Czechoslovak Communist Party was outlined in March. It was given the title "Measures to Improve the System of Planned Management of the Economy."

The "Measures," as they came to be known, basically consisted of a set of rather conservative ideas. Thus, planning would emphasize the five-year period instead of the annual plan; there would

Pres. Gustav Husak took the oath of office after his reelection in May.
UPI

be more intensive preparation of plans; supply and demand would be improved at all levels (national, ministerial, enterprise); and contractual relationships between enterprises would be more strictly enforced. As for labour, supplies of which had almost completely dried up, bonuses would be paid for high performance, and penalties would be imposed for poor quality. There would be stricter control over management than before. In fact, the "Measures" amounted to little more than a codification of existing practice. There was no suggestion of anything resembling the reintroduction of market concepts.

The announcement of the "Measures" was followed in March by a full Central Committee session devoted to ideology. This confirmed the strategy of exhortation and harangues as the instrument for mobilizing the energies of the population. In later months, however, one significant innovation did surface. There was to be much stricter scrutiny of managers, and party members were expected to observe a much higher level of discipline. Severe warnings were issued against those who were caught violating socialist norms, the code name for corruption.

Despite rumours that party General Secretary Gustav Husak, a conservative, might make way for a hard-line successor, he was reelected in May as president of Czechoslovakia for a five-year term. In August and September, however, it became evident that the Czechoslovak leadership was considerably worried by developments in neighbouring Poland. The struggle to establish autonomous trade unions was interpreted as a reversion to the Czechoslovak reforms of 1968 and condemned as a dangerous step. In October the Czechoslovak authorities followed East Germany in closing off the border with Poland and ending free travel.

Intensive harassment of Czechoslovak dissidents, signaled with the trial of six members of VONS (the Committee for the Defense of the Unjustly Persecuted) in October 1979, was maintained. Throughout 1980 there was a steady stream of reports of arrests, beatings, house searches, and other forms of intimidation. Despite this, the opposition Charter 77 movement remained in being and active.

DANCE

The American Ballet Theatre (ABT), as it celebrated its 40th anniversary, changed directors. Lucia Chase and Oliver Smith, co-directors since 1945 (Chase had been ABT's principal patroness and guiding force since its inception), relinquished their joint post to Mikhail Baryshnikov. The anniversary was highlighted by a gala performance at New York City's Metropolitan Opera House (staged by Donald Saddler, an ABT alumnus) that brought together alumni of every generation in excerpts from past roles, in bows, or on a screen in still photographs.

During the year ABT paid tribute to its longtime

MARTHA SWOPE

Natalia Makarova staged and starred in a new version of Marius Petipa's La Bayadère *when the American Ballet Theatre opened its 40th anniversary season.*

creative artists with programs focused exclusively on the works of Antony Tudor, Agnes de Mille, and Jerome Robbins and on those with designs by Oliver Smith. The major new offering was a full-length production of the Marius Petipa classic *La Bayadère*, staged by Natalia Makarova with scenery by Pier-Luigi Samaritani, costumes by Theoni Aldredge, and the traditional score by Ludwig Minkus. Other ABT novelties included several pas de deux: *Rendez-Vous* (choreography by Stephen-Jan Hoff), *Le Retour* (John Meehan), and *Fantaisie Serieuse* (Lorca Massine). Daniel Levans's *Concert Waltzes* was added to the repertory. Among revivals was Tudor's *Dark Elegies* (1937). The first ABT season under Baryshnikov's direction began on December 10 at the Kennedy Center for the Performing Arts, in Washington, D.C. New to the repertory were George Balanchine's *Prodigal Son*; Sir Frederick Ashton's *Les Rendezvous*; a new *Raymonda* (divertissements from Acts I and II) based on the Petipa ballet, staged by Baryshnikov with scenery and costumes by Santo Loquasto and with the music of Glazunov; and *Pas d'Esclave*, a pas de deux (from Act I of *Le Corsaire*), staged by Baryshnikov.

The New York City Ballet (NYCB) featured the

world premiere of *Robert Schumann's "Davids-bündlertänze"* by Balanchine. The NYCB also presented Balanchine's *Ballade* (to music of Fauré), Robbins's *Rondo* (Mozart), and Peter Martins's *Lille Suite* (Carl Nielsen), all new; a newly revised *Suite of Dances* (from Robbins's *Dybbuk Variations* to music of Leonard Bernstein); the company's first production of Robbins's *Fancy Free*, an ABT staple; the New York premiere of Balanchine's *Walpurgis Nacht Ballet;* and a revised *Le Bourgeois Gentilhomme* by Balanchine. Jacques d'Amboise celebrated 30 years with the NYCB.

The Joffrey Ballet, recovering from a period of financial difficulty, returned to its home theatre, the New York City Center, for its first repertory season in two years. The fall engagement included such novelties as a new ballet by Robert Joffrey himself, *Postcards* to music of Erik Satie; *Relache*, a 1920s ballet-cinema concept of Jean Borlin restaged by Moses Pendleton; *Celebration* and *Epode* (dedicated to the ballerina Felia Doubrovska), both by Gerald Arpino; *Night* by the modern dance choreographer Laura Dean; *Helena*, choreographed by Choo San Goh; the first Joffrey staging of Jiri Kylian's *Return to the Strange Land*; and Ashton's *Illuminations*.

Productions by the Eliot Feld Ballet included *Anatomic Balm*, *Scenes for the Theater*, and *Circa*. The Pennsylvania Ballet presented Choo San Goh's *Celestial Images*, and Ballet Repertory Company offered Richard Englund's *Romeo and Juliet*. Ballet West made its New York debut in a repertory that featured *Sanctus* (Bruce Marks-Fanshawe). The San Francisco Ballet offered the world premiere of Michael Smuin's *The Tempest* of Shakespeare, and the Pittsburgh Ballet Theater featured an August

Bournonville program that included a production of *La Ventana* staged by the Royal Danish Ballet's Kirsten Ralov. The Boston Ballet had a New York season in which it offered Pierre Lacotte's reconstruction of Philippe Taglioni's *La Sylphide* (1836) with Rudolf Nureyev appearing as the star at all performances. The Dance Theatre of Harlem added two traditional classics to its repertory: *Swan Lake* (Act II) and divertissements from *Paquita*. The Hartford (Conn.) Ballet, in its first repertory season in its home city, featured the new *Mulheres* choreographed by director Michael Uthoff.

Edward Villella was appointed artistic coordinator of the Eglevsky Ballet. In Chicago Maria Tallchief established a 20-member ballet troupe. Makarova and Company, headed by ballerina Natalia Makarova, made its debut in a Broadway engagement that featured stagings of divertissements from *Paquita* and *Raymonda*, *Sonata No. 5* of Maurice Béjart, Lorca Massine's *Vendetta*, *Ondine* (Barry Moreland), and *Studies* (Maya Murdma). Star dancers, in addition to Makarova, included Cynthia Gregory, Anthony Dowell, and Peter Schaufuss. For its Broadway debut, the Contemporary Ballet Company offered *Night and Day* (William Whitener), *Yerma* (Domy Reiter-Soffer), and *Juice* (Margo Sappington), with casts composed of dancers from such companies as ABT and Joffrey.

Foreign troupes visiting America included the full Royal Danish Ballet, appearing in its 1979 all-Bournonville centenary repertory at the International Dance Festival of Stars in Chicago. The Berlin Ballet featured Valery Panov's *The Idiot*, with Panov, Galina Panova, Eva Evdokimova, and guest star Nureyev, along with Nureyev's staging of *The Nutcracker*. The Ballet National de Marseille, directed

The Berlin Ballet presented the North American premiere of Valery Panov's The Idiot, based on the Dostoyevsky novel, at the Metropolitan Opera House in New York City in July; at right, Rudolf Nureyev, who danced the title role of Prince Myshkin, presents a flower to Jennifer Anne Coen.

UPI

by Roland Petit, made its U.S. debut in Petit ballets, among them *Marcel Proust Remembered*. Others visitors were the Royal Winnipeg Ballet, the Beijing (Peking) Opera (absent from America for 50 years), and the new Munich Dance Project.

The Martha Graham Dance Company returned to the Metropolitan Opera House in a repertory that featured Graham's new *Frescoes*, a new version of *Judith*, a revived and revised *Episodes*, and the evening-long *Clytemnestra*, with Nureyev in the principal male role. Other modern dance events included productions of new works by the Alvin Ailey American Dance Theater (*Phases* by Ailey, *Later That Day* by Kathryn Posin, *Inside* by Ulysses Dove), Nikolais Dance Theater (*Count-Down* by Nikolais), Paul Taylor Dance Company in its 25th anniversary year (*Le Sacre du Printemps—The Rehearsal* by Taylor), Phyllis Lamhut (a full-length *Passing*), Merce Cunningham (*Fractions*, *Inlets*, *Duets*), and Twyla Tharp and Dancers in a three-week Broadway season (*When We Were Very Young* by Tharp).

Robert Schumann's "Davidsbündlertänze," choreographed by George Balanchine, was premiered by the New York City Ballet in June; featured were Peter Martins and Heather Watts.

MARTHA SWOPE

Paul Draper, at 70, created *Tap in Three Movements* for the American Dance Machine, a company specializing in preserving great dances from Broadway musicals. The Spoleto Festival U.S.A. in Charleston, S.C., featured a dance gala based on Shakespeare themes including José Limón's *The Moor's Pavane* (with Soviet defector Aleksandr Godunov dancing the Othello role for the first time) and the world premiere of *The Bloody Crown*, choreographed by Ivan Tenorio and with Alicia Alonso as Lady Macbeth.

The annual *Dance Magazine* awards went to Ruth Page, Patricia McBride, and Paul Taylor and the Capezio Dance Award to Walter Terry. Agnes de Mille was honoured with a Kennedy Center Arts Award. Lucia Chase received the presidential Medal of Freedom.

(*See also* Music; Theatre.)

DEFENSE AND ARMS CONTROL

The year 1980 marked the real start of the "new cold war"—the end of détente and arms control. Two events symbolized this change. In January the Soviets transformed their December 1979 invasion of Afghanistan into a permanent occupation by 100,000 Soviet troops supporting a puppet government, although various Afghan resistance groups continued to wage guerrilla warfare against the Soviet invaders. Then, on November 4, the U.S. elections produced a Republican landslide, putting in power conservative hard-liners pledged to build up U.S. defenses and counter Soviet power. The Republican candidate, former California governor Ronald Reagan, became president-elect, and the GOP gained control of the U.S. Senate.

It was impossible to overestimate the importance of these changes, which marked the end of the U.S. loss of self-confidence that had been a legacy of the Vietnam war. Moreover, the new president and the new Republican senators had won by substantial majorities, and Reagan had chalked up a massive majority in the Electoral College. While defense policy was not the only issue at stake, the results showed that the U.S. public was ready to reject détente and arms control, which had been the policy not only of Pres. Jimmy Carter but also of his Republican predecessors, Gerald Ford and Richard Nixon, and of their secretary of state, Henry Kissinger. The symbols of détente, the strategic arms limitations talks agreements of 1972 and 1979 (SALT I and II), were headed for the scrap heap, and the scene was set for a U.S. attempt to contain the Soviet Union on a scale not seen since 1947.

The decisive point in the change in U.S.-Soviet relations from cooperation to confrontation was the Afghanistan invasion. The change came at a time when the "arc of crisis," from Afghanistan to Turkey, was the scene of fierce fighting over some 3,200 km (2,000 mi). The Soviet occupation had neutralized the Afghanistan armed forces, which had stood at 40,000 personnel and 800 tanks, turning a pro-

Soviet force into a largely anti-Soviet one. But the invasion also put 100,000 troops within striking distance of Pakistan and Iran. Soviet attacks on Afghan refugee camps and guerrilla bases in Pakistan were increasing, posing a danger that the conflict would expand. This danger would increase if, as was likely, the Reagan administration provided military assistance to the Afghan resistance and massively increased military aid to Pakistan.

On the Western border of Afghanistan and Pakistan, Iran continued to resist the Iraqi invasion that had started on September 22. Iraq had seized control of most of Khuzestan Province, with its valuable oil fields, and Iran had suffered considerable losses. Further, Iran's economy was disintegrating. The Iran-Iraq war had also destroyed the assumptions on which the 1978 Camp David accords between Egypt and Israel had been based.

Instability had even spread to Eastern Europe, where the Polish trade unions had challenged the authority of the Polish Communist Party, gaining concessions the Soviet Union would find very difficult to accept. There were fears of Soviet military intervention to enforce the Brezhnev Doctrine, as had happened in Czechoslovakia in 1968, though the Poles would probably meet force with force. The Chinese, now de facto U.S. and NATO allies, saw these events as confirming their prediction that war with the Soviets was inevitable. Equally pessimistically, West Germany's Chancellor Helmut Schmidt likened 1980 to the summer of 1914, when World War I started. If not like August 1914, when the armies met, 1980 certainly looked like July 1914, when the moves that made war inevitable were taking place.

United States

President Carter had kept U.S. defense spending relatively low in real terms, at 5.2% of gross national product (GNP), although inflation raised the dollar amount to $142.7 billion for fiscal 1981. His successor would thus have to request large increases to make up for cumulative defects in U.S. forces caused by underfunding. The forces totaled 2,050,000 (150,000 women), all volunteers, and were insufficient to meet U.S. defense commitments. Moreover, recruitment and retention, especially of skilled personnel, were inadequate, compromising the performance of many units, particularly in the Navy. Reintroduction of the draft was a real possibility, certainly if U.S. forces were involved in even a minor conflict. President Carter's introduction of preliminary draft registration in the summer met relatively little opposition.

Strategic forces were slowly being modernized to maintain the U.S. deterrent. The 1,000 Minuteman II and III intercontinental ballistic missiles (ICBM's) in fixed silos were based on designs 15 and 10 years old, respectively, and the 54 Titans were even older. Development of the new MX mobile ICBM continued to be plagued by technical, political, and cost problems. A total of 200 MX's were planned, each with ten Mark 12A 370-kiloton multiple independently targeted reentry vehicles (MIRV); the Mark 12A was also being fitted to Minuteman III, reducing its circular error probability (CEP; a measure of accuracy) from 275 to 185 m (900 to 600 ft). MX was to be deployed on a shell-game principle, with more silos than missiles and with the missiles moving between silos in trucks on specially constructed roads, thus reducing the likelihood of a successful Soviet strike against them. The basing mode had been changed from an oval road or racetrack system to straight roads so as to take up less land and cut costs, which were expected to rise from $35 billion to $50 billion in 1980 dollars. There were also political problems in securing acceptance of the MX from the states where it was scheduled for deployment. The two states originally designated, Nevada and Utah, were insisting that at least two other states accept MX. The opposition was reminiscent of the 1969 antiballistic missile (ABM) debate, with the difference that the people in the MX deployment areas, and their political representatives, were mostly conservatives who favoured a strong defense.

Other strategic force changes included deployment of the first of 11 giant Ohio-class ballistic missile submarines (SSBN's), each with 24 Trident C-4 submarine-launched ballistic missiles (SLBM's; 7,400-km [4,600-mi] range, 8 × 100-kiloton MIRV). They would replace the ten older Washington- and Allen-class SSBN's with Polaris SLBM's, six of which would be converted to nuclear attack submarines (SSN's) by 1981. The 31 Lafayette-class SSBN's were being retrofitted with the Trident C-4, replacing the Poseidon C-3 SLBM (4,600-km [2,860-mi] range, 10 × 50-kiloton MIRV), but they could not take the larger, follow-on Trident D-5 (11,100-km [6,900-mi] range, 14 × 150-kiloton MIRV/MARV [maneuverable reentry vehicle]).

The ancient B-52 bomber force, dating from 1956 –62, was being upgraded with 3,418 air-launched cruise missiles (ALCM's), specifically the Boeing AGM-86A (4,000-km [2,500-mi] range, one W-80 200-kiloton warhead), to be carried in the 241 B-52G/H's. President Carter revised U.S. nuclear targeting doctrine to accept the idea of deliberately targeting the Soviet Communist Party leadership and control apparatus, a theoretical change that still had to be translated into practice and would need larger U.S. nuclear forces.

In general purpose forces, manpower shortages were compounded by obsolete equipment. New equipment was being introduced, but the attempt to make quality substitute for quantity often led to its being too complicated for reliability. The U.S. Army's new M-1 Abrams tank, with 120-mm gun, was criticized on these grounds; the 152 Abramses supplemented 8,905 M-60 medium tanks dating from 1959 and 1,825 even earlier M-48s. Similarly, the M-2 infantry fighting vehicle (IFV) and M-3 cav-

DAVE FORNELL—SYGMA

On September 19 leaking fuel exploded in an underground silo housing a Titan 2 nuclear missile; 21 air force personnel were injured and one was killed, and debris rained over the nearby areas of Damascus, Arkansas. The missile's warhead was protected from detonation by a fail-safe mechanism.

alry fighting vehicle (CFV) were supplementing the 22,000 M-577, M-114, and M-113 armoured personnel carriers (APC's). The Army of 774,000 personnel was composed of four armoured, six mechanized, four infantry, one airmobile, and one airborne divisions, with, respectively, 18,900, 18,500, and 16,500 personnel plus 324 or 216 tanks. Of these, one mechanized and one airborne division formed the Strategic Reserve in the U.S., where reinforcements for Europe were also based (two armoured, three mechanized, two infantry, and one airmobile divisions). Overseas deployment, largely in NATO-Europe, totaled 206,400 troops, mostly in the 7th Army in West Germany (196,200 troops, 3,000 tanks). Other major deployments were a twice-normal-size infantry division (30,400 troops) in South Korea, where U.S. troop reductions were no longer being considered, and an understrength infantry division in Hawaii. Reserves, totaling 535,000, included a 345,500-strong Army National Guard and Army Reserves of 190,000.

The 528,000-strong Navy had 173 major combat vessels and 74 SSN's. The core of the fleet remained its 14 aircraft carriers; 3 were nuclear-powered and one more was building, but the remaining 11 were elderly. Each carrier had one air wing of 24 new F-14A Tomcats or older F-4J Phantoms, plus 24 A-7E Corsair and 10 A-6E Intruder fighter-bombers as well as reconnaissance, early-warning, antisubmarine, tanker, and other specialized aircraft. The problems of U.S. forces were dramatized in the

abortive April attempt to rescue the U.S. hostages in Teheran. In a major humiliation to a country known for its technologically advanced forces, only eight helicopters were available, and three broke down, forcing cancellation. Nonetheless, the Navy remained the most powerful single fleet in the world, with its 8 nuclear- and 17 conventionally powered guided weapons (GW) cruisers, 37 GW and 43 gun/antisubmarine warfare (ASW) destroyers, and 13 GW and 59 gun frigates. New ship types included Ticonderoga-class GW cruisers (one building and 15 more planned) for fleet air defense, Spruance-class destroyers (30 in service and 5 building), and 7 Perry-class frigates.

The Air Force of 555,100 personnel had 3,700 combat aircraft. New types included 360 F-15 Eagle and 72 lighter F-16 fighter/fighter-bombers, plus 216 A-10 Thunderbolt close-support aircraft. Among older aircraft were 868 F-4 Phantom fighter-bombers and 282 F-111A/D/E/F medium bombers, plus 65 FB-111A's used as strategic bombers.

Formation of a rapid deployment force (RDF) had been announced, but it was only a reorganization of existing forces with improved logistic support. The RDF was based on the 189,000-strong Marine Corps, with its 575 medium tanks, 950 LVTP-7 APC's, 144 F-4N/S fighters, and 80 A-4M, 60 A-6A/E, and 78 vertical/short takeoff and landing (V/STOL) AV-8A Harrier fighter-bombers. These could be transported in 65 amphibious warfare ships.

NATO

Attention within the alliance remained focused on the balance of theatre nuclear forces (TNF). The Warsaw Pact was increasing its already significant superiority over NATO and would enjoy a TNF advantage of at least three to one in arriving warheads until NATO began to deploy new long-range TNF in 1983–84. The NATO allies had agreed to this deployment on Dec. 12, 1979, but only after one of the most divisive debates in the alliance's history. Britain and West Germany had insisted that modernized long-range TNF were vital, while The Netherlands and other smaller members argued that modernization would foreclose the chances of theatre nuclear arms control. Initially, the U.S. was divided between the Pentagon, arguing for long-range TNF, and the Arms Control and Disarmament Agency and President Carter, who favoured arms control. The U.S. eventually backed TNF modernization, but only after Belgium and The Netherlands were allowed to accept it in principle while deferring acceptance in practice.

The new NATO TNF comprised 108 Pershing II IRBM's, all in West Germany, plus 464 long-range ground-launched cruise missiles (GLCM's) in groups of four per launcher. Of the 116 GLCM launchers, 24 were to be in West Germany, 40 in Britain, 28 in Italy, 12 in Belgium, and 12 in The Netherlands. This geographic distribution met the West German principle of nonsingularity: that one other NATO member who did not have nuclear weapons—that is, not Britain or France—must accept GLCM's. By the end of 1980, it was still unclear whether the long-range TNF modernization decision would stand, although the U.S. was now committed to it.

NATO's 1978 long-term defense program was beginning to remedy some of the alliance's worst military defects, but many members, including West Germany, still had not implemented their promised 3% increase in real defense spending. This unwillingness to devote adequate resources to defense was NATO's major problem, since there were no cheap shortcuts, economic or political, for repairing the gap between NATO and Warsaw Pact capabilities. This discrepancy had been cumulative, over nearly 20 years, and had been underestimated until 1978. In addition, NATO had relied too much on its qualitative superiority—now nonexistent—to offset the Pact's numerical advantage and superior reinforcement capabilities during the first month of fighting.

On the crucial Central Front, ready forces were 27 NATO divisions (to 46 Pact divisions), 7,000 NATO main battle tanks (to 19,500 for the Pact), and 2,300 NATO tactical aircraft (to 4,000 Pact aircraft). These forces were insufficient to implement NATO's doctrine of flexible response: a conventional defense phase followed by the use of tactical, and then strategic, nuclear weapons against the Soviet Union. NATO could follow this scenario with forces

WIDE WORLD

Soon after the election of a Republican administration Sen. Charles Percy, expected to head the Senate Foreign Relations Committee, met with Soviet leader Leonid I. Brezhnev in Moscow to discuss arms control.

inferior to those of the Pact, but not as inferior as they had become. In a crisis, the Soviet Union might not be deterred from attacking NATO forces if it believed these could be defeated in a lightning war and if U.S. and NATO nuclear forces seemed inadequate to implement the nuclear part of NATO strategy. Estimates were that NATO could offer a conventional defense for only two to ten days before NATO TNF would have to be used. The increasing fear of Soviet expansion, even—or especially—if motivated by insecurity, was also causing political concern over NATO's military inferiority not seen since the height of the cold war.

DENMARK

The economy dominated Danish politics in 1980. The balance of payments situation continued to deteriorate, and the foreign debt was expected to reach 100 billion kroner during 1981. The budget was unbalanced, and the public sector was still growing disproportionately in comparison with industry and other activities in the private sector. Unemployment figures were rising, reaching 150,000 in October and forecast to reach 250,000 in 1981. Although exports were rising, imports rose even more rapidly. The budget review, published on Oct. 9, 1980, showed a deficit of more than 15 billion kroner, nearly 3 billion kroner more than the

Copenhagen was the site of the World Conference of the United Nations Decade for Women; the conference was marked by a great deal of political squabbling. Here PLO representatives lead a walkout as Jihan El-Sadat, wife of Egyptian Pres. Anwar El-Sadat, begins her address.
WIDE WORLD

forecast of three months earlier. The 1981 forecast spoke of a deficit of over 18 billion kroner (5.59 kroner = U.S. $1).

Under an "economic crisis" bill introduced in May 1980, the government undertook various measures, some in the face of vehement protest when vested interests were attacked. The value-added tax was raised to 22%, taxes on gasoline, fuel oil, and electricity were increased, and adjustments in direct taxation were made, giving Denmark the highest direct taxation in the world.

Oil and other kinds of imported energy posed a big problem for Denmark, which obtained only about 5% of its supplies from indigenous sources such as North Sea oil. A natural-gas grid was under construction, and it was expected that Danish oil production would grow in future years, thus helping to arrest the deterioration in Denmark's terms of trade. The government sought to alter the terms under which the Danish consortium was working in the North Sea sector. Such modification was not easily undertaken, however, because the concession, granted in 1962, was to run for 50 years.

The opposition, of both right and left, was critical of Prime Minister Anker Jørgensen's customary review of the state of the country at the opening of the October parliamentary session. The government and its supporting parties were blamed for Denmark's parlous economic prospects. From the left claims were voiced on behalf of "economic democracy"—compulsory profit sharing and similar measures—while support for the exporting industries was castigated as "taking from the poor and giving to the rich." It was agreed that the foreign debt had to be brought down but that low-income groups should not be affected.

Defense was another difficult matter. Defense expenditure had been accepted by a substantial majority, but the Radical Liberals, previously participants in the existing defense arrangement, opted out of it. The government spoke of a "zero-solution," which meant that Denmark should avoid its NATO obligations to increase defense expenditure by 3%. The Conservatives and Liberal Democrats protested, and it seemed as though the broad majority upholding Danish defense policy within NATO might be jeopardized.

DENTISTRY

To elevate the level of oral health in the U.S. the American Dental Association (ADA) during 1980 continued to focus attention on its multifaceted "access program" launched a year earlier. The program sought to bring comprehensive dental health care to five poorly served population groups: the elderly, the handicapped, the poor, remote-area residents, and the worker without dental insurance. At its annual session in October the ADA resolved to encourage state dental societies to develop access programs that provide reduced-fee comprehensive dental care to indigent elderly persons. The ADA also intensified its work in Congress to have dental care included under Medicare.

William H. Bowen and colleagues at the National Institute of Dental Research in Bethesda, Md., developed a new animal test to measure the ability of certain foods to cause cavities. By feeding rats their essential nutrition through tubes routed directly into the stomach and test foods on a programmed feeder, they found it possible to determine the cariogenicity (decay-producing ability) of many substances. Results showed that certain nonsugary snack foods and lightly sugared breakfast cereals may have the same decay-producing potential as more heavily sugared counterparts. For example, the potato chips used in the experiment demonstrated modest decay-producing potential. "Potato chips are frequently promoted as noncariogenic snacks," the investigators noted. "It may be necessary, on the basis of our results, to reevaluate this opinion." The study also reaffirmed findings of other investigations that chocolate and caramel are less cariogenic than sucrose. In addition it suggested that the cookies used in the study are more cariogenic than sucrose and spur the development of decay-causing bacteria.

Millions of adults who suffer from severe facial pain, backaches, or dizzy spells may be unaware that dental treatment can help them, reported New York City dentist Harold Gelb. Many of the same individuals also suffer from crooked jaws, lopsided faces, and deformed lips. Gelb pointed out that these problems frequently are caused by a misalignment of the temporomandibular joint (TMJ), a location in front of the ear at which the lower jaw hinges. One of the most common causes of TMJ problems is clenching and gnashing the teeth under stress, a practice that often leads to malocclusion or bat bite. Therapy may involve changing the slopes of the teeth or making the teeth higher or lower to bring the chewing muscles into proper working relationship and thus the jaws into balance.

DISASTERS OF 1980

The loss of life and property from disasters in 1980 included the following:

Aviation

January 21, Near Lashkarak, Iran. An Iran Air Boeing 727, engulfed in fog, crashed in the Elburz Mountains; all 128 persons aboard were killed.

March 14, Warsaw. A Polish IL-62 jetliner attempting to make an emergency landing crashed nearly 3 km (2 mi) short of the airport; all 87 persons aboard, including 22 U.S. amateur boxers and officials, were killed.

April 12, Near Florianópolis, Brazil. A Transbrasil Boeing 727 smashed into a wooded hillside during a tropical rainstorm; 54 persons were killed.

April 25, Santa Cruz de Tenerife, Canary Islands. A chartered British Boeing 727 airliner crashed on the slope of the 3,718-m (12,198-ft) Teide Peak; all 146 persons aboard, including 138 British vacationers and 8 crew members, were killed.

June 28, Tyrrhenian Sea. An Italian DC-9 jetliner plunged into the Tyrrhenian Sea; all 81 persons aboard were killed.

July 7, Alma-Ata, Kazakhstan, U.S.S.R. A Soviet airliner with 163 persons aboard crashed while taking off; all aboard died in the second worst air disaster in the country's history.

August 19, Riyadh, Saudi Arabia. A flaming Lockheed L-1011 TriStar jumbo jetliner returned

Twenty-two members of the U.S. Olympic boxing team were among 87 persons killed near the Warsaw airport in Poland when a Polish Airlines jetliner crashed on March 14.
UPI

to make an emergency landing at Riyadh airport; despite efforts by rescue workers, all 301 persons aboard the aircraft lost their lives. The death toll made the disaster the second worst single plane crash in aviation history.

September 14, Near Medina, Saudi Arabia. A Saudi Arabian Air Force C-130 Hercules transport plane carrying 89 persons burst into flames and crashed into the desert; there were no survivors.

December 21, Colombia. A Colombian jetliner crashed in the Guajira Desert minutes after takeoff from Ríohacha, after a bomb exploded in a rear restroom; all 70 persons aboard were killed.

Fires and Explosions

January 1, Chapais, Que. A fast-burning fire, fueled by spruce and pine bough decorations, trapped New Year's Eve revelers inside a crowded club; 46 persons died in the blaze.

May 20, Kingston, Jamaica. A fast-burning fire leveled a wooden two-story home for elderly women. In the worst fire in the history of Jamaica, 144 women were known dead and 11 were missing.

August 2, Bologna, Italy. A bomb explosion at a train station crushed a restaurant, two crowded waiting rooms, and a train platform, claiming the lives of 76 persons and injuring some 200 others. The blast, linked to right-wing terrorists, was the worst terrorist incident in the history of Italy.

August 14, Iraq. An electrical fire in a theatre in a suburb of Baghdad sent panicking patrons to the exits; although the fire was relatively minor, 59 persons were killed in the stampede.

August 16, London. An early morning fire at two adjoining social clubs killed 37 persons; Scotland Yard believed the blaze was started by a home-made gasoline bomb.

August 18, Deh-Bozoorg, Iran. A dynamite explosion occurred when the explosives stored in a private home were inadvertently ignited by a spark from a welder's tool; at least 90 villagers were killed and some 40 others were injured.

October 23, Ortuella, Spain. An explosion in one of three units of an elementary school leveled the structure and killed 3 adults and 61 children aged 6 to 10.

October 31, Gorna Grupa, Poland. A fire that engulfed the third floor of a mental hospital claimed the lives of 50 persons.

November 16, Bangkok, Thailand. An explosion in an army munitions factory detonated some 5,000 rockets, triggering a two-and-a-half-hour blaze and

On May 9 a freighter passing under the Sunshine Skyway Bridge in Tampa Bay, Florida, struck one of the bridge's pilings, plunging cars, a truck, and a bus into the bay. Thirty-five people were killed.
KEYSTONE

destroying a four-block area. Thirty-eight persons were killed and some 350 injured.

November 20, Kawaji, Japan. A fire that was believed started by a smoldering cigarette left near an oxygen cylinder destroyed the Kawaji Prince Hotel; 44 persons succumbed in the blaze.

November 24, Near Ankara, Turkey. An explosion at an engagement party set off a series of blasts that killed at least 97 persons, most of them children and women, including the bride-to-be.

Late November, Southern California. Fires fueled by hurricane-force winds charred more than 34,400 ha (85,000 ac) in San Bernardino, Riverside, Orange, San Diego, and Los Angeles counties. The fires, attributed to a combination of arson, dry vegetation, and the seasonal Santa Ana winds, claimed 4 lives and destroyed over 400 homes.

November 21, Las Vegas, Nev. A fast-burning fire that ripped through the first and second floors of the MGM Grand Hotel killed 84 persons; most died from carbon monoxide poisoning. It was the second most deadly hotel fire in U.S. history.

Marine

January 28, Off the Florida coast. The Coast Guard tender "Blackthorn" collided with the tanker "Capricorn" in Tampa Bay and sank; 26 crewmen aboard the "Blackthorn" lost their lives.

April 22, Central Philippines. The interisland ferry "Don Juan" collided with an oil tanker; 96 persons were known dead of the nearly 1,000 passengers and crew aboard the ferry.

August 22, Near Ciudad del Carmen, Mexico. A run-down ferryboat loaded with a bus, passenger cars, and several cargo trucks sank off the coast of Ciudad del Carmen; at least 50 persons drowned.

September 6, Santo Domingo, Dominican Republic. Twenty-two stowaways concealed in the ballast tanks of a Panamanian freighter were found dead, some drowned, others suffocated; 12 others were rescued.

Late October, Atlantic Ocean. After leaving Philadelphia on October 24, the freighter "Poet" disappeared without a trace; the 34 crewmen aboard were presumed dead.

Mining

March 27, South Africa. A cable supporting an elevator cage snapped and sent 31 coal miners plummeting more than 1,500 m (5,000 ft) down a shaft at Vaal Reef's mine, the world's largest and deepest gold mine; the impact of the crash flattened the cage and killed all aboard.

November 29, Northern Romania. A gas explosion in the Livezeni coal mine in the Jiu Valley claimed the lives of 49 miners and injured 26 others.

Miscellaneous

January 20, Sincelejo, Colombia. Eight bleacher sections surrounding the largest bullring in Colombia collapsed under the weight of some 3,000

GAMMA/LIAISON

Fire broke out in the MGM Grand Hotel in Las Vegas, Nevada, at 7 AM on November 21; 84 people were killed and more than 400 injured; it was the second worst hotel fire in U.S. history.

spectators; at least 165 persons were known dead, and another 500 were injured, many of them trampled or impaled on splintered beams.

March 4, Lagos, Nigeria. When the door of a van in which 68 prisoners were being transported was opened, 47 prisoners were found suffocated.

March 27, Off the coast of Norway. A five-legged floating oil-field platform overturned in gale-force winds in the North Sea; 123 of the 212 men aboard were drowned.

May 4, Kinshasa, Zaire. Nine persons were trampled to death when a huge crowd of people, estimated at 1.5 million, pushed forward to attend a mass celebrated by Pope John Paul II; 72 others were injured in the crush.

Summer, Madhya Pradesh State, India. An epidemic of cholera swept through Madhya Pradesh

Southern California, tinder dry after summer and fall heat, suffered a series of devastating fires in late November, some of which may have been set by arsonists. In Long Beach, above, a pipeline exploded in a residential area.

and claimed the lives of at least 390 persons.

September–October, Northern India. An epidemic of encephalitis, a viral disease spread by mosquitoes, caused the deaths of at least 400 persons.

Natural

January 1, Azores Islands. An earthquake measuring 6.9 on the Richter scale struck the ten-island chain, killing at least 56 persons and injuring 400 others; hardest hit was Terceira Island, where 70% of the buildings in the capital were destroyed.

January, Bihar State, India. A cold wave claimed the lives of at least 79 poor persons who lacked the required food and clothing to withstand temperatures as low as 2° C (36° F).

February, California, Arizona, and Mexico. A nine-day rainstorm blasted Mexico, Arizona, and southern California, where flooding prompted huge mudslides; damage was estimated at half a billion dollars, and 36 persons lost their lives.

March 2, Eastern U.S. A crippling snowstorm that left hundreds of motorists stranded contributed to the deaths of at least 36 persons.

Early April, Central Peru. Heavy rains triggered mud-and-rock slides and caused severe flooding; at least 90 persons were missing and believed dead and some 400 others were stranded.

May 18, Toutle, Wash. The eruption of Mt. St. Helens ripped more than 400 m (1,300 ft) from the top of the 2,950-m (9,677-ft) volcano, which spewed tons of mud, volcanic rocks, and ash; 34 persons were known dead and 53 others were missing and believed buried under debris.

June–August, U.S. A heat wave seared the nation with temperatures soaring above 38° C (100° F) nearly every day in Texas. The Midwest and East were also affected; Missouri experienced the highest death toll in the nation with 311 deaths. The

nationwide death toll was officially put at 1,265 persons, most of them poor and elderly who could not afford air conditioning.

July 23, Northern Vietnam. Typhoon Joe rampaged through the country killing more than 130 persons and destroying newly planted rice fields.

July 29, Western Nepal. A severe earthquake measuring 6.5 on the Richter scale jolted the country. At least 87 persons were killed, 5,600 injured, and some 35,000 left homeless.

July–August, India. Monsoon floods in six states in India ravaged 19,400 sq km (7,500 sq mi); property damage was estimated at more than $131 million, and at least 600 people were known dead.

Early August, Barbados, St. Lucia, Haiti, Dominican Republic, Jamaica, Cuba, and the U.S. Ferocious Hurricane Allen, the second strongest Atlantic hurricane of the century, battered the Caribbean with winds of 280 kph (175 mph) and gusts of 315 kph (195 mph); hardest hit was Haiti, where at least 220 persons died. The cumulative death toll was put at more than 270.

August 14, Japan. A rockfall that sent a dozen rocks measuring more than one metre (three feet) in diameter down Mt. Fuji, Japan's highest peak, struck and killed 12 mountain climbers; more than 30 others were injured.

August–September, West Bengal State, India. Seasonal monsoon rains that caused heavy flooding and triggered landslides contributed to the deaths of nearly 1,500 people in the state.

September 1–3, Arandas, Mexico. A burst dam and flooding waters of the Colorado River took the lives of at least 124 persons.

September 15–16, Central Vietnam. Raging Typhoon Ruth wreaked further damage on Vietnam, which was still reeling from the ravages of Typhoon Joe in July; 164 persons were known dead.

Mid-September, Orissa State, India. Several days of torrential rain caused widespread flash floods and burst a dam that inundated two towns with 3 m (10 ft) of water; at least 300,000 persons were marooned and some 200 others were drowned.

September, Bangladesh. Flooding in 12 northwestern districts of Bangladesh killed 655 persons.

October 10, El Asnam, Alg. A powerful earthquake measuring 7.7 on the Richter scale reduced 80% of El Asnam to rubble in only 30 seconds; 4,000 persons died, 60,000 were injured, and some 300,000 others were left homeless.

November 23–24, Southern Italy. A series of major earthquakes peaking at 6.9 on the Richter scale rocked the cities of Naples, Salerno, Avellino, and Potenza, jolted a total of 179 communities, killed an estimated 3,000 people, and left some 310,000 homeless.

Railroads

January 22, China. An explosion aboard a train destroyed a railroad car and left more than 20 persons injured or dead at a railroad station.

June 30, Near Sofiok, Hung. A train crashed into a bus that entered a flashing railroad crossing and dragged it 800 m (2,600 ft) before stopping; 19 persons were killed and 16 others were injured.

August 19, Near Torun, Poland. A freight train and a crowded passenger train collided head-on; at least 62 persons were killed and 50 others were injured in Poland's worst rail disaster to date.

November 21, Near Vibo Valentia, Italy. A bizarre train crash occurred after a freight train lost 28 of its 41 cars and a southbound passenger train traveling at about 160 kph (100 mph) struck the uncoupled cars; the impact of this crash hurled several boxcars onto an adjacent track, where a northbound train slammed into them. Twenty-eight persons were killed and at least 100 injured.

Traffic

April 7, Near Culiacán, Mexico. A bus traveling from Tijuana to Mexico City careened off the right side of a narrow bridge while attempting to pass a truck and landed in a shallow ditch; 48 persons were killed and 36 others were injured.

May 9, Tampa Bay, Fla. A bus, several cars, and a pickup truck plunged 43 m (140 ft) into Tampa Bay after a ship struck the Sunshine Skyway Bridge and tore away more than 305 m (1,000 ft) of the span; the driver of the pickup truck survived, but 35 persons were killed, most of them from the bus.

May 21, Near Dapoli, India. A bus traveling to Bombay turned over and caught fire; 30 passengers burned to death and 41 others were seriously injured.

June 5, Jasper, Ark. A chartered bus traveling along a dangerous highway on Jasper Mountain in the Ozarks went out of control and slid down a 15-m (50-ft) embankment; 20 Texan tourists were killed and 13 others were injured, some seriously.

June 7, Maguzulu, South Africa. A speeding

Terrorists set off a bomb in the huge Bologna railway station in Italy on August 2; the tremendous explosion reduced much of the station to rubble, killing 76 people and injuring more than 200.
KEYSTONE

WIDE WORLD

Hurricane Allen swept by the northeast coast of Jamaica in August, flattening coastal areas with 100-mile-per-hour winds.

freight train slammed into the side of a bus at an unguarded crossroad; at least 45 persons were killed and dozens of others were injured.

August 3, Near Rio de Janeiro, Brazil. A collision of a bus and a truck on a highway northeast of Rio de Janeiro killed 28 persons. There was only one survivor, a passenger from the bus.

October 15, Near Oaxaca, Mexico. An overcrowded bus plunged to the bottom of the 230-m (750-ft) El Basurero gorge; 23 persons were killed and 18 others were injured in the crash.

December 13, Near Guzmán, Mexico. A trailer truck collided head-on with a bus filled with Roman Catholic pilgrims traveling to a shrine; 37 persons were killed and 18 others were injured in the crash.

DOMINICAN REPUBLIC

During 1980 the Partido Revolucionario Dominicano criticized Pres. Antonio Guzmán Fernández for not implementing its policies before the 1982 elections. Strikes and violence occurred as the economy worsened and the cost of living rose. Taxation and electricity and gasoline charges were raised (gasoline by 30%), state sector wages were frozen, and the availability of foreign currency was curtailed in

a financial package introduced in May in the face of a budget deficit and falling dollar reserves.

Sugarcane rust, heavy rain, and labour and transport difficulties reduced the 1980 sugar crop. Agriculture had not fully recovered from the two hurricanes of 1979, and coffee output also fell. In September Gulf and Western Industries and the government settled their dispute over $64.5 million made by the company's futures market speculations during the 1974–75 sugar boom. The company agreed to set up a 39 million peso nonprofit corporation for the economic and social development of the eastern region, where most of the sugar was grown. In July several hundred Haitian sugarcane labourers, kept starving in a barbed-wire compound before being sent back to Haiti after the harvest, rioted. They were brought under control by soldiers, but protests against this harsh system were renewed.

DRUGS

Seventy-five years ago the U.S. Congress was beginning to fashion the nation's first federal food and drug law—the Food and Drugs Act of 1906, which established what is now the Food and Drug Administration (FDA). Although there have been enormous changes in the drug supply since 1906, one aspect remains the same: a tendency toward overmedication.

In the years before 1906 the problem of overmedication involved substances purveyed as medicines that were often dangerous and totally ineffective, despite the wildly inflated claims made for them. Ingesting such "medicines" in any amount constituted overmedication. Owing to the explosion of biochemical knowledge that took place during and after the 1930s, the ability of the pharmaceutical industry to synthesize important and useful drugs, and the vigilance of the FDA, drugs now do work as claimed and are generally safe when used as directed. Overmedication today results not from taking drugs that do not work but from taking too many drugs that do work. As stated by Commissioner Jere E. Goyan, the first pharmacist to head the FDA, "We Americans take too many drugs. We take an average of six prescriptions a year for every man, woman, and child in this country, and twice that many when you count prescription drugs given in hospitals."

FDA Actions

As a reflection of this concern about overmedication, the FDA succeeded in 1980 in getting the makers of widely prescribed tranquilizers to revise the information they provide to physicians to emphasize that the products are not for "everyday" stress. These tranquilizers, which have the generic name benzodiazepine, are: Valium, Librium, Verstran, Traxene, Azene, Serax, Ativan, and Centrax.

In addition to this action, FDA required that, beginning in mid-1981, pharmacists give patients easy-to-read information along with certain prescription drugs. Such information, called patient package inserts, describes what the drug is for, what side effects may occur, and how to take the drug properly to get the most benefit. FDA already required patient package inserts with certain drugs; *e.g.*, birth control pills. The new program, which would involve ten drugs or categories of drugs, was designed to evaluate the benefits to the public of this form of education and to determine how much the program would cost.

The ten drugs included were the ampicillins, a class of penicillin-type antibiotics; the benzodiazepines; cimetidine, an ulcer drug; clofibrate, used to treat elevated fats in the blood; digoxin, for heart problems; methoxsalen, for skin pigmentation problems; thiazides, a class of diuretic drugs commonly used to treat high blood pressure; phenytoin, for control of epileptic seizures; propoxyphene, a pain reliever; and warfarin, a blood thinner used to prevent blood clots.

New Drug Developments

Through recombinant DNA techniques, it was found possible to produce nonbacterial proteins, such as insulin and growth hormone, by means of bacteria into which nonbacterial genes have been introduced. Human growth hormone is now extracted, at huge expense, from human cadavers. By means of the new DNA technology the gene that codes the production of growth hormone is transferred to a common bacterium, a weakened strain of *Escherichia coli*, and in a matter of hours the bacteria can make millions of copies, from which the hormone can be extracted.

In addition, an entirely new approach to drug development was taking place. In the past the discovery of useful drugs was largely accidental, and many new drugs resulted from modifications of already known drugs. This approach stemmed from limitations of knowledge about the pathophysiology of various disease processes and about the chemistry of enzymes and receptor proteins. It now appeared possible that useful drugs that operate with great precision according to design would soon be available. Among other benefits should be a substantial reduction in unanticipated side effects or adverse reactions to new drugs, as in the case of the new diuretic Selacryn, which had to be recalled for evaluation after it was associated with a number of cases of severe liver damage.

Among the drugs approved for marketing in 1980 was ritodrine hydrochloride, an important new drug for use in halting premature labour. This drug, which acts by relaxing the uterus, could help prevent some of the thousands of premature births—and fetal and infant deaths—that occur each year. Other new drugs included Corgard (nandolol), for treatment of hypertension, and a safer and more effective rabies vaccine that can provide immunity after just 5 injections, compared with the previously required 23.

EARTH SCIENCES

A "great" earthquake is defined as one having a magnitude of 8.0 or greater. Between late 1979 and late 1980 at least one such shock occurred, of magnitude 8.1, on Sept. 12, 1979, in the West Irian region of Indonesia resulting in the deaths of 15 persons. Another, which first was measured at magnitude 8.0 and later downgraded to 6.9, occurred on July 17, 1980, in the Santa Cruz Islands. Several other shocks of lesser magnitude caused fatalities or were of special interest. On Dec. 12, 1979, at least 600 persons were killed and 20,000 injured in Colombia and Ecuador by a shock of magnitude

Eli Lilly & Co., using genetic engineering techniques, began to produce human insulin for diabetics by means of bacteria that had been genetically programmed to produce the substance. Crystals of the insulin, highly magnified, are shown at right. The drug would be especially valuable for persons unable to tolerate insulin from animal sources.

UPI

When Mt. St. Helens in
Washington State
erupted on May 18, it
sent huge clouds of ash
and debris across the
Northwest and flattened
thousands of acres of
nearby timber in an
awesome display of
volcanic force.
WIDE WORLD

7.9. On Jan. 1, 1980, a magnitude 6.9 earthquake in the Azores killed at least 56 and injured more than 400, and on July 29, 1980, 150 people were killed and many were injured in the western Nepal-India border region by an earthquake of magnitude 6.6. The most devastating earthquakes of 1980 occurred late in the year. On October 10 a shock of magnitude 7.7 and a second of 6.5 destroyed as much as 80% of the town of El Asnam in Algeria; death toll estimates ran as high as 20,000, but later figures were closer to 4,000. On November 23 and 24 a broad region of southern Italy experienced a series of shocks that peaked at magnitude 6.9, causing several thousand deaths and widespread damage.

California experienced notable activity in late 1979 and 1980 with a large earthquake on the Mexico-California border, shocks near Livermore in the San Francisco Bay area, and an extensive swarm near the California-Nevada border. The first of these, at magnitude 6.8, was the largest to have occurred in the Imperial Valley since 1940. The region was very well instrumented, and among the excellent records produced was an astonishing ground acceleration at one station of 1.74 times the acceleration of gravity. The ensuing events included two magnitude 6.0 shocks on May 25, followed by a third on May 27 and by more than 100 aftershocks of magnitude 4.0 or greater.

By far the most spectacular and important geophysical event of the year was the eruption of Mt. St. Helens in May 1980. Mt. St. Helens is one of

more than a dozen volcanic peaks in the Cascade Range of the U.S. Pacific Northwest. Prior to March 27 the last of them to act up was Mt. Lassen in California, which erupted for several years beginning in 1914.

Mt. St. Helens is a composite volcano made up of alternate layers of lava and ash, the residues of previous activity. Its last active period began in 1830 and continued until 1857. The current episode can be dated from the recording on March 20 of a magnitude 4.1 earthquake 3½ km west of the summit of the mountain (one kilometre equals 0.62 mi).

Between late March and May 18 the volcano was under intense study by volcanologists, geologists, and meteorologists from many organizations. They recorded a sequence of events that began with an explosive steam eruption on March 27. This was followed by a series of moderate eruptions until April 23, after which came a period of relative quiescence until May 8, when steam and ash eruption resumed, followed by another quiescent period from May 14 to May 18.

Early in the period a nearly continuous fracture system 5,000 m long formed across the summit of the mountain (one metre equals 3.28 ft). As the disturbances progressed, the north flank of the peak began to bulge until it extended more than 80 m out from its original position. These features were watched very closely in hope of some premonitory evidence of a major eruption. Such was not the case, however. A magnitude 5.0 earthquake occurred on the morning of May 18, followed within seconds by an explosion that rivaled Vesuvius, Pelée, and others of the historical era.

As described by Robert L. Christiansen, a geologist of the U.S. Geological Survey (USGS), the earthquake caused numerous avalanches. Very soon thereafter, the entire north face separated along a crack across the upper part of the bulge, and the slope failed in a catastrophic avalanche. Within seconds a large lateral air blast carrying ash and stony fragments in a devastating wave overtook the avalanche. The blast expanded over a width of 30 km east to west and outward more than 20 km from the summit. Everything in a path ten kilometres wide was destroyed, and beyond this the forest was flattened for several kilometres on each side.

The first of four components of the eruption was the directed blast, which swept over ridges and flowed down valleys, depositing significant quantities of ash. Although it was hot, it did not char fallen or buried trees. The second component was a combined pyroclastic flow and landslide that carried the remnants of the north flank uplift across the lower slopes and about 27 km down the Toutle River valley, burying it to depths as great as 55 m. Large quantities of mud, logs, and other debris clogged several valleys around Mt. St. Helens and rendered some shipping lanes impassable in the Columbia River. The third component was a pyroclastic flow of pumice, funneled northward through the breach formed by the destruction of the north flank bulge. This flow dammed the outlet of Spirit Lake, trapping a large quantity of water. Before the lateral blast had reached its full extension, the fourth component, a vertical column, began to rise so rapidly that within ten minutes it had reached an altitude of more than 6,000 m. This column continued for nine hours, produced major ash falls as far east as central Montana, and eventually circled the globe with ash that caused hazy skies and red sunsets. The combination of these events literally blew the top off of the mountain and formed an amphitheatre 1.5 × 3 km in extent where the volcanic cone had been.

After a period of decreasing activity a second major eruption occurred on May 25. Following that date the eruptive activity continued but at a decreased level and, as expected, a volcanic dome formed in the crater due to magmatic action. Although the prognosis for future activity was varied and controversial, the historic evidence indicated that the active period for Mt. St. Helens was likely to continue for some time. As of early October, 34 persons including USGS geologist David A. Johnston, who was manning an outpost eight kilometres north-northwest of the mountain, were killed by the blast or resulting mud flows, and 53 persons were listed as missing. The damage was estimated to be in excess of $2 billion.

Hydrology

In the wake of the Mt. St. Helens eruption May 18, runoff from melted glaciers and snow and possibly some outflow from Spirit Lake caused widespread flooding in the Toutle and lower Cowlitz rivers. Massive volumes of sediment were transported during the flood on the Toutle River, which picked up thousands of logs and destroyed most of the local bridges. About 30 million cu m (25,000 acft) of sediment moved into the lower Cowlitz River. Much of it was deposited, reducing channel capacity by about 85% and significantly increasing flood

A major earthquake struck southern Italy on November 23, killing more than 3,000 people and leveling 90% of the buildings in some towns. In all, 179 municipalities suffered damage, leaving more than 300,000 people homeless.
WIDE WORLD

An earthquake that was felt throughout the country struck Ecuador on August 18; four people were killed when this building collapsed in Guayaquil.
WIDE WORLD

potential. Sediment that moved through the Cowlitz into the Columbia River formed a shoal that blocked shipping lanes for several days.

Evidence continued to accumulate that the acidity of atmospheric deposition, popularly known as "acid rain," was affecting lakes and streams in the northeastern U.S. and southeastern Canada. The acid-producing agents were sulfurous and nitrous oxides created by burning fossil fuels. Most of these gases were entering the air over large population centres, and indeed acidity was highest in samples of rain from Pennsylvania and New York. Many lakes in the Adirondacks were so acid that fish could not spawn. The U.S. and Canadian governments were combining efforts to measure the extent of acid precipitation, locate sources of acid-producing materials, and gain a better understanding of their effects.

A record-breaking summer heat wave in 1980 caused high rates of water loss to the atmosphere in much of the midcontinental and southeastern U.S. High flows from spring rains and high groundwater levels, however, prevented streamflow from reaching record lows except in parts of northern Minnesota and eastern North Carolina. Water was rationed in many regions of the country during the heat wave, primarily because of inadequate distribution systems rather than as a result of inadequate supplies.

U.S. hydrologists expressed growing concern about the future availability and quality of groundwater as a source of drinking water. Increasing evidence showed that this resource, once considered pollutant-free, was locally contaminated nationwide and that contamination at some sites posed a major health threat. The news media also focused on this concern with reports on groundwater contamination from hazardous wastes and with nationwide coverage of the Love Canal problem in New York. (*See also* Environment.)

ECUADOR

Differences of opinion between Pres. Jaime Roldós Aguilera and the president of Congress, Assad Bucaram, reached such a pitch that Roldós called on Congress to convene in extraordinary sessions to discuss constitutional changes giving him more power. When Congress vetoed his bill, on April 10, 1980, he threatened to call a national plebiscite and resign if he lost. By mid-May he had been persuaded to change his mind, however, and a multiparty commission was set up to study constitutional reforms, including the possible creation of a senate.

In August Congress showed its support for Roldós by electing his candidate, Raúl Baca Carbo, as its leader. Yet the president still faced economic and political problems. Party leaders were critical of the government's performance, but popular support for Roldós was strong, despite severe price rises and inflation of about 15%. The bus and truck drivers went on strike in July to protest the rise in the cost of living, but they received only nominal support.

A national development plan for 1980–84 called for investment of 370,572,000,000 sucres, two-thirds from the public sector and one-third from the private. The plan aimed to achieve a growth rate of 6.5% a year, consolidate democracy, promote social justice, and develop the economy with emphasis on agriculture and food production. The economy showed growth in 1980, with oil exports ensuring a trade surplus and rising international reserves. Increased oil exploration succeeded in raising reserves in the jungle region by over 3,000,-000,000 bbl.

EDUCATION

The growing political power of teachers' unions in the U.S. was apparent at the 1980 Democratic national convention, where 433 delegates and alternates belonging to the National Education

Beverly Bimes, a teacher from St. Louis, Missouri, was congratulated at a White House ceremony by Pres. Jimmy Carter on being chosen 1980 National Teacher of the Year. The annual event was sponsored by the Encyclopaedia Britannica companies, Good Housekeeping magazine, and the Council of Chief State School Officers.

WHITE HOUSE PHOTO

Association (NEA) formed the largest single bloc. (By contrast, only 18 NEA members were delegates or alternates to the Republican convention.) The NEA enthusiastically backed Pres. Jimmy Carter's bid for renomination, while the rival American Federation of Teachers (AFT) initially backed Sen. Ted Kennedy, switching to Carter only when Kennedy withdrew from contention. The NEA had never endorsed a presidential candidate before 1976, when it also backed Carter, but with 1.8 million members and representation in every congressional district, it had become an active and influential force in the nation's electoral process. The smaller AFT had long been active in politics and had working relationships with other member unions of the AFL-CIO.

Fulfilling one of the campaign promises that had brought him NEA support in 1976, President Carter in 1979 had signed into law a bill creating the U.S. Department of Education (ED), which officially came into existence in 1980. Headed by a former federal judge, Shirley M. Hufstedler, the new department included some 6,000 employees, most of them transferred from the Office of Education in the former Department of Health, Education, and Welfare, and had a budget of $14 billion. Eventually, 11,000 persons in the Defense Department's overseas dependents schools would also become part of ED. Conservatives generally opposed the new department, in large measure because they saw it as a threat to local control of schools, and during the presidential campaign Ronald Reagan, the ultimately successful Republican candidate, supported its elimination.

The percentage of illiterates in the world continued to fall, but the actual number of illiterates was growing because of the overall increase in population. At the biennial conference of the International Reading Association—a largely North American-dominated body—in Manila, a Swedish reading expert, Eve Malmquist, contended that 50% of the 6- to 12-year-olds in the world were unlikely ever to go to school. She also said there were signs that reading standards in developed countries were dropping and that imbalances between developed and less developed countries were widening. As evidence of the latter, she cited figures showing that Asia, with 56% of the world's population, produced only 20% of the world's books, while Latin America and Africa produced only 2% each.

Primary and Secondary Education

Public school enrollments in the U.S. continued to decline, a trend that was expected to continue until the mid-1980s. Meanwhile, teacher supply and demand were relatively in balance. The number of persons entering teacher-preparation programs had fallen enough to eliminate surpluses in several grade levels and subjects.

Busing for purposes of racial desegregation remained a live issue in U.S. education. During the year the largest court-ordered busing scheme in the quarter of a century since the landmark desegregation decision in *Brown* v. *Board of Education of Topeka* got under way in the nation's second-largest school district. Los Angeles had appealed to state courts and finally to the U.S. Supreme Court to block the plan, but on the day before school opened, a Supreme Court justice refused to intervene on the grounds that the normal flow of state appeals had not been exhausted. Only 27% of the children in the Los Angeles public schools were white, and the district covered a huge area of 1,840 sq km (710 sq mi). Limited busing during the preceding two years had not succeeded in accomplishing desegregation, and meanwhile an estimated 50,000 white students had left the system. Under the new plan, some 80,000–100,000 students were being bused. In a first-of-a-kind suit, the California attorney general claimed that forcing children to attend the Los Angeles schools constituted cruel and unjust punishment. Relief was demanded, though no specific action was requested.

The largest busing plan for a city and its suburbs approved by the Supreme Court would affect 60% of Delaware's public school students. In a new, court-created school district that included Wilmington and 11 nearby districts, students would go to schools other than their nearest neighbourhood school for at least three years. Twice during the year the Supreme Court rejected appeals by school boards for relief from busing. Specific desegregation actions occurred in Cleveland, Ohio (where more than half the students were being bused); Dallas, Texas (which had lost increasing numbers of white students); Chicago (which agreed to develop its own plan after the Justice Department threatened to sue the system); Birmingham, Ala. (which agreed to a limited busing and magnet school plan and some school closings to increase desegregation); and Houston, Texas, and 22 suburban districts. In setting a timetable for Chicago to develop its plan, federal officials said they were studying the largely white suburban schools to see how they related to Chicago's situation.

Despite this activity, many civil rights advocates feared a backlash against what opponents referred to as "forced busing." In its post-election "lame duck" session, the Senate passed a bill—attached as a rider to an appropriations bill for the State, Justice, and Commerce departments—designed to prohibit the Justice Department from using appropriated funds to pursue cases that would result in court-ordered busing. A similar measure was passed by the House. Faced with the threat of a presidential veto, Senate and House conferees dropped the provision from the bill. However, opponents of busing planned to bring up the matter again in the 97th Congress, which would be considerably more conservative. Sen. Strom Thurmond (Rep., S.C.), who would be chairman of the Senate

Judiciary Committee, stated that he planned to seek legislation removing educational matters from the federal courts' jurisdiction.

Shortly before its fall recess, Congress adopted an amendment to another funding bill preventing the Department of Education from enforcing far-reaching federal requirements for bilingual education until June 1981. The plan would have required children to be taught basic subjects in their native tongue until they had mastered English. In its 1974 decision on the subject, the Supreme Court had mandated assistance for the estimated 3.5 million non-English-speaking students in the U.S. but had left the specific procedures up to local districts.

Other matters pertaining to education were before the courts during the year. The Supreme Court indicated that it would review the right of school districts to limit black enrollment in order to discourage whites from moving away. A federal judge upset a 1975 Texas law that excluded the children of illegal immigrants from the public schools unless the parents paid tuition; Texas officials claimed that the ruling would add 40,000–140,000 students to the state's school systems. Modifying a 1971 court order that the Internal Revenue Service lift tax exemptions for segregated private schools, a U.S. district judge ruled that privately operated schools must prove they do not discriminate against minorities if they want to retain their tax-exempt status. A federal appeals judge held that the principal of a church-related school had exceeded his constitutional rights when he expelled a white student for dating a fellow student who was black.

North Carolina became the first state to implement its plan for minimal competency testing before high school graduation. Since 1976, 38 states had set dates after which they would require such tests statewide. Each state determined which competencies were to be included and the required level

Members of a high school football team welcome black students bused to their school on the first day of court-ordered desegregation in St. Louis, Missouri.
WIDE WORLD

French-speaking children attend a bilingual class in La Place, Louisiana. Bilingual education was a federally enforceable right for speakers of any of 70 native tongues.

HARRIS—GAMMA/LIAISON

necessary for passing from grade to grade or for graduation. Those who failed were given remedial work until they could pass.

Criticism of the Scholastic Aptitude Test (SAT), widely used for college entrance, continued to mount, as opponents charged that it was an inadequate predictor of college potential, was inaccurately graded, and was surrounded with excessive secrecy. In an effort to counter its critics, the publisher decided to publish old tests to help students prepare for the current edition. The College Entrance Examination Board said it would make it possible for students to double-check the scored sheets. The publisher also began to provide information on how the tests are constructed and pledged to continue efforts to remove any disadvantage that minority students and females might experience.

Higher Education

The U.S. Congress started to curtail funds for college students, with the aim of saving an estimated $3 billion within the next five years. Benefiting from federal aid that was approved were students eligible for federally guaranteed loans, black institutions and others serving disadvantaged students, and college libraries and projects dealing with language and adult education.

The cost of sending a student to a four-year college in the U.S. reached an average of $6,000 annually, an increase of $500 over the preceding year. According to the College Scholarship Service, the cost of four years of college was higher than the median yearly income of all U.S. families and was

likely to increase. Alexander Astin's annual survey predicted that college costs would reach $20,000 per year if increases continued at the same rate as in 1970–80. Families were responsible for about 56% of all college expenses. Some $14 billion was available in student aid, with 17% from government loans, 57% from government grants, and 7% from state aid programs. The final 19% came from private sources.

The Carnegie Council on Policy Studies in Higher Education predicted a 5–15% drop in college and university enrollments. In its final report, the council, which began its work in 1967, said that students might, in fact, benefit from this development as colleges began to recruit, counsel, assist, teach, and grade more actively and conscientiously and as grading and course planning became more student centred. The times might be difficult for staffs and administrations, however, and a decline in quality and capability was likely. The group's chairman, Clark Kerr, thought the several hundred liberal arts colleges that recruit locally were most likely to suffer from declining enrollments. Although the council projected a decrease in students in the traditional college age range of 18–24, it did suggest that increased numbers of older students, women, and minorities might help to balance that decline. A further conjecture was that the current retention rate might improve.

College graduates in 1980 were not severely affected by the recession. Jobs were available across the board, and majors in certain fields were eagerly sought. These included engineering, computer science, business, health science, and retailing. After

In August Egyptian Foreign Minister Kamal Hassan Ali (left) met with Israeli Ambassador to Egypt Eliahu Ben-Elissar at the Israeli embassy in Cairo, which opened in February.
WIDE WORLD

several lean years, jobs for public school teachers were more plentiful. The "baby boom" generation had now entered the job market, so fewer new graduates were looking for work.

Some 300 black studies programs had survived the cutbacks of recent years, a drop of almost 200 since the peak years of the 1960s. Supporters claimed that black studies were useful to blacks and to an increasing number of whites. They also believed that the existence of such programs influenced other academic departments to include information about the history and culture of blacks, other minorities, and women.

The courts rejected attempts by several states and institutions to refuse university admission to Iranian students or to discourage them from enrolling by charging exceptional tuition. The efforts to exclude Iranians came in response to tensions that arose during the long months when Americans were held hostage in Iran. Some courts attempted to determine the extent to which foreign students are protected by the U.S. Constitution, but the Supreme Court had never clearly ruled on the matter.

EGYPT

Pres. Anwar El-Sadat continued to be isolated in 1980 from the rest of the Arab community as he pursued his policy of accommodating Israel. Sadat seemed intent on respecting the agreed-upon deadline of May 26 for talks with Israel on Palestinian autonomy, but the date passed without substantive progress. The talks were broken off by the Egyptians because of the Israeli government bill presented in the Knesset annexing the whole of East Jerusalem. Kamal Hassan Ali, deputy prime minister for defense and foreign affairs, subsequently said Egypt would tear up the Camp David agreement unless a settlement was reached soon after the U.S. presidential election in November. Sadat had always maintained that the U.S. "holds all the cards" in the Middle East conflict. It was his intention in signing the 1978 Camp David agreement that the

U.S. should become an active broker in the Israeli-Egyptian negotiations. Given the inertia gripping the U.S. administration in the pre-election period, the lack of progress in 1980 appeared explicable. Yet even moderate Arab rulers such as the sultan of Oman, who initially supported the Sadat peace initiative, were puzzled by the lack of progress on fundamental issues concerning the Palestinians.

Egypt was obliged to break off all remaining diplomatic links with the members of the Arab Steadfastness Front—Algeria, Libya, Syria, Yemen (Aden), and the Palestine Liberation Organization—on April 16 in protest against decisions by the hard-line states to tighten sanctions against Egypt. The nuisance nature of these decisions was distressing to the Egyptian leadership. More serious in their view, however, was the line taken by oil-rich Arab states such as Saudi Arabia and Kuwait in cutting economic aid, even though this aid was only a small proportion of Egypt's total requirements and Saudi and Kuwaiti entrepreneurs continued to visit Cairo.

The Iran-Iraq war produced an appeal by President Sadat to Washington to speed up the supply of promised military hardware, including advanced interceptors for the Air Force. The U.S. expressed its support for the Sadat government by sending a military force of 1,400 men to Egypt for the first overseas exercises of the newly formed Rapid Deployment Force. Economic assistance of $715 million a year made Egypt one of the biggest U.S. Agency for International Development (AID) operations anywhere in the world. In addition, the World Bank provided substantial assistance to Egypt's economy at the prompting of the U.S. administration. The U.S. agreed in principle to supply Egypt with some of its most advanced military equipment, including F-16 fighter aircraft. The military supply package included personnel carriers, Hawk antiaircraft missiles, and Chrysler M-60A3 tanks. Since Egypt's military arsenal consisted largely of aging Soviet equipment, the pressure on Sadat from his generals to rearm from U.S. sources was acute. A pan-Arab venture to build weapons and munitions factories in Egypt, headed by a Saudi, had collapsed in the aftermath of the Camp David agreement.

The stabilization of Egypt's relations with its powerful and well-armed neighbour may have had some limited beneficial effects. Ambassadors were exchanged by them in February for the first time. Israel's Foreign Minister Yitzhak Shamir was in Cairo on September 9 at the invitation of the minister of state for foreign affairs, Boutros Boutros Ghali, to discuss strictly bilateral issues. The prospect of some further economic cooperation with the Israelis also seemed likely, although the first steps, including the establishment of air services between the two capitals, were hesitant. Other Arab governments reacted angrily to the two countries' ties by extending the Arab boycott of Israel to any Egyptian entity perceived as trading in or with Tel Aviv, although such sanctions had little more than rhetorical effect.

Domestic Affairs

President Sadat decided in May to become his own prime minister and attempted to streamline his Cabinet. (He had taken similar actions just before the 1973 war.) Six deputy prime ministers were appointed who were to form an inner Cabinet. The most powerful man in this group was undoubtedly Defense Minister Kamal Hassan Ali, who in addition to having responsibility for defense took on foreign affairs and the task of overseeing information. The appointment of Planning Minister Abdel-Razzaq Abdel-Majid as economic czar was intriguing. He was given the task of overseeing planning, economy, trade, and supply. The concentration of all these roles into one job had been sought unsuccessfully by the former deputy prime minister for the economy, Abdel-Moneim al-Qaisouni, in June 1978.

Oil revenues for 1980 were expected to reach about U.S. $2.1 billion, as against $1.6 billion in 1979. To a great extent, they were the reason for economic recovery. Possibly as a side effect of the generally favourable Western response to Sadat's peace with Israel, there was no shortage of help for the Egyptian economy or reluctance on the part of foreign investors from the West to take advantage of the country's "open door" policies.

Sectarian violence increased in 1980, partly because of the Islamic fundamentalism that had swept through Muslim countries in the wake of the Iranian revolution. There were serious disturbances in the Upper Egypt towns of Asyut and Minya in April in which several people were killed. Relations between Sadat's government and the Coptic hierarchy were strained, and allegations of religious persecution were exchanged. There was also a

The deposed shah of Iran, Mohammad Reza Pahlavi, died in Cairo on July 27; a state funeral was held for him on July 29, at which Egyptian Pres. Anwar El-Sadat led the procession.
KEYSTONE

challenge to the government from prominent Egyptians associated with the late president Gamal Abdel Nasser. Their first open letter protested against the treaty with Israel. Liberals were also alienated by a referendum carried out in May, in which Sadat successfully sought changes in the 1971 constitution giving him, among other things, an unlimited number of terms of office. The vote for Sadat was 99%.

In March Sadat offered asylum to the exiled shah of Iran, known to be suffering from cancer. The Shah died in a Cairo hospital in July and was given a state funeral. In November, however, Sadat recognized the Teheran regime.

ELECTIONS

Ronald Wilson Reagan, 69, Republican, was elected on Nov. 4, 1980, as the 40th president of the United States. He was the oldest person ever elected to the office. The popular vote was 42,951,145 for Reagan, 34,663,037 for incumbent president Jimmy Carter, and 5,551,551 for independent John Anderson. Reagan drew 51% of the popular vote cast, Carter 41%, and Anderson 7%. Reagan gained 489 electoral votes, Carter 49. The voter turnout was estimated at 52.3% of eligible voters, the lowest since the 51.1% participation in 1948.

The Republican victory was a triumph for Reagan's strategy of seeking support from traditionally Democratic groups. Except for blacks and Hispanics, all elements of the normal Democratic coalition gave Carter less support than they did in 1976. Reagan's margin was large enough so that Anderson's entry in no way decided the presidential race.

President Carter publicly conceded defeat at about 9:50 PM Eastern time. At that time, polls were still open in California, Washington, Oregon, Alaska, and Hawaii. The early concession brought some criticism from western Democrats, who believed that it discouraged possible late voters.

Congress

The Republicans took 12 Senate seats to gain control of that body for the first time since they won it in the 1952 elections. The Senate lineup for the 97th Congress would be 53 Republicans, 46 Democrats, and 1 independent, Harry F. Byrd (Va.), who had usually sided with the Democrats.

In the House the Republicans gained 33 seats, but the Democrats kept a weakened majority. There would be 242 Democrats, 192 Republicans, and 1 independent, Thomas Foglietta (Pa.), who was expected to caucus with the Democrats. A number of high-seniority Democratic congressmen were defeated, forcing a change in House leadership and in the chairmanship of four committees.

Women won four seats in the House and one in the Senate, bringing the total number of women in the two chambers to 21, a net gain of four seats, with the loss of Rep. Elizabeth Holtzman of New York, who was defeated in a Senate bid. All five newly elected congresswomen were Republicans.

Senator-elect Paula Hawkins (Fla.) was opposed to the Equal Rights Amendment and favoured a constitutional ban on abortion. All four new women members of the House supported the ERA. They were: Rep. Bobbi Fiedler (Calif.), who defeated Democratic Congressional Campaign Committee Chairman James Corman; Claudine Schneider (R.I.); Marge Roukema (N.J.); Lynn Martin (Ill.). Fifteen women won reelection in the House. The 21st woman member of Congress was Sen. Nancy Kassebaum (Rep., Kan.).

Among those who failed to win reelection to the House were Democratic whip John Brademas

President-elect Ronald Reagan and Vice-President-elect George Bush held their first news conference on November 6.
UPI

WIDE WORLD   WIDE WORLD   UPI   WIDE WORLD

Four newly elected senators, all Republicans, bested their Democratic opponents in hard-fought races: (from left) James Abdnor beat George McGovern in South Dakota; Steven Symms beat Frank Church in Idaho; Paula Hawkins beat William Gunter in Florida; and Dan Quayle beat Birch Bayh in Indiana. All the Democrats except Gunter were incumbents targeted for defeat by the Moral Majority.

(Ind.), Ways and Means Committee Chairman Al Ullman (Dem., Ore.), Public Works and Transportation Chairman Harold Johnson (Dem., Calif.), Administration Committee Chairman Frank Thompson, Jr. (Dem., N.J.), and Merchant Marine and Fisheries Committee Chairman John Murphy (Dem., N.Y.).

Thompson and Murphy had both been indicted (and were convicted in December) in the Abscam case, involving bribe offers made by FBI agents posing as representatives of wealthy Arabs. Former representative Michael Myers (Dem., Pa.), expelled from Congress after his conviction in the scandal, and Rep. John Jenrette (Dem., S.C.), convicted of accepting Abscam bribes, also were defeated. Raymond Lederer (Dem., Pa.) was the only congressman indicted in the Abscam case to win reelection.

Robert Bauman (Rep., Md.), implicated in a morals case, was defeated. So was Sen. Herman Talmadge (Dem., Ga.), chairman of the Agriculture Committee, censured by the Senate for "reprehensible financial conduct." He was defeated by Mack Mattingly, former Republican state chairman.

Four new black members, all Democrats, were elected to the House. Gus Savage of Chicago and Mervyn Dymally, former lieutenant governor of California, were the first blacks to represent their districts. Harold Washington of Chicago and George W. Crockett, Jr., of Detroit gained seats previously held by blacks.

A strong effort by independent conservative movements in Senate elections constituted a new development in U.S. politics. The most influential of these groups appeared to be the National Conservative Political Action Committee (NCPAC), which conducted a hard-hitting campaign against six liberal senators it had targeted for defeat, and the Moral Majority, an organization of fundamentalist religious groups formed to combat moral decay. Under federal law, such independent groups were not subject to campaign spending limits.

The six liberal Democratic senators targeted for defeat by the NCPAC were: Birch Bayh (Ind.), John Culver (Iowa), George McGovern (S.D.), Frank Church (Idaho), Thomas Eagleton (Mo.), and Alan Cranston (Calif.); the Moral Majority added Gaylord Nelson (Wis.) to the list. Of the seven only Eagleton and Cranston were reelected. The Moral Majority also was credited with an important role in the election of Don Nickles of Oklahoma and Adm. Jeremiah Denton of Alabama to the Senate. Both were Republicans.

In all, 18 new members were elected to the Senate, 16 of them Republicans. In addition to Senators-elect Hawkins, Mattingly, Denton, and Nickles, they were: Frank H. Murkowski (Rep., Alaska), former Fairbanks bank president, who defeated former state representative Clark S. Gruening for the seat occupied by Sen. Mike Gravel (Dem.); U.S. Rep. Christopher Dodd (Dem., Conn.), son of former senator Thomas Dodd, who defeated Republican candidate James Buckley, former senator from New York; U.S. Rep. Steven Symms (Rep., Idaho), who defeated Church, the chairman of the Senate Foreign Relations Committee; Illinois Secretary of State Alan Dixon (Dem.), who defeated Lieut. Gov. David O'Neal (Rep.) for the seat held by retiring senator Adlai Stevenson III (Dem.); U.S. Rep. Dan Quayle (Rep., Ind.), who defeated Bayh; U.S. Rep. Charles Grassley (Rep., Iowa), who defeated Culver; former state attorney general Warren Rudman (Rep., N.H.), who defeated Sen. John Durkin; Alfonse D'Amato (Rep., N.Y.), who won in a complex campaign against Holtzman (Dem.) and Republican Sen. Jacob Javits, who ran on the Liberal Party ticket; John East (Rep., N.C.), a political science professor, who defeated Sen. Robert Morgan; U.S. Rep. Mark Andrews (Rep., N.D.), who won the seat vacated by retiring senator Milton Young (Rep.); Arlen Specter (Rep., Pa.), former district attorney of Philadelphia, who defeated Pete Flaherty (Dem.), former mayor of Pittsburgh, for the seat vacated by

Two new governorships won for the Republicans were those of Missouri, where Christopher ("Kit") Bond (left) was victorious over the incumbent Democrat who had unseated him in 1976, and Arkansas, where Frank White (right) defeated the liberal Democratic incumbent.

(LEFT) EXECUTIVE OFFICE, JEFFERSON CITY, MO.; (RIGHT) KITTY FRANCIS—ARKANSAS DEMOCRAT

retiring senator Richard Schweiker (Rep.); U.S. Rep. James Abdnor (Rep., S.D.), who defeated McGovern; Washington State Attorney General Slade Gorton (Rep.), who defeated Warren Magnuson (Dem.), chairman of the Senate Appropriations Committee; and former U.S. representative Robert W. Kasten, Jr. (Rep., Wis.), who defeated Nelson, chairman of the Senate Small Business Committee.

Governorships

There were 13 governorships at stake in the November elections. The Republicans retained the three they held previously and captured four from the Democrats, who retained six. The new lineup for the nation was 27 Democratic governors, 23 Republican. The Republican total was the greatest in a decade. In all, six new governors were elected.

Little Rock banker Frank White (Rep.), former director of the Arkansas industrial development commission, defeated Gov. Bill Clinton in Arkansas. Former governor Christopher ("Kit") Bond (Rep.) of Missouri defeated Gov. Joseph Teasdale (Dem.) in a rematch of the contest that saw Teasdale unseat him in 1976. In North Dakota, two-term governor Arthur Link (Dem.) was defeated by Attorney General Allen Olson (Rep.). In Washington, King County Executive John Spellman (Rep.) defeated State Sen. James McDermott (Dem.) for the governorship. McDermott had edged out Gov. Dixy Lee Ray in the primaries.

Two of the new governors succeeded members of their own parties. In Montana, Lieut. Gov. Ted Schwinden (Dem.), a rancher, defeated Gov. Thomas Judge (Dem.) in the primaries and went on to defeat State Rep. Jack Ramirez (Rep.) in the fall election. In Indiana, Lieut. Gov. Robert Orr (Rep.) defeated industrialist John Hillenbrand, a conservative Democrat, to succeed Republican Otis Bowen, barred by law from seeking another term.

State Contests

Republicans gained about 200 seats in state legislatures. They took control of five chambers: the lower houses in Illinois, Washington, and Montana and the state senates in Ohio and Pennsylvania. In Pennsylvania the parties tied, but the Republican lieutenant governor could break the tie to give his party organizational control. There was also a tie in the Alaska Senate, but the lieutenant governor of that state did not have the authority to break a tie.

Voters decided on 346 referendum proposals in 42 states in November. Tax cuts or limitations, many inspired by passage of California's widely publicized Proposition 13 in 1978, had a mixed fate. Massachusetts approved a property tax ceiling of 2½% of assessed valuation—a reduction of about 40%, with effects varying among communities. Arkansas banned tax increases and property reassessments. Montana approved a plan to ease income taxes during periods of rapid inflation. Missouri voted to limit government spending. However, tax curbs were defeated in several other states.

The 1980 elections provided the first popular vote on nuclear power since the Three Mile Island reactor accident in 1979. In Maine on September 23, voters rejected a proposal to shut the state's only reactor and ban new nuclear power plants. In November, Missouri and South Dakota turned down proposed restrictions on nuclear power, and Montana rejected severe limitations on uranium mining. Voters in Washington State approved stringent limits on storage of nuclear wastes, and Oregon voters barred reactor construction without federally licensed dumps for the waste.

Dade County (Miami), Fla., barred public funds for use of any language other than English. This in effect nullified a 1973 action making Spanish an official second language but had no significant effect on schools.

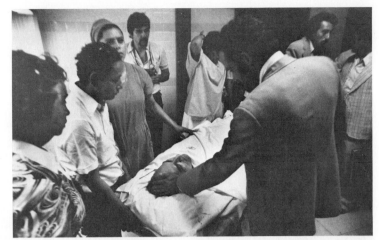

Archbishop Oscar Arnulfo Romero, an outspoken opponent of the political violence that racked El Salvador, was shot and killed as he celebrated mass in a chapel outside San Salvador on March 24. Archbishop Romero had been nominated for the Nobel Prize in 1979 for his efforts to bring peace to his country.
MONTES–GAMMA/LIAISON

EL SALVADOR

Following the military coup of Oct. 15, 1979, the government seemed about to disintegrate as it failed to halt both extreme right-wing acts of violence and left-wing activity. The country moved closer to civil war with the assassination of Archbishop Oscar Romero on March 24, thought to be the work of right-wing factions. Between January and the end of June some 4,000 civilians had been reported killed.

For most of the year Col. Jaime Abdul Gutiérez and Col. Adolfo Arnoldo Majano Ramos were the dominant forces in the junta, although there were a number of personnel changes. The junta, supported only by the Christian Democratic Party (itself divided by its left wing's secession to form the Social Democratic Party), was opposed to both right and left. On January 10 three major left-wing factions and their armed wings united to form the Frente Democrático Revolucionario.

Embassy occupations and guerrilla kidnappings of businessmen continued, and several countries closed their diplomatic missions. In May the junta survived an abortive right-wing military coup mainly because of previous U.S. threats to withdraw its support from a right-wing regime. The U.S. government supported the existing government because of its declared commitment to land reform and human rights. However, although the junta did carry out some reforms, its popular support remained narrow.

In late November six leading leftists were abducted and killed; a rightist "death squad" claimed responsibility, though leftists insisted the junta was involved. A bomb explosion injured several mourners, and at least 11 persons were killed as fighting broke out in the capital. In December the U.S. interrupted its aid program for two weeks following the murder of three American nuns and a lay worker. On December 13 José Napoleón Duarte, a member of the junta, was sworn in as president; Majano had been ousted from the junta a few days earlier. The start of a major leftist offensive was reported at year's end.

Bombs and sniper fire triggered a panic in a crowd of about 75,000 people at the funeral of Archbishop Romero. At least 30 people were killed in the melee.
PATRICK CHAUVEL–SYGMA

Progress was made on a multibridge crossing that would link the Japanese islands of Honshu and Shikoku; the route would comprise six bridges when completed.

ENGINEERING PROJECTS

Two interesting, but totally different, bridges were structurally completed during 1980: the Humber Bridge in England and the Reichsbrücke (Imperial Bridge) in Vienna. The Humber Bridge, the 1,410-m (1 m=3.3 ft) main span of which was the longest in the world, was a suspension bridge across the Humber estuary on the east coast of England, built to encourage regional development by shortening by more than 80 km (50 mi) the distance between the principal towns north and south of the river. The designers, Freeman Fox & Partners, used the same, though augmented, principles that they had introduced for the Severn Bridge (main span 988 m) in England and then enhanced for the Bosporus Bridge (1,074 m) in Turkey.

The crucial design factor for all long-span bridges, if there is to be any attempt to achieve an aesthetically satisfying form, is not the traffic load but the need to counter oscillation of the bridge deck under conditions of sustained wind loading. (The classic illustration of the problem was the failure in 1940 of the Tacoma [Wash.] Narrows Bridge, which broke its back as it shook itself to destruction.) The standard solution in long-span suspension bridges has been a deep truss girder, which, suspended from the main cables, carries the road surface. Truss girders were used in the Golden Gate (Calif.), Mackinac (Mich.), and Verrazano-Narrows (New York City) bridges, the three longest spans in the U.S.

For the Severn Bridge, completed in 1966, the designers substituted an aerodynamically shaped box girder for the truss girder, and this new design was subsequently employed on the Bosporus and the Humber bridges. Many advantages followed. The depth of the box girder at Humber was only 4.5 m as against 10 m or more for the truss girder, thereby generating a structure of great elegance. Second, the required strength and stiffness of the deck were obtained with much less steel; the Humber Bridge required only 4 metric tons per metre of traffic lane as against 7.7 tons for the Golden Gate and 5.8 tons for Verrazano. This smaller steel requirement led to a reduced capital cost, and maintenance of the box girder was easier than for a truss. Together, these advantages made some fixed river crossings viable that otherwise would be ignored for reasons of cost.

The Imperial Bridge across the Danube in the centre of Vienna was a different construction. It replaced the old Reichsbrücke suspension bridge that collapsed in 1976 when the foundations were washed away by floodwater. The new bridge had a ten-span prestressed box-girder superstructure; the two main spans (169.6 m and 150 m long) crossed the Danube itself, the remainder of the bridge crossing a new flood relief channel being excavated. It was particularly noteworthy for the large number of facilities incorporated. Besides a six-lane highway on the top side of the box girders, each box contained a subway track, and where the bridge crossed the island between the Danube and the flood channel a subway station 200 m long was housed; between the two boxes a service duct contained electric power and telephone cables and water and gas mains. Along the outside of the boxes, below the overhang carrying the outer lanes of the highways, cantilevered brackets provided a footpath for pedestrians along one side of the bridge and a cycle track along the other side. It was an exceedingly complex, highly stressed structure with steel reinforcement up to three times more dense than was commonly required. It was also, by common consent, elegant and attractive in appearance.

Buildings

The world recession had some effect on the rate of building in 1980, and there was a notable slowdown in construction in the Middle East. Two spectacular structural failures were the collapse in May of a considerable part of Berlin's prestigious Congress Hall (built in 1957 as a U.S. contribution to that year's international building exhibition, Interbau 57) and that in September of an unfired lining inside a 275-m-high chimney at the Matla power station in South Africa, one of the tallest multiflue chimneys in the world.

Particularly interesting developments occurred in the field of large span-braced dome structures, such as the recently completed stadium at Split in Yugoslavia. The seating areas of the stadium were covered by two double-layer, part-spherical space frames that were crescent-shaped in plan. These roofs had an overall dimension of 215 m and were supported only along the outer edge, which also lay on the circular perimeter of the stadium. The frameworks were built using a system of steel tubes and "ball" joints with screwed connections.

A number of manufacturers offered systems for building braced domes and other forms of braced structures. One of these was being used in the construction of the Spaceship Earth dome at Walt Disney's Epcot City project in the U.S. When completed, this building would appear as a 53.5-m-diameter silver-clad ball supported just off the ground on three sloping legs; display areas would

The Humber Bridge, across the Humber River in northeastern England, was completed in 1980; its main span was the world's longest—1,410 metres (4,626 feet)—and its total length 2,220 metres (7,284 feet).
CAMERA PRESS/PHOTO TRENDS

be contained at several levels inside the dome. In Canada a developer was considering the feasibility of an aluminum-framed braced dome to enclose a controlled environment for combined residential, recreational, and shopping facilities. The structure would have a span of 300 m and a maximum height of 60 m. It remained to be seen whether such an enclosure was a commercially or socially viable proposition.

Ferrocement, the steel-mesh-reinforced cement mortar invented by Italian engineer-architect Pier Luigi Nervi (d. 1979) and originally used in boat-building, hangars, and other utility buildings, was the material chosen to construct five domes up to 16 m in diameter for a mosque in Amman, Jordan, completed in 1980. These onion-shaped ribbed domes had a shell thickness of only 25 mm and were externally finished in graduated shades of blue mosaic. Although the method of construction was labour intensive, significant savings in materials and formwork were demonstrated over traditional reinforced-concrete shell methods of construction.

Roads

Worldwide inflation and the shortage of highway materials continued to hamper road building. In the U.S. the cost of highway construction in 1980 was three times higher than in 1967. The nation's interstate highway system of more than 68,000 km (42,000 mi), which in 1980 was 93% complete, was showing signs of deterioration, especially in the sections built in the late 1950s. Federal funds were made available to the individual states to pay for resurfacing, restoration, and rehabilitation of those roads. Total expenditure for all roads and streets in the U.S. by all units of government in 1979 (the last available figure) was estimated at $35.7 billion.

In Canada much attention was being given to pavement recycling, in which worn-out road material is planed from the road surface and remixed for future use. Canada could soon have a second Trans-Canada Highway, the 4,800-km (3,000-mi) Yellowhead Highway, which runs from Portage-la-Prairie in Manitoba through Saskatoon and Edmonton to northern British Columbia. Designation as a Trans-Canada Highway would make it eligible for a federal-provincial upgrading and maintenance program.

Connection of the long-awaited Darien Gap in the Pan-American Highway system took a step forward in 1980. A special liaison committee was formed by the presidents of Colombia and Panama to study the financial, technical, social, and medical considerations involved.

Five major trans-African highway projects were in progress: the Mombasa–Lagos Trans-African Highway, the Dakar–N'Djamena Trans-Sahelian Highway, the Lagos–Nouakchott Trans-West African Highway, the Cairo–Gabarone Trans-East African Highway, and the Algiers to Lagos Trans-Sahara Highway. Other significant road links in

Africa, completed in 1980, included the 1,200-km (750-mi) Khartoum–Port Sudan road.

In the Middle East Saudi Arabia's massive road-building program was proceeding in high gear. The 64-km (40-mi) four-lane divided highway from Jidda to Mecca was opened to traffic in 1980, as was the 50-km (30-mi) Rastanura–Jubail highway. Construction was under way on the 90-km (55-mi) ring road around the capital of Riyadh.

China was initiating its nationwide road-building program with a 160-km (100-mi) highway from Beijing (Peking) to Tianjin (Tientsin). In Australia a major project was the $4.3 million repair of 755 km (470 mi) of the vital north-south highway between South Australia and the Northern Territory, damaged by flooding.

In the U.K. motorway construction was slowing down. Only 105 km (65 mi) of motorway were opened in 1980, for a total in service of 2,589 km (1,605 mi). Although they represented only 0.7% of the U.K.'s road network, these expressways carried more than 10% of its traffic. The Beaune–Mulhouse Autoroute, connecting the French and West German expressway networks, was opened in September.

Design was begun on the Trans European Motorway, which was to start in Gdansk, in Poland, and pass through ten countries to Adriatic, Aegean, and Black Sea border crossings. More than 250 km (155 mi) of the motorway from Prague to Brno and Bratislava in Czechoslovakia were completed in 1980, with the balance to be opened in 1981.

Tunnels

In Switzerland the 16.3-km-long St. Gotthard tunnel, the world's longest road tunnel, was opened to traffic after an 11-year construction period. The 12.87-km-long Fréjus road tunnel connecting France and Italy was also opened to traffic, after 16 years of construction. In the U.K. the second Dartford tunnel beneath the Thames estuary 25 km east of London was opened to traffic, groundwater problems having caused considerable delay since work was started in 1972.

Normally, a distance of one diameter is preferred between parallel tunnels. At Atlanta, Ga., however, in the construction of twin 6.25-m-diameter subway tunnels at a depth of 17 m below the surface, separation was reduced to one-quarter of a diameter. Steel liner plates were used, and the final surface settlement was 380 mm.

A major event in 1980 was the opening of Hong Kong's first underground railway. Creating a world record for subway construction work, the first 16 km were completed in 4½ years, according to schedule and, it was claimed, within the original budget. In Rome 14.6 km of the new subway were also opened to traffic in 1980. More than 80 cities throughout the world were planning new subway systems, 19 of them in West Germany, which was becoming a world leader in the application of the new Austrian tunneling method. This technique employed spray concrete both for subway construction and in the mining industry.

The technology of cutting rock with high-pressure water jets received a boost when Japanese engineers announced a system combining drill and blast methods with the formation of presplitting slots using fine water jets under a pressure of 4,000 kg per sq cm. It was claimed that tunneling costs were reduced and a much more accurate control over blasting was obtained. Swedish engineers also introduced a practical form of water cannon for splitting boulders.

ENVIRONMENT

Hazardous Waste Disposal

New Jersey Chemical Fire. In a sad footnote to celebrations on Earth Day, April 22, a chemical waste dump in Elizabeth, N.J., exploded into flames, spreading potentially dangerous smoke and ash over a 15-sq mi area, including parts of New York City. Twenty-four thousand barrels of alcohol, solvents, pesticides, and mercury compounds blazed out of control for ten hours. Plans to evacuate Staten Island, Elizabeth, and neighbouring towns were canceled after winds and favourable atmospheric conditions dissipated the poisonous fumes, but parts of New Jersey and New York were placed under a precautionary health alert.

The New Jersey government uncovered and closed the dump in 1979, removing 10,000 drums of the most hazardous substances at that time. State environmental officials announced after the fire that the dump had become even more hazardous to clean up since materials had spilled and mixed.

Love Canal Families Moved. The federal government agreed August 22 to make $15 million in grants and loans available to help relocate 710 families in the Love Canal area of Niagara Falls, N.Y. An unusually high incidence of cancer and other health problems was discovered in 1978 among area residents, whose homes were built over an abandoned canal that had been used for years as

In April an explosion of stored chemicals in an abandoned waterfront warehouse in Elizabeth, New Jersey, sent clouds of toxic gases over nearby residential areas, forcing the issuance of health alerts and school closings in Elizabeth and Linden, New Jersey, and Staten Island, New York.

UPI

a chemical waste dump by the Hooker Chemicals and Plastics Corp. Previously, 239 families had been moved by the state of New York. The federal Department of Justice filed a $124.5 million lawsuit against Hooker, and in 1980 New York State Attorney General Robert Abrams filed a $635 million lawsuit against Hooker and its parent company, Occidental Petroleum Corp., charging them with responsibility for the Love Canal disaster.

New York Gov. Hugh Carey insisted on federal funds for the permanent relocation of the 710 families after the Environmental Protection Agency (EPA) announced in May that an agency study had shown that residents of the area may have suffered chromosome damage. According to the May 16 revelation, chromosome breakage of a sort linked to cancer, spontaneous abortion, and birth defects was discovered in 11 out of 36 people tested. Ordinarily, no one in a sample of that size would be expected to show such damage. The study, conducted to support the government's lawsuit, was criticized by some scientists because the people studied were not selected randomly and because no control group—a group of people unexposed to the Love Canal environment—was studied for comparison. The results of another study, announced May 21, showed that 28 of 35 residents tested had suffered nerve damage. The private study was an attempt to get an objective measurement of the nervous disorders that some Love Canal residents had complained of. The study was conducted under stricter conditions than the federal study had been: no one who had ever worked around chemicals was accepted for testing, and the Love Canal people were compared with a control group of other Niagara Falls residents.

Angry at the government's delay in acting on the situation, frustrated homeowners took two EPA officials hostage for five hours May 19 to press their demands for immediate evacuation of their neighbourhood. Frank Napal, director of the agency's New York office of public affairs, and James Lucas, a physician with the agency's health effect assessment laboratory in Cincinnati, Ohio, were held in the office of the Love Canal Homeowners' Association until FBI agents, United States marshals, and members of the Niagara Falls police force intervened.

Pres. Jimmy Carter declared a federal emergency at Love Canal May 21, allowing the 710 families to leave their homes temporarily at federal expense. The August 22 agreement would give New York a pool of $15 million to help the state buy the Love Canal houses, allowing the owners to leave the area permanently.

"Superfund" Legislation. In an attempt to deal with the problem of paying for cleaning up toxic waste sites like Love Canal, Congress passed legislation December 3 to establish a $1.6 billion "Superfund." The bill authorized the president to take quick action to protect the public health and the environment from dangers posed by the dumping of toxic wastes. The measure also empowered the federal government to sue companies found responsible for dumping such wastes to recover the costs to the fund of remedial action. More than 85% of the fund would come from taxes on the chemical industry.

Pres. Jimmy Carter displays the newly signed Alaska lands bill, finally passed after nearly a decade of wrangling in the Congress. The bill designates those areas available for commercial exploitation and those reserved as wilderness.

TERESA ZABALA—THE NEW YORK TIMES

Residents of the Love Canal area of Niagara Falls, New York, packed up and moved into safe quarters when Pres. Jimmy Carter authorized $3 million to $5 million for their relocation in May. Their homes had been built on the site of a huge chemical dump.
KEYSTONE

Toxic Substance Control. Early in the year the EPA adopted regulations to control the handling and disposal of hazardous wastes. The complex rules, issued two years behind schedule, could cost industry as much as $1 billion per year. EPA spokesmen defended the regulations as "an extremely reasonable program" compared with the costs to society of uncontrolled disposal of hazardous wastes. Regulations published February 26 required companies that produce, transport, or dispose of hazardous wastes to notify the EPA by July, and companies that store, treat, or dispose of such substances to apply to the agency for permits by October. On May 5 the EPA announced rules that defined hazardous wastes and established operating and technical standards for their storage, treatment, and disposal. The regulations included exemptions for small waste producers, which made up 91% of the waste-producing companies, but which together produced only 1% of the nation's toxic wastes.

Air and Water Quality

Mediterranean Cleanup Treaty. Nations bordering the Mediterranean Sea put aside an assortment of political arguments and signed an agreement May 17 to curb pollution of the inland sea. Landlocked except for the narrow Strait of Gibraltar, the Mediterranean had begun to show the strain of its use as a dump by the heavily populated and industrialized nations that surround it. Ninety percent of the sewage that flowed into the sea was untreated; outbreaks of dysentery, viral hepatitis, and typhoid had become common in some areas.

The treaty, signed in Athens by representatives of most of the Mediterranean countries, with the notable exception of Albania, designated a "black list" of toxic substances, including cadmium, mercury,

used lubricating oils, radioactive materials, DDT, and persistent plastics. Signatories agreed to prohibit the discharge of these substances and to limit to certain amounts and places any emissions of a "gray list" that included copper, lead, arsenic, zinc, disease-bearing microbes, crude oils, and some detergents. Experts estimated that it would be 10 to 15 years before pollution cleanup programs had any substantial effect. The cost of cleaning up the Mediterranean could run to $15 billion.

Mexico Oil Spill Capped. An offshore oil well in the Gulf of Mexico was finally capped March 24 after spilling more than 3.1 million bbl of crude oil into the gulf, making it the largest spill ever. Engineers fought for nine months to control the flow, finally succeeding by pumping plugs of cement into the blown well after drilling two relief wells to reduce underground pressure. After Ixtoc 1 exploded June 3, 1979, oil spread to beaches in southern Texas. Private groups and people from the tourist industry there filed lawsuits against Pemex, the Mexican oil company, and Sedco, the American equipment company that owned the Ixtoc drilling platform, for $377 million in damages.

A major oil pipeline break took place in Virginia, where the water supplies of over a half million people were endangered by two kerosene spills in March. An "unscheduled shutdown" of equipment at a Colonial Pipeline Co. booster station northeast of Baltimore, Md., raised pressure in the pipeline until the line ruptured in two places, leaking into the water sources for Fredericksburg, Va., and the Virginia suburbs of Washington, D.C. The accident raised questions about pipeline safety across the nation. The U.S. Department of Transportation had only 16 inspectors to examine some 27,000 mi of oil pipelines.

A whale sports an ironic plea for environmental sanity; students were observing the tenth anniversary of Earth Day in Washington, D.C.

EPA Demands Inspection Programs. In March the EPA announced that it would use its authority to withhold federal money from state and local areas with smog problems unless such areas established annual auto-emission-equipment inspection programs. After the Colorado state legislature missed three EPA deadlines for setting up an inspection program, the agency carried out its threat, halting some $301.5 million in federal highway and sewer funds. The U.S. Court of Appeals stopped the action with a restraining order later in the month.

Then, in September, after the California legislature adjourned without enacting an inspection program, the EPA announced it would cut off some $850 million in federal aid to that state. Environmentalists, auto dealers, service station owners, and government agencies fought a yearlong battle over the issue, and several bills were killed at various points in the legislative process. EPA spokesmen said that no money would actually be held back until January, giving the new legislature, sworn in December 1, time to pass an inspection measure and halt the federal action.

Sulfur Dioxide. The EPA temporarily relaxed its sulfur dioxide emissions regulations March 12, a move taken primarily to allow utilities in Ohio to burn the high-sulfur, "dirty" coal mined within the state. Under the new regulations, utilities would be allowed to average their emissions over 30 days instead of 24 hours to determine whether or not they had met federal air-pollution control standards. The longer averaging period would allow a greater variation in the "dirtiness" of the coal burned, while under the 24-hour period utilities had to use cleaner coal to be sure they met the limits. Environmentalists protested the action as "unwarranted" and threatened to take the matter to court.

Acid Rain Pact Signed. The EPA action was regarded as particularly dangerous by conservationists fighting the acid rain problem. Acid rain is formed when nitrogen and sulfur oxide gases combine with water in the upper atmosphere to form nitric and sulfuric acids. Often carried many miles from their point of origin, acid rain and snow have been blamed for fish kills, stunted forest growth, and damage to food crops. The problem has become an international one, with Canada blaming the U.S. for rising acidity in Canadian lakes and Scandinavia blaming industrial centres in Western Europe for timber losses suffered in the north.

On August 5 the U.S. and Canada agreed to try to curb pollution contributing to the acid rain problem in both countries. The treaty called for vigorous enforcement of existing antipollution laws and established five work groups to prepare a new air-quality treaty.

Public Lands

Alaska Lands Bill. In a historic move the Senate gave its approval August 19 to a bill determining the future of federal lands in Alaska. The bill was a compromise between the strongly conservationist measure approved by the House in 1979 and the development-oriented legislation that emerged from the Senate Energy and Natural Resources Committee. It designated 104.3 million ac of land as components of the National Park, Forest, Wildlife Refuge, or Wild and Scenic Rivers systems, compared with 128.2 million ac in the House bill. Only 24.6 million ac would be closed to oil and gas leasing. In two of the bill's most controversial provisions, the coastal plain of the William O. Douglas Arctic Wildlife Range would be open to seismic exploration for oil and natural gas, and some timbering would be allowed in parts of southeastern Alaska that conservationists wanted placed in the wilderness category, including Misty Fjords and parts of Admiralty Island.

Floor debate in the Senate was marked by bitterness. The bill was not brought up until July 21, after Senate leaders set up a complex time agreement designed to prevent Alaska Sen. Mike Gravel (Dem.) from killing the bill by filibustering it, as he had done with another bill in the closing hours of the 95th Congress in 1978. Senator Gravel opposed the passage of any Alaska lands bill. After environmentalists won important test votes July 22, Alaska's other senator, Ted Stevens (Rep.), threatened to filibuster the measure rather than allow a strong bill to pass. The bill was pulled off the floor and a compromise measure was drawn up in closed-door sessions. After Senator Gravel's attempts to stall the compromise were thwarted by a cloture vote ending debate on August 18, the Senate passed the measure 78 to 14 the following day. The bill then returned to the House for approval, with warnings from the Senate that it would not be able to approve any subsequent revisions that the House might make. Thereupon the House, during its lame-duck session in November, approved the Senate version in a voice vote. The bill was then sent to President Carter, who hailed it as "the greatest land conservation legislation of the century." It was signed into law on December 2.

The present debate over the management of federal lands in Alaska began in 1971 when Congress, in the Alaska Native Land Claims Settlement Act, authorized the secretary of the interior to choose 80 million ac in the state for preservation. The action was to be completed by the end of 1978, but when Congress adjourned without having been able to pass an Alaska bill, Secretary of the Interior Cecil Andrus imposed a temporary ban on development of some 110 million ac. Of this land President Carter designated some 56 million ac as Alaska national monuments, giving them the same protected status as national parks. In February 1980, after the Senate postponed taking up the Alaska debate until July, Secretary Andrus ordered another 40 million ac of federal lands withdrawn because he was concerned that the delay in the debate might make it impossible for Congress to complete its consideration of the legislation before adjourning.

Wilderness Areas Designated. After a long and painful conference, the House and Senate agreed July 1 to establish a 2.2 million-ac wilderness in Idaho. The conference was necessary because the House version of the bill had excluded an area known as West Panther Creek to allow cobalt mining there; the Senate included the 39,000 ac to protect bighorn sheep wintering grounds. In its compromise, Congress included West Panther Creek in the wilderness but designated it a "special management area" with loosened regulations governing mining and subsequent reclamation. The secretary of the interior, however, was directed to take "all reasonable measures" to ensure that mining did not impair bighorn sheep habitat. The new River of No Return wilderness was the largest wild area in the lower 48 states.

A measure designating 1.4 million ac of wilderness in Colorado was based on recommendations made by the Forest Service in its Roadless Area Review and Evaluation study. The measure also designated additional wilderness areas in Missouri, South Dakota, and South Carolina.

The smog in Los Angeles was at the worst October level in ten years when this photograph was taken on October 8; many residents had to seek medical help for smog-related ailments.
WIDE WORLD

Water Resource Policy

The House of Representatives passed a bill Feb. 5 authorizing $4 billion in new water projects. Strongly opposed by the Carter administration and by environmentalists, the bill included a "grab-bag" of controversial projects, many exempted from statutory cost-sharing provisions, many without completed Army Corps of Engineers feasibility studies. In related action, Congress increased the Corps of Engineers budget, funding a number of projects that had been criticized as wasteful and unnecessary.

California Gov. Jerry Brown signed a bill on August 18 authorizing a $5.1 billion expansion of the State Water Project, including construction of the controversial Peripheral Canal. The project, designed to transport fresh water from the state's northern rivers to the water-poor areas of the south, was the most ambitious state water project in the nation.

ETHIOPIA

Political activity during 1980 focused on strengthening the organizational infrastructure for development. The Commission to Organize the Party of the Working People of Ethiopia (COPWE) was created on Dec. 18, 1979, and COPWE's first congress took place in June 1980 with some 1,500 regional representatives participating. A seven-member Executive Committee and a 93-member Central Committee were announced, both chaired by the head of state, Lieut. Col. Mengistu Haile Mariam. At a press conference in September, Mariam stated: "The struggle [for the formation of the party] is not a struggle with civilian/military implications, but a class struggle.. . . the date will not be distant before the formation of the party." He added, "Since it is motivated by a single program, the need for a multiparty system does not arise. The Ethiopian Revolution tolerates no reactionary class posture and will have no place for a multiparty system."

Economic measures were accompanied by strong action to improve cultural, health, and educational facilities. The National Literacy Campaign was awarded a UNESCO prize for meritorious work in literacy in 1980. Seven million participants were enrolled, and over four million had already moved on to postliteracy instruction. The target for eradication of urban illiteracy was May 1981, and the target for total eradication was 1987. A National Children's Commission had been established during the UN Year of the Child (1979); a children's village for 5,000 orphans was created in the Rift Valley Lakes region, and over 350 kindergartens were initiated. Since the revolution, the number of children attending formal school had doubled.

Thirty percent of the population now had access to basic health services, as compared with 15–20% at the time of the revolution. Ethiopia was declared free of smallpox in December 1979, and a nationwide campaign for the control of tuberculosis was launched in 1980. One significant result of the nationalization of rural and urban lands and the creation of Peasant and Urban Dwellers Associations was the virtual end of migration to the cities and its associated problems. The annual population growth rate of Addis Ababa declined from 5 to 3%.

The program for economic and cultural development, initiated in October 1978, moved into its third phase, having achieved an economic growth rate of 5.3% during 1979–80. A total of 6,350,000 ha (15,875,000 ac) was reported under cultivation, with an output, in spite of bad weather conditions

UNICEF distributed drugs and supplementary food supplies to drought victims in Ethiopia in November.
UPI

in some regions, of just under 5.6 million metric tons in 1979. Industrial output grew by 35% during 1978 but by only 11.3% in 1979 as capacity was reached. External trade achieved a high rate of growth in 1979–80 (28.3%), exceeding the planned target by 16%.

Dissident groups in the north remained a problem. The town of Nakfa in Eritrea Province was a rebel focus, and there was guerrilla activity in the Tigre region. Antigovernment activity by Somali-supported groups continued in the south. There was also a Somali Army attack in March, and five major assaults took place between May 27 and July 17 in the Uardare, Wel-Wel, Oubatale, and Shebele areas, well within Ethiopia's Ogaden region. Two further major Somali raids between September 18 and October 9 into the El Kere region of Bale Province were repulsed with heavy losses.

In August the OAU Good Offices Committee, in a six-point resolution, called for the strict application of the 1964 Cairo summit resolution on inviolability of frontiers and the recognition of the Ogaden as an integral part of Ethiopia. In July, following on-the-spot investigations by a UN interagency team, the

Refugees fleeing the fighting in Ethiopia continued to flood into Somalia, taxing that country's ability to provide food and shelter.

UPI

UN Economic and Social Council recommended a grant of 1.5 billion birr for relief in the area (2.07 birr = U.S. $1).

External relations during 1979–80 reflected Ethiopia's association with Eastern Europe and Cuba and the government's desire to strengthen relations with its neighbours. High-level visitors included the East German head of state, Erich Honecker, in November 1979, Soviet Deputy Minister of Defense Adm. Sergey Gorshkov in July 1980, and the Hungarian head of state, Pal Losonczi, in September. Mengistu visited Bulgaria and the Soviet Union during the year. U.S. Ambassador Frederic L. Chapin was recalled to Washington, D.C., at the request of the Ethiopian government in July.

At the same time, Ethiopia maintained an unaligned posture, and in September Mengistu stated his government's willingness to accept all aid for development projects on the basis of "equality and mutual respect." Ethiopia received substantial assistance from the European Economic Community (EEC) under the Lomé agreements and from international agencies and Western countries, notably Sweden. Social assistance included agreements with East Germany for a textile mill and a cement factory, a country loan program from the Soviet Union, and technical assistance from Cuba in the fields of farming, health, and education, with agreements for the supply of cement, fertilizers, and tires.

Relations with Sudan improved. A joint border commission was established, and in March Sudan Vice-Pres. Gen. Abdel Magid Khalil visited Addis Ababa. In May an Ethiopian delegation to Khartoum signed a trade agreement and cultural protocol, and Mengistu paid an official visit there. Similar diplomatic activity strengthened relations with Yemen (Aden; South Yemen), Djibouti, and Kenya.

EUROPEAN AFFAIRS

The year 1980 demonstrated that, in practice, it was easier for the nine member states of the European Economic Community (EEC) to align policies regarding the outside world than to make progress toward internal unity. Internally, 1980 would be remembered for the bitter and protracted dispute over the Community's budget. The refusal of the European Parliament to endorse the draft 1980 budget—because it was held to favour farm spending at the expense of other policies—meant that the Community had to be financed on an emergency basis. It was not until July, amid fears that the financial crisis could lead to collapse of the common agricultural policy, that the European Parliament in Strasbourg finally allowed a slightly amended 1980 budget to enter into force.

Serious as this first major dispute between two major EEC institutions—the European Parliament and the Council of Ministers—proved to be, it was overshadowed by another budgetary dispute. This arose out of the British government's growing dissatisfaction with the imbalance in its payments to and receipts from the EEC budget. Successive Labour and Conservative governments had raised the issue over the previous two years, but no solution had been found. There were suggestions that, unless Britain's annual net budget contributions were reduced, the U.K. government would unilaterally suspend part or all of its budget payments.

At the European Council (the summit meeting of EEC heads of government) in Luxembourg at the end of April, no acceptable compromise was reached. British Prime Minister Margaret Thatcher made it clear that, in the absence of a satisfactory solution to Britain's problem, the U.K. government would not be able to agree to the annual spring farm price increases. In effect, the budget issue became linked with a number of controversial matters including farm prices, fishing policy, and energy policy. It took another month of detailed negotiations to achieve a compromise solution, on May 30. EEC foreign ministers meeting in Brussels agreed on a formula guaranteeing a substantial reduction in Britain's expected net contribution to the EEC budget for 1980, 1981, and 1982. This was to take the form of an increased rebate on gross budget payments by the U.K. and programs of special Common Market spending in Britain itself. At the same time, Britain agreed to a new round of farm price increases, as had been demanded by France and a number of other member states. All parties set themselves the target of concluding agreements on other matters, including fishing policy, energy policy, and a new system for marketing lamb and mutton in the Common Market.

But in September new disagreements emerged about the precise way in which the May compromise should be honoured. It appeared that a final solution might have to await agreement on the level of 1981 EEC farm prices—a subject of acute domestic political importance in France, where Pres. Valéry Giscard d'Estaing would be fighting for reelection in May 1981.

The May agreement did remove the budget wrangle from the agenda of the European summit held in Venice in June, shortly before the Western economic summit there, which also involved the governments of Britain, France, Italy, and West Germany. Venice 1, as the European Council session became known, was dominated by discussion of major world and foreign policy issues including Afghanistan, Iran, and the Middle East.

The Soviet invasion of Afghanistan at the end of 1979 and the continuing imprisonment of the U.S. embassy hostages in Iran were two issues that arose early in 1980 to challenge the coordination of foreign policy among EEC governments. Although common policy declarations of condemnation and unity were readily forthcoming at successive meetings of Community foreign ministers, it proved more difficult to agree on what action the EEC should take. In spite of U.S. pressure, most EEC governments were reluctant to levy economic sanctions against the Soviet Union. Some minor restrictions on agricultural exports were eventually imposed, but the Nine were sharply divided over the U.S.-led campaign for a boycott of the Moscow Olympic Games. In the end, only West Germany refused to send a team to the Games, although

most other governments refused to accord full official status to their athletes. Nor were relations with the U.S. helped by the reluctance of the European Community governments to impose comprehensive trade sanctions against Iran. At a meeting of foreign ministers in Naples during May, the Nine agreed on very partial sanctions against Iran, which were later amended by the British Parliament.

At the December meeting of the European Council in Luxembourg, however, the Nine—without naming the Soviet Union or specifying any measures they might take—issued a strong statement of concern over the situation in Poland. The labour unrest and the threat of Soviet intervention largely dominated the Council's deliberations.

In spite of these setbacks, the priority given to political cooperation among the EEC governments was a striking feature of 1980. The desire to have the European Community act as a major force in world affairs was amply illustrated with regard to the Middle East. The Venice EEC summit issued a major policy declaration on the Arab-Israeli conflict which went further than before in recognizing the rights of the Palestinian people to self-determination and the necessity, at some future stage, of associating the Palestine Liberation Organization in wider peace negotiations. The EEC leaders also hinted that, after sponsoring a fact-finding mission among interested governments in the region, they would launch some kind of Middle East diplomatic "initiative." Israel's reaction was predictably hostile, but the U.S. administration was also markedly cool. Spokesmen in Washington went so far as to say that the U.S. would veto any moves in the UN Security Council that cut across the objectives of the 1978 Camp David negotiations between Egypt, Israel, and the U.S. In face of Camp David, Arab governments were skeptical.

By the time of the Western summit in Venice, the U.S. stand had softened. It became clear that the EEC countries had no intention of putting forward any new resolution on the rights of the Palestinians before the U.S. presidential election in the fall. In August the president of the Council of Ministers, Gaston Thorn of Luxembourg, toured nine Middle Eastern countries to discuss whether there was a basis for future enlargement of the peacemaking process. In September the EEC foreign ministers decided that the initial reaction was sufficiently encouraging to persist with the fact-finding stage of the initiative.

The apparent determination of the European Community to pursue its own policy on the Middle East once again posed questions about the future of the Atlantic alliance. All the EEC governments stressed their desire for the closest possible association with the U.S., but in the course of 1980 doubts were expressed about the stability of U.S. leadership of the alliance. Relations with Washington were not made any easier by a proliferation of trade disputes, many of which were a direct consequence of the serious deterioration in the world economy. There were problems between the U.S. and the EEC over European steel exports and U.S. exports of textiles and chemicals.

The European Community was also involved in difficult negotiations with a number of third world countries over the terms under which they would be free to export into the EEC and with the Japanese government about that country's formidable trade surplus with the Common Market. The EEC resisted any general slide into trade protectionism during 1980, but with unemployment in EEC countries rising to more than nine million in the later months of the year, there were fears for the future of Europe's trade relations with other developed countries. Meanwhile, as was made clear at the Venice summit, the European leaders maintained that any general relaxation of monetary and economic policy to reduce unemployment would not be expedient while inflation remained a serious concern.

Unemployment, recession, and the massive budgetary problems of the European Community were also causes for concern in view of the prospective enlargement of the EEC. Greece was to become the tenth member state on Jan. 1, 1981, and negotiations on applications for membership began to get under way with Spain and Portugal. Spanish entry and the competitive threat to French Mediterranean farmers became a major political issue in France. Speeches by French Premier Raymond Barre suggested that France wanted the EEC to "go slow" in the negotiations with Spain until more progress had been made in solving the European Community's many internal economic, budgetary, and agricultural problems.

The other member states insisted that the talks with Spain and Portugal proceed according to the agreed negotiating timetable, but by October Spain had accepted the prospect of delay until some months after its entry date, provisionally fixed for Jan. 1, 1983. The Ten (as they would be in 1981) intended to open a major long-term review of the Community's budget system and the future of farm spending in particular. The cost of farm policy, and especially unwanted food surpluses, represented the biggest single burden on the EEC budget. Given the fixed limit to EEC revenues, there were fears that the Community would run out of money in 1981.

There was some surprise in February when Turkey announced its intention to apply for full membership in the EEC by the end of 1980. This was reiterated at a meeting in Brussels in May, when the government of Suleyman Demirel secured a number of improvements in its long-standing association agreement with the EEC. However, the matter was thrown into doubt following the army coup d'etat in Turkey in September. The EEC decided not to suspend the association agreement or economic aid but expressed the hope that there would be an early return to democracy.

European members of NATO were divided over

West German Chancellor Helmut Schmidt (left) and French Pres. Valéry Giscard d'Estaing met in the grand ballroom of the Élysée Palace in Paris in February to discuss the Soviet Union's invasion of Afghanistan.
KEYSTONE

the decision by NATO to produce and deploy some 600 cruise and Pershing nuclear missiles in response to the buildup of Warsaw Pact nuclear forces. Norway and Denmark refused to accept any nuclear weapons on their soil, while Belgium and The Netherlands delayed decisions about cruise missile deployment until their governments could judge the progress of U.S.-Soviet talks on European theatre nuclear disarmament.

FASHION

Walking sleeping bags paced the city streets in the winter of 1979–80, in dizzying colours such as hot pink, canary yellow, and cornflower blue. The nylon, down-filled garments, quilted and stitched in large squares or horizontal sections, became a new classic in Paris, London, New York, and Rome.

Under the coat, there was no great fashion change. The straight and narrow skirt with surprise slits alternated with the soft wrap style—with a rounded hem flap instead of the previous square one—or the model with all-around pleats stitched to hip level. The alternative was pants, teamed with knit tops in plain jersey or with big knits, all in the season's colour, deep purple. Silk blouses with narrow fluting at the neckline and cuffs provided a dressier note.

The newest trend in suits for spring was the bicoloured effect, strongest when carried out in black and white. All-around white braid trimming or piping outlined the hip-skimming, collarless black jacket. Top-gathered sleeves or padding widened the shoulder line, and skirts were straight and easy. Black and white journeyed through summer, with particularly vibrating prints seen in London and Milan—designs that undulated with every body movement, bold horizontal or diagonal stripes, and many other references to Op and kinetic art.

Seersucker, with its blistered, crinkled surface, was the choice for blazers, shorts, bermudas, pants, jumpsuits, and narrow skirts with seam slits. Easy to wash, it was ideal in the season's favourite soft pastels, principally pink and evanescent mauves

straight from a Monet summer garden. For full summer it was the all-white look, except for shoes. Plain pumps and sandals with narrow straps drew attention with their technicolour shades and ultrahigh, spiky heels. Bright red was the favourite eye-catcher for open-toed, multistrapped sandals, particularly when worn with the new baggy pants chopped off above the ankle.

There was definitely a new cut for pants. Though second-skin, seam-splitting jeans were still plentiful, the new trousers—also in denim, but more often in plain white cotton—were baggy around the hips and straight in the leg. They actually moved away from the body when the wearer walked. Jumpsuits adopted the same cropped, wide-legged cut and were newest at midcalf level. A newcomer was the flight suit with bagginess at thigh level, then pared down around the leg.

The year's real fashion news was in accessories. With ankles cleared, shoes became very important. In contrast to the still popular spiky-heeled sandals were flat-heeled ballerinas in gold or silver kid or in plain leather studded with gold nails, both types for day wear. Low-heeled pumps, again in kaleidoscopic colours, or jet-embroidered court pumps gave a new balance to evening clothes and silk trousers. But the shape that took the younger set by storm was the flat-heeled Chinese cloth shoe with an ankle strap, made in China. The same shape, but made in Europe, was carried over for autumn in leather, bright red velvet, and satin with an embroidered motif in the front.

As the fad for disco music gave way to country and western, cowboys and Indians were everywhere. Young Hiawathas, male and female, sported wide leather fringe trimming on every available hem or yoke. Fringed moccasins added to the total Indian look, as did beaded headbands over hair parted in the middle with a plait on either side. But the hairstyle that swept all before it throughout the summer was the corn-row look, launched—for Caucasians—by film star Bo Derek in the motion picture *10*. To tiny plaited strands of hair hanging straight down from all over the scalp were added all kinds of finery, such as coloured beads and shells.

As winter approached, the broader shoulder line was emphasized on mannish topcoats with thick padding and on belted models with jutting tippets, fringed scarves piled up on top, or tiered capes. The "preppie" look, reminiscent of '50s college styles, brought a resurgence of plaids for kilts and straight dresses, with an eye-catcher on the hem to draw attention to the new display of leg. The black and white story continued with white silk blouses ruffled at the collar and cuffs and a great deal of black velvet—suits with puffed sleeves, knickers, and plumed pageboy berets—black stockings, of course, and black pumps.

Men's Fashions

Not surprising was the effect that the depressed economy had on men's fashions. Seldom had there been such unanimity, with London, Paris, Cologne, and New York all speaking with one voice to announce the "British look," described by a New Yorker in Paris as "sophisticated English clothing with English details." Throughout the year, both fabrics and fashions were described as the "new-look British classics." Dior named the fashionable patterns for menswear in the 1980s as very British —pin and chalk stripes, houndstooth and herringbone suitings, with a return of the Scottish glen plaid for sports clothes.

Conventional suits and sports jackets and trousers were a little lighter in weight and colour. Nothing was exaggerated; every detail was traditional. Shirts were in softer colours, many in pure cotton or in cotton-polyester blends. The polka-dot tie, sometimes with a matching handkerchief, and diagonal patterned ties were also back in fashion. There was a revival of the double-breasted blazer. Summerweight jackets in alpaca and lightweight wor-

Trend-setter Perry Ellis fashioned pastel linen into a new suit silhouette for spring—exaggerated shoulders on a short-sleeved, cropped jacket over a strapless handknit sweater. The soft, full trousers are hemmed at midcalf. Yves Saint-Laurent drew inspiration from tribal textiles for his fall-winter collection, another of his fantasy looks.

DUSTIN PITTMAN—WIDE WORLD   STEPHANE TAVOULARIS—UPI

AUSTIN REED, LONDON

The well-bred, well-tailored British look was typified in this suit by Austin Reed. The single-breasted, two-button style was cut in striped worsted without affectation.

steds in tartan designs were popular, as were two-piece suits in hairline striped cotton and cotton-polyester cloths. The traditional three-quarter length overcoat returned for winter.

In a year when men's fashion generally stood still or looked backward, what little forward movement there was came in clothes for leisure and pleasure: blousons in a variety of fabrics, both knitted or woven; track suits for jogging; and the inevitable jackets and jeans in true blue and faded denim.

FINANCIAL INSTITUTIONS

Financial markets and institutions experienced unprecedented turbulence in 1980 as the economy was buffeted first by raging inflation and high interest rates, then by the imposition of credit controls and a sharp plunge into recession, and finally by a resurgence of growth accompanied by renewed inflation and a rebound in interest rates to new highs. Landmark financial reform legislation compounded the problems of banks in dealing with an uncertain and swiftly changing business environment.

In March Congress approved the Depository Institutions Deregulation and Monetary Control Act

of 1980, the single most important package of financial legislation passed since the Depression. The law mandated an orderly phaseout of interest rate ceilings on all time and savings deposits over a six-year period, authorized all federally insured banking institutions to offer depositors interest-bearing checking accounts (NOW accounts), and expanded the lending powers of federally chartered savings and loan associations and permitted them to issue credit cards. It also allowed federal mutual savings banks to make a limited amount of business loans and accept deposits from business borrowers, increased federal deposit insurance from $40,000 to $100,000, and overrode state usury limits on mortgage interest rates for at least two years.

A key provision of the new law phased in reserve requirements against transaction (checking) accounts and corporate time deposits for all 40,000 depository institutions in the nation instead of just for banks holding membership in the Federal Reserve System, and it also made the Federal Reserve the lender of last resort for all such institutions. The law thus strengthened the powers of the central bank to control monetary and credit growth.

Observers predicted that the new legislation would hasten the development of a streamlined national banking system, but only after considerable turmoil. By breaking down the distinction between commercial and thrift institutions, for example, it promised to usher in a new era of heated free-market competition. At the same time, the phasing out of interest ceilings and the expansion of interest-bearing checking accounts meant that banks would be forced to pay high money-market rates for funds they had previously obtained very cheaply—a development that promised to squeeze profits and imperil some institutions. The result of these legislated changes was likely to be an industry shakeout and merger wave that would cut the number of financial institutions in half within a decade.

U.S. banks were confronted with the chronic issue of problem loans in 1980. With oil prices up over 20%, non-oil developing countries faced a huge balance of payments deficit of some $50 billion, two-thirds of which they sought to borrow from Western commercial banks. But U.S. banks grew increasingly reluctant to increase their exposure in such markets—particularly at a time when the world economy seemed headed into recession. Internal turmoil and the possibility of Soviet intervention in Poland also raised fears regarding the $30 billion that U.S. and other Western banks had lent to Eastern Europe.

Under Chairman Paul Volcker, the Federal Reserve Board in 1980 continued in its attempt to counter inflation by reining in monetary growth. Implementing a change in operating procedures adopted in October 1979, the Fed sought to control the money supply by controlling the quantity of bank reserves rather than by influencing interest rates—a policy that implied that interest rates would be left free to fluctuate in response to market forces. Rates did indeed exhibit unprecedented volatility in 1980. The prime rate—the interest rate banks charge their best corporate customers—began the year at 15%, climbed to 20% in early April, plunged as low as 10¾% in July, and then vaulted to 21½% in December, a historic peak.

Owing to the roller-coaster pattern of interest rates and credit demand in 1980, there was great variability in individual bank profits. Commercial banks did relatively well overall, however, producing earnings that exceeded the 1979 peak by 12 to 14%. Their total lending increased only 9%, as consumer loans fell by 5%. Business loans, by contrast, expanded by a healthy 11% despite a decline during the spring, and real estate loans were up nearly 8%.

Thrift institutions, on the other hand, experienced one of their worst years in the postwar period in 1980, as rising interest rates on deposits and an uneven flow of funds undercut their ability to meet mortgage commitments undertaken in periods when rates were lower. The nation's 460 mutual savings banks lost about $250 million, while the profits of savings and loan associations plummeted 75% from their year-earlier levels. The Federal Savings and Loan Insurance Corporation spent $1.3 billion in 1980 to rescue, and in some cases to merge, more than 30 savings and loan institutions in deep financial distress.

Meanwhile, the Federal Deposit Insurance Corporation reported that the number of banks on its problem list (both commercial and mutual savings banks) fell by 70 and stood at 217 at year's end. Ten insured banks holding deposits totaling $214.7 million failed in 1980, as compared with ten banks with deposits of $111.2 million in 1979.

As inflation made ordinary savings accounts unattractive, customers who could afford them lined up to buy Treasury bills. The thrift institutions had a bad year in 1980, and the man in the street cited inflation and the bogged-down economy as the chief domestic problems facing the government.

JAMES D. WILSON—NEWSWEEK

Special Report: The 1980 Credit Crunch

by Jane Bryant Quinn and Virginia Wilson

On March 14, 1980, the United States launched its first peacetime credit controls of the modern era. The experiment was short-lived. Controls were eased after only ten weeks and abandoned entirely within four months. The Federal Reserve Board, which administered the program, had only the most general regulations on the books, and the controlled institutions had barely begun to object.

The controls "worked" in that the amount of business and consumer credit outstanding fell abruptly. But in retrospect it appears that the economy was already heading into recession. Rather than being called upon to contain a credit explosion, the controls merely hastened a decline. Economic historians would find this episode an ambiguous addition to the long-standing debate over whether government controls can, effectively, replace market forces in an economy.

The Urge to Act

In the weeks leading up to the imposition of controls, a feeling of impending disaster hung over an influential sector of the financial community. Consumer prices were running at an 18% annual rate. Consumer debt, as a percentage of personal income, ticked up in February, after three months of decline. Interest rates jumped three percentage points in less than a month. The prime business lending rate touched 18% (some banks moved to 20% soon after controls were announced, a high for the modern period). Billions of dollars were being lost in bond values, and seers gloomily predicted the collapse of major savings and loan associations.

The high passions of the 1980 presidential race exaggerated the political reactions to events. The fiscal 1981 budget proposed by Pres. Jimmy Carter in January, $15.8 billion in deficit, was thought insufficiently tight for dealing effectively with resurgent inflation. Critics on the right demanded a balanced budget; critics on the left thundered for wage/price controls. It was thought that only a recession could dampen the inflation emergency—yet more and more economists were predicting faster growth ahead.

Against this emotional, political, and economic background, President Carter launched his selective credit controls, plus some other proposals for tamping down the economy. The controls demanded the following: (1) Banks should not allow 1980 loan volume to grow more rapidly than 6 to 9%. (2) Certain consumer lenders should deposit, in a

non-interest-bearing account at the Federal Reserve, the equivalent of 15% of any credit outstanding above the level existing on March 14 (the base level was modified later, to account for seasonal variations). This rule covered loans against bank credit cards, travel and entertainment cards, overdraft checking, retail charge accounts, unsecured personal loans, and some secured loans. (3) Money-market mutual funds should deposit 15% of their assets, over a base amount, in a non-interest-bearing account at the Federal Reserve. This lowered the interest rate that money funds could pay on savings. It was hoped that this would stanch the flow of savings deposits out of savings and loan associations and into the funds. (4) A 3% surcharge was added to the then 13% discount rate at which large banks borrowed from the Federal Reserve Bank. (5) Reserve requirements were raised on certain bank liabilities, which had the effect of reducing the funds available for lending. (6) Ceilings were put on the interest rates payable by bank holding companies on certain debt instruments of $100,000 or less, thus curbing their ability to raise lendable funds.

Banks were advised that the Federal Reserve would smile on institutions that continued to lend money to home buyers, small businesses, and farmers while restricting credit for commodity speculation and corporate takeovers. Certain secured consumer loans were specifically exempted, among them loans for home buying, home improvements, autos, furniture, and appliances. These exemptions were made because the building and auto industries were already deep into recession.

A Perceived Emergency

Federal Reserve Board Chairman Paul Volcker was not enthusiastic about controls. The previous October 6—in an announcement then referred to as the Saturday-night massacre—he had announced a credit-tightening program to "curb speculative excesses . . . and thereby . . . dampen inflationary forces." He had raised the discount rate to 12%, raised bank reserves, and announced that, henceforth, the Fed would place greater emphasis on controlling the amount of money that banks had to lend than on controlling interest rates. The latter policy is consistent with a more controlled growth in the supply of money, but it allows wider swings in interest rates as demand for credit rises and falls.

The October moves were expected to cap the current inflation cycle and bring on recession. By January and February, however, the Fed's policies were widely perceived as ineffective. The very actions that raised interest rates also raised inflation, because of the way rising mortgage rates are counted in the consumer price index. Adding to the general panic of early 1980 was the fear, in financial circles, that inflation had grown strong enough to overwhelm all the weapons that the Fed could bring against it. The Fed continued to raise the discount rate, but this came to be seen as evidence of failure rather than a determination to succeed.

But a cool look backward supports the case that the Federal Reserve's actions were, in fact, already working. From October 1979 to January 1980, the growth in consumer installment loans plunged at the sharpest rate in recent history. Real retail sales, adjusted for inflation, peaked in September and started down. Retail sales in current dollars turned down just prior to the imposition of controls. Banks were already raising the cost of credit, and retailers were applying tougher yardsticks in granting new credit. It is arguable that the economy was, at that point, on the way down, with or without credit controls. But it was considered too risky to wait. The president chose the path of controls, and they undoubtedly sped the pace of decline.

Results of the Crunch

Consumer credit immediately grew even scarcer and more expensive. Many retailers raised monthly payments, changed the method of computing interest so as to raise the effective cost of credit, and made charge accounts harder to get. Many banks reduced credit lines on overdraft checking accounts and added fees for credit cards; some stopped issuing cards entirely. On the business side, some banks grew cautious about new loans to corporations (although businesses that had obtained credit lines in anticipation of controls were not denied access). Other banks—for example, those in booming cities in the Southwest—appear to have gone on lending to business as usual, on the grounds that their loans were for productive, not speculative, purposes.

The amount of consumer installment credit outstanding fell by an annual rate of almost 6.3% in April, 10% in May, and 7.8% in June. Business loans also fell. The economy plunged sharply in the second quarter (but revived in the third).

On May 6 the Federal Reserve rescinded the three percentage-point surcharge on the discount rate. On May 22 it halved the 15% deposits, in non-interest-bearing accounts, required of lenders and money-market funds. On July 3 the Fed announced that controls would be phased out.

On the consumer side, however, the effects of credit controls lingered on. Retailers and other lenders, who had for some time found their credit programs only marginally profitable, kept the cost of credit up. Fees for bank cards stayed in place, as did higher monthly payments on many charge accounts. Credit became more widely available, but at a higher price. High inflation had been gradually raising the price of consumer credit in any event, but selective credit controls hastened the trend.

MAC NELLY – RICHMOND NEWS LEADER

FINLAND

Sharing as it does an 800-mi frontier with the U.S.S.R., Finland was quietly apprehensive about the deterioration in international relations in 1980. As Pres. Urho Kekkonen celebrated his 80th birthday on September 3, the overwhelming conviction was that the policy he personified—restraint and reconciliation with the Soviet Union—had been vindicated once more. In May he was awarded an International Lenin Peace Prize, and in July he paid an unofficial visit to the Summer Olympic Games in Moscow.

Finland abstained in the UN vote on the Soviet intervention in Afghanistan. While this contrasted starkly with the condemnatory stance of other neutral countries, it accorded with Finland's consistent policy of not taking sides in great power conflicts. Addressing Parliament on February 5, Kekkonen stated: "What has happened outside Europe must not spoil the results achieved here." Acceptance by the Finns of a divisible form of détente differed markedly from the "global" view expressed by Pres. Valéry Giscard d'Estaing during his visit on June 2–3, the first ever paid to Finland by a French chief of state.

Finland was a factor in Soviet propaganda against NATO plans to deploy medium-range missiles in Western Europe and prestock military equipment in Norway for possible use by U.S. Marines. Through the press, the Kremlin appeared to extend Finland's obligations under its treaty with the U.S.S.R. to interception of cruise missiles, as well as more orthodox defense against NATO attacks.

For the second successive year, Finland seemed likely to attain the highest growth rate in the Organization for Economic Cooperation and Development region: official predictions were for a 6% increase in gross domestic product, following the 6.5% recorded in 1979. For the second time in half a year, the markka was revalued by 2% on March 25, 1980. However, the trade balance, comfortably in surplus until mid-1979, plunged into the red, owing to soaring energy import prices and purchases to shore up domestic industry. Trimmed to an annual 7–8% in 1978–79, inflation appeared set to touch 13%, signaling a loss of competitive edge over most other industrialized countries. In August unemployment reached 3.7%, the lowest rate in four years, but it was feared that the spread of the international recession would make this a fleeting achievement. Industrial relations remained touchy, as was shown by the collapse of the centralized incomes formula and a round of springtime strikes by merchant seamen, icebreaker crews, and salaried staff in industry.

FISH AND FISHERIES

With 93 coastal nations claiming a 200-mi exclusive economic zone in 1980, nations whose fishing industries had been based on the exploitation of fishing grounds adjacent to other countries had two choices: they could cut their losses and sell off the costly ships designed to fish such "distant waters," or they could apply for fishing licenses while attempting to negotiate bilateral agreements with the coastal states concerned.

Countries with control over their fishing grounds, such as Canada, South Africa, and Iceland, benefited from the restrictions imposed by their govern-

Striking French fishermen formed a blockade at the harbour entrance at Boulogne, France, in August. They were protesting high fuel costs that were devouring their profits.
KEYSTONE

In January Vice-Adm. Robert H. Scarborough (right), acting commandant of the Coast Guard, showed Transportation Secretary Neil Goldschmidt where Soviet fishing operations in U.S. waters would be curtailed in reaction to the Soviet invasion of Afghanistan.
GEORGE TAMES—THE NEW YORK TIMES

ments. Catch rates began to rise and stocks to recover from years of overfishing. In Iceland and Canada, however, investment in new vessels, combined with better catches, had brought about a surplus of the more popular species such as cod, depressing prices in European markets and causing hardship to fishermen already hard-hit by high fuel costs and interest rates.

On several occasions FAO spokesmen warned that fishing was a resource exploited close to its limit. But if world fish production was to keep up with the growth in demand, it would have to increase by 44 million metric tons over the next 20 years. Half of this amount could be obtained by better management of existing resources. Some 5 million metric tons were lost annually by discarding undervalued species and 6 million through premature spoilage in hot climates. The Asian Bank estimated that sufficient investment could produce an additional 20 million metric tons a year, much of it from fish farming. The FAO believed the day was near when small fish abounding in tropical waters would be used to feed people, not to provide fish meal.

Britain, France, and Spain witnessed mass demonstrations by fishermen. The main factor was fuel costs, which had outpaced the price of fish even when fuel subsidies were provided. Within the European Economic Community (EEC) fishing nations, no common policy on fuel subsidies or other "hidden" subsidies existed. Cries of "unfair competition" were raised in Britain when fish landed by EEC "partners" sold at 15% below prices required to maintain the home fleet. Eventually, £15 million was distributed, pending agreement on the EEC common fisheries policy, promised for early 1981. (Accord was reached in September on fish conservation measures and, in October, on a standardized system for recording and reporting the size and nature of catches.)

When China opened its books to observers from the UN Food and Agriculture Organization, it was found that past estimates of its annual catch had been 2 million metric tons higher than the true figures, which were 3.4 million metric tons of marine fish and 1.2 million metric tons of freshwater fish. But the annual catch of Taiwan had risen to nearly 1 million metric tons, and farmed fish and shellfish production was up 11.7% to 183,000 metric tons. Furthermore, a $220 million fleet-expansion program was announced that would add ten 500-ton purse seiners and 50 new trawlers to the Taiwanese fleet. In Vietnam trawlers donated by Norway as part of a fisheries aid program were found to be in use as naval auxiliaries and were accused of firing on refugees. Norwegian aid worth $20 million was promptly withdrawn.

For the first time, Norway's population was eating more meat than fish. Perhaps this was no bad thing, since the cod quota Norway had set for its fleet was still low, and the Atlanto-Scandinavian herring stocks still showed no sign of recovery. Norway's herring purse seine fleet had been reduced and was now catching capelin for the fish-meal plants. However, new research, announced in 1980, could enable this small fish to be used for human consumption.

The Pacific tuna fishery was still in trouble. U.S. tuna purse seiners continued to complain of restrictions resulting from the limitation on porpoise kills. Costa Rica arrested U.S. vessels found in its 200-mi zone, despite the U.S. claim that ocean-ranging tuna was not subject to such limitation. The U.S. tuna catch in the Pacific amounted to 66% of the total 370,000 metric tons taken by a 17-nation fleet. In December Mexico announced the termination of its fishing accords with the U.S. The two nations had been unable to settle their differences on fishing rights.

Farther north, the Canadian Pacific salmon season was a disappointment, variously blamed on too many boats, the Mt. St. Helens volcanic eruptions, too much logging activity, and a natural cycle. The

Pacific herring roe fishery also encountered trouble when the Japanese market on which it relied raised retail prices steeply, with disastrous effects on demand. Canadian forecasts were speaking of doubled seafood exports by 1985, with a possible target of $2 billion.

At the International Whaling Commission's 1980 meeting, in Brighton, England, yet another proposal for a moratorium on commercial whaling, supported by France, The Netherlands, the U.S., and the U.K., was defeated by the whaling nations—Japan, Iceland, South Africa, Spain, Chile, South Korea, and the U.S.S.R. However, the overall quota for all whale species to be taken in the 1981-82 season was reduced by 13% as compared with the previous year.

FLOWERS AND GARDENS

The National Herb Garden at the National Arboretum in Washington, D.C., was opened to the public on June 13, 1980. A gift of the Herb Society of America, with matching funds provided by Congress, the two-acre garden contained some 7,000 carefully selected herbal plants in a series of gardens. A historic rose garden featured intensely fragrant wild roses, many of which came from Europe. The specialty gardens included an American Indian garden with plants used by Indians of eastern North America as sources of medicines, dyes, poisons, food, and craft materials.

The U.S. Department of Agriculture (USDA) put new rules into effect to prevent spread of the gypsy moth. The new approach would concentrate manpower and funds in heavily infested areas. High-risk areas for 1980 included all of Rhode Island and portions of Maine, New Hampshire, Vermont, Massachusetts, Connecticut, New York, New Jersey, Pennsylvania, and Michigan.

Articles moving from high-risk areas to or through unregulated areas had to be inspected, treated if necessary, and certified pest free. At least nine species of parasitic flies and wasps were being used by the USDA to fight the gypsy moth. Some of these also attack other destructive caterpillars.

The development by pests of resistance to pesticides, the increasing cost of these chemicals, plus their pollution of the environment and possible implication in human disease, drew attention to the need for combined biologic and chemical methods of pest and disease control. The trend was toward "supervised" control in which the level of infestation was carefully assessed prior to the application of a spray program, and monitoring continued throughout the growing season. In England about 2,500 ha (6,750 ac) of commercial orchards were being monitored, chiefly by growers, and this close supervision had brought about an average 35% reduction in the number of insecticide applications. In warmer areas of Europe, a reduction of over 50% had been achieved.

Three roses were 1981 All-America award winners: Bing Crosby, a slightly fragrant hybrid tea with medium-ripe-persimmon orange flowers in the spring and red-orange flowers in the fall, hybridized by Ollie Weeks of Ontario, Calif.; White Lightnin', a grandiflora with pure white, ruffled flowers of intense fragrance, sometimes edged with a light pink blush, hybridized by Herbert C. Swim of southern California; and Marina, a large-flowered, slightly fragrant floribunda, hybridized by Reimer Kordes, of Sparrieshoop, West Germany.

Gypsy, a hybrid pepper (Petoseed Co., Saticoy, Ga.), Apricot Brandy, a celosia plumosa (T. Sakara & Co., Yokohama, Japan), and Blitz, a dwarf hybrid impatiens (Sluis & Groot BV, Enkhuizen, Neth.) were named 1981 award winners by All-America Selections.

Government-controlled tests for purity and performance of cultivars demand that they be demonstrably distinct from each other. The price is the loss of old kinds and, with them, the store of genetic variation accumulated over centuries. To correct this the National Vegetable Research Station in England set up a gene bank. The aim was to store a litre of seed of at least 9,000 vegetable cultivars, plus 3,000 of the more exotic tropical kinds already being stored at centres in Asia.

(*See also* Agriculture; Food.)

The National Herb Garden, displaying some 7,000 herbal plants, was opened to the public on June 13; it is located in Washington, D.C.
GEORGE TAMES—THE NEW YORK TIMES

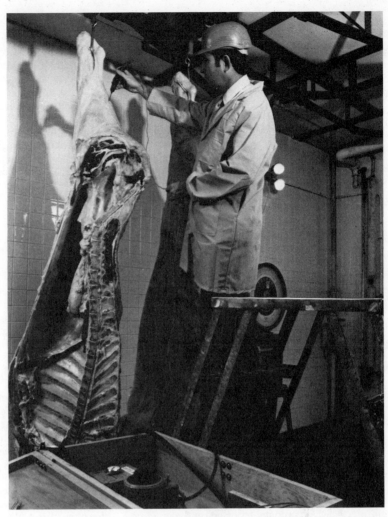

Technologists at the USDA's Science and Education Administration research laboratory in Beltsville, Maryland, discovered that if electric current is applied to beef soon after slaughter, the meat is more tender and weight loss through cooking is reduced.

SCIENCE AND EDUCATION
ADMINISTRATION—USDA

FOOD

Consumers in many countries were becoming increasingly bewildered by the conflicting official and semiofficial pronouncements of experts concerning the presumed effects of foods and food additives on health. The U.S. National Academy of Sciences (NAS) issued a report stating that healthy Americans need not cut their fat or cholesterol intake, and it challenged the previous conclusions of the Senate Select Committee on Nutrition and Human Needs (chaired by George McGovern) that high cholesterol and fat intakes were responsible for heart disease and other chronic illnesses. However, the American Heart Association strongly disagreed with the NAS, while the American Medical Association counseled moderation.

Considerable interest was shown in a U.S. process that made it possible to freeze foods without hardening them. It was claimed that the method could revolutionize frozen-food production. According to reports, it maintains texture, permits refreezing, and conserves energy. A Swiss company developed an ingenious double-walled plastic bag that, upon inflation, closes around a frozen food and keeps it frozen for several hours.

In view of the declining consumption of fresh potatoes, there was much international interest in potato processing. Research in The Netherlands involved the manufacture of french fries (chips) and potato chips (crisps), peeled, canned, and dried potatoes, potato croquettes, and other products. Canadians developed a freeze-thaw process for the production of potato granules, and U.S. workers produced potato puree in flake form. A West German company prepared a protein isolate from potato juice. Improved methods of peeling and deep frying and the use of potato flour in bread and noodles were investigated in Taiwan. Research in the U.S.S.R. included storage conditions for potatoes and potato puree, the use of ionized air to improve potato shelf life, and a method for reducing waste by boiling, freezing, and thawing whole potatoes and then removing the skin from the pulp in a current of hot air.

The biology, cultivation, and food uses of edible fungi were studied in the U.S., as well as in Japan and several other Asian countries. The culture of fungi under water was also investigated. Research on the cultivation and food uses of various types of freshwater and saltwater algae was carried out in Thailand. Soviet workers studied the use of peat as a raw material for the microbial production of protein, fats, and vitamins.

Earlier work on the ultrafiltration of milk and whey began to give results in New Zealand and Europe. West German technologists reported savings in the manufacture of cheese attributable to increased yield and more consistent quality. A Swedish firm developed a continuous process incorporating ultrafiltration for the manufacture of all types of soft cheese. Australian scientists reported that cream from ultrafiltered milk had superior whipping properties.

Whey proteins from ultrafiltered whey became commercially available. They had excellent nutritional properties and good functional characteristics as a substitute for egg white. Progress was made in the utilization of lactose, which constitutes about 5% of whey, and its enzymatic conversion to a glucose-galactose syrup for sweetening proved attractive. Other processes studied included whey conversion to biomass by yeast fermentation and an anaerobic fermentation process to produce methane as a fuel for creamery boilers. U.S. scientists developed two novel processes for the conversion of whey into ruminant feed; in one the lactose was reacted with urea, and in the other it was fermented to lactic acid and converted to ammonium lactate. The latter process was approved by the Food and Drug Administration, and a plant was commissioned to produce 100 tons daily.

Considerable study was devoted to the improved utilization of existing marine resources and to aquaculture. A Swiss company reported on the great potential of many unexploited species, such as lantern fish and deep-sea red crabs, and of underexploited species like squid and octopus, which contain 17–20% protein and only 1–1.5% fat. The need for improved methods of fish filleting was emphasized, since currently used systems wasted more than 50% of the flesh. A process was developed for the better utilization of fish trimmings by isolating a fish protein and spinning it for use as a meat extender.

Abalone were successfully raised from spawn, and a formula diet was developed with a view to the commercial raising of lobsters. Swedish scientists developed a new trout-breeding system that produced 0.5-kg (1-lb) fish from spawn in less than a year. A proposal for whale farming involved capturing pregnant blue whales and raising the young on fertilized atolls.

Increased demand for foods rich in dietary fibre led to numerous new formulations such as bran soups and special pastries. A preparation of soybean bran was developed in Japan, and a British company introduced a similar product.

(*See also* Agriculture; Fisheries.)

FOOTBALL

The Oakland Raiders of the American Football Conference (AFC) became the first wild-card team to win the championship of U.S. professional football when they defeated the Philadelphia Eagles 27–10 in the Super Bowl at New Orleans, La., on Jan. 25, 1981. The game's most valuable player was Raider quarterback Jim Plunkett, who passed for all three of his team's touchdowns, two to wide receiver Cliff Branch and one to running back Kenny King. The pass to King and his subsequent run covered 80 yd, a Super Bowl record. Also outstanding for the Raiders were linebacker Rod Martin, who set a Super Bowl record by intercepting three passes, and the Raider offensive line, which gave Plunkett excellent protection throughout the game.

For Plunkett and the team as a whole the game was a fitting climax to a remarkable comeback season. Plunkett, the 1970 Heisman Trophy winner who began his pro career with several successful seasons with the New England Patriots, had been cast off by both that team and San Francisco and started the year on the Raider bench. But when first-string quarterback Dan Pastorini broke his leg in the fifth game, Plunkett took over. At that time the Raiders had a 2–3 record and seemed unlikely to make the play-offs. But Plunkett led them to an 11–5 regular-season mark and to play-off victories over Houston, Cleveland, and San Diego.

In the conference championship games the Raiders scored three touchdowns in the first quarter and then held on to beat the San Diego Chargers 34–27. The Eagles played tough defensive football to defeat Dallas 20–7 for their first National Football Conference (NFC) title.

The Pittsburgh Steelers failed to become the National Football League's (NFL's) first team to make nine consecutive play-off appearances and win three Super Bowls in a row. Their overwhelming injuries peaked in a week when 35 players needed medical attention. But the 9–7 Steelers had considerable company in their fall from grace. Half of the ten play-off teams in 1979 missed the 1980 Super Bowl tournament. The others were Miami, Denver, Chicago, and Tampa Bay, which fell the furthest by finishing 5–10–1 after playing for the NFC championship in 1979. Los Angeles and Houston, the 1979 semifinalists with Pittsburgh and Tampa Bay, were the first two teams eliminated from the 1980 tournament.

San Diego was the only team to win its division a second year in a row, and Philadelphia was the only other division winner that had been in the 1979 play-offs. The other four division winners were Cleveland, champion of Pittsburgh's AFC Central for the first time since 1971; Atlanta, ending Los Angeles's NFL-record string of seven championships in the NFC West; Buffalo, which leaped from fourth place the previous year in the AFC East; and Minnesota in the NFC Central. San Diego won the AFC West, and Philadelphia the NFC East.

Oakland Raider quarterback Jim Plunkett fades back to pass in the first quarter of the Super Bowl in New Orleans, Louisiana, on Jan. 25, 1981. Plunkett was voted most valuable player in his team's 27–10 victory over the Philadelphia Eagles.
WIDE WORLD

Oakland was the fifth 1980 play-off team that had missed the 1979 tournament, qualifying as an AFC wild-card team with Houston. Oakland and Houston actually tied the AFC division winners with 11–5 won-lost records, but the NFL's tiebreaker rules denied them championships on the basis of conference records or net points in division games. Dallas also settled for wild-card status after tying Philadelphia with a record of 12–4. Los Angeles, the other NFC wild card, finished 11–5, one game behind Atlanta.

The NFL continued its trend toward more passing, passing yards gained, total yards gained, and scoring, as it marked the three highest-scoring weekends in its history. San Diego best exemplified the trend, which had been spurred by rules that made it harder to rush the passer and cover receivers. San Diego quarterback Dan Fouts set NFL records with 4,715 passing yards and at least 300 yd in eight games, and he led the league with 8.01 yd per pass. As a team the Chargers set records with 372 first downs, 6,410 total yards (400.6 per game), and 4,531 net passing yards (283.2 per game).

San Diego's Kellen Winslow led the league with 89 catches, an NFL record for tight ends. Teammates John Jefferson and Charlie Joiner were second and third in the AFC, and Jefferson led the NFL with 1,340 receiving yards. Brian Sipe of Cleveland joined Fouts and Joe Namath as the only NFL passers ever to gain at least 4,000 yd in a season. Sipe led the NFL in efficiency rating. His 30 touchdown passes tied Fouts for the AFC lead, and his .025 percentage of passes intercepted was the NFL's lowest.

In his third season Earl Campbell of Houston won his third NFL rushing championship with 1,934 yd, the second highest total in NFL history. Although injuries kept him out of one entire game and two halves, Campbell set records with 373 carries and four 200-yd games.

But popular coach O. A. ("Bum") Phillips was fired after Houston's play-off defeat against Oakland because critics said his offense lacked imagination. The only coach to lose his job during the season was Dick Nolan of New Orleans, which lost a record 15 of 16 games.

Lester Hayes of the Raiders led the league with 13 interceptions. Buffalo's defensive yield of 256.3 yd per game led the league, and it trailed only Washington in stopping the pass.

Buffalo halfback Joe Cribbs was the AFC's only rookie all-star, but other rookie running backs included Billy Sims of Detroit, who led the league with 16 touchdowns and ranked fifth in rushing; Curtis Dickey of Baltimore, who tied Jefferson and Campbell with an AFC-leading 13 touchdowns; and Earl Cooper, whose 83 catches beat San Francisco teammate Dwight Clark by one for the NFC lead. The .645 pass-completion record of second-year San Francisco quarterback Joe Montana was the NFL's best.

Los Angeles led the league with 174.9 rushing yards per game despite losing two injured halfbacks. Dallas led the NFL with 454 points as Danny White capably replaced retired quarterback Roger Staubach. The Eagles led the league in total defense, allowing 277.7 yd per game and limiting 10 of 16 opponents to fewer than 100 yd rushing. They allowed a league low of 222 points. Also for the Eagles, Ron Jaworski had the NFC's best passer-efficiency rating, but Harold Carmichael's streak of receptions in 127 consecutive games ended, leaving St. Louis's Mel Gray with the NFL's longest at 105.

Atlanta had a nine-game winning streak, the league's longest. Steve Bartkowski led the league with 31 touchdown passes, and the Falcons had the NFL's best rushing pair, William Andrews and Lynn Cain, who gained 2,222 yd. Minnesota clinched its 11th division title in 13 years. Its 230.5 passing

Georgia's Scott Woerner
(right) snags a pass
intended for Notre
Dame's Pete Holohan
during the Sugar Bowl
Jan. 1, 1981, which
Georgia won 17–10.
WIDE WORLD

yards per game led the conference.

New England (10–6) led the AFC in scoring with 441 points and had league leaders John Smith with 129 points, Horace Ivory with a 27.6-yd kickoff return average, and Stanley Morgan with a 22.5-yd average per reception. Other league leaders were Kansas City's J. T. Smith with a 14.5-yd punt return average and the New York Giants' Dave Jennings with a 44.8-yd punting average.

Walter Payton of 7–9 Chicago won his fifth consecutive NFC rushing championship with 1,460 yd and became the NFL's fifth-ranked all-time rusher. He was ejected from a game after one of many incorrect officiating calls that resulted in increased insistence that the NFL use televised replays as officiating aids.

College Competition

The University of Georgia was the only undefeated major college team and clinched a national championship with a 17–10 victory over Notre Dame in the Sugar Bowl at New Orleans on New Year's Day 1981. Georgia, which finished with a 12–0 record and won the Southeast Conference, was led by running back Herschel Walker, whose 1,616 yd rushing were the most ever gained by a freshman. Walker's third-place finish in the Heisman Trophy voting also was the best ever for a freshman. Walker, who ranked fourth in rushing, was first in rushing touchdowns with 15.

South Carolina running back George Rogers won the Heisman, which honours the best college player, and Pittsburgh defensive end Hugh Green finished second. Green won the Lombardi Trophy for linemen, and his teammate, offensive tackle Mark May, won the similar Outland Trophy. Second-ranked Pittsburgh finished 11–1 and led the major colleges' Division I-A of the National Col-

legiate Athletic Association with per-game defensive averages of 65.3 yd rushing and 205.5 total yards. Big Eight champion Oklahoma finished 10–2 with an 18–17 Orange Bowl victory against Florida State and set college records by running for 758 yd and gaining 875 total yards against Colorado on October 4. The third-ranked Sooners' offense ranked second in rushing, third in total offense, fourth in scoring, and first in yardage per pass attempt with 11.8. Florida State was ranked fifth with a 10–2 record. The Seminoles allowed only 7.7 points per game, the best among major teams.

Big Ten champion Michigan (10–2, ranked fourth) allowed only nine points in its last five games, including a 23–6 Rose Bowl victory against Washington. Washington won the Pacific Ten championship without requiring the help of conference sanctions against five schools declared ineligible for academic violations. Rounding out the top ten were 10–2 Alabama, which defeated 10–2 Southwest Conference champion Baylor 30–2 in the Cotton Bowl; 10–2 Nebraska; 10–2 Penn State; 9–2–1 Notre Dame; and 11–1 North Carolina, the Atlantic Coast Conference champion.

But the college season was punctuated by passing. Major college teams had their biggest increase in passing yardage and pass-run ratios since separate offensive and defensive platoons were allowed in 1965, and they set all-time records of 50% of passes completed and 4.65 yd per offensive play. Jim McMahon, Brigham Young's junior quarterback, had the best passing totals in college football history. He set records with 4,571 passing yards, 4,627 total yards, 47 touchdown passes, 53 touchdowns produced, 10.27 yd per pass attempt, and 176.9 passing efficiency points, which gave him a bigger margin over the second-ranked passer than number 2 had over number 22. Brigham Young, the Western Athletic Conference champion, led the country with 46.7 points and 535 yd per game, and its 409.8 passing yards per game broke the old record by 35.6 yd. Tight end Clay Brown led the country with 15 touchdown catches.

Close behind McMahon was senior Neil Lomax of Portland (Ore.) State in the smaller colleges' Division I-AA. He passed for 4,094 yd and set career records with 13,220 passing yards, 13,345 total yards, 106 touchdown passes, and 120 touchdowns produced. He threw eight touchdown passes in his team's 105–0 victory against Delaware State. Portland State won other games 93–7 and 75–0. Other record-setting passers were Dave Wilson of Illinois with 621 yd in one game, Mark Herrmann of Purdue with 9,188 yd in a Division I-A career, and Joe Adams of Tennessee State with 81 touchdowns in a Division I-A career.

Rogers was the rushing leader with 1,781 yd, but Nebraska won the team rushing title with Jarvis Redwine's national high of 7.2 yd per carry. Nebraska also ranked second offensively in total yards and scoring, second in points allowed, and third in yards allowed. Amos Lawrence of North Carolina became the second player to run for 1,000 yd four seasons in a row.

The 1980 game of the 111-year-old Princeton-

The New York Cosmos won the championship of the North American Soccer League by beating the Fort Lauderdale Strikers of Florida.

Rutgers series, college football's oldest, was won by Rutgers 44–13. Yale won the Ivy League by defeating Harvard 14–0. Navy broke its series tie with Army by winning 33–6.

North American Soccer League

The New York Cosmos regained the North American Soccer League championship when they defeated the Fort Lauderdale Strikers 3–0 in the Soccer Bowl at Washington, D.C., before some 50,000 spectators on September 21. Two key factors in the final were the injury to the Strikers' West German ace scorer Gerd Müller five minutes before the halftime break and a goal by the Cosmos' Julio Cesar Romero early in the second half. From that point on the Cosmos were in command, and Giorgio Chinaglia scored twice more to seal their victory.

FRANCE

The year 1980 opened with a political event of significance for the future of France. Georges Marchais, France's Communist Party leader, went to Moscow in January for three meetings with Soviet Pres. Leonid Brezhnev. This ended the estrangement caused in 1976 when French Communists turned away from the U.S.S.R. toward "Eurocommunism." At the meetings it became apparent that the French Communist Party supported all the aims of Soviet foreign policy. Marchais strongly attacked France's Socialist Party; reverting to a Stalinist hard line, he endorsed what appeared to be a definitive split with the Socialists and brought an end to all hopes of a revived union of the left.

Social unrest was reflected throughout the year by a series of strikes—by schoolteachers, sweepers from the Paris Metro (subway), railway workers, post office workers, and electrical workers.

Both the Confédération Général du Travail and the Confédération Française Démocratique du Travail trade union bodies called for a national day of strikes on May 13 in support of social security. There was a massive response from workers in all parts of the country, and the turmoil persisted to some extent in the universities after the death of a demonstrator at the University of Paris VII.

In August and September the strike of fishermen in Boulogne, which spread to most French ports, halted sea traffic for several weeks and aroused anger among tourists and pleasure-boat owners. There were violent incidents at Cherbourg and Calais, where several thousand British tourists were unable to leave, trapped behind a blockade of trawlers, the crews of which were demanding maintenance of employment levels and compensation for fuel price rises. After the Navy had intervened to allow tankers to get through and there had been fierce confrontations, the blockade in most ports was lifted.

In contrast with this turmoil the visit of Pope John Paul II to France from May 30 to June 2 was

Parisians reacted in outrage to a series of anti-Semitic incidents in 1980, including the bombing of a synagogue in which three people were killed. A massive rally and protest march in October in Paris brought together all segments of French society.

a healing interlude that aroused extraordinary fervour. Arriving at Orly Airport, the pope was greeted in Paris by Pres. Valéry Giscard d'Estaing (with whom he later had a private talk). The working session with the French bishops, during which John Paul II gave an uncompromising review of the situation of religion in France, was the most important event of the trip. It was followed by an enthusiastic vigil with young people at the Parc des Princes and a stop at the Sacré-Coeur church. The pope ended his visit at Lisieux.

Unfortunately, calls for peace did not prevent a renewal of violence. In Neuilly in July Shahpur Bakhtiar, Iran's last prime minister under the former shah, escaped assassination, but a policeman and a woman were killed. A few days later Salah al-Bitar, former Syrian premier and co-founder of the Ba'ath Party, was assassinated in Paris. During the previous two years there had been 12 deaths in France in the course of such settling of accounts between rival factions from the Middle East.

Following a series of anti-Semitic attacks in September directed against buildings in Paris belonging to Jews, the violence reached a peak in October with the bombing of a synagogue on the Rue Copernic near the Place Victor Hugo. The explosion of plastic explosive killed four people, caused many serious injuries, and inflicted much damage. There was some uncertainty about the perpetrators of the crime, who might have been neo-Nazis or left-wing

revolutionaries, but the attack provoked a wave of universal indignation.

A demonstration in Paris, organized by the Mouvement contre le racisme et pour l'amitié entre les peuples, an anti-racist movement, was joined by some 200,000 people who marched in a four-hour procession. To the trade unions and left-wing parties that took part were added parliamentarians and groups from the Jewish community. While demonstrations were also taking place outside Paris, Giscard made a statement in the Council of Ministers that amounted to an appeal for the unity of the French people: "Let us together reject the hideous seeds of intolerance, terrorism, and racism."

In the political field the elections to the Senate, which were held on September 28 for one-third of the seats in the upper house, made little basic change in the composition of that chamber. The election did demonstrate (and serve to accentuate further) the deterioration in relations between the Socialists and the Communists.

The task facing the government in 1980 was a daunting one, with inflation rates expected to reach 13–14% for 1980, unemployment rising to 1.5 million, and a considerable balance of trade deficit. At the end of October the government raised its third loan for the year (Fr 10 billion over six years at a record rate of 13.8%, making a total of Fr 30 billion since Jan. 1, 1980), but it predicted that the budgetary deficit for the year, expected to be

Fr 30 billion to Fr 35 billion, would be almost covered by long-term, nonmonetary resources, helping to reduce inflation (Fr 4.19 = U.S. $1).

Foreign Affairs

A sign of the times was the ten-day visit of President Giscard to the Persian Gulf and Jordan in March; included in his itinerary were Kuwait, Bahrain, Qatar, the United Arab Emirates, and Saudi Arabia. In October, en route to Beijing (Peking) to reinforce French relations with China, he again held talks in Abu Dhabi with Sheikh Zaid ibn Sultan an-Nahayan, president of the United Arab Emirates, who promised additional oil exports to France amounting to 2.5 million metric tons a year. However, this visit raised questions about the direction of diplomatic action that appeared to give precedence to commercial interests over other aspects of foreign policy, in particular when it was taken together with Giscard's January visit to India, coinciding with Indira Gandhi's return to power and resulting in the signing of eight agreements on bilateral cooperation; with the official visit to Paris in April of Venezuelan Pres. Luis Herrera Campins and its links to the energy crisis; with that of Mexican Pres. José López Portillo in May; and finally with the sale in October of naval arms worth Fr 14.4 billion to Saudi Arabia after nearly 2½ years of negotiation.

The important meeting in Warsaw in May between Giscard, Brezhnev, and Edward Gierek preceded Giscard's visit to Finland. It confirmed France's desire to carry on the East-West dialogue despite the tension that had arisen in relations between the Soviet Union and the U.S.

However, it was in the strengthening of Europe under the impetus of Giscard that the year's most spectacular progress was made. On May 30 the nine member nations of the EEC (France, West Germany, Belgium, The Netherlands, Luxembourg, Italy, the U.K., Denmark, and Ireland) reached agreement on reducing Britain's contribution to the or-

ganization's budget. Following the 17th meeting of the European Council in Venice on June 12 and 13, Giscard welcomed the fact that the Council (the heads of government of the EEC nations) had "regained its status and its character," adding: "Europe is steadily emerging as one of the independent elements which have their own responsibility in the interplay of the major forces in the world."

FUEL AND ENERGY

Developments in energy in 1980 were dominated by changing circumstances in the international oil market. During the first half of the year the members of the Organization of Petroleum Exporting Countries (OPEC) continued their practice of repeatedly raising the price of oil in leapfrog fashion, having failed to agree on a uniform pricing scheme at their 1979 year-end meeting. Meetings in May and June were only partially successful in achieving agreement, and the leapfrogging continued. At the same time, however, the demand for oil products was softening, the result of a mild winter in the Northern Hemisphere and worldwide conservation. At their meeting in December the OPEC members increased price ceilings for a barrel of crude oil by $4 and set a maximum price of $41 per barrel.

By midyear it was apparent that there was a growing imbalance between production and consumption. Stocks of crude oil and oil products were reaching extraordinarily high levels throughout the world, and sales of OPEC oil began to be made below the official prices even as price increases were being announced. The imbalance continued to worsen during the summer, and by summer's end prices of crude oil and oil products had declined, refineries had cut production to record low levels in the United States, and world stocks had reached all-time highs.

Industry Developments

Thus, when the Iraq-Iran war erupted at the end of September, cutting off imports from both coun-

Pres. Valéry Giscard d'Estaing's travels took him to Beijing (Peking) in October. He reviewed the troops with Zhao Ziyang (Chao Tzu-yang), the new premier of China.

RICHARD MELLOUL–SYGMA

A nuclear breeder reactor neared completion 40 miles south of Lyons, France. A showpiece in France's energy program, it was expected to begin production of electricity in 1983.

In March the Mexican national oil company finally capped the Ixtoc 1 well in the Bay of Campeche, which had blown out of control in June 1979. During the ensuing ten months the well had gushed more than three million barrels of oil into the waters of the Gulf of Mexico, making it the largest oil spill in history. In August the United Kingdom became self-sufficient in oil for the first time, the result of increasing production from the North Sea and a decline in consumption. The U.S.S.R. announced the achievement of a world record drilling depth of 10,000 m (1 m=3.3 ft) in a well on the Kola Peninsula, near the Barents Sea west of Murmansk.

The first large oil discovery off the east coast of North America suggested the possible existence of a major new oil province. The Hibernia Field, discovered by a well drilled in the Atlantic Ocean some 300 km SE (1 km=0.62 mi) off St. John's, Newfoundland, was estimated to contain at least 1,-000,000,000 bbl. Across the continent a significant discovery was made in the Beaufort Sea, 16 km NE of the giant Prudhoe Bay field (which produced its one billionth barrel in January) on the north coast of Alaska. Two wells were drilled from a gravel island one-quarter kilometre from shore and confirmed the expectation that other oil fields would be found near the Prudhoe Bay deposit.

Among events in natural gas were two affecting supplies to the U.S. and some significant new discoveries. In January imports of natural gas from Mexico began under a new agreement between U.S. companies and the Mexican government. The agreement replaced an earlier one reached in 1977 but vetoed at that time by the U.S. Department of Energy on the grounds that the price was too high. The initial price under the new agreement was 40% higher than the vetoed price. In Canada construction began on a portion of the Alaska Highway gas pipeline, intended eventually to carry gas from the Prudhoe Bay field and the Mackenzie River delta via a western leg to a delivery point near San Francisco and via an eastern leg to one near Chicago. The portion on which work was started was the Canadian segment of the western leg, to carry Alberta gas to San Francisco.

In October the Canadian government announced a new energy program designed to insulate domestic energy prices from the world oil prices set by OPEC and to bring Canadian subsidiaries of foreign oil companies under Canadian control through their purchase by the Canadian national oil company. The immediate result of the announcement was to sharpen the already intense controversy between the central government and the provinces (especially the western ones) over the allocation of political power. An unrelated announcement in the same month marked the entry of Canada into the liquefied natural gas business; beginning in 1985 such gas would be exported to Japan for use in Japanese power plants.

tries, the world oil market absorbed the shock with scarcely a tremor. There was no panic buying such as followed the interruption of exports from Iran during that country's revolution. With storage tanks brimming and continued softness in demand it was clear to all that oil-importing countries could withstand many months of the loss of supply from the two warring countries. Saudi Arabia, moreover, announced it would increase its production for an indefinite period, and other producing countries made special arrangements to take care of the needs of those importing nations that had been heavily dependent on Iraqi oil. Nevertheless, as the war dragged on beyond the few weeks military experts had expected it to last, the spot market began to show increasing nervousness.

A facility for the industrial use of solar energy was opened near Madrid.
EFE/PHOTO TRENDS

Initial tests of a gas discovery in the North Sea indicated that it was by far the largest gas field yet found in that oil and gas region and perhaps one of the largest in the world. The discovery was made 110 km off the Norwegian coast in 330 m of water. Continued exploration in the Baltimore Canyon area in the Atlantic Ocean off New Jersey resulted in further promising indications that were tantalizingly short of solid commercial practicability; gas was found in two more wells, adding to the initial discovery made in 1978. Further drilling was necessary, however, to determine whether the size of the reserves warranted investment in production facilities and a pipeline to carry the gas ashore.

The long-term effect of the accident at the Three Mile Island (Pa.) reactor on the future of nuclear power in the U.S. continued to be uncertain. In late February, 11 months after the accident, the Nuclear Regulatory Commission issued the first start-up license for a new nuclear unit to be awarded since the accident. In September voters in Maine defeated by a decisive margin the first referendum proposal to shut down an operating nuclear reactor. On the other hand, several nuclear plants proposed or under construction were canceled or postponed during the year, and no new orders were placed. Elsewhere in the world Swedish voters turned down a proposal to dismantle that country's operating reactors, voting instead to go ahead with plans to double the number of reactors from 6 to 12; and the Soviet Union put into operation a 600-Mw fast breeder reactor, the world's largest.

The shape of things to come in the electric utility industry was heralded in the announcement by a large utility in California that it intended to produce 30% of its output in 1990 from renewable resources, especially solar energy. In Canada the James Bay hydroelectric power complex generated its first power. Begun in 1972, it comprised a mammoth construction project that rearranged the flow of several rivers on the eastern shore of James Bay in Quebec. When completed in 1985, the project would have generating capacity that would make it one of the largest in the world.

Government Policies

Energy legislation and policy made headlines repeatedly throughout the year. In his state of the union address to the U.S. Congress in January, Pres. Jimmy Carter called dependence on foreign oil "a clear and present danger" to national security and announced that he would limit oil imports to a maximum of 8.2 million bbl a day. Although net imports remained below that figure during the first quarter, in March the president used his authority to impose a fee of $4.62 per barrel on imports of crude oil and $4.20 per barrel on imports of gasoline. The action proved to be highly controversial, opponents labeling it a means of raising government revenues under the guise of discouraging imports. Opposition was, in fact, sufficient to result in congressional resolutions that removed the president's authority for the action. Although the legislation was vetoed, both houses overrode the veto in June, the first time in 28 years that a president had sustained a veto defeat from a Congress controlled by his own party.

Carter had mixed success with three key pieces of legislation to further his energy program. In April he signed a bill imposing a "windfall profits" tax on domestically produced oil which he described as "the keystone" of a national energy policy. Under the new law domestic producers of crude oil were taxed at a rate of 30–70% of the difference between the selling price and various specified base prices. Proceeds from the new tax went into a special account to be used for reducing income taxes, assistance to those with low incomes, and energy and transportation programs. The tax was to be in effect for ten years and was expected to result in estimated revenues of $227 billion. Other provisions of the act contained new and expanded tax benefits for individuals and businesses that save energy or produce it, including subsidization of alcohol fuels.

A second measure was defeated. In June the House of Representatives rejected a bill to establish an Energy Mobilization Board that would cut red tape and speed the approval of major new energy projects such as synthetic fuels plants and pipelines. A few days later, however, the third measure, creating a Synthetic Fuels Corporation to bring a commercial synthetic fuels industry into being, was signed by President Carter. The act also provided that the corporation render similar assistance in the development of commercial energy from biomass, solar energy, and other renewable energy resources. The new agency did not get staffed until late in the year; in the meantime the U.S. Department of Energy continued its support of research and development of synthetic fuels. In July it awarded $200 million to approximately 100 companies for work on coal, oil shale, and other sources. Also in July the second largest experimental plant to convert coal into oil went into operation, and West Germany and Japan signed agreements to participate in a U.S.-sponsored commercial demonstration of synthetic fuel production from coal.

Under the Emergency Energy Conservation Act of 1979 President Carter was required to submit a standby gasoline rationing plan to Congress, with the provision that it could go into effect unless Congress did not approve it. The vote on disapproval came in July and narrowly failed. The plan thereby became available, to be called upon in the event of a supply emergency equal to a shortfall in gasoline of 20% or more.

On the international scene in June the leaders of the seven major industrial nations of the non-Communist world met in Venice, Italy, at an "economic summit." They pledged to "break the existing link between economic growth and consumption of oil" through conservation; to increase the use of coal and nuclear energy in the medium term; and to place greater reliance on synthetic fuels, solar energy, and other renewable energy sources over the long term.

Evidence that the international shift to coal was already under way was afforded by a massive backup that occurred during the year at U.S. coal-export facilities in the Norfolk, Va., area. So great was the demand for coal by importing countries that ships were waiting for more than a month to be loaded.

In March Venezuela and the U.S. signed an agreement providing for technical and scientific cooperation between the two countries on energy development projects, the first arrangement of its kind between the U.S. and a less developed country. In August Mexico and Venezuela announced a program of cooperation between the two to ease

The Louisiana Offshore Oil Port, the first U.S. deepwater port to receive supertankers, was scheduled to be fully operational in 1981. The $640 million project features a direct pipeline connection between a pumping station 19 miles at sea in the Gulf of Mexico and inland storage areas.
THE NEW YORK TIMES

UPI

A new entry in the burgeoning field of windmill design was the Giromill, which began generating electricity in August in Colorado.

the crushing financial burden of oil imports on nine of the poor countries of Central America and the Caribbean. Under the plan these nations would pay Mexico and Venezuela the world price for all the oil they needed, but 30% of the payments would be returned as low-interest loans. Also in August the World Bank announced a program to nearly double its lending to less developed countries in order to aid them in maximizing their production of energy from domestic sources.

GERMANY

The West German electorate voted on October 5 for moderation. The coalition government led by Chancellor Helmut Schmidt was confirmed in power with a substantially increased majority. Franz-Josef Strauss, the chancellor candidate of the opposition, lost because most voters considered him too far right of centre.

For the federal chancellor, Helmut Schmidt, it was an impressive personal victory, even though his Social Democratic Party's performance was disappointing. Schmidt fought the election as the head of a coalition that had sworn to stick together, and the 11-year-old alliance emerged with a majority of 45 seats as compared with 10 in the previous Bundestag (lower house of the federal Parliament).

The chancellor made détente, relations with Eastern Europe (the *Ostpolitik*), and foreign policy generally the main issues of his campaign. In the appalling event of war in Central Europe, he said, West Germany would be hit first—and hardest. He claimed that the Eastern treaties, concluded in the early 1970s with the Soviet Union, Poland, and East Germany, had created a more relaxed situation, brought the two German states closer together, and enabled many thousands of ethnic Germans to leave Eastern Europe and settle in the West.

Negotiations between the Social Democrats and coalition Free Democrats on the government's program for the new four-year term were mainly concerned with money. The 1981 budget was to grow by a mere 4.1%, and severe limitations were imposed on further state borrowing, and all government departments were to cut spending.

Defense expenditure could not be increased by 3% in real terms in 1981, as agreed upon by West Germany and the U.S. in 1978. The government said that if it stuck to the 3% target, it would have to cut back heavily on social welfare with the risk of causing domestic unrest. It was admitted that the delivery of vital new weapons systems to the forces, such as the Tornado multirole combat aircraft and the Leopard II tank, would be slowed down. In reply, the U.S. not only insisted that West Germany stick to its target but also requested the Germans to make a hefty financial contribution toward stocking up supply bases for a possible reinforcement of U.S. troops in an emergency.

The federal government found it necessary during the year to build a dike against the rising tide of foreigners seeking political asylum in West Germany. Approximately 150,000 applications had been lodged by the end of 1980, ten times as many as in 1977. Fewer than 10% of them were approved, be-

Soviet leader Leonid Brezhnev (left) and Premier Aleksey Kosygin (centre) greeted West German Chancellor Helmut Schmidt when he arrived in Moscow in June.

VLADIMIR MUSAELYAN—TASS/SOVFOTO

On September 26 a terrorist bomb, placed by a member of a neo-Nazi group, went off near the crowded entrance to the Oktoberfest in Munich. Twelve people, including the bomber, were killed and more than 200 were injured.
UPI

cause most were not fleeing from political persecution but from unemployment and poverty. Well over half of them were Turks, and the rest included large numbers from Pakistan, India, Ethiopia, Afghanistan, and Vietnam, many having paid fees to unscrupulous agents at home for misleading advice. A fundamental reform of the asylum laws was postponed to the next Bundestag, but preliminary deterrent measures were rushed through: applicants would not be given work permits, at least for the first year of their stay in West Germany, nor would they receive children's allowances.

The security authorities had been bracing themselves for a terrorist attack during the autumn election campaign. But when it came, in the shape of a bomb that killed 12 people and injured more than 200 at the Munich Oktoberfest on September 26, it came, unexpectedly, from the extreme right. The bomb was planted by Gundolf Köhler, who was killed in the blast, but he was believed not to have acted alone. Köhler had been connected with an extreme right-wing group called Wehrsportgruppe Hoffmann.

German right-wing extremism in 1980 was disunited but increasingly militant. Some two million foreign workers in West Germany (plus as many dependents) and the influx of foreigners asking for political asylum fostered the distrust and fear of outsiders on which the extreme right fed. In 1980 five explosions were caused on property owned or occupied by Jews or foreigners. In August two Vietnamese were killed in an explosion at a hostel for "boat people" refugees in Hamburg.

Pope John Paul II visited West Germany November 15–19, the first papal visit to the land of the Reformation for nearly 200 years. The event raised a good deal of theological dust. Unflattering references to Martin Luther in a booklet published by the German Roman Catholic bishops caused offense among Protestants. And there was some bitter comment about St. Albert the Great (c. 1200–80), at whose tomb in Cologne the pope paid homage. A Catholic woman theologian denounced St. Albert as a woman hater and a persecutor of Jews.

West Germany supported U.S. policy in the Afghanistan and Iran crises with great reluctance and to the accompaniment of a chorus of criticism of U.S. Pres. Jimmy Carter. In regard to the Olympic Games in Moscow, West Germany held that it was up to the Soviet Union "to create the conditions which will enable teams from all countries to take part," which meant that Soviet troops would have to first pull out of Afghanistan. Not until April 23, when the Soviets had failed to do so, did the federal government grudgingly recommend that the national Olympics committee boycott the Games.

During the year West Germany played a leading role in arranging a big international aid package to Turkey in order to strengthen NATO's southern flank. And it also undertook to place further restrictions on the export of high-technology equipment to the Soviet Union.

On June 30 Schmidt visited Moscow for talks with Soviet leader Leonid Brezhnev. The chancellor's public condemnation of the Soviet invasion of Afghanistan was tough enough to be censored by *Pravda*. Reporting to the Bundestag, Schmidt said that the differences between his government and the Soviet leaders on the Afghanistan issue were not bridged in the Moscow talks but that Brezhnev had offered to open talks with the U.S. on a limitation of nuclear forces in Europe. Schmidt described this proposal as new and constructive.

Throughout the Polish crisis West Germany pursued a policy of noninterference and, indeed, strove to restore stability to Poland by administering powerful injections of hard currency. On October 10 an agreement was signed to grant Poland a DM 1.2 billion ($663 million) credit. West Germany's assistance had an overriding motive—to deter the Soviet Union and, for that matter, East Germany, from military intervention in Poland.

East Germany

Early in 1980 it seemed that the East German government was just as concerned as West Germany that the freeze in relations between the superpowers following the Soviet invasion of Afghanistan should have as little effect as possible on links between the two German states. But the East German attitude changed later in the year with the outbreak of unrest in neighbouring Poland. *Abgrenzung*, withdrawal into the shell, again became the guiding principle of East German foreign policy. On October 13 the authorities greatly increased the minimum amount of money that had to be exchanged at the border by visitors from the West, and in subsequent weeks the normal number of visitors who crossed the borders into East Berlin and East Germany fell by about 60%. This was a blow at the very heart of the West German government's *Deutschlandpolitik*, aimed at increasing contacts between the people of a divided nation.

In late October East Germany announced the temporary suspension of visa-free travel to and from Poland, a clear sign of its increasing nervousness at the possible spread of the "Polish disease." The government also announced that the experiment with summer (daylight savings) time in 1980 was not to be continued in 1981. The time switch, it appeared, saved less energy than expected, and some teachers expressed concern about its effect on schoolchildren. West Germany had long resisted the European Economic Community's efforts to arrange a common summer time throughout the Community, mainly to avoid being on a different time from East Germany. But West Germany did not plan to abandon summer time. There would now be difficulties in timetabling intra-German traffic, and the time difference would be most keenly felt in the divided city of Berlin.

Nevertheless, the East German government was anxious to maintain close economic ties with West Germany. The East Germans needed export surpluses and loans. East German leader Erich Honecker was intensely disappointed that the West German chancellor, Helmut Schmidt, postponed the trip he was to have made to East Germany in August. Later in the year, in November, Honecker visited Austria, his first official visit to a Western country.

GOLF

Although Jack Nicklaus confounded those who thought that his conquering years were over by winning the U.S. Open and the Professional Golfers' Association (PGA) championships, Tom Watson

qualified as player of the year for the fourth successive season. With official winnings of $530,808, Watson became the first golfer to win more than $500,000 in one year and only the third, behind Nicklaus and Lee Trevino, to pass the $2 million mark in career earnings. Watson's most notable victories were the British Open for the third time and the World Series, but Trevino denied him success in the Vardon Trophy for best average number of strokes per round, which Watson had won the previous three years. Trevino's average was 69.73, fractionally better than Watson's and the lowest in 25 years.

When Nicklaus tied for 33rd in the Masters at Augusta, Ga., fears that he was near retirement seemed to be confirmed. Experiments to improve his play seemed to be fruitless, so two months later the whole golf world was astonished when he and Tom Weiskopf tore apart the Baltusrol course at Springfield, N.J., with 63s in the opening round of the U.S. Open. With a final score of 272 Nicklaus beat his own Open record set on the same course in 1967 by three strokes. It was his fourth U.S. Open victory, equaling the record of Willie Anderson, Bobby Jones, and Ben Hogan.

Throughout the championship Nicklaus played

Jack Nicklaus watches his final putt roll home on the 18th green to put the seal on his victory, his fourth, in the U.S. Open.
FRED R. CONRAD—THE NEW YORK TIMES

with Isao Aoki of Japan, who kept the pressure on him until the very end. Aoki's unorthodox swing and method of putting with the toe of the club in the air had fascinated watchers. With a round to go he and Nicklaus were tied and, as Watson, Lon Hinkle, and Keith Fergus, who tied for third, just failed to set a telling pace, Aoki was the last threat. He remained so until Nicklaus scored a birdie on the 71st hole, but Aoki finished only two behind and also broke the old record. Both players won an extra $50,000 each, offered by *Golf Magazine* for breaking the record.

The one sour note of the Open was the failure of Severiano Ballesteros to read correctly his starting time for the second day. He arrived on the first tee minutes late and was disqualified, a pathetic anticlimax to the glory he had achieved by becoming the youngest player and the first from Europe to win the Masters. His victory at Augusta was one of the most masterly in the history of that event. An opening round of 66 gave him a share of the lead with David Graham of Australia, and when he followed with 69 and 68 the rest of the field fell far behind. Jack Newton of Australia sustained his

Amy Alcott's nine-stroke victory in the women's U.S. Open, for a total of 280 strokes, set a record for the competition.
© 1980 DUOMO

challenge bravely and shared second place with Gibby Gilbert.

At the British Open, Watson and Trevino gave swift notice of their intentions at Muirfield, Scotland, with rounds of 68 on an opening day beset with cold and heavy rain. Ideally, the fairest of British championship links should have played fast and firm, but the rain changed all that and made it into a target exercise. On the second morning Horacio Carbonetti of Argentina scored a 64, but 78s on either side of it caused him to miss the cut for the final day. In the third round, Watson went to work with a superb 64, while Trevino, who had appeared to be in great form on the course where he had won in 1972, was taking 71. Aoki's magic returned for one round, but his 63 could not compensate for a moderate start. The previous evening Nicklaus had lost some impetus with a disappointing finish when a 65 seemed probable. An untidy start the next day left him too far behind, and when in the bitter grayness of the last afternoon Trevino missed early shots, Watson was left in almost total command. His total of 271, four lower than Trevino's, had only twice been beaten, by himself and Nicklaus in their historic encounter at Turnberry in 1977. Ben Crenshaw, second the previous two years, finished third and so his frustration continued. Nicklaus shared fourth place with Carl Mason, the leading British player.

A relaxed, confident Nicklaus mastered everyone in the PGA championship at Oak Hill. The only faint challenges came first from Lon Hinkle and finally from Andy Bean, but with 274 Nicklaus won by seven strokes. It was his fifth PGA victory, equaling the record of Walter Hagen, and his 19th major championship as a professional.

As if determined not to be outdone, Watson stormed home in the World Series of Golf at Akron, Ohio, with three rounds of 65 and one 75. Ray Floyd, Jerry Pate, Trevino, and Hale Irwin gave chase, but Watson, playing with enormous confidence, yielded nothing. Nicklaus injured his back in practice before the last round and had to withdraw, but at that point he was six strokes behind. Even he could not have caught Watson, whose golf throughout the year was wonderfully consistent, his swing superbly balanced and strong, and his putting often lethal.

In women's professional golf Amy Alcott won the U.S. Open at Nashville, Tenn., by nine strokes. Her total of 280 was also a record for the championship. Hollis Stacy, champion in 1977 and 1978, was second. On the tour the most successful players apart from Alcott were Beth Daniel—who, in only her second year as a professional, became the first player ever to win in one year over $200,000 in official prize money; Donna Caponi Young; Nancy Lopez-Melton, leading money winner the previous two years; and JoAnne Carner. By her victory in the last event of the year, in Japan, Alcott overtook Daniel in the race for leading money winner.

As the British economy sagged lower and lower, demonstrators gathered at Brighton in October during the Conservative Party's rank-and-file convention to press their demands for jobs and to register dissatisfaction with Prime Minister Margaret Thatcher's economic policies.

UPI

GREAT BRITAIN

In 1980 the British economy became engulfed in its deepest recession since the 1930s, and in August unemployment topped the two million mark. Combating inflation, however, remained the first priority of the Conservative Party government of Prime Minister Margaret Thatcher, and control of the money supply continued to be the chief instrument of her economic policy.

Foreign Affairs

World events impinged heavily upon British politics, in the shadow of the Soviet invasion of Afghanistan and against the background of the drama in Iran, where more than 50 U.S. diplomats had been held hostage since Nov. 4, 1979. These twin crises complicated the government's endeavours to strike a balance between Britain's traditional friendship with the U.S. and its membership in the politically conscious European Economic Community (EEC). The Soviet invasion's Christmas and New Year holiday timing made it difficult for the Atlantic allies to coordinate their response to it. Mrs. Thatcher ordered "100% support" for U.S. Pres. Jimmy Carter when he called for economic sanctions against the Soviet Union and a boycott of the Olympic Games in Moscow.

Lord Carrington, the British foreign secretary, subsequently regretted that his first reaction to the crisis had been to embark upon a tour of South and Southwest Asia (he visited Turkey, Saudi Arabia, Oman, Pakistan, and India) rather than to consult his European counterparts. By contrast the first move made by France and West Germany was to get together in Paris. The result, made worse by some U.S. clumsiness, was a spectacle of allied disarray that left Britain open to the traditional accusation of being a U.S. stooge. Carrington, at the meeting of the EEC foreign ministers in Rome on

Feb. 19, 1980, put forward proposals (which were adopted) for the neutralization of Afghanistan to be accompanied by a withdrawal of Soviet forces. This plan established a more united approach to the crisis by the EEC.

After considerable debate a limited version of the U.S.-proposed sanctions was agreed upon by the EEC on April 22. However, this proposal met with such disapproval in the British Parliament, including a threatened rebellion by Conservative backbenchers (rank-and-file members), that the government decided to further soften its sanctions against Iran.

EEC solidarity was made difficult by the festering issue of the British contribution to the EEC budget, a problem that in the financial year 1979–80 had resulted in Britain, though the third poorest member of the EEC, becoming the largest net contributor to its funds. That net contribution amounted to £1,100 million, and at a rancorous meeting of the European Council in Dublin on Nov. 29–30, 1979, Prime Minister Thatcher had demanded Britain's money back. When the European Council eventually met again in Luxembourg on April 27–28, 1980, Thatcher was offered a rebate worth about £800 million, as compared with the £350 million proposed at Dublin. Still she turned the offer down, partly because the arrangements did not guarantee a sufficient longer term reduction. The matter was settled by the EEC foreign ministers at a marathon meeting in Brussels on May 29–30. A combined repayment of some £1,570 million was agreed upon for 1980 and 1981 with a firm commitment of a similar arrangement for 1982. Thatcher called it a day, and a victory.

British policy within the EEC then concentrated on the long-term reform of the common agricultural policy (from which Britain benefited little) and the structural reform of the organization's budget, which would become unavoidable when it ran out of funds sometime in 1981. Relations in Europe quickly improved, although the "war" with France over British exports of lamb was not ended until September 30 and British tourists made headlines in August when they demonstrated their chauvinistic feelings toward the French after being inconvenienced by an industrial dispute affecting the Channel ports. At the highest level, however, Anglo-French relations took a turn for the better when Prime Minister Thatcher met President Valéry Giscard d'Estaing in Paris on September 19 and, during a similar visit to West Germany in November, both she and Lord Carrington made plainer than ever before Britain's commitment to the European Community.

When the year began, a British Cabinet minister, Lord Soames, was already installed as governor in Zimbabwe Rhodesia to preside over the implementation of the so-called Lancaster House agreement of Dec. 5, 1979, to secure that country's transition to legal independence. After considerable intimidation on all sides, the agreed-upon elections took place on March 4, 1980, and resulted in the choice of a Marxist freedom fighter, Robert Mugabe, to head the first government of an independent Zimbabwe. The result was accepted in Britain with scarcely a murmur, and Prince Charles attended the independence ceremonies in Salisbury on April 18.

Domestic Affairs

The year 1980 began with a major industrial dispute. The strike in the nationalized steel industry was the first in that sector of the economy since the general strike in 1926. The 13-week strike (January 2–April 1) was made more difficult to resolve by interunion rivalries and a lack of confidence in the management of the British Steel Corp. (BSC). The dispute was ostensibly about pay, with the virtually bankrupt BSC's 6% annual wage increase offer—2% of which was largely a consolidation of supple-

ments already being paid and the other 4% for acceptance of cost-reduction measures—adding insult to the injury of proposed closings that would do away with 52,000 jobs by August 1. The two issues, pay and jobs, became intertwined. The government, at the insistence of the secretary of state for industry, Sir Keith Joseph, refused to be drawn directly into the dispute and insisted that the BSC must live within its cash limit of £450 million; in the end the BSC reported losses for the financial year ending in March totaling £1,800 million. In September the government bailed it out temporarily with an additional aid package, bringing the total amount of aid for the financial year ending March 31, 1981, to about £970 million, and in November a major financial reconstruction was promised. Meanwhile, the strike had been settled with an annual wage increase of 15.5%, and the closings went ahead, with production ceasing in Corby and Shotton steel towns. Ian MacGregor was appointed to succeed Sir Charles Villiers as BSC chairman. On December 10 MacGregor announced plans for a further series of closings with the loss of an additional 20,000 or more jobs.

The steel dispute illustrated the difficulties faced by the government in controlling the money supply and in pursuing its market-oriented policies under conditions of deepening recession. It also posed a question as to the limits to social tolerance of rapid structural adaptation in a deteriorating economic atmosphere. Sir Geoffrey Howe, chancellor of the Exchequer, used his budget on March 26 to reaffirm determination to bring down inflation by control of government borrowing and of the growth in the money supply. Extra taxes were imposed on alcohol, tobacco, and gasoline, but for the City of London and the financial commentators the budget's chief importance lay in the announcement of a medium-term financial strategy. This, for the first time, stated the government's monetary targets over a period of four years. In spite of continuing

A bright spot in the year was the celebration of Queen Mother Elizabeth's 80th birthday; the sentimental outpouring proved that the British still loved their "royals."
UPI

Britain's Labour Party meeting in Blackpool September 29–October 3 was marked by clashes between the left and right wings of the party. Later in October party leader James Callaghan resigned and was replaced in November by Michael Foot.

JACOB SUTTON—GAMMA/LIAISON

recession and inflation the path set was a downward one; it would intensify the squeeze on the economy and seemed certain to lead to more unemployment and bankruptcies.

The government could not achieve its targets for financial year 1980–81. The near explosion of the money supply during the summer months was due in part to technical banking reasons, but more fundamental was the cost of public-sector wage settlements and the expensive consequences of the recession itself. By August unemployment figures had exceeded two million and were moving upward. In order to restore the public expenditure limits for 1981–82 the Treasury needed a further £2,000 million of net economies. The Cabinet was unable to agree on departmental cuts on such a scale, which meant that a substantial increase in taxation was required. Howe made a start in November by announcing an increase in the national insurance contribution, the government's first departure from its promises to be a tax-reducing government.

Combating inflation remained the first priority, and at least that was coming down faster than the official forecasts had expected. Announcing measures on November 24, the chancellor reduced the minimum lending rate from 16% (to 14%) in the hope that this would help to relieve the burden of a high exchange rate on Britain's exporting industries. The exchange rate and high interest rates had been the chief causes of complaint from industry, which peaked at the annual conference of the Confederation of British Industry (CBI) in early November.

Further rises in unemployment reported at the time of the chancellor's November package caused a parliamentary furor. Nevertheless, there were no signs yet of abandonment by the government of its stringent monetarism or of adoption of measures to arrest or reverse recession.

The recession affected the atmosphere of industrial relations. After the round of wage increases that ended in August, earnings were ahead of inflation. In the private sector they were up by 20.6%, and in the public sector by 25.6%. The average overall increase was 22%, which compared with a 16.3% increase in prices over the same period. But from early in the year there were signs of a new moderation entering into collective bargaining. The number of working days lost through strikes was at its lowest in 14 years.

At British Leyland, fighting for its existence, workers in February rejected a management offer of a 5–10% pay increase. Management nevertheless imposed the increase in March, causing some 18,400 workers to strike for more than a week in April. Later in the year a 6.8% pay increase was at first rejected, but after a threatened strike was averted the work force accepted the increase. In the private sector there were signs of a willingness to settle for less than 10%, and the 1980–81 wages round started promisingly with two million engineering workers settling at 8.2%; the coal miners, always a key bargaining group, voted for acceptance of a 13% settlement recommended by their leaders.

For the Labour Party the year was one of turmoil. The left-controlled National Executive Committee, in which Tony Benn played a prominent role, kept up a running ideological and organizational battle with the party leadership under James Callaghan. Callaghan resigned as party leader on October 15. It was generally expected that his successor would be Denis Healey, former chancellor of the Exchequer. However, the position went to Michael Foot, a leading left-winger and, at 67, a year younger than Callaghan. Unlike Healey, Foot was broadly in sympathy with the policy decisions taken by the party conference, held in Blackpool on September 29–October 3, favouring Britain's leaving the European Community, a policy of unilateral nuclear disarmament, and an economic strategy of nationalization, state intervention, and trade protection.

The defense issue came to the fore in British politics in 1980, with fear of a nuclear holocaust generated in the Middle East. NATO's decision in December 1979 to deploy cruise and Pershing II missiles in Western European countries aroused new fears of becoming a Soviet target in a limited or preemptive war. The failure of the U.S. to ratify SALT II and the acceleration of the arms race by the U.S. and U.S.S.R. added to alarm. Finally, the government announced in July that it would (as expected) replace the Polaris submarine missile system with the Trident I at a cost of £5,000 million, reopening the nuclear-arms-in-Britain issue. Resentment about additional defense spending at a time of cuts in social spending drew support to the Campaign for Nuclear Disarmament, which in October, after the Labour conference had repudiated defense policies involving nuclear weapons, staged a massive rally in London.

It was a bad year for the newspaper industry. London in November became a city with only one evening paper when the *Evening News* and the *Evening Standard*, old rivals, merged to form the *New Standard*. The job loss was 1,750. More alarming still was the announcement on October 22 that unless buyers could be found for *The Times* and *The Sunday Times*, both would be closed by March 1981, at a cost of 4,000 jobs. (*See* Newspapers.)

The most exciting moment of the year occurred on May 5 when millions of television viewers saw live pictures of the spectacular relief of the Iranian embassy in London by armed and hooded commandos of the Special Air Services (SAS). The embassy had been occupied on April 30 by six terrorists who were demanding a degree of autonomy for the Arabic-speaking Khuzistan Province of Iran and the release of 91 political prisoners there. The gunmen originally held 26 hostages inside the embassy, and it was when one of them (the press attaché) was shot and thrown through the door that the commandos, swinging on ropes and discharging explosives, went in. Five terrorists and one more of the hostages were killed. One terrorist was captured. The successful escapade became a matter of national self-satisfaction.

Northern Ireland

The year brought little hope for Northern Ireland, where sectarian violence continued. Talks aimed at restoring a semblance of local government ("devolution") to the province came to nothing. The Rev. Ian Paisley's Democratic Unionist Party remained adamantly opposed to any form of power sharing or any attempt to achieve closer relations with the Republic of Ireland. The predominantly Roman Catholic Social Democratic and Labour Party, for its part, was equally opposed to any return to local—that is, Protestant—majority rule. When the new session of Parliament opened in November, it became plain from the silence of the queen's speech that the government had shelved its hopes of legislating new constitutional arrangements for the province. Some progress was made during the year in reducing the number of British troops and restoring responsibility for law and order to the Royal Ulster Constabulary, but no end was in sight to direct rule from London with the aid of the British Army.

Despite a hunger strike begun October 27 by seven prisoners at Maze prison near Belfast, the government refused to treat convicted members of the Irish Republican Army as political prisoners. It was feared that there would be a violent reaction if any of the prisoners died, but the strike was called off December 18.

In May and December, in London and Dublin, respectively, Thatcher and Charles Haughey, prime minister of Ireland, met to discuss Northern Ireland, but no positive results emerged.

(*See also* Ireland.)

GREECE

The election of Prime Minister Konstantinos Karamanlis as president of the republic on May 5 and the military reintegration of Greece into the NATO alliance on October 20 were the most significant events of 1980. Both were expected to have long-lasting effects on the country's internal situation and its external relations.

The withdrawal of Karamanlis from day-to-day politics enhanced the electoral chances of the main opposition party, the Panhellenic Socialist Movement (Pasok) led by Andreas Papandreou. Not only did Pasok no longer need to fear this formidable opponent, but the reassuring presence of Karamanlis at the top might also encourage voters to opt for political change. The possibility that the anti-Western Pasok might come to power influenced the speed with which Greece returned to the integrated military structure of NATO, from which it had withdrawn in 1974 in protest against Turkey's invasion of Cyprus. From 1978 Turkey had blocked Greece's reinstatement, demanding a share of NATO operational jurisdiction in the Aegean.

Karamanlis was elected president on May 5 by the Greek Parliament with 183 votes, 3 above the three-fifths majority required on the third ballot. Pasok (93 members in Parliament) refused to vote on the grounds that Parliament, elected in 1977, no longer reflected the current will of the electorate. Pasok accepted the legality of Karamanlis's election, however. Three days afterward, the parliamentary group of the ruling New Democracy Party

Former Greek prime minister Konstantinos Karamanlis (hand on Bible) was sworn into office as president on May 15 while the new prime minister, Georgios Rallis (centre), looked on.
KEYSTONE

met and, in accordance with the democratic procedures adopted in 1979, elected a new leader. The choice went to the moderate foreign minister, Georgios Rallis, who received 88 votes to 84 for Defense Minister Evangelos Averoff-Tossizza, representing the party's conservative wing. Rallis was appointed prime minister the next day, May 9.

The Rallis Cabinet, which took over on May 10, consisted largely of ministers who had served on the Karamanlis team. A few changes suggested readjustments in the unpopular anti-inflationary policies adopted earlier in the year. The new government also took a tougher stand on the question of NATO reintegration. The U.S. was informed that the continued presence of the important U.S. military bases in Greece depended on the early readmission of Greece to NATO's military wing. The Greek threat coincided with a worsening situation in the Middle East and the Persian Gulf area and came just as Turkey's new military leaders were eager to eliminate any distractions on their western flank. In these circumstances, Gen. Bernard Rogers, NATO supreme allied commander, Europe, was able to induce both sides, separately, to agree to negotiate their contested jurisdiction of the Aegean after Greece had rejoined the alliance. The breakthrough was achieved on October 17, and on October 20 NATO had approved Greece's return under a formula that was kept secret but that satisfied the Greeks more than the Turks.

Hopes that the September military takeover in Turkey would ease the resolution of Greek-Turkish differences led to a resumption on October 5 of the bilateral dialogue on the Aegean continental shelf and its airspace. A unilateral Turkish gesture of February 22 had led to the resumption of civil aviation flights across the Aegean, which had been interrupted for six years. The military reintegration of Greece into NATO opened the way for a revision of the U.S.-Greek agreement on U.S. military bases. The new agreement would regulate the status of the U.S. installations as well as the kind of U.S. military assistance Greece would receive. The main Greek concern was that the balance of power between Greece and Turkey not be disturbed.

Greece was scheduled for full membership in the European Economic Community (EEC) as of Jan. 1, 1981. One cause for concern in connection with EEC membership was that the Greek economy was already experiencing some balance of payments difficulties, and the inflation rate threatened to match the 25% leap of 1979. A gentleman's agreement with Greek importers for "self-restraint" held the Greek imports bill (already overloaded with soaring oil costs) in check. Internal economic adjustments in the second half of the year led to increased bank deposits, a slight slowing of the inflation rate, and the elimination of some state subsidies. However, productive investment continued to lag, despite generous incentives, and for the first time in recent years there was a marked increase in unemployment. On November 6 the government granted the trade unions' demand for a five-day workweek, to be introduced on Jan. 1, 1981.

GUATEMALA

The political situation in Guatemala in 1980 continued to deteriorate as polarization between left and right increased. There were occasional acts of violence, causing human rights organizations to protest. The chief victims of right-wing extremist groups were trade union and student leaders and key members of the United Revolutionary Front (FUR), the principal social democratic opposition

SYGMA

Thirty-nine leftist protesters and their hostages were killed in January when fire engulfed the Spanish embassy in Guatemala City during a police raid on the building.

group. In May formation of the Patriotic Liberation Front unified the left-wing opposition.

On January 31 a group of Indian peasants from the Quiché region occupied the Spanish embassy in a protest against repression; police stormed the buildings, and during the raid a gasoline bomb was thrown that resulted in a fire that took 39 lives. Be-

cause the police intervention had occurred against the wishes of the ambassador, the Spanish government severed diplomatic relations on February 1.

In September Vice-Pres. Francisco Villagrán Kramer resigned, charging right-wing elements in the government with adopting a policy of violation of human rights. In February he had withdrawn a resignation he had previously tendered.

No agreement was negotiated regarding Guatemala's claim to parts of the neighbouring British colony of Belize. Britain maintained a military presence in Belize, while Guatemala's foreign minister, Rafael Castillo Valdez, reiterated on November 13 that Guatemala would never permit the unilateral independence of the colony.

GYMNASTICS

Soviet athletes dominated the 1980 Olympic competitions, but spectators could hardly forget that world class gymnasts from Japan and the U.S. did not participate because their respective Olympic committees voted to boycott the Games in Moscow. When the final event was over, gymnasts from the U.S.S.R. had won both team titles, four of the seven gold medals awarded to men, and three of the six gold medals given to women. The latter included one first-place tie. Aleksandr Dityatin, who placed first in the all-around and on the rings, finished second on the parallel bars, the horizontal bar, the side horse, and in the vault; he also won a bronze medal in the floor exercise. Counting the first-place gold medal given to members of the Soviet men's team, Dityatin garnered an unprecedented eight medals during the 1980 Games. Gold medals were also won by Roland Bruckner

Winner of the American Cup gymnastics championship was Kurt Thomas. He scored a perfect 10 on the horizontal bar in the March competition.
WIDE WORLD

(East Germany) in the floor exercise, by Stoyan Deltchev (Bulg.) on the horizontal bar, and by Aleksandr Tkachyov (U.S.S.R.) on the parallel bars. Nikolay Andrianov (U.S.S.R.), the star of the 1976 Olympic Games, retained his title in the vault. And Zoltan Magyar (Hung.), world champion on the side horse, repeated his 1976 Olympic victory by winning a gold medal with an outstanding performance. Dityatin became the first male gymnast to receive a perfect score of ten from Olympic judges. He received the mark for his execution of the vault in the all-around. During that same competition, tens were also awarded to Deltchev on the rings, to Tkachyov on the horizontal bar, and to Magyar and Michael Nikolay (East Germany) on the side horse. Both the male and female gymnasts took advantage of a new rule to earn bonus points by introducing risk, originality, and virtuosity into their optional exercises.

The women's team competition was a replay of the 1976 Montreal Games: the U.S.S.R. team took the gold medal, Romania the silver, and East Germany the bronze. In individual events, however, new names appeared. Yelena Davydova (U.S.S.R.) finished first in the demanding all-around; Nadia Comaneci (Rom.) and 15-year-old Maxi Gnauck (East Germany) tied for second. Comaneci, however, retained her Olympic title on the balance beam but failed to place on the uneven bars. Gnauck won that event and Natalya Shaposhnikova (U.S.S.R.) the vault. Two gold and two bronze medals were awarded in the floor exercise. Nelli Kim (U.S.S.R.) and Comaneci tied for first place with scores of 19.875, and Shaposhnikova and Gnauck shared third-place honours with identical 19.825 scores.

The U.S., which boycotted the Games, had developed its most versatile gymnasts in history. Bart Conner, Kurt Thomas, and James Hartung had already gained recognition as world-class athletes.

Kathy Johnson was generally considered the most polished U.S. female gymnast, followed by Marcia Frederick.

(*See also* Olympic Games.)

HONDURAS

On April 20, 1980, elections for a 71-member Constituent Assembly were held. The Liberal Party unexpectedly gained 52% of the votes but not a clear majority in the assembly, and the Innovation and Unity Party (PINU) held the balance of power with 3.5%; the National Party, linked with the armed forces, had 44.5%. Some three-quarters of the electorate voted, despite an abstention campaign by the left-wing Honduran Patriotic Front, a grouping of about 50 organizations ineligible to take part in the campaign.

The U.S. encouraged civilian rule in Honduras, doubling its economic aid for 1980 to $45 million. It also allocated $3.9 million in military aid, to create in Honduras a buffer state between Nicaragua, El Salvador, and Guatemala.

Relations with Nicaragua underwent a period of strain at the end of 1979 owing to the use of the border area by former members of Nicaragua's National Guard. However, during 1980 diplomatic relations, severed in mid-1979, were resumed. In October Honduras and El Salvador agreed on a treaty ending the state of war that had lasted since the so-called Soccer War of 1969.

The nation's gross domestic product grew by 6.7% in 1979, a decline from 8.9% in 1978. Based on the official cost-of-living index, inflation grew by 8.5%, although the actual rate was nearer to 14%.

HORSE RACING

Among the highlights of the 1980 Thoroughbred racing season were the victory of Genuine Risk in the Kentucky Derby and the triumphs by Spectacu-

Genuine Risk, ridden by Jacinto Vasquez, became the first filly to win the Kentucky Derby since 1915.
UPI

lar Bid in nine starts, all stakes races. Mrs. Bertram R. Firestone's Genuine Risk not only was the second filly ever to win the Kentucky Derby (Regret won in 1915) but also was the only filly ever to compete in all of the Triple Crown events. She finished second to Codex in a controversial Preakness, in which winning jockey Angel Cordero, Jr., was charged with forcing her to run wide on the final turn; and she was runner-up to Temperence Hill in the Belmont Stakes. The stout filly finished third to Plugged Nickle and Colonel Moran in the Wood Memorial. Her other major victory besides the Kentucky Derby came in her last race of the season, the Ruffian Handicap against older fillies and mares.

Despite her unique record, Genuine Risk did not go unchallenged before being named the season's three-year-old filly champion and Eclipse Award winner—Bold'N Determined won 8 stakes races in 12 starts. In the Maskette, the only meeting between the two, Bold'N Determined defeated Genuine Risk by a nose while conceding her four pounds (1 lb = 0.45 kg).

Hawksworth Farm's four-year-old Spectacular Bid earned a third consecutive Eclipse Award as champion of his division and for the first time also was crowned horse of the year. Spectacular Bid won six stakes races in California. The Woodward at Belmont Park was a walkover that climaxed a bizarre series of events in the Triple Crown of handicap races (the Marlboro, the Woodward, and the Jockey Club Gold Cup). Sponsors of the Marlboro were dismayed when Spectacular Bid's owners rejected their horse's 136-lb weight assignment, 4 lb more than his previous high and 13 lb more than the weight assigned rival Winter's Tale. Winter's Tale won the Marlboro easily. The Woodward became a walkover for Spectacular Bid when a leg injury sidelined Winter's Tale for the season and the only two other entrants, Temperence Hill and Dr. Patches, were scratched. Two weeks later, only

minutes before post time, Spectacular Bid himself was scratched from the race because of a leg problem, and Temperence Hill won the Jockey Club Gold Cup to clinch the championship of the three-year-old colt or gelding division. Spectacular Bid retired with earnings of $2,781,607 to surpass the all-time record of $2,393,818 established by Affirmed the previous year.

Temperence Hill, owned by Loblolly Stable, also numbered the Belmont and Travers among his eight victories. The late-running colt had 1980 earnings of $1,130,452, tops for all Thoroughbreds.

Other Eclipse Award winners were SKS Stable's Lord Avie in the two-year-old colt or gelding division; Ryehill Farm's Heavenly Cause, two-year-old filly; Frank Stronach and Nelson Bunker Hunt's Glorious Song, older filly or mare; Dotsam Stable's John Henry, male turf horse; Peter Brant and Joseph Allen's Just A Game II, female turf horse; John M. Schiff's Plugged Nickle, sprinter; and Mrs. Lewis Murdock's Zaccio, steeplechaser. Trainer Bud Delp, owners Mr. and Mrs. Bertram Firestone, jockey Chris McCarron, apprentice jockey Frank Lovato, Jr., and breeder Mrs. Henry D. Paxson also won Eclipse Awards.

In the Triple Crown races for Canadian-foaled three-year-olds, sponsored by the Ontario Jockey Club, Driving Home won the Queen's Plate, Allan Blue was victor in the Prince of Wales Stakes, and Ben Fab triumphed in the Breeder's Stakes. Par Excellance won the Canadian Oaks and Great Neck the Canadian International.

In harness racing, three-year-old champion Niatross won the pacing Triple Crown, established world records on half-mile tracks (1 min 54.8 sec) when winning the Little Brown Jug, and became the first pacer to beat 1 min 50 sec, in a 1-min 49.2-sec time trial. His earnings after the Messenger were $1,825,556.

Toy Poodle and Guiding Beam set a world mile record for three-year-old fillies with 1 min 53.8 sec

Niatross, winner of the Triple Crown of harness racing, was considered to be the best Standardbred horse in the 174-year history of the sport in America.

JERRY COOKE—SPORTS ILLUSTRATED
© 1980 TIME INC.

and also jointly held the season's half-mile track records. French Chef set a new world mark of 1 min 54 sec for two-year-olds. The fastest aged pacer was Pats Gypsy, at 1 min 54 sec. The $2,011,000 Woodrow Wilson pace for two-year-olds went to Land Grant in the richest-ever harness race.

Classical Way set a new world trotting record of 1 min 55.4 sec in a time trial; the Hambletonian went to Burgomeister. The International Trot at Roosevelt was won by Classical Way from the New Zealand mare Petite Evander and the French horse Idéal du Gazeau. J. Simpson, Jr., drove the winning U.S. entry.

HOUSING

New housing starts hit a five-year low in 1980, and the frustrating fact for home builders was that there was clearly a strong housing need that was being blocked by the high mortgage rates that crippled the industry.

New starts surged 33% in June over May as mortgage interest dropped from highs of over 17% in some parts of the country toward a midsummer low of 11.5%. Starts went up another 5% in July, but the figures remained well below those of the previous year, with the July boost bringing new starts to a level still 28% below that of July 1979. However, the summer's modest improvement was reversed when mortgage rates inched upward again in the third quarter.

The irony of the high mortgage rates, at their peak doubling the rates of two years earlier, was that the age group that demanded single-family houses, people in their 30s, had never been larger. Moreover, single individuals had entered the home-buying market in unprecedented numbers. The demographics made home builders optimistic about the decade to come but offered no help in 1980. For the first eight months of the year, total single-family sales of 367,000 new houses were barely enough to work through the inventory that existed when the crunch hit in late 1979. At mid-year, builders had an 11-month supply of new houses on hand, compared with the usual four-to-five-month inventory.

Unemployment in the overall construction industry, the largest sector of the American gross national product, was 15% in the spring. One out of four workers in the residential construction area was out of work. Appliance and building materials companies, closely tied to new home sales, were also depressed. At one point Whirlpool had laid off 4,000 workers.

The clear problem was mortgage interest, combined with the general recession. House prices did continue to rise during 1980, but the price of a median home lagged slightly behind inflation, compared with the 30% jump in house prices over the previous two years. But median mortgage payments rose 48% between 1977 and 1979, according to one survey, and that was before the peak rates of the

Dallas, Texas, provided financial guarantees for homes built within two miles of downtown to draw residents back to the inner city.

spring that meant a buyer with a $60,000, 25-year mortgage loan would pay about $760 monthly.

Rental housing fared no better. It was estimated that only 261,000 rental units would be completed by year's end—46% below the number in 1978 and one-half the number the National Association of Home Builders said was needed just to replace the apartments that were converted, destroyed, or abandoned each year. As a consequence, rents continued upward, and one-bedroom apartments for over $1,000 per month in sections of New York City or San Francisco became common.

Conversions to condominiums did not continue at the pace of 1979, when 115,000 apartments were converted, primarily owing to the same reasons single-family houses sold poorly. Conversions were also blocked by city ordinances in some locations and new state laws designed to preserve the stock of rental apartments.

The way out of the housing bind was not clear by year-end. It seemed, at the least, that the fixed-rate, 25- or 30-year mortgage was a thing of the past. Rates on these loans had climbed as lenders feared

"Oh, oh—there it goes again!"

that inflation would erode any return on long-term loans. And new federal banking regulations in 1980 allowed the move of savings and loan institutions and mutual savings banks, the traditional suppliers of mortgage loans, into more short-term commercial lending.

Variable-rate and renegotiated-rate (or rollover) mortgages, in which interest rates could be ratcheted upward after one to three years, became more common as lenders sought to hedge their investment in mortgages or shorten the time of their commitments. The new mortgage types also allowed banks to start the loan out with a lower interest rate than a fixed-rate mortgage required, and some banks in 1980 began to offer nothing but rollovers. Some banks talked of introducing the "shared appreciation mortgage," which could be made at a lower rate because it gave the lender a portion of the profits when the house was resold.

The problem with rental housing appeared to be even more intractable than the single-family bind. Builders had complained for years that rent-control laws and the return on investment simply made multiunit condominium construction and conversion more attractive than rental building. Even complexes built for rental in 1980 were often earmarked for later condo conversion to make up for early losses.

HUNGARY

The 12th Congress of the Hungarian Socialist Workers' Party was held in Budapest, March 24–27, 1980. The main theme was a frank appraisal of the nation's achievements and shortcomings since the 11th congress five years earlier. Addressing the 767 delegates, Hungarian Communist Party leader Janos Kadar said: "We cannot isolate ourselves from the world economy, but by improving our work we can cushion its unfavourable impact considerably." The congress elected a new 127-member Central Committee that included 32 new faces. The Central Committee in turn named the new Politburo, which consisted of 13 members instead of the previous 15. Kadar was reelected to the post of party first secretary.

At the general election of June 8 a new Parliament of 352 members was elected by 7,462,953 votes from candidates proposed by the Patriotic People's Front (54,070 votes against). More than 100 members were nonparty. In 15 constituencies there were two candidates instead of one, and in two of those, neither candidate received over 50% of the votes and by-elections were held.

The new Parliament on June 27 reelected Antal Apro its president. The new members, one in three of whom had been elected for the first time, chose the country's Presidential Council consisting of the president of the republic, two vice-presidents, one secretary, and 17 members. Pal Losonczi was reelected president and Gyorgy Lazar again was named premier. The Parliament also approved the new government (Council of Ministers).

A two-day parliamentary debate on the country's economic situation ended on September 26. The planners had predicted that by 1980 real income would increase by 25% over 1975, but it rose by only 6%. Hungary's hard-currency exports of $3.4 billion in 1979 were $500 million below its imports.

East German Communist Party leader Erich Honecker presented the Golden Tank award to two brothers in the Hungarian Army after Warsaw Pact maneuvers.
KEYSTONE

At the end of 1979 its debt to Western commercial banks amounted to $7.3 billion, and interest payments were approximately $800 million. To reduce its debts Hungary had to increase exports and reduce imports. In this regard 1980 started encouragingly: exports to the non-Communist world in the first six months increased by a fifth over 1979, while imports were slightly lower.

Closing the debate on the national economy, Kadar spoke of events in Poland: "Hungary wishes to see Poland strong and considers that the Poles, under the leadership of their party, are capable of solving their problems alone." Sandor Gaspar, a member of the Politburo and secretary-general of the Council of Trade Unions, admitted in October that there had been "stoppages in some Hungarian plants due to the incorrect attitude of management."

On July 24 Soviet leader Leonid Brezhnev and Kadar met in the Crimea. In the same month Veselin Djuranovic, president of the Federal Executive Council of Yugoslavia, visited Hungary officially. Laszlo Cardinal Lekai, archbishop of Esztergom and primate of Hungary, visited England from July 3 to 8 as a guest of the archbishop of Canterbury. On September 29 Kadar received in Budapest Agostino Cardinal Casaroli, the Vatican secretary of state.

ICE HOCKEY

After four years in the grip of the heretofore invincible Montreal Canadiens, the Stanley Cup finally found a new home, gracing Long Island for the first time in the hands of the eight-year-old New York Islanders, one of the youngest teams ever to win the National Hockey League (NHL) championship. Having made it to the semifinals four times and the quarterfinals once, the Islanders believed they were ready for the finals. They soon proved that they were by winning the Cup on home ice in Nassau Coliseum against the Philadelphia Flyers four games to two in the best-of-seven series.

The series included two overtime games, the first contest and the last. Denis Potvin's goal decided the opening contest in favour of New York, while Bobby Nystrom, the Islanders' 27-year-old right wing, scored in the final game to win the Cup.

In a year of youth that saw the emergence of 19-year-old Wayne Gretzky, the centre known as "the Great Gretzky," one of the game's finest players—and certainly its most durable—retired. Gordie Howe, 52 years old, announced his retirement a second time, the first having come in 1971 after 25 years with the Detroit Red Wings. Howe had returned to hockey in 1973 to play with his sons Mark and Marty on the New England (now Hartford) Whalers in the then newly formed World

Bobby Clarke (16) of the Philadelphia Flyers checks Bob Bourne of the New York Islanders in a Stanley Cup championship game in May. The Islanders won the cup by beating the Flyers four games to two.
WIDE WORLD

WIDE WORLD

Jim Craig, goalie of the U.S. hockey team, kissed his gold medal after his team's victory in the XIII Olympic Winter Games.

Hockey Association (WHA). He completed his career with 11 NHL records including most regular season games, 1,767, most goals, 801, and most 30-goal years, 14.

During the 1979–80 season the WHA merged with the NHL, ending the long interleague war that had escalated player salaries into six figures. In the first year of the merger the four former WHA teams, Hartford, Quebec, Edmonton, and Winnipeg, fared poorly. Hartford had the most respectable record, finishing with 73 points, while Winnipeg had the worst with 51.

But some of the WHA players did very well, most notably Gretzky, the dazzling centre for Edmonton whom the NHL would not consider a rookie because of his year of play in the WHA. But the young player picked up two major awards, the Hart Trophy as the league's most valuable player and the Lady Byng Trophy as the most gentlemanly player, making him the most youthful double award winner in NHL history.

The rookie of the year was Raymond Bourque of the Boston Bruins, a brilliant defenseman who reminded some Bruin fans of their former idol, Bobby Orr. The league's best defenseman was Larry Robinson, who helped shore up a Montreal team missing its retired goalie, Ken Dryden. Bryan Trottier of the Islanders added the Conn Smythe Trophy to his postseason collection as the play-offs' most valuable player.

Although it was a relatively quiet year for violent on-ice incidents, there were fisticuffs in the stands of New York's Madison Square Garden during the winter when the Boston Bruins jumped over the rail to collar some fans who, they said, had grabbed their sticks and cut one player, Stan Jonathan, with the blade. The fans in turn sued the Bruins, and the matter was in litigation at the year's end. Players

were better protected on the ice because of a new rule making helmets mandatory for all newcomers to the league and requiring all veteran players to wear them unless the player signed an insurance waiver.

The biggest trade of the year was the one that sent massive defenseman Barry Beck, the presumed cornerstone of the Colorado Rockies, to the New York Rangers for Pat Hickey, Lucien DeBlois, Mike McEwen, Dean Turner, and Bob Crawford. The Rangers did not improve noticeably through that trade alone, and the Rockies finished the season tied with Winnipeg for the lowest point total in the league, 51. After the season the Rockies found a new coach, Bill MacMillan, formerly with the Islander organization, to replace Don Cherry. The Rangers also acquired a new coach, replacing Fred Shero with Herb Brooks, coach of the U.S. Olympic team. Brooks was not immediately available, and in the interim his place was filled by Craig Patrick.

There was also trouble in Toronto with a rift between management and players resulting in the dispatching of Lanny McDonald to Colorado. After the season Mike Palmateer, Toronto's goalie, went to the Washington Capitals for Robert Picard, a young defenseman.

The greatest hockey triumph of the year was enjoyed by the players of the U.S. team that won the gold medal in the Olympic Games at Lake Placid, N.Y., handing the Soviet team its first defeat in 12 years. After their victory 12 of the Olympians signed with NHL teams. The sweetest season belonged to Ken Morrow, a defenseman who joined the New York Islanders after the Olympics and went on to add the Stanley Cup to his Olympic medal. (*See also* Olympic Games.)

In the minor leagues the Hershey Bears defeated New Brunswick for the American League championship, while the Salt Lake City Golden Eagles defeated the Fort Worth Texans in the Central League final. The Erie Blades were the Eastern League champions, and the Kalamazoo Wings took the International Hockey League title.

ICELAND

The election of Vigdís Finnbogadóttir to the presidency of Iceland on June 30, 1980, brought to office the first elected woman chief of state in the world. After an intense election campaign that concentrated chiefly on personalities rather than issues, she obtained a narrow plurality of the popular vote, 33.6%, in a field of four candidates, the others all being men. Her closest rival was Gudlaugur Thorvaldsson, the chief state mediator in labour disputes, who got 32.1% of the vote.

On February 8 a new government took office from the previous Social Democrat minority caretaker regime. The new government was formed under the leadership of Independence Party Vice-Chairman Gunnar Thoroddsen, who broke

In June Vigdís Finnbogadóttir was elected president of Iceland, the world's first democratically elected female chief of state.
KEYSTONE

away from his own party along with four other members of Parliament of that party. They joined forces with the Progressive Party and the Peoples' Alliance to form a left-of-centre government.

The economy performed poorly during 1980. Real growth in gross domestic product was approximately 1.5%, but a decline in the terms of trade more than offset this gain, largely because of higher oil prices. Taking this into account, real gross national income was thought to have fallen by about 1%. Unemployment was nevertheless virtually absent. Efforts to fight inflation failed; it continued at a rate of 50–60% a year. The current account of the balance of payments was in moderate deficit in 1980, of the order of U.S. $100 million.

The country's main airline, Icelandic Airlines, a privately owned company and an important part of the local economy, was beset with heavy operational losses during the year owing to intense competition on its transatlantic routes. In the fall it was evident that it would have to give up its transatlantic service unless it received government assistance. The Icelandic and Luxembourg authorities agreed to give it an operational subsidy to continue its service on its main route from Luxembourg over Iceland to the U.S.

Iceland's dispute with Norway over fishing rights around the latter's Jan Mayen Island ended with an agreement reached between the two governments in early May. The agreement contained a broadly stated but definite recognition by Norway of Iceland's 200-mi exclusive economic zone in the direction toward Jan Mayen. It also settled division of the important capelin fish catch between the two countries, though in somewhat vague terms.

There was fairly frequent and intense volcanic activity in Iceland during the year. Four intense but brief eruptions were recorded. On August 17 at Mt. Hekla, the country's best-known volcano, a 6-km (3.7-mi)-long fissure began to emit large volumes of ash but relatively little lava. The other three eruptions were all in the Lake Myvatn area in the north.

ICE SKATING

All four figure-skating titles changed hands at the world championships on March 11–15 in Dortmund, West Germany, contested by 119 skaters from 23 countries. The men's victor, Jan Hoffmann of East Germany, was strong enough in all phases of the competition to outscore Robin Cousins, the runner-up from Great Britain. Having won the European and Olympic titles earlier in the season, Cousins narrowly failed to complete the triple crown because he was unable to trace good enough compulsory figures. His free-skating performance was the best of his career, climaxing three years of superiority in this division with a near-flawless performance that included five triple jumps; he gained maximum six marks from three of the nine judges. Charles Tickner, the 1978 champion from the U.S., finished third.

The women's victory of Anett Pötzsch was her second, her first having been in 1978. After gaining a useful points advantage in the figures, the East German elected not to take undue risks in the free skating, a policy that paid off because Linda Fratianne, the U.S. title defender, was too far behind. Despite comfortably winning the free skating in a program that included two triple jumps, Fratianne could only finish third, close behind Dagmar Lurz of West Germany.

Fans were denied what could have been a great pairs confrontation between the U.S. titleholders, Randy Gardner and Tai Babilonia, and the Soviet

Speed skater Eric Heiden of the U.S. set a new world record with each of his five gold-medal victories in the XIII Olympic Winter Games at Lake Placid, New York, a feat unprecedented in the history of the Winter Games.
WIDE WORLD

Olympic champions, Aleksandr Zaitsev and Irina Rodnina, because of Gardner's injured groin and Rodnina's strained shoulder. Another Soviet pair,

Hungarians Andras Sallay and Krisztina Regoczy won the championship in ice dancing at the competition in Dortmund, West Germany, in March.
UPI

Sergey Shakhrai and Marina Tcherkasova, won the vacant title, followed by Uwe Bewersdorff and Manuela Mager of East Germany and Stanislav Leonovich and Marina Pestova of the Soviet Union. The victory, however, seemed hollow and the event anticlimactic.

The ice dance contest ended on an excitingly high note when Andras Sallay and Krisztina Regoczy became the first Hungarian champions, overtaking the Soviet title defenders, Gennadi Karponosov and Natalia Linichuk, with a superb free dance. Andrey Minekov and Irina Moiseyeva of the U.S.S.R. finished third.

In the third world junior championships at Mégève, France, on January 16–19, Soviet skaters dominated three of the four events. Aleksandr Fadeev gained the men's title, Oleg Makarov and Larisa Selezneva the pairs, and Aleksey Soloviev and Elana Batanova the ice dance. As it had in both previous tournaments, the women's title went to a U.S. skater, Rosalyn Sumners.

Speed Skating

Attempting a fourth successive title, Eric Heiden of the U.S. was unexpectedly defeated in the men's world championship at Heerenveen, Neth., on March 1–2. Hilbert van der Duim of the host country gained a narrow overall points margin over the defending champion. Tom Erik Oxholm of Norway finished third. In the four events van der Duim won the 1,500 m, Heiden the 500 m, Oxholm the 5,000 m, and Mike Woods of the U.S. the 10,000 m.

Natalia Petruseva (U.S.S.R.) became the new women's world champion at Hamar, Norway, on January 12–13, with Beth Heiden of the U.S. second and Bjørg Eva Jensen of Norway third. Petruseva was first in each of the four distances except the longest, the 3,000 m, which was won by Jensen.

The separate world sprint titles for men and women, each contested at West Allis, Wis., on February 9–10, were won, respectively, by Heiden and Karin Enke of East Germany. Each title was decided over four races, two each at 500 m and 1,000 m. Heiden was beaten only once, in one of the 500-m dashes, by his compatriot Tom Plant, who finished third overall behind Gaetan Boucher of Canada. Enke likewise was defeated only once, also in a 500 m, by Leah Poulos-Mueller of the U.S., who finished second overall, just above Beth Heiden.

Three new world men's records were established during the season. Heiden lowered the 1,000-m sprint time to 1 min 13.6 sec on January 13 at Davos, Switz., where, six days later, he covered the 1,500 m in 1 min 54.79 sec. Dmitry Ogloblin of the U.S.S.R. astonishingly bettered Heiden's Olympic time for the 10,000 m with 14 min 25.71 sec at Medeo, U.S.S.R., on March 30. The only new world women's record was in the 1,000 m, reduced to 1 min 23.01 sec on March 27 by Petruseva, also at Medeo.

The second annual short track championships for men and women, in Milan, Italy, on March 22–23, were won, respectively, by Boucher and Miyoshi Kato of Japan. Boucher also led a Canadian team to victory in the men's relay, the women's being won by Italy. These championships, designed especially for indoor rinks, had rules adapted to suit circuits necessarily smaller than those used outdoors. Subject to the success of these tournaments during an experimental period, the intention was for such competition to attain its own world championship status.

(*See also* Olympic Games.)

INDIA

In 1980 Indira Gandhi won back power but lost her son and closest political confidant, Sanjay Gandhi. Voting took place for the Lok Sabha (lower house of Parliament) in the first week of January, resulting in a spectacular victory for Mrs. Gandhi. Of the 525 seats being contested (in a house of 542), Mrs. Gandhi's Congress (I) Party secured 351, Lok Dal 41, Communist Party of India (Marxist) 35, Janata 32, Dravida Munnetra Kazhagam 16, Congress (U) 13, Communist Party of India 10, and others 27. Indira Gandhi personally won in two constituencies, Medak in Andhra Pradesh and Rae Bareli in Uttar Pradesh (from which she later resigned). Sanjay Gandhi won in Amethi. With no opposition group winning more than 10% of the seats, no leader of the opposition was designated.

Mrs. Gandhi was sworn in on January 14 with a Cabinet of 14. Mrs. Gandhi retained the defense portfolio. The first decision of the new Parliament was to extend the statutory reservation of seats in Parliament for scheduled castes and tribes by ten more years.

Emulating the example set by the Janata government in 1977, the Congress (I) regime dissolved as-

LAURENT MAOUS–GAMMA/LIAISON

Indira Gandhi received congratulations from supporters after her Congress (I) Party won a more than two-thirds majority in elections for the lower house of India's Parliament.

semblies in nine states and called for midterm elections. Polling took place at the end of May. Congress (I) won a majority in Bihar, Gujarat, Madhya Pradesh, Maharashtra, Orissa, Punjab, Rajasthan, and Uttar Pradesh—eight of nine.

Soon after this second victory, tragedy struck. Sanjay Gandhi, formidable leader of the youth wing of Congress (I), was killed in an airplane crash in New Delhi on June 23. His death was widely regarded as having a profound effect on the course of national politics.

The Janata Party, which had broken into two the previous year, split further after being routed in the parliamentary elections. A separate Bharatiya Janata Party came into being in April. Jagjivan Ram, the party's former leader, drifted away to join Congress (U). Raj Narain, parting company with Lok Dal, formed the Janata Party (Secular).

Mrs. Gandhi enlarged her council of ministers in installments and filled the vacancies of persons who had left to head state governments. On November 1 the central council of ministers consisted of 20 Cabinet members, 21 ministers of state, and 10 deputy ministers. Even so there were complaints that such key portfolios as defense and steel did not have full-time ministers. Biennial elections were held for the Rajya Sabha (upper house of Parlia-

KEYSTONE

Indira Gandhi's son and political protégé, Sanjay Gandhi, was killed in the crash of the plane he was piloting on June 23; his body was cremated in New Delhi on June 24.

ment) in July. Congress (I) and its allies just managed to secure a majority. In November, 15 by-elections to state assemblies were held, and Congress (I) won ten.

The political impasse in Assam dragged on through most of the year, with students there insisting that all foreigners who had come into that state after 1951 should be detected, deleted (from the voters list), and deported. Discussions held in February and again in September–October failed to yield agreement. Schools and colleges remained closed virtually throughout the year, and offices worked fitfully. A government headed by Anwara Taimor was installed by Mrs. Gandhi on December 6, but the basic problem of the immigrants, most Bengalis from Bangladesh, remained unresolved.

Caste clashes occurred in Bihar and Uttar Pradesh, and a tribal outburst in Tripura resulted in an estimated 550 deaths in June. Virulent religious riots broke out in Moradabad and Aligarh in August. The trouble in Moradabad smoldered for months.

After Mrs. Gandhi's victory the various legal cases against her, her son, and colleagues were withdrawn. The judge of the special court trying one of the cases declared that his court did not have jurisdiction. A major judicial decision during the year was the judgment of a five-member bench of the Supreme Court. It struck down section 55 of the Constitution 42 Amendment Act, which had given unlimited power to Parliament to amend the constitution. The court held that Parliament had no power to change the basic or essential features of the constitution. The court also held as void section 4, which had allowed Parliament to pass legislation that curbed fundamental rights. The preventive detention bill that had been promulgated by the Charan Singh government in October 1979 was enacted into law on September 22 as a National Security Ordinance to legalize preventive detention for up to 12 months.

The Economy

Drought and power shortages in the first half of the year (with an estimated decline of 15 million metric tons in grain production and a fall in industrial growth) spurred inflation. At the end of October the wholesale price index stood 18.1% higher than a year earlier.

Major decisions were taken to improve production and railway movement. Port congestion eased. The reconstituted Planning Commission prepared the outline of a sixth five-year plan (1980–85) involving a public outlay of Rs 950 billion to achieve an overall growth rate of 5.5% (Rs 7.69 = U.S. $1). Revenue receipts for 1980–81 were estimated at Rs 123,560,000,000 (including Rs 2,230,000,000 from new taxation) and disbursements at Rs 133 billion. Amendments to industrial policy were announced in July by means of which production capacities were permitted to be enlarged and restrictions against large plants relaxed. Another major economic event during the year was the nationalization of six banks.

Foreign Affairs

Indira Gandhi's return signaled resumption of her well-understood policies. One of her first statements was to deplore the entry of foreign troops into Afghanistan and to emphasize the need for a solution through discussions. In July India announced recognition of the Heng Samrin government of Cambodia. A large number of foreign dignitaries came to India, some to mend fences and some to reestablish lost links. Among them were the presidents of Bangladesh, France, Bulgaria, Zaire, Cyprus, and Zambia; the kings of Nepal and Bhutan; the prime ministers of Vietnam, Yugoslavia, Denmark, and Mauritius; the chancellor of Austria; foreign ministers Andrey Gromyko of the Soviet Union and Lord Carrington of Great Britain; and Yasser Arafat of the Palestine Liberation Organization.

Mrs. Gandhi visited Tanzania and attended the Zimbabwe independence celebrations in April and the funeral of President Tito of Yugoslavia. In Salisbury she had talks with Pres. Mohammad Zia-ul-Haq of Pakistan and in Belgrade with Soviet Pres. Leonid Brezhnev, Prime Minister Margaret Thatcher of Great Britain, Chancellor Helmut Schmidt of West Germany, and Premier Hua Guofeng (Hua Kuo-feng) of China. A regional conference of Commonwealth heads of government, held in New Delhi in September, was attended by, among others, the prime ministers of Australia, New Zealand, Malaysia, and Singapore and the president of Sri Lanka. The Iraq-Iran fighting placed a heavy burden on India in terms of oil supplies.

There was satisfaction that the U.S. government kept its obligation by sending to India the first installment of uranium fuel for the Tarapur nuclear power plant. The hope was expressed that Indo-U.S. relations would continue to be cordial during the presidency of Ronald Reagan. President Brezhnev visited New Delhi in December and Prince Charles of Great Britain in November.

INDONESIA

In 1980, for the first time since President Suharto formally assumed power following an abortive Communist coup in 1965, political opposition to his stewardship crystallized as Indonesia moved toward national elections in 1982. In foreign affairs, however, the Suharto government continued to command a broad spectrum of support as Indonesia denounced the Soviet occupation of Afghanistan and the Vietnamese occupation of Cambodia. The economic situation, meanwhile, was brightened by a bumper rice crop.

The most important political development of 1980 was the emergence in May of a growing opposition to Suharto's quasi-military government amid indications that the president planned to· run for reelection to a fourth five-year term. Fifty of the nation's prominent political, religious, and military figures joined in submitting a petition to parliament which they described as "an expression of concern." The Group of 50, as they were called, included two former prime ministers, Islamic and Christian leaders, a former defense minister, students, and intellectuals. The opposition also expressed dismay at the widespread graft that continued both in and out of government despite Suharto's repeated promises to stamp out corruption. Also, they claimed that despite the government's annual development plans the country's poor were getting poorer as the rich grew richer. A long-term objective of the opposition appeared to be to get the Army out of government.

In November the political situation took a new turn when the government suggested that a move on the part of the increasingly restive Parliament to convene a special session would be considered by the armed forces as "constitutionally subversive." According to a spokesman for the internal security establishment, the phrase "constitutional subversion" included any effort to amend the present constitution, even under articles provided in the constitution for such amendments. This definition of subversion surprised the government's opposition and puzzled Suharto's supporters. Thus, for example, an amendment barring more than two terms for the presidency would be interpreted as an act of treason, although art. 37 of the constitution provided for amendments by a two-thirds majority of the People's Consultative Assembly.

In foreign affairs Indonesia's relations with the Communist powers grew more distant during the year. In the spring, Indonesia provided a temporary refuge for more than 50,000 "boat people" fleeing Vietnam. At the same time, three years of negotiations between Vietnam and Indonesia over their contiguous sea frontier reached an impasse. Vietnam had laid claim to the Natuna Islands, a small group in the South China Sea that had been historically Indonesian. There were unconfirmed reports during the year of an exchange of fire between Vietnamese and Indonesian patrol boats near the Natunas, where Indonesia was drilling for offshore oil. In 1980 Indonesia's armed forces staged their biggest field maneuvers in history. Indonesia also participated in the Islamic Conference of foreign ministers that condemned the Soviet invasion and occupation of Afghanistan and joined in a conference of the Association of Southeast Asian Nations (ASEAN) that called upon Vietnam to withdraw its estimated 200,000 troops from Cambodia.

In the economic realm an abundance of rice posed a serious storage problem as production of the crop soared to 20 million tons, more than one million tons above the government's estimate. The improving economic outlook was strengthened by a growth rate in the gross national product of 6.5% and an easing of the annual inflation rate to below 20%.

One of these helmets came off the field and off the market when the rules of the game changed.

[advertisement body text]

Here's what we're doing:

Here's what you can do:

Affordable insurance is our business...and yours.

The American Insurance Association ran a series of advertisements in 1980 discussing the industry's position on such issues as industry-wide product liability.

INSURANCE

Money is the raw material of the insurance business, and broad shifts in the cost of money during 1980 led the industry through a very difficult year.

Total damage claims rose at the record-setting pace of the previous year as inflation drove up replacement costs. Underwriting losses (the difference between premiums collected and total expenses and damages paid) during the first quarter of the year ran ahead of 1979 losses by nearly 10%, according to one industry association.

Also, as the prime rate rose toward 20%, pulling rates in money market funds and bank certificates of deposit up toward 15%, holders of whole life insurance increasingly exercised their right to borrow against their policies at low interest rates ranging from 5 to 8%. They evidently used the loans for purchases or reinvested the money at higher rates, draining away money that the insurance companies themselves could have loaned out at rates of prime or above. Policyholder loans outstanding increased by $1,250,000,000 in April, compared with an increase of only $350 million in April 1979. Not only did they take earning power away from insurance companies, but many firms, short of cash, were forced to borrow at high rates in order to meet the policyholder loan demand.

But at the same time, inflation greatly boosted the return on the insurance industry's own investments in securities, bonds, and loans. And as interests began their drop in the spring, policyholder loans fell off. In addition, the price-cutting competition in the property-casualty field that set in after 1979's large investment earnings seemed to have abated during 1980.

By midyear, results were mixed. Though one of the largest insurance companies reported investment earnings up by 23.6% in the second quarter over the same period in 1979 for a total earnings increase of 27.6%, a second large firm reported a profit decline of 9.2%.

While life insurers experienced the hazards of writing whole life policies, in the form of costly policyholder loans, the consumerist attack continued on that type of insurance. The alternative, term insurance, does not build the cash values of whole life, yet the premiums are considerably lower for younger age brackets. Early in the year, to the industry's dismay, Pres. Jimmy Carter endorsed a model Federal Trade Commission regulation obliging companies to clearly spell out the difference in the two types of insurance. It would be up to the individual states to make the changes.

Consumers also heard warnings in 1980 about "dread disease" health insurance policies such as cancer insurance. Two major studies—one by a congressional committee—found that cancer insurance often pays as little as one-third of the medical costs that normal, comprehensive coverage would pay, yet the cancer policies can cost twice as much. Five northeastern states already banned the sale of cancer insurance, and the committee advised the other states to take a closer look at the policies.

Health-related concerns also figured prominently in the growing product-liability field, where a California court awarded $1.2 million to a disabled worker in the first ruling in favour of a shipyard worker exposed to asbestos. Asbestos, once used for fire insulation in ships, skyscrapers, and other construction, can lead to a variety of crippling or fatal diseases. There were some 3,000 suits pending by shipyard workers alone against manufacturers and suppliers. Since asbestos-related diseases appear to develop over time, one of the defendants in the California case, Johns-Manville Corp., sued most of its current and former product-liability carriers to determine how much of the costs they should share.

In the property-casualty area, disasters in 1980 could prove to have greatly compounded the rising rate of claims. Though Hurricane Allen caused less damage than expected when it missed population centres in Texas, the eruptions of Mt. St. Helens in Washington State caused an estimated $1.5 billion in damage. In Miami, Fla., riots touched off by the acquittal of four policemen charged with beating a black insurance executive to death killed at least 14 people and caused an estimated $200 million in property damage.

INTERIOR DESIGN

With the "eclectic aesthetic" popularized in the late 1970s still gaining ground, no particular interior style was considered sacred as the new decade unfolded in 1980. One issue of *Better Homes and Gardens* magazine featured "America's Favorite Furnishings," ranging from Colonial to contemporary styles, while *Architectural Digest* showed a Manhattan apartment that brought together a provocative blend of furnishings and art culled from throughout the world. Jay Spectre, the designer of the sleek city residence, called it the "internationalism" style, a reflection of the increasing worldwide travel being done by Americans.

Architecture's well-publicized Post Modern movement, a reaction to the architectural severity of buildings designed by Mies van der Rohe and his followers, was reflected in rooms rich with historical allusions. Classical pilasters, Palladian arches, and trompe l'oeil murals were among the long-put-to-rest elements that came into play. The "new eclecticism" was a label bestowed on the movement by *New York* magazine.

A proliferation of Chinese furnishings and design motifs was the result of the economic and political alliance between China and the West. Bloomingdale's, the trendy Manhattan retailer, staged a storewide Chinese promotion and offered a remarkable selection of Chinese products. Among the items for the home were scorched bamboo folding chairs, hand-painted dinnerware, straw baskets, and the classic schoolchild's folding stool. San Francisco, Chicago, and New York City hosted an ambitious exhibition of consumer goods and antiquities from the People's Republic of China. Across the U.S., Oriental accessories were appearing in rooms of all styles.

Designers predicted a gradual shift back to formal living. In furniture sales, this was reflected in the popularity of 18th-century English reproductions. After a decade of selling casual, easy-care furniture of rustic oak and pine, retailers found consumers opting for classic pieces such as romantic mahogany dining-room sets with delicate lines and rich surface detailing. At the semiannual High Point, N.C., furniture market, Baker Furniture introduced its second collection of elegant Charleston, S.C., antique reproductions.

For many, the American country look—teaming antique scrubbed pine tables, painted cupboards, quilts, rural pottery, and farm baskets—was synonymous with cozy, comfortable surroundings. It was a decorating style favoured even in city apartments and lofts. Fabrics and wallcoverings with small country patterns appeared in abundance. Two important books celebrating the country look were published: *American Country: A Style and Source Book* by Mary Ellisor Emmerling and *Objects* by John Gruen.

Room sizes continued to shrink in both houses and apartments, and more people found themselves living in confined environments with little architectural character. This provoked enormous interest in dual-purpose furniture and interior design tricks that enhanced limited space. Designers recommended armoires and other vertical storage pieces, equipping rooms so that they could be used for more than one purpose, and turning furnishings on the diagonal so that corner space could be put to good use. Furniture manufacturers responded with a range of ingenious products: triangular tables that fit into corners, chairs and tables on casters that could be easily shifted from room to room, and modular sofas and chairs that could be quickly flipped open into beds. Sofa bed sales continued to grow.

Soaring interest rates on home mortgages gave a boost to the remodeling industry. As more homeowners began to experiment with harnessing natural energy sources, greenhouses and "greenhouse" windows, positioned to take advantage of solar energy, became popular additions. Throughout the country old structures were energetically renovated. The great demand for lofts, created by transforming industrial buildings, reflected a growing preoccupation with the luxury of living in wide-open space. The problems of organizing these vast, wallless spaces gave rise to singularly inventive interior design solutions. In her 4,000-sq-ft Manhattan loft, prominent fashion designer Adri installed a "swimming pool," an enormous platformed whirlpool

The country look was never more popular than in 1980; reproductions of country furniture and accessories and stencil-look wallpaper complete the look in this dining room.

© 1980 BY GREEFF FABRICS, INC.

bath, then coupled it with deluxe exercise equipment. Several closets and a pair of kitchen islands were built on casters to provide maximum flexibility within the space.

In fabrics, velvets and prints were favourites. Corals and mauves were prevalent, as were tapestry-rich colours such as purple, cordovan, oxblood, plum, gold, and ivory.

INTERNATIONAL FINANCE

World price inflation accelerated further in 1980. In the third quarter, consumer prices in 19 industrial countries averaged 11.6% higher than one year before, as against 9.5% higher in 1979. These increases worsened to 12.8% for the United States and 10.6% for Canada. In the 19 countries, the largest consumer price increases between the third quarters of 1979 and 1980 were those of Italy (21.7%, comparing June-through-August quarters), Ireland (18.9%), the United Kingdom (16.4%), and New Zealand (16.3%). The smallest increases were those of Switzerland (3.8%, a slight improvement over 1979) and Germany (5.3%, slightly worse). Japan's prices increased 8.4%, compared with 3.5% in 1979.

After remaining at around 4% in 1977 and 1978, the average annual rate of output expansion in major industrial countries fell to around 3% in 1979 and seemed likely to be still lower in 1980. The average was pulled down by actual declines in output in the first or second quarters in the U.S., Canada, and the U.K.

Exchange-rate regimes changed little from the year before. Of 140 members of the International Monetary Fund (IMF) plus Switzerland on Sept. 30, 1980, 40 were still pegging their currencies to the U.S. dollar, 14 to the French franc, 2 to the South African rand, 1 to the pound sterling, and 1 to the Spanish peseta. Fifteen were stabilizing their exchange rates against the IMF's Special Drawing Right (SDR) and 21 against some other "basket" of currencies. The currencies of Belgium, Denmark, France, West Germany, Ireland, Italy, Luxembourg, and The Netherlands were pegged to each other in the European Monetary System (EMS). Information about one regime (Cambodia's) was still lacking at the end of 1980.

Major adjustments of pegged or quasi-pegged rates were few in 1980. Turkey devalued its lira by 33% in January and carried out several smaller devaluations in the following months. Zaire devalued by 30% against the SDR in February. Greece ended its pegging to the dollar in November and allowed the drachma to float. Israel, where inflation had soared to well over 100%, continued to carry out frequent minidevaluations and, in February, introduced a new currency unit, the shekel, worth ten of the former Israeli pounds. Other countries with exceptionally high inflation rates, including Argentina, Brazil, and Uruguay, also continued their minidevaluations. Chile, in contrast with its past

policy, managed to maintain the rate of 39 pesos per dollar established in mid-1979.

The chief floating exchange rates moved more widely in 1980 than in 1979. High, unsteady, and divergent inflation rates around the world were at work, as well as changing expectations about inflation and the policies responsible. High and unstable interest rates and international interest-rate differentials—themselves largely a consequence of the volatile pattern of inflation—were evidently influencing capital flows and, in turn, exchange rates.

The U.S. dollar stood at a short-term low against the jointly floating EMS currencies at the start of 1980. It then gained some 14% against them by early April. At that time the United States was experiencing soaring interest rates and an intense scramble for funds. A relapse as interest rates softened carried the dollar back in July to about its level of early January. By early November it had regained its level of early April. The dollar's average or "effective" exchange rate against not only the EMS but some 20 currencies in all rose in early April to about 9% above its level at the turn of the year, sank to about 3% below in July, and recovered to about 4% above in early December. While the dollar trended upward against the currencies of continental Europe, it weakened against the pound sterling and Japanese yen.

The fluctuations of the EMS currencies mirrored those of the dollar. The German mark had been depreciating, despite intervention to support it, when official interest rates were raised early in March. Concern was growing about rekindled inflation and about the balance of payments deficit; a current-account deficit had developed in 1979 and grew to record size in 1980. To facilitate financing this deficit, the Bundesbank over the course of the year relaxed its impediments to capital inflows and to growth of the mark's reserve-currency role. (Similar policy shifts, and for a similar reason, occurred in Switzerland and Japan, also.) The mark reached a low of 50.5 U.S. cents on April 7. Next, with U.S. interest rates declining and market conditions disorderly, the mark rose to 55.7 cents by April 29, gaining almost 10% in scarcely over three weeks. It continued rising to 57.2 cents on July 28, then changed direction again and on December 10 dipped below 50 cents for the first time in over two years. On December 31, after a slight recovery, the mark rate stood 13.1% lower than at the end of 1979. The mark's effective exchange rate against 20 other currencies fluctuated less widely. In comparison with its January level, it stood about 8% lower by early December.

The French franc moved against the dollar in step with other EMS currencies: it depreciated to April, appreciated to July, and then sagged again. Its end-of-year dollar rate was 12.3% lower in 1980 than in 1979. Its average exchange rate against the currencies of France's leading trading partners fluctuated only narrowly but was about 4% lower by

FABIAN—SYGMA

Premier Francesco Cossiga (fourth from right) and Pres. Alessandro Pertini (right) of Italy welcomed leaders of Japan, Canada, West Germany, France, the United States, and Great Britain to Venice in June for a two-day economic summit.

early December than at the start of the year.

The Italian lira behaved differently from the other EMS currencies in that it shared only partially in their rise to a July peak against the dollar. Its dollar value was 15.7% lower on December 31 than at the end of 1979. Its average exchange rate drifted smoothly downward to about 9% lower in early December than at the start of the year.

Outside the EMS, the fluctuations of the Swiss franc were similar in time pattern to those of the EMS currencies. Between early January and early April the franc lost 16% against the dollar. At a low of 53.2 cents on April 7, by July it was practically back to its January level. On December 31 its dollar rate stood 10.6% below the end-of-1979 level. The franc's effective exchange rate against other currencies was about 7% weaker in early December than at the beginning of the year.

Switzerland, like West Germany, developed a record current-account deficit in 1980. Swiss authorities also saw an inflationary threat in the weakening of the home currency on the foreign-exchange market (the continued pricing of imported oil in dollars presented one obvious reason). Steps were taken to support the franc, including increases in official interest rates and removal of several barriers to capi-

tal inflows. In April the Swiss National Bank announced its intention of intervening to keep the franc from weakening against the German mark beyond the rate of 95 centimes per mark.

In 1980 as in 1979 the pound sterling showed exchange-market strength that belied its rapid loss of domestic purchasing power. It even reached a seven-year high against the dollar. (Suggested explanations included the benefits of North Sea oil and the relatively high level of British interest rates, which prodded companies and public agencies to borrow abroad and attracted inflows of short-term capital.) The pound rose from a low of $2.07 early in November 1979 to $2.22 at the beginning of 1980 and to a temporary peak of $2.32 in February. After receding to about $2.14 in early April, the rate rose to $2.45 in early November, about 18% above the level of one year before. (By December 31, however, the rate had receded to $2.39, only 7.6% above the end-of-1979 level.) Over the same November-to-November period, the pound gained slightly more against the currencies of Britain's trading partners on average—about 19½%—than against the dollar alone.

Meanwhile, the anti-inflation policy of Prime Minister Margaret Thatcher seemed to be in trouble. The Bank of England was evidently not taking the steps necessary to moderate and stabilize monetary growth. The government announced new methods of monetary control, to take effect in the spring of 1981, that would aim more at controlling the quantity of base money and less at controlling interest rates. In 1980, however, amid exceptional price inflation, Britain slid into the worst recession since the 1930s; unemployment rose to 7.8% in October. The resulting cut in government revenues swelled borrowing requirements. The recession also tended to restrain imports and thus contributed to a string of monthly current-account surpluses.

The Japanese yen fluctuated more widely in 1980 than any other major currency. It had been in a downtrend against the dollar after October 1978 and reached 0.38 of a cent on April 7, about 38% below its earlier peak. It then recovered by 4.8% in three days and by 9.2% in scarcely more than three weeks. After further strength in June and weakness in August, the yen ended 1980 at nearly one-half of a cent, 15.3% stronger than one year before. Against other currencies on average, the yen gained about 19% between the start of the year and early December. Relaxation of restrictions on capital inflows may well have contributed to the yen's renewed strength.

The Canadian dollar ended 1979 at 85.6 U.S. cents, rose above 87 cents at the end of February, sank to just below 84 cents in early April, again passed 87 cents at times in June and July, and sagged thereafter, reaching a 47-year low of 82.7 cents on December 16. At 83.8 cents on December 31, it was 2.1% below its end-of-1979 quotation. The Canadian dollar's average exchange rate was remarkably steady—about the same in early December as at the start of the year (after reaching some 2% higher around midyear).

The Mexican peso trended very mildly downward against the dollar. At 4.32 cents on December 31, it stood 1.5% below its end-of-1979 level. With consumer price inflation rising above 25%, rumours kept recurring that a new devaluation would punctuate the peso's tightly controlled float.

The gold market again saw spectacular instability. After closing the old year at $512 per ounce, the price briefly peaked at $875 in mid-January, slumped to around $480 in March and again in early April, and soared toward $670 in September. Relapsing, it dropped nearly 12% in only three days to a six-month low of $544 on December 11. Exceptionally high interest rates were reportedly diverting funds from the gold market. Closing the year at $586, gold stood 14.5% higher than one year before. In percentage terms the price of silver fluctuated even more wildly early in 1980, briefly exceeding $50 an ounce and then dropping by more than two-thirds.

The International Monetary Fund completed its four-year program of selling off one-third of its gold holdings. Half of that one-third was sold to members at the former official price, the other half at public auctions, the last one being held in May 1980. Profits from all the auctions amounted to $4,640,000,000, of which $1,290,000,000 was transferred directly to 104 less developed countries, with the remainder available for loans to them.

On January 1 the IMF made the second of three new annual allocations of about 4 billion SDR's. Later in 1980 the IMF decided, effective at the start of 1981, to reduce the number of currencies in the basket defining the SDR from 16 to only 5. These are the currencies of the countries whose domestic interest rates are used in calculating the interest rate on SDR's, namely, the United States, West Germany, the United Kingdom, Japan, and France. A more simply defined SDR would presumably be more attractive.

The latest round of increases, amounting to about 50%, in IMF quotas (to which members' entitlements to draw on the Fund are geared) achieved the required volume of approvals late in 1980. In addition, the Fund was preparing to play an expanded role, supplementary to that of the commercial banks and the Eurodollar market, in "recycling" funds from the oil-exporting countries to, in particular, some 40 nonoil less developed countries thought to have limited access to private capital markets and a weak capacity to save and destined to incur further debt. The Fund, according to its managing director, envisaged supplementing its regular resources for this purpose by borrowing funds worth some 6 billion or 7 billion SDR's in the capital markets in 1981 and further amounts in 1982 and 1983.

These developments, along with the Fund's earlier and continuing establishment of special credit facilities to ease the balance of payments problems of less developed countries and along with the above-mentioned use of profits from its gold auctions, testify to the Fund's drift into the business of providing aid to such countries. All this blurs the originally sharp distinction between the purposes of the Fund and of the World Bank. (The Bank, from its side, contributed to blurring this distinction. With an approximate doubling of its capital stock authorized in 1980, the Bank was also authorized to move into financing balance of payments deficits and structural adjustments, thereby diluting its earlier emphasis on financing specific development projects.)

IRAN

In 1980 the Islamic Republic came under increasing stress. Ayatollah Ruhollah Khomeini suffered a worsening heart condition from early January. Despite his illness, he was Iran's sole centre of power and the final arbiter in political matters. Elections for the presidency took place on January 25. In the face of opposition from the Revolutionary Council, Abolhassan Bani-Sadr was elected with 75% of the votes. There was only a 50% turnout at the polls.

General elections for the Majlis (parliament), set up under the constitution approved on Dec. 2–3, 1979, began in March. In a low turnout, the Islamic Republican Party (IRP) was returned as the majority group, with additional support from the Religious Strugglers Party and the Religious Coalition Party. The elections gave the religious establishment under the Ayatollahs Mohammad Hossein Beheshti and Hashemi Rafsanjani a stranglehold on the constitutional organs of government and eclipsed the secular movements led by Bani-Sadr.

The Majlis met on May 28, with the IRP holding 60% of the seats and only 20% falling to the president's side. After a prolonged conflict, Mohammad Ali Raja'i was appointed prime minister in August. He was seen as a mere secular front for the IRP's religious interests. Meanwhile, the Muslim fundamentalists sought to erode the positions of all secular groups. The Teheran headquarters of the leftist Muhajeddin-i Khalq Party was attacked in April and June, and many members of the National Front were isolated from the political mainstream.

The Arabs of Khuzestan, the Turkmen of the Caspian Plain region, and the Baluch were all engaged during the year in elaborating their claims for greater local autonomy. Early in 1980 the Kurds of western Iran put forward claims for increased self-determination. Fighting between groups of Kurds and the Islamic Militia took place in Sanandaj, Mahabad, and Kamyaran, and a combined force made up of militiamen and the regular Iranian Army attacked Sanandaj in April. After some six weeks of fighting, Sanandaj fell to the government in mid-May, at a cost of 1,500 lives. Thereafter, the government held control of most major towns in Kurdistan, but the countryside was firmly in the hands of various Kurdish factions.

The threat posed by the export of the revolution to Shi'ah groups in other Middle Eastern states contributed to Iran's increasing isolation during 1980. In Iraq the attempted assassination of the deputy prime minister, Tareq Aziz, in April by a guerrilla group claiming allegiance to Ayatollah Khomeini set in motion a border confrontation that culminated in the Iraqi decision to attack. In early September Iraq made four demands on Iran as conditions for normal relations. Iran was to withdraw from the islands of Abu Musa and Greater and Lesser Tunb, to renegotiate the agreement of March 1975 signed by the two sides in Algiers, to grant autonomy to the Iranian Arabs of Khuzestan, and to undertake not to interfere in the internal affairs of Arab states. Iran declined to accept these terms, and on September 17 Iraq officially abrogated the Algiers agreement and claimed the Shatt al-Arab waterway.

Iraqi troops had already entered Kurdistan, and on September 22 they pushed into Khuzestan, though neither side declared war. Iranian air strikes at Baghdad, Basra, and the Kirkuk area followed an Iraqi bombing raid on Teheran, but the battle

KALARI–SYGMA

Prime Minister Mohammad Ali Raja'i addressed the Majlis after his election on August 11; his appointment was seen as a defeat for Pres. Abolhassan Bani-Sadr, who had opposed him.

on the ground in Khuzestan became the main theatre of operations. By December the Iraqi offensive had been halted, and fighting was limited largely to artillery exchanges from heavily entrenched positions around the Shatt al-Arab waterway.

Damage to Iran from the war included cessation of oil exports via Kharg Island, destruction of the Abadan refinery, reduction in crude oil output in Khuzestan, closure of some domestic pipeline systems, and disruption of output at the Teheran and Tabriz refineries. Outside the petroleum sector, Iran suffered losses in the petrochemical plants at Abadan, Kharg, and Bandar Khomeini. The iron and steel industry in Ahvaz was also badly hit, and the general cargo ports of Khorramshahr and Bandar Khomeini were brought to a standstill. Large numbers of refugees, up to one million persons in all, were displaced in the fighting. Attempts to end the conflict through the good offices of the UN and the Islamic Conference failed. The Iranian government announced that it would not break off the struggle until all Iraqis had been expelled from Iranian soil and the regime in Baghdad overthrown.

Smoke billows from a burning oil pipeline near Abadan, site of one of Iran's largest oil refineries, after an attack by Iraqi forces in October.

Relations with the international community were overshadowed by the crisis over the U.S. embassy hostages. UN Secretary-General Kurt Waldheim visited Teheran in January to negotiate their release, and a UN commission of inquiry went to Teheran in February. On April 24–25 the U.S., using transport aircraft and helicopters, made an abortive military raid into Iran. But it was not until November 2 that the Iranian Majlis approved conditions for release of the hostages and negotiations began in earnest, with Algeria acting as intermediary. (*See* United States.)

Little progress was made during 1980 in resuscitating the economy. Oil production fell from 2,632,000 bbl a day in the first quarter of the year to 1,565,000 bbl in the second and 1.4 million bbl in the third. After the outbreak of war with Iraq, only minor quantities of oil were produced, mainly from the eastern oil field areas. Iranian financial strength waned as revenues fell; the U.S. retained its freeze on Iranian assets of some $8 billion; and imports surged. Inflation was believed to be approaching 100% by the year's end.

The former shah, Mohammad Reza Pahlavi, died in Cairo on July 27.

(*See also* Iraq; Middle Eastern Affairs.)

IRAQ

Iraq's declaration on Sept. 17, 1980, making void its agreement with the late shah of Iran over passage in the Shatt al-Arab waterway, was the signal for the rapid escalation of border skirmishes into all-out war. Iran rejected Iraq's claim to the waterway, and on September 22 Iraqi jet aircraft mounted the first major strike of the war—an attack on ten Iranian airfields. By mid-November, with the port of Khorramshahr effectively in Iraqi hands and the vital oil-refining complex of Abadan surrounded, there was still no early end to the fighting in sight. The strength of Iranian resistance surprised many observers in the early stages of the war, and the morale of Iran's revolutionary forces was high. Iran also possessed superior weapons, mainly its U.S.-supplied Phantom jets. By contrast Iraq, supplied by the Soviet Union with T-62 and T-72 tanks and MiG-23 aircraft, seemed reluctant to commit them to battle.

With both Iraqi Pres. Saddam Hussein at-Takriti and Ayatollah Ruhollah Khomeini refusing to compromise, prospects for mediation looked bleak. Early attempts under the auspices of the Islamic Conference failed. Iraq's objectives in the war seemed to be threefold: to assert sovereignty over the Shatt al-Arab waterway controlling access to the Iraqi port of Basra; to damage the revolutionary government in Teheran by striking at vital installations; and to destabilize southwest Iran, where many of the population were Arabic-speaking, by supporting the resistance movement seeking to create an autonomous republic in Khuzestan.

Fears that the war would spread into other Gulf countries or involve a preemptive strike on the Strait of Hormuz failed to materialize. The U.S., France, and Britain stepped up their naval forces in the Arabian Sea and the Indian Ocean, but Hussein's strategy was clearly to keep the dispute localized. In the rhetoric manufactured by Baghdad after war had erupted, an Iraqi claim to the Iranian-occupied islands of Abu Musa and Greater and Lesser Tunb at the entrance to the Gulf was asserted. There appeared to be little likelihood of fighting on Iran's southeast flank, however.

On the outbreak of hostilities, Iraq declared *force majeure* (circumstances that could not be controlled) on its oil contracts. Before the war Iraq was the second-largest Arab oil producer, after Saudi Arabia, yielding 3.5 million bbl a day of which 2.8 million bbl were exported. By 1985 refining capacity was expected to be 620,000 bbl a day, but Iranian strikes on refining installations were jeopardizing this target.

As part of an attempt to offer leadership in the Arab world, Iraq pursued a generous foreign aid policy, although it stopped short of "oil gifts" to less developed countries. Strength in external relations and oil wealth enabled President Hussein to take an independent line. He criticized the Soviet intervention in Afghanistan as "unjustified," despite the existing Iraqi friendship treaty with Moscow. At home the separatism of the Kurdish minority was curbed and potential opposition from within the ruling Ba'ath party removed. Early in 1980 Hussein announced what he called the "Arab charter." This appealed for the rejection of foreign influence, better economic collaboration, a peaceful solution to "inter-Arab" quarrels, and, above all, solidarity among Arab states. In 1982 Hussein was scheduled to chair the summit meeting of nonaligned nations in Baghdad. Among his quarrels with other Arab states, Hussein had criticized Yemen (Aden) for allegedly harbouring Iraqi Communists.

IRELAND

Charles J. Haughey succeeded Jack Lynch as prime minister on Dec. 11, 1979, and his efforts to create confidence in his economic and Northern Ireland policies dominated domestic affairs throughout 1980. He was faced with major problems. In common with other Western economies, but more vulnerable because of its dependence on overseas markets and its openness to foreign competition, Ireland faced a year of high inflation, steadily rising unemployment, and low growth and low investment as a result of high interest rates. In addition, industrial unrest, which had led to a record number of workdays lost during 1979, continued to cause major strikes in 1980. One of these closed the national airline at the peak of the tourist season, in June; another, of gasoline-tanker drivers, led to a gasoline famine in August and September that was resolved only after the Army had been called in to distribute fuel to gasoline stations.

Further economic aggravation derived from an appalling summer that ruined crops and left many farmers ruined as well. During 1980 farming costs rose by 20%, incomes fell by 27%, and special relief measures had to be introduced by the government in the autumn. Though the Irish pound (punt) maintained its standing against other European cur-

Iraqi troops posed triumphantly next to a poster of the Ayatollah Ruhollah Khomeini after capturing a military outpost near Khorramshar, Iran, in September.
UPI

UPI

Irish Prime Minister Charles Haughey (right) examines a silver chalice filigreed with gold, part of an 8th-century communion service found in a bog in County Tipperary.

rencies, its fall against sterling, which drove it below 90p in March and below 80p by November, had a further demoralizing effect on the economy, as well as crippling trade.

At the end of January the Supreme Court ruled that it was unconstitutional to discriminate, in any laws, against married couples. The immediate effect of this was manifest in obligatory tax benefits in the budget, introduced on February 27. The budget also made substantial cuts in direct taxation, cutting "pay as you earn" (PAYE) rates and widening tax brackets. Prime Minister Haughey promised action against industrial unrest, but no legislation was introduced. A national wages deal negotiated in the autumn provided a generous raise of more than 15% over a 15-month period and paid no more than lip service to no-strike provisions.

In a marked, but very general, departure from previous policies on Northern Ireland under Jack Lynch and the coalition government of Liam Cosgrave, Haughey turned away from any attempted solution in a Northern Ireland context and sought a Dublin-London basis for moving forward. He initiated this approach at the conference of his ruling Fianna Fail Party on February 17, when he invited Margaret Thatcher's government to join his own in "a joint effort" on Northern Ireland. On May 21 he went to London for his first meeting with the British prime minister, where he repeated the offer. A joint

communiqué issued after the meeting referred to the "new and closer cooperation" and the "unique relationship" between Britain and the Republic of Ireland but did not encourage any belief in a joint initiative.

On November 1 legislation on contraceptives came into force, requiring that they be prescribed by doctors and supplied by pharmacists. Many doctors and pharmacists declined to provide them on moral grounds, and there was widespread uncertainty over what legal action would be taken against the very large numbers of people who, either privately or as organizers of family planning clinics, were in violation of the law. The conservatism of this legislation was echoed by a government decision not to enter all-party negotiations on divorce, which was banned under the constitution.

(*See also* Great Britain.)

ISRAEL

Israel in 1980 appeared, especially to its almost 3½ million Jewish citizens, as a society that was beleaguered from both within and without. Isolated at the UN, the nation had lost count of, and interest in, the seemingly endless resolutions passed by the General Assembly and the Security Council that condemned one aspect or another of Israeli policy and practice. There was in Israel still great admiration for Egyptian Pres. Anwar El-Sadat and belief in his good intentions. But there was also a degree of uneasiness about the future once Sadat was no longer at the helm in Egypt. There seemed in 1980 no one to whom Israel could turn as an automatic ally and friend. It was as if the nation had been contained behind a moat filled with oil and petrodollars. The political and psychological boycott of Israel was almost total in 1980.

The Problem of Disunity

It was a situation that called for the harnessing of all the country's political, economic, and psychological resources. Instead, however, there was an ever widening gulf between the coalition government of Prime Minister Menachem Begin and the popular mood. As the government's parliamentary majorities began to shrink, the credibility of some of its coalition partners was eroded to the point of nonexistence.

This was especially true of the Democratic Movement for Change, led by former army chief of staff Yigael Yadin. When he had joined the Begin government as deputy prime minister, he had commanded a parliamentary group of 15 members and a substantial plurality among voters. But every public opinion poll during the year showed that the voters who had defected to Yadin in 1977 had returned to the Labour Party in 1980.

On a personal level Begin also experienced difficulties. One of his most impressive Cabinet members, Moshe Dayan, had resigned as foreign minister in October 1979; then in May 1980 Ezer

Weizman, the minister of defense and the architect of Begin's election victory in 1977, resigned amid much public recrimination with the prime minister. For Weizman the disagreement centred on cuts in the defense budget that had been proposed by Finance Minister Yigael Hurwitz and supported by Begin. Weizman objected to the cuts on the grounds that they would adversely affect Israel's independent defensive capacity. Against the background of Israel's international isolation, Weizman argued that defense was of greater importance than inflation and that other means, even if politically unpopular, would have to be found to reduce government expenditures.

It was significant that Begin could not persuade either of his two closest colleagues, both considered to be hard-liners, Foreign Minister Yitzhak Shamir and the chairman of the Knesset Defense and Foreign Affairs Committee, Moshe Arens, to accept

The final interim withdrawal of Israel from territory in the Sinai was completed in January 1980 under the terms of the March 1979 peace treaty signed in Washington, D.C.
WIDE WORLD

the defense portfolio. Begin himself kept the post and by year's end still had not resolved the question of cutting defense expenditure. The last days of the year were marked by particular tension as Hurwitz threatened to resign and take his faction out of the governing coalition unless his proposed budget cuts were enacted. This could have precipitated the fall of the government, but on December 21 Begin finally agreed to Hurwitz's conditions.

On November 19 the government survived a no-confidence vote. Subsequently, Weizman, who had voted against the government, was expelled from Begin's Herut Party, leaving the government without a parliamentary majority.

Jerusalem Dispute

It was clearly with an eye to the coming elections that the government supported a bill, introduced into the Knesset (parliament) in May, that affirmed Jerusalem as the capital of Israel. Eventually, its passage created considerable difficulty for Israel in international relations and consolidated opposition.

Jerusalem, at least that part of Jerusalem held by Israel at that time, had become the de facto capital of Israel in December 1949. Despite some protests, the status of Jerusalem was accepted without its having been formally recognized by the major Western powers. This situation remained unchanged when Israel formally annexed East Jerusalem in June 1967, thereby reuniting the city.

In the Camp David discussions with President Carter and President Sadat it had been agreed to leave the Jerusalem question to the end. However, on June 30, the UN Security Council passed a resolution declaring Israel's position in East Jerusalem to be devoid of legal basis and calling on Israel to withdraw from that part of the city and dismantle all settlements established since 1967.

To the surprise of many Israelis, a somewhat differently worded resolution restating the Arab character of East Jerusalem was passed about the same time by Egypt's National Assembly. This was echoed far more forcibly in other Arab capitals.

The Begin government thus was faced by a choice of carrying on with Jerusalem as Israel's de facto capital and waiting for a suitable time when its status could be formalized, or defying its critics with a formal declaration by the Knesset confirming Israel's annexation of East Jerusalem. The bill, introduced by the right-wing Tehya Party, deprived the government of this choice and forced it to decide on formalizing the city's status immediately.

On July 30 the Knesset approved by a large majority, which included many leading members of the opposition Labour Party, an amended version of the "Jerusalem Basic Law," declaring "United" Jerusalem the capital of Israel and seat of its government. Politically, it was an unnecessary law, adding nothing to the already existing Israeli position in Jerusalem. Some saw it as an annoyance, others as a calculated provocation. It produced a

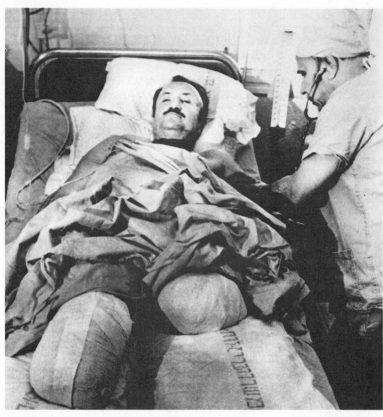

Palestinian Mayor Bassam as-Shaka of Nablus lost both legs when his car was bombed in June in one of a series of terrorist attacks against Palestinians.
UPI

furor of denunciation in the Islamic countries. Conferences calling for a jihad (holy war) against Israel were held in Iran, Libya, and Morocco; Saudi Arabia's Crown Prince Fahd issued a personal call for such a jihad.

Jerusalem's Mayor Teddy Kollek said that he regretted the bill in its entirety. "I think the people of Jerusalem, Jew and Arab, will benefit nothing from this law." However, it served its purpose for Israel's adversaries. Several embassies in Jerusalem were withdrawn as a result of Arab and Islamic pressures. Western governments that had not given a second thought to the transaction of diplomatic business in Jerusalem now had a change of heart.

The Economy

Meanwhile, Israel had become increasingly preoccupied toward year's end with the position of the economy and the future of the Begin administration. The economy suffered from high inflation, but the figures quoted—up to 200% in 1980—were largely meaningless because they resulted from a network of index-linked prices. One leading authority put the actual rate of inflation in real terms at about 20%, slightly higher than that in Britain.

In general, economic or social conditions were not as critical as they had been in the winter of 1966–67 when there had been 100,000 unemployed, when emigration exceeded immigration, when there were real food shortages in some development

towns, and when the morale of the country was at its lowest ebb. Six months later, in June 1967, Israel fought its most successful war, and the economy then began to expand as never before.

In February 1980 the government introduced the shekel in place of the Israeli pound, with ten old pounds making a new shekel. The change made no detectable difference to the economy.

1981 Elections

There was one other development of major significance during the last days of the year. It had been assumed that the Begin government, though unpopular, would probably be returned to power in a spring 1981 election. This was because the only alternative to the Begin government, the Labour Alignment, had been so fundamentally divided that it had been unable to muster an alternative and united administration.

Therefore, when the Labour Party convention met in Tel Aviv in December, it was assumed that it would present a sad spectacle of divided counsels and divided leaders. It turned out otherwise. The party chairman, Shimon Peres, a protegé of Israel's first prime minister, David Ben-Gurion, and a lifelong colleague of Moshe Dayan, was reelected chairman with a 70% majority vote. By the end of the convention Peres had emerged as the undisputed leader who was accepted also by the minority. The public opinion polls had for months indicated a landslide Labour victory in the 1981 elections provided it could resolve its leadership differences. Therefore, the unity displayed at the convention made it seem likely that Labour might emerge from an election with a clear majority for the first time since the establishment of Israel.

(*See also* Middle Eastern Affairs.)

ITALY

Italy in 1980 suffered its worst natural disaster in more than 70 years when an earthquake struck a large area of the south on November 23. It killed more than 3,000 people, injured nearly 8,000, and caused millions of dollars worth of damage. The earthquake had its epicentre in the mountains of Irpinia, east of Naples. Dozens of mountain villages in the predominantly poor region were destroyed, and an area the size of Belgium was devastated. The relief operation was slow to get under way, and hundreds of victims trapped alive under the rubble of their homes died because of the failure of rescuers to move in quickly with heavy equipment to clear the rubble. More than 250,000 people were made homeless. Relief supplies were sent from all over the world, but there was widespread criticism of the lack of a proper civil defense organization to deal with this foreseeable catastrophe.

Naples suffered extensive damage. Hundreds of buildings were declared unsafe for habitation, but many residents refused to be evacuated away from the area to vacation homes along the coast that had been requisitioned for the purpose. The ruins of Pompeii and Herculaneum suffered extensive damage, and hundreds of churches, convents, castles, and historic monuments in Avellino, Irpinia, and Basilicata were destroyed or seriously damaged.

Despite progress by the authorities in the battle against terrorism, 1980 was Italy's worst year ever for terrorist murders. The indiscriminate massacre of 76 persons at the Bologna railway station by a bomb placed in a waiting room shocked the nation. A state funeral was held for the victims, but most families chose private burial ceremonies—a sign of the lack of confidence in the government by ordinary Italians. Responsibility for the bomb was pinned upon neofascists; a prominent Rome psychologist was charged with organizing the attack.

A long series of victims of the Red Brigades and the Front Line, the two main left-wing terrorist organizations, included Gen. Enrico Galvaligi of northern Italy's antiterrorism police force, Mario Amato, a leading investigator into neofascist terrorist crime, and one of Italy's leading journalists, Walter Tobagi of the Milan newspaper *Corriere della Sera*.

The Red Brigades directed a campaign against Italy's antiquated prison system. They kidnapped a Rome judge, Giovanni D'Urso, staged a prison revolt at the maximum security jail at Trani in southern Italy, and murdered several senior prison officials. In December Marco Donat-Cattin, the son of a former Christian Democrat minister, was arrested by French police in Paris. He was wanted by Italian police on charges of armed subversion and was suspected of being a leading member of the Front Line. Earlier in the year the Italian press reported that Premier Francesco Cossiga had tipped off Donat-Cattin's father that a security net was tightening around his son. A full-scale parliamentary investigation into allegations of misconduct by the premier was held, but Cossiga was cleared.

Two new governments were formed during the year, bringing to 40 the number of administrations that have held office in Italy since World War II. But there was no basic change in the direction of policy by the ruling Christian Democrats. More than seven million Italians entitled to vote in the June elections failed to cast a valid vote, reflecting growing disillusionment with the political system. Voting is compulsory in Italy.

Arnaldo Forlani (left) was sworn in as Italy's new premier on October 18 in Rome after the resignation of Francesco Cossiga in September.
UPI

On October 18 Arnaldo Forlani took office as premier at the head of one of the broadest based coalitions since World War II, one that included Christian Democrats, Socialists, Social Democrats, and Republicans. The agreement by the two Socialist parties, which had split in 1947, to work together again was a significant development. The agreement in April by the Socialists to return to government in a coalition with the Christian Democrats, after an absence of six years, marked a move back toward the centre-left type of coalition that governed Italy during the 1960s and early 1970s.

Kidnap crime continued unabated, and more than $10 million was paid in ransoms. Police reported 46 kidnappings during the year, a slight decrease from 1979. On January 16 police in Milan intercepted a consignment of drugs that was the largest ever seized in Western Europe, 80 lb of pure heroin destined for the U.S. market.

Foreign Affairs

Italy's presidency of the European Economic Community from January to June 1980 was interrupted by a government crisis in Rome that caused the postponement of an EEC summit meeting in Brussels in March. Heads of government of the EEC met in Venice in June.

Pres. Alessandro Pertini paid a state visit to China in September. He had to cut short his tour because of the outbreak of the second government crisis during the year. Great Britain's Queen Elizabeth II paid a state visit to Italy from October 14 to 20, after which she was received by Pope John Paul II at the Vatican.

A joint venture was signed in September between Italy's state-owned Alfa-Romeo Automobile Co. and the Japanese manufacturer Nissan for the establishment near Naples of a factory for the assembly of a new Italo-Japanese compact automobile. The venture was strongly criticized because it would allow the Japanese into Italy's large domestic automobile market.

The Economy

The fall of the Cossiga government in September was caused by a parliamentary defeat on a package of economic measures aimed at combating the rise in both unemployment and inflation. The bank rate rose to an all-time high of 16½%, and one of the most severe credit squeezes ever imposed in Italy was put into effect to prevent international speculation against the lira. The increasing cost of oil placed a growing burden on Italy's balance of payments, while the rate of inflation rose to 21%.

A month-long strike took place in Italy's biggest private industry, the Fiat automobile group. Pickets prevented workers from entering the factories. The strike came to an abrupt end in mid-October, however, after tens of thousands of workers from both Fiat and other industries affected by the strike demonstrated in favour of the right to work.

JAPAN

The year 1980 saw an unexpected turnabout in the fortunes of the majority Liberal-Democratic Party (LDP), which had dominated Japanese politics in the postwar era. In mid-May a nationwide survey conducted by Kyodo News Service revealed that 64% of the respondents did not support the government of Masayoshi Ohira. Over half of those interviewed cited domestic issues, particularly concern with inflation.

On May 16 a vote of no confidence against the Ohira Cabinet, sponsored by the Japan Socialist Party (JSP), passed the lower house because 69 LDP members belonging to anti-Ohira factions absented themselves from the floor. On May 19, just seven months after the previous election, Prime Minister Ohira dissolved the lower house and set a general election to coincide with the triennial poll for the House of Councillors. On May 31 Ohira was hospitalized for extreme fatigue, and on June 12 he died unexpectedly, the victim of a heart attack. Chief Cabinet Secretary Masayoshi Ito became acting prime minister.

The unprecedented double election on June 22 attracted a high voter turnout (74.57%). Ohira's untimely death served to unify the LDP, which alone

Representatives of 112 nations attended the funeral of Masayoshi Ohira, prime minister of Japan, who died of a heart attack on June 12 in a Tokyo hospital.
ULYSSE GOSSET–SYGMA

Emperor Hirohito (right) and Chinese Premier Hua Guofeng shared a toast during Hua's visit to Japan in May, the first visit to Japan by a Chinese head of state in 2,000 years.
WIDE WORLD

among the major parties increased its share of the popular vote (47.9%). This was translated into a comfortable majority of 284 of 511 seats in the lower house. With 69 successful candidates, the LDP increased its total in the 252-seat upper house to 135 seats.

On July 15 a dark horse, Zenko Suzuki, 69, was selected to succeed Ohira as president of the LDP, and on July 17 he was elected Japan's 15th postwar prime minister in a special session of the Diet. Suzuki inherited a series of unfolding scandals that had embarrassed Ohira's government. In October 1979 personnel of the Kokusai Denshin Denwa (KDD), Japan's privately owned overseas telecommunications service, had been caught in the act of smuggling expensive accessories while going through customs at the New Tokyo International Airport at Narita. Early in 1980 two KDD employees committed suicide and left notes stating that they had been made scapegoats by Yoichi Sato, former head of the KDD president's office. Sato was arrested on February 24 and was charged with embezzling 15 million yen from the KDD to buy influence from Diet members and to impress foreign customers. A former official and a serving section chief of the Ministry of Posts and Telecommunications were arrested on March 18 on bribery charges. On April 5 the Tokyo Metropolitan Police Department arrested Manabu Itano, former president of the KDD, who had resigned in November 1979, and charged him with misappropriation of 17 million yen from expense accounts.

Meanwhile, on September 19, Health and Welfare Minister Kunikichi Saito resigned "to take political and moral responsibility" for receiving some 13 million yen in political donations from a hospital director under fire for malpractice.

Recession was not evenly felt throughout Japanese industry. In July the nation's automobile production reached an all-time monthly high of 1,039,770 units. Of particular significance for Japanese-U.S. trade, Toyota Motor Sales reported 3,130,392 cars sold in fiscal 1979, including 1,-502,491 exported (an increase of 19.8%). Honda Motor Co. reported its consolidated net sales for the year ended March 31 at 1,307,700,000,000 yen.

On May 7 the Defense Agency disclosed details of a controversial plan for procuring modern weapons systems. The agency envisaged increasing the annual defense budget from the current 0.9% of GNP to a full 1%, at a cost of about U.S. $6.5 billion between fiscal 1980 and 1984. In remarks before the Diet, Justice Minister Seisuke Okuno supported revision of the constitution, in apparent reference to the celebrated art. 9, which renounces war. Opposition parties, labour unions, and citizens' groups criticized Okuno, and on September 3 Secretary-General Yoshio Sakurauchi of the LDP said Okuno had expressed a personal opinion and had "gone to extremes as a state minister." Thus, although public opinion increasingly favoured enlarging Japan's Self-Defense Forces (SDF), the defense issue remained a delicate one.

The Economy

Sharp increases in the price of imported crude oil led to a record $13.9 billion balance of payments deficit on current account for fiscal 1979 (ended March 31, 1980). This represented a deterioration of $25.7 billion from the $11.8 billion surplus in fiscal 1978. As a result, the U.S. dollar soared to a 30-month high in Tokyo on April 1 (253.65

Zenko Suzuki (centre), president of the Liberal-Democratic Party, was named new prime minister of Japan after a vote by the Diet on July 17 to replace Masayoshi Ohira.

yen = U.S. $1), and Japan's foreign exchange reserves fell below $20 billion at the end of March. (Later, in July, the balance of payments returned to the black.)

Strident demands by Americans that Japan reduce its exports of automobiles to the U.S. obscured Japan's softening balance of payments position. On February 13 in Tokyo, Douglas Fraser, president of the United Auto Workers, urged Japan to restrict exports under an orderly marketing agreement. "The impact of the tremendous flow of cars to the U.S. is having serious consequences on the American economy and employment of auto workers," Fraser said. He told Ohira that he wanted to avoid import quotas. Honda decided in January to build an assembly plant in Ohio that would produce 10,000 cars a month. Toyota Motor Co. and Nissan Motor Co. also looked into locating assembly plants in the U.S. In Washington in July, Eiji Toyoda, president of Toyota, stated that his firm envisaged a joint venture with Ford for co-production of 20,000 small cars a month in the U.S. On August 21 Tokyo asked Washington to postpone or reduce scheduled import tariffs on Japanese truck cab-chassis units.

Foreign Affairs

The dialogue between Tokyo and Washington was concerned with longer-range issues, however. In Tokyo in July for Ohira's official funeral, U.S. Pres. Jimmy Carter told Japanese media that the thing to remember was not the trade problem but "the resolution we have to resolve problems working together." On January 14 U.S. Defense Secretary Harold Brown, stopping in Tokyo on his way home from China, had expressed the hope that Japan would increase its defense expenditures, taking into account the current international situation. President Carter used his trip to Tokyo to meet with Chinese Premier Hua Guofeng (Hua Kuofeng). In a rather pointed statement, President Carter called for sharing by the U.S., China, and Japan of "long-range strategic concerns to minimize the threat of a Soviet military buildup."

Meanwhile, Beijing was being represented in Tokyo on the highest level. In late May Premier Hua had visited Japan and had tacitly concurred with Ohira's comment that Japan should increase its defense expenditures, following national consensus and taking financial difficulties into consideration. In the presence of the two prime ministers, Foreign Minister Saburo Okita and his Chinese counterpart, Huang Hua, signed a Sino-Japanese scientific and technological treaty. In Tokyo for the Ohira funeral, Hua stated that his nation would continue to promote closer relations among Japan, the U.S., the nations of Western Europe, and the third world in order to build world peace.

In his annual policy speech to the Diet on January 25, Ohira set the tone for Japanese-Soviet relations during the year. He condemned the Soviet invasion of Afghanistan and stated that Japan would press for immediate withdrawal. Under government pressure, Katsuji Shibata, president of Japan's Olympic Committee, announced on May 24 "with a heavy heart" that his group had voted to boycott the summer games in Moscow because of the Afghanistan situation. Returning from the Venice (Italy) summit meeting of industrial powers in June, Foreign Minister Okita reported that leaders of the seven nations involved had agreed on a condemnation of the Soviet intervention.

In his January policy speech, Ohira had labeled as "an extremely regrettable situation" the Soviet military buildup on the southernmost of the Kuril Islands, northeast of Hokkaido, which were claimed by Japan. Later, a White Paper on defense listed Moscow's deployment of medium-range SS-20 missiles and Backfire bombers in the region and tanks, heavy artillery, and troops on Shikotan in the Kurils, with these forces reinforced by the Soviet Pacific Fleet. The paper admitted that Japan's SDF was inadequate to meet the threat.

The quarrel between Tokyo and Moscow had

been further exacerbated by the indictment, on February 8, of retired SDF Gen. Yukihisa Miyanaga and two serving officers in an espionage case. The Tokyo public prosecutor charged the trio with passing military intelligence concerning China to Col. Yuri Kozlov of the Soviet embassy. Both the army chief of staff and the director-general of the SDF lost their posts over the incident.

JORDAN

Jordan surprised political observers in 1980 by its staunch support during the Iran-Iraq war for Iraqi Pres. Saddam Hussein at-Takriti. King Hussein said on October 5 that military support for Iraq was possible, although an immediate U.S. reaction warning him against taking military action appeared to rule this out. However, the use of Aqaba as a supply route for war materials to Iraq appeared to have been amply proved by Western newsmen.

During 1980 three men acted as prime minister. The death of Sharif Abdul Hamid Sharaf on July 3 was a blow to the king. He was succeeded as caretaker by Qassim ar-Rimawi, a Palestinian and formerly deputy prime minister and agriculture minister. Hussein decided in August to reappoint Mudar Badran, the longest serving prime minister in Jordan's modern history, possibly because he felt a non-Palestinian could help heal a widening breach with Syria produced by Jordan's friendship with Iraq and by Syria's accusations that Jordan was assisting the opposition Muslim Brotherhood in Damascus and other centres. In November Syria

King Hussein of Jordan (right) was greeted by Pres. Saddam Hussein at-Takriti of Iraq during his visit to Iraq in October.
UPI

massed troops on the Jordanian border. Jordan responded by sending its own troops, but after a tense period both countries pulled back their forces.

Hussein's tough mandate to Badran was to end Israel's occupation of Arab territory, including Jerusalem. His Cabinet also included a new ministry (replacing a government bureau)—Occupied Territories Affairs. The royal mandate also stated that Jordan should encourage the European Economic Community to develop a Middle East policy based on "high principles, right, and justice."

The economy was handicapped by huge capital expenditure on major projects such as the Dead Sea potash works and the Aqaba phosphate fertilizer factory, but within five to six years the revenues from such investment might help to close the trade gap. In 1979 exports were a record 120.9 million Jordanian dinars, equivalent to U.S. $404.3 million, but imports were 585.6 million dinars, equivalent then to $1,554,800,000. Crude oil imports from Saudi Arabia made up 11% of the total import bill.

Meeting human needs was to be one of the main aims of the 1981–85 five-year plan, possibly at the expense of heavy industrial investment. In late 1980 government committees were still at the stage of establishing costs and listing priorities. Jordan was unlikely to lose its free-market status for foreign contractors, with the government broadly committed to a liberal policy on repatriation of profits made by foreign companies.

Jordan's relationship with the U.S. appeared to be improving in June, when King Hussein met U.S. Pres. Jimmy Carter. The U.S. administration appeared to have at last accepted Jordan's fundamental opposition to the Camp David accords between Israel and Egypt.

Jordan's acceptability to Western financial markets was shown in mid-1980 by the successful syndication of a $150 million loan for the government. Alia, the Royal Jordanian Airline, raised credits for aircraft finance from both the U.S. Export-Import Bank and the U.K.'s Export Credits Guarantee Department. Inflation was 13.6% in the 12 months ended June 1980, and the domestic economy was fairly liquid, particularly because of the continuing high level of expatriate remittances from Jordanians resident in the Persian Gulf area. The relationship with Iraq produced a gift of $100 million in August for "development and programs to build national strength."

(*See also* Middle Eastern Affairs.)

KENYA

With disagreements over division of the assets of the East African Community still unresolved, nothing of consequence emerged from the meeting of East African heads of state attended by Pres. Daniel arap Moi in Arusha, Tanzania, on Jan. 2, 1980. Recurrent hopes that a solution might be found to the dispute between Kenya and Tanzania that had led to the closing of the frontier between the two

CAMERAPIX/KEYSTONE

*Pope John Paul II visited Kenya during his
11-day, six-nation African tour in May.*

countries also proved vain. Visits by President Moi to West Germany, Britain, and the U.S. in February had a happier outcome in the form of offers of food aid and help with the country's balance of payments. On the debit side were restraints on industrial output resulting from cuts in the electricity supply during February and March, made necessary by the exceptionally low rainfall.

In March Pres. Godfrey L. Binaisa of Uganda visited Kenya, raising speculation that disillusionment with Tanzania's continuing role in Uganda might lead to some rapprochement between Uganda and Kenya. Binaisa's overthrow in May put an end to such ideas, and in September, following a border incursion, Kenya stopped rail and road movement of Uganda's coffee. A meeting of the foreign ministers of Kenya and Ethiopia in Mombasa in April led to an agreement between the two countries to monitor Somali military activities on their respective borders.

Pope John Paul II visited Kenya in May during his tour of the African continent. Also in May, ministers of the African, Caribbean, and Pacific countries met ministers of the European Economic Community (EEC) in Nairobi. Kenya was among a number of countries pressing for restoration of their sugar quotas, since Kenya's own output of sugar was now showing a hopeful surplus.

In spite of help from the U.S., basic foods remained in short supply. Special famine relief arrangements were made to assist the people of the northwest, who had been severely affected by drought and by the unrest along the Uganda-Kenya border. Supplies of food from the EEC helped to reduce the sufferings of these people, but the July rains came too late to enable them to take full advantage of the season for planting crops. Meanwhile, the price of petroleum products soared. The president's visit to several Middle Eastern countries produced no tangible help.

In June President Moi made changes in his Cabinet, the most significant being the appointment of Charles Njonjo, one of the most influential men in the country, to the new Ministry of Home and Constitutional Affairs. In April Njonjo had retired from the office of attorney general, which he had held with considerable effect since Kenya's independence in 1963, and almost immediately afterward he had been returned unopposed to Parliament.

In August one of China's vice-premiers, Ji Pengfei (Chi P'eng-fei), visited Nairobi. President Moi visited Beijing (Peking) in September.

Pres. Julius Nyerere (right) of Tanzania and Pres. Daniel arap Moi of Kenya (centre) were entertained by dancers in January. Moi visited Tanzania to attend a meeting of East African heads of state.

CAMERAPIX/KEYSTONE

South Korea's worst civil unrest took place in Kwangju in May; protesters against government policies took to the streets, fighting government troops, and ten days of rioting ensued. More than 170 persons were killed.
UPI

KOREA

South Korea opened the year with a promise of liberalization; Pres. Choi Kyu Hah announced an amnesty to restore the civil rights of 687 former opponents of assassinated president Park Chung Hee. The move generated enthusiasm among politicians and new hope among students. As the two groups turned to political activism, however, the mood changed—and the country slipped swiftly into stern military rule as before.

The process began in March with student unrest in Seoul; activists expelled by the late Park's regime and readmitted by Choi's agitated for the removal of Park's soldiers from the universities. The agitation expanded to include demands for political reform. By May major disturbances engulfed several universities despite the closing by the Martial Law Command of the National Assembly and the headquarters of both major political parties.

What was widely described as an armed rebellion developed in Kwangju, approximately 266 km (165 mi) south of Seoul. Armed students and other rioters captured the city, gutted one radio and television station, occupied government buildings, and demanded an end to martial law. Troops laid siege to the city and eventually mounted a full-scale military assault to beat the protesters into submission on May 27. According to official estimates 144 civilians were killed along with 22 soldiers and 4 policemen. Some 800 rebels were arrested, while at least 200 armed students escaped. Damage from the Kwangju uprising was estimated at $45 million.

Even before the climactic eruption of violence in Kwangju, the military had decided to do away with the civilian trappings of government. After an emergency Cabinet session on May 17, the military took control of the country, extending martial law, banning all political activity, and closing all universities and colleges. On May 20 President Choi's Cabinet, headed by Premier Shin Hyon Hwak, resigned.

Already political power had passed to the standing committee of the Special Committee for National Security Measures. Military officers were in the majority of those appointed to the standing committee, headed by strong man Lieut. Gen. Chun Doo Hwan. On August 27, a few days after he announced his formal retirement from the Army, Chun was elected president of South Korea with 2,524 of the 2,525 electoral college votes cast. One vote was invalid. There was no other candidate.

The president had appointed on May 21 a Cabinet headed by Prime Minister Park Choong Hoon; they were replaced by Nam Duck Woo and a 20-member Cabinet on September 2. But real power remained with an "inner circle" of close advisers, all generals. A "purification" drive was quickly launched against "corruptors of power" and "social agitators," among them several leading members of the former Park regime. One of them, Democratic Republican Party boss Kim Jong Pil, retired from public life after handing over to the government $36 million worth of corruptly earned assets to avoid prosecution.

The most celebrated case concerned the country's best-known opposition figure, Kim Dae Jung. He was arrested as the student demonstrations swept into the Kwangju region, his birthplace and stronghold. He was put on trial on charges of inciting students and of collaboration with Communists. On September 17, after a 29-day trial, a military court found him guilty of antistate activities and sentenced him to death by hanging. The verdict triggered a worldwide uproar. Japan in particular publicly put pressure on the Chun government to avert an execution; at one point, it threatened to cut off economic relations that were crucial to South Korea. Seoul objected strongly to the pressure tactics, maintaining that due process of the

South Korean Pres. Chun Doo Hwan (left) hears the oath of office taken by members of his Cabinet on September 2; Chun was elected August 27 to replace Choi Kyu Hah, who resigned August 16.
UPI

country's laws would be carried out. By the year's end there was no indication as to whether or not Kim would be hanged.

At the end of September the president released a draft constitution to replace the existing Yushin (Revitalizing) Constitution devised by Park. He also called for new elections for president and Parliament before June 30, 1981. The new constitution reduced the powers of the president in favour of Parliament and limited him to a single seven-year term. On October 22 the nation's voters overwhelmingly approved the draft constitution in a referendum. Five days later the government officially promulgated the document, thereby ushering in the Fifth Republic.

Democratic People's Republic of Korea (North Korea)

Preparation for a leadership change and what looked like an economic policy shift dominated North Korean events during 1980. The highlight of the year was a party congress in October, the first in ten years. In his speech there, Pres. Kim Il Sung proposed direct talks with the U.S. to forge an agreement that would replace the cease-fire pact ending the Korean War in 1953. He wanted the U.S. to withdraw its 30,400 troops from South Korea and then have the two Koreas form a confederation as "the most realistic and reasonable way" to reunify the peninsula. He also declared that his government was ready to establish friendly relations with capitalistic countries as long as they were not hostile to his nation.

One of the chief purposes of the congress, however, was expected to be the nomination of Kim's 40-year-old son, Kim Chong Il, as the new party chief and thus the successor to his father as supreme leader of the nation. However, no official announcements were made at the gathering, but Kim Chong Il headed a committee appointed by the

congress to restructure the all-powerful party Central Committee. He was already secretary of the Central Committee and referred to as "Beloved Leader." He was not formally declared heir apparent, but the congress nevertheless made him the country's second most influential personage by appointing him to three powerful posts: second rank in the party's secretariat, after his father; fourth member of a newly created Standing Committee of the party Politburo; and third-ranking member of the Military Affairs Committee.

KUWAIT

Kuwait adopted a policy of studied neutrality during the Iraq-Iran war, opening its hospitals to the wounded of both sides. Thousands of refugees from Iraq passed through Kuwait in the first days of the fighting. Kuwait's ports provided an alternative to Iraq's blocked Basra and Umm Qasr ports; they had been so used even before war broke out, to relieve congestion.

Parliamentary elections were promised for February 1981, and women were likely to get the vote for the first time. The decision to revive the National Assembly (suspended in 1976) caused some surprise, since during 1980 several politically motivated crimes were committed. Kuwait had cut off official aid to Egypt when it signed a bilateral peace with Israel, but commercial links were maintained. Elsewhere, Kuwait invested in petrochemicals ventures, but instead of simply exporting capital, Kuwait sent management as well.

Oil production decreased from 2 million bbl a day to 1.5 million bbl on April 1, and the possibility of cuts was raised. Oil minister Sheikh Ali Khalifah as-Sabah stressed that Kuwait would drop allowable production only if other members of the Organization of Petroleum Exporting Countries (OPEC) agreed. Kuwait's importance as a financial centre complementing Bahrain in the lower Persian

French Pres. Valéry Giscard d'Estaing traveled to Kuwait in March to meet with Sheikh Jabir al-Ahmad al-Jabir as-Sabah (left), emir of Kuwait. During his visit Giscard endorsed "self-determination" as a Palestinian right.
KEYSTONE

Gulf was confirmed when, in late 1980, the government allowed the Kuwait dinar bond market (shut down in 1979) to reopen.

LABOUR AND EMPLOYMENT

The American Federation of Labor-Congress of Industrial Organizations (AFL-CIO) entered 1980 without the strong leadership of George Meany, its president from the merger of the old AFL and CIO in 1955 until 1979. A long and productive era for American labour ended with Meany's retirement in November 1979 and his death, at 85, on Jan. 10, 1980. Lane Kirkland, AFL-CIO secretary-treasurer under Meany and a former official of the Masters, Mates & Pilots, succeeded to the presidency.

The year was a difficult one for labour. Inflation, heavy layoffs in many industries, widespread plant closings, strong attacks by conservative forces, and, on November 4, political setbacks challenged the unions' efforts to sustain growth and influence.

Union Membership

Heavy layoffs during 1980 affected union membership rolls and treasuries. Those who lost jobs permanently in auto, steel, and other industries dropped from union rolls, while millions of others who were furloughed but subject to recall to jobs were exempt from dues. The United Auto Workers (UAW), the hardest hit, reported more than 300,000 either permanently or indefinitely off its rolls by the fall of 1980. The United Steelworkers had lost 200,000. Meanwhile, financial problems curbed organizing operations.

AFL-CIO's secretary-treasurer, Thomas Donahue, reported that the federation's unions would have to organize 375,000 new workers a year if the AFL-CIO's membership was to stay just even. Preliminary figures indicated that AFL-CIO membership remained near 1979 levels in 1980, at between 13.5 million and 13.8 million. In 1979 all unions and em-

ployee associations had a combined total of 24.3 million. With union representation in factories continuing to drop and membership now rising more slowly among public employees, the total for 1980 was expected to show a modest increase and might reverse growth trends with a decline for the year.

The national work force was continuing to increase faster than union membership. The most recent U.S. Department of Labor report, for 1978, showed that only 19.7% of eligible workers were in unions. Excluding farm workers, the ratio unionized was 23.6%. Unions feared the ratios for 1980 would be a little lower. Organized labour spoke for a slowly declining number of workers.

Not all news was bad for unions in 1980. Unions won major victories in the South, where the ratio of workers unionized was relatively low. The United Steelworkers won bargaining rights for 16,000 shipyard workers in Newport News, Va., after a long strike. The Amalgamated Clothing & Textile Workers settled a long and bitter dispute with J. P. Stevens Co. in Roanoke Rapids and High Point, N.C., and the AFL-CIO hailed the settlement as "an historic breakthrough" in Southern textile organizing. The United Furniture Workers moved its national headquarters to Nashville, Tenn., heartland of the U.S. furniture industry, and reported substantial organizing gains in the area.

Women in Unions

Shortly after Lane Kirkland assumed the presidency of the AFL-CIO, he won approval by the federation's all-male executive council for the election of its first woman member, Joyce Dannen Miller, a vice-president of the Amalgamated Clothing & Textile Workers. She was also president of the Coalition of Labor Union Women, a nationwide organization of women that advocates increased participation of women in unions and politics.

Although the number of women in unions was

growing, women made up only about 28.1% of the total—roughly 6.9 million of the 24.3 million. Only 15% of women eligible for union membership were in unions. Within unions, a few women had been elected to national office as vice-presidents, but not one was the top officer of a major union. The election of Miller to the AFL-CIO council was part of a planned strategy to unionize more women, particularly those crowded into "female job ghettos," including clerical, domestic, sales, and service work. Because of low pay in these areas, the average wage of working women had slipped to only 59% of the average working man's wage, a lower ratio than 25 years earlier.

Settlements and Strikes

Major collective bargaining agreements during the first nine months of 1980 increased wages by 30

Unions scored a big victory in 1980 when employees of ten J. P. Stevens textile plants were unionized after a 17-year battle. Here workers in Roanoke Rapids, North Carolina, cheer the acceptance of their contract.
UPI

to 37%, the actual amount to depend on the national inflation rate through 1982. U.S. Department of Labor reports showed settlements covering 2.9 million workers through September averaged 9.7% in first-year raises (not including cost-of-living adjustments) and 7.3% a year over the term of contracts, usually three years. The figures compared with 7.4% for the first year and 6% over the contract term in agreements signed in the comparable period of 1979. Workers under COLA (cost-of-living adjustment) contracts received 6.1% pay adjustments during the first nine months.

The government said the sharp rise in consumer prices in 1979, 13.3% for the year, caused determined "catch up" bargaining by unions and resulted in higher settlements in 1980. Its 7.5 to 9.5% guideline for acceptable increases remained in effect, but the top limits were strained.

Typically, the United Steelworkers settled in its industries for an average 33 cents an hour in the first year, to be followed by 28 cents in 1981 and 23 cents in 1982. Cost-of-living adjustments could add as much as $2.60 an hour more to pay by 1983 if inflation continued at the 1980 rate.

The United Auto Workers demanded and won from Chrysler a corporate board seat in return for cost-cutting concessions to the financially troubled automaker. The UAW's president, Douglas A. Fraser, became the first U.S. union executive to hold a corporate decision-making appointment.

The Communications Workers of America settled with the Bell System of nationwide telephone companies for 34% over three years for 525,000 CWA-represented employees. The bargaining went to a strike deadline but ended peacefully.

Generally, 1980 was a year for strike-free negotiations. There were some long walkouts, but the first nine months showed fewer stoppages, involving fewer workers, than in the comparable period of 1979. More time was lost, an increase of 1.5 million workdays, because 16 strikes involved more than 10,000 workers (compared with seven strikes in 1979), and some of these were lengthy.

The biggest strikes were in farm equipment, copper, silver, oil, construction, and motion picture and television industries—walkouts in the last of these delaying the start of the 1980–81 television season. Public employee and school strikes erupted again across the country. Strikes by musicians and other artists delayed the opening of the Metropolitan Opera in New York and forced cancellation or delays in symphony orchestra seasons in a number of areas.

Employment

The unemployment rate followed the movements of the U.S. economy as a whole in 1980: it rose to over 6% in the first quarter, the first time it had pierced that level in more than two years. Mirroring the recession, by May it had reached 7.6%, producing the largest quarter-to-quarter jump in joblessness on record, but in the summer it began a slow and hesitant descent that brought it to 7.4% of the labour force by year's end—still substantially above the 5.9% level that prevailed a year earlier.

During the year the unemployment rate for adult men, which is highly sensitive to the business cycle, both rose earlier and declined earlier than that for other groups—increasing by half a percentage point to 4.7% in the first quarter before hitting a peak of 6.7% around midyear and then slipping to 6.2% by year's end. By contrast, unemployment among adult women and teenagers did not start to rise until the second quarter and showed little improvement later in the year. One interesting development was the fact that the jobless rate for men actually rose above that for women during several months, a reflection of the concentrated impact of the recession on manufacturing and construction. Unemployment levels for black and white workers moved from 11.3% and 5.1%, respectively, in December 1979 to 14% and 6.5% at the end of 1980, with the black rate still close to its midyear high of 14.2%.

The roller-coaster course of the economy was also mirrored in the number of the unemployed, which jumped by 338,000 to 6.4 million in January and then shot up even faster to over 8.2 million by July. It then trended downward to 7.8 million in December. The number of discouraged workers—who are not counted as unemployed because they say that a lack of jobs has caused them to give up looking for work—rose to 1.1 million by the fourth quarter, a 300,000 increase over the year. Blacks and women accounted for most of the increase.

Employment, which typically lags behind the overall economy, exhibited a slowing of growth early in 1980. However, it did not actually turn down until the second quarter, when the ranks of the working dropped precipitously, hitting 96.5 million in June—about 1.4 million below the February peak. By December steady job gains had brought the total back to 97.3 million, erasing many but not all of the layoffs caused by the recession.

From an occupational standpoint, deteriorating labour market conditions in two major U.S. industries—housing construction and auto manufacturing—were already pointing to an imminent recession by late 1979. Construction employment leveled off in the final quarter of 1979 and then contracted sharply in the first half of 1980, when the jobless rate for construction workers rose by more than four percentage points to over 16%. Auto industry employment, which actually began to deteriorate in the second quarter of 1979, was down 29% by mid-1980, when the auto industry employment rate climbed above 25%. By year's end, construction employment, which had dropped over 400,000 from its January peak, had recovered by 175,000. More generally, employment in the services-producing sector continued its long-run upward trend in 1980 after dipping slightly for a few months. Mining employment also rose during the

UPI

Joyce Miller of the Amalgamated Clothing and Textile Workers Union was the first woman elected to the 34-member executive council of the AFL-CIO, on August 21.

year, but manufacturing industries by December had called back only 60% of the 1.2 million employees they had laid off during the recession.

The onset of the 1980s provided an opportunity to assess changes in the labour market during the previous decade and to chart probable future trends. Both the civilian labour force and civilian unemployment expanded faster than the U.S. population in the 1970s. The civilian labour force (consisting of persons either at work or seeking work) grew by 22.4 million or 27.5%, while employment ranks climbed by 19.1 million or 24.3%. Women captured 11.5 million of the new jobs, and 6 million were taken by young people aged 16–25.

Looking ahead, experts expected that the labour force would grow by only 14% during the 1980s as a result of the low birthrates that had prevailed since the 1960s. Minority youth unemployment was not expected to improve as rapidly, however, since this group would actually increase slightly. By the same token, the number of prime-age workers—25 to 44—was expected to grow by 36% to 65 million during the 1980s, about half of the total labour force. This development should result in improved productivity and faster economic growth. Women were expected to stream into the labour force in the 1980s at the rate of nearly one million a year.

The structure of employment also changed in the 1970s. With nine out of ten new jobs occurring in the services and wholesale and retail trade sectors, this segment accounted for 67% of all jobs by the end of the decade, while the share of employment claimed by goods-producing industries shrank from 40 to 33%. In the 1980s a similar pattern was expected to unfold.

Employment prospects for new college graduates in the private sector improved only moderately in

The 3rd-century-BC temple of Isis, dismantled from its former site on Philae, which was flooded by the Aswan High Dam, was rebuilt stone by stone on the island of Agilkia, Egypt.

1980. Hiring rose 8%, with demand for engineering majors up a sharp 21% and placements of science, math, and technical students up 10%. But business students saw only a 1% rise in demand, and hiring of liberal arts majors declined by 7%.

LANDMARKS AND MONUMENTS

Growing interest in conservation was reflected in the ratification or acceptance by additional states of the International Convention Concerning the Protection of the World Cultural and Natural Heritage. By mid-1980, 53 nations were giving 1% of their annual contribution to UNESCO to the World Heritage Fund. At its meeting in October 1979 the World Heritage Committee approved 45 nominations to its list of cultural and natural sites, and in September 1980 a further 25 were added. Included in the list were the site of ancient Carthage (Tunisia); Chartres Cathedral and Mont Saint-Michel (France); the Grand Canyon and Everglades and Redwood national parks (U.S.); the ancient city of Bosra (Syria); the Aphrodite Temple (Cyprus); and the mining town of Røros and old wooden buildings (Norway). The committee also approved listing the Auschwitz concentration camp in Poland as a "unique site" but decided to restrict the inscription of other sites of a similar nature.

The first and, in many respects, the largest international conservation campaign came to an end in 1980, 20 years after it was launched to preserve man's cultural heritage in Egyptian and Sudanese Nubia. On March 10 a ceremony was held to mark completion of the transfer of the Ptolemaic and Roman temples of Philae to the neighbouring island of Agilkia farther up the Nile. The campaign had been marked by the dismantling and reassembly of other outstanding monuments, such as the temples of Abu Simbel, also carried out with the aid of international contributions, which amounted to nearly $34 million.

A major salvage program was under way in India following the construction of a dam on the Krishna River near Hyderabad. The most important temple in the area to be flooded, the 7th-century Kudavalli Sangameswaram, was completely dismantled, and the stones were moved to a site 15 mi away. Projects for the rescue of a group of 26 other temples were planned.

In Venice contracts worth $6.6 million were negotiated for the installation of modern sewerage systems in the Venetian area. The municipality also placed a $3.6 million contract for additional water supplies; this would permit the further closing of artesian wells, the use of which had contributed to subsidence. Private committees completed the restoration of the Basilica dell' Assunta on the island of Torcello. The Church of SS. Maria e Donato on Murano was reopened to the public after major restoration work on the building and its famed mosaic pavement. The ruins at Pompeii were reported damaged by the November earthquake in Italy.

The government of Sri Lanka launched a campaign in January 1980 for the restoration of Buddhist monuments in an area including giant stupas, colossal statues of Buddha, and such outstanding sites as Sigiriya (with its mural paintings). Another campaign launched during the year was for the preservation of sites in Malta. These included the Hal Saflieni Hypogeum (late Neolithic), which comprises a series of subterranean rooms carved out of the limestone rock; Vilhena Palace and the bastions of the former capital city of Mdina; Ft. St. Elmo, built by the Knights of the Order of Malta; and the Citadelle on Gozo.

In the U.S. one of the more interesting developments was the award of grants, amounting to $5 million, by the Heritage Conservation and Recreation Service of the Department of the Interior for the preservation of the nation's maritime heritage. Included were the barque "Elissa," to be restored by the Historic Galveston (Texas) Foundation; the "Falls of Clyde," a four-masted, full-rigged ship in Honolulu; various small craft of historic interest; a lighthouse in Navesin, N.J.; and support for the preservation of objects recovered by submarine archaeologists from the Civil War ship "Monitor,"

Thirty-six grain silos that formerly held oats for the Quaker Oats Co. were converted into a hotel (above), the Quaker Square Hilton in Akron, Ohio. In London (below) the famed Covent Garden open market was converted into a shopping centre with restaurants and galleries.
(ABOVE) MARCY NIGHSWANDER–THE NEW YORK TIMES; (BELOW) KEYSTONE

the first ship to have cannons in a revolving turret.

In many European cities derelict buildings and quarters of historic interest were being renovated. In Edinburgh the city council, the biggest owner of empty, derelict historic buildings, turned several over to the Cockburn Conservation Trust for restoration and adaptation to meet contemporary needs. Eighteenth-century terrace houses on Candlemaker Row, for example, were renovated and then sold at a profit. In London the former central market in Covent Garden, restored as a shopping centre after several years of controversy over redevelopment plans, was officially reopened in June. Establishment of a £15 million ($33 million) National Heritage Memorial Fund was announced in April.

(*See also* Architecture; Museums.)

LAOS

Except for a monetary upheaval at the beginning of the year, Laos remained a dutiful and inconspicuous member of the three-nation Indochina grouping throughout 1980. Political developments were dominated by two conferences of Laotian, Cambodian, and Vietnamese foreign ministers, in Phnom Penh, Cambodia, in January and in Vientiane in July. The Vientiane meeting took place in the shadow of stiff opposition from the Association of Southeast Asian Nations to Indochina's Communist thrust under Vietnamese leadership. The conference affirmed the militant solidarity of the three countries and said they were "prepared to discuss with the other countries in the region the establishment of a Southeast Asian region of peace and stability."

Despite the official trumpeting of "complete identity of views" with Vietnam, independent sources continued to talk of popular resentment against the Vietnamese in Laos. According to Thai estimates, there were at least 60,000 Vietnamese soldiers and 100 civilian advisers who controlled all important matters in the country. By late October it was estimated that several thousand Laotians, including government officials, had been arrested during the year for "anti-Vietnamese attitudes"; some had been released. In July Laos signed a new protocol with the Soviet Union to cover road and bridge construction, marking a significant break with the past when China was in sole charge of road works in northern Laos.

Relations with Thailand remained at low ebb, especially after a border incident in June in which a Thai naval officer was killed. Failing to get an apology from Vientiane, Thailand closed the 1,200-km frontier along the Mekong River. As on previous occasions, the closure caused serious food and fuel shortages in landlocked Laos, forcing Vietnam to fill the gap as best it could. Even before the blockade, the economy appeared to be in serious difficulty. The government had introduced major monetary and tax reforms in December 1979. The old kip currency was called in and a new kip intro-

duced. Initially the new kip was worth 100 old kips, which made 1 new kip equal to U.S. 25 cents. A week later it was devalued to 16 to the dollar.

The reform was to be in preparation for the country's first five-year plan, due to begin in 1981. The authorities seemed concerned enough to suggest that they would henceforth be cautious in pushing agricultural cooperatives and would encourage mixed economy on the industrial front. Some basic economic programs were pursued with assistance from international agencies. The UN Development Program and the Asian Development Bank helped to finance an $8.2 million agricultural support facilities project. In May the World Bank's International Development Association provided a concessionary credit of $13.4 million for projects aimed at achieving food self-sufficiency.

LATIN-AMERICAN AFFAIRS

The most important event in Latin-American relations in 1980 was the replacement of the Latin American Free Trade Association (LAFTA) by the Latin-American Integration Association (LAIA) following three negotiating conferences during the year. On August 12 the foreign ministers of the 11 member countries of LAFTA (Argentina, Brazil, Chile, Colombia, Bolivia, Ecuador, Peru, Venezuela, Paraguay, Uruguay, and Mexico) signed a treaty in Montevideo, Uruguay, to set up LAIA.

The treaty was a flexible one, designed to take into account the differing levels of economic development of its members. Three categories of comparative development were created so that the countries under each of the categories would obtain a different tariff treatment. At the head of the group were to be the most developed countries, Argentina, Brazil, and Mexico; the second level would be occupied by Chile, Colombia, Peru, Uruguay, and Venezuela; and the third by Bolivia, Ecuador, and Paraguay.

The treaty also provided for regional and partial agreements, and a significant role was reserved to the private sector in the initiation of agreements. The three main institutions of LAFTA, the Council of Foreign Ministers, the Conference, and the Secretariat, were to continue more or less in the same form for LAIA, with a secretary-general elected for a three-year period.

Many qualified commentators felt that LAIA was too vague to be successful, and a trend was observed during the year favouring the negotiation of bilateral agreements between countries as the best means of promoting trade. An example of this was the drawing up in October by the authorities of Uruguay and Argentina of a list of about 500 noncompetitive products upon which tariffs and other trade restrictions would be eliminated immediately for Uruguayan exports to Argentina and gradually for trade in the opposite direction. Products to be subject to free-trade conditions would be expanded to 1,000 over a two-year period, including vegetable oils, timber, textiles, building materials, hydrocarbons, corn, and wheat.

Political difficulties assumed critical proportions during 1980 among the member countries of the Andean Group (Bolivia, Colombia, Ecuador, Peru, and Venezuela), and economic proposals consequently received less attention. Dissension was created by the military coup d'etat in Bolivia on July 17 when that country was about to return to constitutional rule. The other four members of the Group condemned the coup, and Ecuador broke off diplomatic relations with Bolivia. Venezuela called for a coordinated effort against the new regime by both the Andean Group and the Organization of American States (OAS) and suspended its financial assistance to Bolivia. By October Bolivia appeared to be reconsidering its membership in the Group and arriving at an accommodation with Argentina, Chile, and Uruguay. But later Bolivia denied its intention of leaving the Group, and its representatives attended the meeting of the Commission (the Andean Group's main decision-making body) in Lima, Peru, on October 13 and also a presidential summit conference of member countries in Santa Marta, Colombia, on December 17.

The new Peruvian government was also reviewing certain aspects of the Andean Pact (Fernando Belaúnde Terry of Acción Popular took office as president on July 28 following the impressive victory of his party in the presidential and legislative elections on May 18; these had brought 12 years of military rule to an end). The pact's preoccupation with political affairs was criticized by the Belaúnde administration, which maintained that greater emphasis should be given to economic matters. One of Peru's new policies was to give more encouragement to the entry of foreign investment, and this was expected to contravene the tight restrictions imposed on the latter under Decisions 24 and 103 of the Commission.

There was squabbling over the Andean Group's industrial development programs. A series of meetings attempted to expedite negotiations on the six agreements to be decided upon by the end of 1980 (steel, fertilizers, pharmaceuticals, chemicals, electronics, and communications). The trade liberalization program made steady progress, and the automatic tariff elimination process begun in 1971 was 75% complete at the beginning of 1980. Trade within the region increased significantly as a result, rising from $79 million in 1970 to approximately $1.2 billion in 1979.

There were attempts to revive the Central American Common Market (CACM) during the year; the CACM included Costa Rica, El Salvador, Guatemala, Honduras, and Nicaragua. At a meeting in Managua, Nicaragua, on July 4–5, the economic integration ministers of the member countries agreed on the drafting of a new document to replace the 1960 General Treaty. They urged the governments of Guatemala, Costa Rica, and Honduras to put into effect bilateral payment mechanisms that would alleviate the intrazonal trade deficits of Nicaragua and El Salvador. The ministers agreed to establish the Central American Maritime Transport Commission (Cocatran), with headquarters in Managua, and to strengthen relations with other regional trade associations and also with the Dominican Republic and Panama. A draft resolution supported by Costa Rica, Nicaragua, El Salvador, and Honduras called for a common protective tariff ranging from 35 to 100%, as compared with the existing multiple-tariff system whereby in some cases duties could exceed 300%. Prospects for the reinvigoration of the CACM were improved by the signature in Lima on October 30 of a peace treaty between El Salvador and Honduras, which ended a state of hostility lasting 11 years. Both countries were to negotiate over the next five years to settle their border disputes.

In April Thomas Farer (arm outstretched), U.S. chairman of the Inter-American Human Rights Commission of the Organization of American States, and Andrés Aguilar Mawdsley (right) of Venezuela conferred in Bogotá, Colombia, with guerrillas holding hostages at the embassy of the Dominican Republic. All hostages were later released unharmed after a ransom was paid.
WIDE WORLD

MATTHEW NATHONS—GAMMA/LIAISON

On July 19 Nicaragua celebrated the first anniversary of the Sandinista revolution that ousted Anastasio Somoza from power; in attendance were heads of state from the Caribbean and Central America.

In August the Inter-American Development Bank (IDB) put into effect an increase of $9,-750,000,000 in the bank's resources; it included "callable" capital of $8 billion and $1,750,000,000 for the Fund for Special Operations. The rise was accepted in principle by all member countries. The bank granted loans of about $2.2 billion in 1980 as against $2,030,000,000 in 1979, despite the fact that 19 loans totaling $700 million were frozen between October 1979 and April 1980 principally as a result of delays by the U.S. in making some contributions available. Portugal became the 16th extraregional full member of the IDB on March 25.

Pres. João Baptista da Figueiredo of Brazil paid a number of state visits to neighbouring countries during the year as part of Brazil's drive to improve its relations in Latin America and to increase exports to the area. He went to Argentina in May, and the visit ended a 15-year period of cool relations between the two countries; the improvement was made possible by an agreement on the large hydroelectric plants that both countries were building in conjunction with Paraguay on the Paraná River. During Figueiredo's stay in Argentina agreements were signed concerning cooperation between the two nations in the peaceful use of atomic energy, joint exploitation of the hydroelectric potential of the Uruguay River, and the delivery by Argentina to Brazil of natural gas at the rate of about ten million cubic feet a day. Pres. Jorge Rafael Videla of Argentina paid a return visit to Brazil in August. The most important pact signed then concerned nuclear power, with agreements by Argentina to supply 240 tons of uranium for the Brazilian reactor program and by Brazil to supply nuclear technology. The two countries also agreed on a joint feasibility study for a gas pipeline. The visits were expected to lead to a sharp increase in mutual trade, which amounted to $1.5 billion in 1979.

Figueiredo also visited Paraguay in April and Chile in September.

Other important developments in Latin-American external relations included a trade agreement between Argentina and the U.S.S.R. in July providing for the purchase by the latter of 20 million tons of corn and sorghum and 2.5 million tons of soybeans over five years. During the first half of 1980 the Soviet Union became the biggest purchaser of Argentine grain, receiving more than 50% of Argentina's total grain shipments during that period. Late in July the presidents of Mexico and Venezuela (the region's two largest oil producers) signed an agreement providing for the joint supply of 160,000 bbl a day of crude petroleum at about $32 a bbl to Barbados, Costa Rica, El Salvador, Guatemala, Honduras, Jamaica, Nicaragua, Panama, and the Dominican Republic; this represented the overall consumption of those countries. A total of 30% of the payments was to be returned in the form of five-year loans at 4% interest. The agreement was to be renewed annually and could be extended to other consumer countries.

The IDB reported that the gross national product of the region grew by 6.1% in 1979 to reach $420.7 billion in U.S. dollars of 1978 ($396.3 billion in 1978). Income per head in 1979 was $1,244, a rise of 65% from the 1960 level. At the end of 1979 Latin America's crude oil output amounted to almost 2,000,000,000 bbl, 15% higher than in 1978; it accounted for 6% of the world's total, as against 5.5% in 1978. Proven oil reserves were 74,000,-000,000 bbl at the end of 1979 (Mexico, 64%), as against 54,000,000,000 a year earlier (Mexico, 53%). Agriculture's contribution to the area's gross domestic product fell from 15.7% in 1960 to 10.5% in 1979. The region's share of world trade declined from 7.2% in 1960–62 to 5% in 1977–79.

(*See also* articles on the various countries.)

LAW

A massive bribery and corruption investigation by the FBI resulted in the indictment of six U.S. representatives, a senator, and several other persons in 1980. Four congressmen had been convicted by the end of the year. Cases resulting from the investigation brought disputes over the precise meaning of entrapment. Government agents could not originate the idea of a crime, induce persons to commit it if they were not already inclined to do so, and then arrest them. Several defendants argued that this was precisely what happened.

FBI agents and a paid informer who was a convicted swindler posed as agents for an Arab sheikh and offered bribes for sponsorship of an immigration bill and other favours, often involving aid in plans for multimillion-dollar business ventures. The operation was called Abscam—not from the word Arab, as originally reported, but from Abdul Enterprises Ltd., the fictitious firm invented by the FBI.

Rep. Michael Myers (Dem., Pa.), Mayor Angelo Errichetti of Camden, N.J., Councilman Louis Johanson of Philadelphia, and attorney Howard Criden of Philadelphia were convicted of bribery and conspiracy in the first Abscam trial. A New York appeals court refused to dismiss the indictment against Myers on grounds of entrapment, and the U.S. Supreme Court refused to hear a further appeal. Myers was subsequently expelled from the House of Representatives.

In a separate trial George Schwartz, president of the Philadelphia City Council, and Councilman Henry Jannotti were convicted of conspiracy and extortion. But a U.S. district judge dismissed the convictions on the grounds of entrapment and a lack of federal jurisdiction. The judge ruled that the prosecution had not proved that the officials were predisposed to take bribes and that there was "governmental overreaching amounting to a violation of due process of law." Further, he ruled that there was a question about whether interstate commerce was involved in the FBI's false story about plans to build a $34 million hotel complex in Philadelphia.

Rep. John Jenrette, Jr. (Dem., S.C.), was the second congressman convicted of bribery and conspiracy. Businessman John R. Stowe, who picked up a $50,000 payment, was convicted with him. Jenrette resigned before Congress adjourned.

Rep. John Murphy (Dem., N.Y.) and Rep. Frank Thompson, Jr. (Dem., N.J.), were found guilty a few days after the Philadelphia convictions were thrown out of court. Thompson was convicted of bribery and conspiracy and Murphy of conspiracy, conflict of interest, and accepting an unlawful gratuity. While entrapment did not figure in these legislators' trial defense, their contention that they were denied due process was to be heard in separate proceedings in 1981.

Also indicted were Rep. Raymond Lederer (Dem., Pa.), Rep. Richard Kelly (Rep., Fla.), and Sen. Harrison Williams, Jr. (Dem., N.J.).

DAVID R. FRAZIER—THE NEW YORK TIMES

In July sheriff's deputies raided an Idaho television station in search of videotapes they wanted as evidence; in October Pres. Jimmy Carter signed into law an act of Congress prohibiting such unannounced searches.

In a case related to revelations of the Watergate era, W. Mark Felt, former acting associate director of the FBI, and Edward S. Miller, former chief of the agency's intelligence division, were found guilty of authorizing illegal break-ins during the early 1970s in an effort to find members of the Weather Underground. Felt was fined $5,000 and Miller $3,500; no time in prison was ordered for either. Former president Richard Nixon testified during the trial that he approved a plan to ease restraints on domestic intelligence activities in 1970. But four days later, he testified, he withdrew approval because of objections by FBI Director J. Edgar Hoover.

The Death Penalty

The Massachusetts Supreme Court struck down that state's death penalty law, holding that it was "impermissibly cruel" and discriminated against blacks and other minorities.

The status of Alabama's death penalty law was

In Greensboro, North Carolina, three Ku Klux Klansmen were acquitted in November of charges that they killed five Communist Workers Party demonstrators during a violent clash in 1979.
WIDE WORLD

put in doubt. The U.S. Supreme Court struck down a section that prevented courts in capital punishment cases from finding suspects guilty of lesser offenses. It was left to the Alabama Supreme Court to determine whether other sections of the law were valid. Before the state Supreme Court could act, an appeals court voided a 1977 death sentence because the defendant had been prevented from pleading guilty to a lesser offense.

State supreme courts upheld death penalty laws in California, Indiana, and Maryland. The death sentence in the Maryland case under consideration, however, was voided on a technicality.

Other Significant Cases

Former Central Intelligence agent David Barnett pleaded guilty to one count of espionage. The case involved sale to the Soviet Union of information about the CIA's check on Soviet weapons in Indonesia in the late 1960s. By pleading guilty and agreeing to tell the U.S. government all about his dealings with the Soviet intelligence service, Barnett succeeded in having his indictment restricted to the single count on which he was tried.

Ted Patrick, a professional religious deprogrammer, was sentenced to a year in prison and placed on five years' probation for the kidnapping of a Tucson, Ariz., woman. He also was fined $5,000, and severe restrictions were placed on future deprogramming activities.

Charles F. Dederich, founder of the Synanon drug rehabilitation organization, and two aides were found guilty of conspiracy to commit murder with a rattlesnake. Dederich was found guilty of inducing the other two to put a live rattlesnake in the mailbox of attorney Paul Morantz. Morantz had filed a number of suits for people who contended they were kept in Synanon against their will.

An all-white jury in Tampa, Fla., found four Miami policemen innocent of using undue force in an incident that led to the death of Arthur McDuffie, a black insurance executive. McDuffie died from injuries sustained in a beating inflicted after he was chased and stopped for a traffic violation. The verdict touched off bloody rioting in Miami. (*See* Minorities, American.)

The U.S. Justice Department then began an investigation into possible civil rights violations in the case. Charles R. Veverka, Jr., the first former Miami policeman indicted, was cleared of civil rights charges of covering up police brutality. Veverka, a prosecution witness at the Tampa trial, had been given immunity from state charges.

Bert Lance, former U.S. budget director, was found innocent of making questionable bank loans and of using a partnership with his wife to hide debts. Three co-defendants also were cleared on a number of counts. The government later dropped remaining counts on which the jury deadlocked.

Illinois Attorney General William J. Scott was convicted of underreporting his income for federal tax purposes. The verdict came just one day after Scott lost his primary bid for the Illinois Republican senatorial nomination.

John W. Gacy was sentenced to die in the electric chair in Illinois for the worst mass murder in U.S. history. He was found guilty of 33 slayings and also was convicted of taking indecent liberties with a minor and of deviate sexual assault. The latter charges related to a 15-year-old boy whose disappearance had led to Gacy's arrest. The bodies of 28 victims were found in the crawl space under Gacy's house in Des Plaines, Ill.; one was found in his garage; and four were found in the Des Plaines River.

An Indiana jury ruled that Ford Motor Co. was not guilty of reckless homicide in the 1978 deaths of three young women in the crash of a subcompact Pinto auto. It was the first time a U.S. corporation had faced criminal charges in a product defect case. (*See* Consumer Affairs Special Report.)

Law

Special Report:
Diplomats Under Siege

by Richard L. Clutterbuck

Twenty-six embassies or consulates were illegally occupied in 1979, and another 12 in the first half of 1980. Violation of embassies and the immunity of diplomats is nothing new, but the pattern has changed. Between 1968 and 1975 there were 52 incidents in which diplomats or consuls were kidnapped, but most of the victims were taken to secret hideouts. Now they are more often held in their own embassies. The new pattern, though more hazardous for the terrorists, attracts more publicity —which is usually their primary aim.

New Targets for Terrorism

This pattern began in 1973 when Palestinian terrorists took over the Saudi embassy in Khartoum, Sudan, and held six diplomats hostage. Their demands included the release of terrorists imprisoned in various countries, and when these were not met, one Belgian and two U.S. diplomats were killed. The Sudanese government arrested and convicted the terrorists but, in response to pressure from other Arab countries, released them within a year.

When terrorists took over the Japanese embassy in Kuwait in 1974, they were given safe conduct to Aden and a ransom of $6 million. In 1975 the West German embassy in Stockholm was seized by German terrorists, but this time both the governments involved stood firm, despite the murder of two hostages, and all the terrorists were killed or captured. Later that year, however, when terrorists seized 11 OPEC (Organization of Petroleum Exporting Countries) oil ministers in Vienna, the governments concerned agreed to give way, and it is believed that a huge ransom was paid. The terrorists all went free, and subsequently the plague has grown worse.

The seizure of the U.S. embassy in Teheran by Iranian militants in November 1979 created a new dimension. There is no evidence that Iran's revolutionary leader, the Ayatollah Ruhollah Khomeini, gave it prior authorization. He did approve it after the fact, however, taking full responsibility for holding some 60 diplomats and a number of other hostages (later reduced to 52). Though there have been cases of governments conniving with mobs that attacked or burned embassies (*e.g.*, the U.S. embassy in Libya in 1979), Khomeini became the first national leader in modern times to put his own authority behind the prolonged detention of an accredited embassy staff.

In February 1980 in Bogotá, Colombia, 25 stu-

dents of the M-19 Movement ran across the road from the university and seized the Dominican embassy, where a reception was in progress. One terrorist was shot dead by a security guard, but no one else died. After prolonged negotiations, the 57 hostages, including 14 ambassadors, were released. The terrorists were given safe conduct and a $2.5 million ransom, paid by local businessmen who raised some or all of it from the parent countries of the ambassadors.

On April 30, 1980, six terrorists belonging to the Arab minority in Iran seized the Iranian embassy in London. The subsequent siege and rescue are described below. Five of the six died, but they got the publicity they wanted for their cause.

Rules of the Game

Whether from a big country or a small one, embassy personnel are as helpless as children entrusted to the care of a neighbour if their host decides to incarcerate them or threaten them with murder. Accordingly, over the centuries, rules have evolved governing their rights and responsibilities. Most nations that exchange ambassadors are parties to the Vienna Convention. Under it, the host government accepts responsibility for protecting the embassy (Art. 22), the diplomatic staffs (Art. 29), and their residences (Art. 30). Diplomats, while enjoying diplomatic immunity, are required to respect the laws and regulations of the host country and must not interfere in its internal affairs (Art. 41).

Some embassies, notably those of certain Arab countries, have flagrantly abused their privileges. Diplomatic pouches have been used to smuggle in weapons for terrorists. In Paris in 1978, Iraqi embassy guards shot a French policeman dead in the street outside the embassy. In 1980 several Libyans opposed to the rule of Muammar al-Qaddafi were murdered in London, and Libyan diplomats openly admitted their participation. It has been alleged that the Iraqi embassy in London supported the terrorists who seized the Iranian embassy. Neither this kind of abuse, however, nor allegations that an embassy is being used for subversion or spying can justify the host country in violating it or conniving at its violation. The lawful remedy is to withdraw immunities from individual diplomats or suspend diplomatic relations.

The parent government is responsible for security within its own embassy gates. Though it does not have extraterritorial rights, an embassy is outside the jurisdiction of the host country, whose policemen, guards, or soldiers can enter only if invited. The parent government can place its own armed security guards inside the gates, but a handful of guards cannot keep out a mob, especially if the host country's security forces are either participating or conniving with the attackers.

Outside the embassy, diplomatic staffs in high-risk countries should avoid offering targets for terrorists, observing sensible security precautions in their homes, being discreet about their movements, and avoiding predictable times and routes. They can carry arms and employ armed bodyguards but have a moral duty to observe local law. Escorts or guards outside the diplomat's own car or home should be provided by the host country.

When Precautions Fail

If a host country fails by neglect to provide proper protection for an embassy or its staff, the parent country has no right to intervene, but if the host government willfully participates in or connives at an attack or occupation, this can be regarded as an act of war. The parent government can then justify reply by warlike means, though this may not be wise, as was illustrated by the abortive U.S. rescue mission in Iran in April 1980. The Israeli rescue of hijacked airline passengers at Entebbe, Uganda, in 1976 did prove that operations of this type can be feasible, even in defiance of the local government, but in that case the hostages were at an airfield where the commandos could land and—more important—take off again quickly.

Normally, however, such rescues must be executed by the host country, as in the case of the Iranian embassy in London in May 1980. This incident illustrates many of the problems involved. Iranian security inside the embassy was woefully inadequate. The British had one policeman with a pistol under his coat at the door. The six terrorists posed as bona fide visitors but carried concealed weapons. Once inside, they seized 26 hostages, including the policeman. In response to his "panic button" signal, the first police reinforcements were at the door within three minutes, and a seige was mounted.

No one had been seriously hurt, and the negotiators played for time. This seemed to work well at first, and after six days of negotiation, five hostages had been released. At that point, however, the terrorists lost patience. Realizing that the British and Iranian governments were not going to make concessions, they shot a hostage in cold blood and threatened to shoot another every 45 minutes. The British Army's Special Air Services (SAS) rescue squad then went in, with the agreement of the Iranian government. During the next few seconds the terrorists sprayed the hostages with machine-gun fire, killing one more before the SAS reached the room and rescued the other 19. All the terrorists were killed except one who pretended to be a hos-

UPI

In May a team of crack British commandos freed 19 hostages held in the Iranian embassy in London by Iranian Arab terrorists.

tage, and he was subsequently arrested.

Several such rescues have been carried out, though not often from embassies. Dutch Marines rescued hostages from a train and a school in 1977 and from a government office in 1978, and the German GSG9 squad freed hijacked passengers from an aircraft at Mogadishu, Somalia, in 1977. The Dutch Marines and the GSG9 have much in common with the SAS. The selection and training of that force for a copybook embassy rescue indicate what is required.

The SAS is an elite British Army regiment. Only experienced soldiers are considered for selection. Of those tested, only one in five is chosen, and only a small number of those accepted by the regiment are picked for the rescue squad. They train intensively, and if any man's reactions or skill at arms falters in the smallest degree, he is replaced. They train with live ammunition, with one of their own comrades acting as the hostage, surrounded by figure targets representing the terrorists. The commandos must break in and put lethal shots into every target within a few seconds without hitting the hostage. The resulting confidence and precision the team can muster were proved in London when the decisive moment came.

Such a force may well provide the best deterrent against the growth of diplomatic violations. It is ironic that in this case the diplomats rescued were Khomeini's.

WIDE WORLD

Palestinian guerrillas search through the debris following an Israeli attack on a PLO base near Sarafand, Lebanon, on April 18.

LEBANON

Lebanon continued to suffer in 1980 from a breakdown of government control in the south and from Israeli armed incursions. Polarization into zones controlled by warring factions of Christians and by Palestinian commandos aided by left-wing allies and Muslim extremists was more evident. The resignation of Prime Minister Selim al-Hoss was accepted in July, but his differences of view with Pres. Elias Sarkis prolonged the finding of a replacement government. On October 25 one was formed by Shafiq al-Wazzan, a former justice minister who took the premiership and the interior ministry. However, there was little enthusiasm for the Cabinet of 22, only 5 of whom had served under Selim al-Hoss. Two ministers resigned almost immediately and four more in early December.

In 1981 Lebanon was to receive $22 million in foreign military sales from the U.S. in a three-year program to restore the Lebanese Army. The Army in 1980 was not strong enough to defend against Israeli aggression without the help of Syrian troops, who were serving with the Arab Deterrent Force (ADF), and the UN Interim Force in Lebanon (UNIFIL), monitoring Israeli attacks on the south. The Lebanese government told the UN in October that UN observers had been subject to "continued harassment" by the Israelis, particularly near the village of al-Aadeisse.

During the first nine months of 1980 approximately 1,800 people were killed, some 1,500 for political reasons; about 1,700 were wounded. The killings caused right-wing political leaders to increase their efforts to establish "alternative ad-

ministrations." Palestinian guerrillas were reported in August to have acquired a network of Soviet-made radar sets and electronic surveillance equipment.

About 25 Palestinians and Lebanese died in an attack on August 19 by some 600 Israeli soldiers on Palestinian camps north of the Litani River. The attack was the heaviest incursion into southern Lebanon in two years. Lebanon complained to the UN, and Secretary-General Kurt Waldheim appealed to all parties to cooperate with UNIFIL.

On October 20 the president of the reconstruction and development council, Muhammad Atallah, said that only $153 million of the $400 million pledged for 1980 at an Arab summit in Tunisia in November 1979 had arrived. Lebanon was paralyzed by this financial restraint, Atallah said, because its plans were drafted on the basis of the money's arrival. In July the Cabinet had approved a $295.6 million reconstruction and development program financed by summit aid, almost half of which was for the south. A draft budget for 1981 totaling $1,515,100,000, slightly more than 1980, was also dependent on summit aid.

The Lebanese economy showed its resilience. Exports in the first six months of 1980 totaled $515 million, a 48% rise over the corresponding period of 1979. Building materials accounted for 29%. Reexports (of imported goods) were also up 30% over 1979, with most going to Saudi Arabia. Success was achieved under difficult operating conditions by the national carrier, Middle East Airlines, which made a record profit in 1979 of $15.1 million.

As many as 500,000 Lebanese, including 30–40%

of all industrial workers, had left the country since 1975 to seek work abroad, mainly in Saudi Arabia and nations on the Persian Gulf. Remittances from this source of $100 million a month helped to keep the balance of payments in surplus despite record trade deficits.

LIBRARIES

Internationally, the subjects most discussed during 1980 were Universal Bibliographic Control (UBC) and Universal Availability of Publications (UAP). The UBC program of the International Federation of Library Associations (IFLA), which was accepted by UNESCO and endorsed by national libraries and bibliographic organizations, aimed to promote the exchange of compatible bibliographic records. The IFLA International Office for UBC was responsible for coordinating the work of national bibliographic agencies in this respect.

At the heart of the UBC program was the production of a series of International Standard Bibliographic Descriptions (ISBD's). A general standard (ISBD [G]) was first produced in 1977, and within that framework others had been published covering specific types of publications. In 1980 two more appeared, one for antiquarian books and one for printed music, and work on one for component parts was well advanced.

IFLA's UAP program, which had as its ultimate aim the availability to all of all published documents, continued to be developed as a major element of IFLA's Medium Term Program. Current activity, centred largely on research, included studies of availability from publishers and booksellers and the acquisition, interlending, and retention policies and procedures of libraries, at both the national and international level. These studies would form basic material for the joint IFLA-UNESCO International Congress on UAP, to be held in May 1982.

Since IFLA adopted new statutes in 1976, it had made positive moves toward giving more emphasis to countries outside Europe and North America and especially to library associations from less developed countries. Thus the 1980 conference in Manila, held for the first time in a less developed country, was a milestone in IFLA's history.

In January 1980 the U.S. library press hailed Pres. Jimmy Carter's Nov. 16, 1979, address to the White House Conference on Library and Information Services, where librarians and interested citizens shaped 25 resolutions designed to democratize access to information resources. A follow-up conference was held September 15–17 in Minneapolis, Minn., but the defeats of Carter and other friends of libraries in the November 4 elections clouded earlier optimism. In September a gubernatorial veto in California denied beleaguered public libraries $18 million in relief, and a referendum lowering taxes in Massachusetts would diminish library revenues there. Other major proposals reducing library tax revenues were voted down, however.

As of 1980, some 2,200 libraries shared almost seven million cataloging records in the OCLC, Inc., cooperative on-line network, and the Research Libraries Information Network had 22 members by November. On-line and video technology were key topics at the American Library Association's (ALA's) annual conference, June 28–July 4 in New York City. ALA-accredited library schools with "information" in their names had increased to 34% from 1970, indicating the shift in curriculum. The American Association of School Librarians held the nation's first national conference in this subfield, in Louisville, Ky., September 25–28. Libraries prepared for broad adoption Jan. 1, 1981, of a new and controversial *Anglo-American Cataloguing Rules, Second Edition*. The Library of Congress dedicated its $160 million, 2,112,492-sq-ft James Madison Memorial Building, the largest library structure in the U.S.

Computer terminals were replacing traditional card catalogs in many libraries. In the Evanston, Illinois, Public Library this catalog went on-line on October 6.
SUSAN S. CHERRY, AMERICAN LIBRARIES

In September Libyan leader Col. Muammar al-Qaddafi (far right) celebrated the 11th anniversary of the coup that brought him to power. Syrian Pres. Hafez al-Assad (centre, shaking hands) attended the celebration, held in Lebanon. On September 10 Libya and Syria announced plans to merge into a single state.

WIDE WORLD

LIBYA

Despite Col. Muammar al-Qaddafi's Third International Theory of elected popular committees, Libya remained a centrally directed state organized through centrally appointed revolutionary committees. Qaddafi claimed that one of these, acting without authorization, had urged young Libyans overseas to execute Libyan nationals opposed to the regime who refused to return to Libya by June 11, 1980. Killings took place in Rome (four), Athens (one), Bonn, West Germany (one), London (two), and Milan, Italy (one). France, the U.K., the U.S., and West Germany took action to regulate the activities of the Libyan People's Bureaus representing Libya in their respective capitals.

In oil affairs Libya was aligned with the countries that wanted prices raised and therefore opposed Saudi Arabia. Libya cut oil production more than once during the year. Qaddafi was a would-be friend of revolutionary Iran, but he found it difficult to consummate the friendship. The Iranians could not accept the disappearance at the end of a 1978 visit to Libya of Imam Moussa-Sadr, a Lebanese Shi'ah Muslim leader and friend of the Iranian leader Ayatollah Ruhollah Khomeini.

At the end of 1979 Libyan revolutionary committees seized Palestine Liberation Organization (PLO) offices in Tripoli and organized Palestinian revolutionary committees, turning these against the PLO leadership. PLO/Libyan relations were broken off around the beginning of the year, although the Palestinian struggle remained a theme of the Libyan leader. The relationship with Malta was suddenly terminated on August 28 when the Maltese government expelled a Libyan military advisory team after a Libyan naval vessel harassed a Maltese-licensed oil rig drilling in an area claimed by Libya. Relations with Tunisia improved in the second half of

1980, a significant shift after the disturbances in Gafsa in January, which Tunisia blamed on Libya. Support continued to be extended to King Hassan's opponents in Morocco. Involvement in the Chad civil war expanded in December when Libyan troops occupied that country's capital.

On September 10 Libya and Syria agreed to form what Qaddafi described as an "organic union." As a friend of Syria and so an enemy of Iraq, Qaddafi could logically sympathize with Iran in the Iraq-Iran war, but the war exacerbated relations between Libya and Saudi Arabia (assisting Iraq). Qaddafi went so far as to call for a jihad (holy war) to liberate Mecca, and Saudi Arabia terminated diplomatic relations on October 28.

Libya's economy continued to expand, with oil revenues totaling over $18 billion. The interest in Libya shown by U.S. Pres. Jimmy Carter's brother, Billy, was exploited by the president's political enemies during the U.S. electoral campaign, but the affair soon died away.

LITERATURE

The 1980 Nobel Prize for Literature was awarded to the Polish-born, U.S.-domiciled poet Czeslaw Milosz. (*See* Nobel Prizes.) The Swedish Academy's choice drew attention once again to the difficulty of its task in surveying writing throughout the world to decide what should be counted as "world literature" in order to award the prize—worth $210,000 in 1980.

United Kingdom

Fiction. Several established novelists surprised their admirers. Graham Greene published a grim little novel, *Doctor Fischer of Geneva or the Bomb Party*, about a murderous millionaire. He also republished his film reviews in *The Pleasure-Dome*

and presented a new farce, *For Whom the Bell Chimes*, at a Leicester theatre; it is a play designed for acting, preferably by Hollywood clowns, with no pretension to literary merit. He then published a book about his travels in Africa, Asia, and the Americas and the relationship between his experiences and his fiction; it was called *Ways of Escape*.

Kingsley Amis published a collection of his short stories, very strong on army life, and a fine novel, *Russian Hide and Seek*, with a military background. A serious and sensitive fantasy about Britain under Soviet occupation, it appealed more to left-wing critics than to the conventional anti-Communists. But it was too subtle to be popular.

The contest for the £10,000 Booker Prize was more exciting than usual, enlivened by an element of secrecy and surprise. The principal contenders were senior, ambitious novelists Anthony Burgess and William Golding, both of whom offered historical novels about cruelty and homosexuality. Burgess's *Earthly Powers* is almost a history of the public disasters of the 20th century, narrated by a very old, very brilliant homosexual novelist resembling W. Somerset Maugham. Golding's *Rites of Passage* tells of a 19th-century voyage in which a clergyman dies of shame after sexual involvement with sailors; the strange anecdote bore a universal significance and seriousness, which helped Golding to win the Booker Prize.

Doris Lessing, once a realistic narrator of erotic life and political commitment, offered in *The Marriages Between Zones Three, Four and Five* an essay in metaphysical science fiction. Angus Wilson, too, moved into the world of symbolic fantasy with *Setting the World on Fire*, the tale of two brothers who represent the Apollonian and the Dionysian philosophies of life. Margaret Drabble's *The Middle Ground* is a disquisition on a middle-class, middle-aged woman, with no effort to supply a plot: it was more like a French *roman-fleuve*.

Traditional British realism was well represented by Stanley Middleton with *In a Strange Land*, about a provincial composer, and by Stan Barstow with *A Brother's Tale*, about a provincial English master and a football hero. The scholarly and humorous David Lodge wrote *How Far Can You Go?* about the changing attitudes of British Roman Catholics in recent years, for which he received two of the annual Whitbred Awards for Literature: the fiction category award and a special prize for the year's best book. Iris Murdoch's *Nuns and Soldiers* continued her series of philosophical fables about the nature of love in all its variety. Olivia Manning, who died during the year, managed to complete her Levant trilogy with *The Sum of Things*—a successor to her admired Balkan trilogy.

Simon Raven exhumed a mischievous novel from his youth, *An Inch of Fortune*, long suppressed for fear of libel action; the characters include lightly disguised versions of the duke and duchess of Windsor. Virago, a feminist publishing house, reissued a number of good, half-forgotten novels by women, including F. M. Mayor's *The Third Miss Symons* (1913), Rebecca West's *Harriett Hume* (1929), and Stevie Smith's *Over the Frontier* (1938). Another rediscovery was a previously unpublished novel by John Cowper Powys, *After My Fashion;* it deals with life in rural England and New York City just after World War I, and among the characters is a thinly disguised portrait of Isadora Duncan. Powys's reputation continued to grow, on both sides of the Atlantic.

Also set in post-World War I rural England was J. L. Carr's novel *A Month in the Country*, a nostalgic, mysterious tale centring on a medieval church in Yorkshire; it received *The Guardian* Fiction Prize for 1980. Ted Harriott won the 1980 David Higham Prize for *Keep on Running*, his first novel, about an ex-Nazi fugitive. The judges remarked on the high standard of the "first novels" of 1980, which

Judith Rossner
© THOMAS VICTOR

© THOMAS VICTOR

Thomas Berger

In the world of popular scholarship, Richard Jenkyns scored highly with *The Victorians and Ancient Greece*. It has long been recognized that to understand the great Victorian writers and artists one must know their prayer books, their hymns, and their Bible. Richard Jenkyns reminded readers that such is also true of the ancient Greeks, and he did so with wit and learning.

Poetry. It was a year of many anthologies. The new *Oxford Book of Contemporary Verse* was edited by D. J. Enright, with a preface supporting the ideals of the poetic school known as "The November," skeptical, neat, and unromantic. A new book, called *The Movement*, was offered by a young poet, Blake Morrison. With his own poems Morrison was one of the winners of the Eric Gregory Prize.

Charles Tomlinson offered an important anthology, the *Oxford Book of Verse in English Translation*. Geoffrey Grigson edited the *Oxford Book of Satirical Verse*, overlapping slightly with Gavin Ewart's *Penguin Book of Light Verse*. Valentine Cunningham broke new ground with the *Penguin Book of Spanish Civil War Verse*. However, most of the better poems in it were already well-known, and the new discoveries were less interesting than had been hoped.

United States

Fiction. Only partially filled with the historical fuel that energized *The Book of Daniel* (1971) and *Ragtime* (1975), E. L. Doctorow's *Loon Lake* was an artful but lifeless picaresque novel that followed the crossing paths in 1936 of a very young vagabond and a somewhat older failed poet, both of whom love a tormented beauty and both of whom wind up under the wing of a great tycoon at his Loon Lake estate in the Adirondacks.

The American Indian's heritage has perhaps suffered from overexposure in recent fiction, but Dee Brown (*Bury My Heart at Wounded Knee*) combined his sure grasp of history's sweep with a sharp foreground focus to produce the best of the lot—a lean, incident-rich 18th- and 19th-century saga, *Creek Mary's Blood*. Erica Jong's *Fanny*, a "mock-eighteenth-century novel" from a truly female viewpoint, based loosely on Henry Fielding's *Tom Jones*, is soaked in stale 1970s-chic platitudes that narrator-heroine Fanny is forced to spout smugly at every opportunity. Within the austere severity of her pre-Civil War New England setting, Judith Rossner pierced the central passion and terror of the victim in *Emmeline*, a tale about seduction, out-of-wedlock childbirth, and abandonment, with a Greek-tragedy wallop at the finale. *Bellefleur* is another myth-epic family chronicle, Joyce Carol Oates-style—which means a dark household full of lust, ghosts, disappearances, mystical animals, religious conversions, and ghoulish leaps of Oatesian imagination—all in the Adirondacks.

Thomas Berger returned to middle-class America with *Neighbors*, a comic nightmare-book that has

had been rather overshadowed by the ambitious work of already celebrated writers.

Letters, Lives. The most popular collection of letters was Mark Amory's edition of *The Letters of Evelyn Waugh*. This witty, pious, melancholy, and eccentric novelist was recognized as a serious writer and mysterious human being; his correspondence helped to interpret the mystery. Among other admired letters and diaries were those of Virginia Woolf and John Masefield, Henry James and Cardinal Newman, and William Cowper and Lord Byron. An influential theatre critic and dramaturge, identified with dandyism, left-wing politics, and sexual "liberation," Kenneth Tynan gently expressed his provocative views, for the last time, in his book of profiles, *Show People*.

Among the literary biographies that appeared during the year, those of two poets, W. H. Auden and C. Day-Lewis, attracted much critical attention though neither won universal praise. More familiar subjects for biography were George Orwell, the eccentric left-wing anti-Communist, and Sidney Smith, the witty left-wing clergyman. Bernard Crick's biography of Orwell was received with interest and argument, while Alan Bell's life of Smith was welcomed with general delight.

Eudora Welty
© THOMAS VICTOR

the naked, joyful aggression found only in those old slapstick vaudeville routines—the ones where somebody keeps getting hit on the head with a bladder. The theme of *The Second Coming*, Walker Percy's fifth novel, is tightly bound to the theme of his other four: Why is a person nowadays "two percent of himself"? The answer, always elusive, is clothed in fictional riches that are almost humbling: the spookily precise descriptions of odd physical sensations; the satire on the dead modern South; the rage and the Kierkegaardian comic curiosity. Another comic masterpiece, finally published more than ten years after its writing, was John Kennedy Toole's (1937–69) *A Confederacy of Dunces*, starring Ignatius Reilly, virgin and lute player, rhetorical wreck *in excelsis*.

A number of impressive first novels of high-geared sensibility commanded serious attention. *Blackbird Days*, by Ken Chowder, is a glossy, often fey work, dazzling in its virtuosity and frazzling in its mannerisms—a Harper-Saxton Award winner. *Household Words* was Joan Silber's first effort in American fiction's fastest growing subgenre: the novel of Woman Coping, a sad epigrammatic story about a woman who, groomed for a life of agreeable minutiae, is immobilized and splintered by ravaging forces she cannot control.

Notable major short-story collections included *The Collected Stories of Eudora Welty*, a testament to Welty's masterly evocation of the old South, her genius with dialogue, and her control of brilliant and startling metaphor. *High Crimes and Misdemeanors* features mystical and adventurous stories, some airy, some ponderous, by Joanne Greenberg. In *Side Effects* Woody Allen is at his most impressive self, blending parody, nonstop one-liners, and earthy absurdity.

History, Biography, and Belles Lettres. The long-awaited first installment of Henry Kissinger's *White House Years* finally arrived and, advertising hype aside, it *was* an event, garnering the American Book Award for History. One of the great documents in the history of political statecraft and manipulation, it shows us a Kissinger who knew how to institutionalize his power and who, in the end, outmaneuvered even Richard Nixon. Only a man for whom values are ideology and power is truth could claim that "Cambodia was *not* a moral issue."

In the current explosion of economic panaceas, Ronald Muller offered *Revitalizing America*, a firmly grounded scheme to straighten out the U.S. economy that argues for the enhancement of productivity through worker control of the workplace and the establishment of such "quasi-public" corporations as a development bank to finance experimental industrial projects. *Future Shock* author Alvin Toffler was busy accommodating himself to the future in *The Third Wave*, the Technological Revolution. In *Human Nature and History*, an eloquent defense of historical processes as movers and shapers of mankind, Kenneth Bock added yet another voice to the swelling chorus opposed to sociobiology. On the practical side of social change, Gay Talese may have indeed spent nine years pondering the "social and sexual trends of the entire nation," but the contents of *Thy Neighbor's Wife* are largely determined by which of Talese's subjects were willing to Tell All, thus putting disproportionate emphasis on a relatively small number of sexual case histories.

Woman as Subject continued to attract solid inquiry. In *Women and the American Labor Movement*, Philip S. Foner carefully and exhaustively chronicled women in the trade union movement from World War I to the present; *At Odds*, by Carl Degler, is a major and largely successful attempt to integrate the history of the family with that of women's push for equal rights from the American

Revolution to the present; and in *Powers of the Weak*, Elizabeth Janeway placed important feminist concerns within general social theory by trenchantly arguing that the growth in awareness of the condition of women has already begun to erode the legitimation of power in society, which is the first step toward a new social contract.

In the important domain of New Journalism, Bob Woodward and Scott Armstrong scored with *The Brethren: Inside the Supeme Court*, wherein more than 170 former law clerks—and at least some of the justices—break the U.S. Supreme Court's traditional silence. The result is a searing account of the court's inner workings and dirty linen from 1969 to 1975 that casts doubt on the highest court as a judicious arbiter of anything.

The major literary biography of the year was *Walt Whitman*, by Justin Kaplan, exploring the "rational line of development that led from the journalist-loafer to the incomparable poet." Rich in period colour and demonstrating rangy intellectual grasp, the book shows Whitman influenced by radical Quaker oratory, Manhattan's urban rhythms, sunny Emerson, demonic Carlyle, dark Poe, grand opera, "animal magnetism," phrenology, Egyptology, the Bible, and, above all: "In the city he explored democracy, and in democracy he explored himself."

Lyndon: An Oral Biography, by Merle Miller, offers the lowdown on Lyndon Johnson as hundreds knew him: a crackling projection of his personality and modus operandi, with the former president coming through as a super-Harry Truman, a Kohinoor-in-the-rough. Also noteworthy was Ronald Steel's *Walter Lippmann and the*

Merle Miller
© THOMAS VICTOR

American Century, a conscientious, even eloquent intellectual biography of the Harvard University wunderkind who often applied Freudian thought and moral philosophy to political punditry and who became "without doubt the nation's greatest journalist."

Among the notable belletristic offerings were: *On Language* by double-duty *New York Times* columnist and "libertarian language activist" William Safire, a browser's delight filled with jaunty enthusiasm for puns ("anomie-tooism"), neologisms ("eggsy"—the female version of macho), and the latest jargon in show-biz, drug-pushing, real estate, and espionage—a must for language-lovers of all persuasions; and Mary McCarthy's *Ideas and the Novel*, an insightful defense of the novel as "idea-carrier."

Poetry. Among the poetic offerings the most noteworthy collections were James Merrill's *Scripts for the Pageant*, Lucille Clifton's *Two-Headed Woman*, James Schuyler's *The Morning of the Poem*, and James McMichael's *Four Good Things*.

Canada

Along with some long-established writers, several comparative newcomers brought out new books in 1980. Hugh MacLennan's latest work, *Voices in Time*, places the events of the Hitler era against those of a contemporary Canadian society of the next century in order to illuminate yet a third period of time, the 1980s, when a nuclear holocaust wipes out civilization. *Joshua Then and Now*, by Mordecai Richler, describes a man's search for the truth about himself and his generation as he wanders from Montreal to London to Ibiza to Hollywood and back again. Albert Johnson, the object of one of the Mounties' most publicized manhunts, has been brought to desperate, hunted life by Rudy Wiebe in *The Mad Trapper*.

In a class by itself was the posthumously published *Hear Us O Lord from Heaven Thy Dwelling Place and Lunar Caustic*, by Malcolm Lowry, an evocative exploration of two of the most influential themes in Lowry's writing, his love of nature and the sea and the horrors of the alcoholism he endured. Helen Weinzweig garnered both critical and popular acclaim with her *Basic Black with Pearls*, in which a middle-aged woman's assignations with her (supposed?) lover lead her on a kind of mythic treasure hunt to discover the personal significance of her Jewish heritage, her marriage, and the power of illusion over all. In another novel devoted to religious and social themes, *The Third Temptation*, Charles Templeton demonstrates how piety and publicity, wealth and unworldliness battle in the heart of a popular evangelist and profoundly affect the outcome of his confrontation with a newspaper publisher who is determined to destroy him.

Although apparently based on a real event, Richard B. Wright's *Final Things* becomes a true story of its own as it investigates the rape-murder of a young boy and probes the sources, innocent and otherwise, of this grisly event. Other fine novels produced during the year included *Happenstance*, by Carol Shields; Jan Drabek's *The Lister Legacy;* George Bowering's *Burning Water;* and an ironic description of relations between the U.S. and Canada, David McFadden's *A Trip Around Lake Erie.*

Among first novels were the winner of the $50,000 Seal Book's First Novel Award for 1980, *Odd's End*, by Tim Wynne-Jones; *The Suicide Murders*, by Howard Engel, introducing Benny Cooperman, private eye; and *The Charcoal Burners*, by Susan Musgrave (better known for several volumes of poetry), in which a young woman increasingly loses the will to act through a growing involvement in visions of oblivion. Another poet who turned to fiction was Ralph Gustafson with his collection of short stories, *The Vivid Air*. Other collections showing that the art of the short story was very much alive were those of Hugh Hood, *None Genuine Without This Signature;* Don Bailey, *Making Up*, a further excursion into the meaning of imprisonment both physical and spiritual; and Roderick Haig-Brown, *Woods and River Tales*, 18 stories about people pioneering in the British Columbia wilderness.

Poetry highlights included *Collected Poems, Volume 1 (1940–55)* by Raymond Souster, the first of a projected four-volume collection; Ralph Gustafson's *Landscape with Rain*, lyrical expositions on the nature of things and men; Tom Wayman's *Liv-*

William Golding

ing on the Ground: Tom Wayman Country, which included "Garrison," the poem that won first prize in the U.S. Bicentennial poetry competition; *In Search of Living Things*, by Gail Fox, in which she ventures far into the interior of new lands; and *A Long Apprenticeship*, by Fred Cogswell, in which, with typical modesty and humour, the author attempts to account for himself.

LITERATURE FOR CHILDREN

In 1980 the slogan adopted for Children's Book Week was "Books Alive!" It was an indication that children's book publishing was flourishing. While aspects of contemporary life were reflected in serious fiction and nonfiction, there was also a steady output of fantasy, folklore, and humour.

For Younger Readers

A book that appeals to preschool children is *Truck* by Donald Crews; it is wordless, has a bold, clean use of space, solid blocks of colour, and many vehicles in highway scenes. Paul Showers, in *No Measles, No Mumps for Me*, explains clearly the use of preventive medicine in conferring immunity. An Australian author-illustrator, Pamela Allen, introduces a goat, a kangaroo, and a wombat into a science legend in *Mr. Archimedes' Bath*, which gives accurate facts about Archimedes' discovery about the displacement of equivalent weights in water.

Many of the serious issues that figure in books for older readers are also evident in stories for younger children. Patricia MacLachlan combats stereotypes of old age and blindness in *Through Grandpa's Eyes*, in which a small boy describes a day spent with his grandparents, making it clear that they lead full and active lives. *My Friend Jacob* by Lucille Clifton is a tender story about a black child's friendship with Jacob, a retarded white adolescent, a relationship in which Jacob is not tolerated but appreciated, not pitied but loved. Brock Cole combines fantasy and realism in *No More Baths*, the story of an obdurately dirty child who refuses to wash; she finally capitulates, but when her mother says, "There are worse things than taking a bath, aren't there?" Jessie says, firmly, "Nope." In Bernard Waber's hilarious *You're a Little Kid with a Big Heart*, a girl of seven is given a magic wish; it comes as a shock to both Octavia and her parents when she suddenly becomes 39 and her friends won't play with her. Also amusing, but with its humour in the style rather than the situation, is *Teddy Bear's Scrapbook* by Deborah and James Howe; the toy bear boastfully admits to having been superb at everything he has done. Anecdotes about a legendary black hero are linked into a story in Virginia Hamilton's *Jahdu*, a book that is stunning in its fluent, inventive use of language.

Among the best poetry books were *A First Poetry Book*, an anthology compiled by John Foster with discriminating awareness of children's interests, and *Dogs & Dragons, Trees & Dreams*, a collection of poems by Karla Kuskin. A special kind of poetry book, *The Tamarindo Puppy* by Charlotte Pomerantz, plays with English and Spanish, fusing them deftly into poems that should appeal to children who speak one of the languages and are learning the other.

Of the many adaptations of folklore, two that are outstanding for their illustration are based on tales by the Brothers Grimm. One is *The Fisherman and His Wife*, in which Margot Zemach's paintings are colourful, humorous, and imaginative. The other is Janet Lunn's version of *The Twelve Dancing Princesses*; Laszlo Gal's grave, romantic paintings are remarkable for their meticulous detail and effective composition.

For the 8-to-11 Group

Nonfiction can both stimulate and satisfy children's curiosity; a good example is *Bet You Can't! Science Impossibilities to Fool You* by Vicki Cobb and Kathy Darling; it shows tricky tasks that defy the reader and are related to such scientific principles as the law of gravity. Peter Spier's *People* has handsome drawings and a sprightly text that shows the fascinating diversity of the human race. John Navarra's *Earthquake* describes the causes, measurement, and predictability of earthquakes in a lucid and authoritative book.

Several realistic stories have to do with children who are disabled; one of these is Jan Slepian's *The Alfred Summer*, a touching story about a friendship between a retarded boy and another with cerebral palsy; another is Delores Beckman's *My Own Private Sky*, about the friendship between a shy, fearful boy and an elderly woman who loses a leg in an accident. Both books are surprisingly funny at times, and both have high narrative quality. Patricia MacLachlan's *Arthur, for the Very First Time* is in the same vein: a smoothly written story, funny and compassionate, about a troubled child who gains self-confidence. The protagonist of Ouida Sebestyen's *Far from Home* is illegitimate, motherless, and lonely; the beautifully written story ends on a note that is both hopeful and realistic. Girls are the central figures in Betsy Byars's *The Night Swimmers* and Jean George's *The Cry of the Crow*. In the former the motherless child of a country-and-western singer clings to mothering her two small brothers and is able to be a child herself only after her father's loving friend becomes a substitute mother; in the latter the author's experience as a naturalist and her skill as a narrator produce a trenchant story about a pet crow. In contrast, Judy Blume's *Superfudge* is a lighthearted, witty, episodic story of the problems of having a precocious little brother.

One of the most enjoyable fantasies of the year, Sarah Sargent's *Weird Henry Berg*, is a new variation on an old fantasy theme, the presence of dragons in today's world. Henry's elderly friend, Ms.

Levenson, helps him solve the problem of keeping his pet dragon safe from harm. In *The Frog and the Beanpole* by Charles Kaufman an articulate invisible frog combines his talents with those of a runaway girl to become a smash hit as a circus act. A more intricate fantasy is *The Magicians of Caprona* by Diana Jones; this is in the traditional vein of good versus evil, an adroitly meshed story of two feuding families of spell casters who unite against a common enemy. In another style of fanciful writing, the tall tale *Arthur and the Great Detective* by Alan Coren pokes fun at mystery-adventure stories with a shipboard tale of a boy detective who out-detects Sherlock Holmes.

A major anthologist and poet, Myra Cohn Livingston, has compiled a fine assortment of seasonal selections in *Poems of Christmas*, including selections from many countries. Quentin Blake illustrated a selection of poems from Ogden Nash in *Custard and Company*; the inspired lunacy of his drawings is perfectly suited to the poetry. Aileen Fisher's poems follow the cycle of the year in *Out in the Dark and Daylight*; they are filled with vivid imagery and are fresh and brief.

One of the outstanding books of 1980 was Arnold Lobel's *Fables*: the stories are original, pithy, and funny, each story-page faced by an illustration that is rich in colour, handsome in composition, and creative in concept. Other books in the folk tra-

A Gathering of Days by Joan Blos was awarded the 1980 Newbery Medal.

The 1980 Caldecott Medal went to Barbara Cooney for her illustrations for Ox-Cart Man, *by Donald Hall.*

dition were Alison Lurie's *The Heavenly Zoo: Legends and Tales of the Stars*, a smooth retelling of legends about animal constellations, and *The Trouble with Princesses*, seven stories about New World princesses of the Northwest Coast, told with zest by the eminent Canadian author Christie Harris.

For Older Adolescents

Interest in the disabled is evident in nonfiction as well as fiction: Joyce Mitchell's candid *See Me More Clearly* gives career guidance to the handicapped and makes their problems clear to others. *Listen to Me, I'm Angry* by Deidre Laiken and Alan Schneider gives sensible advice on coping with adolescent anger. Jason and Ettagale Laure interview young people of diverse ethnic and tribal groups in *South Africa: Coming of Age Under Apartheid*.

Among the fictional titles for young adults, two historical titles were notable. Scott O'Dell's *Sarah Bishop* is a dramatic account of a young woman who retreats to the wilderness during the Revolutionary War, while Edith Baer's *A Frost in the Night* describes the eroding security of a Jewish family during Hitler's rise to power. A perceptive contemporary story is Paula Fox's *A Place Apart*, a beautifully written account of disappointed love. In

William Butterworth's *LeRoy and the Old Man*, a black adolescent acquires a new set of values from his grandfather, and in *Maudie and Me and the Dirty Book* by Betty Miles a girl learns how insidious censorship can be. Marilyn Sachs's *Bus Ride*, the story of a first love, achieves remarkable narrative flow with the use of dialogue alone.

One of the engrossing fantasies of 1980 was the subtly written story of four children with supersensory powers, Virginia Hamilton's *Dustland*. In Ursula K. LeGuin's *The Beginning Place* two adolescents cross a time threshold into another world, and in Margaret Cooper's *Solution: Escape* two boys of a future time find they are clone brothers and escape together from the evil scientist who controls their lives.

Two unusual books were published for children but are really for all ages. *Anno's Italy* by Mitsumasa Anno is a stunning pictorial account of a journey, and *Graham Oakley's Magical Changes* is a masterpiece of ingenuity, with cut pages that mix and match. Both are wordless; both are superbly illustrated.

Awards

The Newbery Medal was given to Joan Blos for *A Gathering of Days: A New England Girl's Jour-*

nal, *1830–1831*, by the American Library Association, which awarded the Caldecott Medal to Barbara Cooney for her illustrations of Donald Hall's *Ox-Cart Man*. The International Reading Association chose Ouida Sebestyen's *Words by Heart* as the best book by a new author, and the National Council of Teachers of English gave its award for distinguished poetry to Myra Cohn Livingston. The Laura Ingalls Wilder Award went to Theodor Geisel, who writes as Dr. Seuss.

The international Hans Christian Andersen Awards went to Suekichi Akaba of Japan for his illustrations and to Bohumil Riha of Czechoslovakia for his writing. The Library Association of Great Britain chose Peter Dickinson's *Tulku* for the Carnegie Award and Jan Pienkowski's *Haunted House* for the Greenaway Award. The Canadian Library Association's literary award went to James Houston for *River Runners* and the Howard-Gibbon Medal for illustration to Laszlo Gal for his paintings in *The Twelve Dancing Princesses*.

MAGAZINES

Termed the "fastest growing segment of the print industry" in the U.S., magazines expected their advertising revenues to increase by 41% from 1980 to 1982. This was the finding of "Consumer Magazines in the 1980s," a study issued by Knowledge Industry Publications. Thanks to such promises of growth, approximately 200–350 new general magazines were started in the U.S. each year. Only about one in ten got past the second issue. The success rate for the little magazine, which had about the same number of starters, was somewhat higher, although a total life expectancy of three or four years was average.

The remarkably long-lived *Atlantic Monthly* and *Harper's*, intellectual voices of the U.S. since the mid-19th century, almost ceased publication in 1980. Decreasing readership and editorial focus accounted for the near disasters. Both were saved by last-minute business arrangements. In early summer *Harper's* ceased publication. A month later it started again, thanks to the McArthur Foundation of Chicago and the Atlantic Richfield Foundation, which committed $3 million to its current and future operation. The *Atlantic Monthly* was sold to Mortimer Zuckerman, a real-estate tycoon. Rivaled only by *The New Yorker* and *Harper's* for its literary reputation, the *Atlantic* was not likely to change in content.

Museum Magazine, among the most widely publicized new efforts, offered readers a tour through the treasures of civilization in the world's 24,000 museums. Edited for the general reader, the magazine followed the format of such successful publications as *Smithsonian*, as did another new title, *Science 80*. Issued by the American Association for the Advancement of Science, the latter was an effort to capture the audience that is mildly involved with science but is not knowledgeable

enough for *Scientific American*. And in late 1980 Time Inc. brought out still another popular science title, *Discover*.

"Nonprofit" was a common descriptor for many specialized magazine publishing ventures, such as *Sierra*, *Mother Jones*, *Smithsonian*, and *Black Scholar*. Although this situation was rare for general, large-circulation titles, it could become more common. *Ms.* magazine found salvation in its new nonprofit status during the year. The change allowed it to avoid higher costs by taking advantage of special postal rates and the infusion of tax-deductible grant money from outsiders. The publisher said that the opportunity was offered by the Internal Revenue Service to many publishers.

Among sales in 1980, *Us* proved no competition to *People*, and the *New York Times* finally realized it by selling the magazine to the Macfadden Group for close to $5 million. Rupert Murdoch sold the Los Angeles-based *New West* to the owners of *Texas Monthly* for $4.5 million. *Saturday Review* went to the owner of *Financial World* for an undisclosed amount. Founded in 1924, the *Review* gained fame under long-time editor Norman Cousins, but under its last owner, 28-year-old Carll Tucker, the format was so drastically changed as to confuse readers. As a result the magazine was losing between $500,000 and $1 million a year.

The trend toward specialized magazines was

Among a spate of new science magazines was Time Inc.'s entry Discover, *which began publication in October 1980.*
TIME INC.

Museum Magazine, *a newcomer in 1980 aimed at a broad audience, promised to bring the world's great art to its readership.*

apparent in much of the English-speaking world. In Great Britain, for example, new titles included *Greatest Hits*, which was to be a bimonthly covering 25 years of pop music, and *Rail Enthusiast*, also a bimonthly, which would focus on modern train operations.

MALAYSIA

Police using tear gas dispersed a massive demonstration in January 1980 by more than 10,000 rice farmers who had assembled in Alor Setar, capital of the state of Kedah. At issue was strong resentment of the government's policy of giving the farmers nonnegotiable subsidy coupons in place of supplementary cash payments for the purchase of rice. Ninety-two arrests were made, and a 24-hour curfew was imposed on the town. Despite this violent expression of opposition to government policy, Safirol Hashim from the United Malays National Organization (UMNO)—senior party in the ruling National Front coalition—narrowly won a by-election in April in Bukit Raya, Kedah, against a Party Islam candidate.

Prime Minister Datuk Hussein bin Onn assumed the defense portfolio after a Cabinet reshuffle in September. At the meeting of regional Commonwealth heads of government held earlier in the month in India, he had linked Soviet and Vietnamese occupations of Afghanistan and Cambodia,

respectively, as constituting a common threat in Asia. Malaysia's growing concern with external defense was reflected by the allocation of more than 20% of its budget expenditure for 1981 to its armed forces.

In March Lim Choon Wong, who had been convicted of murdering the chief of police of the state of Perak in 1975, was executed. This was followed by several other executions of men convicted under the Internal Security Act of illegal possession of firearms, despite appeals from the International Commission of Jurists and the Malaysian Bar Council. In April a controversial Trade Union Ordinance (Amendment) Bill was passed by Parliament after the sweeping powers allocated to the minister of labour and manpower, including the subordination of the role of the courts, had been withdrawn.

One of the world's largest natural-gas fields was discovered off the coast of the state of Trengganu in the South China Sea in March. The economic life of the field was estimated at 70 years. In September Malaysian business interests were revealed to be engaged in buying shares in the U.K. firm Dunlop Holdings Ltd.

Tengku Ahmad Rithauddeen traveled to Hanoi in January, the first visit to that city by a foreign minister of a member of the Association of Southeast Asian Nations (ASEAN) since the Vietnamese invasion of Cambodia. He arrived with a mandate for dialogue but failed to induce any measure of compromise on the part of his hosts over their occupation of Cambodia. A return visit to Kuala Lumpur in May by Rithauddeen's Vietnamese counterpart, Nguyen Co Thach, gave some indication of greater flexibility. But a Vietnamese armed incursion into Thailand in June put an end to the prospect of a continuing dialogue. Datuk Hussein bin Onn described the intrusion as a dangerous and irresponsible act when he addressed the opening session of the 13th ASEAN ministerial meeting held that month in Kuala Lumpur.

MEDICINE

Choice of the 1980 Nobel Prize winners for chemistry and for physiology or medicine reflected the importance of two emerging subfields of medical science. The Prize for Chemistry, shared by Frederick Sanger of Great Britain and Paul Berg and Walter Gilbert of the U.S., honoured the three for work fundamental to the progress of genetic engineering, whereby bacteria, for example, can be programmed to synthesize human proteins and other extremely desirable molecules. Some fruits of their basic research also made news during the year. The Swiss firm Biogen, a commercial genetic engineering company, began producing human interferon from bacteria that had been endowed with the appropriate gene. Other firms were experimenting with interferon manufacture using similar techniques. A commercial start was also made on the bacterial manufacture of human insulin, which would be invaluable in the treatment of diabetics who build up antibodies to the insulins of animal origin that are currently in use. (*See* Biology Special Report.)

The Prize for Physiology or Medicine was shared by George Snell and Baruj Benacerraf of the U.S. and Jean Dausset of France. Their work revealed much of the genetic basis of the immunological mechanism responsible for the rejection of grafted organs. Although interest in organ transplants remained high, the most important aspect of their work was the light it shed on the inheritance of resistance to disease and of susceptibility to such common and disabling ailments as rheumatoid arthritis, multiple sclerosis, and diabetes, in which the body's defenses appear to turn against certain of its own tissues. (*See* Nobel Prizes.)

The possibility of the bulk manufacture of interferon by bacteria was particularly welcome in view of a recent renewal of interest in this natural substance, which is produced when viruses invade cells. Apart from its possible use in the treatment of viral infections (which, unlike bacterial infections, do not respond to antibiotics), trials of interferon as an anticancer drug took place during the year. Although some encouraging responses were noted, early results were inconclusive, largely because the small quantities of interferon available and the high cost made adequate trials impossible. Press reports of the very limited experiments that did take place raised false hopes among many cancer sufferers and brought strong protests from some doctors who felt that accounts of such "advances" should be confined to the pages of the medical press until firm conclusions were reached.

In a first for transplant research, a team at Washington University School of Medicine, St. Louis, Mo., transplanted insulin-producing pancreatic is-

lets from one animal species to another (rat to mouse). Previously, islet cells and pancreas glands had been transplanted only between animals of the same inbred strain and, later, between animals of different strains of the same species. The ultimate goal of such research is to allow successful transplantation of animal or human islets into human diabetics.

An attempt at human genetic engineering caused adverse comment and sparked off an investigation. Martin Cline and co-workers of the University of California at Los Angeles (UCLA) treated two women suffering from thalassemia, an ultimately fatal condition in which, owing to a genetic defect, the sufferer is unable to manufacture normal hemoglobin and so develops a progressive anemia. Cline made a laboratory culture of cells containing the gene that initiates the production of normal hemoglobin and then introduced these genes into bone marrow cells (which give rise to the red blood cells) taken from his patients. He then returned the marrow cells to their original owners in the hope that the cells would survive and multiply and give rise to normal red cells. The experiments were performed in Italy and Israel in July, just a few days before a UCLA committee turned down Cline's request for permission to attempt a similar experiment in California. In October Cline revealed what he had done, reporting that both patients were alive and well but not whether they had responded to the treatment. Some critics immediately accused Cline of evading U.S. regulations in order to conduct work that had not yet reached a stage in which human subjects were justified. Cline denied the charge and replied that he was dealing with patients doomed to an early death for whom no other treatment was available.

In January a plan to establish the first test-tube

The recipients of the 1980 Nobel Prize for Physiology or Medicine were honoured for their work investigating the genetic aspects of immunology; they are (from left) Baruj Benacerraf of Harvard Medical School, Jean Dausset of the University of Paris, and George Snell of Jackson Laboratory in Bar Harbor, Maine.

Researchers at the University of Zürich were the first to produce the antiviral protein interferon through gene-splicing techniques. The production of substances such as interferon, insulin, and human growth hormone through bacteria that have had human genetic messages transferred to them is an achievement that has wide implications for medicine in the coming decades.

RALPH CRANE, LIFE MAGAZINE
© 1980 TIME INC.

baby clinic in the U.S. and involving several physicians from the Johns Hopkins University School of Medicine in Baltimore, Md., was approved by Virginia health authorities. The clinic would employ techniques largely developed by British gynecologist Patrick Steptoe and physiologist Robert Edwards whereby a woman rendered sterile by a blockage of her fallopian tubes can have eggs removed from her ovaries by a minor surgical operation. The eggs are then fertilized in the laboratory by her husband's sperm and finally inserted in the woman's womb. As of late 1980 the success rate was poor although the technique did work, as evidenced by the world's first test-tube baby born in England in 1978. When the plan for the clinic was announced, the Virginia Society for Human Life called it "an infamous day in the administration of public health." In the U.K. Steptoe resigned his post as a National Health Service specialist and, with Edwards, established a private clinic for test-tube babies near Cambridge.

In October investigators at the U.S. National Institute of Child Health and Human Development announced the result of a 2½-year study that seemed to offer a far simpler technique for overcoming infertility caused by blocked fallopian tubes. Working with female monkeys whose tubes had been artificially obstructed, they removed ripe eggs from the ovaries by a simple abdominal operation and returned them to the tubes beyond the point of blockage. The eggs were then fertilized during ordinary mating. Eggs are normally fertilized during their passage down the tubes from the ovary to the womb, where conditions (including a proper mixture of hormones) are ideal for the activity of both egg and sperm. When test-tube fertilization is attempted, these conditions must be imitated, as far as possible, in the laboratory, a complication that accounted in part for the technique's limited success.

Some infertility is due to the presence of antibodies to sperm in one of the partners of a marriage, according to a report in the *New England Journal of Medicine*. Antibodies are specialized molecules that attack, for example, bacteria and viruses against which the body has mounted defenses following inoculation or previous infection. It had long been suspected, but not proven, that some people develop antibodies to spermatozoa. A group of researchers in Pennsylvania used sophisticated radioimmunoassay techniques to demonstrate that sperm antibodies indeed were present in 7% of men and 13% of women in a group of 614 people with otherwise unexplained infertility.

Enthusiasm for oral contraceptives continued to decline. Figures published during the year showed that in the U.S. prescriptions for the Pill had dropped from 64 million in 1975 to 49 million in 1978, whereas prescriptions for diaphragms had risen by 140% over the same period. Although medical opinion remained divided concerning the comparative risks and benefits of oral contraceptives, several reports supported the generally accepted view that alternative methods should be recommended to older women, particularly those who smoke cigarettes, since both age and smoking significantly increase the risk of undesirable side effects, notably blood clots.

The tripling in cesarean deliveries in the U.S. during the 1970s was cited by a task force of the National Institutes of Health in recommending that women who previously had delivered by cesarean section be given an opportunity to choose vaginal delivery for subsequent babies. It declared invalid the old dictum "once a cesarean, always a cesarean." Use of the low segment transverse incision has greatly reduced the possibility of rupture of the uterine scar during later vaginal delivery.

Having previously warned women to limit smoking and drinking while pregnant, the U.S. Food and

Drug Administration (FDA) added caffeine to the list. In an FDA study, pregnant rats fed caffeine in doses equivalent to 12–24 cups of strong coffee a day produced offspring with missing toes or parts of toes. In animals whose mothers received the equivalent of two cups a day skeletal growth was delayed. The coffee industry said the FDA warning was premature and lacked evidence from human studies. Rats metabolize caffeine differently than do humans, the industry claimed.

A report by the Food and Nutrition Board (FNB), an agency that recommends dietary standards for the U.S., clashed with dietary guidelines issued earlier in the year by the U.S. Public Health Service and the Department of Agriculture. Whereas the federal government had urged the general public to reduce intake of saturated fats and cholesterol as a means of lowering risk from heart disease, the FNB, an arm of the National Research Council of the National Academy of Sciences, said that it could find no clear-cut cause-and-effect relationship between heart disease and the consumption of such high-cholesterol foods as fatty meat, eggs, and dairy products. In fact, it found no valid reason for healthy adults to decrease dietary cholesterol. The American Heart Association, a 20-year advocate of reducing caloric intake due to fat from 40 to 30%, criticized the FNB findings.

Controversy also beset the field of cancer research. New guidelines for screening tests issued by the American Cancer Society (ACS) recommended generally less frequent routine exams for symptom-free patients. A Pap smear test for cervical cancer need be taken only once every three years instead of annually as had been recommended by the ACS for the past two decades. Dissenting, the American College of Obstetricians and Gynecologists called the advice a disservice to women. An ACS recommendation against annual X-ray screening for lung cancer in cigarette smokers older than 40 was attacked by the Johns Hopkins School of Medicine and the Mayo Clinic.

Reserpine, a drug widely used to control high blood pressure, can cause cancer in animals and may pose a similar risk in humans, the National Cancer Institute (NCI) reported. But it also noted that patients requiring reserpine would have a greater health risk from stroke and related problems if they did not take it. In 1980 an estimated one million Americans used reserpine.

Three studies of humans, including one by the NCI that involved 9,000 persons, found only a minimal risk of cancer occurring from consuming products containing saccharin, an artificial sweetener. The conclusion differed from a 1977 Canadian study in laboratory animals that showed an overall 20% greater risk of bladder cancer for saccharin users. Two other artificial sweeteners, cyclamate and aspartame, again were denied approval by the FDA for human use in the U.S.

Fears that sodium nitrite, a preservative for processed foods, may cause lymphatic cancer were allayed by the FDA. Plans by the government to phase out use of the chemical were shelved after reexamination of 50,000 slides of tissue taken from rats during the original nitrite studies showed insufficient

A team of DNA researchers at UCLA have begun to use genetic manipulation techniques on animals. They were able to incorporate genes conferring drug resistance into fertilized mouse eggs; the techniques might someday be used to eliminate human disease caused by genetic defects.
BRUCE MARGOLIS, TIME INC.

evidence of cancer. Sodium nitrite is widely used in bacon, hot dogs, and sausages to prevent growth of bacteria that cause botulism.

A panel of the U.S. National Academy of Sciences lowered its estimate of cancer risk associated with low-level radiation. It calculated that 67 to 182 additional cancer deaths a year would result in a group of one million people continuously exposed to one rad of radiation, or about 20 times the amount received in a chest X-ray. The panel's estimate in 1979 was 68 to 293 deaths per million people.

An encouraging sign in the disappointingly slow battle against cancer was seen in a paper published in the British medical journal *Lancet* in October. Four British workers showed that, in a study involving some 16,000 men, cancer was more than twice as common among those with a low level of vitamin A in their body fluids. In an appropriately cautious fashion, the authors suggested that a diet high in vitamin A, present in such foods as dairy products and fresh vegetables, might provide protection against the second largest cause of death in the Western world.

A newly recognized and sometimes fatal disease that most often affects women under age 30 during their menstrual periods was linked by the U.S. Center for Disease Control to the use of tampons. Known as toxic-shock syndrome, the condition starts with a high fever, vomiting, and diarrhea. Within days, blood pressure drops sharply, bringing on a potentially fatal shock. The incidence of the disease was low: two or three cases in every 100,000 of the 50 million women using tampons. The relationship between tampons and infection was not clearly understood. Some authorities speculated that the bacterium *Staphylococcus aureus* may have

undergone a mutational change, producing a toxin for which the body has no defenses. Tampons may encourage vaginal propagation of the bacteria, which then may enter tissue through abrasions in the vaginal lining.

Physicians at the Johns Hopkins School of Medicine and Sinai Hospital in Baltimore announced development of a 250-g (9-oz), battery-powered surgical implant that fits in the abdomen of heart patients to deliver automatic bursts of lifesaving electric shock when cardiac arrest or irregular rhythm occurs. The miniature defibrillator, about the size of a package of cigarettes, monitors the regularity of heart rhythms. If irregularity occurs, it waits 15 seconds for the heart to regulate itself and then delivers its stimulus.

Mayo Clinic in Rochester, Minn., announced development of an X-ray scanner that can show human organs, heartbeats, and blood flow in three dimensions. A refinement of computed tomography, it can also detect coronary artery disease, diagnose complex congenital heart defects, assess heart muscle damage after a heart attack, and identify small cancerous lung tumours more reliably.

A new vaccine for hepatitis B proved 92% effective in U.S. tests in immunizing a high-risk group of 549 male volunteers. The results were matched against a control group of 534 men who received placebos.

Elderly Americans who survived to the late 1970s could expect longer lives than previous generations. The National Center for Health Statistics reported that people who turned 50 in 1978, the most recent year for which statistics were available, could expect to live past 77 on the average, a gain of three years over 1950 statistics. Those who reached 65 in 1978 would probably also reach 81, a 30-month in-

Jean Puccio of Washington, D.C., and former Oakland Raiders quarterback Daryle Lamonica were among the witnesses testifying before a congressional Health and Scientific Research Subcommittee on the drug known as DMSO, an industrial chemical that backers claimed was effective against arthritis and a variety of other diseases.
WIDE WORLD

AUTHENTICATED NEWS INTERNATIONAL

Malignant lung tumours can be differentiated from benign ones by checking computerized information on tissue density from a CAT scan, a discovery made by Stanley Siegelman of the Johns Hopkins Medical Institutions.

crease. The death rate for men and women 85 and older fell 26.3% between 1966 and 1977.

Regulation and Legal Matters

In June, by a 5–4 vote, the U.S. Supreme Court ruled in effect that Congress has the right to limit Medicaid payment for abortions to women in danger of death and to victims of rape or incest. The decision came in response to a challenge to the so-called Hyde amendment, which since 1976 had denied unlimited federal funding for abortions. (*See* Supreme Court, U.S.)

In May a U.S. judge ordered the retrial of a case concerning a boy born with congenital defects after his mother had taken Bendectin (called Debendox in the U.K.), a morning-sickness suppressant, during her pregnancy. In the original hearing the jury decided that Bendectin had not been shown beyond a doubt to be the cause of the boy's deformity but awarded the parents $20,000 to cover their medical expenses. Both sides—the parents and Richardson-Merrell, the manufacturers—claimed that the result vindicated their opposing points of view, but the appeals judge held that the verdict was unsatisfactory in law, since either Bendectin was the cause of the boy's defects, in which case the parents were

entitled to damages, or it was not, in which case the parents were entitled to nothing.

The case typified the difficulties surrounding attempts to fix the responsibility for medical mishaps. It also drew attention to the need for codifying the legal relationship between consumers and suppliers of medical aid, so that victims of malpractice are fairly compensated in a way that does not frighten doctors, drug manufacturers, and others from undertaking innovations because of the risk of crippling lawsuits.

U.S. distribution of tetrahydrocannabinol (THC), the active ingredient of marijuana, was approved for cancer patients suffering uncontrollable nausea and vomiting as a result of treatment with anticancer drugs. Authorized to prescribe THC were doctors licensed by the NCI and the Drug Enforcement Administration. Approval of THC as an experimental drug, however, did not change its status as an illegal substance.

In the first code revision in 23 years, the American Medical Association (AMA) approved association with "talents of other health professionals." The revision was expected to relieve the AMA of some of the legal pressure imposed by several antitrust suits charging the organization with conspiracy to prevent chiropractors from practicing their profession for the public good. The new code permitted physicians to refer patients to chiropractors. It also deleted references to patient solicitation, including a ban on advertising by physicians. The ban had been the basis of a suit by the Federal Trade Commission against the AMA charging that the policy discouraged competitive pricing.

MENTAL HEALTH

Fundamental understanding of the roots of mental illness and advances in treatment continued to be discouragingly slow, and 1980 provided only scant cause for expectation that the pattern would soon change.

Schizophrenia, the most commonly diagnosed mental disease, affects about 1% of all adults worldwide, but its cause is still unknown. This ignorance has not been due to any lack of interest in the disease among psychiatrists and medical scientists, for an unending stream of papers in learned journals has advanced a plethora of theories and findings inculpating everything from white bread or an unhappy home life to genetically mediated faults in brain chemistry as possible factors in the disease. Although most of these theories have enjoyed short popularity and then faded from view, evidence amassed during the past two years seemed to support the idea that schizophrenia may be a delayed response to a virus infection.

In October five U.S. researchers published a paper in the British journal *Lancet* that apparently implicated cytomegalovirus (CMV) in the disease. This virus is one of several that infect most people at some time or other but usually without apparent ill effect. It was known, however, that certain viruses can linger in tissues for years, sometimes causing damage long after the original infection, when other factors happen to be favourable. The U.S. study showed that 60 schizophrenic patients, compared with 26 controls, had a high concentration of antibodies to CMV in the cerebrospinal fluid, the fluid that bathes the brain and spinal cord. These results extended findings published in 1979 by investigators in the U.K. that likewise had linked schizophrenia with evidence of viral infection.

The presence of specific antibodies gave evidence of a past infection by the organism concerned and thus suggested a connection between CMV and the disease. The study did not explain why CMV should cause mental disorder in only a small proportion of the people that it infects, although there was growing evidence that abnormal or occasional responses to viral infections may be a factor in several diseases of hitherto unknown origin, including multiple sclerosis and at least some forms of cancer. Nevertheless, it did add some weight to the belief that schizophrenia is due to an organic disorder of the brain and is not (as some psychiatrists maintained) simply the response of a normal mind to abnormal pressures. Should an infective cause for schizophrenia be established, prevention by means of immunization might become possible.

Suspicion that the prevalence of mental disease and disorder was exaggerated was bolstered by a report in *Science Indications*, compiled by the U.S. National Science Foundation, which showed that mental health professionals in the U.S. had contributed more than three-fourths of the world's arti-cles on psychological topics. This figure was markedly disproportionate to the country's size and overall research effort, since the U.S. produced only 40–50% of the world's writings in other scientific areas. It could be suggested that the incidence within a community of reported disorders of the mind bears a direct relationship to the magnitude of the professional effort devoted to the study and treatment of such complaints.

In the autumn a paper appearing in the *American Journal of Psychiatry* went so far as to suggest that major tranquilizers, or antipsychotic drugs—*e.g.*, Largactil, Stelazine, and Serenace—which had been used in vast quantities for more than a quarter of a century and which had greatly reduced the need for prolonged hospital treatment of schizophrenics and other grossly disturbed patients, should be employed only when essential, such as for the control of violence, and then only in small doses and for brief periods. This recommendation reflected a growing concern about the severe side effects that frequently accompany prolonged therapy with these drugs. The most serious of these, so-called tardive (persistent) dyskinesia, takes the form of uncontrollable, involuntary movements of the tongue, lips, hands, and even the entire body which can be both physically and socially disabling. The effects of these drugs on muscular activity were first recognized more than 20 years in the past, but only recently did it become apparent just how frequently they accompany long-term therapy, perhaps troubling more than half of those under treatment for at least ten years.

(*See also* Drugs.)

Pres. Jimmy Carter applauds Patricia Harris, secretary of health and human services, at the signing of the Mental Health Systems Act in October. The act expanded the role of the community mental health centre in serving such segments of society as the elderly and the poor. With President Carter and Harris are Rosalynn Carter and Sen. Edward Kennedy.
WIDE WORLD

MEXICO

In 1980 much of Mexico's domestic and foreign activity was tied to oil development. An oil-for-bauxite contract signed with Jamaica in February exchanged 10,000 bbl a day of Mexican petroleum for 420,000 metric tons of alumina a year and 10% of the shares in Jamaica's South Manchester alumina plant. In April nearly $1 billion was obtained in loans from Canada, West Germany, and France. Pres. José López Portillo visited those countries and Sweden in May. With Canada, an oil supply contract for 50,000 bbl a day was signed, to be increased to a maximum of 100,000 bbl a day, and industrial, agricultural, and mining assistance was agreed upon. Canadian Prime Minister Pierre Trudeau supported the Mexican opposition to a North American Common Market, which was based on Mexico's wish to remain in control of its energy resources. A 100,000-bbl-a-day contract was signed with France, which also agreed to foster cooperation in the prospecting for and development of uranium resources. Sweden in November signed a contract for 170,000 bbl of oil a day from 1981, at which time India also was expected to receive 100,000 bbl a day.

In July and August President López Portillo visited Cuba, Brazil, Nicaragua, Panama, Venezuela, and Costa Rica. In Cuba a communiqué was issued deploring the U.S. blockade of Cuba and the occupation by the U.S. Navy of the base at Guantánamo in Cuba. Mexico and Cuba signed a tourism agreement and a nonintervention treaty. An agreement was signed on August 3 with Venezuela to fulfill oil-import requirements for Central America and the Caribbean on favourable terms.

The Ixtoc well, which had blown out in June 1979, was sealed in March, having discharged about three million barrels of oil into the Gulf of Mexico. In August Mexico and the U.S. signed a cooperation agreement to provide joint action in the future on oil slicks that affected both nations.

President López Portillo stated that Mexico's proved petroleum reserves totaled 60,100,000,000 bbl (oil equivalent), probable reserves 38,000,000,000 bbl, and potential reserves 250,000,000,000 bbl. Current output was about 2.3 million bbl a day, making Mexico the fifth largest oil producer in the world.

Relations with the U.S. were strained in 1980. Mexico linked the exceptionally severe droughts that caused electricity shortages in July and heavy crop losses with U.S. weather experiments to divert hurricanes and stated that in the future permission would be required before such experiments could be carried out over its territory. The cost of nine million metric tons of food imports to make up for the losses was put at 50 billion pesos for 1980 (22.90 pesos = U.S. $1).

A further source of dispute with the U.S. was the "tuna war" in July. Mexico announced on July 7

UPI

Pres. Rodrigo Carazo Odio (right) of Costa Rica greeted Pres. José López Portillo on his visit to Costa Rica in August.

that boats fishing within 200 mi of the coast without permission would be detained. Three U.S. tunaboat crews were later arrested and fined; this led the U.S. to ban all imports of tuna from Mexico (about one-third of Mexico's catch) and also to cancel some fishing concessions. On December 28 Mexico announced that it was terminating all fishing agreements with the U.S.

Relations were also strained with Argentina, because the Argentine government refused to grant safe-conducts to three Peronists; in March the Mexican ambassador was recalled. At home, fighting broke out in May between 60 families of land settlers and 600 Indians near Yajalon, Chiapas State, and 46 people were killed. There were other land occupations, and the 50,000-strong Confederación Nacional de Campesinos took over 150,000 ha (370,000 ac) of land.

Toward the end of October a severe earthquake registering 6.7 on the Richter scale with its epicentre at Huajuapan de León struck across the state of Oaxaca in the southeast up to Mexico City. The quake destroyed or damaged 300 villages, knocked down three buildings in Mexico City, killed at least 65 people, and left 6,000 homeless.

(*See also* Latin American Affairs.)

MIDDLE EASTERN AFFAIRS

The onset of all-out war between Iraq and Iran on Sept. 22, 1980, thrust Persian Gulf security into the centre of Middle Eastern affairs. At the Arab League summit meeting in Amman, Jordan, on November 25–27, Arab disunity crystallized, with Syria, Libya, Algeria, Yemen (Aden), Lebanon, and the Palestine Liberation Organization (PLO) boycotting the meeting. This left the Arab world divided into the Steadfastness Front led by Syria and the somewhat more moderate states led by Iraq and Saudi Arabia.

The Gulf Crisis

In December 1980 the best that could be predicted was a de facto cease-fire in the Iran-Iraq war, which had begun with the crossing of the disputed Shatt al-Arab waterway by Iraqi forces. Iraqi Pres. Saddam Hussein at-Takriti, who gambled on toppling Iran "in days," was by December resigned to a long campaign. Diplomats in neighbouring Gulf countries were predicting ten years of instability in the region as a result of the conflict. Small nations such as Bahrain, whose Shi'ah populations were numerous, could also expect continuing domestic tension because of the pro-Iranian sympathies of their populations. (The Shi'ah branch of Islam is dominant in Iran in contrast with a Sunni majority in most neighbouring countries.)

On a visit to India in December Soviet Pres. Leonid Brezhnev, who was eager to stem the growth of U.S. power in the Gulf, proposed a plan for an international effort to ensure peace in the area. He called for the U.S., China, Japan, and Western European countries to accept "mutual obligations" to promote peace in the region. The obligations would prevent deployment of nuclear weapons and the establishment of bases in the Gulf and "adjacent islands." Outside countries would pledge not to use their military forces or to block trade and would respect Gulf countries' control over their own natural resources.

The Brezhnev proposal was rebuffed by most Gulf states, although they agreed with the Soviet "guarantee" of their right to control their hydrocarbon resources. The plan was immediately seen as a statement directed against U.S. moves to negotiate "access rights" that would allow it to use bases in three countries around the Gulf. Of these Oman at the gateway to the strategic Strait of Hormuz was the most important. At Masirah Island in southern Oman the U.S. was embarking in late 1980 on a major refurbishment of an old Royal Air Force staging airstrip and was locating a regional command centre there. The incoming administration of U.S. President-elect Ronald Reagan was thought likely to continue Pres. Jimmy Carter's policy of stationing a rapid deployment force capability near the Gulf.

The Soviet intervention in Afghanistan in December 1979 produced a climate of acceptance of a U.S. presence near the Gulf. Saudi Arabia and the Gulf states of Bahrain, Qatar, and the United Arab Emirates (UAE), which all had semimonarchical systems of government, showed themselves willing to enter into closer relations with Washington. There were moves in 1980 toward an integrated missile defense system for the Gulf nations based on the Hawk missile, which was made in the U.S. The U.S. was clearly motivated in its friendship for the conservative Gulf states by the need to preserve the oil supply from the area. That this was reciprocated, despite Saudi differences with the U.S. over the wider Middle East peace question, was shown in September when the Saudis requested and immediately received four Boeing airborne warning and control systems (AWACS) aircraft.

Instability in the Gulf was a deep concern of the West, aware that 60% of its oil flowed through the Strait of Hormuz. Even Iran was prepared to allay

The Conference of Islamic States met in Islamabad, Pakistan, in January. They condemned the Soviet invasion of Afghanistan and called for the "immediate and unconditional withdrawal" of Soviet forces.

DEJEAN—SYGMA

KEYSTONE

Refugees from Afghanistan poured into the border town of Peshawar, Pakistan, in February, following the Soviet invasion. Pakistan's resources were soon overwhelmed by the influx.

Western fears in the early days of its war with Iraq by denying that any plan existed to cut off oil supplies through the strait. The loss of Iraqi crude oil, while not an immediate blow to the world oil market, was sure to be felt by early 1981. Limited exports of Iraqi crude were possible through the Banias terminal in Syria, although Iraq's political relationship with Syria remained frigid after the abortive unity proposals of 1979.

Egypt, Israel, and Palestine

With Egypt contemplating a second year of isolation from the Arab camp, there were fears in Cairo in late 1980 that the Reagan administration would feel none of the personal commitment exhibited by President Carter in regard to the peace question. Vice-Pres. Hosni Mubarak of Egypt, who visited the U.S. in early December, specifically warned that for Reagan to give up the framework for peace established during the Carter administration by the Camp David accords would be a serious blow to Egyptian Pres. Anwar El-Sadat. But in mid-December Reagan assured Egypt that his administration would uphold the accords.

In his campaign for the presidency Reagan had hinted that he saw hope in "the Jordanian option." This would mean involving Jordan's King Hussein in talks about the future of the Israeli-occupied West Bank and the Gaza Strip and, to some extent, having Hussein negotiate on behalf of the absent Palestinians. It was apparently a cornerstone of Reagan's policy that the Palestinians were to be excluded from the talks about their future. On the other hand, there were signs of increasing dissension within Israeli Prime Minister Menachem Begin's government, raising the possiblility of the return to power of the Labour Party, generally perceived as being more flexible in its approach to the Palestinian question. The Egyptians were scheduled to receive $1.6 billion in economic aid from the U.S. in fiscal 1981 with a heavy proportion of that as strategic grants, and it had seemed that Reagan might have chosen to bargain with Egypt over it. That the Republican administration was not altogether united on the Middle East question was revealed when the incoming chairman of the Senate Foreign Relations Committee, Sen. Charles Percy of Illinois, was quoted as having told Brezhnev that he favoured a Palestinian state, even one led by the PLO chairman, Yasir Arafat. Later, however, Percy was at pains to explain that he favoured a "Palestinian entity" in federation with Jordan and that he opposed direct negotiations with the PLO until it renounced terrorism and publicly recognized Israel's right to exist in peace as a sovereign nation.

The question of PLO participation in the peace

process became a part of European Economic Community (EEC) policy. On June 13 the EEC called for the PLO to be associated with the negotiations in what was being called the Venice declaration. In July 1981 the EEC and the PLO were expected to have a full ministerial conference. The announcement about this was made on November 13, and the possible site for the meeting was London. The diplomatic preliminaries to this decision included a meeting between the chairman of the EEC Council of Ministers, Gaston Thorn, and Arafat in Beirut, Lebanon, on August 4.

The need for a fresh initiative became apparent to EEC heads of government after the failure of Palestinian autonomy negotiations between Egypt and Israel in July. Israeli Interior Minister Josel Burg, who headed the Israeli team during talks in the U.S., said that Israel would not yield over the status of Jerusalem. On June 30 the Israeli Knesset (parliament) approved a bill that declared all Jerusalem including East Jerusalem to be the united capital of Israel. Egypt reacted quickly with a declaration saying that this move violated the Camp David agreements. A UN Security Council resolution of June 30, sponsored by 39 members of the Islamic Conference and by Egypt, said that all measures that altered the geographic, demographic, and historic character and status of Jerusalem were null and void and must be rescinded. (The vote was 14–0; the U.S. abstained.) The Israeli declaration about Jerusalem angered a number of Arab nations and resulted in Saudi Arabia's strong man Crown Prince Fahd calling for a jihad (holy war) against Israel. Although the call was supported by many Arab countries, the possibility of united Arab action on Palestine looked remote in view of the divisions caused by the Iran-Iraq war.

Moves started in the Knesset in October to introduce a bill annexing the Golan Heights, captured from Syria in the June 1967 war. Members of the Knesset said that they believed Syria's treaty with the Soviet Union and Jordan's support for Iraq in the war strengthened the case for annexation. Geula Cohen, who was leading the lobby for annexation, had also sponsored the bill about Jerusalem. Meanwhile, the situation on the West Bank (of the Jordan River) showed every sign of worsening, with violent student demonstrations continuing in November.

Arab Disunity

The Arab League, which moved its headquarters from Cairo to Tunis in mid-1979 after Egypt's suspension, suffered acutely from Arab disunity. Its secretary-general, Chedli Klibi of Tunisia, whose nomination was opposed by a number of states including Iraq, saw months of preparation for a coherent policy of Arab national development swept away in a few minutes at the Arab summit in November. The Iraqi team suggested that its own proposals for a "decade of Arab joint develop-

ment" be translated immediately into action with the backing of a new $5 billion fund. According to the Iraqi plan, per capita income in Arab countries was to be raised by 13.5% a year, and a fund of between $1 billion and $1.5 billion a year was proposed to meet this goal. Simple arithmetic showed that much more would be needed, but this was the calibre of the Iraqi plan that was added to the summit's agenda on the opening day. A scaled-down version of it emerged two days later as the summit's most important economic conclusion.

Iraq's war with Iran angered Syria, Algeria, Libya, Lebanon, Yemen (Aden), and the PLO, who all boycotted the summit. Lebanon allied itself somewhat uneasily with the others because of its dependence on Syrian military aid.

Syria's quarrel with Jordan, which escalated sharply after the Amman summit, cooled after Saudi Arabia offered mediation. Syrian Pres. Hafez al-Assad accused Jordan of backing the Muslim Brotherhood, an extremist Islamic organization responsible for assassinations in Syria. On December 11 Jordan's information minister, Adnan Abu Odeh, said that Syria had begun withdrawing troops from the border with Jordan. Observers suggested that the main result of the crisis was a stiffening of Israel's fears for its security. By the year's end the Arab cause and, in particular, the ideal of joint Arab action concerning Jerusalem appeared as remote as ever.

Arab International Finance

Increased joint Arab action in international forums such as the International Monetary Fund (IMF) and the World Bank seemed certain in 1981. As the region neared 1981 its major characteristic was oil wealth. Arab banks and Arab money could be expected to play a vital role in "the world economy." On Jan. 27, 1981, the Arab Banking Corporation (ABC), with an authorized capital of $1 billion, was scheduled to hold a formal opening in Bahrain and announce plans to make itself one of the world's top 20 wholesale banks, only five years after the Bahraini authorities had embarked on a plan to make their nation a significant world financial centre midway between Japan and Europe. The arrival of 15 Japanese financial institutions in 1980 in Bahrain made the nation the Middle East's leading financial centre.

At the World Bank-IMF annual meeting in October the Arab oil producers used their financial muscle for political ends. Kuwait and Saudi Arabia withheld participation from loans to the World Bank because of a disagreement over observer status for the PLO at the meeting. Although the absence of Arab funds at the time meant little difference to the World Bank's ability to extend credits, Kuwait and Saudi Arabia were signaling their ability to make such exercises difficult.

(*See also* Energy; articles on the various countries.)

MINES AND MINING

Mining and quarrying in the United States in 1980 were adversely affected by depressed business conditions, which in the case of the steel industry caused extensive shutdowns and curtailment of iron mining in the Great Lakes and other areas. A long copper strike was experienced from midyear into the fourth quarter. Although exploration for uranium continued, plans for building new mines and concentrators were deferred.

On June 30 U.S. Pres. Jimmy Carter signed the synthetic fuels bill, which allotted $25 billion to accelerate development of the synthetic fuels industry. About $20 billion was to go to the new United States Synthetic Fuels Corp., which was to provide loans, loan guarantees, and other financial incentives to encourage production of synthetic fuels from oil shale, coal, tar sands, and other unconventional sources.

The ninth session of the Law of the Sea Conference at Geneva made progress on substantive issues so that a treaty seemed possible in 1981. In the U.S. President Carter signed the Deep Seabed Hard Mineral Resources Act, providing an interim regulatory procedure for ocean mining activities conducted by U.S. nationals.

There were many reasons for increased U.S. coal production, including conservation of petroleum and problems with nuclear energy, but as of 1980 the potential for growth was not being fulfilled. Eastern and Middle Western coals were burdened with regulations and high sulfur, and expansion in the West was hampered by insufficient transportation facilities. The difficulties were expected to be overcome, but no great leap forward was seen in the immediate future. The U.S. Department of Energy released 1985–95 coal production goals as follows: 1985—873.3 million tons per year; 1990—1,247,000,000 tons per year; and 1995—1,558,000,000 tons per year.

As of July 31 copper workers in most U.S. firms were on strike with the expiration of wage contracts. At issue were wages and cost-of-living adjustments, the latter appearing to be more of a problem. After nearly 3½ months five companies had returned to work and six were still negotiating on either wages or noneconomic issues.

A U.S. congressional subcommittee, after a three-week tour of Zaire, Zimbabwe, and South Africa, came to the conclusion that the U.S. should pay more attention to those countries because of U.S. dependence on them for strategic and critical materials. For example, together they possessed 86% of the world's platinum group metals reserves, 53% of the manganese, 64% of the vanadium, 95% of the chromium, and 52% of the cobalt. The U.S. imported heavily from the three countries for its supplies of those metals.

Industry Developments

Atlantic Richfield Co. announced at the end of September that its Montana copper unit would close down the copper smelter at Anaconda and refinery at Great Falls because it would be too expensive to make modifications to meet environmental regulations. The Anaconda smelter produced about 14% of U.S. primary production. In July the Montana Board of Health had adopted air quality standards that were as strict or more so, in some instances, than those set by the federal government.

Placer Services Corp., a subsidiary of St. Joe Minerals Corp., planned to begin gold dredging in 1981 near Marysville, Calif. This would be a renewal of activity in a long-dormant placer mining area. Placer expected to extract 622 kg (1,368 lb) of gold per year for seven years by deeper dredging than

In Australia the mining industry and the government faced a dispute with miners over tax-subsidized housing and protests about the choice of sites for exploration and operations.

BRISBANE COURIER MAIL

had been practiced previously and was rehabilitating two dredges at a cost of $10.4 million.

A significant gold discovery was made in Napa County, Calif., by Homestake Mining Co. The deposit, which could be worked by surface methods, was expected to yield 100,000 oz per year of gold for ten years. The mine and concentrator were scheduled to be operating by 1984.

A new gold mine was planned near Whitehall, Mont., to be in operation in 1982 by Placer Amex Corp. Freeport Minerals Co. and FMC Corp. held groundbreaking ceremonies at the Jerrett Canyon mine near Elko, Nev., in June. Production there was to begin in 1981 with a capacity of 180,000–200,000 oz per year.

Standard Oil Co. (Indiana) planned to spend more than $300 million in the next three years to develop the Cyprus Thompson Creek molybdenum mine in Custer County, Idaho. The operation was to consist of an open-pit mine and concentrator, anticipated to be operational in 1983. The deposit contained reserves of 181 million tons of ore averaging 0.18% molybdenum disulfide.

The New Jersey Zinc Co. ceased production of zinc metal at Palmerton, Pa., at the end of 1980 but planned to continue to produce zinc oxide. The old pyrometallurgical plant had environmental and energy problems that were aggravated by competition from imported metal. It had accounted for 22% of U.S. primary zinc smelting capacity.

St. Joe Lead Co. was building a new lead mine near Viburnum, Mo., that would increase the company's production capacity by 20%, to a total of 5.4 million tons per year. The Viburnum mill was to be modernized and expanded 50% to treat the ore. The project, to be operational in 1983, was expected to cost $25 million. It reflected St. Joe's belief

that lead-acid storage batteries would find widespread use in electric vehicles and in utility load leveling.

Considerable activity in tungsten was taking place in Nevada. General Electric Co., through its wholly owned mining subsidiary, Utah International Inc., was sinking a new shaft in an old mining area near Imlay and building a conversion plant to make tungsten trioxide at a cost of $50 million. The project, to be in operation in 1982, was designed to have a capacity of 91,000 tons per year of the trioxide. Near Fallon, NRD Mining Ltd. rehabilitated an old mine and mill at a cost of $1.5 million and produced its first concentrate early in 1980. Phillips Petroleum Co. was also exploring tungsten deposits in Nevada.

The greatest scene of mine development during the year was in Chile, where nominal production of one million tons per year of copper was to be increased 50% by 1990. The Chilean Copper Corp. accounted for about 850,000 tons of copper annually, nearly all from four big mines: Chuquicamata, El Teniente, Salvador, and Rio Blanco. These mines were being expanded by the government company in order to maintain capacity as the copper content of the ore diminished in the years ahead. The big new mines were to be in the private sector, however, and would require a combined investment of several billion dollars. Chile possessed about 20% of the world's known copper reserves and supplied 13% of the world market.

Zambia, another of the world's great copper-producing countries, had problems with productivity during the year. The result was a 2% decline in production to an annual rate of 360,000 tons per year of copper. The nation's main problem was a shortage of skilled workers.

On June 30 about 39,000 copper workers in the U.S. went on strike across the country. At stake were wages and cost-of-living adjustments. The strike dragged on for months.
WIDE WORLD

MINORITIES, AMERICAN

In a year dominated by presidential politics, a depressed economy, and stalemate in foreign affairs, long-standing American minorities fought to consolidate hard-won gains while new minorities, especially refugees from Asia and the Caribbean, struggled to establish footholds in the United States. The failure of the nation's economy to produce the growth that had earlier helped to ease the passage of minorities into the mainstream contributed to tensions. Gilbert Pompa, director of the U.S. Justice Department's Community Relations Service, characterized 1980 as a year in which "the gains made in the '70s seemed to be in danger of erosion. There was an atmosphere of backlash in the country, based on misperceptions of overcompensation for minority groups."

Immigrants and Aliens

In its courts and bureaucracies, U.S. society confronted a tangle of issues presented in 1980 by an influx of immigration and the continuing presence of illegal aliens. Do the children of illegal aliens enjoy the same right to public education as native children? In April a federal judge in Houston, Texas, ruled that they do—and invalidated a state law that excluded the children of illegal aliens from public schools. Do Haitians seeking asylum represent a claim on U.S. society? In July a federal judge in Miami, Fla., replied with a clear affirmative—and chastised the U.S. Immigration and Naturalization Service for "wholesale violations of due process" in handling Haitians. In early summer, the Carter administration announced a policy decision that granted Haitian and Cuban refugees a six-month "parole" during which no deportation proceedings would be initiated.

For hundreds of thousands of immigrants from Asian countries, 1980 was a year of continuing adjustment to American culture and economics. Sometimes in small groups in small towns, more often in large groups in the cities, Asians enacted their version of the American immigrant saga. In New York City, where there were an estimated 400,000 Asians, whole neighbourhoods began to take on distinctive ethnic aspects, whether Korean, Cambodian, Laotian, Thai, Filipino, or Chinese. In cities that were experiencing continued economic growth, such as Houston, Vietnamese immigrants who constituted a quite visible and significant minority were finding ways to acquire portions of the economic pie. In many areas assimilation was aided by voluntary organizations such as churches.

Blacks

Throughout 1980 blacks in the nation's cities experienced violent and often lethal attacks. At year's end officials in Atlanta, Ga., were still working to find the person or persons responsible for the abduction or slaying of 15 black children. Since July 1979, 11 children from the poorer section of Atlanta had been murdered and 4 had disappeared. In early fall sniper fire killed four blacks in Buffalo, N.Y., within a 36-hour period, and a month later two black taxi drivers were murdered and mutilated. Three young whites in Youngstown, Ohio, were arrested in November for the shooting of a 15-year-old black girl. In Chattanooga, Tenn., four black women were wounded by rifle fire following the burning of crosses in a black residential district. Two out of three Ku Klux Klansmen charged with the shooting were acquitted in July, and a third was convicted on a lesser charge. Following the court action, rioting erupted that lasted for four days.

Several U.S. cities witnessed angry, destructive rioting in 1980. In Chattanooga, Tennessee, violence followed the acquittal of two Ku Klux Klan members charged with shooting four black women. Black leader Jesse Jackson, above, was invited to the city to help cool tensions.
WIDE WORLD

The well-publicized rioting that occurred in Miami in May broke out after the acquittal of four white Miami policemen who had been charged with the fatal beating of a black insurance executive they stopped for a traffic violation. Marvin Dunn, a sociologist at a Miami university, described the acquittal as acting "as a spark after many, many months of trauma involving blacks and justice. It just rocked through this community." An April disturbance in Wichita, Kan., also resulted from an arrest that tapped long-standing resentment toward police behaviour in the black neighbourhoods.

In its annual State of Black America report, the National Urban League (whose president, Vernon Jordan, was seriously wounded by rifle fire during a visit to Fort Wayne, Ind., in May) characterized 1980 as "a year of storm warnings." The report spoke of deepening racial hostilities, took issue with official estimates of unemployment among blacks, and contended that the number of blacks living in poverty had increased during the 1970s from 7.1 million to 7.8 million.

With economic conditions exacerbating the competition for jobs, black leaders in 1980 began to question the efficacy of affirmative-action programs. A New York State assemblyman, Charles Johnson, after holding a series of hearings, concluded that groups such as women, veterans, and the handicapped were more consistently the beneficiaries than blacks and Hispanics.

Hispanics

In the November elections the voters of Miami approved a referendum that prohibited the use of municipal funds for bilingual education and any other public uses. The action symbolized a year in which the prospects for bilingualism in areas with significant numbers of Spanish-speaking Americans were sharply diminished.

The National Council of a La Raza, the Mexican American Legal Defense and Educational Fund, and similar groups were much concerned during the year with issues arising out of Mexican-American relations. The treatment of illegal aliens by both government agencies and employers figured prominently in their concerns. A measure of cautious hope was attached to a June meeting of state governors from both sides of the border. The meeting, convened in Juarez, Mexico, was the first such joint conference ever held, and its agenda included the issues of illegal aliens, pollution, and energy.

The actual numbers as well as the treatment of Mexicans illegally residing in the U.S. continued to be an issue throughout 1980. In February the U.S. Census Bureau released a study that argued that the number of Mexicans illegally in the U.S. was far lower than commonly estimated and might total fewer than two million. In January two U.S. Border Patrol officers were convicted of violating the civil rights of Mexican illegal aliens whom they had beaten. The conviction, in a federal district court in San Diego, Calif., marked the first time that a law enforcement official had been successfully prosecuted for violating the civil rights of an illegal alien.

Women

The Equal Rights Amendment continued to be stalemated in 1980, with three state ratifications needed before the June 1982 deadline. A Chicago National Organization for Women officer predicted that passage of ERA "would take a substantial change in the political climate—and I just don't see that in the works." The Republican landslide in November boded ill for the amendment's passage.

But a number of events in 1980 testified to the cumulative impact of women's activism. In May

Andrea Hollen was among the first women to graduate from West Point, the U.S. Military Academy. Women also graduated from the other service academies in 1980.

UPI

In July Pres. Jimmy Carter signed a bill to establish a commission to look into the government's treatment of the Japanese, both citizens and resident aliens, in the U.S. during World War II.

the four military academies counted women among their graduates for the first time. In July a federal court panel in Philadelphia ruled the Selective Service Act unconstitutional on the grounds that it excluded women.

In a number of academic institutions, women won sex discrimination cases that resulted in promotions, tenure, back pay, and more rigorous adherence to affirmative-action procedures. At Muhlenberg College in Pennsylvania a federal appellate court sustained a lower court decision that reversed the college's denial of tenure to a female physical education teacher. The University of Minnesota in April made an out-of-court settlement that gave $100,000 in damages to a woman chemistry professor. In January the U.S. Supreme Court affirmed a lower court decision that resulted in New Hampshire's Keene State College having to grant back pay and legal fees to a female professor of education.

Native Americans

From Alaska to Maine a number of Native American tribes enjoyed the mixed blessings of success in their battles over land claims and shares in energy production. Maine's Passamaquoddy tribe appeared to have successfully completed a decade-long quest for recognition of their claim to 12.5 million ac of Maine forestland. Subject to final congressional approval, the tribe would receive $81.5

million in payment. The questions that would arise once payment was finally made centred around the issue of how the Passamaquoddy would be able to fashion an existence blending modern economics with tribal tradition.

The encounter of tribal culture with the cash incomes generated by energy production produced among the Inupiat Eskimos of Alaska's North Slope what a University of Pennsylvania researcher called "an alcoholic society." The researcher, Samuel Klausner, attributed the Inupiat troubles to the sudden impact of a cash-wage economy on a hunting-and-gathering culture. Klausner said of the Inupiats: "They need to slow down the cash flow and plan for the day when the oil is gone and no one knows how to catch a whale."

In July the Supreme Court upheld a lower court award of $122 million to eight Sioux tribes in compensation for the illegal seizure of the Black Hills of South Dakota over 100 years ago. The Supreme Court action settled one issue but opened up many others; some Sioux planned to hold out for land rather than money, while others were prepared to accept the money but differed on its manner of distribution and use. Resolution of these and other issues was likely to require years more to resolve.

Homosexuals

After some years of dramatic and occasionally violent forms of activism, the gay rights movement in

1980 made significant progress amid the ponderous churnings of bureaucratic and legal procedure. Most prominent among the institutions forced to reconsider long-standing policy were the armed services and the Immigration and Naturalization Service. In September a federal district court judge declared military standards for homosexuals to be inconsistent and confusing, and he ordered the Air Force to reinstate an airman dismissed in 1975. Two months later the Army, under court pressure, removed homosexuality as sufficient grounds for denial of security clearance to civilians. The Immigration and Naturalization Service, following changes in administrative practice in 1979, was ordered by the Justice Department in September to exclude homosexual aliens only if such aliens voluntarily declared themselves homosexual. The Carter administration had several months earlier endorsed a proposal to eliminated entire the statutory ban on homosexual alien entry into the U.S.

MOROCCO

In the Western Sahara in 1980 the Popular Front for the Liberation of Saguia el Hamra and Rio de Oro (Polisario Front) achieved spectacular military successes in southern Morocco—in the Zag and Assa region in March, at Tan-Tan in September, and around Akka in August and September, around Zak in October, and Rous Lekhyalat in December. Morocco, however, claimed success in the Ouarkziz region in June and September. The Portuguese government recognized the Front on July 26 in order to obtain the release of Portuguese fishermen. Morocco pressured Mauritania to prevent it from recognizing the Front's government-in-exile, the Saharan Arab Democratic Republic (SADR), after the August release by the Front of 45 Mauritanian prisoners.

At the summit of the Organization of African Unity (OAU) at Freetown, Sierra Leone, in July, the Polisario Front had majority support from 26 African states, but the issue was referred to a committee. In an impartial communiqué this group called for a referendum and cease-fire in September, a move seen by Morocco as a victory for its own claims. The U.S. approved the sale of 50 military aircraft to Morocco in February and of another 25 in August. King Hassan sought support for his Sahara policy during visits to Iraq, the Persian Gulf states, and Saudi Arabia in February and to Europe in April. In April, however, a Dutch contract for the reconstruction of El Ayoun port was canceled as a result of parliamentary pressure in The Netherlands. In July Morocco announced an end of phosphate sales to countries that recognized the SADR, and diplomatic relations with Cuba and Libya were broken off.

The war posed strains on the economy, despite support from the Saudis and the Gulf states. Foreign debt rose to U.S. $5 billion, and the trade deficit increased by 12% despite a 52% rise in exports.

The government announced a new energy policy in April, involving an expenditure of $42 million on domestic development in order to cut oil import bills. Oil and gas were found at Essaouira and gas at Mechra Bel Ksiri. Phosphate exports generated 72% of the export earnings from minerals, which in turn were 45% of total export revenue in 1979. Tourism increased by 9% in 1979, with 1.5 million visitors. However, the economy grew by only 3%. In September King Hassan announced a 30% cut in rents for selected social groups, and in August a $400 million improvement plan for Casablanca was unveiled. In early 1980 there were some strikes that resulted in arrests. However, some political prisoners were later released.

Constitutional changes were approved by two nationwide referenda. On May 23 the royal coming-of-age was reduced to 16 from 18, to ease the crown prince's accession to the throne should the king abdicate or die. Then, on May 30, the life of each Parliament was extended from four years to six.

MOTION PICTURES

The outstanding phenomenon of 1979–80 was the extravagant escalation of Hollywood film budgets, out of scale even to current inflation rates. Such films as *Star Trek*, Michael Cimino's *Heaven's Gate* (briefly shown, but withdrawn for reediting), *Flash Gordon*, *1941*, and *The Blues Brothers* all topped $30 million; $20 million came to seem a quite unremarkable budget. Among those films of this "megabuck" class that managed to earn back their cost was the major box-office success of the year, *The Empire Strikes Back*, a sequel to *Star Wars*.

At the other end of the scale, some of the most successful films of the year in commercial terms were comparatively cheaply made, grisly horror films, for which there was a growing vogue among teenage moviegoers. Some of the more notable of these were John Carpenter's *The Fog*, Brian De Palma's *Dressed to Kill*, and Charles Kaufman's *Mother's Day*.

Many directors returned to films more or less based on fact. Stuart Rosenberg's *Brubaker*, starring Robert Redford, was based on the memoirs of a reforming prison warden. In Martin Scorsese's *Raging Bull*, Jake La Motta, the 1940s middleweight boxing champion, was personified by Robert DeNiro in a stunning performance. Even *Urban Cowboy*, a vehicle for the popular star John Travolta, took as its setting the real and raucous background of working-class leisure activities in and near the Texas oil fields. *Melvin and Howard*, odd but well-received, explored a fascinating sidelight of the Howard Hughes legend.

The English-born Michael Apted enjoyed a major box-office success with *Coal Miner's Daughter*, a recreation of the life of country and western singer Loretta Lynn, played by Sissy Spacek, set in locations in Tennessee and Kentucky. Alan Parker, the British director, created his musical, *Fame*, in the

The Empire Strikes Back

setting of New York's School of Performing Arts, following the students for five years, watching their professional progress and their private problems.

Among established Hollywood directors, the veteran Samuel Fuller fulfilled an old ambition with his panoramic view of World War II seen through the eyes of a small and expert fighting detachment, *The Big Red One*. Louis Carlino's *The Great Santini* was a strong portrayal of the dynamics of a family headed by a tough Marine. Hal Ashby achieved a major success with his delicate transposition of Jerzy Kosinski's *Being There*, featuring one of the last and best performances by Peter Sellers.

It was a year of debuts. Woody Allen's script collaborator Marshall Brickman turned director with

Simon, a modern morality cast as farce, which poked fun at the pretensions of science fiction, fake intelligentsia, and other topical targets. David Lynch's first major film, *The Elephant Man*, effectively explored the life of a man trapped by a hideously deforming disease. Actor James Caan directed *Hide in Plain Sight*, a sympathetic and low-key story of a father trying to gain possession of his children from their feckless mother and her criminal husband. Robert Redford's first film as director, *Ordinary People*, was about a similarly human subject, the effects upon his family of a disturbed youth's suicidal urges resulting from the accidental drowning of his brother. Already well established as a director, another star, Clint Eastwood, made a disarmingly modest and self-effacing light comedy *Bronco Billy*, in which he played a somewhat fraudulent Western-style star of a small traveling circus. Robert Altman turned to comedy with *Popeye*, featuring Robin Williams, with Shelley Duvall as Olive Oyl. Two popular singers also made their film debuts, Dolly Parton as an angry secretary in *Nine to Five* and Neil Diamond in a remake of *The Jazz Singer*.

In healthy contrast to the escalating costs of conventional commercial film production, there was marked activity in the production of imaginative, independently produced low-budget films, often financed by grants from public arts funds. Richard Pearce's *Heartland*, based on Elinore Stewart's real-life reminiscences of the hardships of Wyoming homestead life in 1910, was supported by a grant from the National Endowment for the Humanities. Victor Nunez's *Gal Young 'Un* was partly supported by the National Endowment for the Arts and the Florida Arts Council and cooperatively involved the whole Florida community where it was filmed.

The same area of low-budget, independent production produced three outstanding works of inves-

Ordinary People

tigative documentary: John Lowenthal's reexamination of the evidence in *The Trials of Alger Hiss;* Allan Francovitch's inquiry into the history of the CIA's overseas activities in *On Company Business;* and John Harvey's *We Are the Guinea Pigs*, which examined the facts and implications of the Three Mile Island nuclear accident. Made on minimal resources, Ira Wohl's *Best Boy*, a sensitive study of his cousin, a retarded 52-year-old, and the special problems of the man's aged parents, won the year's "Oscar" as best documentary feature.

At the annual awards ceremony of the U.S. Academy of Motion Picture Arts and Sciences, honouring works of 1979, Robert Benton's *Kramer vs. Kramer* won "Oscars" for best picture, director, actor (Dustin Hoffman), supporting actress (Meryl Streep), and screenplay based on material from another medium. The best actress was Sally Field in Martin Ritt's *Norma Rae;* the best supporting actor, Melvyn Douglas in *Being There. All That Jazz* took awards for best editing, art direction, costume design, and adaptation musical score. The best foreign-language film was Volker Schlöndorff's *The Tin Drum* from West Germany.

Some Notable Foreign Films

The British cinema had its share in the "megabuck movies": Stanley Kubrick's supernatural

Urban Cowboy

Popeye

thriller *The Shining*, however, looked wholly American, while *Raise the Titanic* proved a costly and miscalculated folly. Otherwise, there was comparatively little conventional commercial production. One of the last films produced by the Rank Organisation before the announcement that it would abandon production was Nicolas Roeg's effortfully stylish thriller *Bad Timing*. One of the best British films of the year, also a thriller, was John MacKenzie's *The Long Good Friday*, a complex but taut portrayal of the nemesis of a successful East End crook. An admirable feature debut that related popular music to social issues was Franco Rosso's *Babylon*, a lively but pessimistic portrait of black, reggae-obsessed youths in an exciting but hostile South London.

Among the most noteworthy Australian films was Bruce Beresford's *Breaker Morant*, a dramatized recreation of the true story of the court-martial of three Australian soldiers serving with the British in the Boer War and the subsequent execution of two of them as scapegoats (so the film suggested) for High Command blunders. Beresford went on to make an adaptation of David Williamson's play about the behind-the-scenes of football, *The Club*. Stephen Wallace made a striking feature film debut with *Stir*, a realistic prison drama. The first feature production of the Tasmanian Film Corp., John Honey's *Maganinnie*, was an admirable fable of coexistence, the story of a 19th-century Aboriginal woman who carries off a white child and the love that grows up between them.

The outstanding French films of the year were Alain Resnais's *Mon Oncle d'Amérique*, scripted by Jean Gruault, a wise and witty experiment in examining human relationships in terms of the behaviourist theories of the biologist Henri Laborit; and

STEVE SCHAPIRO—SYGMA

Nine to Five

François Truffaut's attractive *Le Dernier Métro*. At once a recollection of Truffaut's own *Day for Night* and a tribute to two of his heroes, Jean Renoir and Ernst Lubitsch, the film was inspired by the recollections of the actor Jean Marais and recounted the adventures of a little Parisian theatre during the German occupation in World War II. Georges Franju's *Le Dernier Mélodrame* also took a backstage subject, the crumbling and demise of a troupe of traveling players.

From West Germany Werner Schröter's *Palermo oder Wolfsburg*, which won the main prize at the Berlin Film Festival in February, was a stylized tragedy about the difficulties of integration experienced by a young Italian worker who comes to the Volkswagen works at Wolfsburg. Rainer Werner Fassbinder turned back to Germany of the 1920s, both for the text and the stylistic influences, in his massive *Berlin-Alexanderplatz*, made as a 16-hour television series but reduced to more manageable length for theatrical distribution.

The major Italian box office successes of the year seemed to be farcical comedies such as Sasellano and Pepolo's *Mani de Veluto*, a Cinderella story about a millionaire industrialist and a beautiful lady pickpocket; Steno's *La Patata Bollente*, a politico-sexual farce; or Bruno Corbucci's *Angencia Ricardo Finzi . . . Practicamente Detective*. Among films of artistic interest, Ettore Scola's *La Terrazza*, probing the disillusion of 1970s intelligentsia, had perhaps the greatest success. A co-production with France, Marco Bellocchio's *Salto nel Vuoto* used the relationship of a middle-aged and slightly eccentric sister and brother to investigate the role of the family in Catholic society. Marco Ferreri's *Chiedo Asilo* was uncharacteristically genial, an odd, gentle picture about an eccentric male kindergarten teacher.

In Sweden the actor Erland Josephson made his debut as director with *The Marmalade Revolution*, in which he himself played a man rebelling against drab middle-class conformism. The year's production was also notable for two superior children's films, Marie Louise de Geer Bergenstrahle's *Not for Children* and Astrid Lindgren's *You're Out of Your Mind Maggie*.

The Polish cinema, which for a year or so had been vividly reflecting the social dissatisfaction that reached a head in the strikes during the summer, continued to echo the prevailing social malaise. Krzysztof Zanussi's *The Constant Factor* described a hero who attempts to discover a constant standard of morality in society and is finally penalized for his refusal to conform to the prevailing corrup-

The Tin Drum
PHOTO TRENDS

PHOTO TRENDS

Kagemusha

tion around him. Another Zanussi film, *The Contract*, used what was superficially a form of absurdist comedy—about a disastrous wedding party—as a criticism of various attitudes of complacency, cynicism, and corruption within the socialist scheme. Andrzej Wajda's *The Conductor* (with John Gielgud in the title role) examined attitudes of provincialism and lack of national confidence through a story about a great Polish expatriate artist and the impact of his return to his homeland. Kazimierz Kutz's *Beads from One Rosary* seemed to echo the spirit of the Polish strikers in its simple tale of a miner who resolutely refuses to leave his old home for the "ideal" new apartment offered him in his retirement.

The outstanding Hungarian film of the year was Istvan Szabo's *Confidence*, a story of two people forced by wartime circumstances to pose as man and wife and the impossibility in those conditions of establishing mutual trust. Already Hungary's most exportable director, Marta Meszaros heightened the exportability of her films by starring in them foreign actresses of box-office appeal: in *On the Move*, Delphine Seyrig; in *The Inheritors*, Isabelle Huppert.

Japan could claim the most important film of the year—perhaps indeed for many years: the greatest living Japanese director, Akira Kurosawa, made a triumphant comeback with *Kagemusha*, a tragedy that, as international critics concurred, achieved a Shakespearean elevation. The story tells of a feudal clan chieftain who uses a double on the battlefield. The leader is killed, and the double—a former thief —takes his place, aspires to his courage and nobility, but is finally discovered and banished from the clan. Made with U.S. financing, the film achieved almost unprecedented visual spectacle.

MOZAMBIQUE

The frontier with Zimbabwe Rhodesia was officially reopened on Jan. 12, 1980, marking the first stage in a new relationship between the two countries, which had been effectively at war for several years. Ten weeks later Lord Soames, governor of Zimbabwe Rhodesia, visited Mozambique at the invitation of Pres. Samora Machel, who had made an important behind-the-scenes contribution to the negotiations leading to Zimbabwe's constitutional settlement. Machel was deeply satisfied by the outcome, which had brought to an end the war between Mozambique and its neighbour.

The invitation to Lord Soames and the discussion that took place between him and the president reflected the growing willingness of the government of Mozambique to contemplate some return to free enterprise and to closer relations with Western countries. In February a group of businessmen representing a number of multinational companies had visited Mozambique and had held discussions with Machel and some of his ministers. The president, while reasserting his commitment to a socialist program, had taken the opportunity to emphasize the benefits Mozambique could derive from the technology and expertise of multinational organizations, the activities of which in Mozambique could be controlled without preventing the companies from making adequate profits.

In an important speech on March 18 President Machel publicly criticized members of his administration and leaders of the Frelimo party for their corruption and inefficiency and dismissed three of his ministers as part of a drive against corruption started in January. The next day he announced the abolition of "people's shops" and said that their services would be provided by small private businesses. This public statement encouraged many who had previously suffered in silence from bureaucratic inefficiency to give voice to their criticisms, but it did not indicate a fundamental change in the political direction that the country had taken. A socialist state was still the goal, but Machel appeared to have accepted that rigid socialist policies must be modified when such action would achieve greater efficiency. On June 16–18 Mozambique changed its currency from the escudo to the metical, at the same value.

Toward the end of May discussions took place between senior defense officers from Mozambique and Zimbabwe with a view to providing mutual assistance. Mozambique was anxious for Zimbabwe's aid in dealing with the remnants of the Mozambican National Resistance (MNR) guerrillas, who continued to operate in the Manica, Sofala, and Tete provinces and who were thought to have a base in Zimbabwe. Although the activities of the guerrillas were crippled by a prolonged Mozambican offensive against them in June, a considerable military force still had to be deployed to keep them in check.

MUSEUMS

Museum activity in the U.S. only partially reflected the problems of world inflation. Both the intense pace of exhibition schedules and the numerous funding campaigns for future construction and general museum support indicated that the importance of the museum in the nation's cultural life was unaltered.

On the West Coast the Seattle (Wash.) Art Museum began a $23 million campaign for new construction, while in Los Angeles the newly organized Museum of Modern Art was given $2 million by its founding trustees to launch a $10 million endowment program. Also, the Los Angeles County Museum of Art announced that it planned to build a new gallery to house the Armand Hammer Daumier collection, the world's largest such archive collection. The Ahmanson Foundation offered the County Museum $4.5 million to fund additional construction for the Ahmanson Gallery.

In the South the High Museum in Atlanta, Ga., was given $7.5 million by an anonymous donor as a challenge grant toward the estimated $15 million cost of proposed new facilities. A new $25 million cultural complex in Miami, Fla., was to include at a cost of $3.5 million the Center for the Fine Arts, a 20,000-sq-ft exhibition area with no permanent collection. Voters in Dallas, Texas, reacted to a carefully planned press campaign and approved the funding of a new Dallas Museum of Fine Arts;

$24.8 million would be the public share of the $40 million building.

In the East the Virginia Museum of the Fine Arts in Richmond received 200 works from Mr. and Mrs. Paul Mellon and $2.2 million toward a $10 million building to house both that collection and the 1,500 Art Nouveau and Art Deco objects donated by Sydney and Frances Lewis. A nationwide campaign, the White House Preservation Fund, was begun to establish a permanent endowment of $25 million to provide the finest U.S. art and antiques to furnish the White House. This would make the White House a major museum and break its traditional dependence upon private and temporary donations for decor. In New York City the Museum of Modern Art presented a $40 million bond issue, offered by the Trust for Cultural Resources, to fund gallery expansion, including a new skyscraper tower on its grounds. After five years of construction the Metropolitan Museum of Art opened its $18 million American Wing, which, when completed, would cover some 150,000 sq ft, about six times the size of the old wing.

In the Middle West the Detroit Institute of Arts moved closer toward its goal of renovation and modernization by 1985 by opening its new graphic arts centre and its new ethnographic galleries. The Grand Rapids (Mich.) Art Museum was to move into greatly expanded quarters in a four-story former government building. In Evanston, Ill., just

On June 11 the Metropolitan Museum of Art in New York City opened its new American Wing to house and display its unparalleled collection of examples of American fine and decorative arts. The Charles Engelhard Court encloses a sculpture garden; the 1822–24 facade of the United States Branch Bank on the far wall originally faced Wall Street.

THE METROPOLITAN MUSEUM OF ART;
PHOTO, HENRY GROSKINSKY

The Corning Museum of Glass in Corning, New York, opened its new building in June; designed by Gunnar Birkerts, the new museum houses the 20,000 glass objects in the Corning collection.

north of Chicago, the Terra Museum of American Art opened. Named for its founder, who donated the museum's building and whose private collection was on permanent loan, the institution was to be devoted to American art of the 19th and early 20th centuries.

Major acquisitions by U.S. museums included the purchase for a reported $1 million by the Whitney Museum of American Art in New York City of the 1958 painting "Three Flags" by Jasper Johns, one of the most expensive works by a living American artist ever bought. The Kimbell Art Museum in Fort Worth, Texas, set a record for a work of Cézanne when it paid $3.9 million for "Peasant in a Blue Smock," and $3.7 million was paid by the Norton Simon Museum in Pasadena, Calif., for a 15th-century Flemish work, "The Resurrection" by Dieric Bouts.

Several important archaeological exhibitions were staged. The Detroit Institute of Arts offered "Treasures of Ancient Nigeria," the largest loan exhibition to the U.S. ever sent from an African nation. "The Great Bronze Age of China: An Exhibition from the People's Republic of China" opened at the Metropolitan Museum of Art and later traveled across the country. Including much recently uncovered material, it marked the first joint effort between scholars in the U.S. and China.

Other Nations

In June a celebration was held to mark the refitting and modernization program of the National Maritime Museum at Greenwich, London, which had taken over ten years to carry out. As a result the museum was now an important research centre for maritime history. It encompassed both arts and sciences and included a picture gallery, historic house, and centre for archaeological research.

The new London Transport Museum in Covent Garden, London, exhibited streetcars, buses, and trains, along with graphic material formerly at the Clapham Museum of British Transport. The new museum was in the building that was originally the Covent Garden flower market.

In Paris plans were well under way for a new museum to be devoted to the art and civilization of the 19th century. It was scheduled to open in 1983. The plans reflected the long-term museological planning of the French government, and when completed the museum would ease the overcrowding currently causing difficulties in the Jeu de Paume and the Louvre. The Jeu de Paume would in the future be used for temporary exhibitions. The new museum would complete the "Louvre-Orsay-Beaubourg" grouping, in which the Louvre would house objects from antiquity to the early 19th century; the Beaubourg (the Centre National d'Art et de Culture Georges Pompidou) most 20th-century material; and the Orsay painting, sculpture, architecture, graphics, and applied arts from most of the 19th century to the early 20th century.

The new museum would occupy the former railway station, the Gare d'Orsay, which was originally built for the 1900 Paris Universal Exhibition. The auction houses and theatre that had occupied the premises since the railway moved were themselves being rehoused. The architects for the interior of the new museum were Colboc, Bardon, and Philippon.

(*See also* Art and Art Exhibitions.)

MUSIC

Zubin Mehta's work with a variable-sounding New York Philharmonic again elicited mixed opinions, the divided views of U.S. critics being reflected with striking clarity when the orchestra visited the 1980 Edinburgh International Festival. Mehta began controversially with the European premiere of Polish composer Kryzstof Penderecki's overtly simplistic Second Symphony, an enigmatic, downbeat piece based entirely on the old Austrian Christmas carol "Silent Night." His choice exasperated widespread sections of the British musical press and posed once again the question as to which direction this one-time enfant terrible of new music was taking. It must have been doubly chastening for the Philharmonic's managers to find press opinion no less scathing in its criticism of Mehta's subsequent bland, slackly managed reading of Beethoven's "Eroica" Symphony.

Elsewhere, Carlo Maria Giulini continued to reign supreme at Los Angeles, the city's Philharmonic continuing its leisurely, largely unadventurous exploration of mainstream European classics under the Italian maestro's elegant baton. If Los Angeles experienced a blending of New World brilliance with mid-European line and warmth, Sir Georg Solti's continuing directorship at Chicago found an admittedly spectacular-sounding symphony orchestra in 1979–80 moving even further from its Fritz Reiner-nurtured Viennese roots and emerging too often as a merely brash and garish instrument. In Boston Seiji Ozawa and Sir Colin Davis drew, respectively, civilized and turgid playing from a generally healthy-sounding symphony orchestra. In Philadelphia outgoing maestro Eugene Ormandy stayed long enough to commit to disc the Philadelphia Orchestra's first digitally engineered recording (an exciting account for RCA of Bela Bartok's Concerto for Orchestra). Eduardo Mata, a rising hopeful in RCA's checklist of house conductors, was to be found tackling Ravel, Stravinsky, and Copland with a newly impressive Dallas Symphony. It was still too early to say whether the appointment of Neville Marriner as principal conductor of the Minnesota Symphony would achieve a similar renaissance there.

In the U.K. the orchestral scene was sadly dominated not by live music but by a headline-making labour dispute of a kind usually reserved for the country's strikebound automobile industry. For weeks before the season of BBC-sponsored Henry Wood Promenade concerts was due to begin at London's Royal Albert Hall, it had been touch and go as to whether Britain's national broadcasting organization would resolve its quarrel over cost cutting and layoffs with members of the Musicians' Union. In the end a potentially magnificent first night, with BBC principal conductor Gennadi Rozhdestvensky directing Sir Edward Elgar's rarely staged oratorio The Apostles, was canceled along with a host of other programs.

Acrimony between the warring parties reached the breaking point with the promotion at the Wembley Conference Centre in northwest London of a widely publicized if slimly attended series of union-sponsored "pirate Proms" that featured renegade members of the BBC's leading symphony orchestra under such guest conductors as Simon Rattle and Sir Colin Davis and such top-line soloists as pianists Cristina Ortiz and Tamas Vasary. Only after weeks had been wiped off the proposed season did the "Proms" go ahead following a settlement of the dispute. Surviving highlights included first performances of Sir Michael Tippett's richly translucent Concerto for violin, viola, and cello and

Beverly Sills's last appearance on the opera stage was a gala at Lincoln Center in New York City; a highlight was the party scene from Die Fledermaus *in which a number of the soprano's prominent friends performed.*

SARA KRULWICH—THE NEW YORK TIMES

The Metropolitan Opera went on strike in New York City after management failed to come to an agreement with the musicians' union; the early part of the season was canceled, but a settlement enabled some performances to take place.

HOWARD HEYMAN—NEWSWEEK

an Eleventh Symphony by the neglected English master Edmund Rubbra.

Other notable events in a season during which U.K. audience attendance slumped (a process exacerbated, promoters argued, by a newly introduced tax supplement on seat prices) were the increasingly frequent and impressive appearances by East German conductor Klaus Tennstedt with the London Philharmonic Orchestra, the celebrations surrounding the 50th birthday of the BBC Symphony Orchestra, and the adoption by the Philharmonia Orchestra under its new general manager, Christopher Bishop, of a Chicago Symphony-style subscription series. By the year's end the last move showed signs of proving a distinct success. John Williams, best known for composing the scores of such motion pictures as *Star Wars*, *Close Encounters of the Third Kind*, and *Jaws*, succeeded the late Arthur Fiedler as conductor of the Boston Pops Orchestra.

Opera

The 1979–80 operatic season was again one of averages, new productions falling on hard times as old favourites were wheeled out for another, often feeble bite at the turnstiles. In New York City the moderate success early in the year of the Metropolitan Opera's *Don Carlo* was completely obliterated by an explosion of anger by the company's orchestra and chorus over pay scales and length of the workweek. This conflict with management led to a move unprecedented in the Met's 96-year history, the peremptory cancellation late in September by Executive Director Anthony Bliss of the entire 1980–81 season. Negotiations continued throughout the fall, however, and settlements were achieved with the orchestra, chorus, and other groups. On December 10, more than two months late, the Met opened its season with a concert of Mahler's *Resur-*

rection Symphony. The first opera, Alban Berg's complete *Lulu*, was given its New York premiere on December 12.

In May 1980 the Paris Opéra and La Scala, Milan, entered into a formal partnership, with shared productions and other activities envisaged. Chief promoter of this arrangement was the Opéra's new administrator-designate, Bernard Lefort, who planned to extend its range by means of an ambitious program of tours and television productions. A European highlight of the year was the staging by the Théâtre des Champs-Élysées, as part of a wide-ranging Stravinsky festival, of *The Rake's Progress* in the brilliantly successful David Hockney-designed Glyndebourne Opera production from England.

A particular pleasure in the U.K. was the revival at the 1980 Brighton Festival in Sussex (by the hitherto little-recognized New Sussex Opera) of the original small-scale version of Mussorgsky's *Boris Godunov*, an imaginative choice whose short run at the Cardner Centre at the University of Sussex garnered universal critical praise and made the more widely publicized attempts of some major professional companies seem sadly lacking in comparison. Covent Garden's Royal Opera and the English National Opera both experienced lean times in 1980, the Garden's weakness for importing big-name casts that failed to jell culminating in a particularly disappointing revival of the Götz Friedrich production of Wagner's *Ring of the Nibelung* and some unimpressive Verdi and Donizetti. At the English National imaginative revivals of Richard Strauss's *Arabella*, Benjamin Britten's *The Turn of the Screw*, *Boris Godunov*, and Puccini's *La Bohème* in the unrivaled Jean-Claud Auvray production were offset by calamitous stagings of Beethoven's *Fidelio* and Offenbach's *La Belle Hélène* and dull ones of Mozart's *Don Giovanni* and *The Magic Flute*.

At the Bayreuth festival Patrice Chéreau's grimly avant-garde *Ring* and *Flying Dutchman* again delighted Wagnerphiles on their annual pilgrimage. Joseph Losey's feature film of *Don Giovanni*, highly thought of and intelligently criticized elsewhere, at last reached London, only to be met with a battery of critical obtuseness from the movie reviewers. Expertly produced by Hal Prince, Stephen Sondheim's semioperatic Broadway hit *Sweeney Todd* also came to London and the Drury Lane Theatre but folded after only a short run. In October soprano Beverly Sills made her last appearance on the opera stage in a special performance in New York of the party scene from *Die Fledermaus*.

Of special interest to serious music from a technical point of view was the appearance of the first widely marketed batch of digitally recorded long-playing records, digitalism being a high-technology system in which musical impulses are encoded directly onto computer tape in the studio without recourse to the supposedly "distorting" medium of analogue tape decks. By the end of the 1970s a number of small U.S. labels had already issued impressive digital material, but it was only with the entry into the ring during 1979–80 of the international names—London Decca, HMV Angel, DG, Columbia CBS, and RCA—that a by now wary public, hooked a few years previously by the false messiah of quadrophony, had a chance to sample (and marvel at) the trueness, clarity, and freshness achieved by a process hailed increasingly as the single most important technological breakthrough since stereo and the introduction of the Dolby noise-reduction system. This did not, however, halt the debate, fueled by steeply rising vinyl costs and higher store prices, over pressing and packaging quality. Too often, collectors believed, top-drawer classical albums at premium prices were being supplied with inferior annotation and flimsy jackets. As far as pressing quality went, Dutch, West German, and Japanese discs were again believed to be leading the field, with the U.K. somewhere in the middle and France and the U.S.—the HMV subsidiaries Pathé-Marconi and Angel especially—falling heavily to the bottom of the pile.

Popular

The year's most significant event was the murder of John Lennon, the former Beatle, who was shot dead by a 25-year-old security guard, Mark Chapman, in New York City on December 8. Chapman had apparently fantasized that he was Lennon, and so he wanted to kill the "imposter." Throughout the world the reaction was extraordinary, reminiscent of the aftermath of the assassination of U.S. Pres. John Kennedy rather than the death of a pop music star.

But then John Lennon was no ordinary pop star. Both in his work with the Beatles, the most popular group in the history of popular music, and in his

The Louise M. Davies Symphony Hall in San Francisco officially opened in September; named after a principal donor, the $27.5 million facility was the city's biggest civic project in 50 years.
UPI

later solo career, he had proved to be a prolific, original, and pioneering songwriter. At 40 he was just reemerging into the music business after five years of inactivity. A new album, *Double Fantasy* (on which he shared the billing with his wife, Yoko Ono), had been released two weeks before his death. It was by no means his greatest work, consisting of pleasant, mellow ballads about the pleasures of retirement and his love for his wife and son, but it showed that Lennon could still write strong songs and, above all, that he could still use the often cliché-filled medium of the popular song to express his feelings with remarkable honesty.

Honesty in his work and a sincere belief in the worth of what he was doing were two of Lennon's strongest characteristics. He could also be sardonic, passionate, bitter, funny, and idealistic. Those qualities, mixed with a love for pop music that began when he heard black U.S. rhythm and blues imports brought into Liverpool by sailors, were reflected in his unpredictable, patchy, but often brilliant work.

It was a sad end to a bad year for the music industry, in which record sales had slumped by 30% and record companies merged, laid off staff, or cut back on their operations. It was ironic, though, that as the major companies contracted, a whole new group of independent firms ("the indies") flourished as never before. The "indies," such as Rough Trade in London or Factory and Zoo in Manchester, England, made no long-term plans for promoting artists and no long-term contracts. Instead, they signed artists for one record at a time, recording them as cheaply as possible and often dividing profits evenly with them.

The British music scene in 1980 was more fragmented than ever, and much British music seemed out of step with American taste, which appeared bland and safe in comparison. The "post-punk" era of optimistic, "do-it-yourself" music continued,

with new bands springing up all over the country but with a far greater degree of musical sophistication than when punk first emerged in 1976–77. Many of the most successful bands consisted of white or multiracial groups reviving or reworking earlier black styles. Thus, The Police, one of the most popular British bands of the year, based their music around reggae rhythms. Ska, the Jamaican style that predated reggae, also continued to be an influence. The Specials, a multiracial band from Coventry, were leaders in that area, mixing cheerful ska rhythms with lyrics that blended social comment with humour. Through their own record label, 2-Tone, The Specials also gave a start to other bands with similar ideas.

Another revivalist form that flourished during the year was rhythm and blues. R&B—the amplified blues style that developed in Chicago during the 1940s and later became one of the basic ingredients in rock 'n' roll—had always remained a major force in popular music. But in the latest revival bands like The Blues Band (led by Paul Jones, once singer with Manfred Mann), or the younger 9 Below Zero, took their mood and inspiration from the white British bands of the mid-1960s "R&B boom," while also reinterpreting earlier R&B material. Nostalgia was also invoked by exponents of "new soul music," which echoed the great gospel-inspired black styles of the 1960s—though mostly without the power or freshness of the originals.

On a more experimental front there was a move toward all-electronic bands, with extensive use made of synthesizers. Gary Numan, with his bleak, futuristic, and theatrical style, became the best-known "electronics" artist, but both The Human League, from Sheffield, and Orchestral Maneouvres in the Dark, from Liverpool, could be argued to have taken the style much further. The finest, and most commercially successful, of the

The Charlie Daniels Band (Charlie at centre) won the Grammy Award for best country vocal performance by a group for their hit "The Devil Went Down to Georgia."
WIDE WORLD

Riding high on the new wave rock crest were the B-52's. While new wave music was abrasive and frequently juvenile, its abundant energy and sense of history made it the most contemporary of popular rock.

COURTESY, WARNER BROS. RECORDS INC.

new bands was Joy Division, whose second album, *Closer*, became the biggest seller for any "indie" label. But the future of the band was in doubt after the suicide of Ian Curtis, the band's singer, just before the album was released.

With all those revivals and experiments providing the year's most adventurous developments in British pop music, the most commercially successful style was Heavy Metal. Attacked by their critics as brash, overloud, and oversimple and for their pounding "head-banging" music, such bands as Whitesnake, Motorhead, or Australia's AC/DC sold records in enormous quantities. The "old wave" of previously established artists still soldiered on, and Cliff Richard—now 40—continued to pack concert halls and make hit singles. A great tragedy among established artists was the death of Led Zeppelin's drummer John Bonham. The most expensive and spectacular shows of the year were provided by Pink Floyd, who went firmly against prevailing trends by performing their concept work *The Wall* at London's Earl's Court. This multimedia extravaganza with its elaborate staging cost the band $2 million.

On the recording front there was a new and impressive album from David Bowie, *Scary Monsters*, on which he proved himself to be still dazzlingly unpredictable but highly commercial. An unexpected move was the departure of Jon Anderson and Rick Wakeman from Yes and their replacement by Trevor Horn and Geoff Downes, who had previously made novelty pop singles under the name Buggles.

In the U.S., also, the record industry faced a slump in sales, but there was little sign of a "new wave" of styles to match the changing scene in Britain. The disco craze began to wane and punk-type groups surfaced in California, but most American pop music seemed bland and predictable compared

with that in Britain. The Beach Boys' patchy performance at the Knebworth Festival and a second poorly received Christian revivalist album from Bob Dylan, called *Saved*, both marked a downturn in popularity for performers who had helped shape the music scene throughout the 1960s and '70s. Paul Simon proved to be in better form with his movie soundtrack album *One-Trick Pony*, while America's finest black artist, Stevie Wonder, returned to form with *Hotter than July*. Bruce Springsteen released his long-awaited double album, *The River*, which justified his reputation as a powerful, passionate singer, drawing on established styles from rhythm and blues to country and western. The latter achieved new heights of popularity during the year, with leading performers including Kenny Rogers, Emmylou Harris, and the Charlie Daniels Band.

(*See also* Dance; Television and Radio; Theatre.)

THE NETHERLANDS

On Jan. 31, 1980, the birthday of her daughter Princess Beatrix, Queen Juliana announced that she would abdicate as queen of The Netherlands in favour of the princess, after a reign of more than 30 years. On April 30, during a combined session of both houses of Parliament in the New Church in Amsterdam, Beatrix swore fidelity to the constitution and was installed as queen.

Elsewhere in Amsterdam serious riots broke out during the ceremony, involving more than 1,500 police and some 1,000 demonstrators. More than 100 police officers and 100 demonstrators were injured. This riot of predominantly young people was a sequel to earlier clashes, such as that on February 29 when a special police task force engaged housing squatters, their sympathizers, and young rioters. The police were met with smoke bombs, stones,

245

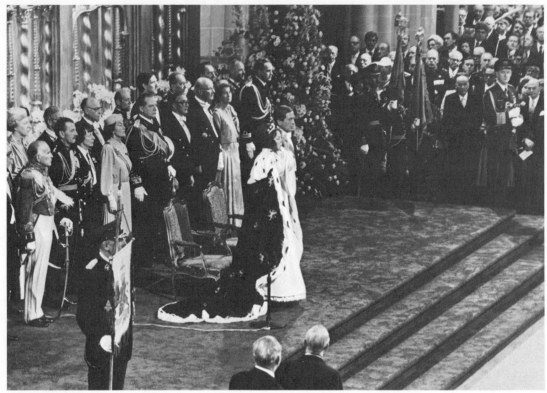

A. NOGUES—SYGMA

On April 30 Princess Beatrix, eldest daughter of Queen Juliana of The Netherlands, was crowned queen in ceremonies in Amsterdam; Queen Juliana had announced her abdication in January.

and iron bars and withdrew; on March 3, however, supported by tanks, armoured vehicles, and water cannons, the police broke down the squatters' barricades and cleared the occupied houses.

On February 20 the minister of finance, Franciscus Andriessen, resigned because the rest of the Cabinet was unwilling to accept economy cuts of 4 billion guilders. A compromise worked out by Prime Minister Andreas van Agt did not satisfy Andriessen. In May the Central Planning Office published the Central Economic Plan. The office's forecast was gloomy: increases in unemployment and in inflation, only a slight growth in production, a decline in profits, and no increase in employment in the near future. In the queen's speech on the opening of Parliament, delivered by Beatrix on September 16, the unfavourable economic situation and the increase of civil disorder received special attention. The budget, prepared by the new minister of finance, Alphons van der Stee, produced a deficit of 12.4 billion guilders.

Although the minister of foreign affairs, Christoph van der Klaauw, had declared that an oil boycott of South Africa would be impracticable, the majority of the lower house of Parliament voted in favour of that policy. A few days later the Cabinet rejected the motion. A vote of no confidence, introduced by the opposition parties in the lower house, failed. Only six members of the Christian Democratic Appeal, the party of the prime minister, supported the no-confidence motion.

Because of the conflicting views of the Dutch Roman Catholic bishops, Pope John Paul II convened a special synod of Dutch bishops, in Rome, from January 14 to 31. Its deliberations were kept secret, only the conclusions being published. One of the issues was the question of married priests and their position in the Roman Catholic Church. As expected, they were to be excluded from performance of priestly functions.

At first the Cabinet was undecided in regard to boycotting the Olympic Games in Moscow, but after the Soviet government sent the Soviet dissident and Nobel laureate Andrey Sakharov into internal exile at Gorky on January 22, the Cabinet and the majority of the lower house demanded a boycott of the Games. The Dutch Olympic Committee, however, voted to go to Moscow.

In November a Chinese delegation visited The Netherlands to discuss the possibility of Dutch assistance in the building of harbours on the east coast of China. At the same time, the Dutch government gave a company permission to build two submarines for Taiwan. The Chinese delegation protested against this decision and left the country at once.

NEWSPAPERS

Newspapers in the United States enjoyed one of their most prosperous years in recent memory. Total daily circulation hit a six-year high of 62,223,040, up 0.4% from the previous year, according to the 1980 *Editor & Publisher International Year Book*. Morning circulation set a record: 28,574,879, a gain of 3.3% over the previous year's all-time high. Evening circulation, however, dropped to its lowest point in two decades: 33,648,161, down 2% from the year before. The number of daily newspapers rose to 1,763, a gain of 7 for the year.

Nearly all of that gain was accounted for by the continuing trend toward morning delivery. There were 382 morning papers, 27 more than during the previous year, as compared with 1,405 evening papers, 14 fewer than a year earlier. A dozen evening papers became morning papers. Six evening papers began issuing editions around the clock, raising the number of such "all day" dailies to 24. (One "all day" paper shifted to morning delivery, and the rest are counted above in both the morning and evening totals.)

One significant exception to the morning trend in 1980 involved the *New York Daily News*, the nation's largest metropolitan daily, with a circulation of about 1.6 million. The circulation had slid by some 500,000 since 1970, largely because the paper's traditional blue-collar readers had moved to the suburbs. To recapture that market the morning *Daily News* launched an evening edition, *Tonight*, with an initial, as yet unaudited, circulation somewhere between 100,000 and 300,000, depending on whose estimates one accepts. *Tonight*, which was aimed at a more affluent audience than the *Daily*

News had ever approached, was part of a $20 million investment the *Daily News* and its parent, Chicago Tribune Co., were making to stop the circulation slide. Tribune Co. executives hoped to attract readers from Australian publisher Rupert Murdoch's evening *New York Post* (circulation 654,000), which had gained readers—though not profits—through an increasing emphasis on crime, sex, and gossip.

The *Daily News*'s owners were also hoping to pick up readers from the staid *New York Times* (circulation 915,000). *Times* officials continued to deny persistent reports that they, too, planned an afternoon edition, but they did begin printing an abridged edition of the paper in Chicago for distribution in nine Midwestern states.

Unlike Britain and some other nations, the U.S. still did not have a truly national newspaper—except, perhaps, for the *Wall Street Journal* (circulation 1.8 million), which concentrated mostly on financial news. In 1980 the *Journal* became the nation's largest daily newspaper of any kind, surpassing the *New York Daily News*. The *Journal* also made one of its most radical format changes since its founding in 1889. The paper was split into two parts, thus raising the maximum number of pages in a single edition from 48 to 56 a day in a move designed largely to accommodate an increase in advertising. However, the change also gave the *Journal* more space for news, much of which it devoted to nonbusiness stories.

The most significant newspaper transaction of the year was the sale of the *Denver* (Colo.) *Post* (circulation 260,000), a leading paper in the fast-growing Rocky Mountain region, to the Times Mirror Co.,

In August the first uncensored newspaper in Poland made its appearance; it was eagerly received at the Lenin shipyard in Gdansk, scene of a successful strike earlier in the month.
WIDE WORLD

Editor William Rees-Mogg (centre) of The Times of London announced in October that the 196-year-old paper would cease publication in March 1981 unless a buyer could be found for it; the paper had long been plagued with labour problems.
POPPERFOTO/UPI

a diversified communications firm known principally as owner of the *Los Angeles Times* (circulation 1,013,000). The firm had a reputation for spending generously to maintain editorial and commercial supremacy in the markets in which it competed, and the Denver paper needed plenty of both. Earlier in the year its circulation had slipped behind that of the rival *Rocky Mountain News* for the first time since the *Post* was founded in 1895.

In London, Times Newspapers Ltd., publishers of *The Times*, beleagured by the sodden British economy and harassed by strikes and other labour difficulties, announced on October 22 that *The Times* and its affiliates were up for sale. They would cease publication for good if no buyers were found by March 31, 1981.

On the legal front a couple of recent setbacks for the press were in effect nullified. In *Richmond Newspapers* v. *Virginia* the U.S. Supreme Court narrowed a year-old ruling that had granted local judges the right to close certain pretrial hearings to the press; some local magistrates had misinterpreted that decision as allowing them to close all kinds of legal proceedings, including trials themselves. In *Richmond Newspapers* the court declared that the First Amendment to the U.S. Constitution requires that all criminal trials must be open to press and public except in rare cases. In addition, Congress passed a law requiring police officers to obtain a subpoena rather than a search warrant, under most circumstances, when trying to obtain evidence from news reporters. This stemmed from *Zurcher* v. *Stanford Daily*, a 1978 decision that allowed police to search newsrooms as long as they had a search warrant.

The Boston *Globe* won three Pulitzer Prizes in 1980, only the second time that had happened in the 64-year history of the awards (the *New York Times* won three in 1978). The *Globe* won the spe-

cial local reporting prize for a series on mismanagement in the local transit system; *Globe* columnist Ellen Goodman won the award for commentary; and *Globe* television critic William A. Henry III was given the criticism prize. The *Philadelphia Inquirer* won its sixth Pulitzer in a row, the general local reporting prize for its coverage of the Three Mile Island nuclear reactor accident. The prestigious Gold Medal for Public Service went to the Gannett News Service for exposing mismanagement of contributions to the Pauline Fathers, a Pennsylvania-based religious order. (The news service distributes stories to member papers of the Gannett chain.) The Pulitzer for national reporting went to Bette Orsini and Charles Stafford of the *St. Petersburg* (Fla.) *Times* for their investigation of the Church of Scientology. Joel Brinkley and Jay Mather of the *Louisville* (Ky.) *Courier-Journal* were cited for their reporting from Cambodia. The award for editorial writing went to Robert Bartley of the *Wall Street Journal*, and the editorial cartooning prize was given to Don Wright of the *Miami* (Fla.) *News*.

NEW ZEALAND

In the face of rising inflation and unemployment, New Zealand consolidated plans to process offshore gas in such a way as to reduce one of its most expensive imports, oil, as much as possible. The plan provided for conversion of the gas to methanol, much of which would then be passed through a NZ$150 million catalyst (NZ$1.02=U.S. $1) to produce 13,000 bbl of gasoline a day, about 30% of New Zealand's energy needs. It was hoped that this, together with other, supplementary plans, would make the country more than 50% self-sufficient in gasoline by 1986.

The public accounts to March 1980 showed a deficit of NZ$1,027,000,000, NZ$69 million more than provided for. The annual budget in June imposed heavier indirect taxes (beer, spirits, cigarettes, domestic air travel, postage) but allowed a rebate for those with low family incomes and a 4% general cost-of-living increase in wages. It did little to hold down inflation, which reached 18.4% for the first quarter of the year—the century's highest.

One of the main thrusts of the government was to restructure and modernize some obsolete domestic industries, and these plans caused increased unemployment, especially in the textile industry. The first moves toward narrowing the range of automobiles assembled inside the country provoked threats from labour unions. But the main industrial tensions resulted from government efforts to limit negotiated pay raises in the battle against inflation.

Government approval for construction of a second aluminum smelter, to process Queensland bauxite using hydroelectricity supplied at a specially negotiated fee, became controversial on economic as well as environmental grounds. The strongest critics contended that provision of more "cheap" power could be a factor in the need to build more river-dam power stations, which would be costlier than ever before.

Inflation, rising costs of commodities, and unemployment were all factors in the government's loss of a "safe" National Party seat in a by-election in September, but a new element at the ballot box warned the government of possible trouble at the general election of 1981. A number of voters who turned against National said that they were protesting against the manner of Prime Minister Robert Muldoon, who came through to them as arrogant and mean when retaliating against criticism.

Major news stories of the year included the breaking up of a New Zealand-based drug ring operating internationally, the Rugby Union's decision to invite a South African rugby team to New Zealand after a 15-year hiatus, and the flooding of farmlands in the Otago district. Only a few New Zealanders participated in the Olympic Games at Moscow, and they had to do so without government assistance or commercial sponsorship. The Soviet ambassador, Vsevolod Sofinsky, was expelled for allegedly supplying money to a political party, and Moscow retaliated by expelling the New Zealand representative there.

NICARAGUA

By the end of 1980 the Sandinista National Liberation Front government appeared to have turned toward the left since taking power after the civil war in 1979. Cabinet changes in December 1979 substituted fairly left-wing Sandinistas for non-Sandinista members in such posts as defense, planning, and agriculture; also, of the two non-Sandinistas appointed to the five-member junta in May, one was said to be more to the left than his predecessor.

Legislative measures nationalized locally owned

On July 19 Nicaragua celebrated the first anniversary of the overthrow of former president Anastasio Somoza Debayle by the Sandinista revolutionaries.
OWEN FRANKEN—SYGMA

banks, insurance companies, and the mining industry and prohibited foreign-owned banks from accepting local currency deposits. Trade controls were introduced with the nationalization of coffee and cotton exports and with state control of seafood exports. Economic interests previously held by the Somoza family and associates were confiscated. The exiled former dictator, Anastasio Somoza Debayle, was assassinated in Asunción, Paraguay, on September 17.

In January the government outlined reconstruction measures in the national emergency and recovery program for 1980, and it was planned to regain 1978 production levels by the end of the year. The plan put forward stringent austerity measures, with a reduction in public expenditure and oil purchase, a construction program, increased exports, and a reduction in the rates of inflation and unemployment. During the 1979 civil war, it was estimated, more than 30,000 people had been killed, damage to the economy exceeded $2 billion, and the foreign debt reached $1.3 billion while reserves declined to $3 billion. Unemployment had risen to 32% of the working population, inflation at the end of December 1979 was running at around 60%, and real gross domestic product (GDP) had fallen by 26% to 1962 levels. During 1980 inflation was expected to decline to 30% and GDP to increase by 18%.

The government negotiated a debt-rescheduling program with a committee of 13 commercial banks representing the 120 debtor banks. In September a breakthrough was reached concerning $582 million in foreign debt contracted by the Somoza administration. However, an estimated $250 million in outstanding private debt remained.

NIGERIA

Nigeria's Pres. Alhaji Shehu Shagari, leading a minority government and faced with inflation, a weak economy, and no accepted census (necessary for revenue allocation among the country's 19 states), experienced a difficult year in 1980. The alliance of his National Party of Nigeria with Nnamdi Azikiwe's Nigerian People's Party (NPP) proved shaky, and an attempt to appoint 19 state liaison officers was not welcomed by the NPP and other parties. Action promised against corruption found an early target in the nearly $5.2 billion allegedly missing from the Nigerian National Petroleum Corporation (NNPC). Amid fears of an "oilgate" national scandal and public disorder, Shagari set up a judicial inquiry into the matter. The July 8 White Paper rejected the allegations as a hoax, but it found the affairs of the NNPC in disorder because of a lack of skilled staff and recommended sweeping reforms. The tribunal also ordered the Royal Dutch/Shell Group, Gulf Oil Corp., and Mobil Oil Corp. to repay to Nigeria over the next three to four years some 80 million bbl of crude oil, about U.S. $64 million in value. (This restitution was to

Alhaji Shehu Shagari, president of oil-rich Nigeria, joined Pres. Jimmy Carter and Rosalynn Carter during a two-day state visit to Washington, D.C., in October.
WIDE WORLD

be based on the respective NNPC and oil companies' shares of actual production, not on the 183 million bbl of the planned level of production.) This was because during the oil glut of 1975–78 the three firms had taken from the country proportionately more oil than allowed by their production agreements as a result of Nigeria's not having taken up its full share during the period of glut. Riots, said to have been instigated by a fanatic Muslim sect (possibly with support from Libya), were reported from Kano in late December. Just before the new year, troops were sent in to quell the disturbance.

On June 27 Shagari announced the establishment of naval and air training academies, as well as increased recruitment to the armed services to make them "second to none" in Africa. Nigeria furthermore pushed for a permanent African Defense Force at the first Organization of African Unity (OAU) economic summit, which was held in Lagos (April 28–29). The summit attempted to improve sharply deteriorating food and agricultural output and establish a common market in the face of falling inter-African trade. Nigeria's trade with the Economic Community of West Africa (ECOWAS) fell 5% during 1978–79.

Despite increasing Japanese, French, and West German competition, Britain maintained the lead in Nigerian trade at 20%. High operating costs and uncertain trade regulations, as well as forced sales of holdings to Nigerian affiliates at low prices, did not encourage new development by other nations, nor did the sudden insertion of Nigerian top executives in foreign banks. Shagari's government attempted to encourage foreign investment by reducing the tax rate on business profits.

Shagari's first budget, presented to the National Assembly on March 18, gave priority to self-reliance and self-sufficiency, to the control of wages (minimum of 100 naira a month for public employees) and prices, and to stemming the migration from rural areas to cities, which was causing agricultural stagnation and, hence, increased food imports. There was a federal deficit of 1.4 billion naira in 1979, with external debts standing at about 360 million naira. Only huge oil revenues of 9.9 billion naira (83% of national revenue) made the 1975–80 development plan possible. Shagari's budget estimated 1980 revenue at 11.9 billion naira (oil accounting for 85%); state allocations totaled 2.5 billion naira and recurrent expenditures 6.5 billion naira (20% higher than in 1979). The recurring surplus of 5.3 billion naira added to the capital budget of 7,623,000,000 naira left a deficit of 2.3 billion naira, to be financed by internal and external loans. The single largest spending item was defense.

Oil receipts maintained their leading role among external assets, accounting for over 90% of total external payments. The discovery of uranium was to be exploited, in partnership with a French firm, by the Nigerian Uranium Mining Co., in which the government had a 60% share.

NOBEL PRIZES

In 1980 U.S. citizens won prizes in five of the six Nobel categories. The Peace Prize, however, went to an Argentine dissident, Adolfo Pérez Esquivel. In 1980 the honorarium accompanying each prize amounted to $212,000.

"The prize is not for me but for my organization and for the cause of human rights and justice in Latin America," Adolfo Pérez Esquivel said when news of the award reached him in his Buenos Aires office. "I accept this prize in the name of Latin America and its workers, in the name of its campesinos and its priests who are working diligently for the peace and rights of all." Pérez has worked most conspicuously for political have-nots, the disenfranchised and brutally repressed people of Argentina in particular.

Pérez, the son of a fisherman, became an architect and sculptor and for many years was professor of sculpture at the Argentine National School of Fine Arts. Barely a decade ago he joined an organization that soon developed an agenda embracing the full spectrum of human concerns. In 1971 he joined the group that was organizing artisans' cooperatives. Within a year it was working for disarmament, nuclear nonproliferation, and social reforms generally. During a 1974 conference in Colombia Pérez was elected secretary-general of Service for Peace and Justice in Latin America.

Pérez himself suffered at the hands of the military junta that overthrew Isabel Perón's regime in 1976. Going to a police station in 1977 to renew his passport, he was detained and then held in La Plata prison for 14 months without being charged. During that time he was tortured.

When Lawrence R. Klein became odds-on favourite to head President-elect Jimmy Carter's economic brain trust, a colleague predicted that the University of Pennsylvania professor would not take the job. He was then building a computer model of the world's economy, a tool designed to project the influence of discrete factors in one nation (*i.e.*, a new British income tax or an Iranian oil price hike) on businesses and whole economies elsewhere. "That's the project that will guarantee him a Nobel Prize," the associate accurately prophesied in 1976. It was Klein who applied the theories of econometrics—the study of dynamic and interdependent cause-and-effect relationships among disparate economic elements—to examine real-world problems and forecast short-term changes in local or international economic conditions. Working first with Arthur Goldberger, Klein used Keynesian theories and new statistical methods to forecast the development of business fluctuations and to study the effects of economic-political measures such as tax or tariff policies. Part of the beauty of Klein's models is their flexibility. New information can be fed to his high-speed computers as it becomes available, and old speculations can be updated with newly observed data.

UPI   WIDE WORLD   DIEGO GOLDBERG—SYGMA

Nobel Prize winners for 1980 included (from left) Lithuanian-born poet Czeslaw Milosz, for Literature; Lawrence R. Klein of the Wharton School of Economics, Philadelphia, for Economics; and Argentine dissident and human-rights activist Adolfo Pérez Esquivel, for Peace.

The winner of the 1980 Nobel Prize for Literature has published poems, novels, essays, autobiography, and criticism. A respected scholar at the University of California at Berkeley, Lithuanian-born Czeslaw Milosz has edited volumes of Eastern European verse and translated many poets—Shakespeare, Milton, T. S. Eliot, Baudelaire, Whitman, and Sandburg among them—into his native Polish. He has also translated the Psalms into Polish, a task that required him to add Hebrew to the languages he already commanded: English, Greek, Latin, French, and Russian.

"His writing is many-voiced and dramatic, insistent and provocative," the Nobel citation reads in part. "He is an author of great importance—captivating and arresting. . . . The world that Milosz depicts in his poetry, prose and essays is the world in which man lives after having been driven out of paradise."

Born in Vilna, Russian Lithuania (now part of Poland), on June 30, 1911, Milosz defected to the West in 1951 after foreign service as cultural attaché for the Communist government. Milosz enjoys only a modest following among the reading public—except in Poland, where his books still circulate clandestinely.

Paul Berg of Stanford University won half the Prize for Chemistry in recognition of "his fundamental studies of the biochemistry of nucleic acids, with particular regard to recombinant DNA," a citation that Berg prefers to interpret as an acknowledgment of the merits of an entire body of work rather than of a single achievement. The other half of the prize was divided between Walter Gilbert of Harvard University and Frederick Sanger of the University of Cambridge, England, for independently developing ways of finding the order in which the individual links are present in the chainlike molecules of nucleic acids. Sanger, who won the Nobel Prize for Chemistry in 1958, is the fourth person to win a prize a second time.

Gene-splicing, or recombinant DNA, techniques were pioneered by Berg. They have become a powerful tool in the production of vital human substances—insulin and growth hormones—for persons needing additional increments for normal functioning. Gilbert's and Sanger's work elucidates part of the basic structure of all life forms.

James Cronin of the University of Chicago and Val Fitch of Princeton University won the Physics Prize for performing an experiment in 1964 that implies that reversing the direction of time would not precisely reverse the course of certain reactions of subatomic particles.

The principle of time-reversal invariance (designated T) states that particle interactions should be indifferent to the direction of time; charge conjugation (C) provides that sets of charged particles should interact the same way if all the charges were interchanged; and parity conservation (P) holds that natural processes do not distinguish between right- and left-handed behaviour. These three symmetries were once thought to govern all the laws of physics, but in 1956 T. D. Lee and C. N. Yang suggested, correctly, that P does not apply to certain processes. Physicists abandoned the view that C, P, and T are independently true but saved the overall concept by proposing that any P violation must be offset by an equal C violation.

Cronin, Fitch, James Christenson, and René Turlay refined earlier measurements of the behaviour of neutral K mesons, uncharged particles formed in large accelerators. One kind of these K mesons decays quickly to two pi mesons, but the other decays slowly to three pi mesons; both processes obey combined CP symmetry. The four scientists, using a very sensitive detector, found events in which long-lived K mesons decay to two, instead of three, pi mesons. This demonstration of CP violations forced another revision of the CPT relation: when CP symmetry is violated, T symmetry must also fail.

Commentators speculate that Cronin and Fitch were not honoured sooner because their finding has only recently been incorporated in cosmology. Earlier theories had foundered because T-inviolability implies that the matter and antimatter formed in a symmetrical big bang should have annihilated one another.

The 1980 Prize for Physiology or Medicine was divided equally among George Snell of the Jackson Laboratory, Bar Harbor, Maine; Jean Dausset of the University of Paris; and Baruj Benacerraf of the Harvard Medical School, Boston. Their contributions underlie much of present knowledge of the hereditary qualities that determine the transplantability of tissue between individuals and that affect the susceptibility of persons to an important group of diseases. Tissue-matching procedures have now become indispensable in bringing together suitable donors and recipients of transplants of skin, kidneys, and other organs, thanks to the work of Snell and Dausset. Benacerraf's findings on "autoimmune" diseases, in which the body's tissues are attacked by its own defenses, have been valuable in guiding studies of such disorders as psoriasis, Graves' disease, and Reiter's disease.

NORWAY

The worldwide recession affected some sectors of the Norwegian economy in 1980. Foreign demand for iron ore, pellets, steel, and ferroalloys fell off. Norway's largest mining company, A/S Sydvaranger at Kirkenes, laid off its 1,000 production workers for the last two months of the year. Rising oil prices and the Iraq-Iran war lessened the demand for oil transport, forcing Norwegian tankers to lay up. Of traditional exports, only aluminum continued to do well. The main stimulus to growth came from the offshore oil and gas industry. Steeply rising oil revenues enabled the government to maintain high public spending, including subsidies to hard-hit industries.

Shipyards booked few orders for new ships but concentrated on equipment for Norway's North Sea oil and gas fields. To stay in the government's good books, the oil companies ordered equipment from Norwegian fabricators. Repair and maintenance of offshore structures provided work and, despite pockets of unemployment, Norway remained an island of prosperity.

A shadow was cast over the offshore industry in March when the dormitory platform "Alexander Kielland" capsized in a storm with the loss of 123 lives. In the debate that followed, it emerged that safety rules were often disregarded; drilling crews worked with unqualified members, and government authorities charged with enforcing safety rules were chronically short-staffed. Some quarters urged the curbing of offshore development; in particular, environmentalists urged that exploration drilling north of the 62nd parallel, to begin in the summer in spite of pollution risks, should be indefinitely postponed. Checks of all floating platforms and a review of safety measures were ordered, but the decision to permit drilling in northern waters was not revoked.

The offshore industry also suffered from labour troubles during the summer. A strike by 2,000 workers on the three Norwegian producing fields—Ekofisk, Frigg, and Statfjord—was ended after two weeks when compulsory arbitration was decreed. However, a strike of 1,500 seamen operating mobile rigs was allowed to continue for over a month, upsetting exploration programs. The delays in exploration may not have been entirely unwelcome to the government. To develop all viable finds at once would put an unbearable strain on the economy.

On the mainland the principal employer and union organizations reached agreement, in April, on a countrywide "framework" for pay rises during the year. It was hailed as a moderate settlement because the general increase granted was low, although low-paid workers got more. But the cost of living rose more than expected following the end (Dec. 31, 1979) of a 15-month price and incomes freeze. Large wage claims by offshore employees affected the attitude of mainland workers in the plant-level bargaining after the general settlement, and by autumn the rate of inflation in Norway was again higher than in many competing countries.

The Labour government's budget for 1981, introduced in October, would tax spending rather than earnings. It was criticized as inflationary because it permitted increased government spending. This was to be financed mainly by larger petroleum revenues, expected to account for nearly one-quarter of total government income in 1981.

The ruling Labour Party was split on economic, energy, and defense policies. A bitter controversy arose over a proposal to stockpile U.S. military equipment in central Norway, said by critics to violate Norway's traditional policy of barring foreign bases on its soil in peacetime. Soviet objections to the plan were expressed at a meeting between Foreign Minister Knut Frydenlund and Soviet leaders in December.

OCEANOGRAPHY

From March to June 1980 an 18-m (60-ft) double-hulled sailing canoe, a replica of the sailing canoes believed to have been used by Polynesian navigators during ancient transpacific migrations, traveled the 4,000 km (2,500 mi) from Hawaii to Tahiti and back again. A unique feature of this voyage was the employment of two methods of navigation. One method was the traditional one: a Hawaiian navigator decided on a course to be steered and recorded his estimates of the canoe's position. The other method was very modern: the canoe carried a location system tracked by satellite.

This system had been developed originally to track freely drifting buoys as they are carried by ocean currents. A number of buoys had been tracked in this manner over long distances in the past several years. In 1979 and 1980 several clusters of buoys were deployed in the tropics. One such cluster, initially placed 600 km (370 mi) north of the Equator near Fanning Island in the Pacific, drifted eastward in the equatorial countercurrent for more than 4,000 km (13,000 mi); some buoys in the cluster finally left the current toward the north at about the longitude of the tip of Baja California. These results showed that this current, a narrow eastward flow only a few hundred kilometres wide and sandwiched between generally west-flowing water, is in fact a single unbroken current.

The equatorial countercurrent and tropical circulation in general are of particular interest because of the manner in which the tropical ocean and atmosphere interact to create large-scale changes in ocean and atmospheric climate. The buoy-tracking experiment was a part of a much larger observational study of tropical circulation that continued during 1980.

For a number of years during the International Decade of Ocean Exploration (1970–80), investigators tracked freely drifting floats in the northwestern Atlantic Ocean by listening to acoustic beacons attached to each float. The floats are ballasted to drift at depths of 1,000–2,000 m (3,300–6,600 ft), and the underwater sound emitted by their beacons may be heard several thousand kilometres away. During the year tracks of these floats were combined with traditional measurements of temperature and salinity to demonstrate the existence of a new feature of deep ocean circulation. One of the floats had become trapped in a small but rapidly rotating lens of subsurface water. Measurements of the temperature, salinity, and oxygen content of this lens revealed that it must have originated many thousands of kilometres away in the eastern Atlan-

tic. A number of similar features were subsequently identified. If they proved commonplace in the deep sea, they could be an important carrier of heat, nutrients, dissolved substances, and pollutants from one place in the ocean to another. An intriguing question was why these small features are not torn apart by ocean currents of large scale.

The passenger ship "Titanic," which sank off Cape Race, Newfoundland, on April 15, 1912, after colliding with an iceberg, was the object of an undersea search carried out during the summer of 1980. Recent developments in high-resolution undersea acoustic imaging, whereby pictures of underwater structures are formed using beams of sound rather than of light, made the search feasible. The complex relief of the seafloor in this region, combined with weather that worsened toward the end of the ship time available, kept the expedition from definitive success. At one point sonar images of the proper dimensions were obtained (the "Titanic" was 269 m, or 883 ft, long), but they turned out to be a submarine ledge rather than the wreck. Further studies were planned for 1981.

Another important achievement was progress in eliminating atmospheric effects from satellite images of the ocean. Such atmospheric features as high clouds are clearly not oceanic, but others such as near-surface layers of moist air may be mistaken for oceanic features. Their removal is essential for proper imagery interpretation. Following application of recently developed methods of subtracting such atmospheric effects, images from the Nimbus 7 coastal zone colour scanner showed very subtle variations in water colour. These were believed to reflect variations in the concentration of phytoplankton and thus to have the potential of making possible oceanwide surveys of this fundamental food source for all higher forms of life in the sea.

Oceanographic research received a boost when a team from Duke University demonstrated the possibility of living and working at great depths by conducting a successful month-long experiment in a diving chamber. They were able to work for 24 hours at pressures equal to 2,132 feet below sea level, 100 feet beyond the previous record for a simulated dive.

JIMMY WALLACE–DUKE UNIVERSITY

OLYMPIC CHAMPIONS, 1980 WINTER GAMES, LAKE PLACID

Alpine Skiing
Men

Downhill	L. Stock (Austria)	1 min 45.50 sec
Slalom	I. Stenmark (Sweden)	1 min 44.26 sec
Giant slalom	I. Stenmark (Sweden)	2 min 40.74 sec

Women

Downhill	A. Moser-Proell (Austria)	1 min 37.52 sec
Slalom	H. Wenzel (Liechtenstein)	1 min 25.09 sec
Giant slalom	H. Wenzel (Liechtenstein)	2 min 41.66 sec

Nordic Skiing
Men

15-km cross-country	T. Wassberg (Sweden)	41 min 57.63 sec
30-km cross-country	N. Zimyatov (U.S.S.R.)	1 hr 27 min 02.80 sec
50-km cross-country	N. Zimyatov (U.S.S.R.)	2 hr 27 min 24.60 sec
40-km ski relay	U.S.S.R.	1 hr 57 min 03.46 sec
70-m ski jump	A. Innauer (Austria)	266.3 pt
90-m ski jump	J. Tormanen (Finland)	271.0 pt
Nordic combined	U. Wehling (East Germany)	432.200 pt

Women

5-km cross-country	R. Smetanina (U.S.S.R.)	15 min 06.92 sec
10-km cross-country	B. Petzold (East Germany)	30 min 31.54 sec
20-km ski relay	East Germany	1 hr 2 min 11.10 sec

Biathlon

10 km	F. Ullrich (East Germany)	32 min 10.69 sec
20 km	A. Alyabyev (U.S.S.R.)	1 hr 8 min 16.31 sec
30-km relay	U.S.S.R.	1 hr 34 min 03.27 sec

Figure Skating

Men	R. Cousins (U.K.)	189.48 pt
Women	A. Pötzsch (East Germany)	189.00 pt
Pairs	I. Rodnina and A. Zaitsev (U.S.S.R.)	147.26 pt
Ice dancing	N. Linichuk and G. Karponosov (U.S.S.R.)	205.48 pt

Speed Skating
Men

500 m	E. Heiden (U.S.)	38.03 sec*
1,000 m	E. Heiden (U.S.)	1 min 15.18 sec*
1,500 m	E. Heiden (U.S.)	1 min 55.44 sec*
5,000 m	E. Heiden (U.S.)	7 min 02.29 sec*
10,000 m	E. Heiden (U.S.)	14 min 28.13 sec*†

Women

500 m	K. Enke (East Germany)	41.78 sec*
1,000 m	N. Petruseva (U.S.S.R.)	1 min 24.10 sec*
1,500 m	A. Borckink (Neth.)	2 min 10.95 sec*
3,000 m	B. E. Jensen (Norway)	4 min 32.13 sec*

Ice Hockey

Winning team	U.S. (beat Finland 4–2 in final)	

Bobsledding

Two man	Switzerland	4 min 09.36 sec
Four man	East Germany	3 min 59.92 sec

Tobogganing (Luge)

Men (single)	B. Glass (East Germany)	2 min 54.796 sec
Men (double)	H. Rinn and N. Hahn (East Germany)	1 min 19.331 sec
Women (single)	V. Zozulya (U.S.S.R.)	2 min 36.537 sec

*Olympic record. †World record.

OLYMPIC GAMES

I. The XIII Olympic Winter Games at Lake Placid, N.Y.

The XIII Olympic Winter Games took place Feb. 13–24, 1980, at Lake Placid, N.Y., which was also the site of the 1932 Winter Olympics. China competed for the first time among a record entry of 37 nations—equaling that at Innsbruck, Austria, in 1976—represented by 1,283 competitors (1,012 men and 271 women). Of the 38 events that were contested, the only new one was the 10-km biathlon. Athletes from 11 nations shared the gold medals, the U.S.S.R. gaining ten, East Germany nine, the U.S. six, Austria and Sweden three each, Liechtenstein two, and Finland, Great Britain, The Netherlands, Norway, and Switzerland one apiece.

WIDE WORLD

In 1980 U.S. speed skater Eric Heiden became the first person to win five gold medals in one Winter Olympics.

The star of the alpine skiing on Whiteface Mountain was Hanni Wenzel of Liechtenstein. Her two gold medals, for slalom and giant slalom, and one silver, in the downhill, equaled the women's record set by Rosi Mittermaier of West Germany in 1976. A remarkable family achievement was completed when Hanni's brother Andreas won the silver medal in the men's giant slalom. Annemarie Moser-Proell, the Austrian genius twice denied a gold at Sapporo, Japan, in 1972 by Switzerland's Marie-Theres Nadig, gained her first Olympic victory in the downhill. Nadig finished third.

Ingemar Stenmark, the Swedish slalom specialist who shuns the downhill, won both the slalom and giant slalom events for men, each time reserving his better effort for the second descent. Third to Wenzel after the first giant slalom run, Stenmark next time gave his opponents no chance with a faultless dash through the gates that finally left the Liechtensteiner three-quarters of a second in arears. In the slalom Stenmark fought back from fourth to win from the U.S. runner-up, Phil Mahre, by half a second. Leonhard Stock was a surprise downhill winner for Austria, many considering him lucky to be chosen at all from a strong national squad. First during both runs, Stock left his compatriot Peter Wirnsberger trailing helplessly in his wake.

The largest number of individual honours in the Nordic skiing, on Mt. Van Hoevenberg, went to Nikolay Zimyatov, the first man to win three cross-country gold medals in one Olympics. The Soviet skier finished the 30 km with a 31-second margin over his teammate Vasily Rochev. Third-place Ivan Lebanov gained the first medal by a Bulgarian in any Winter Olympics. In the grueling 50 km Zimyatov paced himself well to leave Juha Mieto of Finland almost three minutes behind. Mieto was again runner-up in the 15 km, this time to Thomas Wassberg of Sweden; only 0.01 second divided them. Zimyatov completed his triple victory as last-leg racer on the winning Soviet relay team.

Barbara Petzold of East Germany ended the women's 10 km ahead of two Finns, Hilkka Riihivuori and Helena Takalo. Raisa Smetanina of the U.S.S.R. scored a victory in the 5 km with Riihivuori again second. Petzold helped the East Germans triumph in the relay, while the veteran Galina Kulakova's silver as a member of the Soviet second-place team was a record eighth medal in her fourth and final Olympics.

Jouko Tormanen caught a timely updraft from a swirling wind at Intervale when winning the 90-m ski jump for Finland, and Anton ("Toni") Innauer comfortably gained Austria's first 70-m ski jump victory. Another East German, Ulrich Wehling, gained his third straight Olympic victory in the Nordic combination, the first skier in Olympic history to win three golds for the same event. Frank Ullrich of East Germany, with better skiing than shooting, won the 10-km biathlon and finished second to Anatoly Alyabyev of the U.S.S.R. in the 20-km event. Alyabyev was also anchorman in the Soviet biathlon team victory.

The new $16 million ice arena was filled to its 8,500 capacity for the climax in each of the four figure-skating events, three of which featured close finishes. Robin Cousins continued where John Curry had left off to keep the men's title in Great Britain, defeating Jan Hoffmann of East Germany by the slenderest of margins. Hoffmann had amassed an appreciable advantage from his compulsory figures, but Cousins whittled that away with a dazzling free-skating display.

Anett Pötzsch gained the women's title, as her U.S. arch-rival, Linda Fratianne, was unable to eliminate the lead the East German had acquired in the compulsory figures. The eagerly awaited pairs confrontation between the U.S. world champions, Randy Gardner and Tai Babilonia, and the Soviet Olympic title defenders, Aleksandr Zaitsev and Irina Rodnina, was sadly canceled because Gardner had to withdraw from competition after aggravating a groin injury. But any hollowness of the Soviets' subsequent victory was offset by the magnitude of Rodnina's personal achievement, her third gold medal in successive Olympics. The second-place pair, Sergey Shakhrai and Marina Tcherkasova, also of the U.S.S.R., were never serious challengers. Two more Soviet skaters, Gennadi Karponosov and Natalia Linichuk, gained ice dance crowns in a close contest with Andras Sallay and Krisztina Regoczy of Hungary.

OLYMPIC CHAMPIONS, 1980 SUMMER GAMES, MOSCOW

Archery
Men's round T. Poikolainen (Finland) 2,455 pt
Women's round K. Losaberidze (U.S.S.R.) 2,491 pt

Basketball
Winning men's team Yugoslavia (beat Italy 86–77 in final)
Winning women's team U.S.S.R. (beat Bulgaria 104–73 in final)

Boxing
Light flyweight	S. Sabyrov (U.S.S.R.)	Welterweight	A. Aldama (Cuba)
Flyweight	P. Lessov (Bulgaria)	Light middleweight	A. Martinez (Cuba)
Bantamweight	J. Hernandez (Cuba)	Middleweight	J. Gomez (Cuba)
Featherweight	R. Fink (East Germany)	Light heavyweight	S. Kacar (Yugoslavia)
Lightweight	A. Herrera (Cuba)	Heavyweight	T. Stevenson (Cuba)
Light welterweight	P. Oliva (Italy)		

Canoeing
Men
500-m Canadian singles	S. Postrekhin (U.S.S.R.)	1 min 53.37 sec
500-m Canadian pairs	Hungary	1 min 43.39 sec
500-m kayak singles	V. Parfenovich (U.S.S.R.)	1 min 43.43 sec
500-m kayak pairs	U.S.S.R.	1 min 32.38 sec
1,000-m Canadian singles	L. Lubenov (Bulgaria)	4 min 12.38 sec
1,000-m Canadian pairs	Romania	3 min 47.65 sec
1,000-m kayak singles	R. Helm (East Germany)	3 min 48.77 sec
1,000-m kayak pairs	U.S.S.R.	3 min 26.72 sec
1,000-m kayak fours	East Germany	3 min 13.76 sec

Women
500-m kayak singles	B. Fischer (East Germany)	1 min 57.96 sec
500-m kayak pairs	East Germany	1 min 43.88 sec

Cycling
Sprint	L. Hesslich (East Germany)	10.75 sec (best 200 m)
1,000-m time trial	L. Thoms (East Germany)	1 min 02.955 sec*
4,000-m individual pursuit	R. Dill-Bundi (Switzerland)	4 min 35.66 sec
4,000-m team pursuit	U.S.S.R.	4 min 15.70 sec
100-km team time trial	U.S.S.R.	2 hr 01 min 21.70 sec
Individual road race	S. Sukhoruchenkov (U.S.S.R.)	4 hr 48 min 28.90 sec

Equestrian Sports
	Individual	Team
Dressage	E. Theurer (Austria) on Mon Chérie	U.S.S.R.
3-day event	F. Roman (Italy) on Rossinan	U.S.S.R.
Show jumping	J. Kowalczyk (Poland) on Artemor	U.S.S.R.

Fencing
	Individual	Team
Foil	V. Smirnov (U.S.S.R.)	France
Épée	J. Harmenberg (Sweden)	France
Sabre	V. Krovopuskov (U.S.S.R.)	U.S.S.R.
Women's foil	P. Trinquet (France)	France

Football (Soccer)
Winning team Czechoslovakia (beat East Germany 1–0 in final)

One of the most outstanding individual performances in the Games was that of the U.S. speed skater Eric Heiden, the only person ever to win five gold medals in one Winter Olympics. To finish first in each of five widely varying distances within the space of nine days and at the end break the world record for the stamina-sapping, 25-lap 10,000 m seemed like something from schoolboy fiction and was comparable to a track sprinter winning the marathon.

The women's ice speed honours were evenly distributed among an East German, Karin Enke (500 m), a Soviet, Natalia Petruseva (1,000 m), a Netherlander, Annie Borckink (1,500 m), and a Norwegian, Bjøg Eva Jensen (3,000 m). In the nine men's and women's speed-skating events on the fast oval track the previous Olympic records were bettered an unprecedented 106 times.

Ice hockey, which in the early stages threatened to become a monotonous succession of Soviet victories, was suddenly transformed when the U.S. upset the U.S.S.R. 4–3—the first hockey match the Soviets had lost in Olympic competition since 1968

Gymnastics

	Men	Women
ombined exercises		
individual	A. Dityatin (U.S.S.R.)	Y. Davydova (U.S.S.R.)
team	U.S.S.R.	U.S.S.R.
arallel bars	A. Tkachyov (U.S.S.R.)	–
neven parallel bars	–	M. Gnauck (East Germany)
orizontal bar	S. Deltchev (Bulgaria)	–
orse vaults	N. Andrianov (U.S.S.R.)	N. Shaposhnikova (U.S.S.R.)
ommeled horse	Z. Magyar (Hungary)	–
ings	A. Dityatin (U.S.S.R.)	–
alance beam	–	N. Comaneci (Romania)
loor exercises	R. Bruckner (East Germany)	N. Comaneci (Romania) and N. Kim (U.S.S.R.) (tie)

Handball

Winning men's team East Germany (beat U.S.S.R. 23–22 in final)   Winning women's team U.S.S.R. (beat East Germany 18–13 in final)

Hockey (Field)

Winning men's team India   Winning women's team Zimbabwe

Judo

0–kg class	T. Rey (France)	86–kg class	J. Roethlisberger (Switz.)
5–kg class	N. Solodukhin (U.S.S.R.)	95–kg class	R. Van de Walle (Belgium)
1–kg class	E. Gamba (Italy)	95–kg+ class	A. Parisi (France)
3–kg class	S. Khabareli (U.S.S.R.)	Open class	D. Lorenz (East Germany)

Modern Pentathlon

ndividual	A. Starostin (U.S.S.R.)	5,568 pt
eam	U.S.S.R.	16,126 pt

Rowing

Men (2,000–m course)

ngle sculls	P. Karppinen (Finland)	7 min 09.61 sec
ouble sculls	East Germany	6 min 24.33 sec
uadruple sculls	East Germany	5 min 49.81 sec
airs with coxswain	East Germany	7 min 02.54 sec
airs without coxswain	East Germany	6 min 48.01 sec
ours with coxswain	East Germany	6 min 14.51 sec
ours without coxswain	East Germany	6 min 08.17 sec
ghts with coxswain	East Germany	5 min 49.05 sec

Women (1,000–m course)

ngle sculls	S. Toma (Romania)	3 min 40.69 sec
ouble sculls	U.S.S.R.	3 min 16.27 sec
uadruple sculls	East Germany	3 min 15.32 sec
airs without coxswain	East Germany	3 min 30.49 sec
ours with coxswain	East Germany	3 min 19.27 sec
ghts with coxswain	East Germany	3 min 03.32 sec

Shooting

ree pistol	A. Melentev (U.S.S.R.)	581 pt*
mall-bore rifle (prone)	K. Varga (Hungary)	599 pt
mall-bore rifle (3-position)	V. Vlasov (U.S.S.R.)	1,173 pt*
apid-fire pistol	C. Ion (Romania)	596 pt
rapshooting	L. Giovannetti (Italy)	198 pt
keet shooting	H. Rasmussen (Denmark)	196 pt
oving target	I. Sokolov (U.S.S.R.)	589 pt*

*World record.   †Olympic record.   ‡Best Olympic performance.

TASS/SOVFOTO

Soviet gymnast Yelena Davydova, gold medalist.

The Boycott

The issue in the Moscow Games had nothing to do with sport or the Olympic movement. It concerned a country, Afghanistan, which was created over a century ago by Russia and Great Britain to act as a buffer state. At the end of 1979 the Soviet Union invaded Afghanistan, thus threatening the oil of the Middle East. That is how the West saw the situation. The Soviets, on the other hand, maintained that their forces had been invited into Afghanistan by the legitimate government there to help quell a rebellion. Thus began a war of bullets in Afghanistan and a propaganda war between East and West.

Western leaders, most notably U.S. Pres. Jimmy Carter and British Prime Minister Margaret Thatcher, found themselves powerless to intervene militarily, and so instead they sought trade embargoes and a boycott of the Olympic Games due to open in Moscow on July 19. In theory national Olympic committees are independent of governments. Rule 26 of the Olympic Charter says: "NOC's must be autonomous and must resist all pressures of any kind whatsoever, whether of a political, religious or economic nature." In practice the national Olympic committees of the developed nations of the West proved as susceptible to political pressure as the new NOC's from emerging Africa had been in 1976. From the U.S. and Canada to New Zealand came the news that the committees were listening to the political and economic views of their governments.

In the spring of 1980 Lord Killanin, president of the International Olympic Committee, thought that no more than 50 nations would send teams to Moscow, but eventually 81 nations took part. The counterattack against political pressure was led by

and only their sixth defeat in 46 games dating back to 1956. The U.S. went on to beat Finland 4–2 in the final match of the 35-game series to clinch its first Olympic ice hockey gold medal since 1960. The crucial match against the Soviet Union, which finished in second place, was a memorable thriller. Down 3–2 after 22 minutes, the U.S. scored two goals in 81 seconds, one each by Mark Johnson and Mike Eruzione.

II. Reflections on the Olympic Summer Games at Moscow

Cities with names that begin with the letter "M" have spelled death and political disruption for the Olympic Games: Mexico City, 1968, when more than 200 people were killed in demonstrations just before the Games opened; Munich, 1972, when members of the Black September Movement burst in on the Israeli quarters in the Olympic village and 17 men died; Montreal, 1976, when black Africa brought the word boycott into the Olympics; and finally Moscow in 1980, when the great nations of the world played power politics.

PATRICE HABANS—SYGMA

Polish pole vaulter Wladyslaw Kozakiewicz.

OLYMPIC CHAMPIONS, 1980 SUMMER GAMES, MOSCOW

Swimming and Diving

Men

100–m freestyle	J. Woithe (East Germany)	50.40 sec
200–m freestyle	S. Kopliakov (U.S.S.R.)	1 min 49.81 sec†
400–m freestyle	V. Salnikov (U.S.S.R.)	3 min 51.31 sec†
1,500–m freestyle	V. Salnikov (U.S.S.R.)	14 min 58.27 sec‡
100–m backstroke	B. Baron (Sweden)	56.53 sec
200–m backstroke	S. Wladar (Hungary)	2 min 01.93 sec
100–m breaststroke	D. Goodhew (Great Britain)	1 min 03.34 sec
200–m breaststroke	R. Zulpa (U.S.S.R.)	2 min 15.85 sec
100–m butterfly	P. Arvidsson (Sweden)	54.92 sec
200–m butterfly	S. Fesenko (U.S.S.R.)	1 min 59.76 sec
400–m individual medley	A. Sidorenko (U.S.S.R.)	4 min 22.89 sec†
800–m freestyle relay	U.S.S.R.	7 min 23.50 sec
400–m medley relay	Australia	3 min 45.70 sec
Springboard diving	A. Portnov (U.S.S.R.)	905.025 pt
Platform diving	F. Hoffmann (East Germany)	835.650 pt

Women

100–m freestyle	B. Krause (East Germany)	54.79 sec*
200–m freestyle	B. Krause (East Germany)	1 min 58.33 sec†
400–m freestyle	I. Diers (East Germany)	4 min 08.76 sec†
800–m freestyle	M. Ford (Australia)	8 min 28.90 sec†
100–m backstroke	R. Reinisch (East Germany)	1 min 00.86 sec*
200–m backstroke	R. Reinisch (East Germany)	2 min 11.77 sec*
100–m breaststroke	U. Geweniger (East Germany)	1 min 10.22 sec
200–m breaststroke	L. Kachushite (U.S.S.R.)	2 min 29.54 sec†
100–m butterfly	C. Metschuck (East Germany)	1 min 00.42 sec
200–m butterfly	I. Geissler (East Germany)	2 min 10.44 sec†
400–m individual medley	P. Schneider (East Germany)	4 min 36.29 sec*
400–m freestyle relay	East Germany	3 min 42.71 sec*
400–m medley relay	East Germany	4 min 06.67 sec*
Springboard diving	I. Kalinina (U.S.S.R.)	725.910 pt
Platform diving	M. Jaschke (East Germany)	596.250 pt

Track and Field

Men

100–m dash	A. Wells (Great Britain)	10.25 sec
200–m dash	P. Mennea (Italy)	20.19 sec
400–m dash	V. Markin (U.S.S.R.)	44.60 sec
800–m run	S. Ovett (Great Britain)	1 min 45.40 sec
1,500–m run	S. Coe (Great Britain)	3 min 38.4 sec
5,000–m run	Miruts Yifter (Ethiopia)	13 min 21.0 sec
10,000–m run	Miruts Yifter (Ethiopia)	27 min 42.7 sec
Marathon	W. Cierpinski (East Germany)	2 hr 11 min 03.0 sec
110–m hurdles	T. Munkelt (East Germany)	13.39 sec
400–m hurdles	V. Beck (East Germany)	48.70 sec
3,000–m steeplechase	B. Malinowski (Poland)	8 min 09.7 sec
400–m relay	U.S.S.R.	38.26 sec
1,600–m relay	U.S.S.R.	3 min 01.1 sec
20–km walk	M. Damilano (Italy)	1 hr 23 min 35.5 sec‡
50–km walk	H. Gauder (East Germany)	3 hr 49 min 24.0 sec‡
High jump	G. Wessig (East Germany)	2.36 m*
Long jump	L. Dombrowski (East Germany)	8.54 m
Pole vault	W. Kozakiewicz (Poland)	5.78 m*
Triple jump	J. Uudmae (U.S.S.R.)	17.35 m
Shot put	V. Kiselyov (U.S.S.R.)	21.35 m†

the British Olympic Association, which argued that as long as the British government maintained diplomatic relations and trade links with the U.S.S.R., it was right and proper to maintain sporting links and send a team to Moscow.

Highlights of the Games

But those 81 nations that did participate did not include some of the most powerful in the world and must be compared with the 122 that went to Munich in 1972. The track and field results were affected by the absence of the U.S. team, and the swimming events were affected even more by the absence of two out of the four best swimming nations, the U.S. and Canada. Nevertheless, perhaps the two most eagerly awaited events did take place unaffected by the boycott. These were the 800-m and 1,500-m runs.

At the Olympics, the co-holders of the 1,500-m world record were to meet for the first time at that distance. Both were Englishmen: Sebastian Coe of Sheffield and Steve Ovett of Brighton. The two were also matched in the 800 m. One has to go back a quarter of a century to find a parallel: the "Miracle Mile" in 1954 when Roger Bannister, the first man to run a mile in less than four minutes, was matched in the final of the Commonwealth Games against John Landy, the world record holder and only other man in the world to have run a mile in under four minutes. But that race, won by Bannister, was before the days of worldwide television.

Now, in 1980, the world waited for Coe, the man who had broken the 800-m, 1,500-m, and one-mile world records in 1979, to race against Ovett, who in 1980 had taken the mile record from Coe and equaled his 1,500-m mark. Expert opinion was that Coe would take the 800-m gold medal and Ovett the 1,500-m prize. Ovett agreed. Just before he arrived in Moscow he said: "I've got a 50% chance of winning the 800 metres and 90% of winning the 1,500 metres. The 1,500 metres is the one that I am really prepared for. It's the one I want. Steve Ovett is a miler."

Both races turned out to be something of a disappointment. In the 800 m nobody wanted the lead, and so the first lap took an ambling 54.3 seconds, a time good only for a schoolboy. Ovett was in the pack, pushing and shoving to give himself space. Coe trailed, taking no apparent interest in the proceedings. Instead, a third Englishman, Dave Warren, sprang to the front pursued by Nikolay Kirov of the U.S.S.R. As they entered the final straight-

Discus	V. Rasshchupkin (U.S.S.R.)	66.64 m
Hammer throw	Y. Sedykh (U.S.S.R.)	81.80 m*
Javelin	D. Kula (U.S.S.R.)	91.20 m
Decathlon	D. Thompson (Great Britain)	8,495 pt

Women

100–m dash	L. Kondratyeva (U.S.S.R.)	11.06 sec
200–m dash	B. Eckert-Wockel (East Germany)	22.03 sec†
400–m dash	M. Koch (East Germany)	48.88 sec†
800–m run	N. Olizarenko (U.S.S.R.)	1 min 53.5 sec*
1,500–m run	T. Kazankina (U.S.S.R.)	3 min 56.6 sec†
100–m hurdles	V. Komisova (U.S.S.R.)	12.56 sec†
400–m relay	East Germany	41.60 sec*
1,600–m relay	U.S.S.R.	3 min 20.2 sec
High jump	S. Simeoni (Italy)	1.97 m†
Long jump	T. Kolpakova (U.S.S.R.)	7.06 m†
Shot put	I. Slupianek (East Germany)	22.41 m*
Discus	E. Jahl (East Germany)	69.96 m†
Javelin	M. Colon (Cuba)	68.40 m†
Pentathlon	N. Tkachenko (U.S.S.R.)	5,083 pt*

Volleyball

Winning men's team U.S.S.R.   Winning women's team U.S.S.R.
(beat Bulgaria 3–1 in final)   (beat East Germany 3–1 in final)

Water Polo

Winning team U.S.S.R. (won all 5 of the final matches)

Weight Lifting

Flyweight	K. Osmanoliev (U.S.S.R.)	245.0 kg†
Bantamweight	D. Nünez (Cuba)	275.0 kg*
Featherweight	V. Mazin (U.S.S.R.)	290.0 kg†
Lightweight	Y. Rusev (Bulgaria)	342.5 kg*
Middleweight	A. Zlatev (Bulgaria)	360.0 kg*
Light heavyweight	Y. Vardanyan (U.S.S.R.)	400.0 kg*
Middle heavyweight	P. Baczako (Hungary)	377.5 kg
(First) Heavyweight	O. Zaremba (Czechoslovakia)	395.0 kg†
(Second) Heavyweight	L. Taranenko (U.S.S.R.)	422.5 kg*
Superheavyweight	S. Rakhmanov (U.S.S.R.)	440.0 kg

Wrestling

	Freestyle	Greco-Roman
Paperweight	C. Pollio (Italy)	Z. Ushkempirov (U.S.S.R.)
Flyweight	A. Beloglazov (U.S.S.R.)	V. Blagidze (U.S.S.R.)
Bantamweight	S. Beloglazov (U.S.S.R.)	S. Serikov (U.S.S.R.)
Featherweight	M. Abushov (U.S.S.R.)	S. Migiakis (Greece)
Lightweight	S. Absaldov (U.S.S.R.)	S. Rusu (Romania)
Welterweight	V. Raitchev (Bulgaria)	F. Kocsis (Hungary)
Middleweight	I. Abilov (Bulgaria)	G. Korban (U.S.S.R.)
Light heavyweight	S. Oganesyan (U.S.S.R.)	N. Nottny (Hungary)
Heavyweight	I. Mate (U.S.S.R.)	G. Raikov (Bulgaria)
Superheavyweight	S. Andiev (U.S.S.R.)	A. Kolchinsky (U.S.S.R.)

Yachting

Finn class	E. Rechardt (Finland)
Flying Dutchman class	Spain
Soling class	Denmark
Tornado class	Brazil
470 class	Brazil
Star class	U.S.S.R.

away, Ovett clicked into his electrifying top gear and within five strides went to the front to stay. The time was slow: 1 min 45.0 sec, slower than in the Rome Olympics in 1960. And Coe was buried.

He knew it himself, saying: "I knew that my fellow athletes believed that I had blown it in the 800 metres and there was no way back. They wished me well for the 1,500 metres, but I knew that they had already buried me and they were patting down the earth."

Few in the packed Lenin Stadium believed he could win. But, as it turned out, the race was made for him. Again nobody wanted the lead, and so Jurgen Straub of East Germany led the field through a leisurely 800 m in 2 min 4.9 sec. Then Straub drove for the tape 700 m away with Coe in his shadow and Ovett in Coe's shadow. The three entered the final straightaway bunched together, and everyone waited for Ovett's kick. But the pace was too fast for him, and it was Coe who surged to the front to win the gold and regain his self-respect.

In a sense justice was done because both won gold medals. Justice was certainly done when the wizened Ethiopian Miruts Yifter won both the 5,000 and 10,000 m. Yifter had looked old when he won the bronze medal in the 10,000 m in the 1972 Olympics. He looked no different in 1980; balding and deeply lined, he said that he was only 36, but that is old to be the supreme distance athlete of the world. Many people believed that he would have won two gold medals in Montreal in 1976, but he could not compete because of the African boycott. Moscow was his last chance for Olympic glory.

The Ethiopians, Yifter, Mohammed Kedir, and Tolossa Kotu, ran the 10,000 m like a cycling team race, each holding the lead for a while and then dropping back to let his countryman take over. Lasse Viren of Finland, who had won the event in 1972 and 1976, tried a heroic surge with three laps to go, but the Ethiopians packed close behind him and in the last 300 m Yifter let fly with a sprint that won him the gold medal. He gave his opponents the same medicine in the 5,000 m.

Thus, the middle- and long-distance runs were won by true champions with no "ifs" or "buts." The same could not be said about many other events; for instance, the 400-m hurdles, won by the East German Volker Beck, was without Ed Moses of the U.S., unbeaten for years at his specialty and the world record holder.

Of all the major sports swimming suffered most from the boycott. In the absence of the U.S., the East German women won 11 out of 13 gold medals. Led by Vladimir Salnikov, the Soviet men won eight golds.

Women's gymnastics often turned out to be a contest between girls and women. Nelli Kim, a Soviet Asian woman, shared the floor exercises title with Nadia Comaneci of Romania (a girl in 1976; a woman in 1980), who also won the balance beam. But the other two events went to girls: the vault to Nataliya Shaposhnikova of the U.S.S.R. and the parallel bars to Maxi Gnauck of East Germany. And the overall title went to one of the most diminutive gymnasts in Moscow, the Soviet Union's Yelena Davydova. Much of the gymnastics competition was marked by rows about the judging.

These were the joyless Games. The memory of seven months of political war could not be banished, and there was tight security in Moscow. The Soviets said that it was to protect the competitors from outside interference, but to those who spent three weeks in Moscow the security seemed to be designed to prevent any contact with the Soviet people.

After the Games Lord Killanin sounded a warning for the future. As the flame died in the Lenin Stadium, he said: "I would implore the sportsmen of the world to unite in peace before a holocaust descends. Alas, sport is intertwined with politics but, and I do not mind being accused of being naive, sport and the Olympic Games must not be used for political purposes, especially when other political, diplomatic and economic means have not been tried."

U.S.-made T-37 training jets were shipped to Pakistan in March as a dispute continued over the amount and kind of aid to be tendered by the U.S.
WIDE WORLD

PAKISTAN

The shock wave generated by the Soviet military intervention in neighbouring Afghanistan in late 1979 gave Pres. Mohammad Zia-ul-Haq the opportunity to tighten still further the martial-law administration of Pakistan. President Zia had already placed all prominent political leaders under arrest, banned political activities, and imposed press censorship. Air Marshal Ashgar Khan was arrested, released, and rearrested three times in 1980. Begum Nusrat Bhutto and Benazir Bhutto, leaders of the Pakistan People's Party after former president Zulfikar Ali Bhutto was executed in April 1979, were placed under house arrest in October 1979 but released in April 1980.

Using the bogey of a Soviet threat to Pakistan's security, General Zia obtained promises of help from abroad. The U.S. agreed to uphold the 1959 mutual defense treaty, but a U.S. offer of $400 million in military and economic assistance over two years was rejected by Zia as "peanuts." Offers of financial assistance also came from the oil-rich Muslim countries of the Middle East, although no official figures were published. Saudi Arabia was said to have given $100 million, part of which was meant for Zia's islamization program.

Despite the rejection of the U.S. aid package, small arms and spare parts flowed into Pakistan from the U.S., and Pakistan also shopped for weapons in other Western markets. Some of these arms were being funneled into the Afghan insurgency movement through the Afghan rebels, who were finding refuge in Pakistani territory. Zia appealed to international aid agencies for assistance in caring for the growing number of Afghan refugees (over 900,000 by October). Despite denials, Pakistan did little to prevent some refugees from receiving train-

ing and arms and slipping into Afghanistan to take part in the anti-Soviet "freedom struggle."

President Zia organized two Islamic conferences at foreign ministers' level in which the main item on the agenda was the Afghan crisis. The first, in January, took a tough stand by deciding to withhold recognition of the Soviet-backed Babrak Karmal government unless the Soviets withdrew. The second, in May, adopted a more conciliatory approach. A three-member committee was set up to negotiate a political settlement of the crisis.

The economy showed no improvement. The growth rate for 1978–79 was 5.9%, compared with 7% in the previous year. The farming sector improved slightly, but industry suffered as investors shied away because of the unsettled political climate. The trade gap stood at over $2 billion and foreign debt liability at $7 billion. The federal budget for 1980–81 provided for a development outlay of PakRs 26,464,000,000, although resources were estimated at PakRs 19,528,000,000 (PakR 9.90 = U.S. $1).

Relations with China were cordial, but those with India remained strained. India was suspicious of Pakistan's arms buildup and was convinced that, despite official statements to the contrary, Pakistan was going ahead with plans to manufacture a nuclear bomb. The establishment of trade and the exchange of visits and communications were welcomed by both sides, but several rounds of talks in Islamabad and New Delhi failed to make headway toward further normalization of relations. India resented Pakistan's attempts to raise the Kashmir dispute at international forums, despite the Simla accord of 1972 in which both countries had agreed to settle the issue through bilateral talks.

PANAMA

The formal transfer of the Canal Zone to Panama on Oct. 1, 1979, failed to bring the new economic and political age expected by Panamanians. Between 17 and 25% remained unemployed, and all the population suffered from an inflation rate that rose from 10 to 14% during 1980. The national debt approached the U.S. $3 billion mark, and food imports grew while farmers' output declined. Panamanians reacted with strikes and riots. Though there were five disturbances in the two-week period around Christmas 1979, the violence was not confined to this period.

While the depressed economy was the basic cause of the disturbances, the presence of Mohammad Reza Pahlavi, the exiled shah of Iran, provided an additional excuse. Through the personal appeal of Hamilton Jordan, U.S. Pres. Jimmy Carter's special envoy, Panama's strong man Omar Torrijos was persuaded to give the shah asylum on Contadora Island. However, the legal involvements of extradition proceedings, the quarrel over whether Panamanian or U.S. doctors should attend him, and the need for surgery finally impelled the shah to take flight to sanctuary in Egypt.

The pressures from Washington regarding the shah were displeasing to Panama, and there were other irritants, including the U.S. delay in naming members of the new Panama Canal Commission. Students marked the departure of the last governor of the Canal Zone with a riot. Two units of ITT, All America Cables and Radio and ITT Central America Cables and Radio, received notices that their licenses would not be renewed. To Panama's benefit, tolls on ship transits through the canal were raised nearly 30%, but the Organization of American States roundly condemned the increase. Relations with El Salvador were disturbed by the seizure of the Panamanian embassy by Salvadoran militants. In March Pres. Aristides Royo signed an agreement with Japan's prime minister, Masayoshi Ohira, for feasibility studies on a new isthmian canal.

An election, devoid of issues and personalities, was held on Sept. 28, 1980, to fill some of the seats of the National Assembly's Executive Council.

PARAGUAY

By 1980 Gen. Alfredo Stroessner had been in power as president of Paraguay for 26 years, and speculation about a possible successor increased in diplomatic circles, with Gen. Andrés Rodríguez, commander of the General Caballero division, seen as the most likely candidate. The new military government established in Bolivia in July was quickly recognized by Paraguay. Relations were broken off with Nicaragua, held responsible for the assassination of its former president, Anastasio Somoza, in Asunción in September.

There was a serious armed confrontation between troops and peasants in Caaguazú Department in March. Censorship of the press prevented publication of full details of the events, but the Partido Liberal Radical Auténtico, in a paid advertisement in the press, condemned the repression being carried out against peasants in the region. Some estimates put the number killed at between 20 and 50, and some sectors of the church accused the government of executing the peasants after arresting them.

The economy continued to grow, gross domestic product increasing by 9.5% in 1979. Construction continued to be the most dynamic sector, reflecting the impact of the Itaipú hydroelectric project.

On September 17 Anastasio Somoza, exiled ex-dictator of Nicaragua, was assassinated in a hail of machine-gun and bazooka fire as he was being driven in his car through the streets of Asunción, Paraguay, where he had lived since fleeing Nicaragua in 1979. With him in Paraguay was his longtime mistress, Dinorah Sampson (centre).

SIPA PRESS / BLACK STAR

PEOPLE

Among the milestones in the lives of people making news in 1980 were the following:

Births

To actress **Ursula Andress** and actor Harry Hamlin, on May 20, a son.

To actress **Lucie Arnaz** and actor **Laurence Luckinbill,** on Dec. 9, a son.

To singer **Debby Boone** ("You Light Up My Life") and her husband, Gabriel Ferrer, on July 9, a son.

To Kentucky **Gov. John Y. Brown** and his wife, former Miss America Phyllis George, on June 17, a son.

To **Julie Nixon Eisenhower** and her husband, **David,** on Oct. 10, a son.

To **King Hussein** and Queen Noor of Jordan, on March 31, a son.

To **Joseph P. Kennedy II,** son of the late senator Robert F. Kennedy, and his wife, Sheila, on Oct. 4, twin sons.

To actor **John Ritter** ("Three's Company") and his wife, Nancy Morgan, in February, a son.

To actress **Talia Shire** (*Rocky, Rocky II*) and Jack Schwartzman, executive vice-president of Lorimar Productions, in July, a son.

To jockey **Willie Shoemaker** and his wife, Cindy, in July, a daughter.

To **Susan Ford Vance,** daughter of former president Gerald R. Ford, and her husband, Charles, on Aug. 15, a daughter.

To TV's **Henry Winkler** ("Happy Days") and his wife, Stacey, on Sept. 30, a daughter.

To pop-culture watcher **Tom Wolfe** (*The Right Stuff*) and his wife, Sheila Berger Wolfe, in September, a daughter.

Pop singer Debby Boone displays her son, Jordan Alexander, born July 9; Debby's husband is Gabriel Ferrer.

WIDE WORLD

WIDE WORLD

Sheila Kennedy holds twin Matthew Rauch Kennedy, and Joseph P. Kennedy II holds twin Joseph P. Kennedy III; the infants were born October 4.

To Soviet poet **Yevgeny Yevtushenko** and his wife, Jan Butler, on April 8, a son.

Marriages

Cartoonist **Charles Addams,** 68, master of the macabre, to Marilyn Matthews Miller, 53; May 31, Long Island, N.Y.

Entertainer **Lucie Arnaz** (*They're Playing Our Song*), 28, to actor **Laurence Luckinbill,** 45; June 22, Kingston, N.Y.

Nimble-treading, ever young **Fred Astaire,** 81, to jockey **Robyn Smith,** 35; June 27, Beverly Hills, Calif.

Swedish International Tennis Federation world champion **Björn Borg,** 24, to Mariana Simionescu, 23; July 24, Bucharest, Rom.

American Ballet Theatre dancer **Fernando Bujones,** 25, to Marcia Kubitschek; June 8, New York City.

Singer **Karen Carpenter** ("We've Only Just Begun"), 30, to Thomas J. Burris, 39; Aug. 31, Beverly Hills, Calif.

Environmentalist and presidential candidate **Barry Commoner,** 65, to attorney Lisa Feiner, 35; Aug. 26, Madison, Wis.

Political activist **Angela Davis,** 36, to photographer Hilton Braithwaite, 36; July 6, Birmingham, Ala.

Popular daytime talk show host **Phil Donahue,** 44, to actress **Marlo Thomas,** 42; May 22, Beverly Hills, Calif.

Actress **Sandy Duncan** (*Peter Pan*), 34, to dancer-singer **Don Correia** (*A Chorus Line*), 29; July 21, New York City.

Jean-Claude Duvalier, 28, president-for-life of Haiti, to Michèle Bennett, 27; May 27, Port-au-Prince, Haiti.

San Francisco's **Mayor Dianne Feinstein,** 46, to investment banker Richard Blum; Jan. 20, San Francisco.

Automobile magnate **Henry Ford II,** 63, to Kathleen Roberta DuRoss, 40; Oct. 14, in Carson City, Nev.

Actor **Frederic Forrest** (*The Rose*), 42, to **Marilu Henner** ("Taxi"), 28; Sept. 28, New Orleans, La.

Actress **Bonnie Franklin** ("One Day at a Time"), 36, to producer Marvin Minoff, 48; in September, in Los Angeles.

Novelist **Gerald Green** (*Holocaust*), 58, to Marlene Eagle, 46; Oct. 19, New Canaan, Conn.

Actress **Margaux Hemingway,** 24, to French filmmaker Bernardo Faucher, 40; Jan. 1, Ketchum, Idaho.

Actor **Dustin Hoffman** (*Kramer vs. Kramer*), 43, to lawyer Lisa Gottsegen, 25; Oct. 12, Roxbury, Conn.

British actress **Olivia Hussey,** 27, to Japanese pop singer **Akira Fuse,** 32; Feb. 18, Miami, Fla.

Actress **Sally Kellerman** (*The Serial, M*A*S*H*), 42, to Jonathan Krane, 29; in May, in Malibu, Calif.

Courtney Kennedy, 23, daughter of the late senator Robert F. Kennedy, to Jeff Ruhe, 28; June 14, Washington, D.C.

Mukarram Jah Barkat Ali Khan, 45, eighth nizam of Hyderabad and heir to one of the world's largest fortunes, to Helen Simmons, 31; in April, in Perth, Australia.

World Boxing Council welterweight champion **Sugar Ray Leonard,** 23, to Juanita Wilkinson, 23; Jan. 19, Landover, Md.

Tennis champ Björn Borg married Mariana Simionescu in Bucharest, Romania, in civil and religious ceremonies on July 24.

UPI

SYNDICATION INTERNATIONAL/PHOTO TRENDS

Playwright Harold Pinter married novelist and historian Lady Antonia Fraser in London on November 27.

Actor **Malcolm McDowell,** 37, to his leading lady in *Time After Time*, **Mary Steenburgen,** 27; Sept. 29, New York City.

Macho screen actor **Steve McQueen** (*The Hunter*), 49, to model Barbara Minty, 26; Jan. 16, Santa Paula, Calif.

Writer **Norman Mailer,** 57, to former schoolteacher Norris Church, 31; Nov. 11, Brooklyn, N.Y.

French film director **Louis Malle** (*Pretty Baby*), 48, to actress **Candice Bergen,** 34; Sept. 27, Lugagnac, France.

British race driver **Stirling Moss,** 50, to advertising executive Susie Paine, 27; April 17, London.

Playwright **Harold Pinter,** 50, to historian, novelist, and biographer **Lady Antonia Fraser,** 48; Nov. 27, London.

Actress **Linda Purl,** to Desi Arnaz, Jr.; Jan. 13, Los Angeles.

Comedienne **Gilda Radner,** 33, to rock guitarist G. E. Smith, 28; March 26, New York City.

Joffrey II dancer **Ronald P. Reagan,** 22, son of the president-elect, to Doria Palmieri, 29; Nov. 24, New York City.

Rocker **Patti Smith,** to rocker Fred Smith; Feb. 16, Detroit.

Disco queen **Donna Summer** ("Bad Girl"), 31, to guitarist Bruce Sudano, 31; July 16, Los Angeles.

"Doonesbury" creator **Gary Trudeau,** 31, to "Today" show co-host **Jane Pauley,** 29; June 14, New Haven, Conn.

Actress **Raquel Welch,** 39, to film writer and producer André Weinfeld, 33; July 5, Cabo San Lucas, Mexico.

CAMERA PRESS, LONDON
JOY ADAMSON

CAMERA PRESS, LONDON
SIR CECIL BEATON

WIDE WORLD
WILLIAM O. DOUGLAS

Obituaries

Joy Adamson, Austrian-born naturalist who lived for 40 years in Kenya and penned the best-selling book *Born Free*, the story of a lioness that she and her husband raised from a cub and returned to the wild; Jan. 3, Shaba National Reserve, Kenya, age 69.

Yigal Allon, celebrated Israeli military and political figure who first gained note as leader of the commando strike force against the Arabs prior to the establishment of Israel; his 1966 entry into Parliament paved the way for a series of Cabinet posts, including deputy prime minister and foreign minister; Feb. 29, Afula, Israel, age 61.

Mary O'Hara Alsop, U.S. author and composer, best known for two novels written in the 1940s, *My Friend Flicka* and *Thunderhead;* Oct. 15, Chevy Chase, Md., age 95.

Boris Aronson, celebrated Russian-born Broadway stage designer whose original work for such productions as *The Rose Tattoo, Cabaret,* and *Company* earned him six Tony Awards during his career; Nov. 16, near Nyack, N.Y., age 81.

Roland Barthes, influential French philospher and critic, known for his unorthodox analyses of popular culture, typified by his work in semiotics, the exploration of the origins and meanings of signs and symbols; his books include *Mythologies* (1957), *Le Degré zéro de l'écriture* (1953), and *Sur Racine* (1963); March 26, Paris, age 64.

L(ucius) C(hristopher) Bates, U.S. newspaper publisher and civils rights advocate; publisher of the *Arkansas State Press*, he precipitated the historic desegregation of a Little Rock, Ark., high school in 1957; he also served as field secretary for the NAACP; Aug. 22, Little Rock, Ark,. age 79(?).

Gregory Bateson, British anthropologist, author, and philosopher, known for his early work in the 1930s, with his first wife, Margaret Mead, which produced a classic study of the people of Bali, his later contribution to psychiatry of the "double-blind" hypothesis that sought to explain schizophrenia, and recently for his contribution to ecology of the notion that "small is beautiful"; his works include *Steps to an Ecology of the Mind;* July 4, San Francisco, age 76.

Sir Cecil Beaton, noted British portrait photographer, artist, designer, and author; his photographic career was firmly established when he landed a contract in 1930 to supply fashion layouts to *Vogue* magazine; he was soon sought after as portrait photographer of the celebrated, and his own celebrity was sealed when he became the favourite photographer of the British royal family; he provided costume and set designs for a number of plays and films, winning Academy Awards for those produced by *Gigi* (1959) and *My Fair Lady* (1965); knighted in 1972, Sir Cecil produced a number of acclaimed works, among them *The Wandering Years, Cecil Beaton's Scrapbook,* and *Self-Portrait with Friends; The Selected Diaries of Cecil Beaton—1922–74;* Jan. 18, London, age 76.

David Burpee, U.S. mail-order seed mogul, who for 55 years headed the W. Atlee Burpee Co., the world's largest mail-order seed house, and cultivated along the way new merchandising methods and an abundance of new varieties of flowers and vegetables; June 24, Doylestown, Pa., age 87.

Marcello Caetano, former prime minister of Portugal (1968–75) who was ousted in a military coup and exiled himself to Brazil, where he became professor of law at Rio University; Oct. 26, Rio de Janeiro, Brazil, age 74.

Gower Champion, leading choreographer and director in U.S. musical theatre, who began his lengthy career in a dance team with his former wife, Marge Belcher Champion; they gained fame in regular TV appearances and subsequently in films, among them *Showboat* and *Three for the Show;* in 1960 he debuted as a musical director-choreographer in *Bye Bye Birdie,* for which he earned a Tony Award; later musical theatre credits included the critically acclaimed *Carnival* (1961), *Hello, Dolly!* (1964), and most recently *42nd Street* (1980); Aug. 25, New York City, age 59.

Harold Clurman, celebrated figure in American theatre for more than 50 years, who was noted as a director, critic, author, and teacher; in 1931 he founded the Group Theater, which introduced Stanislavsky's Method to the American stage and became known for landmark productions, among them *Awake and Sing* and *Golden Boy;* other directorial credits included *Member of the Wedding* and *Uncle Vanya;* in the 1950s he became drama critic for the *New Republic* and then for *The Nation* and subsequently published several acclaimed works, among them *On Directing* and his autobiography, *All People Are Famous;* Sept. 9, New York City, age 78.

Jacqueline Cochran, U.S. pilot who set more than 200 flying records during her career, including being the first woman to fly faster than the speed of sound; during World War II she served as director of the Women's Air Force Service Pilots, a program that trained more than 1,200 women to fly transport planes; Aug. 9, Indio, Calif., age 70(?).

John Collier, British author and screenwriter known for his macabre short stories, collected in *Fancies and Goodnights*, and for his collaboration on the script for *The African Queen;* other film scripts include *I Am a Camera, Deception,* and *The War Lord;* April 6, Pacific Palisades, Calif., age 78.

Marc Connelly, U.S. playwright, winner of the Pulitzer Prize for *The Green Pastures* (1930), an all-black production; in collaboration with George S. Kaufman he wrote *Dulcy, Merton of the Movies, Helen of Troy, N.Y.,* and *Beggar on Horseback* and as a screenwriter, *The Cradle Song* and *Captains Courageous;* Dec. 21, New York City, age 90.

Dorothy Day, U.S. social activist, a founder of the Catholic Worker Movement, who for more than 50 years worked for social justice; she established 35 settlement houses for the homeless and hungry and fought for civil rights, pacifism, and translation of religious ideals into concrete action; Nov. 29, New York City, age 83.

Karl Dönitz, grand admiral and commander of Germany's U-boat submarine fleet in World War II and a brilliant naval strategist; he was chosen by Adolf Hitler to be his successor, and he presided over Nazi Germany's unconditional surrender to the Allies in 1945; he spent ten years in prison for war crimes after the Nürnberg trials in 1947; Dec. 24, Aumühle, West Germany, age 89.

William O. Douglas, controversial justice of the U.S. Supreme Court who doggedly championed liberal causes and individual rights and who sat on the court for 36½ years, the longest term ever served by a justice; in 1934 he was appointed to the Securities and Exchange Commission and a year later was named to head the agency; in this position he was drawn into Pres. Franklin D. Roosevelt's inner circle and in 1939 was appointed to fill a vacancy on the Supreme Court at age 40; he earned a reputation for unflagging energy, a lightning-quick mind, and a predilection for dissent and worked tirelessly to uphold the U.S. Constitution, whose purpose, as he saw it, was "to keep the Government off the backs of the people"; a staunch advocate of the First Amendment guarantee of free speech and of freedom of the press, he was three times threatened with impeachment proceedings—once for the marriage to his fourth wife, 23-year-old Cathleen Heffernan—but each of these efforts was short-lived; a stroke in 1974 forced his reluctant retirement from the bench the following year; Jan. 19, Washington, D.C., age 81.

Jessica Dragonette, popular singer on radio in the 1920s and 1930s, who for 22 consecutive years brought operetta and semiclassical music to millions of listeners; March 18, New York City, age 75(?).

Richard Drew, U.S. chemical engineer who invented Scotch tape in 1930 while a laboratory technician for Minnesota Mining and Manufacturing Co.; Dec. 14, Santa Barbara, Calif., age 81.

Jimmy Durante, raspy-voiced comedian whose one-liners delivered in butchered diction, honky-tonk piano ballads ("Inka Dinka Doo"), and gentle spirit captured a nation's affection for nearly 50 years in vaudeville, Broadway, radio, movies, and television; it was on radio that Durante inaugurated what was to become a trademark—signing off each performance with a "good night" to the mysterious Mrs. Calabash; Jan. 29, Santa Monica, Calif., age 86.

Peter Farb, naturalist, linguist, and author of a number of acclaimed works on the natural and social sciences, among them *Man's Rise to Civilization, Humankind,* and *Word Play: What Happens When People Talk;* April 8, Boston, age 50.

UPI
JIMMY DURANTE

COURTESY, MICHIGAN STATE UNIVERSITY
ERICH FROMM

KEYSTONE
SANJAY GANDHI

SIR ALFRED HITCHCOCK

OSKAR KOKOSCHKA

ALEKSEY KOSYGIN

Jane Froman, actress-singer who began her career singing with the Paul Whiteman band and went on to appear in the 1935 film *Stars over Broadway* and in several Broadway musical (*Ziegfeld Follies, Artists and Models*); the 1952 film *With a Song in My Heart* portrayed her comeback after serious injuries in a plane crash during a 1943 USO tour; April 22, Columbia, Mo., age 72.

Erich Fromm, German-born psychoanalyst and social philosopher who produced 20 books during his career exploring the emotional problems common in free societies and seeking to promote the use of pyschoanalytic principles to cure societal ills and produce a "sane society"; trained in classical Freudian analysis, he eventually created his own brand of analysis that sought to explain human behaviour by exploring relevant economic and social factors in addition to the unconscious Freudian motives; his works include *Escape from Freedom* (1941), *The Sane Society* (1955), *The Art of Loving* (1956), *Marx's Concept of Man* (1961), and *May Man Prevail?* (1961); March 12, Muralto, Switz., age 79.

Victor Galíndez, Argentine former World Boxing Association light-heavyweight champion (1974–79); Oct. 26, De Mayo, Arg., age 31.

Sanjay Gandhi, Indian politician, the son of Indira Gandhi, whose following he looked to inherit; though politically astute he alienated many by his high-handed and harsh methods, and his death in a plane crash seemed to close the Gandhi dynasty; June 23, New Delhi, India, age 33.

Reginald Gardiner, English-born character actor and comedian whose 1936 Hollywood movie debut in *Born to Dance* was followed by appearances in nearly 100 more films, among them *Androcles and the Lion, The Great Dictator* with Charlie Chaplin, and *Mr. Hobbs Takes a Vacation;* July 7, Westwood, Calif., age 77.

Patrick Emmet Gorman, U.S. labour leader, president of Amalgamated Meat Cutters and Butcher Workmen of North America, a union he served from 1912, presiding over its growth until, through merger in 1979, it became the United Food and Commercial Workers Union, with 1.3 million members; Sept. 3, Chicago, age 87.

Hugh Griffith, Welsh character actor whose greatest fame during a lengthy career in film, theatre, and television was won with his portrayal of the earthy Squire Western in the 1963 film *Tom Jones;* May 14, London, age 67.

Davis Grubb, author of the much lauded 1953 novel *The Night of the Hunter*, eventually made into a successful movie, and of eight other lesser known novels and collections of short stories; July 24, New York City, age 61.

Victor Gruen, Viennese-born architect whose two major shopping centre developments in the 1950s, one near Detroit and the other near Minneapolis, pioneered the development of suburban America; he nonetheless spoke out tirelessly in favour of comprehensive urban planning and against uncontrolled urban sprawl; Feb. 14, Vienna, age 76.

Paul Hall, noted U.S. labour union figure who helped found the Seafarers International Union in the late 1930s and for nearly 25 years served as its president; June 22, New York City, age 65.

Arnold Haskell, British ballet critic, director of the Royal Ballet School, 1947–64; he helped educate British taste and bring the art of ballet to the attention of the masses; Nov. 14, Bath, England, age 77.

Dick Haymes, actor and popular baritone of the 1940s who sang with such big bands as those of Tommy Dorsey, Benny Goodman, and Harry James and who appeared in 35 films, among them *One Touch of Venus* and *Diamond Horseshoe;* March 28, Los Angeles, age 61.

Sir Alfred Hitchcock, celebrated English-born film director and master of the psychological thriller; he established an international reputation in the 1930s with such suspense classics as *The Thirty-Nine Steps* and *The Lady Vanishes* and in 1939 moved to Hollywood, where his first American film, the melodrama *Rebecca*, earned him an Oscar for best film of 1940; numerous other films followed—*Spellbound, Notorious, Strangers on a Train, Rear Window, North by Northwest, Psycho,* and *Vertigo*—as did five other Oscars for best director; a master of technical effect, he was noted for his meticulous orchestration of plot, juxtaposing the macabre and the mundane, and for his heavy reliance on visual image and silence to heighten suspense; in the late 1950s and 1960s he hosted two popular weekly TV shows, "Alfred Hitchcock Presents" and the "Alfred Hitchcock Hour"; despite being a naturalized U.S. citizen, he was knighted in 1980 by Queen Elizabeth II; April 29, Los Angeles, age 80.

Elston Howard, first black to play for the New York Yankees; as catcher and outfielder he was a dependable hitter, with a .274 average; he was named most valuable player in the American League in 1963 and played on nine All-Star teams; Dec. 14, New York City, age 51.

José Iturbi, Spanish-born concert pianist, conductor, and actor who appeared with and conducted a number of American orchestras and in the 1940s helped popularize classical music in the U.S. with appearances in several Hollywood films, among them *The Midnight Kiss, Music for Millions*, and *Anchors Aweigh;* June 28, Hollywood, Calif., age 84.

Eddie Jackson, raspy-voiced comedian and song-and-dance man who teamed up with Lou Clayton and Jimmy Durante in 1923 to form the successful vaudeville trio that launched Durante's career; though the trio disbanded in the 1930s, Jackson and Durante enjoyed a lifelong partnership and friendship; July 16, Los Angeles, age 84.

David Janssen, U.S. actor best known for his portrayal of Dr. Richard Kimble in the long-running (1963–67), Emmy Award-winning television series "The Fugitive"; Feb. 13, Malibu, Calif., age 49.

Howard Mumford Jones, American cultural historian and prolific writer, whose work *O Strange New World*, the first volume of a trilogy retracing the development of American culture, earned him a Pulitzer Prize for nonfiction in 1965; May 11, Cambridge, Mass., age 88.

Ida Kaminska, longtime leading lady of classical Yiddish theatre who for 21 years (1946–68) headed the Jewish State Theater of Poland; emigrating to New York City in 1968, she tried unsuccessfully to establish a Yiddish theatre but continued to perform; she garnered her widest fame for her role in Jan Kadar's 1966 film *The Shop on Main Street;* May 21, New York City, age 80.

Sir Seretse Khama, president of Botswana since the country gained its independence in 1966; July 13, Gaberone, Botswana, age 59.

Oskar Kokoschka, Austrian painter and writer and a leader of the pre-World War I Expressionist movement in art and literature, known particularly for his early psychological portraits, which combined distortion and wiry line to evoke the subject's psyche, and later for his landscapes and urban panoramas; Feb. 22, Villeneuve, Switz., age 93.

Andre Kostelanetz, Russian-born conductor of symphonic and popular music who was for years a fixture on the American music scene; he conducted the country's major orchestras—setting a record for the number of consecutive seasons as conductor of the New York Philharmonic—brought his own blend of classical and contemporary music to millions of listeners in popular radio programs of the 1930s and later in "promenade" concerts in the 1960s, and sold an estimated 52 million records during his career; Jan. 13, Port-au-Prince, Haiti, age 78.

Aleksey N. Kosygin, chairman of the Council of Ministers (premier) of the U.S.S.R. from 1964 to 1980, when he retired; he worked his way to the top of Soviet political life, first joining the Communist Party in 1927; he served in a variety of roles from 1938, and first became a member of the Politburo in 1948; generally thought to be a moderate, he was valued for his pragmatism and administrative skills; Dec. 18, Moscow, age 76.

Louis Kronenberger, longtime theatre critic for *Time* magazine (1938–61) and author who produced a wide range of work, including several acclaimed books on 18th-century England (*Marlborough's Duchess, Kings and Desperate Men*) and several anthologies (*An Anthology of Light Verse, The Viking Portable Reader's Companion*); April 30, Brookline, Mass., age 75.

Jules Léger, Canadian career diplomat, 21st governor general of Canada 1974–79; Nov. 22, Ottawa, age 67.

FRED WARD—BLACK STAR
JOHN LENNON

UPI
WILLARD LIBBY

UPI
ALICE ROOSEVELT LONGWORTH

267

JOHN WILLIAM MC CORMACK

JAMES S. MC DONNELL

STEVE MC QUEEN

John Lennon, British musician and songwriter, who as a member of the Beatles had a profound and far-reaching effect on popular culture as it was reflected and expressed in popular music; his work was versatile and flexible, and many thought his greatness lay in using the format of the pop song to express a variety of messages, from love to societal upheaval; from 1964 to 1970 the Beatles had one hit after another, earning Lennon worldwide fame as the turbulence of the time was both reflected and fueled by his songs. After the disbanding of the group in 1970 he continued to write and work with his wife, avant-gardist Yoko Ono, but dropped out of public life for five years and had returned to music in 1980 only months before he was senselessly murdered; Dec. 8, New York City, age 40.

Sam Levenson, U.S. humorist, author, and television personality, famous for his chatty tales of a poor but happy childhood in a large Jewish family in New York City's Lower East Side; his books include *Everything but Money* and *In One Era and Out the Other;* Aug. 27, New York City, age 68.

Willard Libby, Nobel Prize-winning chemist and atomic scientist who was honoured as a Nobel laureate in 1960 for his development of the "atomic clock," or carbon–14, method of dating ancient archaeological artifacts; he also contributed to the development of the atomic bomb, served on the Atomic Energy Commission under Pres. Dwight Eisenhower, and led the Atoms for Peace project in the 1950s; Sept. 8, Los Angeles, age 71.

Alice Roosevelt Longworth, Pres. Theodore Roosevelt's elder daughter and last surviving child, and widow of Nicholas Longworth, speaker of the House of Representatives from 1925 to 1931; her biting wit, charm, looks, and far-flung political connections ensured her cynosure status in Washington society for nearly eight decades; Feb. 20, Washington, D.C., age 96.

Allard K. Lowenstein, political activist credited with precipitating Lyndon B. Johnson's decision not to run for reelection in 1968 by inducing Eugene McCarthy to run against him in the primaries on an antiwar platform; he served in Congress for one term and with the United Nations from 1977; March 14, New York City, age 51.

John W. McCormack, speaker of the U.S. House of Representatives 1962–70, a U.S. representative from 1928, known for his vigorous anti-Communism and support of social legislation under presidents from Roosevelt to Johnson, a skillful and influential Washington politician for 42 years; Nov. 22, Dedham, Mass., age 88.

James S. McDonnell, Jr., co-founder and chairman of the McDonnell Douglas Corp., the second largest military manufacturing company in the U.S., who helped usher in the space age with the manufacture of the Mercury spacecraft that launched the first American astronaut into orbit; Aug. 22, St. Louis, Mo., age 81.

Marshall McLuhan, Canadian communications theorist, orginator of the phrase "the medium is the message"; his investigations into the nature of communications media and their impact on contemporary life and events were seminal and brought him widespread attention in the 1960s through his books *The Gutenberg Galaxy* (1962), *Understanding Media* (1964), and *The Medium Is the Massage* (1967); Dec. 31, Toronto, age 69.

Steve McQueen, actor who excelled at playing the macho antihero caught in a lonely struggle for survival in a cruel world; in the 1950s he gained note with his television portrayal for three seasons of a bounty hunter in the series "Wanted —Dead or Alive"; in 1958 he broke into film and in 1963 sealed his fame with his performance in *The Great Escape;* numerous other films followed—*The Sand Pebbles, The Thomas Crown Affair, Bullitt, Papillon*—and by the late 1970s he commanded an enormous following and more than $3 million a film; Nov. 7, Juarez, Mexico, age 50.

Carey McWilliams, editor of *The Nation* for 20 years (1955–75) and author of a number of books that championed the rights of minorities and the underprivileged (*Prejudice: Japanese Americans, A Mask for Privilege, Brothers Under the Skin*); June 27, New York City, age 74.

Nadezhda Mandelstam, widow of Soviet poet Osip Mandelstam; her memoirs *Hope Agaist Hope* (1970) and *Hope Abandoned* (1974) revealed the realities of life under Joseph Stalin for dissenters and intelligentsia; Dec. 29, Moscow, age 81.

(Annunzio Paolo) Mantovani, Italian-born conductor of string-filled orchestral "mood" music, whose popularity enabled him to become in the 1950s the first musician in the U.S. to sell one million stereo records; March 29, Royal Tunbridge Wells, England, age 74.

Richard ("Rube") Marquard, Baseball Hall of Fame pitcher whose 1912 record of pitching 19 consecutive victories for the New York Giants still stands; June 1, Baltimore, Md., age 90.

Maria Povera Martinez, American Indian potter who, with her artist husband, Julian Martinez, revived the lost art of making black ware in 1918; her black-on-black pottery, perfectly balanced despite not being thrown on a wheel, is shown in museums worldwide; July 20, San Ildefonso Pueblo, N.M., age 93.

George Meany, labour leader who engineered the 1955 merger of the AFL and CIO and served as its first and, until his reluctant retirement in late 1979, only president; a plumber by trade, he became a professional trade unionist in 1922 and 12 years later was elected president of the New York State Federation of Labor; in 1940 he became secretary-treasurer of the national AFL and in 1952 became its president; the cigar-chomping, gruff-voiced Meany steadfastly fought for basic issues—better pay and working conditions, the right to unionize, limits on corporate profits in any wage-price plan—and also did battle against graft and corruption within the various unions; withstanding the challenges of other labour dons, the stubborn Meany refused to be dislodged from power and since 1955 served as spokesman for most of the ranks of the AFL-CIO, which contained 111 unions and at its height as many as 17 million members; in recent years his power somewhat diminished as membership fell back to 13.6 million, and in November 1979 ill health caused him to step down from his long stewardship of the American labour movement; Jan. 10, Washington, D.C., age 85.

Lewis Milestone, leading Hollywood director of the 1930s and 1940s who earned Oscars for his direction of *Two Arabian Knights* (1927) and *All Quiet on the Western Front* (1930); later credits included *The Captain Hates the Sea, Anything Goes,* and *The Red Pony;* Sept. 25, Los Angeles, age 84.

Henry Miller, U.S. writer who gained notoriety for his book *Tropic of Cancer,* a sexually explicit and somewhat jaundiced view of life in Paris published in France in 1934; attempts to publish his work in the U.S. were successful only in 1964 after a Supreme Court decision declared *Tropic of Cancer* not obscene; his further works *Tropic of Capricorn, The Rosy Crucifixion* trilogy, *The Colossus of Maroussi, The Air-Conditioned Nightmare,* and *Sunday After the War* were less controversial but still unorthodox, as befitted the aging of a Bohemian writer; June 7, Pacific Palisades, Calif., age 90.

Mohammad Reza Pahlavi, deposed shah of Iran, who until he was pushed from power in 1979 by a socioreligious revolution wielded absolute power over his nation, forging its disparate elements into a powerful state with oil revenues as high as $20 billion a year; acceding to the throne in 1941, he brought Iran to a position of eminence in the Middle East and did much to modernize the country, but his tyrannical handling of dissension and his alienation of the powerful Muslim religious leaders led to his downfall; forced into exile in 1979, he ultimately took up residence in Egypt; July 27, Cairo, age 60.

A. S. Mike Monroney, former Democratic representative and senator from Oklahoma who served 30 years in Congress (1939–68) and co-sponsored the Legislative Reorganization Act of 1946, the only major congressional reform in 50 years; Feb. 13, Rockville, Md., age 77.

Sir Oswald Mosley, leader of the British fascist movement during World War II, a pro-Hitler anti-Semite who led a private army of fascists in attacks on Jews in London in the 1930s; with his wife, the former Diana Mitford, he was held in detention during the war; Dec. 3, Orsay, France, age 84.

Louis Muñoz Marín, first elected governor of Puerto Rico (1948–64) who created and implemented Operation Bootstrap, the program that elevated much of the island from the

HENRY MILLER

MOHAMMAD REZA PAHLAVI

MASAYOSHI OHIRA

CULVER PICTURES
JESSE OWENS

PICTORIAL PARADE
JEAN PIAGET

UPI
"COLONEL" HARLAND SANDERS

level of extreme poverty; he was also instrumental in securing commonwealth status for Puerto Rico; April 30, San Juan, P.R., age 82.

A(rthur) C(harles) Nielsen, founder of the A. C. Nielsen Co., a market-research corporation whose television rating system, begun in 1950, became a primary force in network programming; June 1, Chicago, age 82.

John Jacob Niles, U.S. folksinger and folklorist, who collected American folk music and performed it for international audiences and helped keep interest in folk music alive; March 1, Lexington, Ky., age 87.

Masayoshi Ohira, prime minister of Japan, 1978–80, leader of the Liberal-Democratic Party, which has controlled Japanese politics since 1955; active in national politics since his election to the House of Representatives in 1952, Ohira served as foreign secretary and foreign minister and figured prominently in Japan's rapprochement with China; though scandals broke around him, Ohira remained untouched, wielding ever increasing power in his party's factional politics; June 12, Tokyo, age 70.

Jesse Owens, four-time gold medalist in track at the 1936 Berlin Olympics, where he and other black athletes symbolized the repudiation of Hitler's Aryan ideal; March 31, Tucson, Ariz., age 66.

Jean Piaget, Swiss psychologist whose pioneering work on the development of intelligence and understanding in children influenced generations of educators and child psychologists; his writings included *The Language and Thought of the Child* (1926), *Judgment and Reasoning in the Child* (1928), *The Child's Conception of the World* (1929), and *The Construction of Reality in the Child* (1954); Sept. 16, Geneva, age 84.

Katherine Anne Porter, U.S. novelist and short story writer whose *Collected Stories* won both the Pulitzer Prize and National Book Award for fiction in 1966; her writings included such masterpieces of the art as "Old Mortality," and "Flowering Judas" and the novel *Ship of Fools* (1962); Sept. 18, Silver Spring, Md., age 90.

George Raft, U.S. actor who appeared in more than 60 movies, best known for his personification of the suave, tough gangster in 1930s crime pictures such as *Scarface* and *Each Dawn I Die;* Nov. 24, Hollywood, Calif., age 85.

Stanley Forman Reed, justice of the U.S. Supreme Court 1938–57; appointed by Franklin D. Roosevelt, he wrote more than 300 opinions for the court and was considered a moderate and a defender of civil rights; April 3, Huntington, N.Y., age 95.

Duncan Renaldo, Romanian-born U.S. actor best known for his portrayal of the Cisco Kid in seven feature films and the popular 1950s television series; Sept. 3, Santa Barbara, Calif., age 76.

J(oseph) B(anks) Rhine, U.S. psychologist whose investigations into paranormal powers, beginning with his book *Extra Sensory Perception* (1934), led to the flowering of the field of parapsychology; Feb. 20, Hillsborough, N.Y., age 84.

Oscar Arnulfo Romero y Galdames, archbishop of El Salvador since 1977; assassinated while saying mass in San Salvador, the prelate was an outspoken advocate of human rights, denouncing the violence of the extremists of both left and right, and had been nominated for the Nobel Peace Prize; March 24, San Salvador, age 62.

Lillian Roth, actress and singer who entered show business at age 6, appearing in vaudeville, in night clubs, on Broadway, and in the movies; her victory over mental illness and alcohol was described in her best-selling autobiography, *I'll Cry Tomorrow* (1954); May 12, New York City, age 69.

Muriel Rukeyser, U.S. poet whose writings reflected both her dramatic and lyric sensibilities and her lifelong concern with political and social issues; the recipient of many honours and awards, she was widely praised on the issuing of her *Collected Poems of Muriel Rukeyser* in 1978; Feb. 12, New York City, age 66.

Francisco Sá Carneiro, premier of Portugal from 1979, leader of the Social Democratic Party and the Democratic Alliance and a powerful force in Portuguese politics; Dec. 4, near Lisbon, age 46.

"Colonel" Harland Sanders, U.S. businessman who at age

66 founded the Kentucky Fried Chicken franchise business, which by 1963 had 600 outlets. He sold the controlling interest in 1964 but remained associated with the business, his white hair and beard and string ties and white suits making him a readily recognizable symbol of southern cooking; Dec. 16, Shelbyville, Ky., age 90.

Jean-Paul Sartre, French philosopher and author, founder of Existentialism, one of the most influential thinkers of the mid-20th century; with *L'Etre et le néant* (1943; *Being and Nothingness,* 1956) he began to outline his theories of man's existence, which locate him in a godless universe that he must order and harmonize through a series of choices guided by his own instincts and intellect; his literary output was vast, including essays, plays, novels, screenplays, and autobiography; in later years his acute social conscience turned to the radical left, but his last interviews indicated a synthesis and rebirth of hope in progress and community; April 15, Paris, age 74.

Dore Schary, U.S. film producer who produced or supervised the production of more than 300 movies including *An American in Paris, The Blackboard Jungle, Lassie Come Home, Boys Town,* (for which he won an Oscar for his screenplay), and *Bad Day at Black Rock* and several Broadway plays; a human rights activist, he was a leader of the Anti-Defamation League and was New York's first commissioner of cultural affairs; July 7, New York City, age 74.

Peter Sellers, versatile British actor whose uncanny ability to find the telling details of the characters he portrayed made him a most effective and respected member of his profession; although best known for his comedy roles, including the inept Inspector Clouseau, his dramatic skills were considerable, from *Dr. Strangelove* to *Lolita* and *Being There;* July 24, London, age 54.

Jay Silverheels, U.S. actor, a Mohawk Indian best known for his portrayal of Tonto in the "Lone Ranger" television series; March 5, Woodland Hills, Calif., age 62.

Conn Smythe, businessman and sports promoter who in 1928 transformed the lacklustre Toronto St. Pats into the Toronto Maple Leafs, a highly successful team that won seven Stanley Cup championships; after his retirement from ice hockey (he was inducted into the Hall of Fame in 1958), he turned his attention to horse racing, building up a champion stable whose horses won 147 stakes races; Nov. 18, Caledon, Ont., age 85.

Snow, C(harles) P(ercy) Snow, BARON, British scientist, novelist, civil servant, member of Parliament, businessman, lecturer, and critic; he was best known for his 11-novel sequence, *Strangers and Brothers,* which examined and reflected conditions at the executive level in British business and government, and his essay "The Two Cultures," lamenting the dichotomy between the scientific and literary milieus; he was made a life peer in 1964, when he was appointed undersecretary at the Ministry of Technology; July 1, London, age 74.

Gen. Anastasio Somoza Debayle, Nicaraguan politician, member of the family that controlled the government of Nicaragua since the 1930s; like his father before him he consolidated power through the National Guard, ruling through surrogates until his election in 1967; ousted in the Sandinista revolution brought on by the increasing corruption and repression of his regime, he was exiled to Paraguay in 1979; Sept. 17, Asunción, Paraguay, age 54.

William H. Stein, U.S. biochemist who shared the 1972 Nobel Prize for chemistry for his work on the chemical structure of a pancreatic enzyme, ribonuclease; Feb. 2, New York City, age 68.

Donald Ogden Stewart, U.S. playwright and screenwriter who won an Oscar for his screenplay for *The Philadelphia Story;* other works included *Holiday, The Prisoner of Zenda, The Barretts of Wimpole Street,* and *Life with Father;* Aug. 2, London, age 85.

Clyfford Still, U.S. Abstract Expressionist painter of huge canvases in "jagged, flame-like forms," his style arising from deeply held convictions about the nature of art and its function as an expression of human aspirations; June 23, Baltimore, Md., age 75.

PICTORIAL PARADE
JEAN-PAUL SARTRE

CAMERA PRESS, LONDON
PETER SELLERS

UPI
C(HARLES) P(ERCY) SNOW

CAMERA PRESS, LONDON
MARSHAL TITO

A.G.I.P./PICTORIAL PARADE
WILLIAM TOLBERT

UPI
MAE WEST

Milburn Stone, U.S. actor best known for his portrayal of crusty-but-lovable Doc Adams in the television series "Gunsmoke"; June 12, La Jolla, Calif., age 75.

Willie Sutton (William Francis Sutton), bank robber who captured the public imagination by his single-minded devotion to his "craft," his story being told in two autobiographies, *Where the Money Was* (1976) and *I, Willie Sutton* (1953); though he claimed to have garnered $2 million from bank robberies, he spent most of his life in jail; Nov. 2, Spring Hill, Fla., age 79.

Edwin Way Teale, U.S. naturalist and author, winner of the John Burroughs Medal for distinguished nature writing; his history of the four seasons in America—*North with the Spring* (1951), *Journey into Summer* (1960), *Autumn Across America* (1956), and *Wandering Through Winter* (1956)—brought him a wide and appreciative audience; his closely observed and poetically described accounts of natural life reflected a wide knowledge; Oct. 18, Norwich, Conn., age 81.

Tito (Josip Broz), Yugoslav statesman who ruled his country from 1943, becoming its first elected president in 1953; although head of a Communist state, he declared his independence from Soviet control at the outset, consolidating his influence over nearly 40 years of his primacy; he was instrumental in organizing the nonaligned movement in 1961 and remained one of its most influential members; his strong will and charismatic personality enabled him to prevail over the factionalism in his country and pursue his own course; May 4, Ljubljana, Yugos., age 87.

William R. Tolbert, Jr., president of Liberia, 1971–80; assuming the office after having served for 20 years as vice-president, he introduced a number of reforms, but he had inherited a severely inequitable economy and paternalistic and autocratic political system; his repression of dissent led to the coup that took his life; April 12, Monrovia, Liberia, age 66.

Willard R. Trask, U.S. translator, of prodigious learning and output, winner of the National Book Award for his translation of Casanova's autobiography; ranging from the ancient to the modern, from major languages to localized dialects and archaic forms in fiction, poetry, and song, he was an acknowledged giant in his field; Aug. 10, New York City, age 80.

Kenneth Tynan, British drama critic, instrumental in broadening the horizons of British theatre to admit the "angry young men" and other experimental, nontraditional writers; his elegant, acerbic commentaries reflected his deep involvement with the theatrical, and his opinions carried great weight; he wrote for the *Observer* and the *New Yorker* and from 1963 to 1976 was the literary manager of the National Theatre of London; July 26, Santa Monica, Calif., age 53.

John Hasbrouck Van Vleck, U.S. physicist who won the 1977 Nobel Prize for his work on the magnetic properties of solids; Oct. 27, Cambridge, Mass., age 81.

Raoul Walsh, U.S. actor and motion picture director who learned his craft under D. W. Griffith; the more than 100 films he directed included *What Price Glory?*, *Sadie Thompson*, and *The Thief of Bagdad* (all silents) and *High Sierra*, *They Died with Their Boots On*, *White Heat*, *Gentleman Jim*, and *The Naked and the Dead;* Dec. 31, Hollywood, Calif., age 88.

Mae West, stage and movie star whose husky-voiced portrayal of sultry ladies and fallen angels became a part of Hollywood's iconography; best known for films such as *She Done Him Wrong*, *Diamond Lil*, *I'm No Angel*, and *My Little Chickadee*, she was lascivious but good-humoured and in time became something of a parody of her early roles; Nov. 22, Los Angeles, age 87.

Wilhelmina (Behmenburg Cooper), Dutch-born high-fashion model who was one of the best known faces of the 1960s; retiring from modeling in 1967, she opened her own successful modeling agency; during her career as a model she appeared on the covers of 300 magazines, including 28 issues of *Vogue;* March 1, Greenwich, Conn., age 40.

Gen. Agha Mohammad Yahya Khan, former military ruler of Pakistan (1969–71) whose ineffectual handling of the Bengali separatist movement resulted in the disastrous 1971 war with India over Bangladesh and his resignation as the country's third president; Aug. 9, Rawalpindi, Pak., age 63.

French Pres. Valéry Giscard d'Estaing was greeted by an honour guard when he visited Bahrain in March.
KEYSTONE

PERSIAN GULF STATES

Bahrain

Sectarian unrest among the Shi'ah Muslims, who comprise half of Bahrain's native population, continued in 1980 but on a lesser scale than in 1979. The government followed a policy of allowing orderly religious demonstrations but acted to break up disturbances that threatened the peace.

Arab Gulf governments showed support for Bahrain. Kuwait and Saudi Arabia announced participation in a $400 million joint petrochemicals project; Iraq joined a $300 million iron-pelletization project; Abu Dhabi provided funds for power and water projects; and, most important, the government of Saudi Arabia reaffirmed its commitment to a $1 billion road bridge between Bahrain and the mainland.

In continuation of Bahrain's policy of offering the island as a service centre for the Gulf, banks from Japan, the Philippines, and France were permitted to open offshore banking units (OBU's) or representative offices, bringing the total number of OBU's to 58 by July.

Oman

Oman, guardian of the Strait of Hormuz, maintained strict neutrality in the 1980 Iraq-Iran war but was prepared to open its military bases to the West in any general conflagration. A defense pact, with economic aid, was agreed upon with the United States in June.

Sultan Qabus ibn Sa'id's limited support for Egyptian Pres. Anwar El-Sadat's bilateral peace with Israel waned in view of the lack of progress on Palestinian autonomy. Oman's isolation from the rest of the Arab community was less pronounced than in 1979. The Popular Front for the Liberation of Oman, which fought a guerrilla war in the south during the early 1970s, remained an external force supported, among Arab countries, only by Yemen (Aden).

Qatar

Qatar's revenue, $3.8 billion in 1979, was likely to increase substantially in 1980 because of a $2-per-barrel increase in the price of its crude oil that became effective at midyear. The limited capacity of the country to absorb this income led to capital flight abroad, but firm commitments were made to increase investment in domestic industry. Because of a government conservation program, crude oil production in 1980 was expected to be lower than the 506,000 bbl a day achieved in 1979.

With a sizable minority (about 20%) of citizens of Iranian extraction, the government faced the problem of containing religious opposition sympathetic to the revolutionary regime in Iran. The authorities also felt required to act against the large number of illegal immigrants of Asian origin by passing tough sponsorship regulations to eliminate the surplus of floating labour.

United Arab Emirates

Political unity in the Arab world's only working federation came under pressure in 1980, but progress was made. The most powerful emirate governments, those of Abu Dhabi and Dubai, agreed to establish a Central Bank into which a proportion of oil revenues would be paid. Other expressions of greater unity were the amalgamation of government departments in Ras al-Khaimah, the last emirate to join the union (1972), into the federal government and the decision by Abu Dhabi to guarantee a borrowing by Sharjah from international banks.

Social unrest among students was expressed in demonstrations over gasoline prices in February, and there was unease concerning the high proportion of Asian immigrants in the population.

273

On July 28 Fernando Belaúnde Terry (wearing sash), president of Peru, delivered his acceptance speech to Congress in Lima before gathered heads of state from Spain and Latin America.
WIDE WORLD

PERU

Fifteen political groupings contested the presidential and congressional elections of May 18, 1980, to elect the first civilian government to hold office in Peru since 1968. The elections were the first to enfranchise illiterates (13% of voters) and the first to give the vote to those between 18 and 20 years old; 63% of the electorate of 6.4 million were voting for the first time. The two front-running contestants in the presidential election were Armando Villanueva Del Campo of the Alianza Popular Revolucionaria Americana (APRA) and ex-president Fernando Belaúnde Terry of Acción Popular (AP). Although opinion polls predicted it would be a close battle, Belaúnde Terry won easily, with 45.4% of valid votes, a healthy surplus over the 36% required for a candidate to be declared president. On June 18 he appointed a financier, Manuel Ulloa Elías, as prime minister.

On July 28 Belaúnde Terry took office as president of Peru, at the head of the coalition. One of his first acts was to hand back to their former owners the seven Lima daily newspapers confiscated by the military government. Preparations began for the resumption of work on the construction of the Marginal Highway in the jungle, begun during President Belaúnde's first term (1963–68). Road works were a major election promise made by Belaúnde as part of his declared intention to create full employment and increase investment. Other proposals in his economic program included raising agricultural production, developing the jungle region, reducing state participation in the economy and increasing private investment, reducing subsidies and taxes, refinancing part of the external public debt, and seeking long-term loans for financing priority development projects.

Despite the president's initiatives to review labour legislation and reduce inequalities in the distribution of income, together with a quarterly adjustment of wages and salaries in line with inflation (expected to be 55–60% in 1980), labour disputes gathered momentum. Increases in electricity rates, gasoline prices, and bus fares triggered unrest, and in the first half of September there were 30 strikes in progress. In the first municipal elections in 14 years, held in November, the AP appeared to lose some ground to the left.

The Peruvian economy, on the other hand, showed signs of continuing the upward trend begun in 1978 and 1979. The buoyancy of the export sector, an increase in construction and manufacturing activity, and higher tax collections helped the gross domestic product to show an annual growth rate of 3.7% by midyear, and there was a possibility that the official target of a 5% growth rate for 1980 would be achieved. At the end of June there was an overall balance of payments surplus of $516 million. A government decision in September to cut the maximum level of duties on imported goods from 115 to 60% was expected to increase imports.

PETS

In 1979 the three major television networks declared the pet food industry a major advertiser, placing it on par with the automobile industry, soft drinks, and home laundry supplies. Pet food had become a multibillion-dollar industry. Its growth continued in 1980.

The growth of the pet food and pet supply industry did not necessarily signal an enormous growth in the number of pets kept in the United States, but rather that people were taking better care of their pets, maintaining them in a more systematic manner. That trend was likely to continue as pet owning became more restricted by the complexity of community problems. Pet owning was becoming a less casual affair.

Research continued in a number of institutions in 1980 to determine the effects of pet owning. It was determined statistically that people with pets generally live longer than people without pets, that they get ill less often, and that when they do get ill they recover more rapidly. This effect was even more pronounced among people who live outside a family circle.

One important example of this research was published by the University of Pennsylvania in Philadelphia. A group of men and women, each of whom had had one heart attack, was divided into two subgroups. Fifty-three people were chosen who either had pets or would accept one. Thirty-nine non-pet-owning people with the same general medical history were selected as the control group. A time period was established and the two groups observed. Three of the 53 people with pets died of a second heart attack in that time period, while 11 of the non-pet group died. The ratio of 3/53 and 11/39 was too marked to be disregarded, and further research was planned.

In Maryland research was done on high blood pressure. Patients with severe hypertension were placed in rooms with remote-reading blood pressure cuffs attached to their legs. Researchers watched from behind one-way windows as technicians entered the patients' rooms and placed a cat or dog in their laps. As they petted the animals, researchers could watch the readout display of their blood pressure drop.

In Lima, Ohio, in a state institution housing the criminally insane, select wards were designated pet wards. Eighty-five percent of the patients had attempted suicide one or more times. 1980 marked the completion of the sixth year without a single suicide attempt among patients allowed to keep pets.

In the pet world itself the changes appeared to be for the better. The trend toward very large dogs seemed to abate somewhat. The cocker spaniel moved up in popularity to become the third most popular dog by American Kennel Club registration. That moved the German shepherd down yet another notch. In 1978 it had surrendered the number two spot to the doberman pinscher. Poodles remained in first place.

Municipal animal shelters reported a slight drop in the number of abandoned and feral animals they had to deal with. Further study was needed to see if this was a temporary fluctuation or whether the number of these unwanted animals really was decreasing.

Parvovirus Outbreak

The big news in the world of dogs in 1980 traces back to 1977, when a new virus appeared but did not cause a great deal of concern. Then, in 1978, in the area surrounding Louisville, Ky., it exploded into epidemic proportions. It was a true epizootic, and the disease was named parvovirus.

The parvovirus was thought to be a mutation of a cat virus that somehow made the jump from felines to canines. The disease appeared to be closely related to feline distemper or panleucopenia. Feline panleucopenia vaccine works very well in preventing parvovirus infection in dogs, but the federal

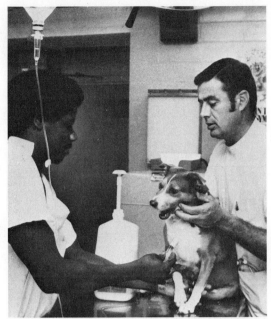

BERNARD GOTFRYD – NEWSWEEK

An outbreak of parvovirus disease took the lives of thousands of dogs in several areas of the U.S. in 1980; a vaccine was available at midyear and helped to halt the outbreak.

Food and Drug Administration (FDA) refused to license the feline vaccine for use in dogs. Veterinarians in many areas were afraid to use the feline vaccine, since as it was unlicensed for use in dogs it could leave them open to lawsuits. The FDA refused to budge on the issue, and a canine vaccine was not licensed until 1980. It remained in very short supply, however, and by midsummer 1980 so many thousands of dogs were dying of the disease that most veterinarians ignored the FDA stand and began using the feline vaccine with good results. By then veterinarians had a better understanding of the disease itself and were able to save 80% of dogs diagnosed early.

PHILIPPINES

A wave of terrorist bombings began in Manila on Aug. 22, 1980, as a challenge to continued martial-law rule by Pres. Ferdinand E. Marcos. Responsibility was claimed by the previously unknown April 6 Liberation Movement, named for demonstrations against Marcos that had taken place on that date in 1978.

Within two months more than 30 bombs had been set off. A U.S. woman tourist was killed by one on September 12, and more than 60 persons were injured. Marcos was attending a conference of the American Society of Travel Agents in Manila when a bomb went off there on October 19. Marcos was not hurt, but more than 20 persons were injured. After an intensive hunt for those responsible, the government announced that 15 persons had

In August former senator Gerardo Roxas (left), president of the opposition Liberal Party, and José Laurel, Jr., chairman of the Ad Hoc Committee of the Nationalista Party of the Philippines, announced the formation of a new movement to try to achieve a peaceful solution to the country's internal problems.
UPI

been arrested and had admitted guilt. In November more than 60 people were charged in connection with 25 bombings.

A group of 72 persons, including leaders of the government before Marcos assumed power in 1972, issued on August 29 a "Covenant for Freedom." It called for an immediate end to what it termed the dictatorship of Marcos, an end to martial law, the holding of free elections, and other changes. Some Filipinos at home and in exile abroad warned, however, that these old politicians lacked the appeal to lead opposition to Marcos, and the bombings showed that new, more desperate forms of opposition were developing.

The New Society Movement headed by Marcos won the first nationwide series of local elections since 1972, held on Jan. 30, 1980. His son, Ferdinand, Jr., a 22-year-old student in the United States, was elected vice-governor of the family's home province, Ilocos Norte.

The best known opposition leader, former senator Benigno S. Aquino, Jr., was allowed to leave prison on May 8 for a heart operation in Dallas, Texas. Aquino had been under a death sentence. In leaving, he promised to "desist from commenting on our domestic political situation or engage or participate in any partisan political activity" while in the U.S. But, beginning with an August 4 speech in New York City, he started speaking out in opposition to the Marcos regime.

Aquino later met in Syria with Chairman Nur Misuari of the Moro National Liberation Front to seek a negotiated end to the Muslim separatist conflict in the southern islands. However, sporadic violence in that region continued, and so did widely scattered violence from the Maoist New People's Army, which the government said was gaining strength.

Despite these problems the Philippines' economy continued to grow at a rate estimated between 4 and 5.8% for 1980. Inflation was cut from 24% in February to 13.8% in September, according to gov-

ernment statistics. Some businesses experienced hard times, however, and the government launched a program to help them and those workers who had lost their jobs. One measure was to set up 12 new export processing zones where Filipino workers could produce goods for export free of taxes. These would compete with similar arrangements in other Southeast Asian countries. As part of this industrial policy the government expanded development of energy resources, including geothermal, hydroelectric, and nuclear, in order to reduce dependence on imported oil. Foreign investment continued to come into the country for energy development as well as other enterprises, showing confidence in economic prospects.

PHOTOGRAPHY

After more than a decade of vigorous growth as an image-making technology, a commercial enterprise, and a cultural force, photography in 1980 showed signs of leveling off, temporarily at least. It was a year of consolidation rather than innovation and of the fruition of numerous trends more than the setting of new directions. In the early months of the year the soaring cost of silver was a sharp reminder that a basic natural resource of the medium was finite. Among books, exhibitions, and auction sales, retrospective and rediscovered work drew more notice than did new talent.

Photo Equipment

In recent years designers and manufacturers of single-lens-reflex (SLR) 35-mm cameras had spent their main effort in developing highly automated models in the medium-to-low price range. In 1980, however, three firms introduced top-of-the-line, professional-quality cameras that attracted much attention.

Nikon's F3 embodied an attempt to combine heavy-duty construction with sophisticated state-of-the-art exposure automation. Somewhat lighter and smaller than previous models of the Nikon F series, it was an aperture-priority camera (user selects the aperture; shutter speed is chosen automatically) with stepless shutter speeds from 8 to 1/2000 sec, a liquid crystal display (LCD) exposure-information readout in the viewfinder, and a behind-the-mirror metering system. A silicon photodiode measured light that passed through thousands of microscopic holes in the reflex mirror and then was reflected downward by a secondary mirror. In the event of battery failure a backup mechanical release lever allowed mechanical shutter operation at 1/60 sec.

Nearly ten years in developing, the Pentax LX included a wide range of accessories that formed a versatile system with many professional, industrial, medical, and scientific applications. Extremely compact, the LX was an aperture-priority, automatic-exposure design using a silicon photocell recessed in the floor of the mirror chamber. The central portion of the reflex mirror was a semitransparent beam splitter that permitted about 15% of the light to pass through to a secondary mirror, which in turn reflected it to the photocell for measuring. Shutter speeds from a full 125 sec to 1/2000 sec were provided in the automatic mode and from 1/75 sec (its synchronization speed for electronic flash) to 1/2000 sec mechanically in the event of battery failure.

The Leica R4-MOT supplied multimode exposure automation (a choice of aperture-priority, shutter-priority, programmed, and full manual modes) plus both "spot" and averaging metering, a feature adapted from its predecessor, the Leica R3. As with the F3 and LX, the Leica R4 also used a secondary mirror behind the main reflex mirror to reflect a portion of the light downward to a photocell on the mirror chamber floor.

As the sale of 110 pocket cameras leveled off or declined, there was rekindled interest in compact 35-mm rangefinder and autofocus cameras. Many new models, from single point-and-shoot designs to more expensive, sophisticated equipment, were introduced in 1980. In many cases only slightly larger than a conventional 110, they all offered the advantage of full-frame 35-mm format and a wide choice of 35-mm colour and black-and-white films. A built-in electronic flash was a commonplace feature, and many designers devised ways to shield the lens with an integral protective cover when the camera was not in use.

Autofocusing technology made some advances during the year. Canon introduced a new system called SST (for solid-state triangulation), the first autofocusing system in a production camera to use a CCD (charge-coupled device) for sensing light. A passive system, it employed two stationary mirrors to place a "standard" image and "reference" image of the subject on an array of 240 sensors. An integrated circuit linked with the array sought the best match between the two images—the point of sharpest focus—and drove a motorized lens-focusing system until that point was achieved. The SST system was first used in Canon's AF 514XL-S super-eight sound movie camera and later shown at the 1980 Photokina exhibition in a prototype autofocus f/4 35–70-mm zoom lens for 35-mm SLR cameras. Also shown in prototype at Photokina was a Ricoh autofocus lens in a K mount. Meanwhile, Honeywell, whose Visitronic module was being used in many current autofocusing compact 35-mm cameras, was developing a new CCD module that was expected to be incorporated in production cameras in the near future.

Although there were no outstanding breakthroughs in lens technology in 1980, the number and variety of lenses for SLR cameras proliferated as camera manufacturers expanded their lines and an increasing number of independent lens makers flooded the market. Manufacturers vied in producing lighter, more compact lenses at lower cost, with the emphasis on zooms that often included a close-up "macro" capacity.

Demonstrated in prototype was a Nimslo 3-D camera that used conventional 35-mm colour print film. It had four lenses that recorded simultaneously. A computerized Nimslo printer integrated the images.

Cultural Trends

Despite a recession and pessimistic predictions, the boom in photographic prints as collectible art

Early photographs fetched high prices at 1980 art sales: this self-portrait by Albert Sands Southworth, c. 1848, was sold for $36,000, a record price.
CHRISTIE'S, NEW YORK

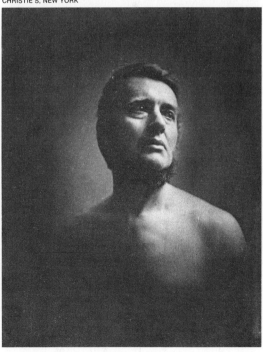

Jean-Pierre Laffont's photograph of Egyptian children in a pottery factory was part of his award-winning study of child labour and child slavery worldwide.

JEAN-PIERRE LAFFONT—SYGMA

objects did not go bust. Landscape photographer Ansel Adams's photograph of "Moonrise, Hernandez, New Mexico," a bellwether among contemporary works, sold in a rare oversize print for $46,000. Signed prints by a growing number of living photographers were commanding $500 prices and higher. The number of serious collectors continued to grow.

As in 1979, many of the outstanding photographic books of the year represented the work of established or nearly forgotten photographers. Of special note was *Photographs for the Tsar*, a collection of colour images made between 1909 and 1914 by Sergey Mikhailovich Prokudin-Gorskii. A pioneer colour photographer, he was commissioned by Nicholas II to document the Romanov empire. Purchased by the Library of Congress in 1948, the remarkable black-and-white colour separation prints and negatives lay almost forgotten in the archives until recently rediscovered and reproduced in full colour. Other outstanding photographic books of the year included *Lisette Model: An Aperture Monograph; Artists: Portraits from Four Decades*, by Arnold Newman; and *Flowers*, by Irving Penn.

For the first time in history the Pulitzer Prize for spot news photography went to an anonymous photographer, for a photograph of the execution of Kurdish rebels in Iran. The Pulitzer for feature photography went to Erwin H. Hagler of the *Dallas Times Herald* for a colour essay on the American cowboy. The University of Missouri School of Journalism and the National Press Photographers Association presented their annual Pictures of the Year awards. Honours for Magazine Photographer of the Year went to David Burnett of Contact Press Images, who also won the top award from the World Press Photo competition. Newspaper Photographer of the Year was Bill Wax of the *Gainesville* (Fla.) *Sun*. Among others also honoured was Jean-Pierre Laffont of Sygma for his "Child Slavery Through the World," a powerful self-assigned documentary essay.

PHYSICS

The year 1980 marked the 49th birthday of the concept of the neutrino. This elementary particle was predicted in 1931 by Austrian physicist Wolfgang Pauli, who described it as a particle with zero rest mass, zero electric charge, and therefore a very weak interaction with matter. The neutrino was necessary to explain the phenomenon of beta decay, in which a neutron in an unstable nucleus transforms into a proton by spontaneously emitting an electron. The electron must be accompanied by a neutrino for momentum and energy to be conserved. Twenty-five years later the neutrino was experimentally observed by U.S. physicists Clyde L. Cowan, Jr., and Frederick Reines in a reaction in which a neutrino is absorbed by a proton to give a neutron plus a positive electron (positron).

Despite 24 years of further investigation the neutrino was still providing physicists with many enigmas, some of which could well have a bearing on the future of the universe. By 1980 it had become generally accepted that there is more than one species of neutrino, but there was some controversy as

 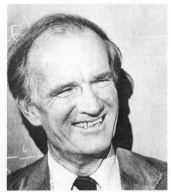

James Cronin (right) of the University of Chicago and Val Fitch (far right) of Princeton University shared the 1980 Nobel Prize for Physics.

(RIGHT) FRANK MCMAHON; (FAR RIGHT) UPI

to exactly how many. In addition, it was not yet clear whether each species always maintains its separate identity or whether they all actually oscillate continuously between identities. The final quandary concerned the mass itself; physicists were not sure whether the rest mass is absolutely zero as originally thought or whether it is small but finite. From estimates based on theories about the origin of the universe, there are possibly a billion relic neutrinos for every proton and neutron in existence; hence, even a small mass for the neutrino would lead to its dominance of the mass of the universe.

Six members (plus their corresponding antiparticles) of a family of light particles called leptons were known as of 1980. One subgroup comprises the electron, the muon, and the more recently discovered tau. In addition, there is thought to be a second group of three leptons, the neutrinos, each of which is associated with one of the first group. The electron neutrino and the muon neutrino have been experimentally observed, but the tau neutrino has avoided detection to date. The possibility that neutrinos can change identities is an intriguing one and could go a long way toward explaining some scientific puzzles. For example, why is the measured flux of electron neutrinos that emanate from nuclear reactions in the Sun only one-third of the value calculated by standard theory? If these neutrinos were free to oscillate between identities, then their chances of being counted by a detector on Earth sensitive only to electron neutrinos would be less than expected.

During the year experimental proof of this possibility was sought using nuclear reactor cores as neutrino sources. One approach was to study the ratio of the products of two kinds of reactions that result when reactor-produced neutrinos, known initially to be pure electron antineutrinos, interact with the nucleus of deuterium (hydrogen-2). The value of this ratio depends on whether all of the interacting neutrinos have retained their original identity or whether some have interacted while wearing a new guise. This experiment, carried out by Reines and co-workers at the Savannah River reactor in South Carolina, produced evidence in favour of neutrino oscillations. Another group, working with the reactor at the Institut Laue-Langevin, Grenoble, France, but using a different approach, came to the opposite conclusion. The two groups were planning more definitive experiments in which neutrino-induced reactions would be studied at a fixed energy but at two or more distances from the reactor core. Different neutrino flight paths would result in different electron neutrino intensities if neutrino oscillations occur.

The mass of the neutrino was under study by teams of scientists at the Institute of Theoretical and Experimental Physics in Moscow and at the University of Guelph in Ontario. The Soviet team was 99% confident that the mass lies between 14 and 46 electron volts (eV). Although the Canadian work was at an early stage, it set an upper limit of 70 eV for the neutrino mass. These values should be compared with a mass of 500,000 eV for the electron, itself a very light object.

It is generally believed that the universe started with a "big bang" and has been expanding ever since. The number of neutrinos that were created in this primordial event is "fantastiquement grand," to quote a French scientist. On the assumption that neutrinos are massless, many cosmological experts estimate that not enough mass exists in the universe to allow gravitational attraction to bring an eventual halt to the expansion. However, if neutrinos have even the feeble mass measured by the Soviets, universal expansion may well be arrested in the distant future and followed by a phase of contraction.

From its beginnings as the unobservable particle predicted by Pauli, the neutrino has become a key feature of astrophysics, cosmology, and theoretical physics, as well as of high-energy physics, in which beams of neutrinos are irreplaceable instruments in their own right. Many theoretical physicists would be delighted if in 50 years' time two other elusive particles, the quark and the gluon, become as solidly established as the neutrino. In the early 1980s the quark, the postulated basic constituent of much of matter, and the gluon, the particle that binds quarks together, were both being sought with the same determination that had accompanied the neutrino hunts several decades earlier.

(*See also* Nobel Prizes.)

"See, it's quite safe, and very therapeutic."

POLAND

The year 1980 began tensely, with the Polish people facing food shortages, rationing of electric power, unsatisfactory public transport, and insufficient housing. At the eighth congress of the Polish United Workers' (Communist) Party (PUWP), held in Warsaw February 11–15, First Secretary Edward Gierek warned that the country faced higher energy and raw material prices and difficult international trading conditions. Real wages over the next five years should not, therefore, rise more than 9–11% and would have to be linked to higher productivity.

The delegates elected the new Central Committee, which in turn elected the new Politburo of 14 members. The premier, Piotr Jaroszewicz, was dropped from the Politburo, and on Febuary 18 the Sejm (parliament) elected Edward Babiuch as the new premier. On March 23 general elections produced the new Sejm, which reelected Henryk Jablonski chairman of the Council of State.

Local strikes of industrial workers started early in the year, becoming more frequent in July when Babiuch increased meat prices. Gierek sought guidance from Soviet leader Leonid Brezhnev, who advised him to reach a compromise with the strikers. On August 14 the entire work force of 17,000 stopped production at Gdansk's Lenin shipyard.

On August 18 Gierek announced his readiness to accept sensible demands formulated by "honest" strikers. Discovering that Babiuch was planning to "promote" him to the presidency of the Council of State and assume the party leadership, Gierek on August 24 convoked the Central Committee, which expelled Babiuch and three of his supporters from the Politburo. Josef Pinkowski was nominated a full member of the Politburo and recommended to succeed Babiuch as head of government. The way was now open to negotiate with the Interfactory Strike Committee (IFSC) formed in Gdansk by Lech Walesa. This organization's demands included the workers' right to organize themselves in free trade unions. On August 31 Mieczyslaw Jagielski, first deputy premier, signed an agreement with Walesa stating that the new self-governing trade unions would "adhere to the principles defined in the Constitution of the People's Republic of Poland" and that they recognized "the leading role of the PUWP in the state." All the strikers' major demands were granted.

On September 1 the Kremlin sounded its disapproval of the historic compromise between the PUWP and Solidarnosc (Solidarity), as the IFSC now renamed itself. At a Central Committee meeting on September 5, Stanislaw Kania revealed that Gierek had been hospitalized after a serious heart attack. The next day Kania was elected party first secretary in his place, and the Central Committee again revamped the Politburo. The Central Committee convoked an extraordinary party congress on October 5, and the Sejm reshuffled the Council of State.

On October 24 the Warsaw District Court registered Solidarity as a legal organization. However, Walesa protested the insertion into the organization's charter of a clause stating that the union recognized the leading role of the PUWP. On October 30 Kania and Pinkowski met Brezhnev and

Nikolay Tikhonov, the new Soviet premier, in Moscow. An understanding was reached on Soviet economic aid to Poland, and in a joint communiqué Brezhnev expressed the conviction that Poland would solve its problems. On October 31 Pinkowski informed Walesa that Solidarity would have free access to all state mass media. Walesa retorted that if the insertion into the union's charter was not deleted, he would order a protest strike. On November 10 the Supreme Court of Poland upheld Solidarity's position, with a compromise: the PUWP clause was removed to an annex.

In November Jerzy Ozdowski, a leading Roman Catholic layman, was appointed a deputy prime minister, the first non-Communist to attain such a high government post. Major personnel changes were made in the local party structure in late November, and the Politburo was again revamped on December 2. Meanwhile, unrest continued, especially in the southern city of Czestochowa and among the railway workers and members of the independent trade union in Warsaw. Both the Central Committee and the Roman Catholic Church urged restraint and an end to disorders. On December 5 leaders of the Warsaw Pact member states meeting in Moscow to discuss the Polish and international situation expressed their confidence that Poland would overcome its difficulties and pledged their support for it within the fraternal treaty membership—an allusion to the disobedience of Hungary in 1956 and Czechoslovakia in 1968. Threats of a strike by the nation's independent farmers abated when the Supreme Court on December 30 postponed a decision on legalization of a new farmers' organization, Rural Solidarity.

POLITICAL PARTIES

Both major U.S. parties reflected the beginnings of a shift to the right that was evident in U.S. politics in 1980. The Republicans nominated conservative Ronald Reagan, who proved victorious in Novem-

ber, and gave him a platform tailored to his views. While the Democrats adopted a series of liberal amendments to their platform, they rejected the candidacy of the amendments' chief proponent, Sen. Edward Kennedy (Mass.), and renominated Pres. Jimmy Carter, whose economic policies had alienated a number of liberal and union leaders.

There also was an unusual independent campaign for the presidency by Republican Rep. John Anderson (Ill.). In addition, there were at least ten minor parties on the ballot in three or more states. Both major parties were concerned with the effect of these campaigns, particularly Anderson's, in draining off possibly decisive votes.

The Primaries

Carter and Kennedy were each entered in 34 primaries. Carter won 24 and took 51.2% of the Democratic primary vote. Kennedy won ten—seven of them in the East—and took 37.6%. Kennedy remained a candidate when the Democratic convention opened but withdrew before nominations began. A third contender, Gov. Edmund Brown of California, never became a serious threat to Carter and withdrew his candidacy April 1.

By the time the Republican convention began, Reagan was the only candidate left in the field. Conservative candidates John Connally, former governor of Texas, and Rep. Philip Crane of Illinois ran into campaign finance problems and withdrew early in the primary season without posing serious threats. Two moderate contenders, Anderson and former UN Ambassador George Bush, together polled about as many votes in the first 13 primaries as Reagan, their conservative rival, but split the vote. Anderson announced April 24 that he would be an independent candidate.

Reagan apparently cinched the nomination May 20 in the Michigan and Oregon primaries. Ironically, Bush, his last remaining rival, scored an upset victory that day in Michigan. But Reagan's share of

Former president Gerald Ford (right) joins George Bush and Ronald Reagan after their nomination at the Republican national convention in July in Detroit.
WIDE WORLD

delegates there and in Oregon put him over the number needed for nomination, according to at least two projections. Bush announced the next morning that he was reassessing his candidacy and withdrew May 26.

Platforms

The conservative wing of the Republican Party, firmly in control of the party's Detroit convention, adopted a platform intended to mute differences with the party's moderates and to focus on attacking the Carter administration.

The Democratic platform was in many important respects shaped by Senator Kennedy. His supporters had drafted a broad range of liberal social and economic proposals with the intent of promoting his candidacy. That candidacy collapsed when Carter's forces won a vote on a rule requiring delegates to give first-ballot support to the man they had backed during the delegate selection process. Nevertheless, the platform amendments had wide support among the delegates. After a dramatic appearance by Kennedy sparked a 40-minute demonstration, Carter yielded on amendments relating to economics except for a call for wage and price controls, which was declared defeated on a voice vote.

The Republican platform endorsed the Kemp-Roth tax proposal, espoused by Rep. Jack Kemp (N.Y.) and Sen. William Roth (Del.) for several years. It called for an individual tax cut of 10% each year for three years. The Republicans also called for a balanced budget, reduction of federal spending to compensate for tax cuts, reduction of federal regulations on business, and speeding of business tax write-offs to stimulate investment. These proposals for stimulating the economy became the heart of Reagan's campaign pledges to blue-collar voters to create more jobs by expanding opportunity. The Republicans pledged themselves to continue existing unemployment benefits and to seek ways to help those whose jobs were threatened by foreign competition.

The Democrats denounced proposals for general, untargeted tax cuts but advocated reductions designed to stimulate business and combat recession. They called for a $12 billion antirecession jobs program—the cornerstone of the Kennedy economic proposals. They also promised to strengthen existing antirecession programs if necessary to reduce unemployment and to create job-training programs specifically designed to help welfare recipients.

The Republicans called for decontrol of wellhead oil prices, an end to the windfall profits tax for newly discovered and hard-to-get oil, ending the right of the federal government to allocate oil products except in emergencies, and easing of overly stringent provisions of the Clean Air Act. They favoured using nuclear power.

The Democrats went on record for a phase-out of nuclear power as other fuels became available. They supported financial incentives for home conservation of energy and promotion of the search for alternate sources of energy.

The Democrats supported the Equal Rights Amendment and adopted a platform ban on use of party funds to aid any candidate opposed to ERA. The Republicans took no platform position on ERA, contending that it was a matter for the states, but otherwise indicated support for equal rights for women.

There was a head-on clash of positions on abortion. Republicans supported a ban by constitution-

Despite a stalwart group of followers, Sen. Edward Kennedy of Massachusetts could not muster the backing to win the Democratic presidential nomination. His speech at the convention in New York City on August 12 was a crowd pleaser, however.
UPI

Running as an independent, Rep. John Anderson of Illinois (left) attracted enough disaffected voters to become a force in the presidential race. With him is vice-presidential candidate Patrick Lucey.

UPI

al amendment and a cutoff of federal funds to pay for the procedure. They pledged to seek appointment of only antiabortion nominees as federal judges. The Democrats opposed overturning court decisions on abortion by constitutional amendment, called for continued use of Medicaid funds for the procedure, and said they recognized a woman's right to choose whether and when to have children.

Both parties promised to increase defense spending. The Democrats called for increases of at least 3% a year for a decade. The Republicans, in a proposal that President Carter sought to make a major campaign issue, called for enough spending to "ultimately reach the position of military superiority" to the Soviet Union. The Democrats supported ratification of the Strategic Arms Limitation Treaty (SALT II); the Republicans said they would support an arms limitation agreement only if it benefited both sides equally and after the U.S. was assured of enough strength to deter conflict.

The Republicans opposed creation of a national health service; the Democrats called for national health insurance with universal coverage. The Republicans opposed federalizing the welfare system; the Democrats pledged an effort to have the federal government assume local government's share of welfare costs by 1982.

Other Candidates

Anderson succeeded in getting his name on the ballot in all 50 states and the District of Columbia. Although election laws in some states—North Carolina and Michigan, for example—required him to file as a third-party candidate, he made it clear that he was not attempting to set up a new party.

Anderson made a significant campaign gain in New York, where he won the endorsement of the Liberal Party, which operated only in that state. It was the first time in the party's 36-year history that

it failed to endorse the Democratic presidential candidate. As his vice-presidential running mate, Anderson chose Patrick Lucey, former governor of Wisconsin and a pro-Kennedy leader during the Democratic primaries.

Candidates other than those of the two major parties were eligible to receive federal campaign financing only if they polled 5% of the total vote in a presidential election, and only retroactively. By competing for the favour of disaffected voters, the Anderson candidacy dimmed the hopes of minor parties of achieving the magic figure.

There were at least ten minor parties on the ballot in three or more states. The parties and their presidential candidates were:

Libertarian, California attorney Ed Clark, on the ballot in all 50 states and the District of Columbia. Strongly advocated self-reliance and a minimum of government interference in private affairs.

American, Percy Greaves, Jr., New York economist; and American Independent, John Rarick, Louisiana, a former congressman. Both parties are descendants of George Wallace's third-party movement of 1968, strongly favouring free enterprise and opposing federal interference.

National Statesman, Benjamin Bubar, former Maine legislator. The successor to the Prohibition Party, with a conservative platform addressing 23 additional issues.

Citizens Party, New York author-environmentalist Barry Commoner. A populist-liberal group, it hoped to become a major force in U.S. politics.

Socialist Workers Party, Chicago steelworker Andrew Pulley, 29. The former Trotskyite splinter of the Communist movement.

Communist Party, veteran radical Gus Hall. The old-line, pro-Soviet Communist movement.

Socialist Party, David McReynolds of New York, an avowed homosexual and strong draft opponent. The party was a weak offshoot of the nation's oldest and most successful radical movement.

Workers World, party founder Deirdre Griswold, New Jersey. Formed 20 years earlier in a split with the Socialist Workers Party.

Right to Life, Ellen McCormack, New York housewife. A single-issue, antiabortion group that gained a permanent spot on the New York ballot by a strong showing in the 1978 elections. Also on the ballot in New Jersey and Kentucky.

POPULATION

According to new UN population projections to the year 2000, developed countries would have low growth rates with modest population increases, while less developed countries would experience high rates. The populations of less developed countries would double, on average, in 35 years and, in some cases, in 20 years. Africa was expected to experience the most rapid growth, followed by Latin America and South and East Asia. Northern America and the Soviet Union would have moderate population increases, and Europe would grow much more slowly.

At the same time, it was observed that the recent trend in the global population growth rate had been downward. According to the International Demographic Data Center of the U.S. Census Bureau, the global growth rate fell from 2.1% in 1965–70 to 1.7% in 1975–79. The decline was characteristic for all areas except Africa. There was speculation that the global growth curve would level off by 2080, when the world's population would have risen from the current 4,500,000,000 persons to an estimated 11,000,000,000 or more. In 1980 China achieved a population of an estimated 1,000,000,000 persons. Countries with over 200 million were (in millions): India (676), the Soviet Union (266), and the U.S. (223).

Birth Statistics

Births and birthrates increased in the U.S. in 1979; the rise resulted from an increase in the number of women of childbearing age, as well as in the rate of childbearing. The estimated number of live births, 3,473,000, was higher than in any of the preceding seven years. The birthrate also rose, to 15.8 per 1,000 population, compared with 15.3 in 1978. The trend continued into 1980; the birthrate for the first six months was 15.6, as against 15.2 for the corresponding period in 1979. The fertility rate in 1979 was 68 live births per 1,000 women 15–44 years of age, 2% above 1978.

Final data for 1978 showed a white birthrate of 14.2 live births per 1,000 population, compared with 14.4 in 1977, and a black birthrate of 21.6, compared with 21.7 in 1977. Fertility rates also dropped; for whites, the rate of live births per 1,000 women of childbearing age was 62.7 in 1978 and 64 in 1977; for blacks, it was 88.6 in 1978 and 89.8 in 1977.

Births to unmarried women continued to increase in 1978, but at a slower rate. There were an estimated 543,900 live births to unmarried mothers in 1978, 5.5% more than in 1977. About half were to women under 20. Some 233,600 births occurred to white unmarried mothers and 293,400 to black unmarried mothers. The ratio of out-of-wedlock

The U.S. Census was taken in 1980, a massive effort that involved mail-in forms and visits from census takers.

FRED R. CONRAD – THE NEW YORK TIMES

childbearing (the number of births to unmarried women per 1,000 total live births) rose to 87 for white women and 532 for black women.

The total fertility rate, a measure of the number of children women would have during their lifetime if current fertility rates remained constant, showed a decline in the U.S. in 1978, from 1,826.3 children per 1,000 women in 1977 to 1,800.2. This would indicate an average of 1.8 children per woman (1.7 for whites and 2.3 for blacks). The estimated total fertility rate for the world was 3.8 children per woman, with the rate in the more developed countries around 2 and in the less developed countries about 4.4. Countries with rates under 2 are considered to be below replacement levels and theoretically will decline in population, while those over 2.5 are above replacement levels and could grow considerably. The fertility rate in northern Europe was 1.8 children per woman, while in Kenya it was 8.

Because of the age composition of the U.S., the population was expected to double in about 99 years, despite current fertility rates. Natural increase, the excess of births over deaths, added some 1,567,000 to the population in 1979. The rate was 7 per 1,000 population and contrasts significantly with some other areas: 29 per 1,000 in Africa, 26 in Latin America, and 18 in Asia. China, with a rate of natural increase of 12 per 1,000 population, had announced a policy of encouraging one-child families and set a goal of zero population growth by the year 2000.

Death Statistics

The provisional count of deaths in the U.S. in 1979 was 1,906,000, and the rate of 8.7 deaths per 1,000 population was a record low. In 1970 the death rate had been 9.5 per 1,000. The world death rate in 1979 was estimated at 11, but there were vast differences between countries, with rates ranging from 6 in Iceland to 25 in Ethiopia.

The 15 leading causes of death in the U.S. in 1979 were:

Cause of death	Estimated rate per 100,000 population
1. Diseases of the heart	331.3
2. Malignant neoplasms	183.5
3. Cerebrovascular diseases	76.9
4. Accidents	47.9
5. Chronic obstructive pulmonary diseases	22.7
6. Pneumonia and influenza	20.0
7. Diabetes mellitus	15.0
8. Chronic liver disease and cirrhosis	13.6
9. Atherosclerosis	13.0
10. Suicide	12.6
11. Homicide and legal intervention	10.5
12. Conditions in the perinatal period	10.4
13. Nephritis, nephrotic syndrome, and nephrosis	7.3
14. Congenital anomalies	6.1
15. Septicemia	3.8

The three major causes of death, heart disease, cancer, and stroke, accounted for 68% of all deaths.

Expectation of Life

Life expectancy at birth in 1979 was 73.8 years for the total U.S. population, a half year more than in 1978 and the highest average ever attained in the U.S. For white women it was 78.3 years; for white men, 70.6; for nonwhite women, 74.5; and for nonwhite men, 65.5. The nonwhite group had made considerable gains in recent years, and the difference between white and nonwhite had narrowed. In 1960 life expectancy for whites exceeded nonwhites by 7 years; in 1979 the difference was 4.5 years. In 1960 white men were projected to live an average 6.3 more years than nonwhite men and white women 7.8 more years than nonwhite women; by 1979 the differentials had fallen to 5.1 years and 3.8 years, respectively.

Infant and Maternal Mortality

There were about 45,000 deaths of infants under one year of age in the U.S. in 1979, with a rate of 13 infant deaths per 1,000 live births. This rate was 4.4% lower than that for 1978 and reflected a substantial decline in deaths during the first month of life. The neonatal rate (deaths under 28 days per 1,000 live births in the same period) fell from 9.5 in 1978 to 8.8 in 1979. The infant mortality rate was a new U.S. low.

Detailed data for 1978 show that the mortality rate for white infants was 12 per 1,000 live births, while that for black infants was 21. In white-nonwhite comparisons, the greatest difference related to immature births; the death rate for nonwhite babies from this cause was over 2½ times that for white babies. Infant mortality is difficult to measure in less developed countries, but UN and other estimates showed rates of over 200 for Afghanistan, Angola, and The Gambia.

There were an estimated 270 maternal deaths associated with childbearing in the U.S. in 1979, with a mortality rate of 7.8 deaths per 100,000 live births. This represented a 19% decline from 1978.

Marriage and Divorce Statistics

An estimated 2,317,000 marriages occurred in the U.S. in 1979, an increase of 3% over 1978 and the fourth consecutive annual increase. It was also the largest annual number of marriages ever recorded, exceeding the previous record high of 2,291,045 in 1946. The marriage rate was 10.5 per 1,000 population. Final statistics for 1978 placed the number of marriages at 2,282,272; of these, 37,462 were nonlicensed California marriages, included for the first time. However, since records of these marriages are sealed and no other information is available, they are excluded from detailed tabulations on marriage characteristics. The average age at first marriage continued to rise, to 21.4 years for brides and 23.2 years for grooms in 1978, compared with 20.5 and

22.4 years, respectively, in 1972. Remarriages accounted for about one-third of all marriages.

There were, provisionally, 1,170,000 divorces in 1979, 4% more than in the previous year and the highest number ever estimated for the U.S. The divorce rate was 5.3 divorces per 1,000 population, up 2% from 1978 and more than 33% above the rate in 1970. The trend continued into 1980, with divorces increasing 2% from January through June. The median duration of marriage ending in divorce was 6.6 years in 1977 and 1978, slightly above the 6.5 years in 1974–76. The average age at time of divorce was 32 for husbands and 29.7 for wives. The number of children under 18 involved in divorce in 1978 was 1,147,000, the largest number ever recorded in the U.S.

PORTUGAL

Pres. António Ramalho Eanes's decision to call elections in December 1979 rested on the Assembly's failure to produce a workable parliamentary majority. The new elections resulted in the emergence of the centre-right Democratic Alliance (AD) as the country's major political party. Nevertheless, the 1976 constitution required both general and presidential elections to be held in 1980. The new AD administration, therefore, had only ten months in office before submitting itself to the electorate again.

The basic objectives of the AD program included: stimulating economic growth by foreign investment to help the country prepare for European Economic Community (EEC) membership in 1983; reversing the four-year decline in real wages; carrying out the 1977 agrarian reform law, which provided for the return of a sizable portion of the nation's collectively owned farmland to previous owners dispossessed by the revolution; and providing increased pensions and social security benefits. A ba-

sic principle was to open the economy to private enterprise, but in April and May the Council of the Revolution, led by President Eanes, declared as unconstitutional laws that would have permitted private banks and insurance companies to compete with nationalized firms. The government finally decided to delay its initiative until after the elections.

The impasse focused attention on the programmed revision of the 1976 constitution. The AD government was adamant that references to the achievement of socialism be removed from the text, the Council of the Revolution abolished, and the revised document made to conform to the requirements of the EEC's 1957 Treaty of Rome. Under the existing constitution, revision required a two-thirds majority in the Assembly. The AD argued for a popular referendum to give Parliament the authority to alter the constitution by a simple majority.

The Republican Socialist Front (FRS), comprising the Socialist Party and smaller socialist groups, was committed to preserving the existing constitution, though it seemed prepared to cede the deletion of references to socialism and a reduced role for the Council of the Revolution. Nevertheless, Art. 83 of the constitution, which stated that "all nationalizations effected since April 25, 1974, are irreversible conquests by the working classes," remained sacrosanct in FRS eyes. There was broad agreement on EEC membership and the changes required from Portugal, but this consensus was set aside during the election campaign, and no party ventured detailed assessments of the issues at stake. The Communist Party showed itself particularly adept at mudslinging. It concentrated on accusing the AD of having quashed a parliamentary inquiry into allegations of improper financial activities by the premier and on his unorthodox private life—Francisco Sá Carneiro campaigned with his Danish-born mistress at his side although he was still legally married

Portuguese elections were thrown into turmoil when Premier Francisco Sá Carneiro was killed in a plane crash while on his way to a political rally in December.
WIDE WORLD

to the Portuguese mother of his five children.

Sá Carneiro stated repeatedly that should President Eanes be reelected in the Dec. 7, 1980, polls he would resign. In April the AD put up 52-year-old Gen. António Soares Carneiro, a right-winger and veteran of the Angola war, as its presidential candidate.

In the October 5 general elections, the AD was able to increase its majority from 6 seats in the Assembly to 18. The Socialists ceased to lose ground, but a major swing against the Communist Party and those further to the left occurred.

On October 8 the official campaign for the presidential election began. The first victim of the presidential campaign was the secretary-general of the Socialist Party, Mário Soares. During the party's congress after the general elections, Soares, blamed for the party's failure to increase its share of the popular vote, resigned after failing to persuade the party to withdraw its support for the reelection of President Eanes. Soares was replaced temporarily by Víctor Constancio, Portugal's brightest economist.

On December 4, only four days before the election, Sá Carneiro was killed in a plane crash. The election resulted in an overwhelming victory for Eanes. On December 22 Eanes designated as premier Francisco Pinto Balsemão, a journalist and lawyer and close friend of Sá Carneiro.

PRISONS

A dangerous atmosphere of tension and unrest pervaded the prison systems of many countries in 1980. Overcowding was often at record levels, particularly in the U.S. and the U.K. Conditions were bad for staff as well as prisoners, and both groups showed their discontent. By far the most serious disturbance of the year occurred in February at New Mexico's state penitentiary at Santa Fe, where a savage outbreak left over 30 prisoners dead, many of them horribly mutilated, and five wings of the prison extensively damaged. (*See* Sidebar.)

Efforts continued to reduce prison populations by speeding up the process of bringing accused persons held in custody to trial, by dealing with as many of the less serious offenders as possible in the community, and by shortening prison sentences where these were unavoidable. Given the high cost of building new prisons, other, less expensive penal methods that produced no worse results had to be pursued whenever it was safe. The French National Assembly adopted a new draft penal code that would restrict the right of examining magistrates to detain suspects without trial, a move designed to reduce the large number of accused held in custody for long periods. However, the measure would also limit the powers of courts to pass suspended sentences. West Germany's Bundestag (federal parliament) passed a bill under which life imprisonment, which hitherto had meant just that, was reduced to a period of 15 years, provided experts were satisfied

that the prisoner concerned was unlikely to commit further crimes.

In the U.K., Home Secretary William Whitelaw, faced with a prison population of 44,000, appealed to the courts to refrain from passing prison sentences for relatively minor offenses or, when this was inevitable, to impose very short ones. But if nondangerous but repeated offenders were to be dealt with in the community, many new facilities were required: accommodation for the single homeless; day centres to train—or at least occupy—such people during the day; and facilities for group work to deal with such problems as alcoholism. Detoxification centres were needed for alcoholic offenders and psychiatric units for the mentally unstable.

On a theoretical level, more penologists had come to question penal systems based on the attempt to rehabilitate the offender. Instead, they favoured a return to a modified "justice model" or, as it was called in European countries, the neoclassical approach. This rejected indeterminate sentences, where release from prison depended on response to treatment, in favour of fixed sentences. Criticism of indeterminacy focused on parole, particularly in Australia, the U.S., and the U.K. Parole is a form of early conditional release from a penal institution, followed by a period of supervision during which recall to prison is possible.

The decisions of parole boards sometimes seemed inexplicable, not only to prisoners and their families but also to the staff whose opinion had been asked. There were increasing demands that parole boards make the reasons for their negative decisions known and possibly appealable. This, however, might involve disclosure of confidential views and prognoses by staff members, including psychiatrists. On the one hand, it was feared that opinions would not be expressed freely once they were no longer confidential. On the other, it was held that decisions about liberty were so fundamental that they had to be made openly.

Beyond that, some critics argued that the element of uncertainty introduced by parole virtually constituted an additional punishment; prisoners continually saw some among their number released while others in apparently similar circumstances were not. Others, however, believed that parole provided a useful flexibility, permitting consideration of new information, not available to the courts at the time of the original sentence.

What the advocates of a penal system based on the justice model wanted was punishment that, with certain exceptions, matched the seriousness of the offense. Lawbreakers guilty of similar offenses should receive the same sentence; penalties should be fixed; and, whenever possible, the victim should be compensated for harm done. Because a rehabilitative system could seem arbitrary, the main aim was fairness.

Among other reasons for the swing away from rehabilitation was the fact that penological research

The New Mexico Riot

"I don't remember anything as bad as this" was how a National Guard officer and veteran of World War II described the Santa Fe, N.M., state penitentiary after the riot of Feb. 2–3, 1980. Thirty-three inmates died in the disturbance, most of them at the hands of fellow prisoners, and much of the prison was destroyed.

According to a report issued in June by the state attorney general, the outbreak began when several inmates, drunk on homemade liquor, overcame their guards and broke through the supposedly shatterproof windows of the prison's control centre. Once there, they were able to open electrically controlled doors throughout the prison.

Eyewitnesses reported that the inmates ran amok, setting fires and destroying equipment. Many were high on drugs taken from the pharmacy. A cellblock designed to protect prisoners at special risk was forced open, and rioters began killing suspected informants. Of the casualties, some died from drug overdose or smoke inhalation. Most, however, were murdered, and many of the bodies bore signs of torture or mutilation. During the riot approximately 700 inmates surrendered to escape the carnage. Remarkably, although 11 guards were taken hostage, none was killed.

The riot was the worst in the U.S. since the outbreak at Attica, N.Y., in 1971, when 32 inmates and 11 prison employees died. The complaints of overcrowding, poor food, and harassment by guards were much the same at Santa Fe as at Attica. Considered a model prison for 800 when it was opened in 1956, the Santa Fe penitentiary housed about 1,100 in 1980, including some regarded as mentally abnormal and very dangerous. It was also understaffed; some of the guards were barely 18 years of age and had had only a few weeks of training.

Unlike Attica, however, where most of the casualties occurred when state troopers and law enforcement officers stormed the prison, the Santa Fe riot pitted inmate against inmate. Police and National Guardsmen waited out the violence until inmate spokesmen offered to exchange the hostages for interviews with reporters. Entering the prison without meeting resistance, they found many rioters in a drugged stupor.

With much of the prison uninhabitable, half of the survivors were moved to other facilities, in some cases outside of the state. Minor disturbances continued to flare among those who remained, partly traceable to the lack of such amenities as the gymnasium, library, and kitchen, all seriously damaged or destroyed. Damage was estimated in the neighbourhood of $25 million.

JOHN BARR–GAMMA/LIAISON

Scenes of horror such as this bloody cell greeted officers entering New Mexico's Sante Fe state penitentiary after a vicious, destructive riot by inmates in February.

tended to show that no one treatment method produced significantly better results than any other. Such results were normally expressed in terms of reconviction rates. Reconviction, however, depended at least as much on the offender's life circumstances and desire, or otherwise, to commit further crimes as it did on the effect of a particular sentence.

Treatment in the community still involved the notion of rehabilitation, so difficult to apply in the harsh circumstances of a penal institution. If two offenders, both having committed similar offenses, got community service orders, for example, the type of community service would vary according to the circumstances of the individual concerned. Probation orders were often combined with a variety of confidence-building schemes, including literacy programs, and heroic efforts to wean drug-dependent offenders away from their addiction were sometimes made. All this was clearly rehabilitative.

(*See also* Crime and Law Enforcement; Law.)

REFUGEES AND MIGRANTS

Africa remained the continent with the highest number of refugees, with approximately five million refugees and displaced persons. The refugee case load grew in early 1980 because of events in the Ethiopia-Somalia region and continued uncertainty in southern Africa. A continued influx gave Somalia the largest refugee problem in the world, with more than 800,000 in 32 camps and (by government estimates) an equivalent number elsewhere in the country. Sudan reported 441,000 refugees in midyear and declared 1980 the "Year of the Refugee." Refugees fleeing civil strife in Chad also entered neighbouring countries, particularly Cameroon and Nigeria. Fresh influxes of refugees from Uganda reached Zaire and Sudan toward the end of the year. In Angola Namibian refugees were again subject to military attacks on their camps by South African forces. Refugees in Djibouti constituted nearly 15% of the population. In Ethiopia assistance to displaced people was hampered by their swelling numbers and by prolonged drought.

At the same time, solutions to several refugee problems in Africa were attained. The mutual repatriation of Zairians and Angolans continued. The United Nations High Commissioner for Refugees (UNHCR) coordinated the voluntary repatriation of Zimbabwean refugees; some 33,000 were repatriated under UNHCR auspices before the national elections. By the end of July more than 51,000 persons had returned home with UNHCR's help. Tanzania announced the naturalization of some 35,000 refugees from Rwanda.

There was a further decline in the number of ref-

ugees in Latin America. In the first half of 1980 about 130,000 Cubans left their country, of whom more than 110,000 were received in the U.S. Costa Rica accepted a limited number for resettlement, and the Peruvian government accepted for permanent resettlement 1,000 of the Cuban nationals who had entered the Peruvian embassy in Havana. Some 35,000 citizens left El Salvador for neighbouring countries. Argentina accepted a number of Indochinese families for resettlement.

In Southeast Asia the mass influx of Indochinese refugees, particularly Vietnamese "boat people," decreased in the second half of the year. The U.S. raised its admission quota for Indochinese refugees to 168,000 for the year, and other nations continued to make places available. Piracy in Southeast Asian waters posed major problems, with refugees being subjected to repeated attacks of rape and robbery on the high seas.

The influx in late 1979 and early 1980 of large numbers of Cambodians into Thailand (in addition to some half a million displaced along the Thai-Cambodian border) necessitated major international assistance in 1980. Some 165,000 stayed in emergency holding centres where they received care and maintenance assistance. Toward the end of the year UNHCR was able to announce a program of assistance to an estimated 300,000 Cambodian returnees in their home country.

The year also witnessed the dramatic escalation of the number of refugees fleeing from Afghanistan into Pakistan, which reached 1.2 million. UNHCR reviewed its program of assistance twice during the year, raising its eventual needs for basic food, shel-

Some 700 Cuban refugees were housed at Eglin Air Force Base in Florida in May as the crowds of refugees clogged port cities and strained available facilities for housing and placement.
UPI

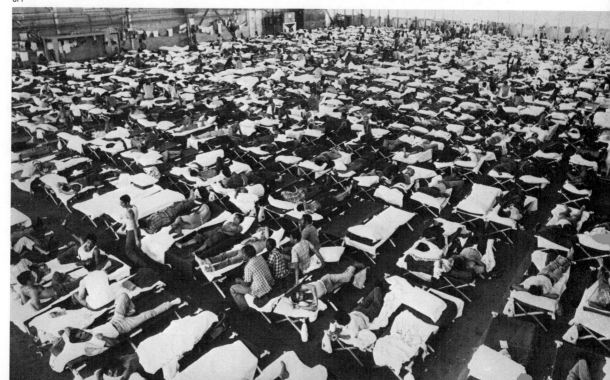

Two of 31 illegal immigrants from El Salvador are comforted by their U.S. rescuers after they were found near death in the Arizona desert. At least 13 of the group died of heat exhaustion.
WIDE WORLD

ter, health, education, water supplies, household items, and self-help for refugees in Pakistan projects to $99 million. During 1980 seven nations ratified the 1951 convention and 1967 protocol relating to the status of refugees, bringing the total number acceding to these instruments to 83.

The U.S. continued to be the single most important destination for migrants from around the globe. The privations endured by some would-be immigrants ended in tragedy. In July 1980 as many as 13 illegal Salvadoran immigrants died of heat exhaustion in the Sonora Desert of Arizona, and 106 Haitians, shipwrecked on a tiny Caribbean islet en route to Florida in the fall, spent weeks with almost no food and water before being forcibly returned to Haiti. Legitimate arrivals under the immigration laws numbered 400,000, in addition to 230,000 refugees, during the year ended in September. The average yearly number of immigrants to the U.S. had risen spectacularly after 1950, from 63,938 in the 1930s and 85,661 in the 1940s to 249,927 in the '50s, 321,375 in the '60s, and 430,628 in the '70s. The ethnic composition and source areas of this flow had also changed markedly. Asia and Latin America now provided 82% of immigrants and Europe 12%; in 1965 the respective figures were 47 and 39%.

On July 15 Hong Kong's commissioner to Britain, Dennis Bray, estimated that legal and illegal immigration to the colony from China in 1979 amounted to 200,000, representing an annual population growth rate of 6%. China's foreign minister, Huang Hua, visiting London on October 1–2, agreed to restrict illegal emigration. Besides intensified patrols by the Hong Kong military and police, new stringent measures included spot checks to control population movements. From October 30 everyone aged 15 and over had to carry an identity card or face a fine of HK$1,000, and from November employers hiring workers without identity cards were liable to fines of HK$50,000 and a year's imprisonment.

RELIGION

The decade of the 1980s began with several strong-willed spiritual leaders asserting their authority in worldly affairs. The headlines were dominated by the names of such men as the Ayatollah Ruhollah Khomeini, the religious and temporal leader of Islamic Iran; Pope John Paul II, whose vision of the mission of the Roman Catholic Church became increasingly clear as he ended the second year of his reign; and the television "superstars" in America's "electronic church," who made concerted attempts to "get out the Christian vote" in the November 4 election.

Although the temperaments and the mind-sets of these men had been shaped by vastly different religious and cultural traditions, all had certain traits in common. They were troubled by few self-doubts or doubts about the validity of their heritages, and they were unawed by the claims to superior wisdom made by the cosmopolitan elite of the secular world.

In its first issue of 1980, *Time* magazine devoted its cover story to the Ayatollah Khomeini, the newsmagazine's choice as its "man of the year" for 1979, "the person who has done the most to change the news, for better or for worse." His audacious attempt to dewesternize Iran and turn that country into a theocratic Islamic state had thrown the Middle East balance of power into chaos and fueled the fervour of Islamic conservatives in other parts of the Muslim world.

Meanwhile, John Paul II, the "pilgrim pope," was no more of a homebody in 1980 than he had been in 1979. In May the Polish-born pontiff was seen by millions of Africans. His messages to them contained attacks on governmental corruption, statements of support for the poor and hungry, and appeals for obedience to traditional church teachings. From May 30 to June 2, the papal entourage went to France, where modern secularism had made deep inroads into the church loyalty of baptized Catholics. Indefatigable, the pope took off on June 30 for a 12-day, 9,000-mi journey to Brazil, the world's largest Roman Catholic nation.

Many progressive Catholics had speculated that the visit to Brazil would be the supreme test to date of the pope's commitment to social justice. In a land of 123 million people, where the gap between the rich minority and the poor majority is wide, the pope deplored acts of violence and class warfare, but he also called for pastoral action "which defends the poor in the face of unjust campaigns that offend their dignity." John Paul also addressed the Brazilians in the language of symbol and gesture. At a reception for members of the church hierarchy, the spiritual leader of world Catholicism made a point of embracing and kissing Dom Helder Câmara, archbishop of Olinda and Recife, a radical who for many years had been a relentless critic of Brazil's military regimes. Similarly, after visiting a squalid squatters' colony in Rio de Janeiro, the pope appeared so moved by the poverty he saw that he removed the gold ring given to him when he

was made a cardinal and gave it to the parish church.

The pope's November five-day trip to West Germany took him into divided territory for Catholics. Although the West German bishops had supported the 1979 Vatican decision that the liberal Hans Küng of the University of Tübingen "can no longer be considered a Catholic theologian," the pontiff still was under attack by theological progressives.

The tireless pontiff apparently would not rest until he personally fulfilled the biblical commandment to carry the Christian gospel to the ends of the Earth. Already announced by the Vatican were plans for a February 1981 papal pilgrimage to Japan and the Philippines and a 1982 trip to Great Britain. Meanwhile, between trips, John Paul set about getting his ecclesiastical house in order.

A strong believer in doctrinal orthodoxy and structural coherence in the life of the church, John Paul began his year by tackling one of his toughest problems: the divisions in the church in The Netherlands, where progressives had allowed several practices that offended Rome. After two and a half weeks of deliberations at a special synod, the Vatican brought the Dutch prelates into line on every major disputed issue. Although many observers predicted church leaders would have trouble enforcing the agreement, the Dutch bishops promised to back clerical celibacy, revive the tradition of individual confession, produce a more conservative catechism, and issue stricter rules governing mixed marriages.

Robert Runcie was enthroned as 102nd archbishop of Canterbury in solemn ceremony at Canterbury Cathedral on March 25; the ceremony was attended by British royalty and government leaders.
KEYSTONE

Hans Küng, a liberal Catholic teaching at the University of Tübingen in West Germany, was advised by the Vatican in 1980 that he could no longer be considered a Catholic theologian and was to cease teaching. Küng had long been known for his unorthodox opinions.
KEYSTONE

In addition, the Vatican reaffirmed its stand on euthanasia, cracked down on "abuses" in liturgical practices that "bewilder" the faithful, and, in preparation for the autumn synod of bishops, published a 115-page document on "The Role of the Christian Family in the World Today." Besides restating familiar church beliefs on abortion, birth control by "artificial" methods, and premarital and extramarital sex, the document called upon Catholics to take a discriminating look at the women's liberation movement.

Politics was often on the pope's mind during 1980. At home and abroad, he constantly stressed that political activism was a proper role for laity but an improper one for clergy. The point was driven home in May when church authorities withdrew permission for Robert F. Drinan, a Jesuit, to run for reelection as a Democratic representative from Massachusetts.

It was ironic that, as the pope was ordering Catholic priests to stay out of politics, conservative Protestant ministers on the U.S. television circuit and in large parareligious organizations were becoming more openly and actively involved in politics than ever before. At the heart of the so-called new Christian right movement were such theological and political conservatives as Bill Bright, founder of the Campus Crusade for Christ, and fundamentalist television preachers like Jerry Falwell of Lynchburg, Va., and James Robison of Fort Worth, Texas.

From their large television audiences, the TV preachers had acquired sources of funds and mailing lists that gave them quick access to millions of voters. The Christian zealots worked in the presidential campaign, but their main targets were liberal incumbents in carefully selected congressional contests. Their key issues were identified in the congressional "report cards" and sample ballots they distributed. Generally, they opposed the proposed

Equal Rights Amendment (ERA) to the U.S. Constitution, the use of federal funds for abortions, the SALT II arms-limitation treaty, and the right of homosexual persons to teach in public schools. With equal fervour, they favoured prayer in the public schools, budget increases to "restore U.S. military superiority for national defense," and intense efforts to "stop or control pornography."

Not all evangelicals supported the "get out the Christian vote" campaigns. Kenneth Kantzer, editor of *Christianity Today* magazine, declared that the Christian gospel should not be identified with "the extreme right wing." David Hubbard, president of Fuller Theological Seminary in Pasadena, Calif., said he would "hate for evangelical Christianity to become a spiritual version of the National Rifle Association." And Billy Graham, celebrated evangelist and friend of many U.S. presidents, told reporters in September that he intended to "remain above, below or beyond the whole political fray." (*See* Religion Special Report.)

On the ecumenical and interfaith fronts, three events stood out in 1980.

On the Greek islands of Patmos and Rhodes in late spring, official representatives of the Roman Catholic Church and Eastern Orthodoxy engaged in the first formal interchurch dialogues since the schism that had separated the two large branches of Christendom in 1054. At the end of the historic gathering, a spokesman said, "It is hoped that steps will be taken that will lead toward the restoration of full ecclesiastical communion between Eastern Orthodoxy and Roman Catholicism."

In late August, Anglican-Roman Catholic relations went through a period of stress when Catholic leaders surprised their Anglican counterparts by announcing that some married Episcopal clergy might be accepted for ordination as Catholic clergymen. Chiefly affected by the ruling would be dissident Episcopalians who had become disaffected in recent

The $18 million "Crystal Cathedral" (Garden Grove, California, Community Church) opened in September.

JOHNSON / BURGEE ARCHITECTS; PHOTO, GORDON H. SCHENCK, JR.

years by the decision of the Episcopal Church in the U.S. to ordain women as priests and its adoption of a new Book of Common Prayer.

The move, regarded as precipitous and unilateral by critics in both churches, did not seem likely to undo the cordial relationship established between Pope John Paul and Robert Runcie, the new archbishop of Canterbury, when the two leaders met in Africa. The future of Anglican-Catholic relations would undergo a new test in 1982 when the pope visited the home of the Church of England.

On a bureaucratic level, some strains developed between U.S. Jewish leaders and officials of the National Council of Churches when the Protestant and Orthodox ecumenical agency began working on a new study document on Middle East relations. Some Jews contended that the working document reflected a pro-Palestinian bias, but intense lobbying efforts appeared to produce a tentative proposal that both sides could live with.

In the United Methodist Church, the rapidly growing influence of women ministers was reflected in the July election of Marjorie S. Matthews as the denomination's first woman bishop. In September she took over her duties as the new spiritual leader of Methodists in Wisconsin.

The expanding interest of religious leaders in biomedical ethics and other science-and-religion issues took symbolic form in May when, in a London ceremony, the £90,000 Templeton Foundation Prize for Progress in Religion was presented to Ralph Wendell Burhoe, a Unitarian-Universalist scholar whose career has been devoted to strengthening the links between science and religion. He was the first North American to receive the award.

Two historic milestones were passed in 1980. The Sunday school movement, started by Robert Raikes in England in an attempt to reach the children of the poor with the Christian gospel, celebrated its 200th birthday. Throughout the world, especially in areas where Lutheranism is strong, observances were held marking the 450th anniversary of the publication of the Augsburg Confession, the basic statement of faith for Lutherans.

Special Report: The New Christian Right

by Martin E. Marty

The morning after the Nov. 4, 1980, national elections in the U.S., a cluster of forces code named the Moral Majority took credit for having helped turn America to a more conservative course. Not only had they supported Republican candidate Ronald Reagan for the presidency and thus helped him win a landslide in the Electoral College, they also had backed a number of aspirants who defeated liberal senators and members of the House of Representatives, along with numerous candidates for statehouses and various lesser offices.

A New Force

Moral Majority was really only a code name used by the media and the public, since the cluster included other vote-seeking organizations like the Religious Roundtable and the Christian Voice. But Moral Majority was both the best financed and the most visible of these sometimes cooperating, sometimes competing groups that made up what might more properly be called the New Christian Right.

Most of the members were of traditionalist Protestant backgrounds, and almost all of them had been brought together by television evangelists, most notably the Rev. Jerry Falwell of Virginia and the Rev. James Robison of Texas.

Two pre-election events served to give visibility to the New Christian Right. While its parties had been working behind the scenes and gathering momentum for a couple of years, they surfaced at a "Washington for Jesus" rally in the spring. Advance criticism against the overt political intentions of this evangelistic rally led the leaders to mute the political sounds and may have served to keep the hoped-for crowd of a million down to about 200,000. But from then on the media began to take the new political force seriously.

In late summer, in Texas, the leaders showed their political finesse and their increasing power by attracting thousands of pastors to a rally and training session. And with them came candidate Reagan, who endorsed them even though, for legal reasons

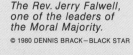

The Rev. Jerry Falwell, one of the leaders of the Moral Majority.

© 1980 DENNIS BRACK—BLACK STAR

A "Washington for Jesus" rally in the spring of 1980 drew more than 200,000 participants and announced to political strategists that the New Christian Right would be a force in the elections.

(of separation of church and state), they were not free to endorse him, their obvious choice. A tape, made at this rally and later released, overheard the president of the Southern Baptist Convention, the largest U.S. Protestant body, announcing that God did not hear the prayers of Jews. Debate over this statement by the Rev. Bailey Smith of Del City, Okla., tended to preoccupy the media and distract from the issues that the rally organizers were bringing forward.

Most of these issues had to do with what they saw as moral decline during the presidencies of two fellow evangelical Protestants, Jimmy Carter and, before him, Gerald Ford. The new militants claimed that liberals, humanists, and leftists in religion and politics had conspired to take God out of the public schools, to teach evolution as an alternative religion, and to create a climate on television and in popular culture that was unfavourable to traditional American moral values. They extended their program to include specific issues: they would defeat the Equal Rights Amendment, abolish the Department of Education, continue to oppose the Panama Canal treaties, limit the rights of homosexuals and women seeking abortions, and prevent the spread of obscene and pornographic materials and images.

The suddenness of the rise of this New Christian Right caught much of the public off guard. It was regionally strong, originating in the Sunbelt and the Midwest. Thus it was underrecognized in the Northeast, which was less familiar with the kind of Protestantism that nurtured the Moral Majority. Even after becoming aware that this force spoke for only a very small minority of the population and even a minority of evangelical, fundamentalist, and Pentecostal Protestantism, the larger public found few means to counter its effective television appeals and its highly technological use of direct mail services.

Uncertain Strength

The Moral Majority was more effective at defeating candidates in primaries—among them Rep. John Buchanan (Rep., Ala.), himself a Southern Baptist minister—than at being noticed nationally. Some of its favoured candidates, among them Rep. Richard Kelly (Rep., Fla.) and Rep. Robert Bauman (Rep., Md.), were subjects of highly publicized personal scandals, and this seemed to deprive the Moral Majority of some of its moral claims. Polls taken before the election showed that most evangelicals joined the public in repudiating the overt intrusion of ministers into partisan politics. Backlash had set in, with evangelical politicians like Sen. Mark Hatfield (Rep., Ore.) and prominent evangelical theologians protesting this intrusion.

Given these trends and countertrends, it was hard to assess the true scope and the potential of the New Christian Right. The rejection of President Carter was so massive, and the public's evident taste for any sort of change in executive and legislative ranks was so consistent, that a tide was created, a tide on which the New Christian Right rode just as much as it helped form the swell. President-elect Reagan in a press conference acknowledged that he would take Moral Majoritarian interests into consideration when forming policy, but he simply included these interests with those of all other backers. Before the election he had already taken some steps that alienated the New Christian Right, and many expected that he would further disappoint these supporters as he took office.

Religion in Politics

The New Christian Right did not represent the first bold entry into politics by fundamentalists, the extreme Protestant conservatives. In *The Politics of Doomsday*, historian Erling Jorstad tells of fundamentalist support for Sen. Joseph R. McCarthy in the 1950s and for Sen. Barry Goldwater and Gov. George Wallace in the 1960s. But these pioneers lacked the instruments of television and computerized direct mail, and Dwight Eisenhower and Lyndon Johnson provided stronger rallying points to counter them than did Carter.

Nor did the New Christian Right pioneer in using religion to affect politics. Nineteenth-century evangelicals had spoken out on both sides of the aboli-

tion cause and promoted the temperance movement. But they gradually retreated into evangelism, concern for personal morality, and life in subcultural pockets. As recently as the early 1970s, the leaders who now shaped the New Christian Right had decried as ungodly the participation of more liberal religious leaders in the civil rights movement and other controversial causes. This meant that they now had to make an about-face—one that they readily acknowledged.

In the 1980 campaigns the main-line Protestants were largely silent. Roman Catholics, who shared some of the New Christian Right's viewpoint of opposition to abortion, were eclipsed by these Protestants. If there was a Jewish vote, it was concerned chiefly with matters affecting Israel. The new religious voice to be reckoned with, then, was that of militant Protestants who evoked nostalgia for a simpler "Christian America," who gained power from the resentment and rage many felt against moral change and those they claimed were responsible for it, and who offered their followers the vision of power to defeat "humanists" and liberals in church and state. They turned out to be far less powerful than they claimed to be, but far more powerful than a caught-off-guard larger public had expected them to become.

Evangelical demonstrators made their position known at the Democratic national convention in New York City in August.

© 1980 MICHAEL O'BRIEN—BLACK STAR

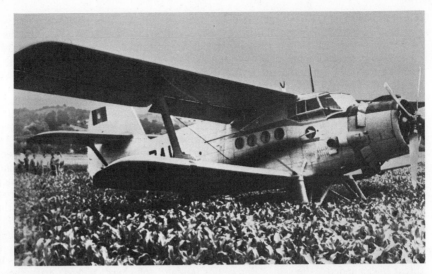

In July, 20 Romanians fled their country in a crop-dusting plane. They landed safely in Austria, where they requested political asylum.

UPI

ROMANIA

During 1980 Pres. Nicolae Ceausescu continued his courageous policy of enhancing Romania's independence and sovereignty while underscoring the Communist characteristics of his country's institutions and its membership in the Warsaw Treaty and the Council for Mutual Economic Assistance (Comecon). On November 5 in an interview for a Swedish newspaper, he boldly called for Soviet troops to be recalled from Afghanistan; at the beginning of the year he had already stood aside from the general Communist endorsement of the invasion.

In September Turkey sued Romania and a Greek shipping firm for $500 million in damages caused by an accident on the Marmara side of the Bosporus in November 1979. As a result of the collision of a Greek cargo vessel and the Romanian 150,000-ton tanker "Independenta," 50 Romanian seamen were killed. The tanker was the first ship of that size built at the Constanta shipyard.

On March 9 a new Grand National Assembly was elected. Out of 15,631,351 citizens entitled to vote, 99.99% went to the polls and 98.52% voted for the candidates of the Socialist Democracy and Unity Front. There were 598 nominations for 369 constituencies.

On March 28–29 the Assembly reelected Ceausescu president of the republic and Ilie Verdet (his son-in-law) premier. Verdet announced the composition of the new Council of Ministers. In addition to the premier, the new 50-member government consisted of 3 first deputy premiers (one of whom was Elena Ceausescu, the president's wife), 9 deputy premiers, 28 ministers, and 9 chairmen of special committees. The new government included only 14 ministers of the 50 in the previous government.

The event of the year was the International Congress of Historians held August 10–17 in Bucharest. The congress, the 15th of the series that started 80 years previously in Paris, assembled 2,700 histori-

ans from 60 countries. For six days in four different halls and in five languages the congress debated different great themes, generally with urbanity but sometimes not without passion. For instance, when a Soviet historian said that the U.S.S.R. was a "voluntary association of sovereign socialist republics," and added rather incautiously that Moldavia (former Bessarabia) joined the U.S.S.R. "as a result of the victorious national revolution," a correction of this historical misrepresentation was unavoidable. When Bohdan Osadczuk-Korab, a Ukrainian-born citizen of West Germany and professor at the Free University in West Berlin, reminded the audience that the so-called "national revolution" was planned in a secret agreement between the U.S.S.R. and Nazi Germany in 1939, he was enthusiastically applauded.

SAFETY

The 1980 edition of the National Safety Council's publication *Accident Facts* reported that the total of accidental deaths and disabling injuries in 1979 had declined about 1% from the preceding year. (A "disabling" injury is one that incapacitates the victim beyond the day of the accident.) The total of accidental deaths decreased about 1,000 from the year before. The death rate per 100,000 was 47, the second lowest on record. There was a 1% increase in deaths and disabling injuries resulting from motor-vehicle accidents, and a 2% increase from accidents in the workplace. These increases were offset by a 4% decline in deaths and injuries from accidents in the home and a 2% decline from accidents in public places. ("Public" accidents include those taking place in transportation other than motor vehicles, in public buildings, and during recreation, such as swimming, hunting, and so on.)

The National Safety Council reported a 7% decline in traffic fatalities in the United States during the decade 1969–79. A study of statistics showed that in 1979 there were 4,000 fewer auto deaths than in 1969. The Council attributed the decrease chiefly to the federally imposed highway speed limit of 55 mph ordered in 1974 in response to the Arab oil embargo the preceding year. Although a long-term decline in the number of traffic deaths followed, an upswing began, the totals exceeding 50,000 in both 1978 and 1979. Officials of the Federal Highway Administration attributed the increase to the growing number of smaller cars, arguing that their safety features were less effective and that the American highway system, designed for larger vehicles, presented safety problems for the smaller cars. Other reasons suggested for the increase were the greater age of vehicles currently on the road and the increasing tendency among motorists to ignore the 55 mph speed limit.

During 1980 Susan B. King, head of the Consumer Products Safety Commission (CPSC), warned of new problems in home safety. "The nature of the threat has changed," she said. "You're not talking about a loose roller skate on the stairs. You're talking about sophisticated problems, unknown hazards—overloads from high-tech appliances, toxic fumes from burning plastics and non-natural fabrics and insulation we all thought was good." Among the new hazards noted by the CPSC were the effects of fumes from formaldehyde, used in a foam insulation installed in more than 500,000 homes in recent years; the widespread use of asbestos, known to be a cause of lung cancer and other respiratory ailments and found in scores of products from oven mitts to washers and dryers; and aluminum wiring, installed in an estimated two million homes and apartments built or remodeled between 1965 and 1973, which the CPSC said was prone to overheating and could cause fires.

Another new home safety hazard noted by the CPSC had been created by the increased use of wood and coal stoves since the Arab oil embargo in 1973 began to increase fuel costs. Annual injuries resulting from stove and fireplace accidents had doubled to about 400, including an estimated 150 deaths. The government was studying minimum safety recommendations for installation of stoves, such as distance or insulation from combustible walls.

The Emerging Hazards Team, a seven-member unit of the CPSC, had the specific task of monitoring trends in accidents. They made use of the National Electronic Injury Surveillance System, a computer network of 72 hospitals across the country that reported product-related deaths and injuries through examining state death certificates. In November, for example, a potential danger represented by automatic garage doors was indicated by a small number of death certificates reporting that children playing "chicken" with the descending doors had been asphyxiated when caught under them. Alerted by the CPSC, manufacturers took steps to correct the problem and warn consumers.

A new consumer product investigated by the CPSC was the hot tub. Alerted by a small number of deaths associated with hot tubs, the CPSC warned consumers to avoid heavy drinking of alcoholic beverages when using hot tubs and to keep the water temperature below 104° F. Pregnant women, persons with a history of heart disease, diabetes, or blood pressure problems, or those taking medications that can cause drowsiness were warned to be particularly careful when using hot tubs.

Lawn-mower manufacturers were successful in November in getting a House conference committee to include a provision delaying the effective date

Safety advisers issued guidelines for the safe use of hot tubs after several deaths were reported linked to their use. Users were cautioned to avoid alcoholic beverages and not to fill the tubs with overly hot water.
PAUL FUSCO—MAGNUM

SCHREIBER—GAMMA/LIAISON

Saudi Foreign Minister Prince Saud al-Faisal (centre) and Oil Minister Sheikh Ahmad Zaki Yamani (right) were under fire from more radical members at a September OPEC meeting in Vienna. Although a pricing compromise resulted, there was no agreement on a long-term strategy.

of new safety standards into an appropriations measure. The standards had been scheduled to go into effect on Dec. 31, 1981. The new provision would delay the effective date until June 1982. Since most lawn mowers are manufactured during the winter months and sold during the first half of the year, the provision would effectively give the industry an additional year to comply with the new standards.

In December 1980 the Consumer Products Safety Commission announced the largest civil penalty in its seven-year history. The $420,000 fine would be paid by the White-Rodgers division of Emerson Electronic of St. Louis, Mo., a manufacturer of thermostats for liquefied petroleum gas water heaters, which had been involved in a number of explosions. More than 600,000 of the heaters sold since 1961 were recalled by the manufacturer.

SAUDI ARABIA

Saudi Arabia maintained neutrality in the opening phases of the Iraq-Iran war in September 1980, but it promised its Western allies that it would do "whatever was needed" to make up for oil production lost as a result of the fighting. At the same time, Saudi Arabia was demonstrating its preparedness to defend its borders in the event of an attack. The U.S. immediately supplied four airborne warning and control systems aircraft at the request of the Saudi authorities, and on October 20 Saudi Arabia announced its intention of seeking to buy them.

Washington's readiness to come to the aid of its main supplier of crude oil reintroduced a note of warmth into its relations with Riyadh, absent since

1979 when Saudi Arabia condemned Egypt's peace treaty with Israel. It made more likely a further resupplying of the Saudi forces with advanced equipment after the U.S. presidential election in November. In the meantime, on October 14, the Saudi authorities signed a U.S. $3.5 billion naval equipment agreement with France providing for the supply of four frigates, two supply ships, helicopters, and training.

U.S. confidence in the stability of Saudi Arabia had been shaken by the events following the temporary seizure of the Grand Mosque in Mecca on Nov. 20, 1979. This incident, and later trouble in the Shi'ah-populated oases of the Eastern Province, where the kingdom's oil was produced, led to fears of a Khomeini-style revolution against the ruling house of Saud. Saudi policy following the Mecca siege was to take limited but sharp reprisals, including imposition of the death sentence on the perpetrators of the sacrilege against Islam. Sixty-three of the men found guilty by an Islamic court of taking part in the attack, including 41 Saudis, were executed on Jan. 9, 1980, by beheading. Subsequently, Crown Prince Fahd outlined plans for major government changes, including a consultative council of 50–70 members to complement the Council of Ministers (Cabinet).

Crown Prince Fahd startled Western observers on August 14 when he vehemently denounced Israel's proposed "annexation" of East Jerusalem and called for a jihad (holy war) against "Zionist religious and racist arrogance." On October 28 Saudi Arabia severed diplomatic relations with Libya after intemperate attacks by the Libyan leader, Col.

Muammar al-Qaddafi, on Saudi Arabia because of its purchase of radar-equipped aircraft from the U.S. (*See* Libya.) Saudi Arabia played an important role in defusing the border confrontation between Syria and Jordan that erupted at the end of November. After a week of intensive diplomacy, Prince Abdullah ibn Abdul Aziz, second deputy prime minister and commander of the National Guard, negotiated a formula under which both countries withdrew their troops from the border.

Saudi sensitivity to media criticism reached the point of open anger in April when British television showed a dramatized version of the execution of a Saudi princess and her lover for adultery. The Cabinet decided on an unofficial embargo of British companies shortly after the program was screened, and on April 23 the British ambassador was asked to leave Jidda. It took a visit by British Foreign Secretary Lord Carrington on August 26 to restore relations.

The major domestic event of the year was the announcement in May of an ambitious third five-year development plan to cover the period up to 1985. Expenditure, equivalent to $235 billion, was much larger than the second plan's $149.5 billion. Perhaps as much as 30% of the plan's allocations was to be committed in the first year. Apart from strict adherence to Islamic social values, the guiding principle would be to ensure the development of human resources, as opposed to emphasis on the construction of infrastructure.

Aramco, the main force in the Saudi hydrocarbons industry, was due to be taken over by the government in 1981. In September 1980 it was announced that the U.S. shareholders in Aramco (Exxon, Mobil Oil, Standard Oil Co. of California, and Texaco) had received full compensation for nationalization in the second quarter of 1980; the amount was reported to be between $1.5 billion and $2 billion. For the first ten months of 1980, direct sales by the General Petroleum Minerals Organization (Petromin) of the Saudi crude oil output of 9.5 million bbl a day were running at about 1,770,000 bbl a day. Oil production had been increased to 9.5 million bbl a day from 8.5 million bbl during the crisis following the fall of the shah of Iran in 1979. From October 1, output increased to 10.4 million bbl a day. The official price of Saudi Arabia's marker crude (Arabian light) was $30.21 a barrel in the third quarter of 1980, against $28.82 a barrel in the second quarter and $27.12 a barrel in the first quarter. A further $2 was added to the price in December. During 1980 the process of saudization of foreign banks within the kingdom continued, with the biggest foreign bank, Citibank of the U.S., becoming the Saudi American Bank on July 11.

On August 19 the world's third worst air accident to that date occurred at Riyadh airport when 301 people died on the tarmac after a Lockheed TriStar burst into flames.

SHIPPING

Early in 1980 the world merchant fleet stood at 675 million tons deadweight (dw) or about 413 million gross registered tons (grt), an increase of nearly 20 million tons dw compared with a year earlier. Both the tanker and the dry-cargo fleets increased in total deadweight capacity, but the overall rate of growth

In October the Dutch cruise ship "Prinsendam" heeled and sank off the Alaska coast after a fire had forced 320 passengers and 150 crew members to abandon ship. All were rescued.

UPI

remained well below the 9–12% prevailing in the first half of the 1970s. Liberia continued to lead the table of world fleets with 160 million tons dw of shipping, followed closely by Japan with 66 million tons dw and Greece with 63 million tons dw. More than two-thirds of the Liberian fleet consisted of tankers. Worldwide, the tonnage of vessels laid up fell to a low of 11 million tons dw; nearly 76% of this represented tankers, mostly in the over-100,000-tons-dw class.

Provisional figures showed that world seaborne trade increased by just under 5% during the year, an improvement over the low of 1.8% for the year before. Crude oil and oil products together accounted for about half the world seaborne trade. Shipments of the three other major bulk commodities, iron ore, coal, and grain, increased by 7½% in volume with shipments of iron ore (the largest bulk commodity after oil) up by more than 8½%.

The first stage of the Suez Canal improvement project was completed. The maximum permitted draft was increased to 16 m (53 ft) and the vessel beam to 43 m (142 ft). The canal could now accept vessels of up to 150,000 tons dw fully loaded, 230,000-tonners partly loaded, and possibly 350,000 tons in ballast. Attempts by the Suez Canal Authority to increase tolls were resisted. There was congestion in the canal as a result of the heavy shipments of grain in transit, and owners of the larger bulk carriers had to face extra daily costs of up to $13,000 because of delays.

A massive program for the modernization of all major ports in India was introduced, with emphasis on facilities for handling containers and bulk commodities such as coal and iron ore. Plans were put in hand for the improvement of U.S. coal export facilities. A new deepwater berth to take bulk carriers of up to 100,000 tons dw was nearing completion at the port of Beilun in China's Zhejiang (Chekiang) Province.

Shipbuilding

Orders placed for new ships in the first half of 1980 confirmed that the market had begun to recover from the acute shortage of new contracts and massive overcapacity that had characterized 1979. After a dramatic reduction from 61 million tons dw at mid-1978 to 53 million tons dw a year later, the world order book recovered in 1980 to reach 67 million tons dw or 32 million grt.

The breakdown of the total world order book for new tonnage showed bulk carriers leading with 12.5 million grt, tankers second at 10 million grt, and general cargo types third at 5 million grt; the remaining 4.5 million grt consisted of fishing vessels and craft for offshore service and supply duties. In terms of tankers, bulk carriers, and dry-cargo ships on order, Japan maintained a large lead with orders totaling just over 26 million tons dw. South Korea was in second place with 4,230,000 tons dw. The types of ships dominating the new order market

KEYSTONE

Auxiliary sails on a new Japanese tanker launched in Tokyo in September can lower energy requirements by as much as one-half; the sails are computer controlled.

were tankers in the 70,000–90,000-tons-dw class, Panamax (suitable for the dimensions of the locks in the Panama Canal) bulk carriers, and product and chemical carriers.

The general feeling that despite the full order books held by the Japanese shipyards there would be at least two or three lean years ahead for the industry found support in Scandinavia and Western Europe. The only hope for the employment of certain sections of shipyard staff was the modernization of existing ships, especially through fuel-saving and pollution-control features.

The interest in repairs was reflected by the provision of additional facilities to handle such work in various parts of the world. Taiwanese ship repairers were installing two new dry docks to accommodate up to 30,000-ton and 75,000-ton ships, respectively. The state-owned Sembawang shipyard at Singapore was scheduled to take delivery in 1981 of a 150,000-ton-dw floating dock as part of a major plan to increase facilities, and the Tuas repair yard at Singapore also invested in a new dry dock, to be ready in 1982, that would take vessels of up to 330,000 tons dw. Ship repair yards in Greece hoped to benefit from the expected increase in the tonnage of tankers passing through the Suez Canal, and they also expected to increase their share of the market when Greece entered the European Economic Community in 1981.

Although U.S. shipyards had orders for just over 1.5 million grt of shipping at mid-1980 and were at that time sixth in the list of top ten shipbuilders in terms of tonnage on order, builders needed new orders if heavy layoffs were to be avoided. Much depended upon the implementation of a long-range Maritime Administration program to rebuild the U.S.-flag dry bulk fleet and the immediate commencement of the subsidized construction of five new dry bulk cargo ships of about 40,000 tons dw each.

SKIING

Although Olympic glamour could not be denied, the season's most prestigious competition was the 14th Alpine World Cup series, which rewarded consistency in events spread over four months. This time a unique family success was achieved by the Liechtenstein brother and sister Andreas and Hanni Wenzel, respective winners of the men's and women's titles, a proud achievement for the tiny European principality of only 25,000 residents.

Ingemar Stenmark of Sweden, foremost in both the giant slalom and slalom, finished a close second in men's competition despite his refusal to race in

any downhill event. The former World Cup champion had a string of 15 giant slalom victories broken by a fall at Waterville Valley, N.H., in late February; until then he had won every World Cup giant slalom since the final race of the 1978 season. Phil Mahre of the U.S. was able to finish third in the Cup competition through sheer all-around ability without specializing. Wenzel was most noted as a slalom racer, but his considerable downhill skills helped win him the title. The best downhill skiers were Peter Müller of Switzerland and Ken Read of Canada, who, conversely to Stenmark, preferred not to race in the slaloms.

Regaining the women's title she first won in 1978, Hanni Wenzel—always stylishly efficient and unwavering in concentration—jockeyed for the leadership with her two main rivals, Annemarie Moser-Proell of Austria and Marie-Theres Nadig of Switzerland, who finished second and third, respectively. Moser-Proell, the defending champion, was eventually thwarted in her bid for a seventh success by flu and a knee injury during the latter part of the winter. She extended her record total of individual events won to 66, spanning 11 World Cup seasons. Wenzel proved best in the giant slalom and Nadig in the downhill, but the highest scorer in the slalom was Perrine Pelen of France. The concurrently decided Nations' Cup was won for the eighth successive time by Austria. Switzerland was runner-up for the sixth straight year, and the U.S. placed third.

André Arnold of Austria won the professional men's title for the third straight year on the North American circuit. His compatriot Hans Hinterseer placed second, and Lonny Vanatta of the U.S. finished third. Jocelyne Perrillat of France captured the women's crown from the defending champion,

The brother-sister team of Andreas and Hanni Wenzel of Liechtenstein continued to triumph in international ski competition. Andreas (left) won the World Cup giant slalom in Oberstaufen, West Germany, in March; Hanni had won the women's version in January in Berchtesgaden.
PHOTOS, WIDE WORLD

WIDE WORLD

Sweden's remarkable Ingemar Stenmark rounds a gate on his way to an Olympic gold medal in the giant slalom at Lake Placid, New York.

Norway's Toril Forland, who placed second. Lyndall Heyer of the U.S. finished third.

The International Ski Federation (FIS) began discussing plans to launch a new alpine combined event comprising downhill and slalom; it would be separate from and in addition to the regular downhill and slalom racing. The proposal was expected to be introduced in the 1982 world alpine championships at Schladming, Austria, and perhaps added to the 1984 Olympic schedule at Sarajevo, Yugoslavia.

Nordic Events

Following the first official Nordic World Cup series in 1979 and with plans for a second in 1981, unofficial standings in a series of 15 major cross-country meetings in 13 countries during 1980 were registered and served as guidance to the season's best performers. Juha Mieto of Finland was thus acknowledged as a decisive victor, with Thomas Wassberg of Sweden runner-up and Lars-Erik Eriksen of Norway third. No comparable women's series was staged. Unofficial ratings were similarly assessed in jumping, involving 104 of the world's leading competitors. The winner was Hubert Neuper and the runner-up Armin Kogler, both Austrians; Stanislaw Bobak from Poland was third.

The largest entry was, as usual, for the annual Vasa race from Salen to Mora, Sweden. Approximately 12,000 skiers took part in the event commemorating the Swedish king's escape on skis from Danish soldiers in 1521. The winner was Walter Mayer of Austria. The organizers, aware that some women had already participated incognito, announced that women would be officially admitted for the first time in 1981.

A 20-km cross-country event for women was proposed by the FIS for future world and Olympic programs, which would bring the number of men's and women's Nordic races to four each. The event was expected to be included in the 1982 world Nordic championships in Oslo, Norway.

Other Events

Professional freestyle skiing gained a new men's champion in Greg Athans of Canada, winner of the World Trophy series in North America. The runner-up was Frank Beddor of the U.S., and another Canadian, Rick Bowie, finished third. Canada's Stephanie Sloan retained the women's title, with her compatriot Lauralee Bowie runner-up; third was Hedi Garharmer from West Germany.

A world endurance record was claimed by an Italian, Ivano Marangoni. He skied 252 km (155 mi) in 24 hours at Lanzada, Italy.

(*See also* Olympic Games.)

SOCIAL SERVICES

Social welfare issues received relatively low priority in the U.S. in 1980 in two important arenas—Congress and the presidential election campaign.

With attention focused on the economy and foreign affairs, social policy took a back seat during the campaign even though the candidates had clear philosophical differences. Republican Ronald Reagan favoured reversing the trend toward greater federal responsibility, while Pres. Jimmy Carter talked of an even greater federal role in meeting social needs. The candidates also differed on where assistance should be focused, Carter stressing the neediest people and communities and Reagan advocating some programs that would benefit those who are not among the poorest.

A cautious, economy-minded Congress shied away from either new initiatives or major reforms in the social welfare field. Typical was its approach to Social Security, which produced considerable discussion about basic changes in funding and eligibility but little action. Two minor cutbacks were enacted—a reduction of disability benefits for workers disabled after July 1, 1980, and removal of prison inmates from the ranks of those eligible to collect benefits.

The 35 million Social Security recipients received an automatic 14.3% cost-of-living increase in their benefits in July. On Jan. 1, 1981, the largest single boost in payroll taxes since the inception of Social Security was to go into effect. The tax rate would rise from 6.13 to 6.65% and taxable earnings from $25,900 to $29,700. This meant that the maximum tax for an individual in 1981 would be $1,975.05, compared with $1,587.67 in 1980.

Congress did make one important shift in social policy. It acted to move low-income children out of foster homes and back with their real families or into new, adoptive families. Nearly half of the 500,000 children in foster care in the U.S. had been there more than two years and about 100,000 more than six years. A new law limited the money that Washington could provide to states for foster care and furnished financial aid for adoption.

Other legislation enacted by Congress included: a $41.2 billion housing and community development bill that reauthorized several programs for low-income housing but did not include apartments for middle-income families; an extension of child nutrition programs, with an increase in the cost of school lunches for middle-income children; an increase in federal spending for mental health services and expansion of those services to groups that had not been adequately served in the past, such as the elderly, severely disturbed children, and the chronically mentally ill.

Other important measures were a three-year extension of revenue sharing, the no-strings grant program, providing $4.6 billion a year to local governments and $2.3 billion annually (in fiscal 1982 and 1983 only) to states; an increase in food stamp expenditures to $9.5 billion for fiscal 1980 and $9.7 billion for 1981 and enactment of several cost-saving changes. Food stamp rolls reached an all-time high of 22.1 million persons in August 1980, and the new spending ceiling made the program the largest of the three main federal welfare programs. Also enacted were a low-income energy assistance program, funded at $1.8 billion annually, and renewal of the Legal Services Corporation. Among the measures that failed to win passage were the Domestic Violence Act, providing federal support to help states care for victims of abuse by family members, and the Youth Employment Act.

One issue that did not produce its usual lengthy debate in Congress was federal funding of abortions. The centre of attention shifted to the U.S. Supreme Court, which ruled in July that poor women do not have a constitutional right to publicly funded abortions. In a 5-to-4 decision, the court upheld the so-called Hyde Amendment, which prohibits federal funding of most abortions. As a result, it was estimated that federal funds would pay for only 2,000 abortions a year, compared with about 470,000 that would be financed if there were no restrictions.

Although social issues were not uppermost among congressional or political concerns, they were the subject of consideration and study in other forums. Among the recommendations given highest priority by the White House Conference on Families were: reform of Social Security to eliminate biases against families; better health care and home care for the aging; development of alternative forms of child care; support for efforts to prevent family violence; services to assist pregnant teenagers and teenage parents.

The Social Security Administration reported that the U.S. was spending an increasingly smaller share of its gross national product (GNP) on social welfare. In 1976 combined federal, state, and local expenditures for social welfare, including Social Security, accounted for 20.4% of GNP; the proportion had fallen to 19.3% by 1978. Meanwhile, the poverty population of the U.S. remained about level. According to the Census Bureau, 25.2 million Americans lived below the poverty line ($7,412 annual income for a nonfarm family of four) in 1979. That was about 11 million fewer than in 1964, when the War on Poverty began, but most of the decline occurred during the 1960s. Between 1972 and 1979, the proportion of Americans who were poor fell only from 11.9 to 11.6%.

In Cape Town hundreds of Coloured (mixed-race) demonstrators, denied permission to commemorate the June 1976 Soweto riots, began a rampage in which at least 40 people were killed. It was one of a continuing series of violent clashes between police and demonstrators throughout the year.

JOHN RUBYTHON—GAMMA/LIAISON

SOUTH AFRICA

Legislation enacted in 1980 abolished South Africa's 70-year-old second legislative chamber, the Senate, and replaced it with a multiracial advisory President's Council of 54 government-nominated members selected from the white, Coloured, Indian, and Chinese communities. No black representatives were included. A separate black advisory council was to be consulted by the President's Council when necessary. The noninclusion of blacks was criticized by the opposition Progressive Federal Party (PFP), and the black, Coloured, and Indian organizations would not cooperate in forming the council. The government then dropped the black advisory council. The President's Council was to become operative on Jan. 1, 1981.

Under the same legislation the Cabinet was enlarged from 18 to 20 and Parliament—the single-chamber Assembly—by 12 members. This change gave the ruling party 11 additional members. A further change was the disbandment of the Coloured Persons' Representative Council, not to be replaced with a nominated Coloured Persons' Council, in view of Coloured opposition.

The concept of a "constellation of states," envisioning the ultimate objective of a "common market" for southern Africa, was furthered by an agreement between South Africa and leaders of the three independent homelands—Transkei, Bophuthatswana, and Venda—in July to establish full regional cooperation. A multilateral bank for southern Africa was to be established and existing development corporations reorganized. The black homelands jointly pleaded with the government to delay such moves until South Africa's internal problems—with particular reference to themselves —had been solved. The semiofficial Bureau for Economic Research, Cooperation, and Development reported that separate economies could not be created for the homelands and advocated drastic structural changes, including joint management of industrial border areas.

The chief minister of the Ciskei, Chief Lennox Sebe, intimated that he was prepared to accept independence for the homeland subject to retention of South African citizenship rights by Ciskeians living outside the homeland and to the transfer of more land to the Ciskei. With nearly half of the Ciskeians living outside the borders of the homeland, Sebe's decision to opt for independence, even on his stated terms, drew sharp criticism from other homeland leaders. Prime Minister P. W. Botha said that it was not government policy to press the homelands to become independent. Provisional proposals to consolidate the Ciskei, issued on October 31, provided for the addition of 100,000 ha (250,000 ac) of land to the territory and the incorporation of the century-old settlers' city of King William's Town, with an estimated population of 22,680, of whom 50% were white. The Ciskei voted overwhelmingly for independence in a referendum held in December.

Tentative steps were taken during the year to relax policies affecting the employment and movement of black workers in "white" urban areas and also affecting restrictions on the sharing of public facilities and racially mixed sports. There was mounting public opposition to the rigid enforcement of the Group Areas Act in such cases as the occupation by nonwhites of flats or other dwellings in "white" areas and of their removal from such areas to make way for whites. A former postmaster general, Louis Rive, was appointed coordinator of far-reaching projects to improve life in the Soweto complex near Johannesburg, with its estimated million black inhabitants.

With the acceptance of the right of black workers to join or form legally recognized trade unions, some registered unions in 1980 admitted black members. In addition to the mixed groups, several black unions sought registration under the amended industrial legislation. For the first time, representatives of black labour sat on the industrial council of the major iron, steel, engineering, and metallurgical industries. Job reservation, the long-standing barrier to the entry of black workers into skilled occupations, was practically abolished. In general, the training of badly needed black skilled workers was encouraged, but in mining, determined white trade union opposition still imposed a colour bar.

The changes raised expectations of more radical reforms. Added emphasis was given to those expectations by the publication of a judge's report on the Soweto riots of 1976 criticizing the government's role. It coincided with a wave of unrest and violence in black and Coloured communities in many parts of the country which originated primarily, as in 1976, in the admittedly inadequate system of nonwhite education. School-class boycotts in Soweto and on a larger scale in the Cape Peninsula, with the accompanying disorders, were followed by similar disturbances in other areas, including South West Africa/Namibia and some of the black homelands. As the unrest dragged on, particularly in the Eastern Cape, it gradually also involved industries and transportation services. In the attempts to restore order, there was a growing loss of life and limb. The government blamed behind-the-scenes agitators and closed down many schools in the affected areas indefinitely. Through the Human Sciences Research Council it set up a commission of inquiry into the educational system.

Efforts continued intermittently to reach an agreement on the future of South West Africa/ Namibia in terms of an internationally accepted independence for the territory. Proposals by UN Secretary-General Kurt Waldheim for a cease-fire in the guerrilla warfare, a demilitarized zone on the Namibia-Angola border to be patrolled by a UN Transition Assistance Group (UNTAG), and a UN-supervised election for a constituent assembly were modified from time to time to meet South African objections. These centred mainly on the composition and functions of UNTAG, the location and monitoring of the South West Africa People's Organization (SWAPO) guerrillas during the cease-fire and transition period, and what South Africa saw as the UN's partiality toward SWAPO.

The negotiations reached a virtual deadlock in midyear. In late October a UN team headed by Brian Urquhart, undersecretary for special political affairs, arrived in Pretoria on a mission to end the stalemate and secure a final timetable for implementing the settlement proposals. The mission sounded out internal Namibian opinion and left the door open for the next move by Waldheim and the Security Council, where there were pressures for mandatory sanctions after the UN initiative failed. Meanwhile, the National Assembly in the Namibian capital of Windhoek, dominated by the Democratic Turnhalle Alliance (DTA), elected a multiparty Council of Ministers with executive powers, headed by Dirk Mudge, DTA leader. Antidiscrimination legislation was adopted, and provision was made for the introduction of compulsory military service for all races. The territory established its own defense department, subject to the South African Defense Force's remaining responsible for security as long as required. Fighting in the "operational area" continued unremittingly, with increasingly heavy losses for SWAPO in border skirmishes and in their bases farther afield.

Newly independent Zimbabwe broke off diplomatic and sports relations with South Africa but

Recognizing that economic growth in South Africa was being stalled because of a lack of skilled workers, the government instituted some training programs for black workers. White labour had long succeeded in keeping blacks in unskilled jobs, to the detriment of industry and mining.
ALON REININGER—CONTACT

maintained economic, tourist, and other ties under special arrangements. Its prime minister, Robert Mugabe, made it clear that his sympathies lay with South African resistance movements. They would receive his support but would not be allowed to use Zimbabwe as a springboard for attacks on South Africa, he declared. Reacting against South African plans for a regional "constellation of states," Zimbabwe joined eight other southern African nations in considering steps to reduce their dependence on South Africa in trade, transport, and communications. The other countries were Angola, Botswana, Malawi, Mozambique, Swaziland, Tanzania, Zambia, and Lesotho. The same countries, with the exception of Angola and Tanzania, set up a commission to consider ways of checking the flow of migrant labour to South Africa, even though it formed an important source of revenue for them.

On September 29 the Appeal Court set aside the conviction and sentence of six years in prison passed on Eschel Mostert Rhoodie in the Transvaal Supreme Court in October 1979 on charges of alleged fraud. Rhoodie had been the secretary of the former Department of Information, the activities of which both in and outside South Africa were the centre of investigation by government commissions and of a political storm in 1978–79.

On March 26 the minister of finance, Owen Horwood, presented the 1980 budget—totaling R 13 billion, with 16% for defense—against a background of strong economic revival stimulated by higher gold prices and the long-term effects of the fiscal discipline of the previous years. Significant indicators were a record balance of payments surplus, increased foreign reserve holdings, buoyant state revenue and tax remissions, and more flexible credit policies.

SOUTHEAST ASIAN AFFAIRS

Defense and security remained Southeast Asia's primary preoccupation throughout 1980. Already alarmed by Vietnam's invasion of Cambodia in December 1978, members of the Association of Southeast Asian Nations (ASEAN) had their worst fears confirmed when Vietnamese troops staged a lightning military strike into Thailand in June.

Vietnamese in Cambodia

ASEAN foreign ministers gathered in Kuala Lumpur within days of the Vietnamese attack on Thailand. Their counterparts from the U.S., Canada, Japan, Australia, and New Zealand also journeyed to the Malaysian capital, demonstrating worldwide concern over the trend of events in the region. Despite earlier differences in policy approaches to Indochina, the ASEAN ministers spoke with one voice in expressing anxiety over the continued presence of Vietnamese troops in Cambodia, deploring Hanoi's failure to heed calls for a political settlement of the Cambodia conflict, noting with grave concern the growing rivalry of outside powers in the region, and

calling for an international conference on Cambodia.

Although the ministers' 23-page communiqué and a separate "joint statement on the situation along the Thai-Cambodian border" proclaimed a strong ASEAN stance against Vietnam, many leaders were worried that the latter, in its isolation, would turn even more toward Moscow and get the Soviet Union embroiled yet more deeply in the region's affairs. That in turn could push ASEAN closer to China, leading to an ominous polarization in Southeast Asia.

The grim scenario received a further boost as ASEAN countries plunged as never before into a flurry of intense international lobbying to keep the Vietnam-backed Cambodian government out of Cambodia's UN seat. They succeeded, but the lobbying did not stop. There were reports of a growing recognition at ASEAN's highest echelons that the deposed Pol Pot regime, which continued to occupy the UN seat, was unworthy of support because of its record of genocide. ASEAN as a body began promoting the idea that a third force or non-Communist alternative should be found in Cambodia so that the security threat posed by the unsettled situation in that country could finally be ended.

The Thai and Singapore prime ministers led the campaign by trying to enlist China's support for the concept. But there were no definite indications that China would give up its backing of Pol Pot. That and the refusal till the end of the year by former Cambodian head of state Prince Norodom Sihanouk to lead a third force left ASEAN leaders unsure of how the overall security problem in the region would develop.

ASEAN and U.S. Support

In line with this sense of uncertainty, a rethinking of ASEAN's relations with the big powers seemed under way. Many government leaders were of the view that the U.S. should become more involved in regional defense than had the administration of Pres. Jimmy Carter. The Philippine government made no secret of its support of Ronald Reagan in the U.S. presidential election. Even before the shift in its leadership the U.S. had started restoring its old military presence in Thailand. By midyear U.S. Department of Defense sources indicated that military assistance to all Southeast Asian countries was being increased. From a peak of $161,750,000 in 1977, such assistance to the five ASEAN countries had declined to $106.6 million in 1979. During 1980 it picked up again and was estimated to reach a total in excess of $147 million. Along with the increased aid there was also an upswing in the sale of weapons to ASEAN countries by the U.S., their principal military supplier.

Relations with the U.S.S.R.

If ASEAN countries moved closer to the U.S. during the year, there was a clear cooling off toward

The refugee problem in Southeast Asia continued to be a serious drain on the economy and social services in Thailand. Attempts were made, as here, to return some Cambodian refugees to their homeland.

PHOTO TRENDS / CAMERA PRESS

the Soviet Union. Singapore took the lead in projecting the view that Moscow was spearheading a new kind of imperialism with Southeast Asia as a prime target. Others did not go quite that far but nevertheless developed reservations about Soviet intentions. China fueled Southeast Asian suspicions by pointing to Soviet gains in Indochina. In October China's Xinhua (Hsinhua) news agency reported that the number of Tupolev TU-95 heavy bombers stationed by the Soviet Union in Vietnam's giant Cam Ranh Bay base had doubled from two to four, that the Soviet Union used the base as a takeoff point for surveillance flights over Southeast Asia, that flights of Ilyushin IL-62 transports from Vladivostok to Cam Ranh Bay had more than doubled, that "well over 20" Soviet warships were sometimes simultaneously serviced at the port, and that the aircraft carrier "Minsk" put into the port for the first time in September.

The Soviet Union for its part was clearly interested in keeping itself on the right side of Southeast Asian countries and in cautioning them against China's tactics. Describing the visit to China in November by Singapore Prime Minister Lee Kuan Yew as pointless, a Moscow commentator said: "To regard Beijing [Peking] as a kind mother who will understand the concerns of ASEAN means cherishing illusions." According to diplomatic circles, the Soviet Union wished to maintain a dialogue with Southeast Asian countries because it was worried that China might gain ground in the region through false pretenses. It was apprehensive also of the return of U.S. influence to the area.

Relations with China

With China itself, Southeast Asian countries maintained close commercial and consular relations, attracted by Beijing's pragmatic shift to economic modernization. However, the view per-

sisted that the long-term threat to the region's stability came from China. Underlying this fear was China's insistence that its relations with and support of the underground Communist groups in most Southeast Asian countries would not be affected by the state-to-state relations it was now fostering with the governments of the region. During his visit to China in November Lee Kuan Yew planned to challenge this position in a banquet speech. But his Chinese hosts persuaded him instead to discuss the matter with national leader Deng Xiaoping (Teng Hsiao-p'ing) in private.

In November Indonesia's First Admiral Suwarso publicly warned that China had finalized plans to expand its naval presence off Southeast Asia, purportedly to counter the growing Soviet naval strength there and to protect its disputed claims in marine oil fields and other resources in the area. He said that such an enlargement of China's fleet would pose a security threat to the ASEAN nations and increase the risk of superpower tension in the region.

Approaches to Japan and Australia

Japan and Australia were the other outside powers that loomed large on Southeast Asia's horizon during the year. ASEAN had running arguments with both countries—with Japan because of its apparent stinginess in regard to promised aid, and with Australia over its protectionist trade and commercial policies. Lee Kuan Yew even had a public exchange of hot words with Australian Prime Minister Malcolm Fraser while they were returning from the Commonwealth regional meeting in New Delhi, India, in September. However, ASEAN countries seemed interested in moving closer to Japan and Australia through the Pacific Community concept, promoted by the latter two countries in tandem with the U.S. ASEAN representatives attended an unofficial seminar held in Canberra in February to discuss the concept.

Economic Developments

The region's relations with Europe, largely confined to trade and commerce, were consolidated in March when an ASEAN-European Economic Community cooperation agreement was signed. It was hailed as a landmark heralding a new stage of formalized arrangements with European countries on an equitable footing. The agreement, to last for five years, offered ASEAN the prospect of liberal terms for trade, investment, and technological cooperation.

Southeast and East Asia together maintained their position as the world's most dynamic growth area. While Japan, Taiwan, and Hong Kong were leaders in their fields, Southeast Asian countries contributed to the overall picture. Singapore led the region with an estimated growth rate of 8%, while Malaysia followed with 7%. Indonesia and the Philippines each registered a rate of growth of about 5%. Thailand alone was in some difficulty owing to a ruinous succession of drought and flood on the one hand and a crushing refugee burden on the other.

In April the Asian Development Bank released its annual report providing final figures for 1979 for the whole of Asia. Growth rates had risen, it noted, in Singapore (9.3% from 8.6% in 1978) and Malaysia (8.1% from 7.4%). They declined in In-donesia (4.9% from 7.2%), the Philippines (5.7% from 5.8%), and Thailand (6.5% from 12%), largely because of a slowdown in agriculture. While the Asia-wide inflation rate (based on consumer price indexes) rose to 11.6%, Indonesia recorded the highest at 21.8% followed by the Philippines at 18.8%.

ASEAN bankers took a major step toward regional industrialization in February when they approved plans to create an ASEAN Financial Corporation and an ASEAN bankers' acceptance market. The wholly ASEAN-owned corporation, with an initial capitalization of $50 million, was intended to provide capital and support services to industrial ventures catering to three or more ASEAN members. The acceptance market's aim was to promote trade within the group.

(*See also* articles on the various countries.)

SPACE EXPLORATION

Clearly the most significant event in manned space flight during 1980 was the record-breaking 185 days spent aboard the Salyut 6 space station by Soviet cosmonauts Valery V. Ryumin and Leonid I. Popov. The pair returned to Earth in the Soyuz 37 spacecraft on October 11.

Ryumin had previously spent 2 days in space in 1977 and 175 days aboard the space station in 1979, giving him a total of 362 days. Neither cosmonaut evidenced any disability on medical examination at the landing site. Physicians were, however, baffled

In July an emergency airlift of weapons to Thailand, including artillery and ammunition, was undertaken by the U.S. to aid the country after Vietnamese troops struck across the Thai-Cambodian border in June.
UPI

by the fact that both men had gained weight. The two men each grew an inch but soon lost it as they adjusted to the Earth's gravity.

During their six months in space Ryumin and Popov performed a number of scientific and technological experiments. Primary among them were the growing of various crystals in the weightless environment in an effort to produce better semiconductor materials and the production of polyurethane foam structures. Among the life science experiments were studies of the production and effect of interferon in human cells. The end of the mission brought the number of Soviet man-hours in space to 45,564, more than double the U.S. total of 22,494.

The Salyut 6, which began its fourth year in orbit on September 29, was visited by five manned spacecraft and six unmanned spacecraft between December 1979 and November 1980. Among them was an improved T model of the Soyuz spacecraft, with Soviet cosmonauts Yury V. Malyshev and Vladimir V. Aksenov aboard. The spacecraft had an onboard computer, an improved and simplified propulsion and maneuvering system, solar-cell power arrays, and a powerful retrorocket for soft landings. The two men tested the T-2 extensively before docking with the Salyut 6. They returned to Earth aboard it on June 9.

Manned space flight by the U.S. was nonexistent during the year, as it had been since 1975. Optimistically, however, the National Aeronautics and Space Administration (NASA) began recruiting for mission specialists and pilot astronauts. A total of 3,465 men and women applied, and 19 were selected in May. Eight were pilots, all male, and 11 were mission specialists, of whom 2 were female.

Experiments for the first operational Spacelab mission late in 1982 were selected by NASA and the European Space Agency (ESA) in May. The 37 experiments were in the fields of atmospheric physics and Earth observations, astronomy and solar physics, materials science and technology, space plasma physics, and the life sciences. Of the total 13 were to be sponsored by NASA and 24 by ESA.

Launch Vehicles

The year was a frustrating one for NASA's trouble-plagued space shuttle. By the end of the year developmental costs of the program had increased by 25% in terms of fiscal year 1971 dollars, or $6.4 billion. The increase could be attributed to insufficient funding of the original program and to unexpected technological problems. In addition to troubles with the main engine of the shuttle orbiter, the problem of bonding the heat-shield tiles to the vehicle proved to be much more complicated and time-consuming than originally foreseen. The magnitude of the problem was illustrated by the fact that there were 31,000 tiles, each of which had to be hand-bonded to the orbiter.

The usually well-informed magazine *Aviation Week & Space Technology*, in its June 16, 1980, issue, made public what had long been known to the intelligence agencies of the West. The U.S.S.R. had under development a huge launch vehicle that seemed destined to play an important role in that nation's interplanetary space programs for decades to come. The vehicle, approximately 90 m (300 ft) long and 15 m (50 ft) in diameter at the base, was designed to be capable of lifting 99,000 kg (220,000 lb) into low-Earth orbit. Also revealed in 1980 was another Soviet launch vehicle, a two-man, reusable space shuttle to be launched by an expendable rocket.

Unmanned Satellites

As 1979 ended, West Germany and France were making plans with far-reaching consequences in the

Soviet cosmonauts Valery V. Ryumin (left) and Leonid I. Popov spent a record 185 days in space in 1980. They worked aboard the Salyut 6 space station.

WIDE WORLD

The U.S. space shuttle "Columbia" fell further behind schedule for its projected launch date. One major problem was the 31,000 silica-fibre tiles that formed a skin over the aircraft to protect it from the friction of passing through the Earth's atmosphere. The tiles refused to adhere adequately to the craft's aluminum skin.

NASA

field of communications satellite technology. The two nations were organizing a joint venture to build, market, and manage a direct broadcast television satellite system. Within the next decade it might comprise 12 to 15 satellites in orbit. Two operational satellites, one each built by West Germany and France, were scheduled to be launched by the end of 1985.

Launched on Oct. 29, 1979, NASA's Magsat satellite proved to be a valuable scientific tool for the U.S. Geological Survey. Data from it helped compile the most accurate maps ever produced of the Earth's magnetic field. Such information is of great assistance to geologists searching for new mineral and petroleum deposits.

A scientific satellite designed to study the ultraviolet and X-ray radiation from the Sun during its maximum period of activity was launched on February 14. Solar Maximum Mission satellite (SMM) provided scientists with data that complemented that obtained by Skylab, which orbited during the period of the Sun's minimum activity. On May 21 SMM recorded a 40-minute solar flare, one of the largest ever detected.

Space Probes

Feb. 22, 1980, was an exceptionally clear day on Mars, and the Viking 1 orbiter probe noted it well. Photomosaics revealed two meteorological features never before seen on the planet. One of them was a sharp, dark line, curving north and east from the volcano Arsia Mons in the Tharsis Ridge. Unsure of what it was, scientists suggested it could be either a weather front or an atmospheric shock wave. Also pictured were four small clouds near the crater Lowell. From shadows cast on the surface, scientists estimated that the largest was about 32 km (20 mi) long. Other measurements indicated that shadows are extremely rare in Viking pictures.

Also during the month the Soviet probe Venera 12, at a distance of 190,373,790 km (118,031,679 mi) from Earth, was commanded to turn its instruments toward Comet Bradfield. The nucleus of the comet was studied by its ultraviolet spectrometer, jointly developed by Soviet and French scientists. Spectral analyses of its data would permit quantitative estimates of such elements as hydrogen, helium, argon, and oxygen in the comet.

Evaluation of images made on March 5, 1979, and returned from Voyager 1 convinced Stephen P. Synnott of the Jet Propulsion Laboratory that Jupiter had a 15th moon. The satellite was numbered 1979 J2 and appeared to be between 70 km and 80 km (43 to 50 mi) in diameter. With a period of 16 hours it circles the planet at a distance of 151,000 km (93,000 mi) above the cloud tops and between the orbits of its sister moons Amalthea and Io. Synnott later discovered a 16th moon some 40 km (25 mi) in diameter orbiting about 56,000 km (34,800 mi) above the planet's cloud layer.

On April 2 Mars Viking Lander 2 exhausted its energy and became an artifact awaiting discovery or recovery by interplanetary archaeologists of the future. After 3.5 years of searching for evidence of Earth-type life forms on Mars, the probe finished its mission with negative results. Since landing on Mars on Sept. 3, 1976, the probe had returned to Earth more than 1,800 pictures of the terrain around it.

The Viking Orbiter 1 was ordered silenced in August during its 1,489th orbit of Mars. Its gas supply for the stabilizing jets was exhausted. The orbiter began a slow tumble that would take it on a 75-year fall to the surface of Mars.

Radar scanning of 93% of Venus by Pioneer Venus provided scientists with the first map of the surface of that planet. Long considered Earth's sister planet, Venus proved to be nothing like the

Earth. The two major terrain features were "continents," one as large as Australia and the other half the size of Africa.

After a journey of 2,000,000,000 km (1,250,-000,000 mi) and more than two years, Voyager 1 passed within 125,000 km (77,000 mi) of Saturn on November 12. Among its many remarkable discoveries were that the planet has at least 15 moons rather than 12; that it has a complex system of major and minor rings, two of which appear to be interwoven in a braided pattern; and that it has a huge encircling cloud of neutral hydrogen gas. After its encounter with Saturn, Voyager 1 continued on a trajectory that would eventually take it out of the Solar System.

At a meeting of ESA held in Paris on July 8 and 9, the decision was made for that organization to develop a probe to study Halley's Comet. The 750-kg (1,650-lb) spacecraft would be derived from the organization's GEOS satellite and would fly through the comet in 1986.

(*See also* Aerospace; Astronomy.)

On Dec. 14, 1979, the French launch vehicle Ariane was successfully tested; a second trial in May was a failure.

GHISLAINE MOREL—GAMMA

SPAIN

In 1980 political developments demanded more than their fair share of the government's energy and led to a feeling of loss of direction and lack of efficient leadership in economic matters. In March, having seen moderate nationalists safely elected to head regional parliaments in the Basque region and Catalonia, the authorities concluded that the autonomy issue had been defused. Earlier, in the February 28 referendum on the issue of devolution (the delegation of powers formerly held by the central government to regional or local authorities) for Andalusia, seven of the eight Andalusian provinces voted in favour of full regional autonomy. A campaign in favour of Andalusia's demands in particular and of speeded autonomy in general was mounted, and it resulted in a decline in the government's popularity nationwide. The Partido Socialista Obrero Español (PSOE) on May 30 moved to censure the policies of the government and lost by only 14 votes. The government's majority was cut to a single vote on June 13, when it defeated an opposition proposal to change Spain's law on referenda; the proposal was aimed at clearing a legal path for reholding the referendum in the Andalusian province of Almeria, the only one of the eight that did not vote for full autonomy.

The summer recess of the Cortes (parliament) was taken up by negotiations among the factions of the governing Unión Centro Democrático (UCD) and with the regionally based parties in order to reengineer a working parliamentary majority. Premier Adolfo Suárez González announced his fifth Cabinet on September 8, including his principal critics in UCD who had lost their posts after the March 1979 elections. Suárez then sought a vote of confidence in the Cortes for a declaration of general policy. The five members of the Partido Socialista Andalusia (PSA) promised support for Suárez on his program for fully autonomous regional governments for Galicia and Andalusia and an accelerated transfer of power to the Basque and Catalan areas, thereby assuring the vote of confidence. Nevertheless, bitter confrontations occurred between Suárez and the leader of the PSOE, Felipe González, while the Basque Partido Nacionalista Vasco (PNV) ended its eight-month boycott of the Cortes and announced it would vote against the government.

Voting in the Cortes on the declaration of general policy was 180 votes in favour and 164 against, but PSA support was conditional on Suárez's fulfilling his part of the bargain on autonomy and government economic support for Andalusia. For Spain's economy Suárez promised to raise gross national product growth from near zero in 1980 to 4 or 5% by 1983. On September 30 the 1981 budget was introduced; government expenditure was to be raised by 23%.

On October 23 an agreement was signed in Madrid between the government and opposition parties. In it the administration agreed to hold a sec-

King Juan Carlos I of Spain visited Libreville, Gabon, as part of an African tour in 1980. He was greeted by Pres. Omar Bongo.

EFE/PHOTO TRENDS

ond referendum on the autonomy question in Almeria, thus allowing Andalusia to proceed to self-government, and to allow the passage of a bill to reform the referendum law (to allow a second poll on the same subject within five years). Elections for Andalusia's regional parliament would be held in 1981. Galicia voted for autonomy on December 21, but only about a fourth of those eligible actually voted. On December 31 the Cabinet voted to restore to the Basque regional government powers of taxation enjoyed before the Civil War.

The Cortes on October 29 passed a new antiterrorism law (298–2, 8 abstentions) in reply to mounting terrorism in the Basque provinces. In 1980 there was on average one political assassination every three days, and in November the UCD in the Basque provinces became a principal target, losing five members in a short space of time. Meanwhile, the "moderate" wing of the Euzkadi ta Azkatasuna (ETA) movement also began to kill.

Faced with a real threat to civil liberties, the right and centre wings of the PSOE pressed to join the UCD in mounting an all-out offensive against terrorism. On November 2, after abstaining from the vote on the new antiterrorism bill, prominent members of the PNV joined forces for the first time with local representatives of the UCD and other major parties in San Sebastian in a demonstration against violence in the Basque country. Supporters of ETA tried to prevent the 50,000-strong march but were forced to flee when the police intervened.

In June the government announced that it would seek membership in NATO in 1981. This brought protests from the Socialists and Communists. The government argued that with Spain's treaty with the U.S. running out in 1981, Spain should take part in its own defense; NATO membership was to be conditional on the solving of the Gibraltar dispute with Great Britain.

Spain finished its first round of preliminary entry negotiations with the European Economic Community (EEC). The second, more detailed discussions were postponed from July to November, when Spain's new EEC minister, Eduardo Punset, took office. Spain accepted that agricultural negotiations would be delayed but asked if it could borrow from the European Investment Bank in advance of its EEC membership. (*See* European Affairs.)

SRI LANKA

In 1980 Sri Lanka welcomed foreign investment in fields lacking local capital, technology, or expertise and permitted a major role for the private sector. Protection from imports was given to some local industries. A 12-member Sri Lanka Aid Consortium, meeting in Paris in July, pledged more than $1 billion in new aid (a 42% increase over 1979). A general strike threatened to paralyze the economy, and the government proclaimed an emergency on July 16. The emergency, approved by Parliament, was ended on August 15. On October 16 former prime minister Sirimavo Bandaranaike was expelled from Parliament and deprived of her civil rights for alleged abuses of power. Fearing possible disorders, the government again declared an emergency on October 14.

A major legislative effort in tackling the country's ethnic problems was the passage in August of the district development bill, introduced after a presidential commission decided against a separate Tamil homeland. It provided for decentralization and the association of people of various regions through 24 elected district councils.

In international affairs Sri Lanka's policies were closer to those of the Association of Southeast Asian Nations (ASEAN) than to those of its northern neighbour, India. Sri Lanka condemned Soviet action in Afghanistan, did not accord recognition to the Heng Samrin government in Cambodia, and opposed militarization of the Indian Ocean.

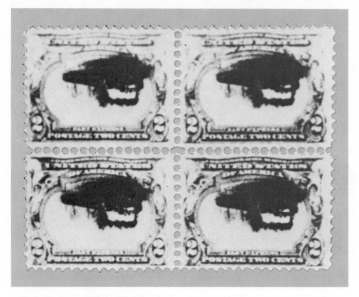

This block of four U.S. stamps with upside-down centres due to a printing error brought $240,000 in an auction in New York City in April, a record-high price.
WIDE WORLD

STAMPS AND COINS

A new world record price for a single stamp was established in April 1980 by Robert A. Seigel of New York City when he auctioned the only known example of the British Guiana 1856 one-cent stamp for $850,000. The buyer's identity was not disclosed. Classic stamps advanced steadily in value, but the overstretched market in the British "Seahorses" stamps of King George V reacted adversely when too many were released for sale almost simultaneously.

Sotheby Parke Bernet stamp auctions made an increasing impact on the U.S. stamp market and claimed two records: $240,000 for a mint block of four of the 1901 two-cent Pan-American Exposition stamps with inverted centres; and $240,000, again, for the only known cover with three clear impressions of the "Running Chicken" cancellation created by the postmaster of Waterbury, Conn. This identical cover was sold in 1976 for $45,000.

In May, Harmers of San Francisco held a four-day sale of the Sandra Ilene West collection of German stamps in the firm's London offices and realized £1,005,443, a new record for a single-country collection. The Bavarian section made £314,843 on the first day.

In May the UN Postal Administration announced the discovery of forgeries of the 1954 three-cent United Nations Day stamp. They were printed by photo-offset rather than the steel engraving (recess) process used for the genuine stamps. It was the first recorded forgery of a UN stamp. There was no worldwide issue during 1980, but the U.K. and many Commonwealth territories marked the 80th birthday of Queen Elizabeth, the queen mother, by issuing special stamps.

Coins

Coin collecting during the year was greatly influenced by the drastic changes in the prices of silver and gold bullion. After reaching highs of $50 and $880 per troy ounce, respectively, in the spring of 1980, silver and gold dropped quickly to $12 and $460. Before the decline the value of a U.S. silver dime, 1964 and earlier, had risen to about $3.50, that of a pre-1936 silver dollar to about $38.50, and that of a $20 gold coin to about $850. Many of the common-date silver and gold coins, especially those

The U.S. entered the gold medallion market in 1980 with a one-ounce gold medallion honouring artist Grant Wood ($645) and a half-ounce medallion honouring singer Marian Anderson ($322.50).
PHOTOS, WIDE WORLD

in somewhat worn condition, were melted and the metal reclaimed.

Continuing inflation and the purchase of rare coins as investments forced prices to new highs during the early part of 1980. However, the influence of the business recession was the cause of some weakening in the rare coin market by midyear.

As expected, the U.S. Treasury did start to sell gold medals to the public in one-ounce and half-ounce sizes in 1980. The purchase of these pieces through the Post Office was coordinated with the changing gold market, making transactions a bit complex. During the first two months that the medals could be ordered only about 332,000 of the 1.5 million pieces struck were sold, and the original September 30 deadline for ordering was extended to Dec. 31, 1980. The Susan B. Anthony dollar, released in 1979, continued to be unpopular, largely because its size caused it to be confused with the quarter. A "P" mint mark was placed on all coins struck at the Philadelphia Mint in 1980 except the cent.

Paper money of all kinds and numismatic books continued to increase in popularity with collectors, resulting in higher prices for both. An 1890 $1,000 U.S. "Treasury Note" reportedly sold for a record price for paper money of $100,000. At a California auction in June 1980, an 1869 *American Bond Detector* realized $3,200; a two-volume work on coinage in The Netherlands that brought $1,600 a year earlier was sold for $2,900; and an unusually fine first edition of *Heath's Counterfeit Detector* brought a record $650 for that series of books.

False collector coins continued to plague the marketplace. In addition to known false rare and expensive coins, the certification service of the American Numismatic Association in Colorado Springs, Colo., discovered counterfeits of such pieces as the 1972 doubled-die cent, 1926 $20 gold coin, and the popular 19th-century U.S.-type coins of various denominations.

During the year a number of countries issued new coins of interest to collectors. Coins relating to the 1980 Olympic Games in Moscow included issues by the Soviet Union, China, Hungary, Isle of Man, Jamaica, and Western Samoa. Belgium issued a 1980 silver 500-franc coin in observance of the 150th anniversary of its independence. Canada's 1980 silver dollar portrays a polar bear on an Arctic ice floe with the northern lights above. Canada also issued a 1980 gold coin containing one-half ounce of fine gold. Another 1980 gold coin was the $200 of Australia, containing about 0.295 troy ounce of fine gold and depicting the koala.

The medal authorized by the U.S. Congress in May 1979 honouring movie actor John Wayne was released by the Mint in March 1980. Orders for the two sizes of the portrait medal, which bears no other legend than "John Wayne—American," approached 500,000, making it the most popular mint medal of all time.

STATE GOVERNMENTS, U.S.

Continuing their recovery from the 1974 Watergate-related debacle, U.S. Republicans added four governorships and a modest number of legislative seats during 1980 elections. The results were particularly important because these newly elected officials would be redrawing congressional and legislative district boundaries based on 1980 census results.

Of the 13 governorships contested, Republicans won 7, wresting the statehouse from Democrats in Arkansas, Missouri, North Dakota, and Washington. That put the 1981 gubernatorial lineup at 27 Democrats and 23 Republicans.

For 1981 Democrats controlled both houses of 28 legislatures, while Republicans dominated in 14. All states were solidly Democratic except Arizona, Colorado, Idaho, Indiana, Iowa, Kansas, Montana, New Hampshire, North Dakota, Pennsylvania, South Dakota, Utah, Vermont, and Wyoming (where Republicans had a majority in both houses); Delaware, Illinois, Maine, New York, Ohio, and Washington (where each party controlled one chamber); Alaska (where Republicans controlled the House but the Senate was tied); and Nebraska (which has a nonpartisan, unicameral legislature).

(*See also* Elections.)

Amid signs of increasing disenchantment with government and taxes, belt tightening and retrenchment marked state organization during 1980. Although the Michigan governor vetoed a similar measure, Delaware and Illinois (late in 1979) approved new "sunset" laws, bringing to 34 the number of states providing for periodic termination of state agencies unless specific reauthorization is made. Arkansas voters rejected a proposed new state constitution. Alaska, California, and Mississippi reorganized various executive departments, and Illinois voters, following a 1978 Massachusetts lead, reduced the size of the lower house of the state legislature by one-third, from 177 to 118.

Government Relations

The ongoing tension between federal and state governments flared up during the year over finances and distribution of power. As a nationwide recession cut markedly into state revenue collections, the federal government proceeded with a cutoff of funding to states under general revenue sharing ($2.3 billion), countercyclical assistance ($1 billion), and Law Enforcement Assistance Administration (LEAA) grants ($600 million). State revenue sharing was scheduled to resume in October 1981 but might be vulnerable to future budget cuts.

As U.S. Pres. Jimmy Carter made efforts early in the year to cut federal expenditures, he began withholding federal highway aid to states, already hard hit by a decline in maintenance funds as a result of a drop in gasoline consumption. Arkansas, Maine, New Mexico, and Vermont obtained court injunc-

On March 10 Dave Treen was sworn in as governor of Louisiana, the first Republican to hold the post in over a hundred years.
WIDE WORLD

tions ordering the resumption of federal funding but not before lengthy delays had occurred.

Smoldering resentment over federal control of lands, especially in Western states, grew in intensity during the year. Arizona, New Mexico, Utah, Washington, and Wyoming formally joined Nevada in the "Sagebrush Rebellion," approving laws calling for state takeover of unreserved land currently controlled by the federal government. About one-third of the nation's land area was owned by the U.S., 90% of it west of the Rocky Mountains. Yet the revolt appeared to be spreading eastward: Ohio became the first state to revoke its "automatic consent" statute that gave formal state approval to federal land purchases under Article I, Section 8, Clause 17 of the U.S. Constitution.

Several state leaders predicted that federal-state tensions would worsen in future years as the nation looked to Western lands for development of alternative energy sources. The governors of Nevada and Utah provided a foretaste of that conflict when they informed Congress that they opposed construction of the MX missile system in their states because of economic and environmental problems.

Some disputes were resolved amicably, however. State attorneys general lobbied Congress successfully for a $1.6 billion "superfund" to cover cleanups of chemical spills and toxic wastes. The U.S. Supreme Court settled two boundary disputes, favouring Ohio over Kentucky in one conflict and Nevada over California in another. The latter ruling allowed continued operation of four casinos in the Lake Tahoe region claimed by California, where gambling is prohibited.

Finances and Taxes

After two years of sizable budget surpluses and tax cuts, the effects of inflation and recession caught up with state governments during 1980, prompting cost cutting and some tax increases. That latter trend was countered by an anti-government-spending drive predicated on the success of California's Proposition 13 in 1978, which reduced property tax burdens markedly without destroying essential services as predicted by opponents.

Tax relief was approved in Arizona, Arkansas, Massachusetts, Montana, and Utah. Massachusetts voters endorsed "Proposition 2½," a measure limiting property taxes to 2.5% of property value. Delaware, Idaho, and South Carolina adopted a state revenue collection lid, bringing to 17 the number of states with a statutory spending cap. Alaska, its coffers overflowing with oil revenue, attempted to eliminate income taxes for long-time residents; when a court declared that the measure discriminated against newcomers, state voters abolished the entire tax in September. A survey by the Tax Foundation revealed that 16 states increased taxes during the year, raising an additional $850 million, while 7 enacted $430 million worth of tax trimming.

Figures accumulated in 1980 showed that state revenue from all sources totaled $247.1 billion during the 1979 fiscal year, an increase of 9.8% over the preceding 12 months. General revenue (excluding state liquor and state insurance trust revenue) was $208 billion, up 10%. Total state expenditures rose 10.2% to $224.3 billion, creating a surplus of $22.8 billion for the year. General expenditures, not including outlays of the liquor stores and insurance trust systems, amounted to $200.5 billion, up 11.5% for the year. The largest state outlay was $77.7 billion for education. Other major outlays were $38.9 billion for public welfare, $21.2 billion for highways, and $15.6 billion for health and hospitals.

Some Legislative Actions

Rhode Island lawmakers established alcoholism as a disease, with treatment eligible for health-insurance compensation. Colorado and Kentucky joined 19 states in legalizing laetrile as a cancer treatment. Nevada approved a law providing rape victims with up to $1,000 in medical care and counseling, provided that the crime is reported within three days. A federal judge declared Alabama's mental health commission had allowed "indefensible conditions" to infect state facilities and ordered the system into receivership by the state governor.

Although court-approved cutoffs of government funding for elective abortions took effect during 1980, controversy on the subject continued unabated in the states. Tennessee became the 16th state to call for a U.S. constitutional convention to overturn the U.S. Supreme Court's 1973 decision, which struck down antiabortion statutes in several states. Louisiana, Massachusetts, Rhode Island, and South Dakota passed new restrictions, typically requiring pregnant women to sign an "informed written consent" document and wait 24 hours before receiving the abortion. New Jersey's governor vetoed a similar law. Kentucky joined states abolishing public funding for abortions, but Michigan's governor vetoed a bill forbidding funding except when necessary to save the mother's life. Illinois attempted to prohibit abortion unless a physician deems it "necessary."

Even though 11 states had decriminalized possession of small amounts of marijuana, a hardening of attitudes toward the drug was noticeable during 1980. Kentucky's governor vetoed a legislature-approved bill that would have established a ten-year prison term for conviction of marijuana possession. Although Arizona, Colorado, Georgia, Michigan, New York, Rhode Island, and South Carolina joined 18 states allowing prescription of marijuana for treatment of cancer and glaucoma, an attempt to outlaw sale of drug paraphernalia through so-called head shops took hold nationally. Alabama, Colorado, Connecticut, Delaware, Florida, Idaho, Indiana, Louisiana, Maryland, Nebraska, New York, and Virginia passed laws shutting down the shops; similar laws were vetoed in Tennessee and declared unconstitutionally vague by federal judges in Georgia and West Virginia. Reversing a short-lived trend, several states raised the legal age for consumption of alcohol: Florida, New Jersey, and Georgia to 19, Nebraska and Rhode Island to 20, and Illinois to 21.

With the U.S. Supreme Court clearly unenthusiastic about its 1976 decision allowing resumption of the death penalty, the debate over capital punishment continued inconclusively during 1980. The high court voided the death law of Alabama on technical grounds, and court delays led to another year without any executions in the U.S. New Mexico and Connecticut approved new capital punishment laws, bringing to 39 the jurisdictions providing the death penalty, but New York's governor for the fourth consecutive year vetoed a death law for his state. The Massachusetts Supreme Court declared that state's capital punishment law unconstitutional. To soften criticism of the brutality of traditional execution methods, four states—Idaho, New Mexico, Oklahoma, and Texas—had

GOVERNORS OF THE STATES
(With Party Affiliations and Current Terms)

Ala.	Fob James (D),	1979–83
Alaska	Jay S. Hammond (R),	1978–82
Ariz.	Bruce Babbitt (D),	1979–83
Ark.	Frank D. White (R),	1981–83
Calif.	Edmund G. Brown, Jr. (D),	1979–83
Colo.	Richard D. Lamm (D),	1979–83
Conn.	William A. O'Neill (D),	1980–83
Del.	Pierre S. (Pete) du Pont (R),	1981–85
Fla.	Bob Graham (D),	1979–83
Ga.	George Busbee (D),	1979–83
Hawaii	George Ariyoshi (D),	1978–82
Idaho	John V. Evans (D),	1979–83
Ill.	James R. Thompson (R),	1979–83
Ind.	Robert D. Orr (R),	1981–85
Iowa	Robert D. Ray (R),	1979–83
Kan.	John Carlin (D),	1979–83
Ky.	John Y. Brown (D),	1979–83
La.	David C. Treen (R),	1980–84
Maine	Joseph E. Brennan (D),	1979–83
Md.	Harry Hughes (D),	1979–83
Mass.	Edward J. King (D),	1979–83
Mich.	William G. Milliken (R),	1979–83
Minn.	Albert H. Quie (R),	1979–83
Mississippi	William Winter (D),	1980–84
Mo.	Christopher S. (Kit) Bond (R),	1981–85
Mont.	Ted Schwinden (D),	1981–85
Neb.	Charles Thone (R),	1979–83
Nev.	Robert List (R),	1979–83
N.H.	Hugh J. Gallen (D),	1981–83
N.J.	Brendan Byrne (D),	1978–82
N.M.	Bruce King (D),	1979–83
N.Y.	Hugh L. Carey (D),	1979–83
N.C.	James B. Hunt, Jr. (D),	1981–85
N.D.	Allen I. Olson (R),	1981–85
Ohio	James A. Rhodes (R),	1979–83
Okla.	George Nigh (D),	1979–83
Ore.	Victor G. Atiyeh (R),	1979–83
Pa.	Dick Thornburgh (R),	1979–83
R.I.	J. Joseph Garrahy (D),	1981–83
S.C.	Richard W. Riley (D),	1979–83
S.D.	Bill Janklow (R),	1979–83
Tenn.	Lamar Alexander (R),	1979–83
Texas	William P. Clements, Jr. (R),	1979–83
Utah	Scott M. Matheson (D),	1981–85
Vt.	Richard A. Snelling (R),	1981–83
Va.	John N. Dalton (R),	1978–82
Wash.	John Spellman (R),	1981–85
W.Va.	John D. (Jay) Rockefeller IV (D),	1981–85
Wis.	Lee Sherman Dreyfus (R),	1979–83
Wyo.	Ed Herschler (D),	1979–83

provided for death by lethal injection; during the year, however, the American Medical Association house of delegates declared that physicians should not cooperate in that execution method.

New York enacted a tough one-year mandatory prison sentence for conviction of carrying a loaded, unlicensed handgun in a public place. Eight states barred police searches of newsrooms before a federal law preempted the matter, declaring the practice illegal nationwide. Police strip searches, which often victimize women stopped for minor traffic offenses, were regulated in Illinois, Iowa, and Connecticut.

Illinois and Michigan made fraud by computer a state felony. Rhode Island downgraded prostitution to a petty misdemeanour in order to speed courtroom trials. Arizona, Kansas, Kentucky, Minnesota, Missouri, and Vermont approved new laws prohibiting abuse of the aged, bringing to 24 the number of states outlawing mistreatment of the elderly.

Sparring over nuclear plant construction continued during 1980 with decidedly mixed results. Oregon voters approved a measure to ban plant construction until safe disposal of fuel rod waste becomes practical; Missouri and South Dakota voters rejected similar proposals. Maine voters defeated a referendum that would have shut down the state's single nuclear plant. Washington approved, but Montana rejected, a plan to regulate nuclear waste disposal. Montana and Vermont voters enacted prohibitive restrictions on uranium mining. A federal judge again told California that its attempts to ban nuclear-plant construction pending waste disposal improvement were illegal because the federal government had preempted the field.

Connecticut and New York approved gross receipts taxes on oil companies doing business within their borders, but federal judges invalidated state laws prohibiting the companies from passing the costs on to their customers. Kentucky and North Dakota helped in construction of the nation's first large-scale commercial synthetic fuels plants. Late in 1979, a reluctant Massachusetts became the 50th state to allow right turns at red lights, thus avoiding a federal Department of Energy fund cutoff.

A study published in 1980 indicated that the benefits of oil price decontrol would hardly be spread evenly: eight states (Alaska, Texas, California, Louisiana, Oklahoma, Wyoming, New Mexico, and Kansas) stood to receive a $128 billion windfall over ten years from increased severance taxes and other revenue associated with decontrol.

Although soaring market interest rates prompted numerous states to amend or cancel their usury ceilings, the federal government preempted state interest regulation during 1980, first by executive order and later by legislation. States would have until April 1983 to override the federal standards, which set relatively high interest ceilings in an attempt to avoid disruption of commercial transactions.

Connecticut, Hawaii, New Jersey, and New York joined states establishing or expanding the scope of "plain English" regulations, which required simple, understandable language in such documents as insurance forms and leases. Colorado outlawed solicitation by means of automatic-dialing telephone equipment. Fearing interruption of farm produce transportation following the bankruptcy of two major railroads, South Dakota arranged to purchase 457 mi of Milwaukee Road track; Iowa, Montana, and Wisconsin officials sought similar purchase and operation options.

Owners of this house set it afire after the government ordered it removed from public lands in Wyoming. Across the West the "Sagebrush Rebellion" was spreading, a movement to remove what Westerners saw as undue government restriction of land use and ownership.

JANA BURKHALTER—CASPER STAR-TRIBUNE

STOCKS AND BONDS

Investors in the U.S. experienced a bull market as stock prices rose steadily for most of 1980 and carried many indexes to all-time highs despite a continuing recession, record high interest rates, and international political problems in the Middle East. Standard & Poor's 500-stock index, the New York Stock Exchange (NYSE) composite index of all its common stocks, the American Stock Exchange market value index, and the index of over-the-counter stocks all established historic highs.

The Dow Jones industrials displayed a roller-coaster behaviour in 1980, rising in January from a level of 870 to 890 before beginning a slide that ended in mid-April at a level of about 759.13. From mid-April there was a steady climb to a high of 960 in August, and then after much backing and filling a peak of 1,000.17 was hit in November. At the year's end the index closed at 963.99.

Stocks traded on listed exchanges and over-the-counter surged to a record $1.4 trillion in market value, appreciating about $350 billion during the year despite two sharp setbacks.

On the New York Stock Exchange the record of 8,155,915,314 shares traded, set in 1979, was eclipsed on September 25, and volume for the year totaled 11,350,000,000 shares, an increase of 39%. Average daily volume was about 44,870,000 shares, up from just under 32 million shares a day in 1979. The average daily transaction volume in government securities alone was 18,100,000,000, up from 13,200,000,000 in 1979 for a 37% advance. The NYSE composite, with a top of 81.02 on November 28, finished at 77.86, up 25.7%.

The five most active stocks on the NYSE for 1980 were IBM with a turnover of 134 million shares, Texaco Inc. with 126 million, Mobil Oil Corp. with 103 million, AT&T with 93 million, and Gulf Oil Corp. with 88 million. Automobile stocks were among the biggest losers, falling more than 15%.

Volume on the American Stock Exchange rose to a record 1,630,000,000 in 1980, a 47.8% increase over the 1,099,990,000 traded the prior year. In the over-the-counter market volume was so hectic that on some days it exceeded that on the NYSE. For the year, unlisted trading volume neared 6,700,000,000 shares, more than half the 1980 turnover on the NYSE and up more than 80% from 1979. The Amex Index was up 41.2% for the year, and the over-the-counter index 33.9%.

Mutual funds did well in 1980. The Investment Company Institute, a trade group, estimated in a year-end report that mutual fund shareholders numbered more than 11 million, a record high. Aggregate assets of mutual funds doubled between 1978 and 1980 to about $138 billion. Investors bought more shares of common stock mutual funds than they redeemed in 1980, the first year in which that had happened since 1971. Growth funds had a net inflow of $667.6 million in 1980. Money market funds, which invest in U.S. Department of the

UPI

Soybean futures plunged on the Chicago Board of Trade commodities market after the announcement of the U.S. grain embargo against the Soviet Union in January.

Treasury bills and such short-term securities as large certificates of deposit issued by banks, were particularly successful, with assets increasing from $11 billion in 1978 to $45 billion at the end of 1979 and $76 billion in 1980. Securities firms projected record profits for the year of $2.1 billion pretax, according to the Securities Industry Association. This was nearly double the 1979 pretax income of $1.1 billion. Gross revenues were $15 billion, up from $11.3 billion the previous year. Corporate underwritings were $55 billion, compared with $36.6 billion in 1979.

The Standard & Poor composite index of 500

The New York Futures Exchange, a subsidiary of the New York Stock Exchange, opened in August in an attempt to capture some of the market in financial futures.

JIM COLBURN–PHOTOREPORTERS

New York Stock Exchange stocks began the year at 110.87, approximately 11% above the corresponding figure for 1979, rose to 115.34 in February, dipped to 102.97 in April, and then briskly advanced to 107.69 in May, 114.55 in June, 119.83 in July, and 126.51 in September, when it was 16.4% ahead of the prior year. By the year's end the index had reached a level of 135.52. The 400 stocks in the industrials sector of the index rose from 124.72 in January to 130.91 in February, then dropped during March and April before moving ahead to 120.80 in May, 128.80 in June, 135.23 in July, and 143.73 in September. Public utility stocks, by contrast, fluctuated within a very narrow range about the levels of the previous year. Railroad stocks performed unusually well, climbing from 58.64 in January to 80.64 in September, when the index was 44% above its level in the same month of 1979.

U.S. government long-term bond prices, as inversely reflected by their yields, were well below the levels of the previous year throughout 1980. The average yield in January was 10.03%, nearly 19% higher than in the corresponding month of 1979. The yield rose to 11.87% in March and then, following the sharp drop in the prime rate, slid to 10.83% in April, 9.82% in May, and 9.40% in June. The yield recovered at 9.83% in July and moved ahead to 10.94% in September, at which time it was 26% ahead of the previous September figure. Treasury bond yields peaked at 12.5% in early November and rose to 12.8% by mid-December before ending the year at about 11.8%. The Dow Jones Municipals, a weekly average of 20 20-year bonds, began the year with yields of 7.5% in January, rose to 9% by the end of February, peaked at 9.5% in March, and then slid to 8.6% in April and 8.5% in May and June. It rose again to 9% in July, 10% in September, and 11% by the year's end. This index also reflected the radical upward movement of interest rates generally throughout the year.

U.S. corporate bond prices were substantially lower during 1980 than at any time in 1979. The average price fluctuated from 44 in January, down 16.6% from the previous January, to 37.3 by March, rose briskly to 47.4 in June, and thereafter slipped to 41.1 in September. Yields were well above earlier years, ranging from a high of 12.96% when the prime rate peaked in March to a low of 10.58% in June. Despite the unfavourable market conditions, a total of $40.9 billion of corporate bonds were publicly offered. The previous record had been $37.5 billion in 1975.

Trading of options on the major futures exchanges rose impressively in 1980 with the volume for all contracts on the Chicago Board of Trade at 45.1 million, up 33% from 1979. The gain on the Chicago Mercantile Exchange was up 11.5% at 22 million contracts. High interest rates eliminated many small investors from futures markets in 1980, but financial institutions were not deterred.

On March 27, later referred to as "Silver Thursday," a near collapse of silver prices shook all the markets. The great silver crash of 1980 involved the brothers Nelson Bunker Hunt and W. Herbert Hunt, who appeared to have cornered the market in silver before sustaining very heavy losses. Silver prices dropped from more than $50 per ounce in January to $10.80 per ounce in late March. By acquiring control of huge amounts of silver for future delivery, largely on credit, a handful of speculators had pushed the price of silver to incredible levels during the fall and winter of 1979–80. When the commodity exchanges suddenly restricted trading and raised margins, the price dropped sharply and the collateral for billions of dollars of debt vanished almost overnight.

SUPREME COURT, U.S.

The Supreme Court in 1980 broke some new legal ground but for the most part continued its task of defining limits of previously stated principles. The court was often divided; many major decisions were made by a 5–4 vote or by a consensus of opinions reached by varying lines of reasoning.

Decisions in criminal cases strengthened some defendants' rights and weakened others. The milestone Miranda decision, requiring police to inform a suspect of his rights before questioning him, was affirmed in two cases presenting possible challenges.

In one, a new guideline was provided for police questioning. The justices explained that interrogation, under the Miranda decision, includes any words or actions that the police should know are likely to bring an incriminating response. Other chance remarks by police officers are not included. The case that brought the decision involved an officer's chance remark that he hoped a murder gun was not found by children from a nearby school for the retarded. The remark caused the suspect to lead police to the gun. The court found that there was no violation of the suspect's rights. In the other major Miranda rights case, the court decided that putting an informer in a cellblock with a suspect and instructing him to report on incriminating statements was a violation of right to counsel even if the informant was not told to ask questions.

A defendant who testifies at his own trial can be questioned in court about why he failed to turn himself in to police. The court ruled that such questioning does not force self-incrimination. A crime victim can identify an accused person in court even if the suspect was arrested illegally, it was decided. The victim's knowledge of the crime was held to be independent of the circumstances of arrest.

A limit was placed on the power of federal courts to prevent misconduct in prosecution. The courts cannot keep illegally seized evidence out of a trial unless the defendant's rights were violated. The decision involved the illegal search of a Bahamian bank official's briefcase in which evidence was found that implicated a U.S. citizen in tax evasion.

The court ruled that police must have a warrant to make a routine arrest in a suspect's home. Though previous rulings on the constitutional ban against unreasonable searches and seizures dealt only with evidence, it was decided that the rule applies equally to seizure of a person by arrest.

A Texas life sentence for a third-offense theft of $120.75 was found not to be cruel and unusual punishment. The offender did not challenge the constitutionality of the third-offense law but contended the sentence was grossly out of proportion to the crime. The court said this was a matter for the state legislature to decide.

The right of the public—and specifically of reporters—to attend criminal trials in almost all cases was enunciated in a Virginia dispute over an order for a closed trial. The Supreme Court decreed that if a trial is closed because of extraordinary circumstances, the judge must spell out his reasons in writing. The decision appeared to undercut the famed Gannett ruling of 1979 allowing the closing of pretrial hearings upon a defendant's request. That ruling was based on only the Sixth Amendment. It guarantees the right to a public trial, but the court held that the right concerned only the defendant. The 1980 rulings said that under the First and Fourteenth amendments, the trials must be open. Some of the six opinions in the case also hinted that the rule may apply to other public bodies. Chief Justice Warren E. Burger, in his opinion, cited First Amendment guarantees of free speech, freedom of the press, and right to assemble. (The Fourteenth Amendment orders states to grant the same freedoms allowed in the federal constitution.)

States can require shopping centres to let people circulate petitions and otherwise exercise free speech, the justices ruled. However, they found nothing in the federal constitution that requires such access.

An Illinois village was forbidden to enforce an ordinance limiting door-to-door solicitations for charity to groups that could prove they spent at least 75% of their proceeds for charitable purposes.

The court's ruling that new life forms can be patented came in a suit by the developer of a new bacterium that digests oil spills. The ruling was a boon for the budding science of genetic engineering, which permits modification of genes to produce entirely new organisms. (*See also* Biology Special Report: The Business of New Life.)

Patentholders were given the right to prevent

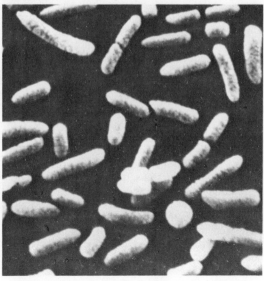

In 1980, in a ruling with wide implications, the U.S. Supreme Court judged that life forms created in the laboratory can be patented. The subject of the ruling was laboratory-modified bacteria of the Pseudomonas genus.
WIDE WORLD

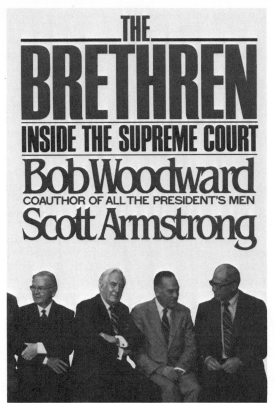

COURTESY, SIMON & SCHUSTER, INC., NEW YORK

A controversial study, The Brethren, *by Robert Woodward and Scott Armstrong, took a look behind closed chamber doors at the Supreme Court.*

others from selling ingredients that would be used in patent infringements, even if the ingredients themselves were not patented. The ruling involved sale of chemicals.

A financial printer who profited from advance knowledge of a stock takeover bid was cleared of charges that he violated Securities and Exchange Commission regulations. The court ruled that trading on the basis of nonpublic, "inside" information can be forbidden only if the trade violates a previously established relationship of trust with another party to a transaction.

California's system of allowing wine producers to fix wholesale prices for transactions in that state was ruled illegal under the Sherman Antitrust Act.

In two decisions, the justices ruled that persons affected by a class-action lawsuit can bring an appeal to force the suit to go on, even if the individuals who started the suit settle with the defendant.

The right of Congress to order 10% of federal contracts set aside for minority businesses was affirmed. It was the first time the court specifically approved the awarding of federal benefits on the basis of race. It was not clear, however, whether the same right extended to state and local governments.

The court upheld federal legislation severely restricting Medicaid payments for abortions. The law bans payments for abortions for needy women except in cases where a mother's life would be in danger or in cases of rape or incest that were reported promptly to police or to health officials. The opinion said that states can adopt a similar cutoff or can continue financing abortions for the needy without federal matching funds. The justices said it was not the function of the courts to decide whether the action of Congress on the issue was wise social policy. Nor is the cutoff discriminatory, they ruled. A woman's right to have an abortion was affirmed, but the court said that this did not imply that government must provide her with funds for the procedure. The ruling would cut off funds for abortions for an estimated 250,000 to 300,000 women a year.

Much of the court's attention was devoted to cases brought under the Civil Rights Act of 1871. The scope of possible civil cases under the act was enlarged dramatically when the court ruled that it protects citizens against all state violations of federal law—not just violations of civil rights law. The 1871 act allows individuals to sue for injunctions or for damages.

The court also ruled that a citizen has the right to be compensated for attorney fees if he wins such a suit. In a separate case, the court decided that the fees must be paid to a successful plantiff even if his case never goes to trial.

In addition, the possibility of civil suits under the 1871 act was enlarged when the court ruled that local governments, such as cities, were reponsible even when they were acting in good faith. The new ruling was an enlargement of one in 1978 in which the court decided that cities did not have absolute immunity for all official actions.

States had a right, however, to give parole officers absolute immunity for lawsuits arising from a decision to let a convict out of prison, the court held. The ruling was based, however, on the narrow ground that the death of a California girl at the hands of a recently paroled man did not amount to a violation of her right to due process—that is, that it was in no way an act of the state. There was no decision on the broader question of whether the immunity would hold if a violation of rights could be proved.

The Environmental Protection Agency can enforce clean water standards for an entire industry even if some companies contend that they cannot afford to comply, the court ruled. The decision reversed a Court of Appeals verdict that would have forced the EPA to consider economic hardship. This was not the intent of Congress, a unanimous opinion held.

It also was decided that zoning regulations passed to preserve the environment do not necessarily amount to a violation of the constitutional rights of property owners. The opinion upheld the right of a city in the San Francisco Bay area to pass an open-space ordinance but did not rule on the merits of the legislation.

The secretary of the interior is not required to keep indefinitely 2.4 million ac of desert land set aside for possible irrigation by the state of Idaho, the court said. Idaho was given the right in 1908 to receive three million acres for irrigation. Interest lagged until 1974, when new technology made irrigation feasible. Idaho was refused 27,400 ac it requested in that year on the grounds that the land had since been granted for other purposes.

The right of an administration to dismiss public employees solely because of their political affiliation was severely limited. In a New York case, dismissal of two holdover Republican assistant defenders by an incoming Democratic defender was ruled illegal. The court indicated that in order to fire for political reasons, the executive doing the firing must prove that affiliation with a certain party is essential for discharge of the employee's responsibilities. This would be true, for example, of a speech writer for an elected official.

The ban against private fund raising by presidential candidates who accept public financing of their campaigns was upheld. The law made $29.4 million available to each of the two major party candidates in 1980.

The court allowed the state of California to continue an investigation of the way officials of the Worldwide Church of God handled church funds. The state's attorney general charged misuse of large amounts of money for the personal benefit of the church's leader, Herbert W. Armstrong, and others. The state argued, in effect, that churches are

"If you have to ask how much, you can't afford one!"

DOUG MARLETTE—THE CHARLOTTE OBSERVER

charitable trusts that can be held accountable for proper use of their money. The argument was opposed by a wide range of civil rights and church organizations. The Supreme Court declined to hear an appeal from a lower court ruling allowing the investigation.

The Supreme Court ruled that it had no jurisdiction to hear a challenge to Florida law that bars members of the Ethiopian Zion Coptic Church from using marijuana as part of religious ritual. The ruling left open the possibility of further court action by the church. However, the Supreme Court's stand was consistent with its refusal four years before to hear a challenge to the right of Tennessee to outlaw snake handling and drinking of poison as religious practices.

SWEDEN

Two events overshadowed all others in Sweden in 1980. In a national referendum on March 23, Sweden said a cautious "yes" to nuclear power. In the referendum, 58% voted for the use of not more than 12 nuclear reactors over 25 years, while 38.7% favoured a shutdown of all reactors in 10 years. (Another 3.3% returned a special blank ballot paper indicating that they disapproved of the referendum.) After a year of discussion and contention, the referendum ended a great deal of political and economic uncertainty.

But any optimism that might have been generated was wiped out just over a month later with the ending of 42 years of more or less unbroken labour peace. The dispute, which at its height saw one-quarter of the work force of four million either on strike or locked out, threw into question the much vaunted "Swedish model" of a highly centralized wage-bargaining structure.

The labour crisis of April and May shook a nation that had become used to industrial peace. Since the Saltsjöbaden Agreement of 1938, centralized wage negotiations had always ended peacefully, but in 1980 they deadlocked almost simultaneously in the public and private sectors. On April 25, 14,000 employees in the public sector struck, and 12,000 others were locked out four days after an overtime ban by 1.2 million workers in support of a 11.3% pay increase had gone into effect. All air traffic into and out of the country was grounded; shipping and haulage were disrupted; and the Stockholm subway and Göteborg tram system were halted. Hospitals treated only emergency cases. Mail was delayed, television blacked out except for newcasts, and radio restricted to one channel.

In the private sector, on May 2 the Swedish Confederation of Trade Unions (LO) added a series of selective strikes to an overtime ban already in effect in support of an 11.3% pay increase. The Swedish Employers Confederation (SAF) responded with a lockout of 750,000 workers, originally set to last one week but later extended until May 18. Practically all industry in Sweden shut down, and

110 major stores and 60 hotels were forced to close. On May 9 the transport union stopped gasoline and oil deliveries to 80% of the country's suppliers.

Agreement was reached two days later after two government-appointed mediation commissions, one for the private and one for the public sector, presented the employers and the unions with final offers. These gave a 7.3% increase to public sector employees and 6.8% to those in private industry.

On August 25 the first extraordinary session of the Riksdag (parliament) since World War II raised the value-added tax from 17.1 to 19% (from 20.63 to 23.46% at consumer price level), the highest in Europe. Then, on September 16 the government presented a 6.3 billion kronor package of public spending cuts (4.16 kroner=U.S. $1). These two measures were expected to reduce the estimated budget deficit for 1981–82 by more than 7 billion kronor. There were strong protests, and on October 22 Thorbjörn Fälldin's coalition government survived Sweden's first no-confidence vote by one vote.

On November 17 the automotive concern Volvo, Sweden's largest company, merged with the industrial and trading conglomerate Beijerinvest, the fifth largest company in the country. The new group would have a turnover in the 40 billion kronor range and employ 75,000 people.

Swedish voters went to the polls on March 23 for a referendum on the future of the nuclear power industry in their country; results showed the power of the antinuclear bloc.

PATRICK ZACHMANN/RUSH–KATHERINE YOUNG

SWIMMING

The Games of the XXII Olympiad, held from July 19 to Aug. 3, 1980, in Moscow, failed to produce the major aquatic competition that had always been an Olympic highlight. Joining the United States in a boycott to protest the Soviet Union's invasion of Afghanistan, swimmers from Canada, West Germany, Japan, and several other nations supported their Olympic committees' ban on participation. The boycott gave the aquatic events a heavy East German and Soviet flavour. Swimmers from those two nations alone won two-thirds of all of the medals and 20 of the 26 golds.

Many new world swimming records were set during the year. Seven were by men (three by U.S. swimmers) beginning with 3 min 51.20 sec for the 400-m freestyle by the Soviet Union's Vladimir Salnikov at the U.S.S.R. indoor championships in Leningrad on February 24. The women were far more prolific, as they set 14 world marks led by Tracy Caulkins of the U.S.; she lowered her 200-m individual medley time to 2 min 13.69 sec at the third annual U.S. Women's International Competition at Austin, Texas, on January 5.

The male swimmers of the Soviet Union and the East German women completely dominated all rivals at the Olympic Games. The Soviet men placed first and second in the 200-, 400-, and 1,500-m freestyle and the 400-m individual medley. It marked the first time any Soviet male swimmer had won an Olympic gold medal. Salnikov won three events and became the first man ever to break the 15-min barrier for the 1,500-m freestyle, winning in 14 min 58.27 sec on July 22.

Surpassing their 1976 Olympic medal output of 18 medals, the East German women's team won 26 medals (11 gold, 8 silver, and 7 bronze). Led by Barbara Krause, who won three gold medals and set two individual world records in the process, the East Germans finished first, second, and third 6 times in 11 individual events. They were one-two in another, two-three in still another, and gained a lone first-place finish in two more events. Krause became the only woman ever to break 55 sec in the 100-m freestyle, swimming the distance in 54.98 sec in the preliminary competition on July 20. In the finals a day later she won the gold medal in 54.79 sec. Teammate Ines Diers achieved a fine Olympic performance, winning five medals (two gold, two silver, and one bronze).

Sergei Kopliakov broke the listed world mark in the 200-m freestyle by swimming the distance in 1 min 49.81 sec in the Olympics on July 21. However, awaiting approval by the governing body for amateur aquatics, the Fédération Internationale de Natation Amateur, was a world record for that event of 1 min 49.16 sec by Rowdy Gaines at the U.S. indoor championships at Austin, Texas, on April 11. At the Austin competition, also on April 11, Par Arvidsson of Sweden set a world mark for the 100-m butterfly of 54.15 sec. He also won this event

World Swimming Records Set in 1980			
Event	Name	Country	Time
MEN			
200-m freestyle	Rowdy Gaines	U.S.	1 min 49.16 sec
400-m freestyle	Vladimir Salnikov	U.S.S.R.	3 min 51.20 sec
400-m freestyle	Peter Szmidt	Canada	3 min 50.49 sec
1,500-m freestyle	Vladimir Salnikov	U.S.S.R.	14 min 58.27 sec
100-m butterfly	Par Arvidsson	Sweden	54.15 sec
200-m butterfly	Craig Beardsley	U.S.	1 min 58.21 sec
200-m individual medley	William Barrett	U.S.	2 min 3.24 sec
WOMEN			
100-m freestyle	Barbara Krause	E. Ger.	54.98 sec
100-m freestyle	Barbara Krause	E. Ger.	54.79 sec
100-m backstroke	Rica Reinisch	E. Ger.	1 min 1.50 sec
100-m backstroke	Rica Reinisch	E. Ger.	1 min 0.86 sec
200-m backstroke	Rica Reinisch	E. Ger.	2 min 11.77 sec
100-m breaststroke	Ute Geweniger	E. Ger.	1 min 10.20 sec
100-m breaststroke	Ute Geweniger	E. Ger.	1 min 10.11 sec
100-m butterfly	Mary T. Meagher	U.S.	59.26 sec
200-m butterfly	Mary T. Meagher	U.S.	2 min 6.37 sec
200-m individual medley	Tracy Caulkins	U.S.	2 min 13.69 sec
200-m individual medley	Petra Schneider	E. Ger.	2 min 13.00 sec
400-m individual medley	Petra Schneider	E. Ger.	4 min 39.96 sec
400-m individual medley	Petra Schneider	E. Ger.	4 min 38.44 sec
400-m individual medley	Petra Schneider	E. Ger.	4 min 36.29 sec
4 × 100-m freestyle relay	East German national team (Barbara Krause, Caren Metschuck, Ines Diers, Sarina Hulsenbeck)	E. Ger.	3 min 42.71 sec
4 × 100-m freestyle relay	East German national team (Rica Reinisch, Ute Geweniger, Andrea Pollack, Caren Metschuck)	E. Ger.	4 min 6.67 sec

peted in the Moscow Olympics. The championship started two days after the completion of swimming in Moscow in the hope that the competitors would swim faster than the medal winners in the Olympics. The swimmers generally failed to respond, however, setting two world marks in the 200-m butterfly and one in the 200-m individual medley. On July 30 Meagher lowered her butterfly world mark by 0.64 sec, clocking 2 min 6.37 sec. A day later in the same event for men, Craig Beardsley set a world mark of 1 min 58.21 sec, and on August 1 William Barrett set a new record of 2 min 3.24 sec in the 200-m individual medley.

Canada honoured its Olympic team at its national championships in Toronto. There, Peter Szmidt on July 16 swam the 400-m freestyle in a record 3 min 50.49 sec, lowering by 0.71 sec the record set by Salnikov in February.

In addition to Krause's records at the Olympics the East German women set an additional seven world marks during the year. They included: Rica Reinisch, 100-m backstroke, 1 min 1.50 sec (preliminaries) and 1 min 0.86 sec (finals); Reinisch, 200-m backstroke, 2 min 11.77 sec; Ute Geweniger, 100-m breaststroke, 1 min 10.11 sec (preliminaries); Petra Schneider, 400-m individual medley, 4 min 36.29 sec; 400-m freestyle relay, 3 min 42.71 sec; and 400-m medley relay, 4 min 6.67 sec.

Diving

Unable to compete in Moscow, U.S. and Canadian divers did manage to meet the future Olympic medalists in a series of three international competitions during April and May in Canada, the U.S., and Mexico. Winner of the men's 3-m springboard in all three competitions was Carlos Giron of Mexico, who also won the 10-m platform in Mexico. Brian Bungum of the U.S. and Bruce Kimball of

at the Olympics, though in a slower time. Mary T. Meagher lowered the women's 100-m butterfly record to 59.26 sec, also at Austin on April 11.

The U.S. outdoor championships at Irvine, Calif., from July 29 to August 2 were designated as the U.S. Olympic team selection. A team was chosen to honour those athletes who would have com-

Tracy Caulkins set a U.S. record in the 100-metre breaststroke during the U.S. Women's International Swimming Competition in January in Austin, Texas. She also set a world record in the 200-metre individual medley.
UPI

Vladimir Salnikov of the Soviet Union won the gold medal in the 1,500-metre freestyle event in the 1980 Moscow Olympic Games with a record time of 14 minutes 58.27 seconds.
EASTFOTO

the U.S. were the winners in the 10-m platform in Canada and the U.S., respectively. In the women's events Jennifer Chandler of the U.S., Carrie Irish Finneran of the U.S., and Milagros Gonzalez of Cuba were the 3-m springboard winners. Melissa Briley of the U.S. won the 10-m platform in the U.S. and Canada, and Guadalupe Canseco of Mexico won the event in Mexico.

At the Olympics the men's gold medals went to Aleksandr Portnov of the Soviet Union in the springboard and to veteran Falk Hoffman of East Germany in the platform event. In women's competition Irina Kalinina of the Soviet Union won the springboard and Martina Jaschke of East Germany the platform. (*See also* Olympic Games.)

SWITZERLAND

By the end of 1980 Switzerland appeared to have come through the economic blizzard almost unscathed, with a high national income, low taxation, small budget, practically full employment, and inflation below 5%. Economic activity showed growth, with the gross national product increasing by about 3%.

No parliamentary elections and no political surprises troubled 1980. Public discussion revolved around popular initiatives, referenda, and draft laws proposed by the government. In the spring a popular initiative proposing the separation of church and state at the federal level was rejected by 79% of those voting. At the same time, 86% of the people approved a constitutional amendment authorizing the government to purchase and stock in peacetime primary supplies for a potential emergency (it already had this authority in wartime).

In the fall a plebiscite involved, besides the grants of some supplementary sources of revenue to the federal government (largely at the expense of subsidies to the cantons), the heatedly controversial question of whether or not the wearing of safety belts in automobiles should be enforced by law. The results of the financial proposals were largely favourable to the federal government, but the compulsory safety belt won only narrowly. The French-speaking cantons, in contrast with most of the German-speaking, all voted massively against what they considered an inadmissible interference with individual freedom.

The growing deficit of the federal budget was of major concern and was expected to exceed SFr 1 billion in 1981 (SFr 1.66=U.S. $1). The largest item in the budget was expenditure on national defense. Against Socialist opposition it was fixed at SFr 1,550,000,000, of which SFr 1.2 billion was earmarked for the Skyguard and Rapier air defense weapons. Another concern was future energy supply. As of 1980 the country possessed sufficient stocks, but in anticipation of future needs the government was working out a comprehensive strategy and sought a new constitutional article to give it the necessary authority.

Aware of the criticism leveled against it, especially by international organizations, the government sought to persuade Parliament and the people to increase the country's contribution to development aid. While the Organization for Economic Cooper-

Usually placid Switzerland experienced an outbreak of civic violence in 1980; young demonstrators staged a series of outbursts beginning in May.
KEYSTONE

ation and Development aimed at a rate of 0.32% of each member's gross national product, Switzerland lagged behind with 0.19%, although private credits —by banks and industries—raised this figure to 4%. At the end of 1980 the federal Parliament approved the extension of credit of SFr 1,650,000,000 (out of government funds) for a period of three years.

SYRIA

Rapidly deteriorating relations with its neighbours dominated Syria's politics in 1980. Pres. Hafez al-Assad's regime was also shaken by the most violent civil disturbances in its ten-year existence. A union with Libya declared on September 10 appeared to be foundering by November, although it had brought quick rewards for Assad; it was reported that Libya had paid off U.S. $1 billion of Syria's weapons debt to the Soviet Union. Syria continued to drift into the Soviet camp with the signing of a friendship treaty in October. The war between Iran and Iraq brought into the open Syria's polarization in the extreme Arab grouping known as the Steadfastness Front. Syria led Libya, Algeria, Yemen (Aden), Lebanon, and the Palestine Liberation Organization (PLO) in a boycott of the Arab summit in Amman, Jordan, on November 25–27.

Relations with Jordan, which had been improving in 1979 with the start of a number of joint economic ventures, slipped into tension in late 1980. Saudi mediation was necessary to defuse a border crisis. By December three Syrian divisions—at least 30,000 men—had been massed on the border, while

two divisions were assembled on the Jordanian side. On December 4 Saudi Arabia's second deputy prime minister, Prince Abdullah ibn Abdul Aziz, said that President Assad had agreed to withdraw Syrian forces gradually from the border. But Jordan had apparently rejected Syria's two basic demands: that Jordan end its support for the Muslim Brotherhood in Syria and abandon its alleged plans to usurp the PLO's right to be sole representative of the Palestinians. Jordan's point of view was that King Hussein could not accept these conditions because the charges were themselves "senseless."

President Assad had cause to worry about the Muslim Brotherhood, an extremist group. Membership in the Brotherhood was made a capital offense in Syria on July 9. There had been violent incidents in Hamah and Aleppo in March, and individuals close to the regime had been assassinated. The security forces had some success against the Brotherhood, but by year's end it was unclear how much it had been permanently weakened.

In 1979 Syria had had ambitions for a political union with Iraq, but the project ended with the discovery in mid-1979 of a coup attempt in Iraq in which Syria was alleged to be involved. The Soviet intervention in Afghanistan in December 1979 hastened the split, with Syria defending the move and Iran, Saudi Arabia, and moderate Arab states attacking it. Contacts were still being maintained with Baghdad, however, and on December 22 the two countries reportedly agreed on the resumption of crude oil pumping from Kirkuk in Iraq to Banias in Syria. A major cause of the unease with Syria felt in

In October Syrian Pres. Hafez al-Assad (right) and Soviet leader Leonid I. Brezhnev signed a 20-year treaty of cooperation in Moscow. At the time, Brezhnev declared that the Soviet Union had no intention of intervening in the Iran-Iraq conflict.
WIDE WORLD

Baghdad and other capitals was the 20-year friendship and cooperation treaty with the Soviet Union, signed by Soviet Pres. Leonid Brezhnev and Assad on October 8 during the latter's visit to Moscow. The treaty stipulated that Syria and the Soviet Union would consult each other immediately should the security of either be threatened. Union with Libya proved more difficult. Problems arose in November when Libya's leader, Col. Muammar al-Qaddafi, expressed a desire to see Syria adopt Libya's form of government by committee.

Continued economic hardship seemed likely in 1981. Economy Minister Muhammad al-Atrash said the investment budget was to be cut drastically, from S£14,000 million in 1980 to between S£8,000 million and S£10,000 million in 1981 (S£3.925=U.S. $1). Syria was about to embark on its fifth development plan (1981–85). It was admitted that the fourth plan had been too ambitious and had emphasized industry at the expense of agriculture. In an attempt to stop a drift to the cities, investment and technical and vocational training in country areas would be stressed.

TAIWAN

In 1980 the international status of the Republic of China suffered a further setback when the International Monetary Fund and the World Bank voted in April and May, respectively, to replace Taiwan by the People's Republic of China. Nevertheless, Taiwan continued to prosper and to enjoy political stability and economic growth. Only about 20 countries—most of them in Central and South America—maintained formal diplomatic representation in Taipei. At the same time, trade relations were being established with more countries than ever before, including several Eastern European

countries. The Nationalist regime's determination to maintain its independent status was reflected in its increased defense budget and in the statements of its leaders and people for the celebration of the 69th year of the republic. The new year was termed the year of self-reliance.

The economy of Taiwan depended largely on foreign trade. Total two-way trade reached U.S. $30,877,000,000 in 1979, with a favourable balance of $1,329,000,000. In the first half of 1980 Taiwan's exports rose 29% to $9.3 billion, but it experienced its first trade deficit in four years, amounting to about $220 million. This was attributable chiefly to increasing imports of crude oil and machinery and, especially, to the rise in the price of oil. Total trade in 1980 was expected to reach $40 billion, with little or no surplus. Per capita income in 1980 rose to more than $1,800 from $1,720 in 1979, the highest in Asia after Japan.

When U.S. Pres. Jimmy Carter announced, in December 1978, his intention to recognize the Beijing (Peking) government "as the sole legal government of China," he also declared that the people of the U.S. and Taiwan would "maintain cultural, commercial and other [unofficial] relations." To this end, the U.S. established a quasi-governmental agency, the American Institute in Taiwan, and its Taiwanese counterpart, the Coordination Council for North American Affairs, was set up in New York and other major cities. After arduous negotiations, the "unofficial" U.S. and Taiwanese institutes signed an agreement on Oct. 3, 1979, granting customary privileges and immunities to each other's representatives.

During 1980 the so-called unofficial relations between the U.S. and Taiwan progressed smoothly. In January, after a year's moratorium, the U.S. Defense Department approved Taiwan's request to buy about $300 million worth of weapons, despite the usual protest from Beijing. Partly as a test of U.S. intentions toward them, the Nationalists continued to seek U.S. approval to purchase high-performance fighter planes.

Aided by large loans from the U.S. Export-Import Bank and private U.S. banks and by new investments on the part of U.S. corporations, bilateral trade with the U.S. continued to grow in spite of derecognition. In 1979 it rose 22% to $9,030,000,000, making Taiwan the eighth-ranking trade partner of the U.S. The U.S. was Taiwan's chief trade partner, followed closely by Japan. In the first six months of 1980, Taiwan's exports to the U.S. reached $3.2 billion, 26% above the same period in 1979, while imports from the U.S. rose nearly 50% to $2.2 billion.

While the long-standing hostility and suspicion between the rival governments on Taiwan and the mainland continued, unofficial and indirect contacts began to expand. Two-way trade through Hong Kong showed a considerable increase. Beijing ceased its campaign to isolate Taiwan economically; in April it announced that goods from Taiwan were exempt from import duty. Chinese industrial experts, scientists, scholars, and athletes from both sides met at international conferences and meetings in third countries. All this indicated some loosening-up by both sides and a reduction of tension in the Taiwan Straits.

TANZANIA

Under a new constitution and for the first time since the 1964 revolution, elections were held in Zanzibar on Jan. 7, 1980, for the National Assembly. Pressure for an end to union with mainland Tanzania continued, however, because critics of the government regarded the union as the main cause of the island's economic problems. In July, 16 people were arrested and accused of plotting to overthrow the regime, but in October Aboud Jumbe was overwhelmingly elected president of the Revolutionary Council, a post that he had previously held by nomination.

Elections in mainland Tanzania on October 26 resulted in more than half of the members of the National Assembly, including several former ministers, losing their seats. This reflected the electorate's concern about the failure of the country's economy to deal with the problems created by the high price of oil and the cost of the war in Uganda. Pres. Julius Nyerere was reelected for another five-year term. He appointed Cleopa David Msuya prime minister in succession to Edward Sokoine (retired because of ill health).

Relations with Tanzania's neighbours remained uneasy. Nyerere's criticisms of Britain's handling of the elections in Zimbabwe caused embarrassment to the eventual victor, Robert Mugabe. In March Tanzania began to withdraw its troops from Uganda, but unsettled conditions there made it necessary to retain half the original invading force. Nyerere

In February the $203 million North Link Railway went into operation in Taiwan, the latest stage in a projected island-wide railway system.
KWANG HWA FILM
SYNDICATE/AUTHENTICATED NEWS
INTERNATIONAL

agreed to this arrangement subject to wholehearted efforts being made by Uganda to restore law and order and to hold elections. Nevertheless, the continuing presence of Tanzanian troops in Uganda aroused suspicions in Kenya about Nyerere's motives, while in Uganda itself, although there was no lack of appreciation of the contribution made by Tanzania's armed forces to the country's stability, there were fears that their presence might promote the interests of Milton Obote's Uganda People's Congress Party. Nor was Tanzania's own shaky economy helped by having to pay the returned soldiers, and unrest in the Army over pay led to the arrest of 30 officers in May.

TELEVISION AND RADIO

In some form television and radio service was available in all major nations in 1980. Approximately 828 million radio sets were in use, of which about 456.2 million, or 55%, were in the United States. There were about 425 million television sets, of which 169 million, or 40%, were in the U.S.

The Soviet Union, with 75 million television sets, ranked next to the U.S., according to estimates published in the 1980 *Broadcasting Yearbook*. Japan was third with 27.8 million. Other *Broadcasting* estimates included: West Germany, 20.5 million; United Kingdom, 18 million; Brazil, 16 million; France, 15 million; Italy, 12.6 million; Canada, 11 million; Spain, 8.4 million; Poland, 7 million; Mexico, 6 million; East Germany, 5.2 million; The Netherlands, 5.1 million; Australia, 5 million; and Argentina, 4.5 million.

More than 6,790 television stations were operating or under construction throughout the world. Approximately 2,200 were in the Far East, 2,110 in Western Europe, 1,130 in the U.S., 920 in Eastern Europe, 180 in South America, 105 in Mexico, 96 in Canada, and 45 in Africa. Radio stations totaled about 15,800, mostly of the amplitude modulation (AM) type but with a growing proportion of frequency modulation (FM) stations. In the U.S. there were 9,238, of which 4,546, or 49%, were FM.

Programming

A strike by the American Federation of Television and Radio Artists and the Screen Actors Guild stopped almost all U.S. program production from July 22 until October 3, forcing the three commercial television networks to delay the start of the 1980–81 prime-time season. In the meantime they presented reruns of current hits, interspersed with a large number of specials. One of the most notable specials was NBC's "Shogun," a 12-hour, $22 million miniseries based on James Clavell's best-selling novel set in feudal Japan. Shown over a five-night period starting September 15, "Shogun" became one of the highest-rated programs in television history, with an average A. C. Nielsen Co. rating of 32.6 and a 51 share of the audience. (Each rating point is equal to 1% of television homes, which in September numbered 77.8 million in the U.S.; each share point equals 1% of all homes with their TV sets turned on at the time the rating is taken.) NBC estimated that some 125 million viewers watched all or some part of "Shogun," as compared with 130 million in 1977 for "Roots," the ratings record holder for a miniseries.

In preparing for the new season the networks dropped more than a dozen weekly series. These included "Galactica 1980," "The Ropers," "Angie," and "Goodtime Girls" on ABC; "Hawaii Five-O" and "Barnaby Jones" on CBS; and "Hello Larry," "The Big Show," and "United States" on NBC. In their places the networks scheduled a mixture of comedies, dramas, and magazine or information shows, including "Too Close for Comfort," "But I'm a Big Girl Now," "It's a Living," and "Those

In July the Screen Actors Guild and the American Federation of Television and Radio Artists went on strike, forcing the postponement of the fall television season. The strike lasted 94 days, the longest ever in the industry.
WIDE WORLD

NANCY ELLISON–GAMMA/LIAISON

Most-talked-about television actor of the year was Larry Hagman as the villainous J. R. Ewing of "Dallas." "Who shot J. R.?" became a catch-question in the summer of the year.

Amazing Animals" on ABC; "Ladies' Man," "Enos," and "Secrets of Midland Heights" on CBS; and "Hill Street Blues," "Flamingo Road," "Harper Valley PTA," and "Speak Up America" on NBC. *Broadcasting* estimated that, even before the 1980–81 season began to unfold, the networks were spending a combined total of $1 billion a year on prime-time programming.

For the week that ended November 23, only one new series ranked among the top 20 programs in the ratings: ABC's "Too Close for Comfort," a comedy, which placed ninth. The highest rated programs of the week were "Dallas," a vastly popular "nighttime soap opera" on CBS; "The Dukes of Hazzard," a comedy drama, also on CBS; and "60 Minutes," a CBS News magazine show that was the highest rated program of the 1979–80 season.

The highest rated program of the year—and of any year since the early days of television, when programs often played with little or no competition in their time periods—was the November 21 episode of "Dallas," when the identity of the culprit who had shot John Ross Ewing, the rich, ornery, wheeler-dealer star of the show played by Larry Hagman, was finally revealed. "Who shot J. R.?" had become a national, even international, catch-question during the summer, after his shooting in an episode at the end of the 1979–80 season. The November 21 story, in which Kristin, J. R.'s con-

niving sister-in-law, admitted doing the dirty deed, was watched in 53.3% of all TV homes and by 76% of all homes that had their sets turned on during that time. CBS estimated that 83 million people watched the show. The 53.3 rating exceeded the previous record for a series episode, a 45.9 rating, set Aug. 29, 1967, when "the one-armed man" was finally caught in the concluding episode of "The Fugitive." It also topped the record held by the final installment of the "Roots" miniseries, which scored a 51.1 rating and a 71 share on Jan. 30, 1977. In Britain the "Dallas" installment attracted the BBC's highest rating of the month.

Among other programs attracting attention in 1980 was "Playing for Time," a drama shown on CBS on September 30. The showing was widely protested in advance because of its casting of the actress Vanessa Redgrave, an outspoken Palestine Liberation Organization supporter, as a Jewish inmate in a Nazi death camp. The program scored a 26.2 rating and a 41 share of audience, with its viewers estimated at 41 million.

Networks and stations continued their efforts to improve programming for children, playing down violence and racial and sexual stereotypes and adding informational broadcasts and news reports designed for young audiences, especially in the Saturday morning and Sunday schedules. During the daytime, game shows and soap operas continued to predominate. In an effort to break the mold NBC introduced a 90-minute variety program, "The David Letterman Show," but apathetic audiences led to its being cut to 60 minutes and finally canceled and replaced by game shows.

In the 32nd annual Emmy awards, the Academy of Television Arts and Sciences voted "Lou Grant" the outstanding drama series and "Taxi" the outstanding comedy series, both for the second year in a row. Ed Asner of "Lou Grant" and Barbara Bel Geddes of "Dallas" were named outstanding lead actor and actress in a drama series, and Richard Mulligan and Cathryn Damon, both of "Soap," best lead actor and actress in a comedy series. Johnny Carson of "The Tonight Show with Johnny Carson" received the annual special award of the Academy's governors.

Sports continued to rank among the most popular television fare and became increasingly expensive. *Broadcasting* estimated that television and radio networks and stations paid $207,241,350 for rights to broadcast college and professional football games in 1980, or about $6 million more than in 1979, and $80,225,000 to broadcast major league baseball games, an increase of almost $26 million over 1979. Philadelphia's victory over Kansas City in the sixth and final game of baseball's World Series was watched in 40% of all U.S. television homes, making it the highest rated World Series game in history.

NBC had paid $87 million for rights to cover the Summer Olympic Games in Moscow but withdrew

A storm of controversy surrounded "Playing for Time," with PLO-supporter Vanessa Redgrave (second from left) playing a Jewish woman forced to entertain her Nazi captors at Auschwitz by singing with a prison orchestra in order to stay alive. A powerful story and a strong supporting cast made the show memorable; despite Redgrave's politics her performance was superb.
UPI

—at a cost put at $16.1 million after insurance claims had been collected—because of the U.S. boycott of the Games after the Soviet invasion of Afghanistan. The winter Olympics at Lake Placid, N.Y., however, was a boon for ABC, which had acquired the TV rights there. ABC's prime-time coverage drew ratings in the 20s, and its broadcast on February 23, the day after the U.S. hockey team defeated the Soviet Union, gained an average audience of 22,050,000 homes, said to be a record for Olympics broadcasts.

News and public affairs, which normally represented about one-fourth of television programming, increased substantially as a result of coverage of state political primaries, the Republican and Democratic conventions, the ensuing campaigns for national, state, and local offices, and the election returns on November 4. As is usually the case, however, TV audiences were relatively small. The coverage of the Republican convention on ABC, CBS, and NBC had a combined rating of about 22 and a 45 share of audience; with the Democratic convention the combined rating was 27 and the share 55. On a normal evening, when entertainment programming was offered, combined network ratings were in the 50s and the share was above 80.

The only televised debate between Pres. Jimmy Carter and Ronald Reagan brought a departure from this trend. Carried on ABC, CBS, and NBC, the debate drew a 58.9 rating and an 84 share. But on election night, when all three networks were carrying the returns, the ratings dropped again. For the hours from 7 PM to 11 PM Eastern time, they averaged 46.3, with the share at 67. On the whole, however, the public's appetite for news remained strong, and two new national television news services were formed to help serve it, both distributed by communications satellites.

Music and news remained the basic format in radio programming. A study by *Broadcasting* found

that, among the 10 highest rated stations in each of the top 50 U.S. markets, "contemporary," or currently popular, music was featured by 32.2%, "beautiful music" by 15.7%, and various forms of rock music by 15%. News or news and talk were basic formats at 7.4% of the stations.

PBS introduced a fall schedule that included 11 new programs. One of the most ambitious was "Cosmos," a 13-part series with Carl Sagan, the astronomer, as host. Another was "The Body in Question," also a 13-part series, exploring mysteries

Richard Chamberlain and Yoko Shimada starred in the enormously popular miniseries "Shogun," which aired on NBC in September.
NBC PHOTO

Masterpiece Theatre offered a five-part dramatization of Pride and Prejudice, *with Elizabeth Garvie (standing) as Elizabeth Bennet.*
COURTESY, PUBLIC BROADCASTING SERVICE

of the human body. Other new entries included "From Jumpstreet," on black musical heritage; "Vikings!," tracing the travels of the Nordic sailors; "This Old House," offering information on refurbishing houses; and "Matinee at the Bijou," presenting classic films, newsreels, and old cartoons. A possible blow to PBS was the BBC's agreement to sell U.S. rights to its programming—a PBS staple for many years—to a new cable-TV network.

A British television documentary about a member of Saudi Arabia's royal family, "Death of a Princess," provoked enormous controversy not just within the medium but at the highest government levels. The two-hour dramatized documentary, by filmmaker Antony Thomas, told how Princess Misha'al had reportedly rejected her arranged husband, who was her cousin, in favour of another man, with the result that in 1977 she had been accused of adultery and executed. The Saudi royal family made substantial efforts to stop the film from being shown, but Associated Television (ATV), the main backers, broadcast it as scheduled on April 9. British Foreign Secretary Lord Carrington said he regretted its showing but said he had no powers to intervene in such matters. On April 23 Saudi Arabia expelled the U.K. ambassador in Riyadh and halted the appointment, then in process, of a new Saudi ambassador to the U.K. However, the atmosphere cooled over the months, and by the end of the summer diplomatic relations had been reestablished. In the U.S. PBS was urged to cancel the program but went ahead and achieved a network-record audience.

Stricter standards for drama documentaries were imposed by the Independent Broadcasting Authority (IBA), partly as a result of "Death of a Princess" but mainly because of the showing of a U.S. series, "A Man Called Intrepid," about Britain's wartime espionage activities. Col. Maurice Buckmaster, head of Britain's World War II Special Operations

Executive, described the series as "a travesty of fictionalized espionage activities," and his criticisms were supported by many others who had been involved in the series' subject matter. The Independent Television (ITV) companies promised to change their editorial processes to ensure stricter controls.

The year's drama in Britain was notable for a large number of successful adaptations of well-known novels, including Fay Weldon's adaptation of Jane Austen's *Pride and Prejudice* (BBC), Simon Raven's adaptation of Nancy Mitford's *Love in a Cold Climate* (Thames), Alan Plater's adaptation of J. B. Priestley's *The Good Companions* (YTV), and Philip Mackie's version of Emile Zola's *Thérèse Raquin* (BBC). Vera Brittain's autobiographical *A Testament of Youth* (BBC) was adapted by Elaine Morgan. London Weekend Television's (LWT's) "Why Didn't They Ask Evans?" was the first TV adaptation of a work by Agatha Christie.

(*See also* Advertising; Telecommunications.)

TENNIS

Increasing spectator attendance and increasing earnings by the leading players were outstanding features of 1980. The U.S. Tennis Association estimated that Björn Borg (Sweden) and John McEnroe (U.S.) each earned more than $1 million during 1979 in prize money alone; the three leading women were Martina Navratilova (Czech.) $747,548, Chris Evert Lloyd (U.S.) $564,398, and Tracy Austin (U.S.) $541,676. Attendance at the French championships at a refurbished Stade Roland Garros, Paris, set a record, more than 222,000. At the Wimbledon championships in London, despite persistently wet weather, spectators numbered more than 333,000, and at the U.S. Open championships there were more than 331,000, a record. The International Tennis Federation (ITF) in 1980 named Borg and Navratilova as world champions, based on their 1979 performances. Raul Viver

(Ecuador) and Mary Lou Piatek (U.S.) were designated world junior champions.

Men's Competition

Guillermo Vilas (Arg.) won the Australian singles for the second straight year when on January 2 in Melbourne he beat John Sadri (U.S.) 7–6, 6–3, 6–2. This was the last event in the Grand Prix for 1979. That title was won by McEnroe for a bonus of $300,000. Borg won ten tournaments for second place. In the subsequent Masters' Tournament in Madison Square Garden, New York City, Borg beat McEnroe 6–7, 6–3, 7–6 in the semifinals. In the same round Vitas Gerulaitis (U.S.) defeated Jimmy Connors (U.S.) 7–5, 6–2. In the final Borg beat Gerulaitis 6–2, 6–2.

The eight-tournament series organized by World Championship Tennis (wcT) again maintained its own identity while being incorporated in the Grand Prix. In the eight-man wcT finals at the Reunion Arena in Dallas, Texas, in May, Connors beat McEnroe 2–6, 7–6, 6–1, 6–2 in the final.

The West German championship, in Hamburg, was won by Harold Solomon (U.S.). He beat Vilas in the final 6–7, 6–2, 6–4, 2–6, 6–3. Vilas won the Italian championship in Rome, defeating Yannick Noah (France) 6–0, 6–4, 6–4. Borg won the French championship for the third successive year and for the fifth time in all, a record in both cases. In the final he beat Gerulaitis 6–4, 6–1, 6–2.

Björn Borg won a tough battle with John McEnroe for the Wimbledon men's singles championship, his fifth consecutive victory.
CENTRAL PRESS PHOTOS

KEYSTONE

Evonne Goolagong Cawley took first place at the women's singles competition at Wimbledon in July; she defeated Chris Evert Lloyd.

Borg also set a record in the Wimbledon championships. He won for the fifth consecutive year, a feat not achieved since the abolition of the challenge round system in 1922 required the defending champion to play all rounds. Borg beat Brian Gottfried (U.S.) in the semifinal. McEnroe won his semifinal against Connors 6–3, 3–6, 6–3, 6–4 to reach the final for the first time. In the final Borg beat McEnroe 1–6, 7–5, 6–3, 6–7, 8–6 after a memorable contest. McEnroe saved seven match points during the 18–16 tiebreaker in the fourth set. McEnroe's prowess earned him a standing ovation as a loser of heroic mold.

In the U.S. Open Borg reached the final after five set matches against Roscoe Tanner (U.S.) and unseeded Johan Kriek (South Africa). McEnroe reached the final after a perilous five-set semifinal against Connors, 6–4, 5–7, 0–6, 6–3, 7–6. In the final McEnroe beat Borg 7–6, 6–1, 6–7, 5–7, 6–4 to take the title for the second straight year.

In doubles competition two Australians, Peter McNamara and Paul McNamee, won their national open title at the start of the year. The French championships had unexpected winners in Victor Amaya (U.S.) and Hank Pfister (U.S.), who won the final against the revived partnership, outstanding in 1976, of Brian Gottfried and Raúl Ramírez (Mexico). McNamara and McNamee won at Wimbledon. In the final they beat another revived partnership, Bob Lutz (U.S.) and Stan Smith (U.S.). Lutz and Smith won the U.S. title, beating the defending champions, Peter Fleming (U.S.) and McEnroe, in the final. A doubles tournament endorsed by ATP at Sawgrass, Fla., in September was won by Gottfried and Ramírez against Lutz and Smith.

In the Davis Cup participants agreed upon a change in the competition format, to take effect in 1981. Zoning was abolished for the 16 leading nations, which would compete in an elimination tournament against one another. The remaining nations would maintain their zoning, American, Eastern, European "A," and European "B," with the four zone winners qualifying for promotion to the upper group in the following year. The 8 first-round losers of the top group would compete to determine which 4 would drop out of the top 16 in the following year. The 16 nations exempted from zoning for 1981 were, in draw order, West Germany, Argentina, Romania, Brazil, Great Britain, Italy, South Korea, New Zealand, Japan, Sweden, France, Australia, Switzerland, Czechoslovakia, U.S., and Mexico.

The U.S. had a brief tenure as champion nation in 1979. In February 1980 the U.S. beat Mexico in Mexico City 3–2. In March, however, Argentina beat the U.S. 4–1, José-Luis Clerc and Vilas each taking two singles against McEnroe and Gottfried. By so doing Argentina won the American Zone. Australia beat Japan and New Zealand to win the Eastern Zone. An unexpected result was a win, 3–2, by South Korea over India. South Korea then lost 5–0 to New Zealand. In the European Zone "A" Italy and Sweden were finalists. Borg was unfit and could not play for Sweden. Italy beat Sweden 4–1 in Rome. Czechoslovakia won the European Zone "B." In the semifinal round they beat France 5–0 in Prague. In the other semifinal Romania beat Great Britain 3–2 at Bristol. Because of complaints about the behaviour of Ilie Nastase in this contest, the Romanian was subsequently suspended for 18 months from Davis Cup play. Against a team thus weakened, Czechoslovakia beat Romania 4–1 in Bucharest. At the interzone stage Czechoslovakia beat Argentina 3–2 in Buenos Aires, and Italy beat Australia 3–2 in Rome. In the final at Prague, Czechoslovakia beat Italy 4–1.

Women's Competition

Chris Evert Lloyd announced at the start of the year that she would not play again until she felt her former urge to win. Her absence proved brief. In the Colgate Series championships in Landover, Md., in January, the climax to the 1979 women's equivalent to the Grand Prix, Austin beat Evert Lloyd 6–3, 6–0. Navratilova beat Austin 6–2, 6–1 to win the tournament. A little later Austin again beat Evert Lloyd, 6–2, 6–1, in the final of the first of the Avon championship series in Cincinnati, Ohio. Evert Lloyd subsequently withdrew from the series. The ten-tournament series was dominated by Navratilova, but in the climactic event in Madison Square Garden, New York City, Austin beat Navratilova 6–2, 2–6, 6–2 in the final.

Evert Lloyd returned to competition in May, winning the Italian championship, staged in Perugia, with a final win 5–7, 6–2, 6–2 against Virginia Ruzici (Rom.). She beat the same opponent 6–0, 6–3 to win the French championship in Paris, her fourth French title in five attempts.

In the Wimbledon tournament Evert Lloyd beat Navratilova, champion in 1979 and 1978, 4–6, 6–4, 6–2 in the semifinals. Evonne Goolagong Cawley (Australia) beat Austin 6–3, 0–6, 6–4 in the other semifinal. In the final Cawley won 6–1, 7–6. She had won the title once before, in 1971.

Evert Lloyd won at Flushing Meadow to take the U.S. Open title for the fifth time in six years. In the semifinals she beat Austin 4–6, 6–1, 6–1. In the final she beat Hana Mandlikova (Czech.) 5–7, 6–1, 6–1. In her semifinal Mandlikova, aged 18, beat Andrea Jaeger (U.S.), aged 15 years 3 months, 6–1, 3–6, 7–6. With Austin 17 years old, the average age of three of the semifinalists was only 17 years 2 months.

In doubles Kathy Jordan (U.S.) and Anne Smith (U.S.) had notable success. After winning the French championship they beat Rosemary Casals (U.S.) and Wendy Turnbull (Australia) 4–6, 7–5,

Third-seeded Chris Evert Lloyd won the women's singles title at the U.S. Open championships in New York in September.
WIDE WORLD

UPI

John McEnroe avenged his Wimbledon loss to Björn Borg by beating him in the U.S. Open championships in New York in September.

6-1 to win at Wimbledon. Pam Shriver (U.S.) and Betty Stove (Neth.) beat them in the semifinals of the U.S. Open only to lose to Billie Jean King (U.S.) and Navratilova 7-6, 7-5 in the final.

The 1980 Federation Cup, staged in May in Berlin, involved the sacrifice of women's events in the West German championships. It was won by the U.S. for the fifth consecutive year and for the ninth time out of 18. For the second consecutive year the U.S. did not lose in any round, and wins by 3-0 were made over Poland, New Zealand, U.S.S.R., Czechoslovakia, and Australia. The U.S. team comprised Austin, Evert Lloyd, Jordan, and Casals. In the Wightman Cup the U.S. (Evert Lloyd, Andrea Jaeger, Kathy Jordan, Anne Smith, and Rosemary Casals) beat Great Britain (Virginia Wade, Sue Barker, Anne Hobbs, and Glynis Coles) 5-2 at the Royal Albert Hall, London, to record the 42nd U.S. victory in 52 contests.

TEXTILES

Throughout the world the textile industry continued to experience an exceptional depression in sales, forcing the closing of companies in Europe, the U.S., and Asia. The troubles in the oil-producing countries of the Persian Gulf added to the general depression and suggested that worse was to follow, since rising oil prices must inevitably lead to more expensive oil-based fibres and higher energy costs. The less developed nations of Africa were building plants to make textiles from their own raw cotton, and as these began to come on stream, the arrival of their low-priced products on world markets was certain to increase pressure on the textile

industries of the industrialized countries.

The year opened with an earlier upward trend in textile production still evident. As recession spread, production rates deteriorated patchily, but wool tended to gain ground, if only gradually, at the expense of other fibres, notably man-made fibres where oversupply was substantial. World production of wool in the 1980-81 season was estimated by the Commonwealth Secretariat at 1,584,000 metric tons clean, compared with 1,579,000 tons in 1979-80. Wool prices fluctuated only modestly. Reserve price support by grower organizations assisted stability, with sales from stocks relieving shortages. As the year closed, the wool market maintained strength without large accumulations of stock.

For the first time in more than a decade, output and consumption of raw cotton were roughly in balance during the 1979-80 season. Although the area harvested was smaller than in 1978-79, yields reached a new peak, resulting in a record production of nearly 66 million bales, 5.5 million bales more than in the previous season.

The average price of raw cotton in Liverpool during 1979-80 rose steadily from the low point of around 77 cents per pound to nearly 84 cents by the end of 1979. After touching 98 cents in February 1980, it declined to 83 cents in June, but by the end of the season it had moved up to nearly 93 cents, reaching 100 cents by the end of August and a peak of 103.8 cents in early September.

The Japanese silk industry spent an anxious year, as the apparently irreversible trend away from the kimono saw stocks rising despite decreased production. There was uncertainty as to the future of the government silk subsidy in the prevailing economic climate. In July 1979 China had raised the price for 3A 20/22 denier to 49.20 yuan, announcing at the same time a price of 51.70 yuan for 1980.

Man-made fibre producers were turning their attention to new and comparatively expensive fibres with special properties. A range of hollow fibres made from all manners of polymers was under development in all the technically advanced countries, including Eastern Europe. Their immediate application was as filter media for kidney dialysis equipment, but their potential could reach far beyond such specific use.

Electrets were being developed in The Netherlands and the U.S. and probably in other countries. These fibres, having very strong and almost permanent electrostatic charges, could be used as filter media for removing solid matter from smoke or other fumes. Polymer scientists sought new synthetic polymers with much greater strength or improved heat resistance. The aramids made in the U.S. offered greater weight-for-weight strength than steel. One application for the new fibres was as an alternative to asbestos in the clutch plates of high-performance cars, and they were also used in cordage to anchor deep-sea drilling platforms.

THAILAND

The year dawned with a rising crescendo of criticism against Prime Minister Kriangsak Chamanand's administration, primarily over economic issues. Opposition parties in Parliament planned a no-confidence motion for the end of February. There were clear indications that Kriangsak would have trouble winning the slender majority with which he had survived a similar motion in October 1979. Steep rises in the prices of domestic fuel and electricity had caused nationwide disaffection, and economic frustrations in turn sparked a higher crime rate, especially gang robberies. The prime minister was also criticized for his open-door policy toward Indochinese refugees.

Persuaded by his close supporters that he had lost the confidence of Parliament and that his clinging to office would only create tension and perhaps violence, Kriangsak resigned on February 29. Parliament thereupon elected Defense Minister Gen. Prem Tinsulanond to succeed him. The 37-member Cabinet Prem introduced after two weeks of deliberations was the least military-dominated government in Thailand in recent years. It also placed heavy emphasis on economic policies by appointing highly rated banker Boonchu Rojarsthien as deputy prime minister for economic affairs.

Once the government was settled in office, security became its principal concern. Border tension with Vietnamese-dominated Cambodia and Laos persisted throughout the year, reaching a climax on June 23 when regular Vietnamese forces crossed the border and occupied three villages and two temporary refugee encampments in Thailand before they were repulsed. The Thai Foreign Ministry said that the incursion was "planned, premeditated, and carefully thought out," and Thailand played a central role in the successful attempt at the UN General Assembly in September to deny the Cambodian seat to the Vietnam-backed Heng Samrin regime in Cambodia. Thailand also made strenuous efforts to persuade other countries to support its stand that Vietnam must withdraw its troops from Cambodia. Prem himself toured Southeast Asia early in the year and China in October. Other ministers visited the U.S., the U.S.S.R., and several European capitals. After one visit, Deputy Foreign Minister Arun Bhanupong went so far as to say in November that if the Soviets did not rein in the Vietnamese, Southeast Asian countries would consider forming a military alliance.

Despite its popularity, the government was criticized because of General Prem's retention of his army post beyond the retirement age of 60. In September Parliament adopted legislation extending Prem's tenure as Army commander in chief for up to five years. Oppositionists called it a throwback to authoritarian rule. Some opposition groups also tabled censure motions against the ministers of commerce and interior on charges of mismanagement. The government preempted the challenge by closing the special session of Parliament that was to debate the motions. On November 23 Adm. Sangad Chaloryu, chairman of the National Policy Council and leader of a military coup in 1976, died. At the year's end he had not yet been replaced.

Thailand also had to cope with unusual natural disasters during the year. In the early months, in the severest drought the country had experienced in 25 years, some 240,000 ha (600,000 ac) of rice fields were ruined. Consequently, a steep decline in the country's vital rice exports was expected. Then, in

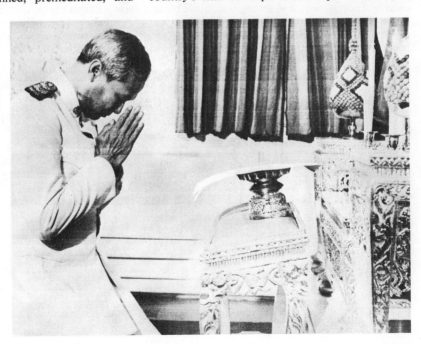

After being elected by Parliament, Gen. Prem Tinsulanond was formally appointed prime minister of Thailand by King Bhumibol in March, to replace Kriangsak Chamanand, who resigned February 29.
UPI

the second half of the year, the country was ravaged by its worst flood in five years. Floods overran vast areas of Bangkok as well as the lower northern region and the central plains, the traditional rice bowl.

The fiscal 1981 budget adopted by Parliament in September showed a 28% increase over 1979–80 to 140 billion baht (20.26 baht = U.S. $1). Nearly 20% of the total was allocated to defense, which, the government said, would remain a top priority.

THEATRE

Like the presidential election, the U.S. theatre in 1980 reflected the country's growing conservatism. The nation's stages were dominated by Broadway, a Broadway that was producing traditional works. Consequently, the accounting reports were rosier than the artistic ones.

For example, the trend in recent years toward reviving old musicals swelled to oppressive proportions. On Broadway there were revivals of *West Side Story*, *The Music Man*, *Camelot*, and *Brigadoon*. Fortunately, audiences proved not quite the gulls they were supposed to be. Of all those shows only *Camelot* was a real hit and that only because its star, Richard Burton, was a gilt-edged box-office attraction. None of the revivals was outstanding, and even *West Side Story* demonstrated itself to be, if a landmark in terms of dance, not really a great work. The blitz of revivals crowded out new musicals, which are the lifeblood of Broadway. Of the few that were produced the only real hit was *Barnum*, while *A Day in Hollywood/A Night in the Ukraine* was moderately successful.

Conservatism also set the tone among dramas, but in that area it was sometimes beneficial. Audiences were demanding and getting well-made plays, unlike some of the indulgent modern dramas of recent years. Even Harold Pinter's latest, *Betrayal*, was comprehensible. Indeed, *Betrayal* was our old

friend the romantic triangle. Pinter did put modern clothes on this story of a wife, her husband, and his best friend. He arranged the scenes in reverse time sequence so that the play began at the end and worked its way to the beginning. None of this, though, altered the play's basic orthodoxy.

Other established playwrights who had new works on Broadway included Arthur Miller (*The American Clock*), Tennessee Williams (*Clothes for a Summer Hotel*), Edward Albee (*The Lady from Dubuque*), and Howard Sackler (whose *Goodbye Fidel* was his first play since the Pulitzer Prize-winning *The Great White Hope*). They were all rudely rejected. More than ever it seemed that Broadway's commercial system was inimical to artistic thriving. In other countries, though their work is criticized, such established artists are not often subjected to that kind of humiliating commercial test.

Dramas that did make a mark on the season were straightforward and effective but artistically unambitious. The British import *Whose Life Is It Anyway?* was a problem play, the problem being one's right to death. The case in point was a young man, paralyzed in a motorcycle accident, who wanted his hospital physician to pull the plug. Because the playwright, Brian Clark, gave the fellow a marvelous black sense of humour, audiences enjoyed the play as if it were a comedy while being effectively struck by its point.

Another successful problem play during the year was Mark Medoff's *Children of a Lesser God*, dealing with a romance between a man who teaches speech to those born deaf and one of his students. This play took many of the season's prizes, including the Tony Award for best play. Other honours were won by Lanford Wilson's *Talley's Folly*, the year's Pulitzer Prize winner. *Talley's Folly* was most definitely not a problem play. Rather, it was a valentine, a romance between an immigrant Jewish accountant from St. Louis and a barren young heiress

A Day in Hollywood/A Night in the Ukraine *spoofed both Hollywood's classic musicals and Marx Brothers madness; it was directed and choreographed by Tommy Tune.*
MARTHA SWOPE

MARTHA SWOPE

David Merrick's 42nd Street, *a redo of the 1933 Ruby Keeler-Dick Powell movie, was choreographed and directed by Gower Champion, who died of cancer hours before the show opened on August 25.*

of the local Missouri aristocracy. The author had for 15 years been the U.S. theatre's unsung poet of the Midwest. Suddenly, in 1980, Wilson was not only produced but produced twice. His other play, *The Fifth of July*, was related to *Talley's Folly*—they are part of a cycle. But their relationship is tenuous, and *The Fifth of July* is a talky play without the sunny warmth of *Talley's Folly*.

All these dramas, *Children of a Lesser God*, *Talley's Folly*, and *The Fifth of July*, originated at nonprofit institutional and regional theatres before being transferred to Broadway. Such a routing had become familiar in recent years as private producers looked to such theatres for tryouts, while the institutions in turn hoped to derive income from shares of Broadway transfers. The relationship was born of mutual economic need. Dwindling interest in the theatre by governmental and private foundations put the institutional theatres in economic crisis, but even so their intimacy with Broadway was unhealthy. The idea behind nonprofit regional theatre was to decentralize the U.S. stage and provide alternatives to Broadway. These institutions should be presenting what Broadway will not or cannot present: classics, and unusually modern or sombre plays.

Wilson's pair originated at New York's Circle Repertory Company before being staged at the Mark Taper Forum in Los Angeles, where *Children of a Lesser God* began. Other Broadway transfers from the Mark Taper were Steve Tesich's *Division Street* and a new comedy, *I Ought To Be in Pictures*, by Neil Simon. As the most commercially successful playwright in the history of the Western theatre, Simon did not need help from theatre supported by federal tax waivers. Although one could sympathize with the financial plight of the Mark Taper Forum and other regional theatres, their production of patently commercial plays only made them seem less necessary.

Hand-holding with Broadway was not the only worrisome development for the regional theatre in 1980. Artistic directors resigned, were fired, or went unreplaced at such established places as the Guthrie Theatre in Minneapolis, Minn., the McCarter Theatre in Princeton, N.J., and the Hartford Stage Company and the Hartman Theatre Company, both in Connecticut. Even Canada's venerable Stratford (Ont.) Festival found itself in leadership trouble.

Stratford's 1980 season was as ambitious and successful as ever. No fewer than 15 productions were mounted, an astounding number economically and artistically. The Shakespeare plays included

Twelfth Night, *Henry V*, *Titus Andronicus*, *Much Ado About Nothing*, *King Lear*, and *Henry VI*. Additionally, there were productions of Chekhov (*The Seagull*), Carlo Goldoni (*The Servant of Two Masters*), and Eugene O'Neill (*Long Day's Journey into Night*). The Festival presented such new plays as D. L. Coburn's *The Gin Game* and John Guare's *Bosoms and Neglect* and even a musical classic (*The Beggar's Opera*).

Yet, shadows fell across the season. Robin Phillips, Stratford's artistic director, had been unhappy with his board of trustees for bowing to governmental pressure on various issues. Phillips finally resigned and was replaced by John Dexter, a respected British director who was also artistic head of New York's Metropolitan Opera. Fierce Canadian nationalist reaction followed the choice of a foreigner to head Stratford, and the government refused to issue Dexter a work permit, effectively precluding his directorship.

But back in New York City there was a new beginning for the most troubled institutional theatre of all, the Vivian Beaumont in Lincoln Center. It had been closed for three years, ever since Joseph Papp withdrew to concentrate on his Public Theater in downtown Manhattan. Somehow convincing the right people, Richmond Crinkley became administrator of a new Lincoln Center Theatre Company, leaving the Folger Theatre in Washington for the job. Instead of finding an artistic director he hired an "artistic directorate," composed of playwright Edward Albee, directors Ellis Rabb and Robin Phillips, the Romanian avant-gardist Liviu Ciulei, conductor Sarah Caldwell, and writer-comedian Woody Allen. The Beaumont reopened in the fall with the first revival of Philip Barry's *The Philadelphia Story* since its Broadway premiere in

1940. The new company's inaugural season was to include *Macbeth* and a new play by Allen. Whether that first season would be successful was less important than that the most visible regional theatre in the United States was now, in fact, visible.

Great Britain and Ireland

Theatre in Great Britain fought hard against the double dangers of a sagging economy and the ravages of inflation. The pledge to protect the arts against inflation given by Norman St. John-Stevas, the arts minister of the United Kingdom, bore fruit with an increase in the Arts Council grant of 12% (with £21 million earmarked for drama), or a real reduction of only 4¼%. The National Theatre (NT) gave 909 performances before 564,000 paying patrons. The NT announced annual seasons starting in 1982 in Bath, whose 175-year-old Theatre Royal was thus saved.

Peter Hall's National Theatre production of *Othello*, starring Paul Scofield, represented Britain at the biennial European Common Market's Europalia Festival in Brussels, while Peter Shaffer's *Amadeus* continued to break all box-office records. At the Olivier the NT staged Brenton's new translation of Bertolt Brecht's *The Life of Galileo* in a production by John Dexter; Brenton's epic drama of *The Romans in Britain*, produced by Michael Bogdanov, which attracted much abuse for its political bias and scenes of violence; and Bogdanov's dazzling adaptation of *Hiawatha*. Popular at the Lyttelton were David Storey's *Early Days*, with Ralph Richardson; Bernard Pomerance's *The Elephant Man*; Harold Pinter's *The Caretaker*, with Warren Mitchell; and Lillian Hellman's *Watch on the Rhine*, featuring Peggy Ashcroft. The Eugene O'Neill season continued with *The Iceman Cometh*

Tony Award-winner Children of a Lesser God, *by Mark Medoff, dealt with the relationship between a speech therapist and his deaf wife, portrayed by John Rubinstein and Phyllis Frelich.*

MARTHA SWOPE

*Neil Simon's latest entry
was I Ought To Be in
Pictures, starring Ron
Leibman and Dinah Manoff.*

MARTHA SWOPE

and *Hughie*, at the Cottesloe, where Bill Bryden staged Arthur Miller's *The Crucible*, and Athol Fugard's *A Lesson from Aloes* played with its original South African cast.

With the Royal Shakespeare Company (RSC) taking the SWET (Society of West End Theatres) top awards the Aldwych had a record season. David Edgar's nine-hour, two-part version of *Nicholas Nickleby* was named best play, and other awards for the play went to Roger Rees as best actor for his role as Nickleby, to David Threlfall for his best supporting performance as Smike, to Suzanne Bertish as best supporting actress in several roles, to Trevor Nunn and John Caird for direction, and to John Napier and Dermot Haynes for design. Two other SWET awards to the RSC went to Judi Dench (best actress in a revival) as Juno in Trevor Nunn's moving recreation of *Juno and the Paycock*, and to Willy Russell, author of *Educating Rita*, at the Warehouse, for the best comedy.

Transfers from Stratford included, at the Aldwych, *Twelfth Night*, with Cherie Lunghi as Viola and John Woodvine as Malvolio, *The Merry Wives of Windsor*, with Woodvine as Falstaff, and *Othello*, with Donald Sinden and Suzanne Bertish in the leads; and at the Warehouse, *The Caucasian Chalk Circle*, with Jane Carr as Grusha. New plays included works by Barrie Keefe, Howard Barker, Ron Hutchinson, and Peter Prince, and *No Limits to Love* by David Mercer. Outstanding at the Aldwych was *The Greeks*, a three-part epic adaptation of Aeschylus, Homer, Sophocles, and Euripides, notable for Lynn Dearth's Electra and Janet Suzman's Helen. The Old Vic's controversial *MacBeth*, starring Peter O'Toole, put the company in the black despite unfavourable notices.

A few commercial West End shows originated in fringe or regional theatres, such as Andrew Davies's *Rose*, with Glenda Jackson (in Coventry), Ronald Harwood's *The Dresser* (in Manchester), Alan Ayckbourn's *Season's Greetings* (in Scarborough), Rodney Ackland's *Before the Party* (in Oxford), Tom Kempinski's *Duet for One*, which won Frances de la Tour the SWET award for best actress in a new play (at the Bush), Frederick Lonsdale's *The Last of Mrs. Cheyney* (at the Chichester Festival), Noel Coward's *Private Lives* (in Greenwich), Michael Frayn's *Make and Break* (at the Lyric in Hammersmith), Pinter's *The Hothouse* (in Hampstead), and the smash hit *Pal Joey* (at the Half Moon).

Among musicals *Sweeney Todd*, though a box-office failure, secured two SWET awards, as best musical and, for Denis Quilley in the title role, that for the best actor in a musical. Gemma Craven won the equivalent actress award for *They're Playing Our Song*. Other musicals included *Tom-foolery*, *Colette*, *The Streets of London* (transferred from the Theatre Royal, Stratford East), *The Biograph Girl* (from Brighton), and *Oklahoma!*

At the Royal Court Jonathan Pryce won the SWET award for best actor in a revival for his portrayal of Hamlet. New plays at the Royal Court included Paul Kember's *Not Quite Jerusalem*, Sam Shepard's *Seduced*, and the 18-year-old Andrea Dunbar's *The Arbor*. Other noteworthy productions were Miller's *The Price* at the Shaw, Michael Frayn's *Liberty Hall* at Greenwich, Shepard's *Buried Child* at Hampstead, the return of Frank Dunlop to the Young Vic with *King Lear*, the world premiere of *Mayakovski* by East German writer Stefan Schütz at the Half Moon, Charles Marowitz's *Hedda* at the Round House, and Edward Dukes's one-man show *Jeeves Takes Charge*, which won a special SWET award for most promising newcomer.

The Abbey Theatre, Dublin (with a grant of I£800,000), continued its Sean O'Casey season with *The Shadow of a Gunman* and *Red Roses for Me*, while *Juno and the Paycock*, starring and staged by Siobhan McKenna, also went to the English Theatre in Vienna. At the 22nd Dublin Festival were Hugh Leonard's *A Life*; new plays by Bernard Farrell, J. Graham Reid, Neil Donnelly, and Stewart Parker; and Maureen Charlton's *Nora Barnacle*, about James Joyce's wife, which created a minor theatrical scandal. Earlier, Joe Dowling had staged *Faith Healer* by Brian Friel, who joined forces with fellow Ulsterman Stephen Rea to found the northern Irish "Field Day" company and launch a tour of his own highly praised historical drama *Translations*.

(*See also* Dance; Music.)

TOURISM

International tourist arrivals in 1980 were estimated at 280 million–290 million (excluding some 600 million excursionist arrivals) and receipts of the destination countries at $89 billion (excluding international fares and domestic tourism). Among source countries, West Germany continued to lead, with about 28 million departures and over $20 billion spent abroad in 1980. The U.S. remained the second most important source (24 million departures, primarily to Canada and Mexico); there was some increase in travel by Americans to the U.K. in the first half of 1980, following a drop of 11% in 1979, and to Austria, but travel to other European countries declined. France, with about 16 million departures, was the third major source of international tourists, and U.K. departures were at a level similar to that of France. Japanese tourism slowed in 1980, as did outgoing tourism from Canada, The Netherlands, and the Scandinavian countries. Relative to population, Austria continued to lead in terms of tourism expenditure abroad (about $400 per capita), while Switzerland led in tourist departures abroad (averaging about 1.5 per resident per year).

The countries of the Organization for Economic Cooperation and Development continued to be the leading sources and destinations of international tourism, spending about $4 billion more than the $62 billion they received in 1979. The less developed countries apparently expanded their share as sources and destinations; most notably, Mexico's incoming tourism grew by 14% in 1979.

The U.S. remained a leading destination ($8.3 billion tourism receipts, 260 million tourist nights in 1979). It registered considerable increases in tourism from Europe in 1980, owing to reduced transatlantic fares and favourable prices of tourism services resulting from the weakness of the dollar. Florida, which had been primarily a winter resort for Americans, attracted many summer tourists, especially from the U.K.

Data for 1980 indicated increased competition for international tourists—by destinations, carriers, tour operators, and travel agents. The 1979–80 winter season in Europe was generally successful, but the summer and autumn seasons were affected by accelerated inflation, unemployment, and tighter credit, and the outlook for the winter season was problematic. Tourism to West Germany shot up (by about 10%) following a slight increase in 1979: the decennial Oberammergau Passion Play (May–September 1980) attracted large numbers of tourists, many of whom continued their pilgrimage by

Foreign tourism to the U.S. was up in 1980, especially from nations in strong monetary positions vis-à-vis the U.S. dollar. Here a Japanese tourist chooses postcards in New Orleans.
CHRISTOPHER HARRIS

Sales of electronic toys were expected to reach $750 million in the U.S. in 1980, about 10% of the entire U.S. toy market.
MARIO RUIZ

visiting Rome or Jerusalem. Austria reported an 8% increase, following an 11% decrease in 1979. Latin America celebrated its "Tourism Year," with increases recorded in Brazil (40%) and Colombia (16%). The Caribbean also gained in popularity. In the Far East, Japan reported a 23% growth in tourist arrivals, Thailand 26%, Singapore 10%, and Hong Kong 3%, while decreases were recorded for South Korea and Taiwan, following increases in 1979. Australia expected a 20% increase in arrivals.

Political events affected tourism in many countries in 1980. Philippine terrorists tried to disrupt the conference of the American Society of Travel Agents in Manila in October. In Spain bombing incidents on the Costa Blanca and Costa del Sol, combined with steep price rises, caused a decline in tourism from many countries. Other Mediterranean destinations enjoyed increases, especially Portugal (up 50% following a rise of 34% in 1979), Cyprus and Malta (up 20%), Italy (up 7%), and Tunisia (up 6%). Tourism in Egypt (up 16%) and Israel (up 8%) was assisted by the opening of direct air and land links between the two countries in early 1980. Greece, where tourism had grown 16% in 1979, reported a drop in the first half of 1980, as did Yugoslavia. The strikes in Poland, the change of regime in Turkey, and election violence in Jamaica also affected tourism in those countries. The U.S.S.R. had hoped for 300,000 foreign visitors for the Moscow Olympic Games, but the partial boycott cut Western tourism considerably.

Petrodollars were an important source of financing for new and upgraded facilities. The growth in tourism from Arab countries was now a major source of revenue for many resorts. In parallel with the building of giant and luxury hotels and greater use of private aircraft and yachts, demand increased for facilities for popular tourism, spurred by the growth of camping, backpacking, and youth

hostels. Self-catering holidays and time-sharing or condominium projects were increasing in importance.

TOYS AND GAMES

Following the avalanche of first-generation microprocessor-based games and toys that arrived on the market in 1979, toy merchants in all parts of the world found themselves with unusually high inventories at the beginning of 1980. Prior to the 1979 Christmas season there had been widespread overstocking by retailers, and when this was followed by a drastic downturn in consumer spending, many toy manufacturers found themselves caught between investment in new technology and the world slump in trade.

In the U.S. retail sales of electronic toys were estimated at $500 million in 1979, representing about 10% of the total U.S. toy market. Optimists predicted that this figure would increase by 50% in 1980, and at the New York Toy Fair in February more than 300 electronic items were offered to trade buyers. However, increased competition, even though it resulted in substantial reductions in the prices of handheld microprocessor-based games and other electronic toys, did not persuade buyers to loosen their purse strings.

U.S. observers of the toy trade saw 1980 as a "back-to-basics" year. Consumers spent more time in their homes, a result of which was improved demand for staple games such as Monopoly and Scrabble; against the normal pattern, retailers were selling board games well during the summer season.

The spectre that had been haunting the toy industry in recent years was the decline in the birthrate in the Western world, and while this had halted in a number of countries, there remained for the toy manufacturer an equally serious problem arising from the comparatively early maturing of children's tastes. This shortening of the period during which children were the recipients of toys resulted in the preschool sector of the industry currently accounting for about 50% of the world toy market. It was significant that such companies as Fisher-Price and Lego, which specialized in preschool toys, were those that were less seriously affected by the world depression.

The boom in roller skates that had begun in the U.S. in 1979 moved across the Atlantic in 1980, and skates were one of the few bright spots in European sales during the summer months. In general, however, the consumer emphasis shifted to the traditional staple items, especially those with a low price tag. An example in the United Kingdom was the success achieved by one manufacturer, Thomas Salter Ltd., in selling £750,000 worth of rub-on colour transfers.

A fad that grew to major proportions in the U.S. during the year was the riding of mechanical bulls. More than 400 of these $7,000 devices were in-stalled in country and western bars and nightclubs throughout the nation, drawing large crowds and testing the skills of would-be cowboys with bucking action that increased in violence on a scale of one to ten. The original model was in Gilley's Club in Pasadena, Texas, which was popularized in the movie *Urban Cowboy*.

It was a difficult year for the leading British toy manufacturers, especially those whose production was geared to a high percentage of export business. Apart from high interest rates, particularly onerous for an industry whose products are heavily committed to the Christmas sales period, the increasing strength of the pound seriously affected the profitability of many firms. At the beginning of the year Lesney Products Ltd. announced a loss for 1979 of £3.6 million, increased to £6 million by mid-1980. Early in the year Europe's largest toy company, Dunbee-Combex-Marx Ltd., revealed a deficit of £18 million. This failure was in the main due to the fact that the company came to grief in the U.S.,

---

Game Playing

"It's constant decision-making, a funneling effect of everything you've done before." It satisfies "the need to escape from the ever more unpleasant reality." "It is very definitely antireligious . . . it leaves them so open to Satanic spirits." "It's all a part of the irresponsibility that college undergraduates normally have, and it shouldn't be begrudged them."

The observers were not addressing drug addiction, sensitivity enhancement seminars, or conversion to an exotic religious cult. They were talking about playing games. The first three statements referred to Dungeons and Dragons, a role-playing adventure guided by rule books and the roll of special dice. The fourth came from a Stanford University student who had been waging a night-long computer-programming battle called Wheel Wars.

Games that emphasize fantasy and conflict or that pit one's mental abilities against an electronic computer have become extremely popular with adults and children alike. Among the more recent best sellers is Simon, a computerized memory game that razzes and rewards its human opponent with lights and sound. The continually swelling ranks of war gamers support annual conventions and a spate of periodicals. Requests for the most popular of the fantasy games, Dungeons and Dragons (D&D), are keeping games shops and campus bookstores depleted; the game is grossing an annual $2.5 million for its inventor, a former shoe repairman from Wisconsin.

To explain this appeal, some observers do not look beyond the games themselves. Their novelty supposedly lies in their ability to allow one to exercise intellect or imagination or in their freedom from the competitiveness of traditional board games. Analysts who favour economic explanations cite the attractiveness of games in a society with in-creased leisure time but little money for expensive amusements. Others point to growing social and psychological pressures. Game worlds can offer the player physical and intellectual power and a social structure more congenial than that of the real world.

Persons of high intelligence have not proved immune to the lure of game playing, although they may invent their own kinds. One of the most arcane is played on U.S. campuses by "subcultures" of bright computer-science undergraduates who call themselves hackers. For solitary entertainment, these young adults spend long hours hacking—inconsequentially toying with complex programs—at the terminals of university computers. Together, they fight Wheel Wars, using ruthless strategies to frustrate opponents' tinkering with their programs or even to block opponents' access to terminals.

Do games actually sharpen wits and nourish the imagination? Or are they intellectual "black holes" that absorb one's time and talents and return nothing? Some former Wheel Wars players consider themselves lucky to have escaped with their sanity. Do their experiences foreshadow a newly emerging form of aberrant behaviour, comparable to alcoholism or compulsive gambling?

Anyone asking such questions must also consider the true purpose of human play. As one ex-hacker concluded: "To me, as one matures, the highest forms of play cease to be consumptive and begin to be productive. . . . there is nothing wrong with consumptive play in an appropriate setting and appropriate circumstances. Middle-aged adults enjoy Great America. . . . nonetheless, I don't believe it is the highest form of play that they should be capable of."

where it had acquired subsidiaries that it failed to integrate.

Far East toy manufacturers continued to dominate the export field, particularly with electronic and radio-controlled items. But there was a growing awareness, especially in Hong Kong, that there would be a slowing down of demand in their best markets, the U.S. and Europe, and to compensate for this extra efforts were made to sell toys in the Middle East and South America.

TRACK AND FIELD

Although diminished in scope and performance by international politics, the Olympic Games dominated a productive 1980 track and field season. Forty-one world records were broken or equaled before, during, and after the Olympics, which were held in Moscow without the presence of the United States and several other nations.

Men's International Competition

Record breaking started on April 23, and by the time of the Olympics (July 24–August 1), 17 new world marks had been established. Three more were recorded during the Olympics but only one after the Games despite a busy two-month schedule.

Poland's Wladyslaw Kozakiewicz began the pole vault festivities with a new record of 5.72 m (18 ft 9¼ in) on May 11. France contributed the next three records as Thierry Vigneron cleared 5.75 m (18 ft 10¼ in) on June 1 and again on June 29, while Philippe Houvion made 5.77 m (18 ft 11 in) on July 17. Kozakiewicz then won a stirring Olympic competition with his second record of the year, 5.78 m (18 ft 11½ in).

The hammer throw records were set by three Soviets. Yury Sedykh, the 1976 Olympic titlist, threw 80.38 m (263 ft 8 in) on May 16, lost his record in the same competition to Juri Tamm, who threw 80.46 m (264 ft), and regained it later that day with 80.64 m (264 ft 7 in). Then, after Sergey Litvinov upped the standard to 81.66 m (267 ft 11 in) on May 24, Sedykh had his final turn in the Olympics on July 31. On the very first throw of the meeting he reached 81.80 m (268 ft 4½ in), regaining the global mark and becoming the first two-time Olympic hammer winner in 48 years.

The 1976 Olympic high-jump champion, Jacek Wszola of Poland, opened the season with a new high of 2.35 m (7 ft 8½ in) on May 25. Just a day later the mark was matched by Dietmar Mogenburg of West Germany. That record stood until the Olympics, when Gerd Wessig of East Germany became one of the least expected Olympic winners with a jump of 2.36 m (7 ft 8¾ in).

Particularly keen was the double battle between Britain's Sebastian Coe and Steve Ovett in the 800-m and 1,500-m runs. Coe, who set world marks in the 800 m, 1,500 m, and one mile in 1979, added the 1,000-m mark with a 2-min 13.40-sec performance on July 1. But he lost his mile record in the same

Oslo meet when Ovett ran the distance in 3 min 48.8 sec. Two weeks later Ovett equaled Coe's 1,500-m time of 3 min 32.1 sec.

Coe, the world record holder and believed to possess more natural speed, was the favourite in the 800, while Ovett, the stronger of the two, was favoured in the 1,500. But Ovett was the surprise winner in the 800 at 1 min 45.4 sec. Surprised and disappointed, Coe made up for the unexpected loss six days later when he won the 1,500-m handily with Ovett third behind East Germany's Jurgen Straub. It was a tactical race, and the time was a modest 3 min 38.4 sec.

With Coe and Ovett splitting victories it was left to Miruts Yifter to become the only men's double track and field winner of the Games. The little Ethiopian, of unknown age but thought to be at least 38, won the 10,000 m in 27 min 42.7 sec and then the 5,000 m in 13 min 21 sec. He succeeded Lasse Viren of Finland as gold medalist in both events, Viren achieving no better than a fifth in the 10,000.

Joining Sedykh as the only other successful defending champion was East Germany's Waldemar Cierpinski. He took 2 hr 11 min 3 sec to become the second runner ever to win the Olympic marathon twice.

Olympic records fell in 7 of the 24 events: the three world record events (high jump, pole vault, hammer throw) plus the 20,000-m and 50,000-m

Britain's Sebastian Coe set a world record for 1,000 metres on July 1 in Oslo with a time of 2 minutes 13.40 seconds.
KEYSTONE

walks, the long jump, and the shot put. Maurizio Damilano of Italy captured the shorter walk in 1 hr 23 min 36 sec, while Hartwig Gauder of East Germany was the 50,000-m champion in 3 hr 49 min 24 sec. The long jump was won by Lutz Dombrowski of East Germany. His leap of 8.54 m (28 ft ¼ in) was the second longest ever and the best at low altitude. Vladimir Kiselyov of the Soviet Union established a new Olympic shot put record of 21.35 m (70 ft ½ in).

Other Olympic winners were: 100 m, Alan Wells, U.K., 10.25 sec; 200 m, Pietro Mennea, Italy, 20.19 sec; 400 m, Viktor Markin, U.S.S.R., 44.60 sec (a new European record); 3,000-m steeplechase, Bronislaw Malinowski, Poland, 8 min 9.7 sec; 110-m hurdles, Thomas Munkelt, East Germany, 13.39 sec; 400-m hurdles, Volker Beck, East Germany, 48.70 sec; 4 × 100-m relay, U.S.S.R., 38.26 sec;

In New Zealand on January 26, Mary Decker of the United States set a women's mile record at 4 minutes 21.68 seconds.
UPI

4 × 400-m relay, U.S.S.R., 3 min 1.1 sec; triple jump, Jaak Uudmae, U.S.S.R., 17.35 m (56 ft 11 in); discus, Viktor Rashchupkin, U.S.S.R., 66.64 m (218 ft 8 in); javelin, Dainis Kula, U.S.S.R., 91.20 m (299 ft 2 in); and decathlon, Daley Thompson, U.K., 8,495 points.

The Soviet Union and East Germany captured more than half of the medals for the 24 events. The U.S.S.R. won 8 events and 15 other medals, while East Germany had 6 golds and 8 other prizes. (*See also* Olympic Games.)

All world record action in 1980 occurred in Europe, with no new marks being set in the U.S. for the first time in 35 years. Only one U.S. athlete achieved a new world record, Edwin Moses lowering his own 400-m hurdle standard to 47.13 sec on July 3.

Ferenc Paragi of Hungary threw the javelin 96.72 m (317 ft 4 in) on April 23 to begin the parade of records. The decathlon mark fell twice, Thompson earning 8,622 points on May 18 and Guido Kratschmer of West Germany topping that with 8,649 on June 14. Only Ovett was able to break a record in an unexpected post-Olympic letdown. He captured sole ownership of the 1,500-m prize, running the distance in 3 min 31.36 sec on August 27.

Women's International Competition

The pattern in women's participation paralleled that of the men. Thirteen women broke 17 records in nine individual events, and three relay records were established.

Eastern Europeans dominated competition throughout the year, including the Olympics. The U.S.S.R. accounted for nine of the world records and won 7 of the 14 Olympic events. East Germany scored with eight world marks and five Olympic gold medals. All but one of the 20 records were established in Europe, mostly in the Eastern sector. The lone exception was the first new mark of the year. Mary Decker of the U.S. ran the mile in 4 min 21.68 sec in New Zealand on January 26.

The most honours were won by Nadyezhda Olizarenko of the Soviet Union. She lowered the 800-m record to 1 min 54.85 sec on June 12 and then knocked it down to 1 min 53.42 sec in winning the Olympics. Tatyana Kazankina, another Soviet middle-distance star, won in the Olympics and broke the 1,500-m standard twice, but neither record was set in the Games. Kazankina ran 3 min 55 sec on July 6 and created the sole post-Olympic record with a 3 min 52.47 run on August 13.

East Germany's Ilona Slupianek extended the shot put record to 22.36 m (73 ft 4¼ in) on May 2 and to 22.45 m (73 ft 8 in) on May 11 and later won the Olympics. Olga Kuragina of the Soviet Union twice bettered the pentathlon standard, first scoring 4,856 points on June 20. She raised the figure to 4,875 points on July 24 in the Olympics but despite her record-shattering performance finished only third. This unusual finish was made possible by a

UPI

Alberto Salazar, running in his first marathon, was victor in record time in a field of 14,000 runners in New York City.

unique sequence of events in which the pentathlon record was broken three times in just 1.6 sec.

Kuragina was the first to finish the 800-m run, the concluding event in the pentathlon. As she crossed the line in 2 min 3.6 sec, she achieved her 4,-875 record. But when Olga Rukavishnikova finished in 2 min 4.8 sec, her total was 4,937 points. Kuragina's mark had lasted only 1.2 sec. The new figure remained a record for even less time as Nadyezhda Tkachenko finished in 2 min 5.2 sec for 5,083 points.

Among the other record setters only Evelin Jahl and the East German 4 × 100-m relay team were successful in the Olympics. The foursome ran a record-equaling 42.09 sec on July 9, 41.85 sec on July 13, and 41.60 sec in the Olympics on August 1. Jahl of East Germany threw the discus 71.50 m (234 ft 7 in) on May 10.

Non-Olympic winners who set new world bests were Grazyna Rabsztyn of Poland, 12.36 sec for the 100-m hurdles on June 13; Karin Rossley, East Germany, 54.28 sec for the 400-m hurdles on May 17; Maria Vergova, Bulgaria, 71.80 m (235 ft 7 in) in the discus July 13; Ruth Fuchs, East Germany, 69.96 m (229 ft 6 in) in the javelin April 29; and Tatyana Biryulina, U.S.S.R., 70.08 m (229 ft 11 in) in the javelin July 12.

Non-record-breaking Olympic winners were: 100 m, Lyudmila Kondratyeva, U.S.S.R., 11.06 sec; 200 m, Barbel Eckert-Wockel, East Germany, 22.03 sec; 400 m, Marita Koch, East Germany, 48.88 sec; 1,500 m, Kazankina, 3 min 56.58 sec; 100-m hurdles, Vera Komisova, U.S.S.R., 12.56 sec; 4 × 400-m relay, U.S.S.R., 3 min 20.2 sec; high jump, Sara Simeoni, Italy, 1.97 m (6 ft 5½ in); long jump, Tatyana Kolpakova, U.S.S.R., 7.06 m (23 ft 2 in); shot put, Slupianek, 22.41 m (73 ft 6¼ in); discus, Jahl, 69.96 m (229 ft 6 in); javelin, Maria Colon, Cuba, 68.40 m (224 ft 5 in).

U.S. Competition

Not allowed to compete in the Olympics, U.S. athletes climaxed their season with the so-called "Olympic Trials" at Eugene, Ore., in late June. Only Moses and Decker produced world marks, and only two national standards were bettered at the Trials; Henry Marsh ran the 3,000-m steeplechase in 8 min 15.68 sec, and Jodi Anderson long jumped 7 m (22 ft 11½ in).

Decker enjoyed the best season, adding four U.S. 1,500-m records and one 3,000-m mark to her world mile figure. Her best times were 3 min 59.43 sec in the 1,500 and 8 min 38.73 sec in the 3,000. Another successful performer was discus thrower Lorna Griffin. After breaking the U.S. record four times in 1979, she did it another five times in 1980, finally reaching 63.22 m (207 ft 5 in).

Additional U.S. records for women were made by Jan Merrill with 15 min 30.6 sec for 5,000 m; Joan Benoit, 2 hr 31 min 23 sec, and Patti Lyons-Catalano, 2 hr 30 min 57 sec, in the marathon; Sandy Myers, 56.40 sec and Esther Mahr, 56.16 sec for the 400-m hurdles; and Louise Ritter, 1.95 m (6 ft 4¾ in) for the high jump.

U.S. males were not as productive. In addition to the steeplechase, national records were set in the 10,000 m, 27 min 29.16 sec by Craig Virgin; high jump, 2.32 m (7 ft 7¼ in) by Jeff Woodard (record equaled); and in the discus 70.98 m (232 ft 10 in) by Mac Wilkins.

Indoors, Steve Scott set U.S. bests for one mile (3 min 53 sec) and 3,000 m (7 min 45.2 sec); Larry Myricks long jumped a world best 8.38 m (27 ft 6 in); and Ron Livers extended the triple jump to 17.07 m (56 ft). For the women Decker lowered the world 1,500-m figure to 4 min 0.8 sec, while Ritter high jumped 1.93 m (6 ft 4¼ in) for a national best.

The University of Texas at El Paso led the way in team competition, winning the men's National Collegiate Athletic Association outdoor and indoor tournaments and becoming a power in women's track while capturing the indoor Association for Intercollegiate Athletics for Women (AIAW) title. California State at Northridge won the AIAW outdoor.

TRANSPORTATION

Three major considerations dominated the transport scene in 1980: the economic recession, energy, and deregulation. The recession brought the bleakest year in international aviation history and difficulties for those transport activities (*e.g.*, bulk movement of iron and steel) most closely geared to economic activity. The temporary shortage of fuel oils and the corresponding rise in prices in the early part of the year provided a reminder of the need to find alternative energy sources for the 1990s and beyond—a reminder later underlined by the outbreak of hostilities between Iraq and Iran. The liberalization of competition was spreading from the North American domestic air market and the North Atlantic to other routes (*e.g.*, London to Hong Kong) and to surface transport.

Aviation

The world airline industry faced a disastrous financial situation in 1980 as economic depression reduced traffic while fuel prices continued to cause concern. In the U.S. it was the second full year of deregulation, the relaxation of economic regulation of airlines by the government following passage of the Airline Deregulation Act of 1978.

The U.S. airlines lost more than $1 billion in the second half of 1979 and a further $475 million in the first half of 1980. There was improvement later in the year, but in late December the U.S. Air Transport Association (ATA), representing almost all of the nation's scheduled carriers, estimated that the airlines' operating loss for the year would be between $150 million and $200 million. This would be the largest loss in the 42 years since ATA began keeping records. The notable exception among the trunk carriers was Delta, which managed to record a significant profit.

Among the regional carriers, which benefited considerably from deregulation, USAir, Air Florida, and Southwest achieved excellent results.

With losses thought likely to continue for one or two years, the main concern of the U.S. industry was financing the acquisition of new aircraft. According to the ATA, airlines needed to spend $4.4 billion per year up to 1990 on new aircraft. Actual expenditure was running at less than half that figure in 1979 and at only $1 billion in the first nine months of 1980. To generate the necessary capital, a rate of return on investment of 13–15% was needed, a figure achieved in only one year of the past 20.

All U.S. trunk carriers except United and Northwest experienced a traffic decline in the first ten months of 1980 as compared with the corresponding period of 1979. Traffic, at 304,000,000,000 revenue passenger-kilometres (189,000,000,000 revenue passenger-miles) overall, was 5% below the 1979 period. Most trunk carriers' load factors were down significantly in the ten-month period—by a disastrous nine percentage points in the case of United. Braniff, following a major cutback of the extra capacity it had operated immediately following deregulation, increased its load factor marginally. Some observers believed that the instability that had followed deregulation was beginning to subside.

Regional carriers in general benefited from the new regulatory environment, but it was the commuter carriers that showed the strongest growth rate. The commuters' revenue passenger-kilometres increased 35% in 1979 compared with 1978, and a further increase of at least 10% was anticipated in

Airline services between Beijing (Peking) and London began on November 17 with the arrival of the first flight from China at Gatwick Airport.
KEYSTONE

UPI

Atlanta International Airport opened in September, a $500 million terminal complex (the world's largest) with 134 jet gates, designed by a consortium of architects.

1980 in strong contrast to the industry's general performance.

Traffic of international scheduled airlines during the year was about 3% above that of the previous year, according to a preliminary assessment by the International Air Transport Association (IATA) in October. At the same time, it was estimated that capacity had risen by 8%. IATA members' operating revenue in 1980 was forecast by the association's director general, Knut Hammarskjöld, at $23.7 billion, representing an increase of 21% over 1979. However, operating costs rose 27% to $25.1 billion, leaving the airlines with an operating loss before interest of $778 million and a loss after interest of $1.4 billion. Despite this bleak picture, Hammarskjöld believed that the industry was at the bottom of a trough and that recovery could well be evident within two to three years. Fuel costs for IATA members averaged about $1.22 per gallon in 1980, nearly three times the figure for 1978. The IATA predicted that fuel would constitute 31% of members' operating costs on international scheduled services in 1981.

Total world traffic in 1979, as recorded by the International Civil Aviation Organization, was 532,900,000,000 passenger-kilometres (331,100,-000,000 passenger-miles), an increase of 9.9% over 1978. Charter traffic, included in that total, declined 5.8% to 102,200,000,000 passenger-kilometres (63,500,000,000 passenger-miles). The number of scheduled passengers in 1979 was 155 million, 10.4% more than in the preceding year.

Railroads

In the U.S., government regulation of the railroads was significantly loosened by passage of the historic Staggers Rail Act of 1980. The act, which Pres. Jimmy Carter called the "capstone" of his efforts to get the federal government "off the backs" of private industry, became law on October 14. It marked the culmination of an 18-month drive to reduce the load of government regulation that had controlled the industry for 93 years. The law did not totally deregulate the railroads but allows for a measure of ratemaking freedom—including the ability to offer contract rates—and it removes the Interstate Commerce Commission (ICC) from many aspects of day-to-day rail operations.

In addition to landmark deregulation legislation, 1980 also witnessed a dramatically quickened pace in the rail merger movement. The nation's two largest rail systems resulted from mergers in 1980. On November 1, the Chessie System and the Family Lines merged to form CSX Corp. The combined system operated 27,000 mi of line serving 22 states, the District of Columbia, and Ontario, Canada. The Burlington Northern and St. Louis–San Francisco merged on November 21. The surviving railroad— the Burlington Northern—had 29,226 route miles in 25 states and two Canadian provinces.

Other changes in the rail map took place in 1980 as the fates of two bankrupt Midwestern carriers—the Chicago, Rock Island and Pacific and the Chicago, Milwaukee, St. Paul and Pacific—were decided. The 133-year-old Rock Island began liquidation on January 25. The Milwaukee Road operated a pared-down 3,600-mi core system. The Milwaukee's lines west of Miles City, Mont., were abandoned as its trustees worked to develop a reorganization plan. Sales of Rock Island and abandoned Milwaukee lines were negotiated during the year with states, railroads, and nonrail companies. Meanwhile, other railroads were given interim authority to operate over sections of track from both systems.

While rail deregulation and a revised rail map promised to affect the future of the industry, the railroads had to face a more immediate impact—the downturn in the nation's economy. The result was a drop almost across the board in rail traffic.

Motor vehicles and equipment—the fourth most important commodity in terms of revenues—paced the decline with carloadings down 24% in 1980 compared with 1979. However, strong traffic in grain, which was up 10.1%, and coal, up 8.6%, bolstered an otherwise depressed traffic picture.

The high volume of grain and coal loadings — which generally travel long distances—caused the anomaly of an estimated record 915,000,-000,000 ton-miles for the industry, while carloadings as a whole declined 5.4%. Those railroads that primarily carry coal and grain, however, were less severely affected by the downturn.

Railroads' financial performance also closely reflected the recession. This was evidenced by a drop in second-quarter ordinary income, which plummeted to $183.8 million, compared with $446.4 million for the same quarter of 1979. By the close of the first nine months, however, the picture had brightened considerably, with ordinary income totaling $613.1 million, compared with $554.4 million for the first three quarters of 1979.

In passenger railroading, the National Railroad Passenger Corp. (Amtrak) reported an increase in ridership as Americans continued to feel the impact of spiraling fuel prices. August 1980 saw 2.2 million passengers ride Amtrak trains—the most since the corporation began operations in 1971.

Roads and Traffic

Efforts were made to hasten completion of major transcontinental routes and to fill in missing links. Notable completions were the Beune to Mulhouse Motorway linking the French and West German national expressway networks and the 4.2-km (2.6-mi) Ahmed Hamidi tunnel under the Suez Canal

New Yorkers took to their feet and bicycles when a nine-day transit strike in April stranded millions of commuters. The city's businesses lost an estimated $100 million a day during the strike.
PHOTO TRENDS

British Rail put into service in 1980 an Advance Passenger Train capable of achieving speeds of 250 kilometres per hour (155 miles per hour); the train leans dramatically on curves.
KEYSTONE

linking Africa and Asia. Autoroute 26 connecting the North Sea coast to the south of France was opened to traffic.

Unorthodox materials were being used, both to renew existing pavements and for new construction. The Trans-Sahara Highway was being constructed of low-moisture laterite, and the world's first highway to be paved with sulfurous materials (3.3 km [2 mi] long) was completed at San Antonio, Texas. Recycling of the existing pavement (using hot-mix methods) could save up to a quarter of the cost of complete replacement; this method was used to rebuild the Edens Expressway in the Chicago area and to renew 87 km [54 mi] of U.S. highway in New Jersey.

Despite economic difficulties, world road traffic continued to grow, particularly in those countries that were neither "Western rich" nor "less developed poor." In Poland, for example, the current growth rate was 13% per year. The world's road vehicle fleet reached 400 million units. Efforts continued to reduce reliance on hydrocarbons for fuel. Of particular note during the year were General Motors' proposal to mass produce an electric car during the mid-'80s, the mass production of an electric light van by Diahatsu, the announcement by Gulf and Western of a breakthrough in battery technology, and the mass production (for Brazil) of alcohol-powered cars.

Urban Mass Transit

During the 1970s, 21 new rail transit systems were opened, and most of the pre-World War II systems were extended. The total route length in operation in 1980 was about 3,500 km (2,175 mi) serving 3,400 stations. Operating speeds ranged from 19 km per hour (12 mph) on the Budapest, Hung., system to 70 km per hour (43 mph) on San Francisco's Bay Area Rapid Transit; the average was 34 km per hour (21 mph). As of 1980 there were 90 cities with rail transit systems in operation or under construction, and this number seemed likely to top 100 by 1990. Some 800 route-kilometres (500 route-miles) were currently under construction, and a further 1,800 route-kilometres (1,100 route-miles) were planned.

Light rail transit (LRT) and tramway technologies were under consideration in about 100 cities. The key difference between these two systems is that LRT uses formal railway signaling whereas vehicle separation on tramways is a matter for the driver. There were 45,000 trams (streetcars) running on 290 systems, ranging from the huge network in Leningrad to the tiny system in Bex, Switz. The first stage of the Tyne and Wear system in the U.K. opened in August.

Despite the large investment being made in urban rail systems, buses were a more important form of urban public transport and would continue to be for many years to come. Roughly 800,000 buses in the world's towns and cities carried one billion journeys each day. Bus manufacturing was more stable than in 1978–79, and the traditional major manufacturers consolidated their positions. Structural problems, possibly attributable to the highly complex federal specifications, were reported in many of

Locomotives of the Burlington Northern and St. Louis–San Francisco lines "clasped hands" to symbolize the merger of the two lines, approved in 1980.
WIDE WORLD

the new buses purchased by the U.S. government for several U.S. bus systems.

The decline of the trolley bus seemed to have been halted as systems were introduced by such countries as Switzerland, South Africa, Brazil, and Canada that either had good electricity supplies or were excessively dependent on imported oil. Currently there were 20,000 trolley buses operating in over 200 systems, the largest being in Moscow. Perhaps the most interesting technological developments were in the field of hybrid systems (trolley/battery and trolley/diesel), which offered the prospect of a greater routing flexibility and the possibility of avoiding overhead wires in sensitive and difficult areas.

(*See also* Aerospace; Automobiles; Energy; Engineering Projects; Ships and Shipping.)

TUNISIA

Pres. Habib Bourguiba, continually confronted with a watchful and active opposition, had to show both firmness and a spirit of accommodation. At the end of December 1979, Prime Minister Hedi Nouira delivered a violent attack on Islamic unity purists, and in February 1980 the government closed all university faculties. In March, however, several opponents belonging to the Mouvement des Démocrates Socialistes joined the government Parti Socialiste Destourien. In July six Marxist-Leninist students were freed, and in August trade union leaders were granted some freedom from restriction.

Hedi Nouira underwent surgery in March following a stroke and went to Nice, France, for his convalescence. Appointed "coordinator of government activity" on March 1, Mohammed Mzali became prime minister on April 23. A few days earlier Hassan Belkhodja was appointed foreign minister. There was a minor government reshuffle on December 3, in the direction of further liberalization. Restricted to living under observation, Mohammed Masmoudi, an important political personality, went on a hunger strike in July and was granted complete freedom in August.

During the night of January 26–27, the regime faced a commando attack by 50 men sent from Libya via the "Qaddafi route," generally used by the Polisario Front guerrillas of the Western Sahara. This armed group attempted to seize the mining town of Gafsa in a surprise attack. Although the Libyan government professed astonishment at being suspected of involvement in the incident, Tunisia recalled its ambassador from Tripoli and then its workers in Libya; it also exposed a Libyan scheme to implicate Algeria in the affair. After France had sent three warships into the Gulf of Gabès, the French embassy at Tripoli and the French consulate at Benghazi were sacked by Libyan mobs.

After the Gafsa affair, the U.S. speeded up the delivery of arms to Tunisia. On March 10 the trial of captured Gafsa commandos began before the Court of State Security, and on March 27, 15 of them were condemned to death. When their appeal was rejected, 13 were hanged (two had been sentenced in absentia).

Before the deterioration of Tunisian-Libyan relations, Bourguiba had attempted to strengthen existing ties with Algeria and Morocco (Mzali paid the latter an official visit in June) and with France, the former colonial power. There were numerous comings and goings between Paris and Tunis during the year. As a result of French Prime Minister Raymond Barre's visit in October, it was decided to create a Franco-Tunisian development bank and to release, as of Jan. 1, 1981, French credits blocked in Tunis. Queen Elizabeth II also paid a visit to Tunis in October.

TURKEY

The minority administration formed on Nov. 12, 1979, by Suleyman Demirel, leader of the right-of-centre Justice Party, was overthrown by the armed forces in a bloodless coup on Sept. 12, 1980. In spite of an extension of martial law in February, political violence claimed some 2,000 lives, including those of Nihat Erim, prime minister of the country from 1971 to 1972, and other prominent figures.

Muslim sectarian violence broke out between the Sunni majority and the Shi'ah minority (known in Turkey as Alevi). The armed forces suppressed leftist-led workers in Izmir in February and occupied the Black Sea coastal town of Fatsa in July, so ending a "liberated zone" run by revolutionary leftists.

Agreement among the political parties proved impossible. Demirel failed to secure an early dissolution of Parliament; the Republican People's Party (RPP) leader, Bulent Ecevit, failed to agree on an alternative coalition with Necmettin Erbakan, leader of the Islamic National Salvation Party (NSP), but, with the help of NSP votes, achieved the dismissal of Demirel's pro-Western foreign minister, Hayrettin Erkmen, on September 5. Parliament failed to elect a president of the republic to succeed Adm. Fahri Koruturk, whose term of office expired on April 6. On September 6 a rally by Erbakan's Islamic fundamentalists in Konya challenged the government and provided the immediate cause of the military takeover.

Demirel was more effective in economic management. On January 24 he introduced new economic measures, including a one-third devaluation of the Turkish lira against the U.S. dollar, the limitation of multiple exchange rates, the abolition of price controls and of most subsidies, and the promotion of exports and of foreign investment. These and later measures found favour with Turkey's Western creditors. On April 15 the Organization for Economic Cooperation and Development pledged Turkey $1,160,000,000 in fresh aid, and on July 23 it recommended the rescheduling of Turkey's existing debts. The International Monetary Fund agreed to extend to Turkey standby credits of $1,162,500,000 over three years.

Demirel's foreign policy was pro-Western. The Soviet invasion of Afghanistan was condemned and the Olympic Games in Moscow were boycotted. On February 6 it was announced that Turkey would apply for full membership in the European Economic Community. On February 22 Turkey announced the resumption of civil air traffic with Greece. Turkish objections to the return of Greece to NATO were resolved through negotiations by October 20.

After the military takeover the foreign and economic policies of the Demirel government were continued by a National Security Council headed by the chief of the general staff, Gen. Kenan Evren, and including the services' commanders. Parliament

UPI

Gen. Kenan Evren led a bloodless military coup that ousted the government of Suleyman Demirel on September 12.

was dissolved; political activity was banned; leftist and rightist unions and associations were banned; and more than 6,000 people, including party leaders, were detained. On September 21 a mainly civilian Cabinet was formed under retired Adm. Bulent Ulusu, commander of the Navy until August 8.

A constitutional instrument issued on October 27 transferred Parliament's powers to the National Security Council, General Evren officially becoming head of state. Priority was given to the struggle against terrorism, with the promise that a new democratic constitution would be submitted to a popular referendum at a later date. Terrorist incidents were fewer, the most notable being the hijacking of an airliner by Islamic fundamentalists on October 13. The crew and passengers were rescued and the terrorists arrested. Ecevit resigned from the leadership of the RPP on October 30.

UGANDA

In 1980 Uganda's border with the Sudan was reopened and relations between the two countries improved, but stable government remained elusive. Pres. Godfrey L. Binaisa tried unsuccessfully to encourage foreign investment to revive Uganda's ex-

Joyous supporters greeted former president Milton Obote upon his return to Uganda after nine years of exile in Tanzania. Obote again became president after the December elections.
KEYSTONE

port crops. In February he dismissed Paulo Muwanga, minister of the interior, for banning three newspapers reporting Uganda's lawlessness. Pres. Julius Nyerere of Tanzania threatened to withdraw his troops from Uganda if steps were not taken to restore order quickly. Kenya observed Nyerere's intervention with dismay and in March promised Uganda aid if Tanzanian troops were withdrawn. Later, clashes took place between Tanzanian troops near Kampala and some of the local population. The cost of maintaining the Tanzanian troops—£60 million in 1979–80—was also of concern to Uganda.

In April Binaisa induced the National Consultative Council to endorse his proposal that political parties should not be permitted to participate in the forthcoming elections but that candidates should stand instead as representatives of the Uganda National Liberation Front. His triumph was short-lived. On May 10 he dismissed Brig. David Oyite Ojok, army chief of staff and an associate of former president Milton Obote, charging that Uganda's new Army was looting and killing Ugandan citizens. Ojok refused to accept dismissal and was supported by Muwanga, now minister of labour. Nyerere refused to intervene, and Muwanga then headed a six-man Military Commission that removed Binaisa from office on May 11. The commission appointed a new Cabinet, replacing several supporters of Binaisa with adherents of Obote and including Ojok. Otema Alimadi continued as foreign minister and announced that Uganda would remain nonaligned.

On May 27 Obote returned to Uganda and soon announced that he would lead the Uganda People's Congress in the forthcoming elections. In the north and east he was warmly welcomed, but many Buganda could not forgive him for overthrowing their traditional leader, the kabaka, in 1966; in western Uganda attitudes varied. Obote's opponents became increasingly hostile, and in June the Uganda Patriotic Movement was set up under Yoweri Museveni, vice-chairman of the Military Commission, to challenge him. Former president Yusufu Lule, expected to lead the Democratic Party, was prevented by the Military Commission from returning to Uganda because he refused to deny statements he had made at the time of his overthrow in 1979. In his place, Paul Semogerere was elected Democratic Party leader in June. Also in June Kenya called for Tanzanian troops to be withdrawn from Uganda and replaced by Organization of African Unity, UN, or Commonwealth forces.

Meanwhile, famine in the northeastern district of Karamoja, due to drought and the depredations of armed bandits, brought suffering and death to thousands. For a time in July even external relief organizations had to stop work in the area because of attacks by armed gangs in search of food, while Kampala's crime rate became more serious because of the violence caused by rival political groups and by individuals.

The target date for national elections, September 30, could not be met and, later, Cabinet members opposed to the Uganda People's Congress refused to support a proposal by Muwanga regarding the number of seats in the new Parliament because it favoured areas where Obote's supporters were strong. Agreement was eventually reached, however, and Ugandans went to the polls on December 9–10 to vote in the country's first national election since 1962. Amid charges of massive fraud and intimidation, Obote's Uganda People's Congress won 68 of the 126 seats in Parliament to 48 for the Democratic Party. As a result Obote became the nation's president for a five-year term and was inaugurated on December 17.

The Summer Olympic Games opened in Moscow on July 19 despite the absence of athletes from 65 nations who were boycotting the competition because of the Soviet invasion of Afghanistan. Security was tight throughout Moscow, and incidents were few.

SIMON—GAMMA/LIAISON

UNION OF SOVIET SOCIALIST REPUBLICS

The major change in Soviet leadership in 1980 was the resignation of 76-year-old Aleksey N. Kosygin as premier in October. He was replaced by his deputy, Nikolay A. Tikhonov, a man only one year younger than himself. Kosygin's ill health for four years, culminating in his death in December, had meant that Tikhonov had often headed the government. The new premier worked closely with Pres. Leonid Brezhnev during the post-World War II reconstruction of the Ukrainian city of Dnepropetrovsk and had amassed great experience in the economic bureaucracy. He was made a full member of the Politburo as recently as November 1979. His appointment was seen as an indication that the post of premier had been downgraded to that of an economic functionary. All the members of the Politburo except one were senior to Tikhonov.

The Summer Olympic Games were the year's major domestic event and were well organized. The Soviet Union carried off the largest number of gold medals. The Games were overshadowed, however, by the U.S.-led boycott, which resulted in the withdrawal from competition of many leading nations—the U.S., West Germany, and Japan, for example. (*See* Olympic Games.) The U.S. action was taken in response to Soviet intervention in Afghanistan. U.S. Pres. Jimmy Carter also prevented the export of 17 million metric tons of grain to the U.S.S.R. and halted sales of high-technology products such as computers and oil-drilling equipment. The embargo on the latter, however, was quietly dropped during the summer. The eight million tons provided for under the terms of the U.S.-Soviet grain agreement were delivered, but this agreement was to expire in 1981. The Soviets were able to purchase most of the shortfall in other markets but in so doing forced up the price. One U.S. source estimated that President Carter's embargo cost the U.S.S.R. an extra $1 billion. In July the U.S.S.R. signed an agreement with Argentina to purchase 4.5 million tons of forage cereals annually over the next five years.

Since the Soviet Union was unable to import all the extra fodder it needed, meat production suffered, as did the output of butter, milk, and cheese. This led to considerable problems for the urban population. Meat was often unavailable in Moscow, Leningrad, and Kiev, usually the three best provisioned cities in the nation. Many labour strikes were reported during the year, the most significant being in Gorky and Togliatti, both with large automobile plants. The Soviet authorities vehemently denied that the closing of the plants on May 8 and 9 amounted to a strike. They claimed that workers were merely celebrating Victory Day. This, however, would account for the stoppage on May 9 but not on May 8.

The widespread shortages of food, the poor quality of some consumer goods, and the unavailability of others led to an expansion of the black market. The government turned a blind eye to some of its activities because it was satisfying consumer needs but dealt severely with some black marketeers. For example, Yuza Kobakhidze, a Georgian, was shot for corruption. Many officials throughout the country were found guilty of accepting bribes. A huge caviar fraud came to light in April. According to reports, about 200 officials of the Ministry of Fisheries had been arrested during the year and accused of being involved in the fraudulent export of caviar in tins marked as herring.

Nikolay Tikhonov succeeded Aleksey Kosygin as chairman of the Council of Ministers (premier) after Kosygin's retirement in October.
WIDE WORLD

Not since 1977 had Soviet dissidents been treated so harshly. In order to ensure that no demonstrations took place during the Olympic Games, a campaign was launched, beginning in 1979, to clear dissidents, beggars, and ne'er-do-wells from the streets of Moscow and other cities accommodating the Games. Many living farther away were also arrested because it had been their custom to travel to Moscow to publicize their grievances and to contact the world press. The Committee of State Security (KGB) was successful in intimidating the vast majority of dissidents and their sympathizers. Only the hard core were arrested since the political police resorted to arrest only if all other methods failed. By late summer 252 arrests had been documented. These actions, carried out despite international protests, revealed that the Kremlin had given up all hope of SALT II being ratified by the U.S. Senate. Since Soviet relations with the U.S. were at a low ebb, the Politburo obviously believed that there was little more to lose.

The KGB came up with a neat solution to the problem of what to do with the dissident physicist and 1975 Nobel Peace Prize winner Andrey Sakharov. They exiled him to Gorky and provided him with an apartment without a telephone. His wife was free to remain in Moscow. Sakharov was stripped of his Soviet decorations but remained a member of the U.S.S.R. Academy of Sciences. There was no legal foundation for the measures adopted.

The number of Jews granted exit visas reached a peak in 1979 when about 50,000 left, but numbers began to drop thereafter. A much more restrictive policy was adopted in the wake of the U.S.-led boycott of the Olympics. If Jews found it increasingly difficult to leave the U.S.S.R., Germans and Armenians did not. The number of Armenians leaving was unprecedented, exceeding 1,000 a month by midyear. The Armenians were mostly those who were drawn to the Soviet Union after World War II when Stalin conducted a vigorous campaign to attract them to Soviet Armenia.

The Economy

The far-reaching changes in the management of the national economy announced in July 1979 appeared to have had little impact. The industrial growth target of 4.5% in 1980 was unlikely to be met because during the first nine months of the year industrial output grew only by 4%. National income was only 3.8% above that of 1979. In the important energy sector oil production rose 3%, and it was possible that the target of 606 million metric tons would be achieved. Coal output declined 0.7% from the previous year. The real income of the population rose 3%. The harvest was again disappointing, only about 181 million tons, far short of the target of 235 million tons. Owing to the shortage of fodder, meat production declined 5% from 1979. The output of animal and vegetable fats, sausages, and tinned fruit was also below that of the previous year.

The 1976–80 plan would not be fulfilled. Growth of industrial output for the period would be about 25%, far short of the target of 36%. Average annual agricultural output over the five years had exceeded the 1971–75 period only by 9%. Given the huge investment in agriculture (one ruble in three went into agriculture or agriculture-related industries), this was very disappointing. Since the Soviet population had risen by about 4%, the people's diet had not improved significantly.

The Soviet Union's hard currency debt dropped $1 billion to $16.2 billion in 1979. It was likely that the U.S.S.R. would again show a surplus in its hard currency trade in 1980. Soviet sales of gold plummeted during the year, and only 25 tons instead of the usual 1,400 tons had been sold by November. This revealed that earnings from oil, natural gas, and mineral exports had remained buoyant.

The Soviet Union warned its partners in the Council for Mutual Economic Assistance (CMEA, or Comecon) that it was rapidly approaching the limit of its capacity to meet their energy needs. Whereas in 1970 other Comecon countries obtained 70% of their energy needs from the Soviet Union, this figure was expected to drop to 50% in 1990. Over the period 1976–80 Comecon countries imported Soviet oil at about 40% below the world price, and this was estimated to have cost the U.S.S.R. 5 billion rubles.

Foreign Affairs

Relations with the outside world deteriorated throughout 1980. The Soviet Union came to the conclusion that nothing positive could be expected from relations with the U.S. as long as President Carter remained in office. Carter was particularly incensed by Soviet intervention in Afghanistan after the U.S. had reportedly warned Moscow five times that such a move would seriously affect détente. The zigzags in the president's foreign policy left the Soviets bewildered. They completely miscalculated U.S. and world reaction to their Afghanistan move. A UN motion in January calling for the withdrawal of foreign troops from Afghanistan was passed by 104 votes to 18, an unprecedentedly heavy defeat for Soviet diplomacy. Once in Afghanistan, the U.S.S.R. discovered that the task of subduing the Muslim rebels was much more difficult than it had imagined. The decision to intervene apparently took Ministry of Defense personnel by surprise. Pres. Babrak Karmal of Afghanistan visited Moscow in October and received assurances of continuing Soviet aid.

As hopes for the ratification of SALT II faded, incomprehension about U.S. motives reigned in Moscow. The Soviets hoped that a dialogue could be started with Ronald Reagan when he entered the White House. SALT II would probably have to be renegotiated, but the U.S.S.R. was eager to reach

an agreement. Andrey Gromyko, the key figure in Soviet foreign relations, knew that if relations with the U.S. were bad, so were those with its allies. The revolution in Iran had not benefited the Soviet Union as much as it had expected; one Soviet offer of arms was publicly rejected by Teheran. The Iraqi attack on Iran further complicated the situation. Iraq had a treaty of friendship with the U.S.S.R. and continued to receive Soviet arms through the port of Aqaba. The war drew Jordan closer to Iraq, and if that continued Jordan might establish closer relations with Moscow. Syria found itself isolated and hastened to support Iran, the only other Muslim country to do so being Libya. This finally led Syria to accede in October to the Soviet wish for a treaty of friendship. Thus, the Soviet position in the Middle East improved.

France's Pres. Valéry Giscard d'Estaing became the first Western head of state to meet President Brezhnev after the Soviet intervention in Afghanistan. Giscard decided to meet the Soviet leader in Warsaw in May, but Brezhnev gave nothing away, and any diplomatic gain from the meeting accrued to the Soviet side. The U.S.S.R. had further cause for gratification when the French Communist Party (PCF) sided with it over Afghanistan. PCF leader Georges Marchais traveled to Moscow to heal the breach that had occurred as a result of the PCF's support for Eurocommunism. The latter phenomenon was still alive but was restricted to the Italian and Spanish Communist parties. Both criticized the Soviet move into Afghanistan, as did Romania, which called for withdrawal. West German Chancellor Helmut Schmidt visited Moscow on June 30–July 1 and forcibly argued Western views on Afghanistan and the need for NATO to modernize its nuclear weapons. The discussions became heated, and Brezhnev was critical of Schmidt's support for U.S. policy.

The Soviets found the year's events in Poland deeply embarrassing, since the leadership was sensitive about any manifestation of worker discontent. Independent labour unions were anathema to the Communist Party of the Soviet Union. A propaganda campaign was launched, blaming the trouble in Poland on the West and accusing Western governments and labour unions of interfering in Polish internal affairs. Elements in West Germany were accused of launching a "massive anti-Polish campaign" using Nazi methods and propaganda to stir up unrest. The Soviet media on occasion accused the West of pouring "millions of dollars" into Poland to support anti-Communist groups. They served notice that the U.S.S.R. would not countenance the Polish independent union Solidarity's receiving money from abroad and also did not favour Poland's borrowing money from the West. The new Polish party leader, Stanislaw Kania, won support in Moscow for his policy of trying to whittle away piecemeal the concessions forced on the party by the strike.

Human rights advocate and Nobelist Andrey Sakharov, shown with his wife, Yelena, was sentenced to internal exile in the city of Gorky in January for his continued criticism of Soviet policies.
ZAL—SYGMA

Relations with China deteriorated. The border talks that began in October 1979 foundered on the rocks of Afghanistan. China then launched a campaign calling for the withdrawal of Soviet troops. In October it blamed the U.S.S.R. for an incident during which a Chinese peasant and a Soviet soldier were killed, the first official report of shooting on the Sino-Soviet border since 1969.

Soviet-Japanese relations reached a new low in November when the Soviet chairman of the U.S.S.R.-Japan Friendship Society accused the Japanese of limiting contacts between the two countries, of impeding the expansion of economic relations, and of raising a hullabaloo about a "supposed Soviet military threat." The Soviet Union had become alarmed at recent developments, especially the Sino-Japanese treaty of friendship. Ongoing disputes over fishing boundaries, Japan's boycott of the Olympics, its refusal to allow a crippled Soviet submarine to be towed through its territorial waters, and the amendment of the Japanese constitution to permit the expansion of the armed forces all left a bitter taste in Moscow.

The second Helsinki Final Act (of the Conference on Security and Cooperation in Europe) review conference opened in Madrid in November with the Soviet Union on the defensive. Led by Leonid Ilichev, who had previously spent years negotiating with the Chinese without giving or gaining an inch, the Soviet delegation attempted to reduce significantly the amount of time devoted to examining the human rights record of the member countries but was not wholly successful. Evidently the U.S.S.R. regarded the conference as an embarrassment but had decided to attend so as not to bring détente officially to an end. Western powers attacked intervention in Afghanistan and the Soviet Union's human rights record and argued that détente had to cover all aspects of the Helsinki Final Act.

UNITED NATIONS

Among the year's highlights in the United Nations, observers could point to the striking progress made in fashioning a new treaty on the law of the sea, a special General Assembly session on international economic goals, and a spate of old and new political problems.

Law of the Sea

During a five-week meeting of the UN Conference on the Law of the Sea, which ended August 29, delegates in Geneva prepared an informal draft treaty incorporating the results of arduous negotiations since 1973. The most significant progress was made in devising a unique voting formula to be used by the Council, executive organ of the projected International Seabed Authority. The agreement spelled out how the Council would allocate the still-untapped mineral wealth below the deep oceans. It classified substantive issues that required decisions into three "tiers," each needing a different majority for approval.

The one major issue that the conferees left before them for a six- or seven-week session scheduled for New York City in March 1981 was how to settle disputes about overlapping maritime boundaries beyond the territorial seas. UN officials anticipated signing ceremonies to take place in Caracas, Venezuela, before the end of 1981.

Economic Assembly

On September 15 the General Assembly concluded a special session devoted to international economic problems. At those meetings the member nations agreed on the goals of an international development strategy for the 1980s, but they were unable to reconcile their differences about ways and means of achieving them. The agreed-upon strategy reaffirmed a long-standing UN aim to have developed states allocate, by 1985, 0.7% of their gross national product for official aid to less developed countries and to aim at a higher target (1%) as soon as possible thereafter. The Assembly also hoped that the less developed countries would increase the growth rate of their gross domestic products to an annual average of 7%.

Despite agreement on goals, West Germany, the United Kingdom, and the United States differed with the majority on how best to negotiate to achieve Assembly objectives. The majority suggested a new global conference; the three dissenting nations preferred to continue working through established specialized agencies, the International Monetary Fund, and the World Bank.

The Assembly's regular session, September 16–December 19, discussed the issues again. Indeed, in his inaugural address as Assembly president, Baron Rudiger von Wechmar of West Germany criticized his own country and other developed nations for failing adequately to support the economic objectives of the third world. He called it "appalling" that "rich" states were not meeting UN guidelines (West Germany was contributing under 0.35% and the U.S. 0.19%).

Afghanistan

On January 7 the Security Council voted on a resolution calling on all foreign (*i.e.*, Soviet) troops to withdraw immediately and unconditionally from Afghanistan. The draft received 13 favourable votes but was not approved because of a Soviet veto. On January 9 the Council requested the General Assembly to meet in emergency special session on the problem. The Assembly met the following day and on January 14 voted 104–18–18 for the "immediate, unconditional and total withdrawal of foreign troops" from Afghanistan. On November 20 the Assembly overwhelmingly (111–22–12) repeated its call for the U.S.S.R. to withdraw. The resolution, though similar to the earlier one in not naming the Soviet Union, was somewhat less stern.

Iran

A UN commission of inquiry, created on February 20 "to hear Iran's grievances and to allow for an early solution of the crisis between Iran and the United States," suspended work on March 11, unable to arrange to free the U.S. hostages seized on Nov. 4, 1979. On May 24 the International Court of Justice ruled unanimously that Iran "must immediately release each and every one" of the hostages and that none could be kept in Iran for trial or to participate in a trial as a witness. In addition, the court held, 12–3, that Iran was obliged to make reparations to the U.S.

On April 25, after learning that the U.S. had unsuccessfully attempted to rescue the hostages by military force, UN Secretary-General Kurt Waldheim called for "restraint, reason, and reinvigorated efforts to solve the problem" peacefully. Iran called the U.S. operation an act of aggression, but the U.S. defended it in a letter to the Security Council as an exercise of its inherent right of self-defense, adding that the mission was occasioned by mounting dangers to the hostages' safety.

The UN Security Council voted January 7 in favour of a resolution calling for the immediate withdrawal of foreign (Soviet) troops from Afghanistan; the Soviet ambassador, Oleg Troyanovsky, vetoed the resolution. Seated in the back section (left, striped tie) was the foreign minister of Afghanistan.
UPI

Iran-Iraq War

On September 22 Iraq invaded Iran. Waldheim repeatedly offered his good offices to settle the conflict, and he and the Security Council tried diligently throughout the year to arrange a cease-fire.

Two goodwill missions to stop the war proved fruitless, one undertaken in September by Pres. Zia-ul-Haq of Pakistan on behalf of nine Islamic states and a second in November, when, acting on Security Council instructions, Waldheim named former Swedish prime minister Olof Palme as UN mediator. Palme ended a week of talks with the parties on November 24. He reported that, although he did not expect rapid results, he anticipated that in the long run the need of both nations for development and construction would bring the war to an end.

Israeli-Arab Relations

The UN was preoccupied throughout the year with border attacks and reprisals between Israel and its Arab neighbours, with Israeli unwillingness to surrender occupied Arab territories, and with the security of the UN Interim Force in Lebanon (UNIFIL). Israel lodged several protests about terrorist actions launched, it claimed, from Lebanon-based Palestine Liberation Organization (PLO) strongholds. Israel's retaliatory raids were in turn excoriated by Lebanon.

In April an engagement between Muslim insurgents and UNIFIL resulted in the deaths of two Irish soldiers serving with the UN. In a unanimously agreed-upon statement issued through its president on April 18, the Security Council strongly condemned the "cold-blooded murder" of the two UNIFIL soldiers. On April 24 the Council reaffirmed UNIFIL's need to enjoy free movement in the area up to internationally recognized boundaries. It strongly deplored violations of Lebanese sovereignty, Israeli military intervention in Lebanon, all acts of violence contrary to the 1949 armistice agreements, and the provision of military assistance to the "so-

called *de facto* forces." UNIFIL came under attack by PLO forces on August 12, and on September 17 the secretary-general appealed for all parties to cooperate with UNIFIL and to abstain from further acts of violence against it.

Several UN bodies called throughout the year for Israel to dismantle its settlements in Arab territories occupied since 1967, including Jerusalem, and pressed the claims of Palestinians for a homeland in the Middle East. Starting on February 22, the Security Council held a series of meetings on the subject of the occupied lands, and on March 1 it unanimously called on Israel to withdraw from them. On April 30 the U.S. vetoed a Council resolution that would have affirmed the Palestinian people's right to establish an independent state in the area. U.S. delegate Donald McHenry explained his vote by saying that, although the Palestinian issue was central, Middle East solutions had to be negotiated. On May 8 and 20 the Council called on Israel to rescind its "illegal measures" expelling two Arab mayors and a judge from their posts on the West Bank. Then, on June 30, the Council declared that Israeli measures to alter the character and status of Jerusalem had no legal validity, were a flagrant violation of the fourth Geneva Convention relating to the protection of civilians in time of war, and constituted a serious obstruction to achieving a comprehensive, just, and lasting peace. It also reaffirmed the "overriding necessity" to end the Israeli occupation. The vote was 14–0, with the U.S. abstaining.

The General Assembly had its turn at dealing with these questions when, at the request of 90 member states, it met on July 22 in emergency special session. It reaffirmed (112–7–24) on July 29 the Palestinian people's right to establish their own independent state and called once more on Israel to withdraw from occupied lands. It also asked the Security Council to consider imposing sanctions on Israel if it did not comply. On December 15 the General Assembly adopted several anti-Israeli reso-

In January Mexico was chosen to fill a seat on the Security Council reserved for a Latin-American nation; Mexican Ambassador Porfirio Muñoz Ledo made the acceptance speech.
UPI

and June 27 the Council condemned South Africa for military operations against Zambia and Angola, which South Africa characterized as essential to protect Namibia from SWAPO incursions.

Other Matters

On November 13 the Assembly elected Panama (111–24) to the Security Council on the 23rd ballot. Costa Rica had been its leading opponent until Panama convinced members that, because U.S. President-elect Ronald Reagan opposed the Panama Canal treaties of 1979, Panama needed the seat to defend its national interests. Ireland, Japan, Spain, and Uganda also were to begin terms on the Council in January 1981. The other members were East Germany, Mexico, Niger, Tunisia, and the Philippines, which were to serve until the end of 1981, and the permanent "big five": China, France, the U.K., U.S., and U.S.S.R.

UN membership increased to 154 with the admission on September 16 of the new nation (formerly British-ruled) of St. Vincent and the Grenadines. Zimbabwe had become the 153rd UN member when it was admitted during the Assembly's special economic session on August 25. The UN had long concerned itself with the problems of Zimbabwe (formerly Southern Rhodesia), which achieved independence on April 18.

UNITED STATES

In an election that major polling organizations had described as "too close to call," Republican Ronald Reagan overwhelmingly defeated Democrat Jimmy Carter on November 4 to become the 40th president of the United States. Reagan carried 44 states with a combined total of 489 electoral votes; Carter won 6 states and the District of Columbia, with 49 electoral votes. Reagan won 43.2 million popular votes, or 51% of the total; Carter won 34.9 million (41%); and independent candidate John Anderson won 5.6 million (7%). Carter's percentage of the vote dropped below his 1976 share in every state by at least two percentage points. (*See* Elections.)

After his election Reagan began the process of choosing his Cabinet and other top aides. His most controversial selection was Alexander Haig, former supreme commander of NATO forces in Europe, as secretary of state. Haig's role as Pres. Richard Nixon's chief of staff in the last days of the Watergate crisis seemed likely to cause opposition to him in the Senate confirmation hearings. Among the other appointments were Donald Regan, chairman of Merrill Lynch & Co., as secretary of the treasury; Caspar Weinberger, a former secretary of health, education, and welfare, as secretary of defense; and William French Smith, Reagan's personal lawyer, as attorney general.

The Republicans also scored significant gains in congressional elections, capturing control of the Senate and picking up 33 additional seats in the

UNITED NATIONS–KEYSTONE

U.S. Ambassador to the UN Donald McHenry voted in March in favour of a Security Council resolution condemning Israel for establishing settlements in occupied Arab territories; later the vote was said to have been a mistake.

lutions; it again called for Security Council sanctions, rejected the Camp David agreement, and censured Israel for annexing East Jerusalem. On December 16 the Assembly repeated its call for a Palestinian state led by the PLO.

South Africa

On November 24 Waldheim reported to the Security Council that South Africa had conditionally agreed to a cease-fire that could end 15 years of guerrilla war in South West Africa/Namibia in 1981 and bring independence to the territory, which the UN considered was illegally occupied by South Africa. The report envisaged South African and Namibian leaders conferring with guerrillas of the South West Africa People's Organization (SWAPO) in January 1981 in an effort to dispel mutual mistrust. Should that meeting be successful, a cease-fire would come into effect in March and a UN peacekeeping force would patrol a demilitarized zone 50 km (31 mi) wide on either side of Namibia's northern border with Angola. An assembly would then write a constitution for an independent Namibia in October 1981.

One U.S. diplomat called the report "very much a step in the right direction," but a SWAPO observer pointed out that it "only calls for a pre-implementation conference. It is," he said, "South Africa's success, to win a stay of execution." On April 11

As the year drew to a close, negotiations to free the hostages in Iran intensified. Deputy Secretary of State Warren Christopher (right) was assisted by Algerian intermediaries including Redha Malek (left), Algerian ambassador to the U.S.

WIDE WORLD

House. The Senate lineup for the 97th Congress would be 53 Republicans and 47 Democrats. That was the largest number of Republican senators since the 71st Congress (1929–31), when the GOP had 56 seats. The Republican Senate majority was the first since 1954 and ended the longest one-party dominance of the Senate in U.S. history.

As in previous countings of the nation's population, controversy over its fairness and accuracy marked the 1980 census. In a ruling handed down on September 25, U.S. District Court Judge Horace Gilmore of Detroit held that the 1980 census had undercounted the population of the nation's minorities and ordered that the figures for them be revised upward before release of the data. Subsequently an appeals court permitted release of national and state totals by year's end, but the suit, brought by Detroit and supported by dozens of other cities, remained in the courts. Preliminary data confirmed the shift in the U.S. population toward the so-called Sunbelt states of the South and Southwest.

Foreign Affairs

A reason often cited for President Carter's failure to win reelection was his inability to obtain the release of the U.S. hostages held captive in Iran since a band of Iranian militants seized the U.S. embassy

---

Hostages Freed

After 444 days the U.S. hostages in Iran were freed on Jan. 20, 1981, the same day that Ronald Reagan took the oath of office as U.S. president. The 52 Americans were released after agreement had been reached concerning the return of Iranian assets impounded in the U.S.

---

in Teheran on Nov. 4, 1979. The hostage issue was Carter's main foreign-policy concern during the year, but none of his efforts bore fruit.

U.S. spirits were lifted briefly on January 29, when Canada announced that six other Americans working at the U.S. embassy, who had been sheltered by Canadian embassy personnel since the takeover, had been flown out of Iran secretly the previous day. The six received an emotional welcome on their arrival in Washington, and thousands of Americans sent messages of gratitude to the Canadian government.

Iranian Pres. Abolhassan Bani-Sadr announced on February 11 his nation's conditions for release of the hostages. He demanded that the U.S. acknowledge "past crimes"; recognize Iran's right to obtain extradition of the deposed shah, Mohammad Reza Pahlavi, and take control of his fortune; and promise not to interfere in Iran's internal affairs. Twelve days later a U.N. commission arrived in Teheran to review Iranian grievances against the former shah and try to secure the hostages' release. Nothing came of this mission, and on April 7 Iranian leader Ayatollah Ruhollah Khomeini announced that the hostages would remain in the militants' custody until the Iranian Majlis (parliament), to be elected in the spring, decided their fate.

On the same day, Carter severed diplomatic relations with Iran and ordered all its diplomatic personnel still in the U.S. to leave the country. He also imposed an embargo on all U.S. exports, except for food and medicine, bound for Iran. The president announced additional sanctions on April 17, banning all imports from Iran and prohibiting travel there by U.S. citizens. In addition, he made military equipment previously purchased by Iran and impounded after the embassy takeover available for sale to other nations and asked Congress for the authority to use frozen Iranian assets to pay reparations to the hostages and their families.

The most dramatic development in the hostage crisis began to unfold on the night of April 24, when eight U.S. Navy Sea Stallion helicopters took off from the U.S. aircraft carrier "Nimitz" in the Gulf of Oman and headed for a secret base in the salt desert of eastern Iran. Owing to mechanical failures, only five of the helicopters finished the trip intact. Carter ordered the 180 commandos and airmen to abort the mission and return, but when one of the remaining helicopters maneuvered to refuel, it crashed into a C-130 transport plane and exploded in flames. Eight men died.

Contrary to their threats, the militants did not retaliate against the hostages. But they did claim to have moved some of them to Qom, Kerman, and other cities around Iran in order to make a repeat rescue attempt impossible. The failed mission also had repercussions in the U.S. government. Secretary of State Cyrus Vance, who had opposed the rescue mission from the start, resigned in protest. His successor, Sen. Edmund Muskie (Dem., Maine), was confirmed by the Senate on May 7.

The abortive rescue was followed by a lull in diplomatic efforts to free the hostages which lasted through the remainder of the spring and summer. On July 11, however, Iran released hostage Richard Queen, a vice-consul, because of an undiagnosed illness that was later found to be multiple sclerosis. Then, on July 27, the shah died in Cairo.

Hope for the release of the hostages began to rise again in the waning days of the presidential election campaign. In a televised debate with Reagan on October 28, Carter reiterated that he was prepared to unfreeze Iranian assets under U.S. control and send Iran items it already had bought and paid for if the hostages were released. Five days later the Majlis endorsed a special commission's conditions for freeing the hostages. The terms were similar to those announced earlier by Khomeini: the U.S. must relinquish the property and assets of the shah, cancel all financial claims against Iran, release the frozen assets, and promise not to interfere in Iran's internal affairs.

Carter's loss to Reagan, which appeared to surprise Iranian leaders, clouded the hostage question once again. Negotiations continued, however, with Algerian diplomats acting as intermediaries between the two nations. After a visit to Iran in late November, the Algerians reported that the 52 hostages "are in good health." Much of the difficulty apparently centred around the ability of the U.S. government to return the frozen Iranian assets, since various U.S. individuals and firms had brought suit in U.S. courts claiming part of this money as compensation for losses suffered in the Iranian revolution.

Iran was not the only country in the Middle East that aroused concern in the U.S. in 1980. The nation's policymakers were deeply disturbed by the Soviet invasion and occupation of Afghanistan. In a nationwide television address on January 4, Carter announced that 17 million metric tons of grain ordered by the Soviet Union would not be delivered because of the invasion. He also suspended the sale of high-technology equipment to the U.S.S.R., severely curtailed Soviet fishing privileges in U.S. waters, and delayed the opening of new U.S. and Soviet consular facilities.

Throughout the year, to show solidarity with the hostages in Iran, the citizens of Hermitage, Pennsylvania, raised a new U.S. flag for each day of captivity. The total number of days reached 444 before the final release on Jan. 20, 1981, inauguration day.

Moreover, Carter said that the U.S. would consider boycotting the 1980 Summer Olympic Games in Moscow if the Soviet Union continued its "aggressive actions" in Afghanistan. But the Soviets refused to withdraw their forces. Under strong pressure from the White House, the U.S. Olympic Committee voted 1,604 to 797 in April in favour of a resolution to boycott the Moscow Olympics. A number of other countries, including Japan and West Germany, took the same action. (*See* Olympic Games.)

The simmering border dispute between Iran and Iraq that erupted into open warfare late in September came at a time when the U.S. was moving to bolster its military presence in the Arabian Sea and Persian Gulf areas. The U.S. negotiated agreements for access to air and naval bases at Mogadishu and Berbera in Somalia, at Mombasa in Kenya, and on Masirah Island in Oman. Plans also were announced to expand the existing U.S. base on the British-owned island of Diego Garcia. Military construction bills providing funds to build the new and expanded facilities cleared Congress in mid-September. At about the same time, the U.S. massed an unprecedented number of ships and troops in the Indian Ocean. One apparent purpose of this show of naval force was to warn the Soviet Union against any attempt to send troops into Iran from neighbouring Afghanistan and thereby imperil Western access to Middle Eastern oil supplies.

The rising turmoil in the Middle East and the failure of the mission to rescue the U.S. hostages in Iran raised questions about the state of U.S. military preparedness in general. Disturbed by reports that the all-volunteer armed forces were below par, Congress approved legislation in June providing for

the registration of some four million young men aged 19 or 20 for the draft. A subsequent proclamation by Carter required all men born in 1960 and 1961 to sign up between July 21 and August 2 for any future military conscription. Although antidraft groups staged numerous protest demonstrations, Selective Service System Director Bernard Rostker said on September 4 that 93% of the men subject to draft registration had registered.

Government officials disclosed in August that Carter had adopted a new strategy for the U.S. to employ in fighting a nuclear war with the Soviet Union. Detailed in Presidential Directive 59, it gave priority to attacking military targets in the Soviet Union and lessened a previous emphasis on all-out retaliation against Soviet cities and industrial complexes. Administration officials believed that the Soviets would be less inclined to launch pinpoint nuclear attacks designed to destroy American land-based missile forces if the U.S. could deny them eventual victory in the nuclear war by similarly destroying vital Soviet military capabilities without resorting to all-out retaliation.

In a speech given in August at the Naval War College in Newport, R.I., Secretary of Defense Harold Brown said that the nuclear policy revision "is not a new strategic doctrine . . . not a radical departure from U.S. strategic policy over the last decade or so." But in a surprising statement Brown said that the U.S. land-based Minuteman nuclear missile force might already be vulnerable to a Soviet first strike. This was seen as a major reassessment of U.S. vulnerability.

Pentagon officials said that the new assessment of the Soviet threat to the U.S. land-based nuclear strike force came from recent intelligence reports.

Protesters demonstrated against the possibility of new draft legislation in January in New York City. In July 19- and 20-year-olds were required to register for a possible future draft.
MAXINE ORRIS—KEYSTONE

Brown emphasized plans to build the mobile MX missile and the cruise missile as a way of reducing the increased vulnerability to a Soviet first strike.

(*See also* Defense.)

Domestic Affairs

The troubled state of the nation's economy aroused widespread concern in 1980 and was generally considered a major reason for President Carter's defeat in his quest for reelection. As of October consumer prices had risen 12.6% from the previous year, as measured by the U.S. Bureau of Labor Statistics' Consumer Price Index; 7.6% of the nation's work force was unemployed; and sales of new single-family homes had declined to an annual rate of 548,000 units.

Interest rates were unusually volatile throughout the year. The prime lending rate—the interest that financial institutions charge their most credit-worthy corporate customers—climbed to a record high of 20% in April. It then declined in stages to 11% in July and August before heading upward again. In mid-December it reached 21%.

These sharp fluctuations sapped the confidence of both businessmen and consumers. The automobile industry was especially hard hit. After an initial recovery at the start of the year, U.S. auto sales took a sharp turn for the worse as higher interest rates and car prices kept potential buyers out of the market. Sales volume for November was 8% below that of November 1979.

Ford and the United Auto Workers union asked the International Trade Commission for temporary protection against Japanese automobile imports while the U.S. industry was carrying out its massive conversion to small, fuel-efficient cars. But the commission turned down the request in November, saying that imports were not the major cause of injury to the domestic automakers. It held that the recession, higher gasoline prices, and the shift in consumer demand to smaller cars were primarily responsible for the U.S. auto industry's economic problems.

The 96th Congress spent the first half of 1980 trying to deal with economic issues and the second half avoiding them. It was not a productive combination. Congress discovered that it could do little to alleviate the nation's fiscal troubles, while at the same time it ended up achieving little in the way of other major legislation.

Confronted by an aggressive Republican Party and concerned about its own reputation as the party of "big spenders," the Democratic-controlled Congress began the year by attempting to cut programs in order to balance the federal budget. But hopes of achieving a balance were soon dashed by the recession combined with spiraling inflation. And these new economic problems did not encourage Democrats to resume working for some of their favourite programs.

As campaign pressures mounted, Democratic

UPI

Edmund S. Muskie became secretary of state in May, replacing Cyrus Vance, who resigned after the abortive mission to free the hostages in Iran in April.

leaders were forced to delay until after the election Congress's consideration of the budget and other key spending bills. Once more the other bills were delayed as well. With the scheduling of a lame-duck session, the Democrats hoped that the post-election climate in Washington would be more favourable for them. By the year's end, however, the Democrats found that their scheme had backfired. Instead of rewarding them for their restraint, the voters had taken from them their control of the White House and Senate and put them in a substantially weakened position in the House. Consequently, many of the top-priority bills advanced by the Carter administration and the Democratic leaders in Congress earlier in the year made little progress during the lame-duck session and died at adjournment. (*See* Congress, U.S.)

It is notable that, while the 96th Congress was

THE 13 EXECUTIVE DEPARTMENTS

Secretary of State	Edmund S. Muskie
Secretary of the Treasury	G. William Miller
Secretary of Defense	Harold Brown
Attorney General	Benjamin R. Civiletti
Secretary of the Interior	Cecil D. Andrus
Secretary of Agriculture	Bob Bergland
Secretary of Commerce	Philip M. Klutznick
Secretary of Labor	Ray Marshall
Secretary of Health and Human Services	Patricia Roberts Harris
Secretary of Housing and Urban Development	Moon Landrieu
Secretary of Transportation	Neil Goldschmidt
Secretary of Energy	Charles W. Duncan, Jr.
Secretary of Education	Shirley M. Hufstedler

concerned with the continuing debate over defense spending, unlike such debates in earlier years this one was not over where to cut the defense budget but about how much to add to it. Both houses of Congress approved defense spending bills larger than the president had requested, the first time this had occurred during the post-Vietnam war era.

What many had believed would be the major foreign policy debate of the year never materialized. On January 3 Carter asked the Senate to delay its debate on ratification of the second strategic arms limitation treaty with the Soviet Union (SALT II). It was clear that the Soviet invasion of Afghanistan had eliminated any possibility of the treaty's ratification during the session.

Perhaps the most significant energy measure to be approved during the year was Carter's windfall profits tax, which was proposed to tax a portion of the oil companies' expected profits resulting from the decontrol of oil prices. The most important environmental bill passed during the session was the Alaska lands measure. The lame-duck Congress handed the Carter administration one last environmental victory with the passage of a bill to set up a $1.6 billion "superfund" to clean up toxic waste dumps and chemical spills. (*See also* Environment.)

Two major transportation deregulation measures streamlined the government's regulation of the trucking and railroad industries. For the first time, both houses of Congress voted to prohibit the Department of Justice from bringing lawsuits that would require the busing of students for the purpose of school desegregation, but the provision was dropped in conference committee.

Congress's image was tarnished following reports in February that eight of its members had been implicated in an FBI "sting" operation called Abscam. Seven of them subsequently were indicted in connection with the undercover investigation, in which FBI agents posed as representatives of wealthy Arabs willing to pay for political favours. By the year's end four of the seven had been convicted, and one of those, Rep. Michael Myers (Dem., Pa.), was expelled from the House. (*See* Law.)

Mt. St. Helens, a volcano in southwestern Washington State that had been dormant since 1857, erupted in 1980. A series of minor eruptions that began on March 27 culminated in a major explosion on May 18 that left 34 people dead, 32 others missing, and damage estimated at $2.7 billion. It was the first volcano to erupt in the contiguous United States since volcanic activity ceased in Mt. Lassen in northern California in 1921. (*See* Earth Sciences.)

A summer-long drought and a record-breaking heat wave caused widespread suffering in the Great Plains, the South, and the Southwest. The final toll from the heat wave was 1,265 deaths and nearly $20 billion in damage. Only three other summers in this century had caused more heat-related fatalities in the U.S. Crops and livestock suffered extensive damage from the combined effects of heat and drought.

A massive, five-month-long boatlift known as the "freedom flotilla" brought approximately 125,000 Cuban refugees to the U.S. beginning April 21. About 80,000 of them settled in Dade County (Miami), Fla., which already had a sizable Cuban community. Other refugees were placed in makeshift camps in Florida and other states until they could find U.S. sponsors. The latest influx of Cubans, coming at a time of recession and high unemployment, aroused considerable resentment in the Miami area and elsewhere, especially when it became known that the refugees included criminals who had been released from Cuban jails and ordered to leave the country. These undesirables were blamed for outbreaks of violence in the resettlement camps.

(*See also* Cities and Urban Affairs; Minorities, American; State Governments, U.S.; Supreme Court, U.S.)

Unemployment lines lengthened in Detroit during the year as automakers laid off hundreds of thousands of workers. The entire industry was slumping, unable to match the competition from foreign cars.

UPI

Special Report: Emptying the Attic

by Kyle Husfloen

Collecting, as a pastime, is not new. Its roots are as old as recorded history. But until fairly recently, collecting tended to be far removed from the everyday life of ordinary people, a rather exclusive hobby suitable only for those with leisure time and surplus income that they could afford to spend extravagantly.

As the 20th century draws to a close, it is apparent that this situation has changed dramatically. No longer are the wealthy the only ones with time and resources to search out works of art or antiques, whether to satisfy some personal aesthetic taste or to meet the need for ostentatious display. Since the early 1960s there has been an astounding growth of collector interest at all levels of society. Furthermore, this interest has spread beyond the field of antiques to include the much broader area of what are loosely described as collectibles.

Collectibles and Antiques

For all that it is a commonly used term, "collectible" is difficult to define precisely. In general, a collectible can be any artifact from the recent past that, when first produced, was a mundane item used in the course of daily homelife or commerce. "Antiques," on the other hand, are more historic pieces and by legal definition are at least 100 years old. With age, they have developed a certain aura of exclusivity.

It should be pointed out that the two terms often overlap, and strict interpretation is open to debate. Many pieces well under 100 years of age are sold as antiques. Using current market values as a guideline can also be misleading, since many collectibles will sell for much more than truly antique pieces. For example, an 18th-century handwritten American land deed, an antique in the strictest sense and certainly an intriguing historic relic, may sell on the collecting market for a fraction of the cost of a rare piece of Depression-era glass, mass-produced in the 1920s and '30s. It is apparent that age alone cannot be used to judge desirability and demand in the current market.

Another popular collecting field relates to "collectors' items." Again, interpretation of the term may be open to debate, but for purposes of discussion, collectors' items may be said to encompass the new and very recently made products, such as limited edition plates, that have been and are being produced to appeal directly to the collecting mania. They are ready-made collectibles, marketed as having all the best qualities of true antiques and collectibles but without any age criteria.

Milk Bottle Madness and Other Phenomena

Clearly, collecting is a well-established and pervasive phenomenon, but what lies behind its incredible popularity? What conscious or subconscious motives drive millions to search out and accumulate a myriad of artifacts, many with seemingly little intrinsic value? Items ranging from milk bottles to Christmas seals are being collected, and each collectible has its own dedicated core of enthusiastic and well-informed aficionados. What is the magic lure that compels such pursuits?

Probably the major motivation is a desire for self-expression and personal fulfillment. In a computerized age, it seems increasingly difficult to find a creative outlet for one's energies. How can a person express his or her individuality while still remaining within the bounds of accepted social behaviour? Collecting is one way.

In the 1950s, when Marion I. Levy picked up his first apple parer at a "your choice 50¢" table in a local flea market, he was amused by the Rube Goldberg aspect of the strange apparatus. Although that first parer was purchased only as a curiosity, Levy became fascinated by the mechanical ingenuity that had gone into devising this 19th-century utensil. Pursuing his interest, he discovered that parers had been produced in a wide variety of shapes and styles. By 1980 Levy had acquired a significant collection of unusual old parers; he had done extensive research into their history and development and had become a leading authority on the subject. Meanwhile, as other collectors entered the field, many of those 50-cent apple parers were bringing prices in the $25 to $50 range.

Other reasons for collecting, related to the need for personal self-expression, are nostalgia and individual aesthetics.

Many people, young and old alike, have found the hectic pace of modern life bewildering and frustrating. They seek to recapture a bit of their own past or some fragment of a bygone era that they have heard or read about. "The Good Old Days" seem to offer a respite from atomic age pressures, whether the "Good Old Days" in question are the 1920s or the 1950s. Hence, many devotees have found a pleasurable obsession in preserving the everyday items made obsolete by modern technology and economics. Take, for example, the more than

COLLECTION OF RON VILLANI; PHOTO, BILL ARSENAULT

200 members of MOO (Milkbottles Only Organization). Glass milk bottles are a thing of the past, but the members of this collecting group have taken up the task of preserving them and studying their history and evolution. To disseminate information on this collectible, MOO even publishes a monthly newsletter, *The Milking Parlor*.

Perhaps it was nostalgia that led John C. Tibbitts to begin collecting old dog-license tags. His involvement began when, as a comic gift, he prepared a mounted plaque displaying the tags of his former pet. Soon, however, he became entranced by the various sizes and shapes of these bits of metal, and before long he was advertising for tags in a national collectors' publication. This led to the discovery that he was not alone. The International Society of Animal License Collectors (ISALC) was already in operation, with over 100 members scattered around the United States. Dog-license tags date back at least to the mid-19th century, and all the latest research information and data on new discoveries are presented in the club's newsletter, *Paw Prints*. For serious collectors like Tibbitts, dog-license tags have a number of virtues. They are abundant, easy to display and maintain, and relatively inexpensive. Recent dog tags sell for less than 50 cents apiece, though more unusual and scarce ones from the 19th century can bring $15 or more.

It was aesthetic appeal that attracted Marian D. Kealey to old eyewash baths (commonly called eyecups). When her father brought one home from a bottle-digging expedition at a garbage dump, Kealey was captivated by the way the old glass refracted light. Hunting for more examples, she, too, discovered that she was not alone in her pursuit. There had even been a monthly newsletter for collectors—the *Eye Wash News*—but it had ceased publication in 1975. As Kealey continued her search, she delved into historical research, eventually publishing a feature article on the subject in a national collectors' magazine.

The Profit Motive

One final factor that has played an undeniable part in the rapid growth of the collecting hobby is investment potential.

For many years, fine antiques have been touted as prime investments, rivaling blue chip stocks. However, few people have the interest or the financial means to consider seriously, for example, the purchase of an 18th-century American highboy at around $100,000. On the other hand, many a collector who has concentrated on less expensive antiques or some of the newer collectibles has witnessed a great financial appreciation for a collection started only a few years earlier.

Although investment-minded persons often ask, "What is a good collectible investment that is sure to appreciate in the future?", most dedicated collectors put such considerations near the bottom of their list of reasons for collecting. To collect anything, one should first find it personally appealing. For most people, collecting is an expression of individual interests and desires. Mass media promotion has certainly tended to stress the investment aspect, and in today's unsteady economy this may be natural. But those for whom it is a primary concern cannot truly be classified as "collectors."

In the end, then, it is apparent that there can be no simple answers to what is collectible and why people collect. Every facet of the collecting hobby has expanded tremendously in recent years and will undoubtedly continue to do so. Citizens of the 21st century may well consider, among their "unalienable rights," "Life, Liberty and the pursuit ..." of collectibles.

URUGUAY

Through most of 1980 preparations for the general election of 1981 continued, and in May the executive submitted to the Cabinet the draft of the projected constitution; it provided for a restricted parliamentary democracy under a Council of National Security. A Constitutional Tribunal would resolve cases of conflict between authorities and of governmental infringement of ethics. Both the Blanco and Colorado parties were legalized; to achieve the same status other parties would have to have gained 2% of the vote in the preceding election.

In September the ban on the political activities of 50 people was lifted. However, the ban continued to affect many who had been politically active in Uruguay. An opposition newspaper, *El Día*, called for restoration of rights for all citizens, not just for an obscure 50. The draft constitution was submitted to a popular referendum on November 30. It was rejected by 879,765 votes to 642,279; 80% of the electorate voted. On December 3 the government called off the general election projected for 1981, while promising to restore democracy.

Economic growth trends continued in 1980, though they were affected by a slowdown of Argentina's economy. The Salto Grande hydroelectric complex was scheduled to be completed early in 1981; the 300-Mw Palmar project was under construction. Price increases slowed as a result of a programmed annual 16% cut in customs duties from Jan. 1, 1980, but industrialists feared the increased competition from abroad.

VENEZUELA

Opinion polls showed that in 1980 the popularity of Pres. Luis Herrera Campins plummeted. Opposition came from the business sector, which called for reduced government intervention in the economy while criticizing its bureaucracy and inefficiency, and also from the labour unions, which demanded a greater part in determining economic policy and company management, particularly in the public sector. Both called for an end to the recession (gross domestic product grew by only 0.7% in 1979) through a strategy designed to increase employment and raise the consumption levels of the poor.

Some improvement was expected in growth in 1980, but the rate would remain low because of reduced oil production, from an average of 2,350,000 bbl a day in 1979 to 2,140,000 bbl in 1980. The government attributed the recession to deliberate policies that it had instituted to cool the overheated economy after the expansionism of the mid-1970s and took only limited steps to stimulate the economy by introducing financial incentives for the construction industry.

External trade, however, continued to benefit from high oil prices, and a trade surplus of about $6.7 billion was expected in 1980 as compared with one of $3.4 billion in 1979; the nation's current account was forecast to register a surplus of $2.4 billion against a deficit of $2.1 billion the previous year. The government continued to borrow heavily on the international capital markets, principally to consolidate short-term debt contracted by state

French Pres. Valéry Giscard d'Estaing (left) greeted Venezuelan Pres. Luis Herrera Campins as he arrived in Paris for a three-day visit.
KEYSTONE

agencies. A senator and former president (1974–79), Carlos Andreas Perez, was censured by the Congress in May as "politically responsible" for the financial corruption involved in the purchase of the Norwegian ship "Sierra Nevada" in 1977 through a Swiss intermediary.

An economic cooperation agreement was signed with Mexico for the provision of oil to nine countries in Central America and the Caribbean; under the scheme oil would be sold at market prices, but 30% of the income would be returned as low-interest loans for the development of alternative sources of energy. Venezuela's role as political stabilizer in the region and its support for democracy and social justice was again proved when the military took power in Bolivia in July on the eve of that country's planned return to democratically elected government. Venezuela cut off aid of $40 million to Bolivia and, with the other member countries of the Andean Pact, condemned the coup.

Relations with Cuba sank to an all-time low following the decision of a Venezuelan military tribunal to acquit four men (two Cuban and two Venezuelan) accused of blowing up a Cubana airliner off Barbados in 1976. As a result Cuba withdrew diplomats from Caracas in October but stopped short of breaking off diplomatic relations.

As a member of the Organization of Petroleum Exporting Countries (OPEC), Venezuela again took the line of the doves, favouring small, gradual increases in the price of oil. Venezuela also pressed for the transformation and enlargement of the OPEC Special Fund into a development bank for financial aid to third world countries. In October the members of the Group of 77 less developed countries elected Venezuela to chair the group's deliberations for 1981, in place of India.

VIETNAM

For Vietnam 1980 was another year of tribulation, with a war it seemed unable to bring to a close, continuing isolation from much of the world, and yet more economic setbacks. At the end of what the government had hoped would be the first peacetime development plan, the nation lay trapped under military priorities.

One million out of a national labour force of some 20 million were soldiers. Up to 200,000 troops were stationed in Cambodia opposing a Khmer Rouge force estimated at about 30,000. As many as 100,000 men were massed along the Thai-Cambodian frontier where the resistance forces, apparently with substantial assistance from China and Thailand, were at their strongest. Vietnamese operations aimed at "wiping out" the remnants of the deposed Pol Pot regime in Cambodia evidently did not gain their objective.

The most serious escalation of the fighting took place in June, when Vietnamese units struck across the Thai border into the refugee camps. Several of the camps, controlled by either the Khmer Rouge

or the Free Khmers, were suspected of turning out guerrillas who would later be sent back to Cambodia. The thrust into Thailand, however, enabled Hanoi's adversaries to focus on its reputed expansionist policy. The non-Communist countries of Southeast Asia charged Hanoi with taking the first steps toward annexing Thailand. In August and again in October there were reports of Vietnamese troop movements to the Thai border. On each occasion, adversaries accused Hanoi of territorial ambitions threatening all Southeast Asia.

Although the Southeast Asian nations were not in complete agreement over the Vietnam-Cambodia problem, they all held that the first step toward any solution should be the withdrawal of Hanoi's troops from Cambodia. As Vietnam saw it, this was impossible. Therefore, its efforts to seek a common ground with at least some Southeast Asian countries did not make much headway.

Nor did the year see any improvement in Vietnam's relations with the West. In November 1979 U.S. pressure had led the World Bank to announce that it would make no loans to Vietnam in 1980. U.S. opposition continued during the year with a trade embargo in which Washington's close allies were asked to join. For its part, Hanoi kept making statements that it was ready to establish full relations with the U.S. A group of prominent but unofficial Americans issued a statement calling for normalization of relations. China remained Vietnam's most implacable foe. Both sides accused each other of border violations throughout the year. In September China said that tension along its borders with Vietnam had grown so much that it was impossible to resume peace talks with Hanoi (begun in 1979 and last held in March 1980).

One result of this virtual ostracism was that Hanoi found itself moving even closer to the Soviet Union. In July party chief Le Duan and Premier Pham Van Dong led a delegation to Moscow for the first Hanoi-Moscow summit since the two countries signed their friendship treaty 20 months earlier. Apart from attaining "a complete identity of views on all questions," the two governments signed economic assistance agreements covering, in particular, energy resources on the continental shelf off southern Vietnam. (Some European countries were already engaged in offshore oil prospecting in the area at Hanoi's invitation.)

Despite the aid provided by the Soviet Union, Vietnam's economy remained in a shambles. The damage suffered during the war with China in 1979 proved too heavy to be repaired quickly, and the continuing war in Cambodia demanded all the attention and resources the nation could mobilize.With all available technical and managerial expertise going to the military, economic activity was left largely in the hands of unskilled workers and managers. In some industrial sectors 70% of the work force was female. None of the targets set by the 1976–80 state plan was achieved. In the all-important agricultural sector, output was expected to be 17 million tons or less of grain—four million tons short of the goal for 1980. Also contributing to the shortfall were a series of typhoons and alternating floods and droughts.

With fears of another attack by China dominating Hanoi's thinking, one official said in May that the thrust of the next state plan (1981–85) would be to "militarize the whole country." This was to involve a high priority for food production, less emphasis on heavy industry, and reliance on massive Soviet aid.

The leadership structure in Hanoi underwent a quiet upheaval, presumably to ensure greater effectiveness than the aging hierarchy of the war years was able to provide. A formal announcement in February marked the rise of a new cluster of stars. The most notable newcomers on the political front were Foreign Minister Nguyen Co Thach and Nguyen Thanh Le, who took over as head of the party Central Committee's foreign affairs section. On the military front, top leadership was provided by a new defense minister, Gen. Van Tien Dung; Gen. Chu Huy Man, head of the Army's political section; and Gen. Le Trong Tan, army chief of staff. Late in December the National Assembly adopted a new constitution establishing a collective presidency, to consist of a Council of State headed by a chairman. However, supreme power was said to be consolidated in the hands of Le Duan and the party's secretary for organization, Le Duc Tho.

WEATHER

From June into September, the United States received a harsh reminder that the prolonged stress of a summer heat wave can be more destructive than

such short-lived, violent phenomena as tornadoes and hurricanes. The year's heat wave began in mid-June, when temperatures rose above 100° F (38° C) in southwest Texas. By mid-July the heat wave had spread northward and eastward to the Ohio Valley and mid-Atlantic regions, covering much of the eastern United States into early September.

Temperature records were shattered in more than half a dozen states, and on one day, July 13, three cities broke their maximum temperature records: Augusta, Ga., with 107° F; Atlanta, Ga., with 105°; and Memphis, Tenn., with 108°. Temperatures in Dallas, Texas, reached at least 100° each day from June 23 through August 3.

A post-heat-wave report from the National Oceanic and Atmospheric Administration (NOAA) assessed the toll Americans paid the 1980 heat wave: at least 1,265 lives and nearly $20 billion. In this assessment NOAA scientists found that heat-related summer deaths were seven times greater than normal, electrical energy use rose to a record 5.5% above normal, crops and livestock suffered greatly, hundreds of miles of major highway buckled from the heat, and, in many areas, water resources were seriously jeopardized.

Most of those who died from the heat wave were either elderly or poor and lived in non-air-conditioned homes or apartments. The greatest number of fatalities, 311, occurred in Missouri even though other states had higher temperatures for longer periods. Of course, these figures could not assess the heat wave in terms of indirect casualties. Scientists have observed, for example, that death rates from heart disease and similar conditions also increase sharply during heat-waves.

The Atlantic hurricane season spawned only one

A dramatic view of Hurricane Allen was provided by GOES-D, a weather satellite stationed 22,300 miles above the Equator. Hurricane Allen was moving northward and westward through the Gulf of Mexico on August 7. Also visible is Hurricane Isis in the Pacific south of Baja California.

NATIONAL OCEANIC AND ATMOSPHERIC ADMINISTRATION, U.S. DEPARTMENT OF COMMERCE

The research vessel "Oceanographer" took part in STREX, a six-week study of storm activity in the Gulf of Alaska, where storms are spawned that dominate the North American atmosphere for days at a time.

storm, Allen, that made landfall in the United States. Allen was distinguished by the lowest central pressure—an indicator of a hurricane's relative severity—recorded in an Atlantic storm since the Florida Keys Labor Day hurricane of September 1935. The 1980 Atlantic season also saw storms forming unusually close to the African coast and such rare postseason storms as Karl, which appeared in the North Atlantic in late November.

New Status for Satellites

A presidential directive late in 1979 bade NOAA develop a transition plan for developing a fully operational, land remote-sensing satellite program, which would join the agency's existing responsibility for operating environmental satellites. During 1980 NOAA, with representatives from the National Aeronautics and Space Administration, the Departments of Agriculture, Interior, State, Energy, and Defense, and other concerned organizations, cooperated in planning such a system. At the same time, NOAA's National Environmental Satellite Service moved to a higher level in the agency and was renamed the National Earth Satellite Service, reflecting its broad charter for operating satellite systems that watch the land, air, and sea environments.

Two satellites in the NOAA environmental series were launched during the year. NOAA-B, intended to be polar-orbiter NOAA-7, suffered a partial booster failure in May, which placed it into a highly elliptical orbit that would ultimately bring it back to

burn up in the Earth's atmosphere. In September GOES-D was placed in geostationary orbit some 22,300 mi above the Equator at 100° West Longitude. In that position, about halfway between the western and eastern geostationary weather satellites, scientists began testing a satellite sensor capable of profiling the atmosphere's temperature and humidity from geostationary altitudes.

Weather Modification

The second phase of NOAA's Florida Area Cumulus Experiment (FACE 2) completed its third summer of experimentation over southern Florida during the year. Scientists were analyzing rainfall data to answer one of the weather modifier's persistent questions: Does cloud seeding produce a net increase in rainfall over an area, or does it increase rainfall at one point while somehow suppressing it nearby?

Meanwhile, a potential follow-on project, PACE (Precipitation Augmentation for Crops Experiment), entered its first phase, in cooperation with the Illinois Water Survey and area universities. Focused on the Midwest, PACE examined the possibility of applying the cloud-seeding techniques learned in Florida to the rather different kinds of cumulus clouds found over the corn belt.

A related effort, undertaken by NOAA and Colorado State University, sought to evaluate the operational weather modification programs run by Utah and North Dakota. Utah, the second driest state in the U.S., conducted what may have been the largest wintertime cloud-seeding program in the U.S., to increase mountain snowpack. North Dakota had been the site of weather modification projects since the 1950s, most of them aimed at decreasing hail and increasing rainfall. Scientists hoped the state programs would benefit from the evaluation and that lessons learned there could be applied to solving weather modification problems in geographically similar areas.

Perhaps the largest modification of the global atmosphere was a natural one that began in May with the massive eruption of Mt. St. Helens, in Washington. The volcano injected tons of dust and other material into the upper troposphere and stratosphere, raising the question of how such material would affect sunlight reaching the Earth's surface, and climate. Preliminary indications were that the volcanic debris would have minimal effects on climatic trends, although it could produce a very slight, temporary, cooling of the planet's surface. (*See also* Earth Sciences.)

Major Storm Experiment

In November scientists from the United States and Canada, using the large storms in the Gulf of Alaska as a laboratory, began exploring how the atmosphere and ocean interact during some of the most violent weather in the Northern Hemisphere. Called STREX (Storm Transfer and Response Experiment), the six-week-long study focused on the exchanges of energy and water vapour across the ocean-atmosphere boundary, extending from several thousand feet in the air to several hundred feet beneath the sea.

The experiment was managed jointly by NOAA, the University of Washington, and the Atmospheric Environment Service of Canada. Elements of the experiment included an array of research ships and instrumented buoys in the path of the large cyclones (low-pressure systems) that rage across the Gulf of Alaska. Crucial data for the study came from a squadron of research aircraft, flying patterns across the advancing storm fronts at altitudes as low as 150 ft. In addition, satellites provided high-data-rate imagery of North Pacific cloud cover, as well as relaying the positions of the drifting buoys used in the experiment. The STREX array of ships and buoys was roughly centred on Ocean Weather Station "Papa," at 50° North Latitude, 145° West Longitude. This station, occupied by a Canadian Coast Guard weather ship, provided the only vertical soundings of the atmosphere available for the Gulf of Alaska. But weather ships are a vanishing species, and one of the imperatives behind Canada's participation in STREX was to evaluate alternative methods of getting weather information from this area—an area that feeds western Canada much of its serious weather.

WORLD TRADE

International trade grew rather slowly in 1980, increasing at only a 3% rate, compared with the 7% growth of 1979. This slowdown was largely due to

A huge shipment of Toyotas symbolized trouble for U.S. automakers, who sought cutbacks in foreign-made vehicles shipped to the U.S. as their sales lagged and workers had to be laid off.
J. P. LAFFONT—SYGMA

the rising world oil bill, the U.S. recession, and slower growth in virtually all industrialized countries. Higher oil prices also meant a drop in domestic investments and a curb on domestic growth through government anti-inflation policies.

Ironically, these factors combined to improve the U.S. balance of trade deficit in 1980. It was estimated that by year's end the difference between the value of what the country imported and the value of its exports would amount to a total of $32 billion, compared with a $37 billion trade deficit in 1979. The deficit decline followed the second quarter recession in the U.S. and fuel conservation in response to the 130% rise in world oil prices since 1978.

Oil imports for the first ten months of the year were 2,060,000,000 bbl, 23% below the 2,550,-000,000 bbl imported during the same period in 1979. The U.S. recession meant fewer imports even as exports continued to the stronger European economies. Britain was the sole exception to European performance in the first half of the year, with gross national product declining about 2% from the previous six months and unemployment at the worst levels since World War II.

However, the improving U.S. trade balance contributed to a strong U.S. dollar, which could only spell trouble for Europe, since world oil prices were pegged to dollars. European countries had actually experienced a declining cost of oil from 1975 to 1978 because their currencies rose against the dollar. Indications were that European central banks in 1980 were obliged to adopt stringent controls on monetary growth to keep their own currencies from eroding against the dollar and to avoid inflation.

The possibility that such policies would lead Europe into recession during the last half of 1980 or the first half of 1981 was viewed with some misgiving. The United States traditionally runs a large payments surplus with Europe—estimated at $24.5 billion in 1980—and this makes up for the fact that the U.S. imports more from Japan and OPEC (Organization of Petroleum Exporting Countries) nations than it sells to them. Recession in Europe would cut into U.S. export sales and trim the sums repatriated by U.S. multinationals doing business in Europe. But economists were cheered somewhat by the fact that the Western economies had not marched lockstep into recession in 1980 as occurred during the last recession, which had been one factor contributing to the duration of that downturn.

Inflation fighting and reducing world oil consumption remained the top priorities of the industrialized nations in 1980, as elaborated at their annual economic summit in Venice in June. Also addressed at Venice was the potential for a rise in protectionism as hard-pressed industries struggled to retain their domestic market shares in the face of stiff import pressure.

Trade Protectionism

Protectionism did develop a following in the U.S. during the year, a trend resisted by economists who feared that import restrictions on the U.S. market would lead to retaliation by other nations and choke off world trade. The Carter administration in September raised the minimum price of foreign steel by 12% to bolster sales by the U.S. steel mills. In addition, Douglas Fraser, president of the United Auto Workers, whose membership had long opposed barriers to foreign imports as inflationary, reversed that position and joined the Ford Motor Co. in asking for restrictions to protect the ailing U.S. auto industry.

Their target was Japan, which in 1980 expanded, primarily through exports, by 4.8%. Japanese automakers claimed over 20% of the U.S. car market in midsummer—four out of five of all foreign cars sold in the U.S. Japan also captured 9% of all auto sales in West Germany, double its share of the year before. But the U.S. International Trade Commission in November turned down the UAW and Ford Motor Co. appeal for restrictions against the Japanese. Japanese trade officials applauded the ruling,

Advertisements for both foreign-made and domestic products became a common sight in China's big cities in 1980. The opening of China for consumer goods promised a vast new market for U.S. manufacturers.
WIDE WORLD

OLIPHANT © THE WASHINGTON STAR

"When it comes to wanting to blow the hell outa the Ayatollah, I'm as patriotic as anyone. But I don't see embargoing our dear Russian friends over some little misunderstanding."

and they added that they would attempt to cool the export fervour of their auto industry.

Paying the Oil Bill

Of course, the rising cost of fuel in 1979 and 1980 was the main cause for Japan's growing share of worldwide auto sales with its line of small, fuel-efficient cars. Conflicting signs in late 1980 made it difficult to predict just how fast oil prices would continue to rise and how quickly OPEC would increase the surplus trade balance that drained the major industrial nations of $114 billion in 1980.

The war between Iran and Iraq—both OPEC members—seemed to have foreclosed the possibility of any new pricing agreements within the organization until the hostilities ceased, in particular putting off plans for a long-term pricing strategy. Yet the Middle Eastern friction also cut Iranian and Iraqi oil production and cut into the world oil surplus that had caused spot prices to fall below contract levels before the outbreak of the war.

There was little fear that rising oil bills would force any countries to default on their foreign debts, since the heaviest borrowing among the less developed countries was among relatively strong economies like Brazil and South Korea. But it was clear that oil costs were forcing many less developed nations to settle for low or no growth, thus making them poor markets for exports. There was a call by Robert S. McNamara, retiring in 1980 after 12 years at the head of the World Bank, to increase lending authority and aid more health and education projects in those countries.

Politics and Trade

The U.S. policy of mixing politics with trade—termed linkage—continued in 1980. The most-favoured-nation status granted to China, a free-trade advantage not enjoyed by the U.S.S.R. even during the better days of détente, did increase trade with that country to the United States' advantage. But Pres. Jimmy Carter's efforts to hobble the arms race by curbing U.S. weapons sales appeared to lead only to more arms exports by other producers including Israel and France. And the freezing of Iranian assets, including military equipment already paid for but not yet delivered, had not led to release of the American hostages at year's end, though it seemed that this action would bear fruit when Iran needed to bankroll its war with Iraq.

But the most criticized linkage was the curtailment of grain sales to the U.S.S.R. in response to the Soviet invasion of Afghanistan in December 1979. Though supported by the majority of the American public, the move led to Soviet grain deals with other countries, notably Argentina. Support by U.S. allies for the grain boycott was lukewarm. The export limits agreed to by Canada and Australia, for example, were about equal to their total exports of the same commodities to the Soviets in the previous year.

The Soviet Union, meanwhile, was having some success forging new trade links with Europe. In the works was an $11 billion pipeline to supply Siberian gas to six European countries. It was estimated that the pipeline project would eventually double West

German reliance on Soviet gas to 30% of West German gas imports.

In all, Europe's tendency to increase trade ties to the Soviet bloc without seeking political concessions ran counter to the U.S. linkage approach. Ronald Reagan's election seemed unlikely to ease this impasse with the allies, since his campaign rhetoric emphasized linkage even more strongly than President Carter's had.

YOUTH ORGANIZATIONS

Big Brothers/Big Sisters

The Big Brothers/Big Sisters of America organization comprised nearly 400 member agencies in 1980. Through its 150,000 matches between adult volunteers and children, it provided the opportunity for concerned, civic-minded adults to offer their services to the community. Young people, many from single-parent homes, were given the opportunity to develop a high-quality, individual relationship with an adult volunteer who served as both role model and friend. As always, the huge backlog of young people awaiting a match made the recruitment of adult volunteers a major priority for the year.

Boys Clubs of America

Of the more than one million young people being served by the Boys Clubs of America, Jace L. Smith, 16, of the Massillon Boys Club of Ohio was

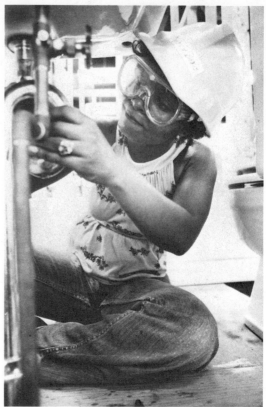

COURTESY, SOUTHWEST-BELMONT AREA YWCA, PHILADELPHIA, PA.

In Philadelphia the YWCA sponsored training courses in such nontraditional jobs for women as plumbing to help them break into the lucrative building trades.

Boy of the Year Jace Smith explained the Boys Clubs' new service mark to Pres. Jimmy Carter during a White House reception in September.
COURTESY, BOYS CLUBS OF AMERICA

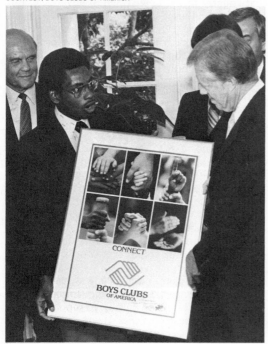

chosen Boy of the Year. He met with Pres. Jimmy Carter in Washington, D.C., in September. The March meeting in Milwaukee, Wis., of over 500 young men participating in the Keystone Clubs was judged the most successful to date. Speakers representing sports, the media, and politics addressed the gathering. These clubs promote leadership development and service to the less fortunate in local communities. The Boys Clubs emblem got a new look in 1980. Created by Saul Bass/Herb Yager & Associates, the stylized clasped hands symbolized the opportunities provided for young people and adults to connect with one another through contemporary Boys Clubs programs.

Boy Scouts of America

The 50th anniversary of Cub Scouting was observed in 1980, with special activities nationwide highlighting the home-centred emphasis of the Cub Scout program. In March the 30 millionth Cub Scout was registered in the movement. The Boy Scouts of America received a gift of $2.1 million from the Max C. Fleischmann Foundation of Reno, Nev. The funds were to be used for improving facilities at four national high-adventure bases. The bases offer young people 14 years of age and older the opportunity to explore wilderness areas while backpacking, snorkeling, canoeing, and sailing. The number of community organizations using the Scouting program continued to grow, with more than 345 types of organizations using the program through chartered Cub Scout packs, Boy Scout troops, and Explorer posts.

Camp Fire, Inc.

Camp Fire's broad objectives for 1980 committed the agency to studying the changing role of volunteerism. This included a major mass-media recruitment campaign seeking new adult volunteers and a commitment to ongoing volunteer staff development. Revision began on youth program materials to reflect inclusion of both boys and girls from birth to 21 in the Camp Fire program as well as Camp Fire's commitment to nonsexist programming for all children. Seeking to improve those conditions in society that affect all youth, the Camp Fire, Inc., board of directors resolved to support the deinstitutionalization of status offenders. Camp Fire is part of an effort to help youth who have been placed under the jurisdiction of the juvenile courts. Camp Fire also endorsed and supported the International Year of Disabled Persons and pursued a direction of mainstreaming and involving disabled youth in Camp Fire programs.

4-H

More than five million young people, rural and urban, from every cultural and economic background participated in 4-H programs in 1980. The 4-Hers, both boys and girls between the ages of 9 and 19, participated through learn-by-doing educational projects and activities. They contributed to energy conservation, environmental improvement, community service, food production, and many other areas. In addition, 4-Hers participated in programs that aid youth employment and career decisions, health, nutrition, and family relationships. Nearly 566,000 4-H adult and teen volunteer leaders assisted with programs. Young people participated through clubs, special-interest groups, camps, instructional television, and school enrichment programs. The 4-H Expanded Food and Nutrition Education Program reached youth primarily in disadvantaged areas of cities.

Future Farmers of America

President Carter presented his Energy Efficiency Award to the Future Farmers of America (FFA) "in recognition of outstanding contributions to American economic and national security through exemplary leadership in a national effort to achieve energy efficiency." Over one-fourth of the nation's 8,000 FFA chapters accepted the "President's Challenge" last year and conducted energy conservation and production programs for agriculture and agribusiness in their communities. President Carter presented a plaque to the Alamosa, Colo., chapter for having the most outstanding program. The FFA National Hall of Achievement, which records the history of the organization, was dedicated at the National FFA Center in Alexandria, Va.

Future Homemakers of America

Future Homemakers of America (FHA), sponsored by the Department of Education and the American Home Economics Association, is a vocational student organization made up of junior and

First Lady Rosalynn Carter greeted Girls Clubs award winners during the national conference designated "Girl Power: Our Natural Energy Resource."

COURTESY, GIRLS CLUBS OF AMERICA

senior high school students. FHA has 52 state associations, including the District of Columbia and Puerto Rico, with a combined membership of 400,000 in more than 12,000 chapters in rural, urban, and suburban settings. Chapters function as an integral part of the home economics program, with projects and activities developed jointly by students and teacher/advisers within the framework of the home economics curriculum. In planning and completing the projects members can practice life skills such as decision making, value clarification, working together, sharing, carrying responsibilities, and developing understanding.

Girls Clubs of America

Girls Clubs of America (GCA) received a major grant from the U.S. Department of Labor for Teen Women Employability Programs in 17 member clubs. The program seeks to raise the skills, aspirations, and prospects for employment of nearly 1,000 girls. Funding was also obtained to begin a

national creative children's theatre program entitled "Acting You." Training workshops were conducted around the country, and a series of program workbooks and materials were developed. GCA continued to hold "Today's Girls: Tomorrow's Women" conferences to call attention to the needs and concerns of today's girls and young women in the areas of human sexuality, juvenile justice, education, and employment.

Girl Scouts of the U.S.A.

Program conferences were held in ten states during the fall to introduce Girl Scouts and volunteers from more than 300 Girl Scout councils nationwide to the totally revised and updated Girl Scout program for girls aged 6–17. At the White House in June, new materials for teens (12–17) and younger girls (6–11) were previewed by honorary Girl Scout president Rosalynn Carter. Mrs. Carter was presented with a framed set of the 76 new Junior Girl Scout proficiency badges, including such topics as

The sail training ship "Young America" took 42 Cadette and Senior Girl Scouts on a whale-watching wildlife study expedition along the East Coast in May.
COURTESY, GIRL SCOUTS OF THE U.S.A.

"energy saver" and "computer fun." Other new additions to the Girl Scout program for teens included a new highest award, the Girl Scout Gold Award, and a comprehensive handbook called *You Make the Difference.*

Young Men's Christian Associations

The YMCA, the largest voluntary, youth-serving organization in the world, topped the ten million-member mark for the first time in its U.S. history. The two fastest growing segments of members in the U.S. were families and women and girls. The 1,855 local YMCA's and branches offered a multiplicity of services ranging from traditional programs such as camping and parent-child activities to nontraditional work with troubled youth. One major new thrust was the cardiovascular health program with its emphasis on keeping people well. An increasing number of businesses and industries were turning to the YMCA to provide such programs for their employees. The YMCA was also pioneering mainstreaming programs that provide opportunities for handicapped and nonhandicapped children to participate together.

Young Women's Christian Associations of the U.S.A.

To realize the primary goal to help women and girls fulfill their individual potential as citizens contributing to their communities, the YWCA's service programs addressed, particularly, societal conditions affecting women and third world persons with a focus on racial justice, public policy, health, physical education, and recreation. Highlights of the ongoing programs offered in 1980 by over 400 member associations were: ENCORE, the national YMCA's post-mastectomy group rehabilitation program; job-training sessions; hot lines for battered wives and for teenage pregnancy counseling; rape crisis services; adult day care; senior citizens' programs; arts, crafts, and recreational programs; programs to recognize the accomplishments of women in corporate and community life; world affairs discussion groups; and refugee support programs.

YUGOSLAVIA

For Yugoslavia 1980 was the year of transition from the Tito into the post-Tito era. The collective bodies to head the nation and the Communist Party, which had been set up and were already functioning during Tito's lifetime, took over completely during his illness, which began in December 1979. After Tito's death on May 4, 1980, the president of the collective presidency was Lazar Kolisevski until May 15, when he was succeeded by Cvijetin Mijatovic for 12 months as head of state and commander of the armed forces. World leaders attended Tito's funeral on May 8 in Belgrade. They included Soviet Pres. Leonid Brezhnev, China's Chairman Hua Guofeng (Hua Kuo-feng), West German Chancellor Helmut Schmidt, and British

Prime Minister Margaret Thatcher. U.S. Pres. Jimmy Carter was criticized in the U.S. and elsewhere for not attending the funeral personally and for sending Vice-Pres. Walter Mondale instead, but he paid Yugoslavia a visit in June after the Western leaders' summit in Venice, Italy, and specifically reaffirmed U.S. support for Yugoslavia's independence and integrity.

Yugoslavia's relations with the Soviet Union became strained as a result of the Soviet invasion and occupation of Afghanistan in December 1979, which Yugoslavia condemned. Relations with the Soviet Union's closest ally, Bulgaria, also deteriorated early in 1980 over Macedonia, but they improved, and in November Yugoslavia's foreign minister, Josip Vrhovec, visited Sofia. Relations with the Soviet Union also improved later in the year. In July a top-level Supreme Soviet delegation visited Yugoslavia, and in September Yugoslavia signed a long-term trade agreement with the Soviet Union that envisioned an increase in mutual trade in 1981–85 to $26 billion from $11 billion in 1976–80. The Soviet Union committed itself to ordering in that period nearly 100 ships worth $1.3 billion from Yugoslav shipyards. Relations with Albania improved despite ideological differences, and the two countries signed a trade agreement in July.

In February Yugoslavia agreed to an economic cooperation pact with the European Economic Community (EEC) in Brussels. It allowed duty-free access to EEC markets for a wide range of Yugoslav goods, leaving mostly textiles, steel products, ferrous metals, and alloys still subject to tariffs. Yugoslavia was granted a $280 million credit by the EEC for the completion of its east-west highway linking Austria and Greece. To service and repay its estimated $15 billion debt, Yugoslavia was obliged to raise a number of credits and loans in the West. The Yugoslav dinar was devalued by 30% against major Western currencies in June. A partial price freeze was also introduced in June but lifted in October. The rate of inflation in 1980 averaged 30%. Shortages of various foodstuffs and consumer goods occurred.

During Tito's illness a crackdown began on political dissidents despite a marked absence of public political dissent. In January a law was passed in the federal republic of Serbia enabling the government to fire seven Marxist philosophers for criticizing the Yugoslav system. In June seven people were sentenced in Zagreb to terms ranging from 5 to 15 years for allegedly plotting sabotage. A group of 50 Albanians (mostly young people) was tried during the summer for alleged separatism.

In July sharp press attacks were made on Milovan Djilas, a former vice-president and for many years Yugoslavia's leading dissident, for publishing abroad articles and interviews critical of the Yugoslav system, including a "critical portrait" of Tito. Also during the year a group of Yugoslav intellectuals demanded the abolition of the article of the

Pres. Jimmy Carter visited Belgrade, Yugoslavia, on June 24, where he was greeted by Pres. Cvijetin Mijatovic. Carter assured Yugoslavs of continuing U.S. support; he had provoked criticism for not attending President Tito's funeral in May.

CHRISTIAN VIOUJARD—GAMMA

penal code dealing with hostile propaganda. A group of Croatian intellectuals in Zagreb demanded amnesty for all political prisoners. Legal proceedings were started against two Croatian dissidents, Gen. Franjo Tudjman and writer Vlado Gotovac, for giving interviews to Western journalists.

ZAIRE

With the inflation rate at 100%, the task of reviving the country's economy was one of the main concerns of Zaire's government throughout 1980. Another problem was the widespread discontent of the people, whose standard of living had declined steadily for years while a handful of the country's leaders amassed wealth. The discontent provided fertile ground for dissidents, and there were rumours that agents from countries hostile to Zaire were attempting to stir up trouble. The government acted firmly against any suspected agitators, but its repressive measures only led to further suspicion and hostility. The situation was aggravated by the low price paid for copper, the output of which had been cut drastically in 1979, and by the high cost of petroleum products.

In one respect Zaire was fortunate. A number of Western powers, fearing the further spread of Communist influence in Africa, were determined to support the regime however little they respected its policies. To this end, representatives of the country's main creditors had met in December 1979 and agreed to recommend the rescheduling of Zaire's external public debt, which would fall due in 1980. In April 1980 the government of Zaire signed an agreement with representatives of 122 commercial bank creditors making the rescheduling proposals effective.

In January 1980 Zaire's power to draw on a standing fund set up by the International Monetary Fund (IMF) was suspended when it became known that the 1979 budget deficit had seriously exceeded the limit set by the IMF. An IMF mission visited Kinshasa with the object of reviewing Zaire's economy and suggesting new criteria for the operation of the standing fund arrangement. The Consultative Group for Zaire, consisting of representatives of nine industrial countries, together with the IMF, the World Bank, and the European Economic Community, met in Paris at the end of May and decided to recommend additional aid, the nature and extent of which would be subject to further discussion. On May 20 Amnesty International published a report claiming that about 1,000 political detainees were being held in Zaire, many of them without trial. Nguza Karl-I-Bond, the foreign minister (and prime minister from August 27), declared that the report was an attempt to influence the discussions of the Consultative Group for Zaire. The evidence did not seem to support his statement, however.

In return for the various measures of assistance, the country's creditors insisted that the government take more effective measures to control the situation and restore order. On January 18 Pres. Mobuto Sese Seko announced a number of changes in his Executive Council. He himself relinquished the portfolio of national defense and veterans' affairs in favour of Lieut. Gen. Babia Zongbi Malobia, but he retained the portfolio of territorial security. Speaking on February 4, the president affirmed that as long as he lived there would be no biparty or multiparty system.

At the same time, efforts were made to reform the Army with the assistance of Belgian and French advisers, together with a number of Chinese instructors. In February it was reported that Zaire had signed an agreement on military matters with Egypt aimed at an exchange of technical knowledge and reciprocal training of troops. The following month Mobutu visited Romania, where he signed a treaty of cooperation, and later in March he visited China, where he had talks with some of the country's leaders.

None of these measures brought any immediate improvement in the conditions of the ordinary people. The cost of food remained high and jobs were scarce. Rioting in January at the Institute for Applied Technology in Kinshasa was followed by a month-long strike by students, culminating in demonstrations in April protesting the inadequate support provided for higher education. This led to closure of the National University in Kinshasa, along with several other educational centres. In the course of a visit to Zaire early in May for the consecration of several new bishops, Pope John Paul II

During his visit to Zaire in May, part of a six-nation African tour, Pope John Paul II celebrated Mass before a million people at the People's Palace in Kinshasa.

GIANSANTI-FABIAN—SYGMA

cautioned the congregation against hasty africanization of church ceremonial. His visit was marred by the deaths of nine people and the injury of many more when huge crowds flocked to attend his celebration of mass.

ZAMBIA

In 1980 Zambia was again forced to import corn (maize) from a variety of sources; in May Pres. Kenneth Kaunda announced a £300 million, ten-year plan to raise the country's level of food production. The achievement of independence by neighbouring Zimbabwe was celebrated, but it led to further criticism of the government, which could no longer attribute shortages to Rhodesian hostility. Although rumours of an attempt to assassinate Kaunda in February were denied, Kaunda himself admitted that he had thwarted an attempted coup in October. He imposed a curfew on most of the towns in Zambia, and this was followed by the arrest of several leading businessmen and former government officials. In a separate operation, more than 40 members of a heavily armed gang were captured after a gun battle near Lusaka. Kaunda accused South Africa of involvement, but the charge was denied.

Low prices for copper meant that reserves of foreign currency remained disastrously low. On January 23 the government nationalized stores of diesel oil and gasoline held in Zambia by five international companies. On April 1, at Lusaka, Zambia was one of nine southern African countries pledging economic cooperation and efforts to improve transport and communications.

ZIMBABWE

Zimbabwe became independent at midnight April 17–18, 1980, with the Rev. Canaan Banana as its first president. This was the culmination of three and a half months of intensive preparation under the direction of the British governor, Lord Soames. The cease-fire that had come into force at midnight on Dec. 28, 1979, marked the official end of the civil war in Zimbabwe Rhodesia. The soldiers of the Patriotic Front were given a week in which to assemble in camps supervised by troops of a Commonwealth monitoring force, and many thousands of them, though not all, responded to the governor's appeal.

On January 13 Joshua Nkomo arrived in Salisbury from Zambia after three years in exile, and Robert Mugabe, leader of the Zimbabwe African National Union (ZANU), the larger section of the Patriotic Front, returned to Rhodesia from Mozambique a fortnight later. Against a background of recriminations, resulting at times in violence between the various parties that were to contest the elections at the end of February, and of criticism of the handling of the highly volatile situation by Lord Soames, a beginning was made toward repatriating an estimated 200,000 refugees from

Zambia, Mozambique, Botswana, and other neighbouring countries. Under the supervision of British soldiers, a start was also made toward integrating some of the former guerrillas into the existing Rhodesian Army.

When the elections took place (results completed March 4), 94% of the electorate cast their votes. Mugabe's ZANU (PF), with 63% of the total vote and 57 of the 80 seats contested by black candidates, won an overwhelming victory. Nkomo's Patriotic Front was second with 24% of the vote and 20 seats. Mugabe's victory caused apprehension among many of the white citizens, but he was at pains to reassure all sections within the country of his good intentions toward them. On March 5 he agreed to form a coalition with Nkomo's party, and Nkomo accepted the portfolio of home affairs. Only three other members of his party were given ministries, but two white ministers were appointed to Mugabe's Cabinet.

Some whites were worried by Mugabe's insistence that he had been elected to introduce changes and that the main areas of change would be in land settlement, in the restructuring of the civil service to open opportunities for the promotion of blacks, and in the fields of health and education. Several

hundred white members of the Army and police refused to serve under Mugabe, and many whites began to leave the country. On the other hand, fears that Zimbabwe would be seriously affected by Mugabe's Marxist ideology were partly allayed by his application for membership in the Lomé Convention, linking African and other less developed countries with the European Economic Community (EEC). The foreign minister, Simon Muzenda, also announced in March that Zimbabwe intended to maintain close and friendly relations with Britain. In April the minister of mines, Maurice Nyagumbo, reassured those who feared nationalization of the mines by stating that the government's policy would be to encourage private ownership with a view to increasing output and profits.

The task of reconstruction facing Zimbabwe after years of civil war was enormous. Once an exporter of corn (maize), Zimbabwe now had to import large quantities. Finance for rehabilitation was threatened by the fall in income from the tobacco industry—the main earner of foreign currency as well as the chief employer—because of overproduction throughout the world and a consequent decline in prices. However, substantial development loans from Britain, France, West Germany, and the U.S.

At midnight April 17–18 the former British colony of Southern Rhodesia became the independent nation of Zimbabwe; Prime Minister Robert Mugabe (light suit) and Pres. Canaan Banana met with members of the newly chosen Cabinet in Salisbury.

W. CAMPBELL—SYGMA

promised to ease the pressure somewhat.

The formation of the new Army was beset by problems. The members of the two branches of the former Patriotic Front were not at ease with each other, and neither group found it easy to cooperate with the former Rhodesian Army. Erstwhile guerrillas, still in camps, were restless at the delay in reintegrating them into the life of independent Zimbabwe, and violent incidents involving armed members of the guerrilla forces became more numerous. In July Parliament agreed to extension of the state of emergency for a further six months. Lieut. Gen. Peter Walls, the former Rhodesian commander in chief, had been asked by Mugabe to stay on after independence to integrate the guerrilla forces into the Army. However, he was relieved of his post as chief of the joint high command on September 15, as a result of derogatory remarks made while on leave about the risk of civil war in Zimbabwe and the fairness of the elections, and was barred from returning to the country.

At the end of September Mugabe ordered the Army and police to act against dissidents. Army units moved into areas where armed troublemakers had been most in evidence, and in November fighting broke out in Bulawayo between members of the two guerrilla forces who had supported Mugabe and Nkomo. Order was restored only after about 50 people had been killed, some of them civilians. In July white civil servants were given assurances about the security of their appointments and promotion prospects.

Mugabe also announced that Zimbabwe would not provide a base for African National Congress guerrillas wishing to operate against South Africa. Nevertheless, the prime minister ordered closure of the South African mission in Zimbabwe because, he claimed, Pretoria was recruiting mercenaries to fight against Zimbabwe. The South African government then withdrew all senior members of its diplomatic staff from Salisbury. A further blow to the government came with the arrest in August of the minister of manpower, Edgar Z. Tekere, on a charge of murdering a white farmer. On December 8, after a month-long trial, Tekere was found guilty but freed on the grounds that he had been suppressing terrorist activities.

In October the government regretfully announced its intention to introduce regulations to control the activities of visiting journalists. An example of the difficulties faced by the government was provided at the beginning of November. It was reported that Mugabe—contrary to his previous statements on land—had announced the government's intention to take possession of some white-owned farms without compensation because Britain had failed to fulfill its preindependence promise to pay white farmers for land needed by the government. The land thus taken would be allocated to Africans living in reserves or on less fertile land. Almost at once it was explained that the speech, delivered in Shona, had been misinterpreted and that the prime minister had stated only that it might be necessary to seize vacant and unused land if the international community did not provide the aid Zimbabwe so urgently needed.

On November 4 Zimbabwe signed the Lomé Convention. This would enable the country to draw upon aid from the EEC and to export specified quantities of sugar and beef to EEC countries on favourable terms.

ZOOS

Two authoritative reports published in 1980, *World Conservation Strategy*, prepared by the International Union for Conservation of Nature and Natural Resources, and *Global 2000*, a study initiated by U.S. Pres. Jimmy Carter on the future of the environment, estimated that approximately 600,000 to one million species of plants and animals would become extinct by the end of the century.

Such prognostications increased awareness among zoo scientists, directors, curators, and councils of their fundamental and increasingly urgent obligations to propagate and sustain in captivity species that might otherwise disappear. Papers given at the third international conference on "Breeding Endangered Species in Captivity," held in San

The first emperor penguin chick bred and hatched in captivity peeks at the world from the safety of his father's embrace at San Diego's Sea World.
UPI

Diego, Calif., in November 1979, and published in the 1980 *International Zoo Yearbook*, emphasized these obligations. They also stressed some of the difficulties inherent in long-term wild-animal propagation and reintroduction schemes.

The emphasis given to various manipulative techniques, such as artificial incubation, cross-fostering between related species and individuals, artificial insemination, and semen banks, indicated the direction that research was taking. Also stressed were the needs for data collection, careful record keeping, and cooperation and coordination; these points were also underlined at the international symposium on "The Use and Practice of Wild Animal Studbooks" organized by the International Union of Directors of Zoological Gardens and held in Copenhagen in October 1979.

In mid-August the first captive birth outside China of a giant panda occurred at Chapultepec Park Zoo in Mexico City. The parents, Yin-yin and Pe-pe, had been given as young animals to the people of Mexico by China in 1975. Despite the utmost care, at eight days old the cub died, inadvertently suffocated by its mother. Among the first or rare breedings reported by zoos during 1979–80 were: yellowhead jawfish (*Opistognathus aurifrons*), San Diego, Calif.; Coahuilan box turtle (*Terrapene coahuila*), Dallas, Texas; Santa Catalina Island rattleless rattlesnake (*Crotalus catalinensis*), Fresno, Calif.; scarlet-headed blackbird (*Amblyramphus holosericeus*), Philadelphia, Pa.; Hispaniolan conure (*Aratinga chloroptera*), Santo Domingo, Dominican Republic.

Other outstanding propagation news included the recording of the 70th cheetah birth at Whipsnade, England, and the rearing of the rare Tahitian blue lory (*Vini peruvini*) at San Diego, Calif., and in a private collection in England. Under schemes based on captive-bred stock various species that had become rare in the wild state were reintroduced into their natural habitats. These included rhinoceros iguanas (into Dominica), Houston toads (the Houston, Texas, region), Arabian oryx (Jordan and Oman), and badgers (Norfolk, England).

Although artificial insemination had already resulted in successful births in a number of animals, two important such achievements were announced in 1980: the birth of a puma in London (to act as a prototype for further work on the rarer large cats), and the rare Speke's gazelle in St. Louis, Mo. Late in the spring the U.S. National Zoo in Washington, D.C., artificially inseminated its giant panda Ling-Ling with sperm from its companion Hsing-Hsing, but the effort failed to produce offspring.

Recent new zoo buildings and exhibits included a magnificent walk-through aviary in Melbourne, Australia, the imaginative North American Living Museum in Tulsa, Okla., and the well-equipped veterinary hospital and pathology unit in Jersey, Channel Islands. *Great Zoos of the World* (1980), edited by Lord Zuckerman, president of the Zoological Society of London, dealt comprehensively with the history, present collections, and future policy of 24 selected zoos and included a long introduction by Lord Zuckerman on the rise of zoos and their future.

The first large cat to be born from artificial insemination, Bonny, a puma, takes a walk with her mother at the London Zoo; preservation of endangered species might someday necessitate widespread use of artificial fertilization techniques for big cats such as snow leopards.

THE TIMES, LONDON

80
FOCUS

THE GLOBAL VIEWS OF PRESIDENT SADAT

by Anwar El-Sadat

Since the time I was very young, my great interest was in politics. Even as a boy in secondary school in Cairo and on vacation at home, in my own village of Mit Abul-Kum, in the heart of the Nile Delta, I started reading newspapers and books on current affairs and recording what I read. In fact, my hobby was politics. At that time Mussolini was in Italy. I saw his pictures and read about how he would change his facial expressions when he made public addresses, variously taking a pose of strength, or aggression, so that people might look at him and read power and strength in his very features. I was fascinated by this. I stood before the mirror at home and tried to imitate this commanding expression, but for me the results were very disappointing. All that happened was that the muscles of my face got very tired. It hurt.

Later on, I was reading Machiavelli. I suppose everyone who has any interest in politics has read him and what he says about the art of political maneuvering. It is a classic source of teaching for diplomats and statesmen. Of course, I was fascinated by parts of this book. But when I thought of putting his teaching into practice, I felt that I would only be cheating myself. I felt awkward inside, just the way my face had hurt when I tried to project the soul of the "new Roman Empire" by imitating Mussolini's gestures.

Politics is only one aspect of life. It is just like everything else we do. For the politician, as with the lawyer, the doctor, or the farmer, there are certain ethics which must be upheld, ethics which impose limits on any efforts to make a success or to have influence in this life. To have any real influence one must be true to his inner self—at work, at home, at school, or in the Ministry of Foreign Affairs. When I reach peace with myself, I find that I am strongest. But at moments when I have not found this inner peace, I am very weak. At those times I try to avoid doing anything until this sense of inner peace returns.

I first felt that inner peace in my village of Mit Abul-Kum, where I still have my living roots, deep in the soil of that Nile community. But I really found this peace in Cell 54, a bare damp room in Cairo Central Prison, where I spent 18 months for revolutionary activity. I was in solitary, where I could not read or write or listen to the radio. Suffering builds up a human being and gives him self-knowledge. It made me know God and his love. Thus I learned in Cell 54 to value that inner success which helps a man to be true to himself.

Democracy is not merely laws and provisions; it is a mode of daily life. Democracy is essentially a matter of ethics, and in a democracy we must stand ready for a daily test of ethics. When we call now for measures to insure ethical democratic practice, this is not a cunning device to impose ties and restrictions or a relinquishing of democracy. Rather our call comes from a profound and sincere belief that a free society bears the responsibility of protecting itself. I will fight for democracy and ethics whatever position I hold, so that on the day ordained by God I can give an account of my performance with an easy conscience, at peace with myself.

I have often said that the new Egypt, indeed any country, should be a state founded on faith and science. I did not intend this as a slogan whose glitter would attract the masses but as a genuine appeal linked to the roots of democracy and freedom. Science is the emancipation of the human mind to accomplish good and achieve progress for the sake of man, free of bonds and chains. Faith is a commitment to principles, values, and ethics upheld by religions which before and after the advent of divine religions have unceasingly toiled to liberate human dignity.

Religion was never a bond. God in his glory favoured man by enabling him to think, released his capacities and created him in his own image. The U.S. Declaration of Independence, which followed the British bill of rights, states that the natural rights of man bestowed on him by God are the rights to life, to freedom, and to happiness. Hence, freedom is a natural right, but its practice depends

on the consent and agreement of the community. Otherwise chaos prevails.

Let me illustrate this point about faith. I have been asked about it many times. I remember a reporter in London in 1975, who questioned most intently on this. Go back for a moment to 1972 and the early part of 1973, when everyone in the world thought that the Arabs were of low significance, either militarily or politically or in any other way. The fabulous victory of Israel in 1967 and the dimensions of the Arab defeat had confirmed that im-

pression. At that time in Egypt I was planning the October war against Israel. I had turned to war only after my peace initiative had failed. That was in February 1971, when I offered to conclude a peace treaty with Israel. After that there was no alternative to war. Sometimes one has to swallow a bitter pill so that he may regain his health. It was clear to me that Egypt was a hopeless case unless we proved that we were fit to live, that we could fight, that we were not a dead body.

In October 1973 Henry Kissinger was in the State

Department [as U.S. secretary of state]. Henry told me later that he had called Abba Eban, the foreign minister of Israel, who was roving about the United States collecting money. Kissinger was then the diplomatic star of the whole world. He had realized détente between the two superpowers; he had made the first of his mysterious voyages to China. Now he wanted to do something in the Middle East. So he said to Eban, "Why don't you be generous? You are the victorious side. Why don't you take some initiatives on your side to get peace?" That was on Thursday, the fourth of October.

Eban answered him: "Why don't you recognize the fact that you know nothing about the Arabs. We know everything about the Arabs. Ours is the only way to teach them and deal with them—let me tell you that. Why should we make peace now, when the Arabs will not be important for 50 years."

Forty-eight hours later the war started. When Kissinger woke Nixon to tell him, they both believed that the Israelis would crush our bones. Most of the world believed it. Most of the Arabs believed it. Of course the Israelis believed it. So when they telephoned Kissinger after war broke

out, they told him: "It's only a matter of 48 hours." Two days later they talked to Kissinger again and told him: "Give us another 48 hours. We need time because it was Yom Kippur and we didn't completely mobilize, but we don't need any armaments or munitions."

Another 48 hours passed. Then it was Moshe Dayan who called Kissinger on the telephone. He said, "S.O.S. Please, Mr. Kissinger, send us 400 tanks." Kissinger called Golda Meir to confirm this request, and she said, "Yes, it was a decision by the Cabinet."

Remember that scenario. They had lost 400 tanks on the Egyptian front and one-third of their Air Force. And do you know what Kissinger told me he said? "Mrs. Meir," he told her, "we shall send you the 400 tanks. But whatever happens after that, you have lost the war. Be prepared for that." And this was at a time when everyone in the world was convinced that any Arab force starting a war would be crushed. I answer by recalling the reporter's question in London about faith and science. For my actions in 1973 came from a conviction given me by faith. I knew at the beginning what the

A Visit with President Sadat
by Frank Gibney

At 62, Anwar El-Sadat is a rare phenomenon among late-20th-century statesmen: a man who knows his own mind, keeps his own counsel, and acts on his own hunches. He is also one of the world's few remaining political leaders to whom that much abused word charisma might be justly applied. It did not always seem so. Like Harry Truman, Konrad Adenauer, and a few celebrated others, Sadat was a late bloomer, politically speaking. For almost two decades he played a courteous second fiddle to his old friend Gamal Abdel Nasser. In the end Sadat was the only member of the original revolutionary officers' group not to be purged by Egypt's moody dictator. As a result, since the Egyptian Revolution of 1952, Sadat has been able to observe the workings of Egypt's government and its problems from a variety of vantage points: as Cabinet minister, secretary-general of the Islamic Conference, speaker of the National Assembly, editor of the government newspaper al-Gomhouria, and, finally, as vice-president.

A Revolutionary Presidency

When Sadat succeeded to Egypt's presidency in 1970, few people would have taken bets on his political longevity. Egypt was still suffering in every way from the disastrous defeat by Israel in 1967. The economy was in ruin. A power struggle for the ultimate succession was going on among Nasser's other old subordinates, several of them agents of the Soviet Union. But Sadat acted with surprising swiftness. On one hand he removed political trou-

blemakers from office. On the other he repealed the repressive edicts of the Nasser era, which had kept Egyptians in a state of personal fear and economic stagnation. In 1972 to the world's surprise he denounced the one-sided treaty of alliance with the Soviet Union and in one week sent 17,000 Soviet military and political advisers packing.

Equally surprising was Sadat's sudden "October war" against Israel in 1973, which, as noted in his autobiography, In Search of Identity, he contends was, paradoxically, a necessary prelude to any kind of lasting peace in the Middle East. After the ensuing cease-fire, when later peace measures seemed to be faltering, he startled everyone again, his own people included, by his unprecedented visit to Jerusalem in 1977, when he addressed Israel's Knesset in a personal effort to break the deadlock in negotiations. U.S. Pres. Jimmy Carter's Camp David accords between Egypt and Israel were the outgrowth of Sadat's initiative.

There are still many problems involved with consummating the peace between Egypt and Israel, and Egypt's fellow Arab nations continue their formal boycott as an indication of their displeasure with Sadat. At home, however, his popularity continued. He received a striking vote of confidence in the 1979 elections. Although Egypt's staggering economic problems are by no means solved, new oil revenues and advances in both the agricultural and industrial sectors have for several years given the nation a healthy growth rate of 7 to 9%. An "open door" policy encourages foreign investment, and an computers would tell me, if I relied on science only. If I were to feed the computers with the information on the balance of power between us, the characteristics of the Israeli armament and the characteristics of our armament, the computer would tell me: "Don't even think of starting any action against Israel or you will be crushed." I knew that, but I took my decision because I had faith in our course of action. The computer alone would have advised me either to stalemate or commit suicide. But I knew both the limits and the possibilities of what God gives us in our life. So I took this action. I took it out of my inner conviction that it was the only thing to do. And before taking this course I discussed it with all our commanders—not just the chief of staff but all of them, including many low-ranking officers, so they would know what was to happen. For we had a problem there. Not only did the lower commanders not know what was about to happen but they all had a complex about the Israelis, rather like the Vietnam complex in America. And this complex I had to attack.

The October war of 1973 was for us in Egypt a historic transformation—from despair to hope,

from complete lack of self-confidence to the regaining of that confidence. After the cease-fire we initiated an ambitious program of building and reconstruction despite the economic crises which beset us. Our economy at that time was below zero because of the burdens and responsibilities of constant military preparation. Despite these obstacles we succeeded in restoring our economic path from total isolation to an open-door policy.

And since that time we have worked wholeheartedly for peace. My peace initiative when I visited Jerusalem in 1977 was not a television show or an offer of surrender, as some adolescents in the Arab world alleged. It was a unique and historic event that challenged in one confident plunge a fearful block of spite, bitterness, and bad feelings which had piled up and multiplied over a period of 30 years. Let that October war be the last of the wars.

Without that initiative the Camp David summit would never have materialized. And without the persistence and wisdom of President Carter we would never have found a path leading to a real and lasting peace.

Yet other Arabs came out with statements say-

---

economy that under Nasser had approached Soviet state-controlled totalitarianism is moving quickly in the direction of free enterprise and association with the West.

The author of these changes is a tireless propagandist for them—constantly explaining, exhorting, and admonishing as he makes his unending round of parliamentary meetings and talks with foreign leaders and prays at the mosques of Egypt's countryside. He is able to do so much because of intense self-discipline and the bulwark of a very private, family-centred life. He and his wife, Jehan, a strikingly handsome woman with a magnetic presence of her own, live simply (but well) either at one of their houses outside of Cairo or, in the summer, at their beach villa at al-Mansurah outside of Alexandria. They spend a great deal of time with children and grandchildren. Sadat exercises by walking at least one hour a day. Almost every evening he looks at a film: his only recreation. He spends a great deal of time by himself, thinking and planning.

A visit to Sadat is a memorable experience. There is a magnetism about him that communicates itself in the confines of a drawing room as surely as it does in his constant public appearance, where his power as an orator plays no small part in his success. He received me in the rambling, comfortable house at the Qanater, some ten miles up the Nile River from Cairo.

As always impeccably tailored, with a dark blue suit and a large Windsor knot in his tie, he was missing only the pipe that he smokes almost continually. That was because on Thursdays, the day we met, he fasts—abstaining from food and tobacco from dawn to sunset, in the Muslim tradition.

Sadat is gifted with an innate sense of theatre. In

a sense almost every conversation is a performance. His English is at once expressive and explicit. He often impatiently searches for words in the middle of a sentence. He is a learner, as well read in Western history and literature as in his own. His talk is peppered with references ranging from the Magna Carta to Franklin D. Roosevelt, and he entertains German visitors with quotations from *Faust*. (He learned German in a Cairo prison.) He is an enthusiast with a sense of history.

Sadat's own confidence of success comes from his conviction that he has at last made Egypt a government of institutions. He has certainly done much in that direction. Only time will tell whether the machinery of government that Sadat has rebuilt can govern on its own, without dependence on the transitory charisma of a single leader.

Frank Gibney, vice-chairman of the Encyclopaedia Britannica Board of Editors, was the founding president of TBS-Britannica, Tokyo.

ing: "Alas, the Camp David agreements have not restored Jerusalem to us nor have they established a Palestinian state." They attacked the agreements and tried to boycott us.

To them I say: Should not the people concerned sit down to talk at issue with someone, do you just let it go—or do you sit down and discuss it with the side concerned? Regrettably many of our Arab brothers can never face up to responsibility. They weep over Arab solidarity, but Moscow Radio draws up their slogans for them. Their uncompromising position is a splendid thing for Israel's hawks.

Ninety percent of the Israeli people are for peace. I told the Israeli people when I visited there that the exercise by the Palestinians of their right to self-determination poses no threat to Israel or its security. Indeed it is the only sure way to peaceful and harmonious coexistence. By contrast, the policy of building Israeli settlements in Arab-occupied territories is a serious obstacle to peace. It is ill-founded, ill-conceived, and illegal. In the Egyptian-Israeli peace treaty we set a model for security arrangements that protect the legitimate interests of all parties. Such measures are applicable to other fronts as well.

Here, in fact, was a radical difference between Menachem Begin [prime minister of Israel] and myself. Begin believed that signing a peace agreement concluded the whole affair. I replied that this was only the premise of the arduous stage of entrenching and assuring peace.

We do not accept Israeli sovereignty over Arab Jerusalem. When I spoke to the Knesset in the heart of Israel in 1977, I said that Arab Jerusalem must become Arab again. Eight hundred million Muslims do not accept Israeli sovereignty over Arab Jerusalem. This is a fact. Yet to those dwarfs who criticize us in Arab countries, I say again: I will continue to sit down with the Israelis and talk to these issues and work to reduce our disagreements, in the interests of peace.

There are those, like the insane Khomeini in Iran, who want to say that Islam is opposed to peace. Is Islam against peace, when the very greetings exchanged among Muslims are those of peace? God Almighty is Faith and omnipotent Peace. Life hereafter is peace. Believers should choose peace. This is Islam. This is the faith of our Egyptian people.

Let us review the recent history of Egypt by decades. With nations we should speak in terms of decades. The '50s was our time of glorious victory. We had our July 23 Revolution in 1952. We nationalized the Suez Canal. We became a nonaligned power. We witnessed the Iraqi revolution and the fall of the Baghdad Pact, despite its support by America, Britain, and the West. We thought our victory complete.

Yet the '60s became our time of defeat. We had to cope with the effects of the Israeli victory of 1967. And in our economy with crass stupidity we had copied the Soviet pattern of socialism. Our socialism was coloured with Marxism. Where free enterprise was regarded as "odious capitalism," naturally individual effort came to a standstill. This resulted in the passivity of the people from which we still suffer.

The '70s marked the end of our suffering. In 1975

RICHARD MELLOUL—SYGMA

we reopened the Suez Canal. We began to develop the oil of Sinai and the Red Sea—without this source of energy our country would have gone bankrupt. We could see the end of our suffering, but we had to work to create the conditions for the '80s. Now in the '80s we shall reap the fruits of our suffering and our hard work. We are just starting to do this.

In this decade of the '80s, 80% of Sinai will have been returned to us. It is rich in minerals. We have the new oil that has been discovered. In 1975 we still imported oil. We are now exporters rather than importers. We now have an income of $2 billion a year from our oil sales; by 1985 we hope this figure will be $12 billion. This year, 1981, I shall be opening the Suez Canal for the third time. The first was the original opening by the khedive Ismail in 1869. Then I reopened it in 1975 after it had been closed for eight years. Now we have the third opening. It is a completely new canal. We worked silently for five years, widening and deepening that canal. I have already opened the tunnel under the canal to Sinai after six years of work. This project is a masterpiece, one of the wonders of the world.

We live most of us in this narrow Nile Valley, occupying only 4% of Egypt's total land area. We have lived on this narrow 4% when we were a population of 17 million, then 20 million, then 30 million, now 42 million. There is rich soil elsewhere in Egypt, and we are reclaiming it, notably in the New Valley. Let us be grateful to God for the potential provided us. Yet we are truly racing against time.

The public sector, the state, cannot do this alone. We need modern agricultural companies using modern technology. But according to past concepts of socialism in this country, the land had to be parceled into state farms. God be praised, this era is over. In the past debates were held over whether owning five lorries [trucks] would amount to capitalism, with the result that no one bought any. In the past, when the government was expected to meet every need, people's attitudes were negative. That belongs to a dead era of impoverishing socialisms. Now we have an open-door policy for our economy—and democratic socialism.

Yet we all must continue to face the problems of foreign intervention. The Soviet invasion of Afghanistan was not unexpected. I had been cautioning against such developments all along. For throughout the '70s you Americans really suffered from your Vietnam complex. It was this which gave the Soviets their freedom of action. In Africa and the Middle East they have built three belts of security for themselves. They built them right under your nose. You gave them the opportunities. The first belt stretches from Angola to Mozambique. The second belt runs from Afghanistan through the anarchy of Iran, then South Yemen, Ethiopia, and finally Libya. The third belt is now under construction. Libya and Syria are starting a union together.

The Soviet Union has already signed a treaty with Syria. This would be automatic in the case of Libya. Look at the map. These three belts are clearly seen. They threaten us. We are a small country. But if the Soviets try to consolidate these belts, I shall fight.

If you in America do not again take up your responsibilities, as the first superpower of the world and the one which supports peace, all of us are doomed. We shall see the Soviet Union in the Persian Gulf as well as in the Mediterranean. We shall see them putting their puppets everywhere. And we know what it means to be a puppet of the Soviet Union. They foreclose people's dreams. They cancel out all logic. For they themselves are robots. It is only the heads of the Party who can act. They do everything.

In the "people's democracies" there is no orderly transfer of power. There are only coups. See how Stalin came after Lenin. Then there was Malenkov for only a few months—and where is he now? Khrushchev came and ousted him. Then Brezhnev took over. But he will be ousted in the same way.

Yet we still have the upper hand. The forces of peace can win. Despite all these puppets, all these countries that depend on the Soviets, they are despised and hated. They are despised and hated in the Arab world because they do not have the support of the people. I have dealt with the Soviet Union for a long time. I know that if you check them, they will pull back. In 1972 I abrogated Egypt's treaty with the Soviet Union, because they violated it. We had 17,000 of them here in Egypt, but in 1972 in one week I ordered them out.

For three years I have told the Americans this. I have said to the United States and the Western European nations that I will give them facilities to defend their position in the Persian Gulf. For the collapse of the oil facilities there could mean the collapse of Western civilization. Without this oil the factories will stop. Look at all your tanks in NATO. Without oil they are scarecrows. But we are ready to give the United States every facility to reach the Gulf states, to protect their interests.

When I was in Washington, someone in your Congress asked how much money it would cost to build a base on the Red Sea. He asked if I wanted an American base there and I said we would not. Why should we have *your* bases there? It could bring on hate for you and for me. If Johnson or Dulles had asked me this question, I would have told them, "Go to hell." Your use of *our* facilities, however, is different. This we give you on a basis of partnership—air, naval, and military facilities. But America should drop the Dulles mentality for the '70s and the '50s and cease thinking of "bases."

Of course to share our facilities with you and to cooperate in other economic matters is not only in your interest. It is in our interest. To whom will we send our oil, if not the West? Who will give us the know-how to rebuild our countries? Who will in the end share with us the nuclear energy to replace oil, if Western civilization collapses?

The Soviet Union will not give us these things. I worked with the Soviets for almost 20 years. They may have the technology to build airplanes and reach the Moon, but they have no technology for the consumer. They have new technology in the military field only. It is not deep-rooted. We have had Soviet factories here. We have now hundreds of Soviet factories which were built for us by the Soviet Union and quickly become out of date, because the Soviets have no technology at all, apart from the military.

In the '80s there must be a new peaceful order in the world. And I have a hunch that we in Egypt can participate in it. To protect this order the United States must accept its responsibilities. You Americans did not ask me for facilities to reach the hostages in Iran. But one day I came and said that I was ready to give the United States such facilities. I remain ready to offer any facilities that will help you reach the Gulf states. For the face of the United States has changed for us from that of the policeman, who represented imperialism and colonialism, to that of the peacemaker.

We should have a new order in the international economy. As I told Henry Kissinger, long before the prices of oil rose so high, why don't we call the producers and the consumers of oil together. Let us sit down together and agree upon what we need to build up our countries. Let us regulate oil prices and commodity and food prices. To whom can the oil-producing countries send their oil? Who will give them the know-how they need, if the West collapses?

If it is God's will, I hope I may help make this contribution. Let us agree, producers and consumers, on a certain level, on certain ratios we can become one family. Because all of us need each other.

That is the dream I have for the '80s. Let us hope the day will come when I can tell the whole world about my idea. Let us hope for the time when, instead of confrontation, we have *complementations*.

When I first came to power in 1970, I had to stand by myself. Our people had been taught unfortunately to be totally dependent on their leader. This was indeed their custom. When they become confident of their leader, they give him freedom of action to the extent that they ultimately become totally dependent on him. That was the situation after Nasser's death.

Gamal Abdel Nasser and I had been friends since we were 19. We were young cadets and officers together. When I was sent to jail for the first time in 1942, he took charge of the Free Officers group which I had started. I was in jail for six years. I was released in time to take part in our July 23 Revolution in 1952. It was I who gave the ultimatum to the king in Alexandria, asking him to leave. When this revolution actually took place, the dream I had had since my childhood was realized.

KARL SCHUMACHER – THE WHITE HOUSE

The Camp David agreements between President Sadat and Israeli Prime Minister Menachem Begin marked a historic turning point in relations between their countries.

We had three foes to fight against in our revolution: the king, foreign colonialism, and our own irresponsible party system, which had become dissolute and hopelessly corrupt. Four years later, in 1956, the British evacuated this country and at last ended the shameful era when the secretary for Oriental affairs at their embassy in Cairo was the real ruler of Egypt, fawned upon by pashas and party leaders.

Yet for all our successes in achieving independence, the revolution failed to establish sound democratic practice. A one-party system was set up, which turned into a totalitarian regime under the name of socialism. Nasser regarded everyone with suspicion. Anxiety gnawed continually at his heart. It was only natural, therefore, that he bequeathed a legacy of suspicion to his colleagues and to everybody. The hate that prevailed in Egypt for 18 years before I assumed the presidency was a destructive force. We still suffer from its consequences.

But Nasser was my friend. I never quarreled with him but stood by him alike in victory and defeat. In the months before he died, we spent many hours together in his home and at my house near the pyramids. "Anwar," he told me, "look to the succession of power." At that time we had just seen two surprise changes in international politics. Prime Minister [Edward] Heath in England had called an election suddenly and, to his surprise, lost. In Lebanon, according to the constitution left them by the French, they had had another election and Suleiman Franjieh won it by one vote—he was one of the bad ones. We made comparisons with Egypt. I joked with Nasser. "Gamal," I said, "what will your successor do—this poor man who will have to succeed you. What will he do in place of this giant?"

We both laughed. I was not even considered. For I had already had two heart attacks. It was clear that I would not succeed him and, indeed, would probably die before him.

Events turned out otherwise, and I did succeed him. But if we had not been close friends and not spent so much time together that last year, I would have missed many details. In particular there was our relationship with the Soviet Union. The Soviets would have denied facts or asserted things that never happened between them and Nasser. But I knew everything.

Politically and economically Nasser had left me a pitiable legacy. We had no real relations with any country except the Soviet Union. Many of our own people in the political leadership were Soviet agents. Economically we were almost bankrupt thanks to the Yemeni expedition, the Israeli defeat of 1967, and the Marxist application of socialism. We had had socialist slogans in place of social democracy. Two months after I came to power, I abolished the state sequestration of private property. In May 1971 I ordered the detention centres closed, and I put an end to arbitrary arrests. I ordered the Ministry of Interior to burn the recorded tapes of individuals' private conversations. This was a symbol of the restoration to the people of their long-lost freedom.

All this was not easy. The Soviets tried to create havoc for me. They left me not one moment of peace in those first months. So I had to use lots of power in the first stages. For some years I was—I can say without boasting—the sole guarantor of the country's security. But now everything is changing. With the help of my aides, my friends, and the cadres whom I have trained, we have now built a state of *institutions*. So I could retire at this moment. I should like to remain another year or two to achieve with my political party what I have achieved with my aides. But if I were compelled to retire now, by illness or by death, I would not be sorry. They could now carry on.

The vice-president and the acting prime minister know every small detail in the workings of this country—inside and out. We have developed a sense of teamwork. We now have a pension and retirement system, which protects our people against disease or disablement and helps their survivors after death. We have a clear view before us.

All this took me ten years to do. Our very constitutional referendum was in my opinion a turning point in our democratic course. When the majority

decided to join the National Democratic Party, the political party I deemed it my duty to establish, they were attracted by tangible achievements. They were attracted by our May 15 revolution, which eliminated corrupt centres of power; by the expelling of the Soviet military experts from Egypt; by the October victory; by the peace initiative.

I stepped into the political arena to establish a genuine democracy that would achieve in tangible realities, not merely in words, man's freedom, his dignity, and prosperity. For the same purpose I welcomed the establishment of an opposition party. We call for a patriotic honest opposition, to say "no" when it finds fault with our decisions, to help the majority redress any deviation in its course, but by resorting to proof and not defamation, to facts and not to rumours like the deceitful parties of the past. For no man is above the law. We are all responsible to the people.

This could have taken 50 years, or it might not have been achieved in my lifetime. In a lifetime of a nation, what are 20, 30, or 50 years? But all this took ten years, and I am proud of it.

Politicians are replaced. Why not? This is life. Our good friend President Carter was defeated by the vote of the American people. That is democracy. The will of the people must always be respected.

There are two species of people who do not always realize this: artists and politicians. They both want to stay on stage. The artist stays on the stage and won't leave it until the audience throws eggs at him. The politician waits in the limelight until the people in the streets throw stones. A wise politician knows when to leave. Take the case of my friend Walter Cronkite. When he came to interview me a year ago, he had already decided on his retirement, but he didn't tell me. "You rogue," I joked with him later, "why didn't you tell me then?" But I admire a man who can decide on his retirement at the climax of his success.

For my part, my only will to the Egyptian people is: keep what I have created with you—the spirit of the Egyptian family. We have been a family for 7,000 years. Whenever the spirit of the family is neglected, we lose our direction and face a miserable end. Whenever we stick to the family tradition, we shall succeed. This is the tradition of this soil. Family ties, family values, family tradition.

Egypt is now one of the happiest countries in the world. We are not self-supporting. We are still suffering from certain difficulties, from lack of services and in other ways. But because we struggle against the difficulties, we are happy. The more you struggle to succeed, the more you take out of life. God Almighty has taught us that Allah changes not the condition of a folk until they change what is in their hearts.

I have brought this country back to realize what is the mainstream of our culture: the Egyptian family and its ties. For that I am a most happy man.

DANGER SIGNALS FROM THE ARC OF CRISIS

by R. W. Bradnock and K. S. McLachlan

With a suddenness that has severely jolted the international community, instability and uncertainty have spread across Asia Minor and Southwest Asia. The so-called northern tier states, Turkey, Iran, Afghanistan, and Pakistan, have been profoundly destabilized by ethnic and religious conflict within their borders, and this conflict has already brought intervention by the big powers in its wake.

There are grave risks that the underlying tensions within this arc of crisis will prove contagious. Neighbouring oil-exporting states in the Persian Gulf, notably Iraq, have already been drawn into active involvement, but the threat of major upheaval extends well beyond the immediate area, to the Indian Ocean and the Indian subcontinent. The Iranian revolution that reached a climax in February 1979 signaled a clear warning that there was a danger of prolonged turbulence in the strategically vital region stretching from Turkey to Pakistan, designated by Zbigniew Brzezinski, national security adviser to U.S. Pres. Jimmy Carter, as the "arc of crisis."

Yet the situation was scarcely new. Historically the region has been one of endemic instability, and it was only during the 1970s that there appeared to be growing maturity and credible signs of authority.

That this authority was more apparent than real was demonstrated by the events that followed the exile of the shah of Iran in January 1979. His departure removed the chief prop to stable government in the region, and governmental authority that had seemed secure was shown to have been built on foundations of sand. In all four states, enforced modernization by rulers with scarcely any claim to democratic legitimacy had failed to win the acceptance of societies still cast in a traditional mold.

International pacts and agreements, whether within the region (such as the Regional Cooperation for Development among Turkey, Iran, and Pakistan) or beyond it (the Central Treaty Organization, or CENTO), never proved effective vehicles for either joint economic development or mutual defense. Indeed, the four states have little in common, even in respect of Islam. Iran has a predominantly Shi'ah population and now a Shi'ah government. Pakistan is officially a Sunni state, though it has a significant Shi'ah minority. Turkey has long been officially secular, and Afghanistan has a Marxist government that is ideologically opposed to Islam though grudgingly tolerant of its practice.

Internal Problems

The rise of nation-states during the 20th century and the crystallization of firm frontiers has divided ethnic, linguistic, and religious groups who formerly migrated freely across the borderlands. In an area of poor and marginal environments, pastoral nomadism was one of the few possible economic responses. Containment and control of these peripheral areas of tribal occupation proved precarious, even during periods of strong central government. As the erosion of central authority accelerated in the late 1970s, so cohesive tribal organizations in the border regions were reestablished. At times they were expressed in traditional forms, as when tribal hierarchies reemerged in place of government structures. Occasionally, they were manifested in modern political form as a party system claiming formalized regional autonomy.

The convulsions that have shaken these four Islamic countries have potentially different implications for each one's future internal structure. They also have unpredictable though profound implica-

tions for the future relationships of these countries with each other and with their neighbours.

Iran

In Iran the decline of central government authority was accompanied by revolts in those areas where specific ethnic groups of Sunni Muslim faith inhabited coherent territories on the geographic fringes of the country. For the most part these groups reacted in self-defense against the rampant Shi'ah Muslim nationalism of the Khomeini government. Regional movements for autonomy sprang up in Kurdestan, Baluchistan, Khuzestan, and the Turkmen Sahra of the eastern Caspian plain. De facto autonomy was seized less dramatically but just as effectively by a number of tribal groups in the inaccessible mountain zones of the Zagros, including the Qashqa'i and the Bakhtiari. The arm of the new civil administration simply failed to reach these areas.

The most destabilizing elements of the revolt against the alliance between Shi'ah Islam and Iranian nationalism came from those groups, such as the Kurds, the Arabs, and the Baluch, whose lands spread across political frontiers. While none of them claimed total autonomy, they did articulate

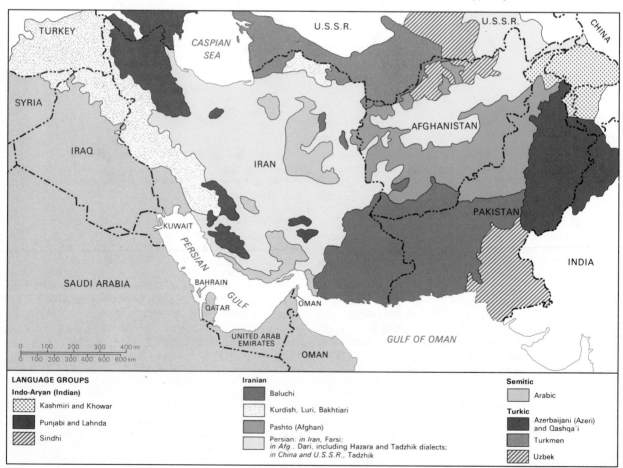

LANGUAGE GROUPS

Indo-Aryan (Indian)
- Kashmiri and Khowar
- Punjabi and Lahnda
- Sindhi

Iranian
- Baluchi
- Kurdish, Luri, Bakhtiari
- Pashto (Afghan)
- Persian: in Iran, Farsi; in Afg., Dari, including Hazara and Tadzhik dialects; in China and U.S.S.R., Tadzhik

Semitic
- Arabic

Turkic
- Azerbaijani (Azeri) and Qashqa'i
- Turkmen
- Uzbek

Anti-Khomeini factions in Tabriz, Iran, present a continuing problem in the unification of the country; linguistic and ethnic factions are present throughout the region (see map on p. 396).

specific demands for regional self-administration, including rights to linguistic and religious freedom. Two main factors have given strength to the Kurdish revolt and have precluded a settlement with Teheran. First, the Kurds worked within the framework of the Kurdish Democratic Party. This unity implied a pan-Kurdish movement. Second, the Kurds proposed a federal and democratic political structure for Iran. Arab, Baluch, and Turkmen groups presented similar programs. These had to be taken seriously, because all the tribal or party organizations could draw support, both intellectual and military, from related and sympathetic groups outside Iran's borders.

The Islamic republican regime in Teheran was profoundly hostile to the various claims for provincial autonomy. It did not wish to give up any power, to permit deviations from the Shi'ah line of the Ayatollah Ruhollah Khomeini, or to allow, in the provinces, an unfettered democracy that might prove attractive to the Iranian heartland. The Iranian government declared a holy war against the Kurds and designated them traitors. Few concessions to the Kurds or the other minorities were likely to be made by the government, despite the military weakness of the Iranian army and the Islamic militia. Continuing warfare appeared inevitable as the minorities pressed their demands, ensuring political dislocation within the country and opportunities for involvement in Iranian affairs by outside interests. Thus Iraqi backing of Kurdish and Arab movements contributed to the war of September–October 1980.

The alienation of almost half the geographic area of the country from the central government had severe economic side effects. Among the most serious were loss of agricultural output from the rainfed lands of the west lying within Kurdestan, disruption of the southern oil fields and the main Gulf ports by guerrilla action, failure of the important cotton-growing area in the Turkmen region, and diversion of funds and personnel away from development of the vital productive sectors of the economy.

Turkey

Although Turkey's internal problems in 1980 were less severe than those of Iran, the difference was only a matter of degree. Economic failure had precipitated a political crisis that threatened civil war, leading to a military coup in September 1980. The rapid rise in energy prices after 1973 hit Turkey particularly hard, and by 1980 the country's total foreign exchange earnings were scarcely large enough to cover its import bill for petroleum. Turkey's balance of payments deteriorated rapidly, leading to shortages of goods and accelerating inflation that reached to 80% in 1980.

To obtain help from international financial institutions such as the International Monetary Fund, Turkey was forced to embark on an economic stabilization program that included large devaluations of the Turkish lira and a sharp reduction in public-sector indebtedness. These measures increased domestic economic distress. A growing number of workers, estimated at three million, were unemployed, with the highest concentrations in urban areas. After 1974 there had been a growing exodus of peasant families from the land, concentration of a rapidly expanding population in the western provinces, and unrestrained proliferation of urban slum districts. At the same time, employment opportunities in industry and services were declining.

Political polarization in Turkish society grew apace from 1974. Democracy continued to exist but ceased to work. Legislation needed to run the state was rarely passed. On the streets and in the university campuses, right- and left-wing factions fought a bloody war that resulted in more than a thousand deaths in the first half of 1980 alone. From the 1960s, the left wing had gained strength as a result of poor management of the economy and the many strains in a rapidly changing traditional society. Governments tacitly supported anti-left-wing activities, including violence, and a pattern of extralegal and extraparliamentary confrontation between extreme left and right established itself. Insecurity was made worse by sharp economic contrasts between a relatively prosperous and urbanized west and a backward and neglected east, the former europeanized, the latter conservative and mainly attached to its Islamic or Turkish nationalist legacy.

Violence in political life was exacerbated by the Kurdish problem. There are some seven million Kurds in Turkey, mainly in 18 provinces of the southeast. They represent approximately 15–16% of the total population and have kept their ethnic and linguistic identity despite oppression by the majority group. As Kurdish nationalism spread in Iraq and, particularly, in Iran after 1979, Turkey's Kurds were encouraged to seek concessions from and recognition by the central authorities. After years of neglect, the Kurds had good reason to feel they had little to lose except their poverty and subservience if they joined the general Kurdish movement in adjacent territories.

The aggregate effect of these factors—Turkey's economic difficulties; the political cleavages between Communist left and fascist right, Muslim fundamentalism and secular political parties in the Kemalist tradition, Turkish elites and Kurdish nationalists; the geographic division separating Anatolian east from Mediterranean west—was an internal security problem of mammoth proportions. By 1980 the situation had hardened to such an extent that no immediate solutions were apparent. Despite the military coup of September, further chaos and insecurity appeared to threaten this western wing of the arc of crisis.

Afghanistan

Of the four states in the crescent of crisis, Afghanistan had been least touched by the forces of modernization and least effectively brought under any form of central governmental authority. Virtually accepting Soviet hegemony in 1973, Pres.

398

Mohammad Daud Khan led Afghanistan away from its earlier balancing act between the superpowers and attempted to assert his own central authority over the country. Subsequent attempts to distance himself from the Soviet Union contributed to his ultimate downfall, and the succession of puppet regimes, first under Nur Mohammad Taraki and then, from December 1979, under Babrak Karmal, pursued an ever more vigorous pro-Soviet Communist line. Alone in the region, the Afghan government of 1980 was attempting to undermine the role of religion and to assert a secular, Marxist ideology throughout the country.

What may have seemed a difficult situation to the Soviets at the end of 1979, when they invaded Afghanistan in force to quash rebel tribesmen battling the Kabul government, appeared almost insoluble as 1980 drew to a close. Far from being brief and effective, the Soviet armed presence turned out to be protracted and was seemingly unable to cope with continuing unrest and armed resistance. Unlike its neighbours, Afghanistan had never really known a powerful and effective central government. Always a marchland, it is still occupied by tribal

Despite a military takeover in September 1980, the Turkish government was unable to control the fighting between leftist and rightist factions.
ABBAS—GAMMA/LIAISON

Afghan guerrillas, members of the Islamic revolutionary movement, pause in prayer before engaging the Soviet Army in a skirmish; the fighting in Afghanistan seems likely to drag on indefinitely.

groups, fiercely independent of each other, practicing a nomadic pastoralism for which the politics of settled agricultural or urban society has no relevance, and clinging to their Islamic faith and group identity with extraordinary tenacity. For them the new Islamic movements to east and west had no particular significance. Their struggle, unlike that in Iran, had become a fight against an invader.

Yet while the problems facing the Soviet army appeared enormous and the base of popular support for the Communist regime seemed to become ever narrower, the implications of Soviet dominance in the country remained profound. Unable to fight a united battle or to agree on a civilian government in peacetime, Afghanistan appeared certain to remain a battleground of warring interests in the immediate future. For the global powers it remained a crucial piece of the southwest Asian jigsaw puzzle. The question of who controlled it was of fundamental significance for Iran, for the Persian Gulf, for Pakistan, and ultimately for India. Internally it remained the space in which nomadic tribes attempted to assert their own control and the right to retain their own patterns of living. At the end of 1980 it seemed there could be no winners in Afghanistan, only losers.

Pakistan

The rise of a new Islamic self-awareness and power in the western countries of the crescent of crisis was reflected in the political changes that overtook Pakistan after 1977, but the reflection was distorted by Pakistan's unique historical, cultural, and economic background.

Born out of the partition of British India in 1947, with Islam as its sole *raison d'être*, Pakistan has always regarded the Islamic faith as the touchstone of its national identity. In its 30-year history, religion has repeatedly proved to be the only significant factor contributing to the national integration of an otherwise extremely diverse country. In 1971 even that was insufficient to contain the regional and cultural pressures that led to the secession of Bangladesh and the emergence of Pakistan in its present form.

Yet despite the fundamental role of Islam throughout Pakistan's history, the replacement of Zulfikar Ali Bhutto's government by that of Gen. Mohammad Zia-ul-Haq in the coup of 1977 represented a real break with the established pattern of Pakistani government. In contrast to all his predecessors in power, General Zia asserted that Pakistan was to abandon the pursuit of Western-style economic and political goals and embark on the process of transforming its society into one based entirely on Islamic principles. The preceding 30 years were seen by the new government as a period of apostasy, and the secularization of government, encouraged by all major Pakistani leaders from Mohammad Ali Jinnah through Mohammad Ayub Khan to Bhutto, was looked on with contempt.

In part, the reversion to Islam was a possible op-

399

tion for General Zia because of the political and economic failures of previous governments. The tribal and ethnic minorities of the west and northwest had never become wholeheartedly integrated into the national polity. Democratic politics had frequently been betrayed by party factionalism and the assertion of regional or pressure-group self-interest. Ideologically defined groups fought with each other and among themselves. The dismemberment of Pakistan in 1971 was significant not merely in itself but also as an omen of what the country's future might be: subjection to India in the east and ultimately to the Soviet Union in the north; possible further defection of tribes such as the Pashtun and Baluchis in the west; and continued failure to provide the kind of economic growth that alone could sustain the drive to some form of secular westernization.

In this context, it is perhaps no surprise that General Zia should have seen a call for a return to the "true principles" of Islam as the proper path for his new government. Such a call might be perceived as resolving some of Pakistan's major and apparently insoluble problems. Failure to meet the expectations aroused by the much proclaimed programs of development could be deflected by the assertion that these goals themselves were inappropriate for an Islamic state. At the same time, while traditional sources of economic and military aid—the U.S. and

Western Europe—might be discouraged by the new political trends, the newly rich Arab oil states could now be wooed on quite a different footing. This newfound unity with major countries in the Muslim world might itself be seen as a protection from possible interference in Pakistan's internal affairs by either India or the Soviet Union.

Despite the support that General Zia obtained from the Arab world, the political future of Pakistan remained far from clear. The Soviet presence in Afghanistan was matched by strong pro-Soviet political forces inside Pakistan. The strength of Zia's own position was still far from secure. And, while disaffection in Baluchistan quieted during 1980, it remained near the surface.

Through 1980 General Zia continued his struggle to find ways of neutralizing political opposition internally while retaining some credibility externally. Signs that a continued Soviet presence in Afghanistan would force a reassessment of his broad strategy of external relations surfaced at several points. Outwardly, the civil situation in Pakistan remained calm throughout the year, but 1980 might well prove a turning point in Pakistan's history.

The Spillover Effects: the U.S.S.R.

Unfortunately, the minorities problem that was wracking the region was not confined to the northern tier states themselves. Spillover effects were

The hundreds of thousands of Afghan refugees who have poured over the Pakistan border since the Soviet invasion in December 1979 are straining Pakistan's resources and present a political problem.
KEYSTONE

many and serious. In 1980 the U.S.S.R. had a Muslim population of 50 million, mainly concentrated in Azerbaijan, Turkmeniya, Uzbekistan, Kazakhstan, Kirgiziya, and Tadzhikistan adjacent to the Soviet Union's southern border. Although Islam is not a dominant force in these territories, neither is it dead, despite many years of Communist control and official discouragement.

With the Muslim states showing a more rapid rate of population growth than other areas of the Soviet Union, the proportion of Muslims could rise from the current 20% to 40% or more by the year 2000. The Russian leadership could not contemplate with equanimity a revitalization of Islamic sentiment stimulated by the ayatollahs in Iran. This was vividly attested to by the rapid withdrawal of Soviet troops of Central Asian origin after the initial invasion of Afghanistan.

The Arab States of the Gulf

In 1980 the full impact of the Iranian revolution had yet to be felt. There were many indications that problems arising from the upheaval in Iran could damage the prospects for long-term stability in the region. Small but influential communities of Iranians existed in most of the Arab states around the Persian Gulf. Some were trading groups established for generations; others comprised recent immigrant labour. Their sympathies lay with Ayatollah Khomeini and the Iranian revolution, and there was a not unreasonable fear in the minds of the indigenous Arab populations that the Iranians among them represented a third column actively engaged in subverting the established order.

Iranian religious emissaries active in these communities have been expelled in recent months, the most notable example being Ahmed Abbas Muhri, who was expelled from Kuwait in September 1979. Bahrain and the United Arab Emirates were equally affected, and the former was particularly at risk since Iranian claims to sovereignty over Bahrain had been resurrected by Ayatollah Rouhani, a senior Iranian cleric. During a tour of the gulf in April 1980, the then Iranian foreign minister, Sadegh Ghotbzadeh, suggested that all Arab states in the area were formerly under the aegis of Iran and could still be deemed to be so. Continuing vigorous calls by the Iranian hierarchy to export the revolution to adjacent regions, including one by Ayatollah Khomeini's nominated successor, Ayatollah Hussein Ali Montazeri, in February 1980, did little to diminish Arab apprehensions.

However, the main threat to the Arab world arising from the Iranian revolution was not so much political as religious. Iran had gained little from its political campaign for the reversion of Bahrain to Iranian control or from its militant retention of the islands of Abu Musa and the Tunbs, seized by the shah's regime in 1971. Its appeal to Shi'ah communities in the Arab world was much more insidious and effective. Iraq's Arab population is almost equally divided between Shi'ah and Sunni Islam (the Kurds are mainly Sunni), with approximately 5.8 million Shi'ah concentrated in the south of the country. Scattered among the other states of the Persian Gulf and the Arabian Peninsula are a further 2 million–3 million Shi'ah, many of whom are Arab rather than immigrant Iranian. Shi'ah majorities exist in Bahrain and Yemen (San'a'; North Yemen). Elsewhere in the Arab world, there is a large minority of Shi'ah in Lebanon, while Shi'ah communities in Syria exert a virtual stranglehold on the government. In all, there are approximately 85 million–90 million Shi'ah in the world. Most significantly, there are appreciable Shi'ah groups in all the oil-exporting states of the Middle East.

The appeal of the Iranian revolution to the Shi'ah elsewhere in the region arises not simply from the historical cleavages between the two main branches of Islam, although these go back to AD 661 and the assassination of Ali, son-in-law of the Prophet Muhammad. Nor is Shi'ah exultation over the rise to preeminence of their leaders in Iran the main ingredient. Most Shi'ah minorities are resentful over the poor treatment afforded them by ruling Sunni elites. Nowhere is this more true than in Iraq, where the Shi'ah have good reason to feel oppressed and neglected, but this is also perceived to be the case in countries as different as Lebanon and Saudi Arabia. In Lebanon the Shi'ah occupy the least fertile land and have the fewest privileges in education and commerce. In Saudi Arabia the Shi'ah are scarcely represented in government at any level, have benefited least of any indigenous group from oil wealth, and are found largely among the labouring rather than the proprietor classes.

Social and economic resentments compound religious differences and open up a receptive audience to the revolutionary spirit engendered in Iran. This is inevitable, regardless of whether or not the Iranian religious authorities seek to export their revolution as a conscious policy. And, as the Shi'ah hierarchy consolidated its position in Teheran, the likelihood of an official drive to spread Khomeini's doctrines throughout the Shi'ah world would be enhanced and the threat to the internal stability of Arab states with Shi'ah minorities increased. Shi'ah riots occurred in the Eastern Province of Saudi Arabia in December 1979; sectarian assassinations affected Shi'ah and Sunni communities in Lebanon throughout 1980; and there were riots in Shi'ah areas of Iraq in December 1979.

It is a measure of Shi'ah importance in the current situation that the deaths of two Shi'ah leaders, the Imam Moussa Sadr of Lebanon and Mohammed Baqr as-Sadr in Iraq, were at the heart of Irano-Arab conflicts and have led to Shi'ah militancy within the respective communities. In the case of several Arab regimes, the rise of stiff Shi'ah opposition could exacerbate their existing political instability, which derives mainly from their lack of popular mandate and legitimacy. Among the Arab states in the Gulf, only Iraq had made significant conciliatory gestures to its Shi'ah population by way of general elections and specific improvements in living standards. Indeed, Iraqi fears of Iranian interference in its affairs were acute enough to encourage what was in many ways a preemptive military strike against Iran in September 1980. Equally, in the eastern part of the region, the Shi'ah minority in Pakistan forced a significant change in government policy regarding imposition of the *zakat* tax (roughly analogous to a tithe), and the Sunni-dominated government was forced into an awareness of the importance of the Shi'ah.

The Western Countries

For the West and, indeed, for all those countries that draw substantial proportions of their oil supplies from the Persian Gulf states, the effects of the crisis in Iran and the Middle East have already been apparent in erratic oil supplies and uncertain pricing of petroleum on the international market. Other problems loom for the oil industry. The Persian Gulf contributed one-third of world oil production and accounted for two-thirds of the oil entering international trade in 1979. The crucial importance of the area's oil has tended to grow rather than diminish over time. Thus the possibility that the Iranian revolution might be exported represents a double threat: such an eventuality would bring political

chaos to neighbouring oil-exporting states, and it would disrupt oil production.

Just as alarming would be a drop in oil production in the Arab states as the oil exporters attempted to placate Iran by trimming output or as Arab governments opted for the Iranian model of oil conservation. From 1979 Kuwait clearly chose to minimize its oil output and to eschew rapid domestic growth through industrialization. It is not impossible that, encouraged by the Iranian experience in oil pricing during 1979 and 1980, Kuwait could reduce its production from the 1979 level of 1,945,000 bbl per day to a level of 500,000 bbl. Reductions in output in Kuwait or any other Arab state would cause further disarray in the international oil market and open the way for a new price explosion.

The U.S. purchased one quarter of its oil imports from the Persian Gulf area in 1979, representing approximately 12% of its entire consumption. Its interests in the region go far deeper than oil supply, however. In defining the "arc of crisis," Brzezinski had strategic considerations strongly in mind. In this context, the danger signal transmitted from the northern tier countries was that Afghanistan had already fallen to the U.S.S.R. and other countries might slide the same way. The U.S. had to respond to the regional problems and the individual crises within each state by shoring up its own political and military position and supporting its local allies.

The Kurds represent an ethnic group without a country; in Iran they have continued to demonstrate and to fight for autonomy, including linguistic and religious freedom.
CAMERA PRESS/PHOTO TRENDS

In view of the bitter differences between the U.S. and Iran over the seizure of the U.S. embassy in late 1979 and the holding of diplomatic personnel hostage, the position of the U.S. in Iran remained extremely weak. At the same time, the U.S. position in Afghanistan was entirely undermined by the Soviet invasion. Pakistan, wary of accepting U.S. aid, edged toward an uneasy neutrality, rejecting a U.S. offer of arms as too small to be of value and emphasizing its commitment to the nonaligned bloc. The U.S. also made moves to reach an accommodation with Turkey and to assist its economic and political recovery. To the south of the crescent of crisis, it sought to create a set of staging posts and bases that would enable it to bring its military power to bear should this be required. Arrangements were made for the use of the former Soviet base at Berbera in Somalia. Facilities in Egypt and Oman were also available to U.S. forces, and the existing U.S. base at Diego Garcia was expanded to provide further underpinning for the U.S. position in the Indian Ocean.

Perhaps the greatest threat to world stability arising from the crises of 1979–80 lay in a paradox. On the one hand, the weakness of the four countries of the arc invited intervention by the great powers. On the other hand, for a number of reasons, neither the U.S. nor the U.S.S.R. was able to improve its position or to protect its vital economic interests. By February 1979 the eclipse of U.S. influence in Iran appeared to open the way for the Soviet Union, which had long felt the need to draw its strategically placed neighbour into its sphere of control. In fact, however, the U.S.S.R. had less political sway, less commercial access, and less reason for satisfaction with the situation in Iran than had been the case during the shah's regime. In Turkey, too, the U.S.S.R. had been unable to profit from the sharp decline in U.S. involvement and Turkey's desperate economic plight.

While control of Afghanistan might give the U.S.S.R. a long-term advantage in its relations with Pakistan, in the short term those relations worsened dramatically. In Afghanistan itself, the outright invasion of a country that was already an economic satellite and political client put the U.S.S.R. under great odium. Furthermore, at least in the short term, the area of real Soviet influence was reduced rather than increased as large parts of the country slipped into rebellion. At the end of 1980, the Soviet-supported government in Kabul controlled only the lowlands and the towns.

For the U.S. the situation was little better. The main political and economic patron of Turkish, Iranian, and Pakistani regimes in the recent past, the U.S. by 1980 was alienated to a greater or lesser degree from all three states. From being a serious competitor for the favours of the Afghan government in the period prior to 1973, the U.S. had become an insignificant political and economic factor well before the coup that brought the Marxists to power in 1978. The promotion by the U.S. government of a settlement of the Palestine problem through the Camp David accords, marked as it was by insensitivity to Muslim sentiment concerning both the future of the Palestinian refugees and the status of Jerusalem, damaged U.S. credibility in the eyes of Islamic nations, including both the northern tier countries and the Arab states, especially Saudi Arabia. Failure of the U.S. to secure release of the hostages in Iran, and particularly the disastrous outcome of its military expedition to free them, further eroded its strength and influence in the region.

Throughout 1980 the two superpowers struggled to restore their positions and reimpose stability. In doing so, they converted local difficulties into international problems and raised the spectre of a major superpower clash in the area. Since instability appeared to have reasserted itself as the political hallmark of the region, the potential for conflict with worldwide implications seemed certain to persist. It was this danger that constituted the most threatening outcome of the turmoil in the crescent of crisis.

Conclusion

The outside world tended to view the deterioration in economic conditions and political security in the northern tier states purely in terms of its international impact. Danger signals were read largely as threats to the world's oil supply or as warnings of a slide by the superpowers into conflict. Within the countries of the region, the causes of and effects flowing from their domestic crises were matters of more concern than the international implications. But the two aspects of the crisis were inseparable.

There were few remedies that promised immediate relief, and the passage of time appeared to be worsening the situation. In Iran oil resources needed to support continuing large-scale exports were running down. In Turkey overseas indebtedness had become a burden on the future. In Pakistan the rate of economic growth had dipped seriously below the rate of population increase. In Afghanistan destruction of the agricultural base by military action and an exodus from the land was eroding one of the few bases for productive economic life.

In most cases, economic failures were matched by political chaos. There was a growing tendency toward national disintegration as minority ethnic and religious groups, resentful of national regimes that failed to hear their cultural voices and respond to their economic aspirations, laid claim to autonomy. With the resurgence of powerful traditional forces and the emergence of so many problems without easy solution, it could be many years before the arc of crisis ceased to pose a threat to regional and international stability.

Keith S. McLachlan is senior lecturer and Robert W. Bradnock is lecturer in geography with special reference to South Asia at the School of Oriental and African Studies, University of London.

FOUNDATION FOR SURVIVAL

by Brij Khindaria

The bone-jarring shocks dealt to the Western industrialized market economies in recent years have raised the spectre of a chain of periodic global recessions that could make the 1930s crash look like a tempest in a teapot.

This may sound exaggerated, but it is the considered view of an alarming number of specialists. It has been voiced in such respected institutions as the International Monetary Fund (IMF), the World Bank, and the Organization for Economic Cooperation and Development. It is also the opinion of the Independent Commission on International Development Issues—known as the Brandt Commission from the name of its head, former West German chancellor Willy Brandt. In its 1980 report, "North-South: A Program for Survival," the prestigious independent panel paints an apocalyptic picture: "The world community faces much greater dangers than at any time since World War II. It is clear that the world economy is now functioning so badly that it damages both the immediate and longer-run interests of all nations."

Why has such a gloomy view taken hold among so many moderate and sober thinkers? At a time when humanity has such an unprecedented fund of knowledge and resources, why do economic crises proliferate, and why do people die of hunger, poor sanitation, or simple ignorance? There are no easy answers, but it is obvious that the economic crises of the West and the state of the world's less developed nations are intimately related.

Even a cursory analysis of the various stalemates in current international economic negotiations raises warning flags about likely economic upheavals if nations persist in beggar-thy-neighbour rivalry. These deadlocked negotiations are not only between poorer and richer nations but also between Western market economies and centrally planned economies and within those two groupings. The need is for boldness and enterprise—bold actions that break with tradition where necessary—to sustain the global economy by bringing equity to the world's three billion people in 120 underprivileged nations without damaging the richer Western and Eastern economies. In the words of the Brandt Commission: "The North-South debate is often described as if the rich nations were being asked to make sacrifices in response to the demands of the poor. We reject this view. The world is now a fragile and interlocking system, whether for its people, ecology or its resources. The world can become stronger by becoming a just and humane society. If it fails in this it will move towards its own destruction."

A World Economy on Its Knees

What has brought the world economy to its knees? Some of the answers lie in three crippling blows dealt to it in recent years, and especially in 1979 and 1980.

The worst was the realization that the leading industrial nations no longer know how to manage their internal economic affairs. Inflation and unemployment continue to spiral; spending on wages, salaries, and social welfare is reaching crippling proportions; unit costs of industrial outputs are rising; and severe jitters characterize foreign markets and foreign exchanges. Almost every government is

BRUNO BARBEY—MAGNUM

reduced to patching up problems with stopgap measures. In this volatile environment, business and industry face extraordinary uncertainties.

The effects of this drift in economic management were sharply aggravated by the oil price rises of 1979 and 1980. The oil price increases of 1973–74 were neutralized by subsequent gradual drops in real prices because of recession, inflation, and energy savings, but 1979's doubling of the real price for oil more than made up for lost ground. At the same time, there were growing fears of turmoil in the Persian Gulf area, forestalling all Western efforts to bring some predictability to the pricing and supply policies of oil exporters.

Turmoil in the Third World

The second blow came from the growing inability of regimes in less developed countries, whatever their political colour, to maintain domestic law and order and industrial peace. With the overwhelming majority of their populations living in grinding poverty, third world governments cannot allow their people to think that their nation's resources are being exploited by foreign companies or governments. There is an awareness that within every less developed country lurks an ayatollah eager to wreak vengeance on governments seen to be in collusion with foreign exploiters. As a result, Western

405

governments and transnational corporations can no longer rely on sympathetic local regimes to protect their economic interests.

Internal social and economic tensions have also increased the risks of political instability in less developed countries, and the future seems bleaker still. UN agencies predict that less developed countries will contain at least 800 million destitute people and more than one billion unemployed by the year 2000. Clearly, the Western industrialized nations, which together sell 40% of their exports to less developed countries, stand to lose heavily from third world misery—even if by some miracle they manage to put their own economic houses in order.

The third blow for the global economy was the heightened tension between the Western allies, led by the U.S., and the Soviet bloc, especially following the Soviet occupation of Afghanistan in late 1979. As a result, the world is becoming an unsafe place for any less developed country wishing to play one bloc against the other to gain economic concessions. Each superpower is more willing to twist arms to get support, and neither hesitates to gain influence by encouraging destabilization of unsympathetic governments. Such interference can only lessen the ability of weak and mismanaged states to solve their economic problems. Again, the real loser is the world economy.

The North-South Dialogue

Given this background of turmoil, strife, and uncertainty, how can the world's economic, social, and political systems be saved? Clearly, all parties must talk and keep talking, instead of retreating into autarchy and confrontation.

Many eminent world personalities, experts, and institutions have made suggestions for keeping international economic tensions within manageable proportions, and many of these suggestions have found their way into what has come to be known as the North-South dialogue. The North includes all the world's industrialized nations—both market and centrally planned economies. The South includes all the less developed countries, which in formal negotiations use the designation Group of 77 (although the Group contains 119 states). The North-South talks are less a dialogue than a series of uncoordinated but formal negotiations on a bewildering variety of subjects—monetary, financial, and trade relations, the use of science and technology for development, food, health, education, transport, communication, and environmental issues.

Although it failed to produce a real breakthrough, 1980 was an active year in North-South negotiations. The most important event was a special session of the UN General Assembly held in New York City from August 25 to September 13. The session had two main aims. One was to establish a program for "global negotiations" on all problems in economic relations between less devel-

NORBERT NORDMANN—TIME INC.

In 1980 former West German chancellor Willy Brandt presented his commission's report on the state of relations between rich and poor nations: a serious problem growing worse.

oped and industrialized countries. The other was to decide the shape of the International Development Strategy for the Third UN Development Decade (1980–90). Another significant conference was a joint meeting of the IMF and the World Bank held in Washington, D.C., from September 29 to October 4. The meeting laid the foundation for substantive policy changes by the two institutions, both of which have become important forces for development in the past decade.

The Special Session. The special session was a disappointment for all participants. It failed to decide on the topics for global negotiations, the forums where the negotiations should be held, how they should be organized, and how quickly they should be completed. Nor was the International Development Strategy approved, although substantive negotiations on it were completed.

The main reason for the failure was timing. In mid-1979, when the decision was made to convene the special session, it appeared that the price of oil would continue to rise in real terms. The top priority of Western diplomats was to get OPEC to talk, if not about pricing policies, at least about oil supplies. They had already scored some success in persuading several oil-importing less developed countries to think again about giving OPEC automatic diplomatic support. But recession in the West dashed third world hopes of gaining economic concessions, and third world solidarity again became a powerful slogan. This was especially true as OPEC steadfastly refused to discuss energy unless the West pledged to begin negotiations on all the South's economic demands.

An oil glut began to appear in the spring of 1980, and by the time the special session took place, OPEC had temporarily lost much of its ability to frighten the West. The West is understandably reluctant to demonstrate any unnecessary flexibility toward the South. Fulfillment of the South's demands would change the world's trade and monetary structures so fundamentally that the Western nations would lose control over the decision-making process. Hence, the Western attitude at the special session was one of slow-moving caution.

The key third world demand for more say in running the world's economy is a legitimate one, but placing a large part of economic decision-making power in the hands of 120 disparate and, in many cases, unstable nations carries incalculable dangers. The stability of the world economy depends heavily on Western economic health. Until economic links among the less developed countries become much stronger and more self-sustaining, every blow to the West is a blow to the less developed nations as well.

The Global Negotiations. At the special session India, speaking for the Group of 77, said the global negotiations should deal with all the "major issues in the fields of raw materials, energy, trade, development, money, and finance." The detailed agenda suggested by the Group of 77 ran to four pages and covered almost every imaginable issue. In contrast, the West suggested an agenda dealing only with food security, energy, and trade problems, including financing of balance of payments deficits. But the session never got around to discussing the agenda. It became deadlocked over how the global negotiations should be conducted.

Less developed countries want a powerful central body to initiate and monitor negotiations on various themes held in forums of its choice, including existing UN specialized agencies. The separate sets of talks would be closely coordinated, and the central body would hold final negotiations to reach a balanced package deal. Industrialized countries want to reduce any central body's role to a minimum and to hold decentralized negotiations in various specialized agencies without attempting to tie up all the strands into a package.

The Group of 77's position is based on the disputable belief that simultaneous negotiation of such complex and disparate themes is feasible and that some kind of grand package deal can be achieved. It reflects the Group's eagerness to get as much as possible from the industrialized countries in return for any OPEC concessions on energy issues. With equal conceptual fuzziness, the industrialized countries want to limit the negotiations to the ills that most threaten their own economies or that they— rather than the third world—believe to be important for third world development.

The International Development Strategy. The International Development Strategy for the Third UN Development Decade, starting on Jan. 1, 1981, fell far short of third world objectives, mainly because Western governments felt they could not make long-term commitments while recession and economic distress prevailed at home.

The Strategy, which is not obligatory, sets modest goals. Industrialized countries are asked to raise official development assistance from the current average annual level of about 0.36% of gross national product (GNP) to 0.7% by 1985 and 1% by 1990. (The target in the 1970s Strategy, 0.7%, surpassed by a few countries, although the average level for the 1970s was 0.31%.)

The goal for the less developed countries as a whole is to achieve an average yearly growth rate of 7% of gross domestic product (GDP). (The target in the previous Strategy was 6% and the rate actually achieved was 5.5%, although the poorer countries managed only 3.2%.) Exports should be increased by at least 7.5% each year and imports by at least 8%. (The 1970s target was 7% for both exports and imports; in actuality, exports rose by only 4.5% per year, while imports increased by 9%.) The savings target is set at 24% of GDP per year by 1990 (compared with a 1970s target of 20% and actual savings of 21.5% in 1980). The target for growth of agricultural production is 4% per year, while that for manufacturing output is 9% (compared with targets of 4 and 8% in the 1970s and actual rates of 2.9 and 6.8%, respectively).

Issues Under Debate

Energy remains the most difficult problem for all oil-importing countries, less developed and developed, but it has never been discussed substantively at any North-South negotiation. Apart from its own problems with OPEC, the West has been trying to get OPEC to contribute more toward third world development. In fact, OPEC has been more generous than the West in percentage terms, although the proportion fell from a 1975 peak of 2.7% of GNP to 1.28%, or $4.7 billion, in 1979. This was still small compared with the $27 billion increase in the poor countries' 1979 oil bill, however, and third world indebtedness (because of oil bills, more expensive manufactured imports from the West, and falling commodity prices) is an urgent problem.

Foreign Debt. The foreign debt of oil-importing less developed countries stands at about $300 billion, compared with $114 billion in 1973. Many countries are so deeply in debt that interest payments and service charges alone swallow half their yearly export earnings. The less developed countries have had current account deficits averaging $30 billion, or 4% of their combined GNP, for six years running, and commercial banks are seriously concerned about the risk of default.

A major challenge facing the banking system is finding ways to relend to needy countries the $100 billion oil exporters are expected to place on world capital markets annually during the 1980s. The difficulty lies not in finding borrowers but in setting terms that do not slow their economic growth. The IMF, which lends to cover balance of payments deficits, is facing mounting third world criticism for placing onerous conditions on loans. Both the IMF and the World Bank are increasing their lending capabilities. The World Bank also has an energy development fund of $13 billion, to which it may add another $12 billion.

Energy. The energy outlook for less developed countries is bleak. According to World Bank estimates, their oil import bill rose from $7 billion in 1973 to $67 billion in 1980 and is expected to reach $124 billion in 1985 and $230 billion by 1990. The real energy crunch has not yet come. It will take shape in the 1980s when industrialization in the third world brings a much larger demand for commercial energy. To make more oil available to the third world at sensible prices, industrialized countries may have to change their life-styles.

If oil is beyond their reach, less developed countries may have to turn massively to nuclear energy. This conjures up a nightmare of dangers, ranging from poor security standards and unsafe waste disposal to uncontrollable proliferation of nuclear weapons.

Food. The UN Food and Agriculture Organization estimates that food aid must be increased to 18 million tons by 1985 from the current 10 million-ton level if widespread starvation is to be prevented. Less developed countries now buy 50 million tons of cereals each year, or two-thirds of total world imports, making them a force to be reckoned with for the cereal traders of the U.S., Canada, and Australia. Third world and Eastern European needs have converted food into a weapon, but it is dou-ble-edged. Thus the U.S. banned cereal exports to the Soviet Union as punishment for the Afghanistan invasion, but a drop in foreign demand means less income for North America's farmers.

Trade. To help the poorer nations, both the European Economic Community and U.S. have elaborate schemes involving very low import duties on thousands of third world products. However, imports of third world-made manufactured goods are still discouraged by most Western nations because they compete with ailing domestic industries. This is the biggest problem in North-South trade.

The third world believes there is ample evidence to show that more people in industrialized countries have lost their jobs because of technological advances than because of cheap imports. Furthermore, one U.S. worker in 20 is employed because of trade with less developed countries. The third world also sells far fewer manufactured goods than it buys. Between 1970 and 1977, less developed country imports of such goods rose from $32 billion to $141 billion, while exports increased from $6 billion to $30.9 billion.

Raw Materials. Raw materials account for almost all the exports of 19 less developed countries and more than 85% of the exports of 76 others. Only seven less developed countries can claim that raw materials make up less than half their exports. So there is severe pressure on third world governments to seek better prices and gain more control over raw material resources. Oil, copper, and bauxite have already been nationalized in most countries, and the UN Conference on Trade and Development (UNCTAD) is currently conducting negotiations to improve producers' incomes through international commodity arrangements for

Famine continues to be a basic problem in less developed countries. The UN Food and Agriculture Organization estimates that food aid must be nearly doubled by 1985 if widespread starvation is to be avoided.
UPI

at least 18 major raw materials.

Industry and Technology. The UN Industrial Development Organization estimates that official development assistance (ODA) must total at least $400 billion between now and the year 2000 if less developed countries are to obtain a 25% share of world manufacturing output, instead of the current 10%. Although it will be difficult to attain, the ODA figure constitutes less than 10% of total investment needed. Private investors find many less developed countries unattractive because of restrictive legislation, poor infrastructure, lack of skilled workers, and lack of legal protection for their technology. Yet without such help, third world markets will not become wealthy enough to buy more Western-made goods.

Transnational Corporations. The six countries that supply almost three-quarters of the third world's manufactured exports (South Korea, Hong Kong, Mexico, Singapore, Yugoslavia, and India) succeeded partly because of help from transnational corporations. Most less developed countries remain mistrustful of transnationals, however, because their power rivals that of many governments and because they are controlled from abroad. According to the UN Centre on Transnational Corporations, such companies now control almost one-third of all world production; in 1976 total sales of their foreign affiliates, at about $830 billion, nearly equaled the GNP of all oil-importing countries. The UN is currently preparing an International Code of Conduct for Transnational Corporations.

Economic and Technical Cooperation. Less developed countries plan to hold several economic negotiations among themselves during the 1980s. The experience of the past decade has been that they have much to learn from one another, and they also wish to take advantage of each other's markets. Successful cooperation will help them gain bargaining power and correct historical distortions whereby many of them have better links with the West than with their neighbours.

Cooperation for Survival

How much money would make a difference in development? The Brandt Commission makes the following points: (1) One half of 1% of a year's total world military spending would pay for all the farm equipment needed to make the world's poorest countries self-sufficient in food by 1990. (2) Half a day's military expenditure would finance eradication of malaria in less developed countries. Even less could end onchocerciasis (river blindness), which debilitates millions in Africa. (3) The cost of one tank would provide 1,000 classrooms for 30,000 children. It could also protect 100,000 tons of rice from destruction by pests. (4) The price of one warplane could pay for 40,000 village pharmacies.

The third world already has more power than the industrialized countries are willing to admit. It lies in the teeming masses of human beings still living in misery, although their countries are crammed with natural resources and unexploited wealth. They are waiting to get their most basic human right—dignity—and that patience is wearing thin.

The Brandt Commission suggests some emergency measures to solve the most urgent problems. It calls for a summit of some 25 world political leaders to revive the faltering North-South dialogue, and it suggests levying a tax on trade or air travel or arms transfers to ensure funds for development. To those who say that such an international tax would be unworkable, the commission replies that the same thing was said of the national income tax.

The financial and technical means to feed, clothe, and house all the world's people are available, but do we have the political will, intellectual genius, and humanitarian drive to do so?

Economic cooperation today is no longer a matter of philanthropy, or even of interdependence and mutual interest. It means our survival and that of the environment in which we live. Only bold moves can put the doomsday forecasters out of business.

A writer on North-South relations and correspondent of the Financial Times *(London), Brij Khindaria is a specialist in the work of international organizations and the role of private enterprise in economic development.*

FERMENT IN CENTRAL AMERICA

by Peter Calvert

Central America was in ferment in 1980. In Nicaragua the year-old Government of National Reconstruction struggled to maintain the unity forged in the revolution against the Somoza dictatorship. El Salvador's moderate military junta found itself increasingly helpless in the face of terror from both the right and the left. Fearing contagion, Guatemala's military regime became ever more repressive, while Honduras began tentative steps toward a return to civilian government. Even democratic and prosperous Costa Rica was experiencing economic difficulties. Meanwhile, the United States looked on nervously, unsure of which way the tide was running. Long dismissed as a cluster of banana republics firmly under U.S. control, Central America was a relative newcomer among the world's hot spots. But the sources of the current unrest reached back to the beginnings of the region's independence movement and beyond.

Central America is the term given in geography to the land bridge connecting North and South America, a volcanic region formed by the collision of continental plates. In politics it has a more restricted meaning, referring to the countries between the southern frontier of Mexico and the Isthmus of Panama, specifically the five countries of Guatemala, El Salvador, Honduras, Nicaragua, and Costa Rica. Panama, which because of its past history is classified as a South American country, has so much in common with the Central American republics that it is normally considered together with them.

Common Colonial Heritage

All this area lay within that part of the world claimed by Spain under its agreement with Portugal in 1494, and the five countries of Central America proper once formed the captaincy general of Guatemala, with its capital at Antigua (Guatemala). This, in turn, was a subordinate unit of the viceroyalty of New Spain, with its capital at Mexico City. When Mexico became independent in 1821, it took the provinces of Central America with it. After the short-lived episode of the Mexican Empire, the provinces seceded from Mexico to become a separate Central American republic.

The enlightened and imaginative government of the republic proved too liberal for the taste of many of its citizens. In 1838 an insurrection led by an illiterate mule driver from Guatemala, Rafael Carrera,

MICHEL PHILIPPOT—SYGMA

411

began the disintegration of Central America into the five countries in existence today. Since then, almost every generation has seen an attempt to reunify Central America, but none has gotten further than the moment of formal establishment before being destroyed by a revolt in one or another of the states. Nevertheless, the tradition that the five states were once one country and ought to be once again, coupled with the fact that they are relatively small by the standard of the mainland Americas, has meant that writers have tended to treat them together, emphasizing what they have in common rather than what separates them.

What they have in common is their relatively small size, their common Spanish colonial heritage, predominantly rural economies dominated in each case by the production of food crops and one or two tropical export crops (coffee in El Salvador and Costa Rica, coffee and cotton in Guatemala, bananas in Honduras), an unusual degree of vulnerability to natural catastrophes such as earthquakes and hurricanes, and a 19th-century history of dictatorship and political turmoil. But even such generalizations can be misleading unless seen in perspective.

Take, for example, the question of size. It is true that the Central American countries are relatively small by American standards; however, compared with many ancient or historic nations and many current member states of the United Nations, they are not. Guatemala, for example, is roughly the same size as mainland Greece, and El Salvador, the smallest of the mainland states, is only slightly smaller than Belgium. Moreover, one of the consequences of disunification—and one of the factors that has made reunification so difficult—has been the tendency to emphasize those factors that keep the countries apart. Hence, during their relatively long independent existence of nearly a century and a half, the states have become less and less like one another.

U.S. and Other Influences

In the 19th century, an age dominated in world politics by sea power, Central America was seen by the great powers less as a land bridge than as an obstacle to travel. For the Spaniards it had always been both: an essential link in the chain of communication that ran from Spain to Cuba, onward to the Isthmus, and from there southward to Callao, Lima, and the southern continent. With the rise of the United States, and particularly after its acquisition of California, a new power developed an interest in the strategic route across the Isthmus. The Spanish-American War (1898) brought an urgent awareness of its importance to the U.S. public. But it was not until the early 20th century that politics and technology were brought together to make the dream of an interoceanic canal a reality. The separation of Panama from Colombia (1903), and the

(Left) Salvadoran guerrillas teach young boys to handle rifles. (Opposite) The polarization of society into pro- and antigovernment factions, each carrying grudges for atrocities committed on both sides, bodes ill for the rebuilding of the country. From January to June 4,000 civilians died in political violence.

LEFT, UPI; RIGHT, ETIENNE MONTES—GAMMA/LIAISON

treaty that gave the U.S. unfettered control of the canal, also gave the U.S. a vital strategic interest in Central America and its political stability. Disturbances in the area immediately to the north of the canal carried the risk that European powers might intervene there, with unpredictable consequences for the defense of the Canal Zone, now under virtual U.S. sovereignty.

The collapse of Spanish authority in the region had left one mainland colony in British hands: Belize, then rather misleadingly known as British Honduras. In the middle years of the 19th century it had seemed for a time that British influence would be extended into the Mosquito Coast of Honduras itself, but any moves in this direction were ended voluntarily by Britain in 1860. In the early 20th century German influence in Guatemala was strong but was not seen in the U.S. as a strategic threat. Instead, interest focused on disturbances in Nicaragua, which offered the only serious alternative site for a canal across the isthmus. In 1910 a change of government there brought Nicaragua clearly within the U.S. sphere of influence, just as World War I decisively put a stop to any lingering possibilities of European expansion within the Americas.

By 1920 the U.S. was unquestionably the dominant power in the area, and soon afterward its control over Nicaragua was reinforced by military occupation. Contingents of U.S. Marines had already occupied nearby Haiti and the Dominican Republic in the course of the war. It was the height of irony that U.S. withdrawal from Nicaragua in the era of Pres. Franklin D. Roosevelt's Good Neighbor Policy was to have consequences for the Nicaraguans at least as undesirable as the occupation itself. Control of the Nicaraguan National Guard that had been formed by the U.S. to keep peace fell into the hands of the elder Anastasio Somoza. This enabled him to take power in 1936 and to found the dynasty that retained political control of the country, the largest in Central America, down to 1979.

Regional Divergences

By this time, the political and social fortunes of the Central American states had begun to diverge sharply. Costa Rica, immediately to the south of Nicaragua, had had a series of liberal and enlightened presidents going back to the 1880s. Supported by a relatively well-to-do population of medium landowners, they had introduced mass education, abolished the death penalty, and laid the foundations for a democratic government that became the strongest in the region and at times one of the strongest in the Americas. After World War II there were fears of a return to a more authoritarian form of rule, but the revolution of 1948, led by José ("Pepe") Figueres, reestablished competitive party government. Further, it destroyed the basis of the

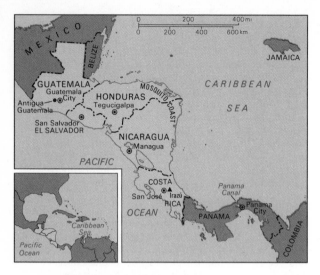

leap to the support of the U.S. after the Japanese attack on Pearl Harbor in 1941. Small and poor, they were of only modest assistance in the global conflict, although their strategic significance for the U.S. remained. But their adherence to the Allied cause was to have far-reaching consequences. The presence of U.S. forces during the war and the dissemination of the ideals of the Allies created a desire for change that was all the more keenly felt because it had come relatively late. At the end of the war, peaceful revolutions in Guatemala and El Salvador ended the dictatorships there. In these and other Central American countries, the tension between the ideals of democratic government and the actuality brought the first stirrings of the unrest that has become the dominant political fact of Central America in recent years.

Roots of Unrest

The factors leading to this unrest can be viewed on two levels, economic and political. The fundamental economic problems are those of most small, underdeveloped economies in a world of big enterprise, with producers dependent on the whims of the world market and the great majority of the people existing, as their ancestors have for centuries, at or near a subsistence level. And in an area prone to natural disasters, subsistence is something that can be put in hazard at any moment—as by the eruption of Mt. Irazú in Costa Rica in 1963, the Managua (Nicaragua) earthquake of 1972, or the hurricane in Honduras in 1974. Central Americans are often described as fatalistic. They really have no option, when their weak and underfinanced governments have no spare capacity to meet a crisis without outside help that may or may not materialize.

militarism so endemic in the region by the drastic step of abolishing the armed forces.

In the three northern states, the 1930s saw the emergence of conservative dictatorships, accompanied by the first steps toward economic modernization. In El Salvador control of the economy remained in local hands, in the persons of the members of a tightly knit oligarchy (the so-called 14 families). At the other end of the scale, in Honduras, modernization took the form of an "enclave economy" on the northern coast, where the big banana plantations of the United Fruit Co. were virtually autonomous. The bulk of the people were only indirectly affected by the changes going on around them.

These very dissimilar countries were the first to

In contrast to many of its neighbours, Costa Rica enjoys a relatively prosperous and politically stable climate. Agricultural exports form the backbone of the economy.
CARL PURCELL

In 1978 the National Guard of Nicaragua fought a losing battle against Sandinista guerrillas despite a heavy military presence; here they search a family suspected of harbouring the rebels.

The fundamental political problem is the traditional weakness of government, jealously fostered by those who fear strong rule, interrupted by the recurrent establishment of dictatorship as a method of achieving some movement. Yet, in a very real sense, both the fear of strong government and the urge to establish dictatorships are irrelevant. The most important changes in the daily lives of Central Americans during this century have taken place without reference to either. Improvements in medicine, transport, and communications, rural electrification, the spread of the sewing machine and the bicycle all have been beyond the control of the region's governments. Paradoxically, the spread of such innovations has tended to increase, rather than decrease, the contrasts between rich and poor.

There is also the problem of militarism. With the sole exception of Costa Rica, the armed forces of Central America have remained strong, to the extent that they have preempted the effective growth of political parties and organs of civilian participation, such as trade unions. Further, the armies are locked into a tradition that makes them fearful of cooperation with neighbouring states. Each sees the others as rivals and as convenient scapegoats for its own failures. The most striking example of this has been the long-standing Guatemalan claim to Belize,

which was revived in the 1930s and which has blocked that colony's advance to full independence for more than a decade. Understandably, the citizens of Belize are unwilling to risk finding themselves under the control of an alien dictatorship. Accordingly, they have sought guarantees of safety, which Britain has not been able, and the U.S. has not been willing, to provide.

Because the change and ferment after World War II occurred during a period of U.S. hegemony in the region, the U.S. has been unable to avoid involvement in the troubles that have ensued. In the immediate postwar period, it was the target of unrealizable expectations. In the more recent period, it has been blamed on all sides for every political and economic shortcoming.

The Cuban Model

It has been noted that the first wave of unrest in the postwar period resulted directly from the impact of the ideas of the Allies, the Atlantic Charter, and the UN Declaration of Human Rights. The emergence of democracy was stifled by military officers of limited imagination. Most notable was the case of Guatemala (1954), where a right-wing revolt, aided by the Republican administration in the U.S., forestalled the possibility of a land reform that could have broadened the basis of ownership.

This incident was crucial in the radicalization of those who created the second wave of unrest in the area, this time centred on the Cuban revolution of 1959. Though the Cuban government does not appear to have assisted revolutionary movements in the mainland states directly, there can be no doubt of the effect of its example and its encouragement. Throughout the region, left-wing elements had been affected in some degree by the heady optimism of the early days. In Guatemala itself, not one but three guerrilla movements emerged seeking to emulate the Cuban example.

U.S. efforts to isolate Cuba after the "missile crisis" of 1962 received powerful support from the military regimes that had seized power in the area. In El Salvador in 1960 and in Guatemala and Honduras in 1963, military juntas had taken over in an effort to forestall what they saw as a threat to themselves and to their social and institutional position. Ironically, however, it was not until after U.S. interest had been diverted by the war in Vietnam and the problems of superpower rivalry that the local political elites found themselves with a virtually free hand. They took advantage of it to crack down ruthlessly, not only on armed dissent but on every sign of political opposition. Beginning between 1967 and 1973 in Guatemala, armed right-wing gangs appeared, bent on eliminating enemies of the government. They were subsequently imitated in El Salvador, where their activities culminated in 1980 with the assassination at mass of the outspoken Archbishop Oscar Romero of San Salvador.

The emergence of the new, independent states of the Commonwealth Caribbean actually helped to foster a rapprochement between the U.S. and Cuba itself. At the same time, the crisis in mainland Central America, where right-wing governments were now firmly entrenched, grew and spread. One special grievance was eliminated. In 1968 a left-wing military regime emerged in Panama dedicated to renegotiating the terms of the U.S. presence in the Canal Zone. Ten years later, climaxing the most successful diplomatic action of Pres. Jimmy Carter's administration to date, the U.S. Senate ratified an agreement transferring the Canal Zone back to Panama.

Meanwhile, the situation in Nicaragua had reached the breaking point. Exasperated beyond belief by the ruthless self-seeking of the Somoza regime, which had not scrupled even to profit from the Managua earthquake, the citizens formed a coalition of all social groups and interests to overthrow the dictatorship. Months of fighting followed in city and countryside against the still-loyal forces of the National Guard before Somoza's regime was finally toppled in 1979. This event, and the expectation of real far-reaching social change under the new provisional government, in turn played a major part in bringing the crisis in El Salvador to a head. Certainly Somoza's fall marks the most important change in the political balance of the region in the last 36 years.

Elusive Unity

The future of the area in general, and of El Salvador in particular, is also closely bound up with the future of the most recent attempt to unify the region: the Central American Common Market (CACM), formed in 1960. Because the economies involved are very similar and the opportunities for diversification and trade are limited, the organization enjoyed only partial economic success during its first seven years. Nevertheless, in political terms, it did offer hope for better cooperation for the future.

Unfortunately, anger in El Salvador over the treatment of Salvadorans seeking work in Honduras, along with Honduran irritation over the pressure of Salvadoran immigration led to the outbreak in 1969 of the "Football War," so called because feelings had been exacerbated by an international soccer match between the two nations. Despite the small size of the forces involved and the brief duration of the war—it lasted less than two weeks—some 2,000 people were killed. Honduras broke off all trade with El Salvador and seceded from the CACM, disrupting the delicate trade balance between the interlocked economies of the five nations and crippling the hopes for regional cooperation that the organization had begun to engender. As of 1980, no peace treaty has been signed between the two countries.

It seems, therefore, that the future of Central America must be sought in diversity rather than in unity. This does not preclude restoration of the CACM. On the contrary, the organization could only benefit from increased diversity among its members. But, as so often before in Central America, politics has proved to be most powerful where most locally based, and generalizations about the future are likely to prove even more misleading than those about the past.

Peter Calvert is reader in politics at the University of Southampton and the author of Latin America; Mexico; The Mexicans; *and* Emiliano Zapata.

THE MEDIA AND THE THIRD WORLD: A FAIR SHAKE?

by Rosemary Righter

Ever since the first messenger was killed for bringing bad news, politicians have held in precarious balance the state's need for information and their natural distaste for criticism. Information shapes our world and will shape it more comprehensively still as the age of the computer advances. Much of that information comes as news and commentary: reality sifted, selected, and interpreted by the press. In Western societies, although the sparring between government and press continues, it has slowly become accepted that an open, democratic society requires a freely informed public if it is to function effectively. After World War II, the Universal Declaration of Human Rights enshrined that recognition as a universal principle. Freedom "to seek, receive and impart information and ideas through any media and regardless of frontiers" was formally listed as an essential individual right.

Inevitably, this doctrine of the "free flow of information," recent and imperfectly respected as it is, has been exercised most conspicuously by the international press, based in those Western countries where the concept developed. Equally inevitably, it has come under attack from a number of political leaders of third world countries. In the 1970s these leaders began to allege that the doctrine served as a convenient mantle for "cultural imperialism," enabling the rich countries to perpetuate an inegalitarian world order and to impose their views, their cultures, and their market economies on the vulnerable societies of the less developed world.

When, in 1976, the nonaligned governments issued their call for a New World Information Order as "an integral part of the overall struggle for political, economic and social independence," few in the West noticed. Those who did were united in viewing it as a serious threat to the free flow of information. They were right in one important respect: the call for a new "balance" involved not only the pattern of news flows but the content of news. At UNESCO, in 1974, the new majority formed by the emerging states had dismissed the principle of the "free flow of information" as outmoded, "belonging to the 19th century." For some it was not only outmoded but a fraud, practiced on them by the handful of countries whose news agencies, networks, and newspapers set the international agenda in terms of their own interests.

The Third World's Grievances

Since 1976 demands for the establishment of a "new order" have multiplied in almost every inter-

417

These Iranian schoolboys were assembled for foreign reporters, after which they began chants of "death to America"; an Iraqi bombing attack had killed 17 children in their village. The media have frequently been willing accomplices in this type of manipulation of events.

national forum, above all at UNESCO and the United Nations itself. There the question of communications—and their control—is rapidly becoming one of the most intractable areas of disagreement between the less developed countries and the West.

Two basic claims underlie the third world challenge. The first, which must be taken very seriously, is that the news and views of less developed coun-

tries should be enabled to reach the outside world directly. The facts are clear enough. Although more than 100 national news agencies exist, around 80% of the international news circulated worldwide is supplied by only four: Reuters, the Associated Press, United Press International, and Agence France-Presse. Many third world leaders feel that their affairs are sparsely and poorly reported by these agencies. To remedy the situation, they are seeking to build up their own media to serve national audiences and to compete for attention in the international marketplace.

It is the second claim that makes the issue politically explosive. This is that the role of the media must be altered radically. At home, the press must be used for the general good (as governments perceive it), as a tool for mobilizing the masses for development and the task of nation building, and as an instrument for propagation of the national ideology. It is not only the Western press that is under attack; the model of a free press itself is being rejected as alien and undesirable.

Such an approach goes well beyond the more familiar arguments of national leaders that their societies are too vulnerable to permit an independent press to function freely. And it leads naturally to the effort, at the international level, to establish controls on the activities of the "transnational" media and on the flow of news across frontiers.

News and Economics

From the outset, the attack on the information structure has been explicitly linked with the campaign, launched in 1974, for a New International Economic Order. The demand for a fairer share of the world's resources which that campaign embodies has been accompanied by outspoken distrust of Western financial power and economic prescriptions; as negotiations have stalled, it has been marked by growing bitterness. To the extent that the economic struggle sought to break the chain of dominance forged by the industrialized West, it was bound, eventually, to focus on the press. Western reporting of third world affairs is widely held responsible for the miserly attitude to trade, aid, and financial reforms taken by Western leaders. Above all, it is blamed for public indifference to the issues at stake.

However quixotic the belief that Western publics, given better information, would rush to lobby their governments in favour of a new economic order, there is force in the charge that the international media fail to report and explain pressures for change. Parochialism, of course, is not confined to the Western press. Worldwide, newspapers allocate only a quarter of their space to foreign news. Television and radio tend to be hemmed in still more tightly by the pressure of time and by editors' perceptions of market tastes.

The news agencies merely offer the basic ingredients for this thin diet. But because they claim to provide an international service, they bear the brunt of the third world's offensive. At one extreme, they stand accused of deliberate manipulation of the news in the service of vested interests. More moderate critics charge that they lack objectivity—the very basis of their claim to credibility—because they select news in terms of their main markets, judge events through Western eyes, and therefore subject the less developed world to an unrelenting one-way flow of Western ideas and preoccupations. Their third world coverage concentrates on calamity and political turmoil, neglecting or treating only superficially the steps taken in the struggles against poverty, hunger, and illiteracy which are the constants of development.

There is another side to the coin. National censorship all too frequently sees to it that publics are not "swamped" by alien (or embarrassing) news. In fact, the agencies provide far more stories about economic and social development than the press of the less developed countries cares to use. And, in a sense, the agencies are being criticized for failing to do what they have never attempted. On combined budgets of less than $400 million, the "Big Four" cannot cover the globe.

But if this is so, the justification for third world access to the international news flow is all the greater. The exchange of news may well be an essential precondition for better North-South understanding. The key question is: what news? Western editors are not merely obstructive or fanciful when they fear they are being asked to accept propaganda, to deceive their publics in the name of some larger good. The "new information order," as it is being promoted, is more likely to produce a "guided" press in the service of a kind of cultural nationalism than a richer and more diverse flow of news. The end result may be national monopolies established in the name of the struggle against international monopoly. In the list of demands that make up the call for a new information order, the missing ingredient is the very concept of press freedom.

A Rising Debate

Yet the complaints are not just the invention of tinpot dictatorships, nor are the proposals mere international rhetoric. They are becoming institutionalized and embedded in international politics.

The first moves toward the "new news" originated in UNESCO, the body of the UN committed by its constitution to promote "the free flow of ideas by word and image." In 1970 UNESCO turned its focus of attention away from technical assistance to the media, emphasizing instead the content of news and the role of the media in society. It announced a major international communications program, with the express purpose of assisting governments to use the media more effectively for development purposes. This change in policy was largely ignored by Western governments.

They were finally alerted, in 1976, by three events: the call for a New World Information Order issued by the nonaligned nations; the first of a series of UNESCO intergovernmental conferences on communications policy, held in Latin America; and a UNESCO "declaration" on the media, which came before its General Conference that autumn.

The declaration was something of a fluke. It arose not out of UNESCO's communications program but from a Byelorussian proposal of 1972 aimed at bringing pressure on foreign broadcasters beaming programs to the Soviet Union and Eastern Europe. But because of its timing, what began as a narrow East-West quarrel rapidly developed into a symbol of North-South disagreement on the media's role. The 1976 draft, in the name of such worthy goals as the promotion of peace and the fight against apartheid, imposed duties on the media and required states to use their power to see that the media conformed. The key paragraph said that "States are responsible, in the international sphere, for all mass media under their jurisdiction."

The proposed declaration challenged Western assumptions in two ways. It advocated the setting of international standards for and state control of the media; and its existence forced debate on Western governments, which do not believe that questions of news content and news values belong on the intergovernmental agenda at all. The declaration thus came to symbolize the growing pressures against the free-flow principle. In the confrontation that resulted, genuine grievances became obscured by the rhetoric of freedom versus sovereignty.

At the 1978 General Conference of UNESCO, to the surprise of most observers, the challenge of the declaration was deflected by the negotiation of a new text that switched the whole focus of the original, eliminating all references to state control and emphasizing human rights, diversity of news sources, the free flow of information, and access to news sources. The result was widely interpreted as a victory for the West.

So, in a sense, it was, although the final document was little more than an exercise in squaring the circle. In Western eyes, the fact that the basic issues were not addressed was an advantage, since it avoided the pretense that a UN resolution could reconcile the fundamental conflict between those who view the press as an instrument of state power and those who see it as a guarantee against the abuse of power. But to win agreement on the new text, Western negotiators assured the third world nations that their aspirations for "a new, more just and more effective world information and communication order" would be taken seriously, and they promised aid for communications development. A little time was thereby purchased.

The phrasing of the assurance, which took days to negotiate, was deliberate. By now, the proponents of a New World Information Order had formulated some of its key elements in such a way that Western negotiators believed acceptance of the slogan meant, by implication, acquiescence in the concept of state control of the media. The most explicit formulation had come from Mustapha Masmoudi, who as Tunisia's secretary of state for information had chaired the nonaligned governments' information group in 1976. By 1978, as Tunisia's representative at UNESCO, he had become the chief negotiator for the third world voting group. Some

months before the General Conference, UNESCO had provided him with "nonaligned experts" (coming, it turned out, from Cuba, Vietnam, and East Germany) to assist him in setting out the goals of the "new order."

Masmoudi's paper began by redefining communication as "a social goal and a cultural product and not as a material commodity." Each nation "should choose its information in accordance with its own realities and requirements" and should have power to regulate the collection, processing, and transmission of news across national frontiers. "Abuses" of the right of access to information should be prevented and, to that end, "appropriate criteria" should be devised to ensure that news selection was "truly objective." In the same way, "the right of those receiving information" (the public) should be regulated "to ensure free and balanced flow of information." The new "news" would, of course, be "an essential corollary of the New International Economic Order."

The MacBride Report

Masmoudi had a target audience. At the height of the confrontation over the media declaration in 1976, the director-general of UNESCO, Amadou Mahtar M'Bow, was invited by the General Conference to conduct a survey of communications problems. His response was to set up an independent International Commission for the Study of Communication Problems, to report to him in 1980. The 16 members, including Masmoudi, met eight times over two years under the presidency of Sean MacBride, Irish statesman, lawyer, holder of both the Nobel and Lenin peace prizes—a man with a rooted belief in the power of the media and the possibility of channeling that power in the cause of world peace.

Nothing escaped the MacBride Commission's purview. It was to look at the totality of communications, considered, M'Bow suggested, as a "sociocultural problem" with "political, ideological and philosophical" dimensions. But its mandate was not entirely open-ended. The members were to seek ways of establishing a new information order and, while they were at it, to consider how the media could be better used for objectives ranging from education to "safeguarding peace."

Born in controversy, the commission could not have been expected to resolve the dichotomy between two approaches to information, but the report that finally surfaced in 1980 was a hybrid that actually sharpened the controversy. Voluminous, indigestible, and ambiguous as it was, it could not obscure the internal contradiction between its professions of respect for the principle of freedom and the didactic and paternalistic character of many of its recommendations. MacBride replied to Western critics by pointing to the pieties scattered throughout its 500 pages, to its condemnation of censorship and its insistence on free access to news

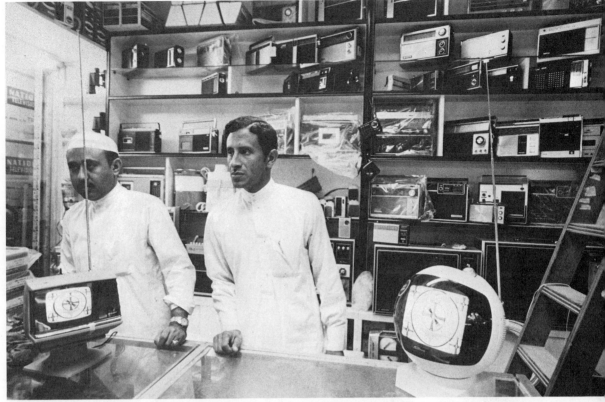

ALAIN NOGUES—SYGMA

Many nations that are dissatisfied with the media coverage given their countries by Western newsmen are building up their own communications networks so that they may control the content of the news.

sources for journalists. But where it proposed action, the report betrayed a passion to regulate which impinged directly on the practices of free reporting.

Journalists, it said, must be free; at the same time, they should promote friendly relations between states, foster cultural identity, enhance the dignity of nations and peoples, respect national sovereignty, and support just causes such as disarmament and liberation movements. Governments, it said, should formulate "comprehensive communications policies . . . linked to overall social, cultural, economic and political goals." Communication was to become "an instrument for creating awareness of national priorities."

According to MacBride, the commission was concerned "that freedom of information as a doctrine has sometimes been 'misapplied' or 'narrowly interpreted.' " One aspect of the report's proposed remedy was that "effective legal measures" should "circumscribe the action of transnationals [including news organizations] by requiring them to comply with specific criteria and conditions defined by national legislation and development policies." Who was to decide whether or not a news report so conformed? The recommendation constituted an open invitation to governments.

In a report that was intended to be interpreted and used, what mattered was not so much the quality of its analysis as the hostages it offered to governments and to UNESCO, whose future strategies it was intended to influence. To governments, which by nature love the idea of centralized planning, the report offered encouragement in harnessing news to the service of national policy. To UNESCO, it suggested that the policy of helping governments to do this should be strengthened. Further, it encouraged UNESCO, as an intergovernmental body, to continue concerning itself with international standard setting and with the content of news. Characteristic of the report's ambiguity was its failure to define what a New World Information Order actually meant. But on balance, its proposals for reform were weighted in favour of the many forces, at both the national and the international level, that aimed to limit the public's freedom of choice in the name of the public good.

Belgrade, 1980

With such ammunition it was perhaps inevitable that the next UNESCO General Conference should mark the watershed between the uneasy truce that followed agreement on the 1978 declaration and the next stage of the campaign for a New World Information Order. The détente had been fragile anyway. Western promises of assistance to third world communications had, with limited exceptions, remained promises, although efforts had been made by at least some of the international media to improve the quality and sensitivity of their third world reporting.

Western hopes before Belgrade had been that pressures for a "new order" could be rechanneled. But the heart of the essential, never articulated, bargain was that the West was prepared to help build up the third world's media if its leaders would refrain from seeking to define the New World Information Order. That bargain fell apart at Belgrade. A small group of less developed countries, led by Iraq, Cuba, Tunisia, and Venezuela, pressed toward a definition. They insisted on including a statement of principles in a resolution on the Mac-Bride Report, and Venezuela pushed through a resolution asking the UNESCO secretariat to prepare a fuller definition of the "new order" with a view to producing another declaration. In fact, a secret text had already been prepared, calling for regulation of international news agencies and for the right of states to use the media for propaganda and to take measures to "protect" themselves against reporting that was deemed "irresponsible," "distorted," or likely to harm national interests.

By the end of the conference the West—again unprepared and without a positive strategy—had agreed to accept a central role for UNESCO in communications; had agreed to the new international program; had been forced to accept increases in UNESCO's budget; had accepted defeat when they tried to divert funds from communications research to technical projects; and had concurred, without a vote being taken, on the MacBride resolution, which included a number of "basic considerations." Strikingly absent from these considerations were references to the free flow of information and ideas or to freedom from censorship and government control. Only Switzerland, the U.K., West Germany, and the U.S. resisted compromise, and only the U.K. maintained its opposition to the end. The net result was that a "New World Information Order" would now be defined by politicians.

A gun battle breaks out in the streets of El Salvador. Third world nations complain that the only images of them presented internationally by the major Western news sources are those of political turmoil and natural disaster.
ASLAK AARHUS—GAMMA/LIAISON

Western newsmen were expelled from Afghanistan soon after the installation of Babrak Karmal in 1979. Coverage of the Soviet invasion thenceforth was sketchy and second-hand.

BORREL—SIPA PRESS/BLACK STAR

Shaping the New Order

The technological revolution in communications looming in the 1980s meant that changes in news flows and news structures were inevitable. The world was moving toward a "new order" of some kind. It was in this context that international moves to regulate the media were most disturbing. It was natural for Western governments to hope to avoid a potentially rancorous ideological debate, but the chief lesson of the 1970s was that absentees have no influence.

If, in the 1980s, governments moved further toward shaping their national media to official ideologies (as had already happened in revolutionary Iran), the "new order" threatened to bring with it a positive manipulation of the media that went far beyond mere censorship. Much more was at stake than the fortunes of the Western press. At issue was the ability of citizens, in less developed countries as in the West, to make their opinions heard and to choose on the basis of knowledge. This fundamental right of access, which so much of the rhetoric obscured or ignored, was imperiled as the decade began by a mistrust of Western values and lifestyles that made freedom itself a suspect word, synonymous with entrenched privilege.

Rosemary Righter is development correspondent of The Sunday Times, *London. She is the author of* Whose News? Politics, the Press and the Third World *and co-author of* The Exploding Cities.

AMERICAN INGENUITY– DOES IT STILL THRIVE?

by Neil P. Ruzic

The pursuit of ingenuity in the United States is faltering. Fewer new technological enterprises have been started in recent years, and national productivity actually decreased for the first time in 1980. But if Yankee ingenuity is not entirely well, it is still very much alive. The U.S. still produces more Nobel laureates each year than the rest of the world combined. It continues to lead the world in computers, communications, space technology, electronics—where it was first to develop the transistor, integrated circuits, and microminiaturized circuits—chemicals, construction, agriculture, and medicine. It also leads in the exciting new fields of biological innovation, including recombinant DNA or "genetic engineering."

Meanwhile, social innovation takes its usual back seat to both physical and biological technologies. But that is a commentary more on humanity in general than a divergence between Americans and other nationals in comparative degrees of ingenuity.

Energy

While physicists struggle with diverse methods of controlling the ultimate power source—nuclear fusion—engineers are at work on fuel cells, hydromagnetic power, the extraction of oil from shale, new catalysts, synthetic fuels, and a variety of methods for harnessing the wind and sun.

Giant commercial sailing ships are returning to the oceans to fight increases in diesel fuel costs. These new cargo vessels are wind-assisted diesel-powered craft, saving 10 to 40% of a typical fuel bill. Under computer control, sails and engines work together to keep a ship cruising at a constant 12 knots. Instead of tacking to catch the wind, as did the old clipper ships, the new vessels use wind power whenever possible to reduce engine load; but the engine never stops completely, and the ships travel in straight paths. In most designs the sails are set in winds up to 40 knots, folding up within two or three minutes in heavier winds.

The design pioneered by Dynaship Corp. of Palo Alto, Calif., sets or furls the sails with power rollers located inside hollow masts. The rollers and rotation of the mast itself are controlled automatically from the bridge—no seamen climbing yardarms here. The first new U.S. sail-freighter was scheduled to be the 450-ton "Patricia A." Four sails ranging from 16 to 50 ft in width will assist the 170-ft freighter across the Caribbean starting in April 1981.

The U.S. National Aeronautics and Space Administration (NASA), which has an active program to transfer ingenious ideas from the space program to

424

private use, built the world's largest wind-turbine generator at Boone, N.C. At wind speeds of 25 mph on a tower high over the Smoky Mountains, its 200-ft rotor produces 2,000 kw, enough to power several hundred homes.

Meanwhile, private U.S. inventors developed two ingenious methods to speed up the wind for wind turbines. Since the power in the wind is proportionate to the cube of its velocity but only to the square of the rotor diameter, it pays to increase wind speed and use smaller, faster rotors. One method, devised by Alfred Weisbrich of Windsor, Conn., employs a stack of hollow toroids as the top of a building, silo, or tower. Each toroid is shaped something like an automobile wheel without the tire. The ambient wind is entrained and accelerated around the channel formed by the flanges of each "wheel." Two wind turbines are placed there, mounted on a circular track, to keep the rotors headed into the wind.

The other wind augmenter, pioneered by Pas Sforza of Huntington, N.Y., uses a delta wing to build up vortices of air. The delta wing, in the shape of an isosceles triangle, is inclined about 22° to the ground. On a stationary surface, such as a large roof, vortices strong enough to be termed miniature tornadoes are created toward the base of the triangle even when the wind is moderate. In a typical design twin rotors are placed at these focal points, where they turn in opposite directions atop the delta roof. Both the toroidal arrangement and the delta wing increase wind velocity by more than 50%, resulting in about a fourfold increase in electrical or mechanical power.

Among the many designs for generating solar power are saltwater ponds used as heat exchangers. As the Sun's radiation heats the pond, the salt dissolves, making the heated water heavier and keeping it at the bottom. A top layer of fresh water remains relatively cool through evaporation and a cooling system. Southern California Edison Co. planned to employ this design in a station that would generate 5,000 kw by mid-1981.

Transportation

The "Gossamer Penguin," the world's first completely solar-powered manned airplane, flew for the first time on April 29, 1979. Designed by Larry Mauro of Santa Clara, Calif., the craft was fitted with 500 solar cells, a helicopter battery, and a small electric motor.

While solar cells have a long climb on the efficiency scale ahead of them, the dream of efficient electric automobiles for long distances is at hand. The breakthrough was the successful laboratory testing of a new battery at Lawrence Livermore National Laboratory. The battery uses air, water, and aluminum plates. Instead of being recharged it is refueled periodically with tap water. Recharging consists of replacing the aluminum plates, which are consumed in operation. This would have to be done every 1,000 to 3,000 mi, depending on their thickness. The Livermore engineers were working on a design that would allow the plates to be replaced in 15 minutes.

Most electric cars are powered by batteries that have to be recharged overnight after driving about 150 miles. The new aluminum-air battery, weighing just under 1,000 lb, would allow long-distance driving. A five-passenger electric car moving at 55 mph would stop to "refuel" (with about six gallons of water) approximately every 250 mi.

Meanwhile, at Garrett-AiResearch in Torrance, Calif., flywheels were being adapted to electric cars to give them improved acceleration and start-stop capabilities. A car sponsored by the U.S. Department of Energy featured a unique continuously variable transmission and all-fibreglass chassis.

Transportation research inches forward every day with progress made in high-strength plastics, hovercraft, hydrofoils, fast submarines, automobiles with computer-controlled injection for greater fuel economy and fewer pollutants, wheelless 300-mph rail cars, and vertical- (and short-) takeoff-and-landing aircraft. Air buses, of which the Boeing 747 was the first, were being designed to carry 1,000 or more passengers.

Ocean Exploitation

The need for desalination in freshwater-poor regions like the Caribbean is obvious. But the scarcity of fresh water is becoming worldwide. The U.S. is expected to require 29,000,000,000 gal of desalinated water a day by the year 2000.

Reverse osmosis and vacuum stills are in use today, but more cost-effective methods are needed. One ingenious idea for a solar still, developed by Philip Youngner at St. Cloud (Minn.) State University, boils water at 150° F (65° C) at reduced pressure. The water is heated in a solar pond and then passes through an intricate piping system that creates a vacuum in a vertical pipe by the falling motion of entrapped air bubbles in the water. A specially designed bellows pump lifts the distilled water to a heat exchanger, where it is cooled by indirect contact with ambient ocean water. Energy for the pumps is expended only when the procedure is being started. Afterward, no energy is required other than the warmth of the solar pond. The result is distilled water projected at less than $2 per 1,000 gal, a remarkable improvement over conventional desalinators.

Many designs for seafarms are being proposed. One grows shrimp in a symbiotic relationship with seaweed. The seaweed adds to the water oxygen that the shrimp require while using the shrimp metabolites and carbon dioxide as nutrients. Seaweed is grown for its gels of carrageenan and agar, used as additives in some 10,000 food products as thickeners, emulsifiers, and stabilizers.

Not only does the seaweed contribute oxygen to the system but it also provides shade, hiding places, and a portion of their diet to the shrimp. By grow-

In Boone, North Carolina, a huge wind turbine—each blade is 100 feet long—generates enough electricity for 500 average households; it was built by the General Electric Space Division.

427

ing two crops in the same structures at the same time, profitability of the seafarm is approximately doubled.

The oceans also are being exploited for the nodules found on the seafloor that are rich in manganese and nickel; for ocean thermal energy conversion, in which the difference in temperature between the cold bottom layers and warm surface is used to produce electricity and distilled water as a by-product; and for growing food crops on land by gradual adaption to salt water. With some 80% of the Earth's animal life living in the oceans, pharmacologists are entering the sea in diving masks to search for new drugs. Anticancer substances from sea invertebrates, antibiotics from sponges and coelenterates, immunosuppressive activity in tunicates, and prostaglandins from the common sea whip are among the examples of marine drugs.

New ocean devices worthy of mention include underwater robots and a new compact seawater hydraulic motor. The motor, developed by Westinghouse Electric Corp., uses seawater as the working fluid rather than oil, thereby eliminating pollution and fire hazards. The motor can be used under water for such purposes as drilling holes in the seabed for installing dock pilings.

Space and Communications

NASA was finding more and more uses for its Landsat remote-sensing satellites, which acquire voluminous data about features on the Earth's surface from orbital altitudes above 800 km (500 mi). The satellite's exceptional utility results from its sensitive onboard detectors, which pick up energy emitted from features on the land. Landsats make agricultural inventories, prospect for new oil and mineral resources, monitor pollution, and improve the accuracy of maps.

Bell Laboratories introduced designs for sending electronic mail and other information as packets of digital data by using narrow microwave beams from satellites. Xerox completed technical specifications for "Ethernet," a communications network that would link various manufacturers' machines within offices.

Cable television, picturephones, interoffice communications, and the electrical transmission of newspapers are examples of American ingenuity at work. Mobile radio telephones soon will be widespread following the recent innovation by AT&T of using a series of low-power transmitters, each serving a limited area of "cell," instead of relying on a single powerful radio transmitter to link local mobile-home users with regular telephone lines. The new system permits a number of mobile-phone conversations on the same channel at the same time but through different cells, without interference. As a vehicle travels from one cell to another, its calls are handed off automatically to the new cell. A computer assigns channels in such a way that the low-power transmissions do not overlap.

Computers and Robots

Probably the prime beneficiary of the U.S.'s early lead in space technology has been the computer. The great scientific discoveries of the past two decades, in antibiotics and contraceptives, in pulsars and astrophysics, in the chemistry of new materials, in the fundamental knowledge that spurs tomorrow's progress—all would have proceeded, if at all, on a much lower level of awareness without space-stimulated computer technology.

Computers take over more jobs daily. Approximately 200,000 microcomputers, called "microprocessors," already have been sold for home use. They could become as standard as the telephone. They can answer personal correspondence, cross-index journals, keep a log of people talked to on the phone, dim and brighten living room lights, open and close the drapes, balance the checkbook, keep track of investments, update the Christmas card list, collate menus, play electronic games, report on water seepage, and lock the front door at night.

Computerized robots today work the assembly lines in much of the nation's automobile and aircraft factories. Rows of sleek, smoothly articulated arms swing out, surround a car, dip forward with pneumatic air bursts, and weld metal to metal. At McDonnell Douglas in St. Louis some two dozen acres of milling machines noisily grind grooves, slots, and intricate patterns in airframe parts to a tolerance of 0.0025 in. All those machines work virtually alone, watchdogged by master computer-robots that make decisions.

Construction

Housing developments might be built better and more economically if they were prefabricated at a factory at the development site. In this regard Leon Blachura of Clarkston, Mich., obtained a patent for a "house leveler." He envisions newly built houses being carried and lifted into place by big cranes, set down on prepared foundations, and leveled by jacks built into perimeter frames. A developer might start by placing houses farthest out, working in toward the factory along semifinished roads. When all houses were completed, the factory could be converted into a community building.

NASA developed a flat electrical wire for spacecraft that is now being used along baseboards and under carpets in wiring homes and offices. Because it is very thin, the wire can be mounted on the surface of walls and floors instead of inside them. One version of the wire is so thin it can be completely hidden by paint. Installation costs are reduced significantly by using such wire, especially in remodeling projects.

Also derived from space technology is an improved inorganic paint for coastal bridges that are subject to extreme corrosion from seawater spray. Zinc-rich coatings with both organic and inorganic binders have been tried in the past. But organic

The "Gossamer Penguin," the world's first solar-powered aircraft, flew for the first time in 1979; exploiting the possibilities of fuel from nonfossil sources is the wave of the future.

paints do not last as long and require a finish coat, while inorganics normally are more difficult to apply but require only one coat. The unique inorganic zinc-dust coating developed by NASA for painting spacecraft gantries is formulated with a potassium silicate water-base binder loaded with zinc particles to provide uniform coverage in a single coat. One gallon of the paint covers 375 sq ft, almost double the usual coverage for inorganic paints. And the paint is expected to last about twice as long. It is being tested on the Golden Gate Bridge in San Francisco.

Also affecting construction, a "glue revolution" is under way in the United States. Nuts and bolts, nails, and rivets are being replaced by synthetic superadhesives—epoxies, silicones, cyanoacrylates, anaerobics, and hotmelts—emerging from the nation's polymer chemical laboratories. Half the shoes made in the U.S. are put together with these new adhesives. They stick fenders to hoods and hold computer frames together.

Safety

"Firefly," a lightweight, portable fire-fighting module designed for combating shipboard or dockside fires, is being manufactured by Aviation Power Supply Inc. of Burbank, Calif. It can be mounted on a light truck for use by local fire departments or transported by helicopter to hard-to-reach fire scenes such as forests, high-rise buildings, or offshore oil rigs. Within a compact package it has everything needed for fire fighting: its own pump, which delivers 2,000 gal of water per minute; a fast-starting gas turbine; hoses; monitors; nozzles; protective suits; and other equipment.

A patent was granted to D. G. Dalziel of Lake Forest, Ill., for a telescoping and pivoting arm to swing out from under the belly of a helicopter. The craft thus could reach places otherwise inaccessible, such as alongside tall buildings or mountain overhangs. Harnesses, cages, or life vests could be attached along the arm to reach endangered people.

Among the many security devices being developed to fight crime is one produced by Sentry Products Inc. of Santa Clara, Calif., called SCAN, for Silent Communications Alarm Network. It is a signaling device that looks like a pen and emits a silent, ultrasonic alert signal. The signal activates a series of receivers interconnected with a constantly monitored master console, such as in a school principal's office. An outbreak of violence in a high school triggered the development of SCAN.

Defense

Among the few ingenious but nonclassified recent devices for military defense is the radar-foiling airplane appropriately called "stealth." Rather than a single invention, stealth is a series of design improvements. The smaller a plane, the less surface it presents to radar, and so stealth aircraft are small. Because engine pods and other projections and sharp angles reflect radar well, stealth is ultra-streamlined. Since radar picks up metals easily, stealth is made of a nonmetallic composite of graphite, epoxy resins, and asbestos filaments that absorb and diffuse radar waves. The design also insulates hot engine parts to shield them from infrared or heat-seeking missiles. The exhaust nozzles are bent at odd angles to disperse the fumes so as to confuse heat sensors. Finally, computerized devices send out confusing radar signals.

Recombinant DNA

By far the hottest field in biology is "genetic engineering" or "gene splicing," achieved by recombinant DNA (deoxyribonucleic acid) technology. In this process a gene from the DNA of one organism is combined with the DNA of another. For example, the DNA for a desired product is inserted into the DNA of a laboratory strain of a common bacterium. The bacterium, following directions from the new DNA, then produces the new product.

U.S. biologists are applying this technology in several ways. For instance, instead of crossbreeding to improve crop plants, they are performing gene-splicing experiments that can have several desired effects. These include increasing food yield, reducing water requirements, speeding growth so that two crops can be raised in a single season, and developing bacteria capable of nitrogen fixation in order to eliminate the need for fertilizer. To grow fuel, genes are being recombined so that alcohol can be produced from vegetables without recourse to the low efficiency of fermentation. Nonrenewable raw materials can become renewable ones through recombinant DNA techniques for the manufacture of plastics and organic chemicals. Gene splicing even offers potential solutions for tranforming the genes responsible for toxic wastes into harmless or useful materials.

Most successes so far have been for treating disease. For example, insulin—which when derived from cattle causes allergic responses in 20% of diabetics using it—has been produced that is identical to that made by the human body. Human interferons, natural defense products made by the body in reponse to viral infections, also are under investigation, and synthetic versions of these substances are being developed by means of recombinant DNA technology.

Antiviral Drugs

Researchers are out to kill viruses that cause everything from the common cold to some kinds of cancer. One of the most promising approaches concerns "immunopotentiators," which increase natural defense mechanisms.

For instance, Newport Pharmaceuticals International Inc. of Newport Beach, Calif., developed a new drug called "Isoprinosine." It enhances cellular immunity, potentiates the antiviral action of interferon in the body, and inhibits the growth of viruses in a cell by blocking the translation of viral messenger-RNA (ribonucleic acid) on the host cell.

Health Devices

One of the most effective spin-offs from the U.S. space effort is the cardiac pacemaker that can be charged. An outgrowth of miniaturized solid-state circuitry developed for spacecraft, some 30,000 pacemakers are implanted in the chests of heart patients each year. These pacemakers formerly had to be removed surgically every couple of years for recharging. Now they are rechargeable through the skin by inductance. Once a week the patient simply wears a charger vest for an hour to recharge his pacemaker. Because recharging can be done frequently, only one cell is required and the size of the pacemaker is half its former thickness, weighing only two ounces.

Also introduced recently was an advanced cardiac pacing system that allows a physician to reprogram a patient's implanted pacer without surgery. Called "Programalith" and made by Pacesetter Systems Inc. of Sylmar, Calif., the system has a two-way communications capability, permitting the device to be fine-tuned to the patient's changing needs. The device uses technologies originally designed to send coded instructions to unmanned satellites and to receive messages back from them.

Other examples of ingenuity in medicine and health care include an improved physician's portable "black bag," consisting of an electronic vital signs monitor, electrocardiogram recorder, equipment for minor surgery, along with the usual stethoscope and drugs. O. A. Battista, president of Research Services Corp. of Fort Worth, Texas, patented "Landel" disposable contact lenses, wound and burn dressings, bioassimilable bone dressings, and high-foam dental creams in which millions of tiny bubbles trap bacteria and food particles so that they can be flushed away efficiently.

Stimulants of Innovation

Turning toward social innovations, Battista is starting an "Olympiad of knowledge." Similar to the Olympic Games of sports, his proposed annual knowledge competition would encourage and recognize competitive achievements of human minds and discover solutions to problems facing mankind.

The annual IR-100 competition, started by Neil Ruzic, gives recognition to the developers of the 100 most significant new technical products of the year. The products themselves are on display each year for a month at the Museum of Science and Industry in Chicago.

Ruzic's "Island for Science" is a subtropical island base established to work out practical ideas for improvement in near-ocean living conditions. U.S. innovators associated with the new facility include those described earlier working on augmented windmill systems, shrimp and seaweed mariculture, solar desalination, and marine pharmaceuticals.

Economics

Often working independently and surreptitiously, many Americans have established an "underground economy" in the face of high inflation and taxation. It consists of barter arrangements between professionals, nonrecorded tips, under-the-table cash payments for services, and black-market activities—all designed to elude the tax collector. While nothing to be proud of, it is an example of ingenuity that cannot be ignored. Economists estimate that this subterranean economy in the U.S. is as large as 27% of the gross national product. That would approximate $700 billion.

Legal economic innovations include the variable-rate mortgage to help the beleaguered home buyer; interest rates are tied to an index of lenders' cost of money. An affiliate of the First Boston Corp. developed a novel way for corporations to issue bonds in a fast-fluctuating market. Securities are sold to investors on a trial plan. Instead of putting down the full purchase price for a bond, an investor pays only 25%. After six months or so he or she has the option of completing the purchase or losing the down payment.

Work sharing has proliferated among companies hit by decreased production. About 2.2 million workers in 1980 shared work schedules with co-workers. For instance, at Pan American Airways flight attendants fly one month and then are laid off one month but retain their seniority.

Peace

Satellites that make inspection possible render treaties between nations more meaningful. Another suggestion in the interest of peace is to turn the entire armed services of the United States into a combination defense force and peace corps. With peace—and defense—as its mission, the military would continue its armed presence but in times of relative peace would "wage peace" on other countries that invited it to do so. Following a "declaration of peace" on a country, the U.S. would pursue its objectives there with all the men, machines, money, and fervour formerly expended only for war.

If American ingenuity can devise nuclear and thermonuclear bombs, it can and should be harnessed—fast—toward peace on Earth.

Neil P. Ruzic, founder of Industrial Research, Oceanology, *and other magazines, is president of Island for Science Inc., Beverly Shores, Indiana. He is the author of eight books on the practical applications of science and holds the first U.S. patent for a device to be used exclusively on the Moon.*

The electronics explosion of the last 25 years has made possible such innovations as robot "workers" on the automobile assembly line, capable of a high degree of accuracy, and tireless.

DAVID FRANKLIN—TIME INC.

Asides

Not all the news events of 1980 made prominent headlines. Among items reported less breathlessly in the worldwide press were the following:

Irma Loyear left the cleaning service business to enroll in the art department of the University of Wisconsin at Superior. When she was elected homecoming queen, other female students were understandably disappointed. But the crowd at the coronation ceremony thought she was terrific. They jumped up and shouted "Irma! Irma!" as the 76-year-old beauty smiled.

Before taking her life in San Francisco, one of Mary Murphy's last decisions concerned her faithful ten-year-old dog. Fearing Sido would be lonely without her, Murphy stipulated in her will that the mutt be put to sleep. When this news became public, the Society for the Prevention of Cruelty to Animals (SPCA) took the matter to court. After noting that "even stray and abandoned dogs have rights," the judge ruled that Sido could live out her years with the head of the local SPCA.

JIM WILSON—NEWSWEEK

Tombstones can be expensive in more ways than one, as Bernard Gladsky of Baltimore, Md., found out in February. When his father died in 1977, he commissioned Kirby L. Smith to carve the tombstone inscription. It read: "Stanley J. Gladsky, 1895–1977, abused, robbed and starved by his beloved daughter." Gloria Kovatch charged her brother with libel and sued for $500,000. Gladsky insisted that the engraving was done in jest, but added his sister had once sent their father to the hospital on a bus while he was suffering from malnutrition and dehydration. A Superior Court jury awarded Kovatch $2,000.

Texas criminal law stipulates that any person convicted of three felonies must receive a life sentence. William James Rummel argued that in his case such a sentence constituted a "grossly disproportionate" punishment; as such, it violated the U.S. constitutional provision against cruel and unusual punishment. Rummel was convicted and served time for an $80 credit card fraud and for the forging of a $28.36 check. He then accepted a $120.75 check after falsely promising to repair an air conditioner. The third felony led to his life sentence. In March the U.S. Supreme Court ruled 5–4 that the Texas law did not violate the U.S. Constitution. Justice William Rehnquist explained that states have a valid interest in imposing such a sentence on those "who by repeated criminal acts have shown that they are simply incapable of conforming to the norms of society." In Texas, prisoners serving life sentences are eligible for parole after 12 years.

Joseph Kamoo, a Swiss inventor, applied for a patent for a technological improvement of Muslim prayer rugs. Since Muslims perform their daily prayers facing Mecca, it is important, but sometimes difficult, to know how to line up the rectangular mat in the proper direction. Kamoo's rug has a map and compass that permit believers to align their rugs properly no matter where they are. The rug map is simply rotated around the compass until the needle points to the city where the believer happens to be. When that is done, the rug is facing Mecca.

Cosmetic firms, usually in fierce competition for new fragrances, showed no interest at all in Arthur F. Isbell's patented aroma. Though two small bottles of chemicals have to be mixed to produce the smell, that inconvenience was not the real problem. They simply didn't think the aroma would sell. Hunters and wildlife photographers, on the other hand, think it's great. Human odours, which alert animals to danger, seem to be effectively masked by Isbell's artificial skunk bouquet.

Western observers, getting their first peek at the actual proceedings of Chinese divorce courts, were afforded a rare glimpse of the human comedy and tragedy in that formerly closed society. When Yao Yitian, a 52-year-old editor, began to recite a litany of abuses he had endured during 18 years of married life, the spectators were quite reserved. He testified that domestic tensions had become so great that the mere sound of his wife's voice made him wince in pain. But the spectators started smiling when his shrewish wife, Chen Zhengyu, who was vehemently contesting the divorce, sought to bolster her case on Marxist principles. She reminded the judge that the late Chairman Mao Zedong had often insisted that in a socialist society there could be no progress without strife. This application of one of Mao's most famous axioms brought down the house in gales of ironic laughter.

Winning a million dollars in the Massachusetts state lottery should be a thrilling experience. But the very first winner of the Big Money Game didn't even smile when his name was announced during a live television broadcast. He was already dead. In another drawing in September the winning ticket belonged to Wilfred Madelle, Jr. He didn't attend the drawing either, but a lottery spokesman said Madelle will get the money. Not immediately, but after he leaves the Worcester County House of Correction, where he has been doing time for breaking and entering. He regrets the breaking, but he's happy about entering. The lottery, that is.

William Wilcox, a movie projectionist in Illinois, was so determined to have his unborn son named after him that he took the matter to court. His estranged wife was equally insistent that their son would not be named William Earl Wilcox IV. Circuit Court Judge Robert C. Buckley made some preliminary rulings, and then continued the case. Before the couple returned to court, Tammi Wilcox gave birth to a lovely daughter.

Sex discrimination can be financially rewarding, as in the case of two California men who went to dinner at the Ojai Valley Inn in 1976. Both were refused seats unless they wore staff-supplied neckties with their leisure suits. The men finally complied under protest, then sued the restaurant for sex discrimination. Only males, they noted, were obliged to wear the ties. A Superior Court judge dismissed the case, but a higher court reversed the ruling. After listening to testimony, a jury awarded Robert Hales $13,000 and Irving Losner, whose stay in the hotel had been much briefer, $5,000 in damages. However unhappy the men might have been about the neckties, they were certainly delighted with their suits.

UPI

Chicken-man Ted Giannoulas gained national renown as the mascot of the San Diego Padres baseball team. Flapping his wings, wiggling his tail, leaping through the air, rolling on the ground, and threatening to bite off the heads of umpires, he won everyone's heart. But not, apprently, the hearts of his sponsors at radio station KGB. He was fired by the station after he began to moonlight in his costume at other events, and another man was given his outfit. Giannoulas, unfazed, devised a new chicken-man costume and was promptly brought to court by KGB for wearing a costume "substantially similar" to its own. The case finally went before Superior Court Judge Raul Rosado, who ruled that Giannoulas could continue to perform in his by-then nationally known suit. Discounting an ancient Roman proverb that clothes made the man, Rosado felt that the man, not the outfit, made the act.

Legionnaire's disease terrified a lot of people until it was finally identified by medical sleuths. Early in the year flight attendants aboard Eastern Airlines planes flying between New York and Florida got another scare. Some 95 attendants reported 170 cases of "red sweat," mysterious red spots on the skin that seemed to exude a bloodlike liquid. Eastern ordered its flight supervisors to board flights to look for clues. The National Institute for Occupational Safety and Health also sent representatives to help. On March 19 Eastern Airlines happily reported that the ominous red spots were nothing more than tiny flecks of red ink that came from letters stenciled on the rubber life vests used by the attendants who demonstrated their use before takeoff.

433

Occupational hazards vary from job to job, but in the U.S. neither mining nor police work heads the list of most dangerous professions. Miners have an on-the-job death rate of 56 per 100,000, while policemen have a rate of 35 per 100,000. But, according to a study conducted by the International Association of Fire Fighters, an average 68 out of 100,000 fire fighters die in the performance of their duties.

A November issue of the *Journal of the American Medical Association* carried a report on an unusual side effect of silicone implants used to enlarge the breasts. The topic had been raised by an airline stewardess who had undergone such surgery. According to Dr. Charles C. Fullett, implants inserted at sea level would expand to twice their normal size at 5,500 m (18,000 ft) and to three times their size at 9,150 m (30,000 ft) if the airplane lost its cabin pressure.

Sotheby's, the famous London auction house, sent one of its experts on Oriental art to the home of an elderly couple to see what antiques would be acceptable for auction. The man was clearly startled when he spotted a red and white Chinese bottle in the bedroom that had been converted into a lamp. The foot-high bottle was a rare 14th-century creation that Sotheby's auctioned off in 90 seconds for $672,800.

When A. James Manchin, West Virginia's secretary of state, heard about the case of Mary Marvich, he wondered aloud if lunatics had taken over the U.S. Department of Immigration and Naturalization. Marvich had been told that her application for citizenship could not be approved until she supplied the name of the ship that carried her to the U.S. But Marvich claimed she could not remember. Little wonder, since the 107-year-old woman had emigrated from the Balkans in 1894.

When android C3PO won a leading role in *Star Wars*, his silicon-chip brain had not been programmed to include swinging a rhythmical baton. But that had to change when John Williams, who composed the prizewinning score of the blockbuster movie, was named to succeed Arthur Fiedler as conductor of the Boston Pops. On opening night, C3PO moved to the podium and without batting an electronic eyelash conducted the 100-member orchestra in a moving rendition of the movie's theme song.

WIDE WORLD

"It's a little bit spooky," was Edward Galland's startled reaction when he first saw Robert Shafran. The two were brought together after students at New York's Sullivan County Community College greeted Robert with a "Hi, Eddy," when he first appeared on campus. Both young men were born on July 12, both are the same height, and both have brown curly hair and brown eyes. What's more, both were adopted through the same agency. The two were still seeking positive proof that they were twins when Edward's mother got a phone call from a David Kellman. He said: "You're not going to believe this ... but I think I'm the third." If one picture (of Robert, David, and Edward) is worth a thousand words, the three do indeed appear to be triplets.

WIDE WORLD

When 260 squatters refused to leave a luxury apartment building in Amsterdam, a judge issued an order for their removal. The defiant squatters, however, swore they would not be evicted without a struggle. A huge crowd was on hand to witness the showdown. Some 2,000 policemen arrived with dogs, horses, water cannons, armoured personnel carriers, and army sharpshooters positioned in cages on hydraulic platforms. The first serious problems came when the angry crowd began to attack the police with cobblestones, bags of paint, and homemade firebombs. They were finally subdued by tear gas. The police then moved forward to assault the building. To their chagrin, they found only one squatter in the building. He was armed with a bouquet of flowers.

When he retired from the U.S. Army, Vietnam veteran James Tobin signed up as a civilian pilot with his old employer. His first assignment was to fly a load of light weapons from the Picatinny Arsenal in Dover, N.J., to the Aberdeen Proving Grounds in Maryland. The plane was traveling 320 kph (200 mph) at 2,745 m (9,000 ft) when a flashing light indicated a rear door of the U-21 Beechcraft was not properly closed. Leaving his co-pilot at the controls, Tobin went to investigate. The moment he touched the latch he was sucked through the open door and somersaulted into space. Incredibly, one of his feet was firmly caught by a holding line attached to the door. When the co-pilot saw Tobin dangling in midair, he made a very careful emergency landing. Tobin went to the hospital with a broken right arm, possibly pondering the old saying that no one really ever knows what to expect on the first day of a new job.

American pollsters spend huge sums of money and countless hours trying to predict the outcome of the U.S. presidential election. In gauging public opinion these experts generally count themselves lucky if they come to within three percentage points of the actual vote count. Perhaps Nepali astrologers know something American pollsters don't. About a score of the kingdom's astrologers reached a consensus on April 21 that a national referendum would carry with 55% of the vote. Eleven days later the referendum was endorsed by 54.79% of the voters.

Aetna Life & Casualty thought April Fools' Day an appropriate occasion to publish some of the most unusual claims it had received during the 1970s. One fellow who couldn't sleep because of buzzing mosquitoes got out of bed in the middle of the night and gave his bedroom a thorough spraying. The next morning he discovered he had used an aerosol can of red enamel paint.

A first-class counterfeiter will spend countless hours trying to duplicate authentic government currency. A 26-year-old man in Hamilton, Mont., had no such ambition. He took a genuine $20 bill, changed the figure to $22, substituted a drawing of a cigar-smoking man in a Panama hat for the engraved likeness of Andrew Jackson, and photocopied it on rag-bond paper. He also used the name Alaska Jack for that of the U.S. treasurer. A cashier at the court of Judge Herbert Kester accepted the bill as payment for a $20 traffic fine. No one was saying whether or not the cashier gave the jokester $2 in change.

Edwin Robinson was struck by lightning in June and lived to tell an incredible tale. After a truck accident in February 1971, he began to lose his sight and hearing. More than eight years later, during a midsummer thunderstorm in Maine, he picked up his aluminum cane and went outside in search of his pet chicken. That's when it happened. A bolt of lightning knocked him unconscious. Twenty minutes later he awoke, got to his feet, and realized that something wonderful had occurred. His head was "clear as a bell." For the first time in almost a decade Robinson no longer felt what seemed to be a tight band around his head. As his eyesight, hearing, and even the hair on his head he had lost through baldness began to come back to him, the 62-year-old former truck driver hoped he could travel to Virginia to see his four grandchildren.

When textile workers at the Darlington Manufacturing Plant in South Carolina voted for union representation, the owners shut down the plant "for economic reasons." The matter went all the way to the Supreme Court before both sides agreed to a settlement. Milliken & Co. offered $5 million in back pay, and the workers accepted. Some would receive as little as $50, others as much as $36,000. Money belonging to workers who had died would go to their beneficiaries. Everyone seemed relieved to have the matter finally settled. It had, after all, been in litigation for 24 years.

Diplomatic immunity is rooted in solid principles, but flagrant violations of the privilege can be infuriating. In 1967 the Soviet Embassy in Canada asked Wallace Edwards's firm to print a magazine to be sold at the Expo '67 exhibition in Montreal. After he completed the job, Soviet officials refused to pay the $26,000 bill. When asked to help, Canadian government officials shied away from a confrontation with the Soviets, claiming that all embassy personnel have immunity. But Edwards wanted his money and finally found a law firm willing to tackle the issue and Canada's bureaucracy. Lawyer Ron Manes felt "that if a country descends into the commercial arena to participate in our capitalist system, it must play by the same rules as everyone else and pay its just debts." In October Edwards won his first battle. The Toronto sheriff ordered the Soviet freighter "Stanislavsky" seized. Then Soviet embassy bank accounts in Ottawa were frozen by court order. Only then did the Soviet officials agree to pay the debt and an additional $10,000 in interest. They also handed over a supply of caviar and vodka and footed the bill for Edwards's victory celebration at the Royal York Hotel. "You've got to have a little fun in life," Edwards remarked, as he patted the 36,000 Canadian one-dollar bills he had demanded and finally got.

Sally Lippman was very grateful when a friend suggested that a visit to a New York disco might help relieve the loneliness she felt after the death of her husband. Sally went and loved it. In time she met and fell in love with 28-year-old Yiannis Touzos. When they decided to get married in June, disco habitués hoped that would not end 80-year-old "Disco Sally's" nights out on the town.

A healthy big toe is worth $8,657.50, according to calculations worked out by an arbitrator for the Illinois Industrial Commission. Members of the Cook County Board, none of them a known expert on big toes, must have thought the figure was just about right because they approved an award of $3,463 as compensation to a former assistant state's attorney who sustained a 40% injury to his big toe while hurrying to answer a phone.

Presidential invitations are hard to come by, especially if you happen to be the owner of Eddie's Standard Service Station. So when Edward Finkelstein received a White House invitation, he jumped at the chance to visit the nation's capital. He didn't get much from the special briefing for several hundred VIP's, but he had lunch with Missouri Sen. Thomas Eagleton. Finkelstein said he enjoyed every minute of it and felt just fine when other senators passed by and patted him on the shoulder—even though "they didn't know me from Adam." Actually, they didn't know him from another Finkelstein named Edward who should have received the invitation. But the St. Louis, Mo., publisher had only one listing in the phone book, so the White House chose the Finkelstein with two: one a residence, the other an office. The latter was Eddie's gas station.

Undecided voters were beset on every side during the U.S. presidential election, but none perhaps so persistently as Reagan Carter, the owner of a welding shop in Beaumont, Texas. He honestly could not decide which candidate he preferred. But with a name like his, it's not surprising that employees right next door couldn't give him much sympathy. They worked for the Nixon Ford Motor Co.

David Berkowtiz, the notorious "Son of Sam" killer, was sentenced to 315 years in prison for killing six persons in New York City in 1977. After the Bureau of Disability Determination certified that Berkowitz was unable to hold a job because of "a mental impairment," he began to receive $300 a month from the Social Security Administration. From his prison cell in Attica, N.Y., Berkowitz said he had faked insanity during his trial and now wanted to be declared legally sane so he could personally manage his own finances.

Miss Piggy's film debut as an eyelash-fluttering temptress trying to win the love of Kermit the Frog was a smashing success. Bruce Collin, a Cincinnati, Ohio, businessman, was so taken with her performance in *The Muppet Movie* that he helped launch a campaign to have the superstar nominated for an Oscar as best actress of the year. Collin was not at all surprised when 38,000 fans sent letters praising Miss Piggy for her sensitive interpretation of a very difficult role. Apprised of this development, Miss Piggy wrote to Collin to say: "I feel I am but a humble actress/singer and I do not believe it is my place to comment on this wise, perceptive, discerning and tasteful Oscar campaign."

Students at Yale University, harassed by upcoming midterm examinations, decided to filch a highly revered moose head from the university's Ezra Stiles College. They then fashioned a crude ransom note addressed to the president of Yale. It read, "Dear Bart: We have your moose. Cancel midterms or we'll eat him. The Moose Liberation Army." President A. Bartlett Giamatti, unintimidated by such tactics, contemptuously responded: "Let them eat mousse."

Two hours after being shot in the abdomen, 24-year-old Margarette Maddox of Chicago gave birth to a 4-lb 4-oz baby boy. When doctors at Michael Reese Hospital examined the newborn infant, they found bullet fragments in the child's elbow and thigh. After surgery, the child was reported doing well.

Big Ben, perhaps the most renowned of London's many famous landmarks, was the subject of a BBC overseas broadcast on April 1. Foreigners who wrote letters of protest had probably never heard of April Fools' jokes. The Big Ben clock wasn't really going digital.

Brazil's program for reducing its dependence on OPEC oil includes the use of sugarcane alcohol as automotive fuel. The same sugarcane alcohol provides the kick in Brazil's rumlike *cachaca*, a potent and popular drink. Small wonder, therefore, that some Brazilians began to drink the fuel. Government officials figured out a way to make the fuel undrinkable; it is planned to poison the alcohol with a small quantity of regular gasoline.

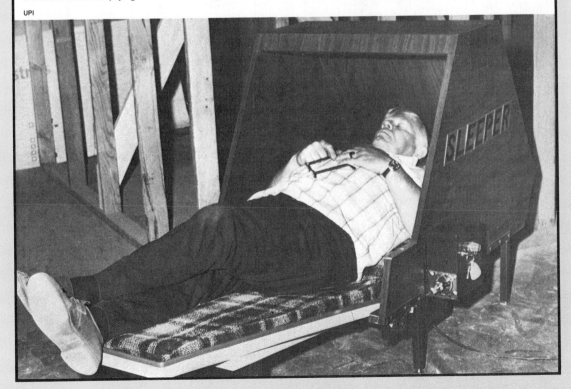

Weary travelers stranded at airports for long hours may soon be blessing Grant Russell for inventing the Sleep-a-Matic. The chairlike contraption opens into a 1.8-m (6-ft) daybed when quarters are inserted into the coin slot. A high-pitched tone rouses the sleeper when the selected number of 15-minute periods has elapsed. Russell seems to have thought of everything—except, perhaps, how to dislodge bone-weary travelers who simply ignore the buzzing or continue to sleep on despite the noise.

UPI

*A variety store advertises the industrial solvent **DMSO**, used by some to treat arthritis.*

JEAN-CLAUDE LEJEUNE

*A fitness group works through a **Jazzercize** routine in unison.*

New Words

Language constantly changes. New words and word meanings are forever coming into the vocabulary; old ones die out. The new words are often only passing fads. One group uses a word, but the novelty may never gain wide acceptance. The word dies when the group gives it up or changes if it is given fresh meaning.

Sometimes, however, a new word does become a part of the living language. How do dictionary makers know when that has happened? And how do lexicographers go about giving a new word recognition in a reference work as part of the English language?

Dictionary and reference-set staffs and individual professionals employ continuous word-watching systems. Readers and editors record and analyze the language as it is actually spoken and written. Almost everything printed in English—books, magazines, newspapers, catalogs, and even business forms—is sampled. Each marked item is recorded and filed along with the content of its usage. These citations are tangible proof that each word was used in a particular way to convey a particular meaning at a particular time.

The following list of new words and meanings contains a sampling of the continuing change and growth of our language. Some of the entries may be forgotten next year; some may last as long as man himself.

alcomobile *n:* automobile with an engine that is designed to burn alcohol rather than gasoline

average radius *n:* on waterless planets, a reference point analogous to sea level on Earth that serves as the basis for measuring heights of mountains and depths of valleys

coyote *n slang:* one who smuggles Mexican nationals into the U.S. to avoid immigration procedures

DMSO *n abbrev:* dimethyl sulfoxide, an industrial solvent with pharmaceutical applications, including alleged arthritis relief

exit poll *n:* an attempt to predict the outcome of an election by interviewing voters as they leave the polling place, before votes are officially tabulated

freebase *n:* an illicit drug, a preparation of cocaine treated with ether for greater potency

giveback *n:* in labour-management negotiations, nonwage concessions involving reductions in benefits or increases in productivity on the part of union members

grid lock *n:* the ultimate traffic jam, in which streets are so clogged with vehicles that all intersections become blocked and traffic is paralyzed in all directions

hacker *n slang:* a computer-programming addict, especially a person who obsessively makes small, insignificant changes to a computer program solely for enjoyment

hit list *n slang:* a roster of enemies or issues to be eliminated or neutralized

hortitherapy *n:* the use of gardening as a therapeutic aid for, *e.g.*, the blind, aged, or handicapped

hot tub *n:* deep, usually wooden tub in which one or more users sit in water heated above blood temperature in order to relax and ease tensions

Jazzercise *n:* fitness exercise program that uses jazz dance movements set to music

medicant *n:* medical jargon

mini-musical *n:* scaled-down musical comedy for live presentation, with a small cast, simple sets and costumes, and minimal (or no) story

niphophile *n:* snow lover

ochlotheocracy *n:* mob rule with religious connotations

penem *n:* one of a class of synthetic antibiotics that are chemically similar to the penicillins and cephalosporins

preppie *adj:* characteristic of preparatory schools, especially clothing and accessories of traditional styles and cut; also **preppy**

radioimmunoglobulin *n:* a preparation of antibodies to tumour cells combined with a radioactive substance such as radioiodine, used as an antitumour agent in cancer therapy

retronym *n:* a word that is coupled with an adjective to retain its original meaning; *e.g.*, natural turf, hardcover book

scriver *n:* street artist, one who creates ephemeral works such as chalk drawings on sidewalks

sinsemilla *n:* marijuana prepared from the unpollinated female cannabis plant

spherand *n:* ligand, or coordinating molecule, which contains spherical cavities that can incorporate certain ions but reject others

ten or **10** *n slang:* the best or most desirable item in a given category, as rated on an imaginary numerical scale with ten as the highest score possible

victimology *n:* the study of victims (as of crime or societal inequities) and their needs

videodisc *n:* flat disc resembling a grooveless phonograph record that contains recorded video and audio information in optical form that can be played back using a laser

videodisc player *n:* a device that plays back via speakers and screen the information recorded on a **videodisc**

wheel *n slang:* computer user, often a **hacker** who has obtained access to a large computer

wheel war *n slang:* game played between **hackers** at separate terminals of a large computer with the object of frustrating others' attempts to interact with the computer

ORMOND GIGLI

Two students show off the clothes and accessories that make the clean-cut **preppie** look.

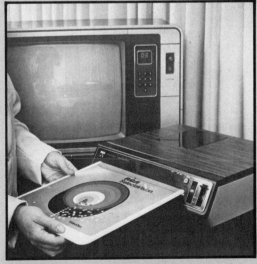

COURTESY, RCA

A **videodisc** provides both picture and sound through a **videodisc** player.

BIOGRAPHIES

The following is a selected list of men and women who influenced events significantly in 1980.

Anderson, John Bayard

A major surprise in the 1980 campaign was John B. Anderson's strong showing in the early Republican primaries, which led to his independent candidacy for president.

Anderson started the long campaign as a respected but little-known ten-term congressman from Rockford, Ill., where he was born on Feb. 15, 1922.

A conservative at the start of his political career, he stood out from the pack by taking liberal positions unpopular with the conservative constituency other GOP hopefuls were trying to attract. But he gained support from young people, independents, Democrats, and moderate Republicans. Many Democrats crossed over to vote for Anderson in the "open" primaries, enabling him to finish a strong second in Vermont, Massachusetts, and Illinois.

This encouraged Anderson to become an independent candidate, though he failed to win a single primary. Unlike previous independent or third-party candidates, he had no single issue to use as a rallying point. His "national unity" campaign was based on the idea that he offered a respectable alternative for those who could not accept Ronald Reagan or Jimmy Carter. Patrick Lucey, a Democrat and former Wisconsin governor, became Anderson's vice-presidential running mate.

Despite opposition from the Democrats, who feared he would take votes away from Carter, Anderson fought his way onto the ballot in all 50 states. The polls showed him at about 15% in early September and threatening to hurt Carter in the Midwest and Northeast. The League of Women Voters invited Anderson to participate in the first presidential debate in Baltimore, Md., which Carter avoided because of Anderson's presence.

Thereafter, Anderson's support began to decline as voters became convinced that he could not win. The campaign went heavily into debt and almost collapsed when Anderson was not included in the second and final presidential debate in late October. On election day, Anderson pulled 5.5 million votes, or 6.5% of the national total, which qualified him to receive $4 million in federal funds. Reagan overwhelmed Carter, and the so-called "Anderson factor" proved to be of little consequence. However, in the 20th century, only Theodore Roosevelt (1912), Robert La Follette (1924), and George Wallace (1968) had won higher popular vote percentages as independent or third-party candidates.

Ballesteros, Severiano

In common with many fine Spanish golfers, Severiano Ballesteros entered the game as a caddie, at Santander in northern Spain. Born at Pedrena, near Santander, on April 9, 1957, he was one of four golfing brothers who were nephews of Ramón Sota, a professional golfer. Ballesteros turned professional in 1974 at the age of 17. Within a year it was clear that he had exceptional talent. In 1976 he led the European Order of Merit and delighted huge crowds at Birkdale by tying for second with Jack Nicklaus behind Johnny Miller in the British Open championship.

The power and flair of his golf, fearless play, and striking looks made Ballesteros the most exciting young golfer to emerge since Nicklaus was a similar age. He and Manuel Pinero won the World Cup for Spain in 1976, and he and Antonio Garrido repeated the feat the following year. During 1977 and 1978 Ballesteros remained the leading money winner in Europe and won tournaments in ten or more countries. These included Japan, Britain, New Zealand, and, most notably, the Greater Greensboro Open in the U.S., but he was not tempted to compete regularly on the U.S. circuit.

Ballesteros's career reached its first great peak when he won the 1979 British Open at Lytham, with Ben Crenshaw and Nicklaus three strokes behind, and became the youngest champion of the century. His victory was based on well-nigh uninhibited attack. Immense drives were unleashed, rarely finding fairways, but the rough was so trampled by the crowds that even the wildest shots were not costly, and his short game and putting were superb for their skill and confidence.

Many Americans claimed that he would have been nowhere on a course in the U.S. This was probably true, but he showed that he had the control and judgment to adapt his game at Augusta, Ga., in April 1980 with one of the most commanding victories in the history of the Masters. None of the established U.S. golfers was in sight of catching him. His driving was rarely wild, and his approach shots and putting were almost faultless.

At that time Ballesteros's horizons seemed limitless, but unfortunately he mistook his starting time for the second round of the 1980 U.S. Open and was disqualified. This was a setback, and later he did not excel in the British Open. In five years, however, he had won £230,000 official money in Europe.

Bani-Sadr, Abolhassan

Abolhassan Bani-Sadr was elected first president of the Islamic Republic of Iran on Jan. 25, 1980, with 75% of the popular vote. The nation's religious

JACQUES HAILLOT—CAMERA PRESS

leader, Ayatollah Ruhollah Khomeini, administered the oath of office on February 4. Two days later Khomeini appointed Bani-Sadr chairman of the Revolutionary Council, Iran's policy-making body. As president of the republic Bani-Sadr was appointed commander in chief of the armed forces on February 19.

Bani-Sadr's presidency was an uphill struggle against enemies in the clergy seeking to reduce him to a figurehead and also against inexperienced departmental executives. He was forced to accept Mohammad Ali Raja'i (q.v.), not a man of his choice, as prime minister on August 11, and soon the two men were at odds, the president refusing to accept one-third of the prime minister's Cabinet nominations. A climax was reached on October 31, when Bani-Sadr wrote Khomeini a letter (first published in Stockholm on December 8) complaining that his incompetent ministers were a greater danger than Iraq's aggression (begun on September 22) and that their rivalries should be stopped before Iran lost both the war and the revolution; the president also noted that he had warned of the worsening economy and of the need to reorganize the armed forces, without avail. Some indignant members of the Majlis (parliament) on December 16 demanded his punishment for revealing "military secrets."

Bani-Sadr was born on March 22, 1933, at Hamaden, a village near Abadan, the younger son of Ayatollah Seyed Nasrollah Bani-Sadr. He studied theology and economics at the University of Teheran and spent four years at the Institute of Social Research. He was a leader of the antishah student movement in the early 1960s and was imprisoned twice for political activities. Wounded in the unsuccessful uprising of June 1963, he emigrated to France, where he continued his studies and also taught at the Sorbonne in Paris. A fervent Islamic nationalist and revolutionary economist, he began to publish the results of his studies in the early 1970s.

Bani-Sadr joined Khomeini's entourage during the latter's exile in France, and the two returned to Iran together on Feb. 1, 1979. Bani-Sadr was appointed deputy minister of economy and finance in Mehdi Bazargan's government in July 1979 and became full minister in November of that year. In August and September 1980 the president was fortunate to escape injury in two helicopter crashes near the Iraq frontier.

Queen Beatrix

In a broadcast to the Dutch nation on Jan. 31, 1980, Queen Juliana of The Netherlands, who had reigned since September 1948, announced her intention to abdicate in favour of her eldest daughter, Crown Princess Beatrix. Three months later, on April 30, Beatrix was crowned queen at a special session of both houses of Parliament.

Beatrix Wilhelmina Armgard, princess of Orange-Nassau and of Lippe-Biesterfeld, was born

at Soestdijk Palace in Baarn on Jan. 31, 1938, the first child of the then Crown Princess Juliana and Prince Bernhard of Lippe-Biesterfeld. After the outbreak of World War II, the royal family in May 1940 took refuge in England. Princess Juliana and her daughters Beatrix and Irene then went to Ottawa, where they stayed throughout the war.

After the German surrender the family returned to The Netherlands in August 1945. Beatrix enrolled in 1956 as a student at the State University of Leiden. She attended lectures and tutorials in sociology, jurisprudence, economics, parliamentary history, and current international affairs, and was graduated in 1961.

On June 28, 1965, Queen Juliana and Prince Bernhard announced the engagement of Beatrix to a West German diplomat, Claus von Amsberg. The following November Parliament passed a bill authorizing the marriage—a procedure necessitated by a provision in the constitution that excluded from the succession all members of the ruling dynasty and their descendants who married without the consent of Parliament. Princess Beatrix's choice of a former member of Hitler's army displeased many Dutch people, but within a short time von Amsberg succeeded in winning the sympathy of a great number of them. Although the marriage ceremony in Amsterdam on March 10, 1966, was accompanied by widespread and violent demonstrations, these were mainly directed against prevailing political and social conditions and probably only to a lesser degree reflected opposition to the marriage. There were also some antimonarchist demonstrations during Beatrix's coronation, but when the couple later toured The Netherlands, they were received everywhere with great enthusiasm.

Queen Beatrix and Prince Claus had three children: Prince Willem-Alexander Claus George Ferdinand (born April 27, 1967); Prince Johan Friso Bernhard Christiaan David (born Sept. 25, 1968); and Prince Constantijn Christof Frederik Aschwin (born Oct. 11, 1969).

Beckwith, Charles A.

He is something of a mystery to the country he serves, as is the U.S. Army unit he commands. The unit, formed in 1977 and called "Blue Light," is an elite antiterrorist outfit based at Ft. Bragg, North Carolina. Its commander is Col. Charles A. Beckwith, a tough, gravel-voiced combat veteran, who in 1980 led an attempt to rescue the Americans being held hostage at the U.S. embassy in Teheran, Iran.

For much of his career Beckwith specialized in commando operations and "special warfare," assignments that made him a rather shadowy figure in the army hierarchy. When journalists tried to find out something about him in the wake of the rescue attempt in Iran, the Army's records department would provide only the following: Born Jan. 22, 1929. Attended college. Commissioned 1952. Assignment "classified." Serial number 258–364046.

Despite such secrecy some details of Beckwith's career have surfaced. He entered the Army in 1953 and was an early volunteer for the Special Forces. As a major in Vietnam in the 1960s, he became commander of the "Delta Project," several hundred Indochinese troops under the direction of the Special Forces. On one operation with the unit, Beckwith was seriously wounded; he impressed a field surgeon with his toughness when he sat up in his litter and demanded immediate trauma treatment because, he said, "I'm bleeding to death."

"He was right," the surgeon was quoted as saying later. "A few more minutes and he would have been dead."

After his service in Vietnam, Beckwith was assigned to the Special Warfare School at Ft. Bragg and was named commander of Blue Light. When the attempt to free the hostages was made in April, Beckwith was the assault commander. With about 90 of his Blue Light troops, he helicoptered at night to a spot in the Iranian desert, from which the next phase of the assault on Teheran was to have been launched.

But then things started to go wrong. Three of the eight RH–53 Sea Stallion helicopters developed mechanical problems. One chopper collided on the ground with a C–130 cargo plane, which exploded in flames. Eight men were killed and five injured, and the hostages remained hostages. But criticism of the operation did not seem to touch on Beckwith himself, and he faded back into his customary obscurity.

Blake, Eubie

To say that Eubie Blake has had a remarkable career would be an understatement; it would be far closer to the truth to say that he has had *several* remarkable careers. He has worked at various times over the years as a pianist, singer, composer, vaudeville performer, musical director, recording artist, concert and jazz-festival performer, record-company founder, and talk-show guest. No less remarkable was the fact that Blake in 1980 at the age of 97 was still active musically, playing the piano a number of hours each day in his Brooklyn, N.Y., home and even performing occasionally in public.

James Hubert Blake was born on Feb. 7, 1883, in Baltimore, Md., the son of former slaves. He demonstrated an early talent for music, and his formal instruction in piano and organ included rigorous training in the classics. But the young Blake developed a passion for ragtime, which his mother considered indecent music and forbade him to play at home. So he went elsewhere to perform, making his first public appearance at one of Baltimore's notorious sporting houses at the age of 15.

In 1915 he formed a prolific and long-standing partnership with singer/lyricist Noble Sissle. After touring the vaudeville circuit for a number of years,

KATHERINE YOUNG

the pair scored a triumph in 1921 with *Shuffle Along*, the first Broadway musical to be composed, produced, directed, and performed solely by blacks. They followed this success with *Elsie* in 1923 and *Chocolate Dandies* the next year. Their compositions included such favourites as "Love Will Find a Way" and "I'm Just Wild About Harry." Blake also scored the music for *Blackbirds of 1930*, which starred the famous black performer Ethel Waters.

From the 1930s to the 1950s Blake experienced diminishing popularity, but he and his music returned to prominence with the release of several recordings during the 1950s and 1960s. He then launched a series of appearances that included concerts and jazz festivals throughout the U.S. and Europe. He crowned this revival of interest in his music with a triumphant return to Broadway with *Eubie!*, a show based on *Shuffle Along* that opened to popular and critical acclaim in 1978.

Bush, George

Some conservatives were unhappy when Ronald Reagan (*q.v.*) chose George Bush to be his vice-presidential running mate on the 1980 Republican ticket, but Bush's appeal to middle-of-the-road voters helped create the Reagan landslide.

The polls did not give Bush much chance in May 1979, when he announced that he would be among those challenging Reagan for the GOP nomination. He had held many top government jobs and was well known in party circles, but he was relatively unknown to the general public. He worked long and hard to build name identification. He also recruited an excellent campaign organization, which enabled him to upset Reagan in the Iowa precinct caucuses and become an instant "front-runner." But that ended abruptly when Reagan came back to win the New Hampshire primary.

Bush stayed in the race long after the other challengers quit. He won major primaries in Pennsylvania and Michigan, demonstrating that he could attract voters in the vital northern industrial states. He was a logical choice to balance the ticket, but his opposition had angered Reagan while his moderate stance on many issues antagonized the GOP right wing. But after Reagan's unsuccessful attempt to get former president Gerald Ford to be his running mate, the shocked Detroit convention learned that Bush had been chosen.

Bush was born June 12, 1924, in Milton, Mass., the son of Prescott Bush, a wealthy investment banker and U.S. senator. After graduation from Yale University, he began selling oil-drilling equipment in Texas and later founded his own company. He became involved in Texas politics and served two terms in Congress (1967–71) between unsuccessful tries for the Senate. Pres. Richard Nixon appointed Bush ambassador to the UN. In 1974 he became Republican national chairman, helping the embattled GOP survive Watergate. Ford named Bush to head the first U.S. liaison office in Beijing (Peking) and then to be director of the Central Intelligence Agency.

Carter, Billy

It began, perhaps, as just another sibling rivalry: the younger brother—unappreciated, resentful—taking his revenge on the prim, proper, and overachieving firstborn. But in this case, the older brother, Jimmy Carter, was president of the United States. From the day Jimmy Carter was elected in 1976, it was clear that brother Billy would be a problem. While Jimmy was trying to live down the redneck image of the white Southerner, Billy appeared to revel in it.

Things might have remained at that relatively harmless level except that Billy Carter became involved with a foreign government—the regime of Libya's Muammar al-Qaddafi—whose relations with the U.S. were, at best, strained. In 1978 Billy Carter became Libya's most prominent American apologist. However, the case did not achieve the status of a major political issue until July 14, 1980, when papers were filed in federal court revealing that Billy Carter had agreed "under protest" to register as a Libyan agent and admitted receiving $220,000 from Qaddafi's government. (Billy claimed the money was a "loan" and that he had only a business relationship with Libya as an oil broker for a U.S. firm, Charter Oil Co.) Questions immediately arose about the extent of the president's knowledge of Billy's activities and whether they had affected U.S. foreign policy.

After a series of public hearings, a subcommittee of the Senate Judiciary Committee concluded that while Libya had sought out Billy in hopes of influencing the U.S., that hope soon faded. The subcommittee's report, which was also critical of the president's and the administration's handling of the case, said: "[Billy Carter's] conduct was contrary to the interests of . . . the United States and merits severe criticism."

William Alton Carter III was born March 29, 1937, in Plains, Ga. In 1979, in the midst of his dealings with Libya, he entered an alcoholic rehabilitation centre in California. Neither that experience nor the furor over his Libya connection seemed to dampen his determination to remain independent of his brother. For his part, the president was tolerant and stoic, but when he was defeated for reelection on November 4, some observers thought the voters, in some measure, had responded to the antics of his younger brother.

Carter, Jimmy

During 1980, an election year, Pres. Jimmy Carter delegated most of his preconvention campaigning to surrogates, chiefly First Lady Rosalynn Carter and Vice-Pres. Walter Mondale. Most of Carter's attention was occupied by problems in foreign policy, principally the American hostages held by Islamic militants in Iran and worsening U.S.-Soviet relations following the Soviet invasion of Afghanistan.

Following the failure of preliminary sanctions against Iran to secure the release of the Americans, Carter severed diplomatic relations with that country April 7, formally banning American exports to Iran and expelling all Iranian diplomats from the U.S. The president unsuccessfully urged American allies to support economic and political sanctions against Iran. Later in April Carter widened the U.S. sanctions, warning that military action remained the only American option if the hostages were not released. On April 25 he announced that an airborne rescue attempt scheduled for the previous day had been canceled after the helicopters involved in the operation developed engine trouble in a staging area in the Iranian desert. Eight Americans had been killed and several others injured in the subsequent withdrawal of the U.S. force. Reaction to the news of the attempted rescue was generally unfavourable. On April 28 Carter accepted the resignation of Secretary of State Cyrus Vance, who had been unable to accept the president's decision to attempt the rescue operation. Although Carter continued to defend the mission, he acknowledged June 12 that military measures were no longer being considered to obtain the release of the hostages. In September the Ayatollah Ruhollah Khomeini announced terms for the release of the American hostages, including the unfreezing of Iranian assets in the U.S. and the return of the shah's wealth. Although these terms were formally approved by the

Iranian parliament in November and substantially agreed to by the Carter administration (with the exception of the matter of the shah's wealth, over which it said it could exercise no control, except through the courts), the hostages had not been released by year's end.

On January 4 President Carter announced a sharp reduction of U.S. grain sales to the Soviet Union in response to the Soviet invasion of Afghanistan. Other measures included the suspension of sales of high technology equipment and the possibility of a boycott of the 1980 Summer Olympics in Moscow. With the exception of France, most of America's European allies supported Carter's actions. On February 8 the president issued his plan on draft registration. Under the controversial new plan, women as well as men were to be registered. On February 12 it was announced that the president had ordered an amphibious strike force to the Arabian Sea in mid-March as a demonstration of the U.S. ability to protect the Persian Gulf region. The decision of the U.S. Olympic Committee in mid-April to support the Carter boycott was viewed as a major victory for the administration, but both the grain embargo and the new draft registration plan were extremely unpopular measures that hurt the president politically.

On August 5 government officials announced that President Carter had adopted a new strategy to be used by the U.S. in fighting a nuclear war with the Soviet Union. The new strategy, detailed in Presidential Directive 59, gave priority to attacking military targets in the Soviet Union, and lessened a previous emphasis on all-out retaliation against Soviet cities and industrial complexes. Administration officials asserted that the new strategy lessened the chance of nuclear war by giving U.S. forces the capacity to initiate a limited nuclear strike against military targets. Critics of the new strategy argued that the existence of such a capacity would prompt military planners to think in terms of limited, winnable nuclear war.

In an extraordinary statement issued March 3, President Carter disavowed the U.S.-backed United Nations Security Council resolution calling for Israel to dismantle its settlements in the West Bank and Gaza Strip. The president announced that the U.S. vote, the first cast by this country against Israel on the question of the settlements, was a mistake based on a communications failure between the U.S. delegation and the White House. Carter's announcement, widely viewed as prompted by domestic political concerns, generated a great deal of unfavourable criticism of the administration, particularly from the Israeli government, which remained unconvinced of American intentions on the matter of the settlements, despite the president's disavowal of the UN resolution.

Carter entered the Polish crisis in late August, urging leaders of major Western nations to respond positively to expected requests by Poland for sub-

UPI

stantial economic aid once workers' unrest subsided. At Labor Day speeches kicking off his postconvention election campaign, the president praised Polish workers, prompting charges by the official Soviet news agency Tass that Carter was interfering in the internal affairs of Poland.

Following Cuban Pres. Fidel Castro's offer in early April of safe passage to Cubans wishing to leave the country, many refugees began to arrive in Florida. By early May their numbers had grown so great that President Carter, while pledging that the U.S. would welcome the refugees, declared a state of emergency for the regions of Florida most affected by the unexpected wave of immigration.

On July 14 the president's brother, Billy Carter, registered with the Justice Department as an agent for the Libyan government, disclosing that he had received more than $220,000 in payments from that country in 1980. Later that month a special panel to investigate Billy Carter's role as a Libyan agent was established by the Senate. Growing controversy about possible White House involvement in Billy Carter's affairs resulted in the president's delivering a report to the Senate panel and holding a televised news conference to answer questions about his brother. The Senate panel's report, issued October 2, while critical of administration handling of the Billy Carter case, found no illegal or clearly unethical activity by government officials.

The worsening economy continued to be Carter's major problem domestically. On June 1 the president admitted the recession had come more quickly and had been more serious than the administration had anticipated. Despite campaign predictions that the economy was on its way to full recovery, voter dissatisfaction with continued high inflation and growing unemployment was viewed by administration officials as a major cause (along with frustration over his failure to secure the release of the American hostages in Iran) of President Carter's defeat by his Republican opponent, Ronald Reagan, in November.

Chun Doo Hwan

For almost ten months after the October 1979 assassination of South Korea's longtime president Park Chung Hee, government leadership in the country remained in a state of flux. By August 1980, however, it became clear that a relatively obscure officer, Lieut. Gen. Chun Doo Hwan, was working his way to the top in ways identical to those Park himself had used two decades earlier.

First, he took charge of the investigation when his mentor was shot dead and arrested all suspects, including his own nominal superior, Army Chief of Staff Gen. Chung Seung Hwa. Then, heading a group of younger officers, he took control of the military in a coup. He was also promoted to full general. Like Park he let a figurehead, Pres. Choi

Kyu Hah, stay in office for almost a year while he himself remained chairman of a special committee wielding all power. On August 27, five days after formally retiring from the Army, Chun was elected president of the country.

Chun was born Jan. 18, 1931, the sixth of nine children in a rural family in Naechonri in southeastern Korea. His father, a farmer of modest means, was said to have given intensive tutoring to his children in Confucian ideals. After graduation from the Taegu technical high school in 1951, in the middle of the Korean War, Chun entered the Korean Military Academy. He was in the first class to receive the full four-year course of instruction. He emerged an infantry officer and, after four years in front-line rifle units, joined the Special Forces in the U.S.

Quick promotions marked his subsequent career. He commanded the White House Division in Vietnam and was at different times chief of the Capital Garrison Command in Seoul, commander of the famed 1st Airborne Special Forces Group and later of the 1st Infantry Division, and, from March 1979, commanding general of the Defense Security Command. The post was to prove the springboard to political power.

Chun, respected in Korean military circles for his professional competence and reputation for honesty, was a nationalist steeped in his country's traditional virtues. A soccer enthusiast, he captained the Military Academy team. In 1958 he married Lee Soon Ja, daughter of Brig. Gen. Lee Kyu Dong, then chief of staff of the Military Academy.

Church, Sam, Jr.

When Sam Church, Jr., was a boy, homes in the West Virginia coal country boasted pictures of three heroes: Jesus, Franklin D. Roosevelt, and John L. Lewis. The president of the United Mine Workers, Lewis had improved the miner's lot and made the UMW a power in national economic and political affairs. Stepping down after four decades as president, he was succeeded by a protégé, W. A. "Tony" Boyle, who was found guilty of the murder of a reform candidate for the presidency after a disputed election between the two men.

The U.S. Department of Labor supervised new elections, and reform candidate Arnold Miller won the top job in 1972. But he proved to be an inept administrator and negotiator who was unable to keep wildcat strikes from closing unionized mines. The UMW lost members, influence, and effectiveness. Then Miller suffered his second heart attack in late 1979 and resigned. He was succeeded on Nov. 16, 1979, by Sam Church, Jr., his vice-president and executive assistant, who was the son of a disabled miner and for eight years a miner himself.

At the first national union convention Church chaired, the membership gave him several votes of confidence. He won the right to name his own vice-president, and his proposal to double union dues was approved. The rank and file were clearly willing to trade some local autonomy for better national representation and effective leadership.

Early in 1980 Church began hiring the first of 100 new organizers to rebuild union membership. He also began amassing a strike fund worthy of the name. With new contracts in the offing, he meant to go to the bargaining table with the wherewithal to call strikes selectively. Observers expected him "to play off company against company" in the time-honoured Lewis tradition.

Forbes and other business journals cautiously applauded his election, believing he would restore discipline and end the wildcat strikes. Church says he enjoys management's respect because "I don't throw them the curves and I don't consider them the enemy. . . . Both the union and the industry have a job to do and that is to produce coal."

Born on Sept. 20, 1936, in Matewah, W.Va., Church attended college briefly and then went to work in a Baltimore, Md., sugar warehouse. He went to the mines in 1965 and held a series of local union jobs before being called to union headquarters in 1975.

Craig, Jim

Jim Craig was giving one last tug on the nation's heartstrings. The United States had just defeated Finland 4–2, winning its first Olympic gold medal in ice hockey since 1960. Craig's teammates were a pantomime of pandemonium on television sets throughout his country. But Craig was at the side of the rink, scanning the stands, and the words millions of Americans saw on his lips were, "Where's my father?"

For weeks, strangers asked Craig if he had found his father. "That impressed me," he said. "People really cared." In a country so cool toward ice hockey that its professional National Hockey League does not have a network television contract, people rallied for two weeks around the amateur stickhandlers who helped them forget about the embarrassment of Iranians holding American hostages and the danger of the Soviet troops in Afghanistan. Indeed, the gold-medal victory against Finland February 24 was somewhat of an anticlimax after the U.S. team had defeated the Soviet Union 4–3 two nights before.

In that victory goalie Craig made 36 saves against the same players who had consistently beaten NHL all-star teams. As he did so often, he shut out his opponents in the final period, when the U.S was overcoming a 3–2 deficit.

It was the youngest U.S. Olympic hockey team ever. Craig, born May 31, 1957, in North Easton, Mass., had just finished college. His Boston University team had been national champion in 1978, and he had been an all-American as a senior in 1979, completing his college career with a three-year record of 55 wins, 6 losses, and 3 ties. But for two weeks in February, the rest of the country knew little of Craig's past record. It knew him as an out-

WIDE WORLD

standing hockey player and a loving son who greeted his father after games and who missed his mother. She had died three years earlier. Toward the end of the Finland game, Craig was thinking about how proud she would have been. So when it ended, he had to make eye contact with his father.

That done, he joined his teammates at centre ice, accepted the gold medal, and unwound by dancing on the Lake Placid, N.Y., rink, kissing his medal, and waving his index finger. Within a week he was playing for the NHL Atlanta Flames in their first home sellout of the season, and on June 2 he was traded to his hometown Boston Bruins.

Falwell, Jerry

A new force appeared on the U.S. political scene in 1980 as fundamentalist Protestant ministers successfully organized their followers as political activists for conservative causes and candidates. These politicized evangelicals claimed credit for the election of Ronald Reagan (*q.v.*) as president of the U.S. and the defeat of liberal senators and congressmen across the country. While their claims may be exaggerated, most of the liberals targeted by the loose alliance of conservative political action committees and fundamentalist religious groups were defeated.

Their most notable success came in Alabama, where Republican Jeremiah Denton was elected to the U.S. Senate and Rep. John H. Buchanan, Jr., himself a conservative Baptist minister, was beaten in the Republican primary because he was not far enough to the right to satisfy the evangelicals. In Oklahoma Don Nickles won an upset victory in the Republican primary and was elected to the Senate with strong fundamentalist support.

Best known of these religious groups is Moral Majority Inc., founded and led by the Rev. Jerry Falwell, minister of the Thomas Road Baptist Church in Lynchburg, Va. Born in Lynchburg in 1933, Falwell was an outstanding high-school student and athlete. He graduated from a Bible college in Missouri in 1956 and then returned to Lynchburg to found his own independent Baptist church, in an abandoned soft drink-bottling factory. Six months later his first religious program appeared on local television. By 1980 his "Old Time Gospel Hour" was carried by almost 700 television and radio stations and was heard by some 18 million people each week. His church claimed 17,000 members, more than one-quarter of Lynchburg's population.

Falwell's religious-political crusade focused on what were described as "family issues." The Moral Majority opposed abortion, homosexual rights, and the Equal Rights Amendment and supported school prayer, increased defense spending, and a strong anti-Communist foreign policy. Falwell viewed the issues as more important than individual candidates and personally avoided making a formal endorsement of anyone, though he publicly announced that he would vote for Reagan.

Foot, Michael

In November 1980, at the age of 67, Michael Foot became leader of Britain's Labour Party following the retirement of James Callaghan. His choice by a majority vote of Labour members of Parliament, with 139 votes to 129 for Denis Healey, was in many ways a surprising outcome of some months of divisive internal conflict within the party. A late entrant in the contest, persuaded to run only by the insistence of his friends, Foot himself said he had never expected to become party leader.

A long and active political career in the Labour Party began for Foot when at the age of 21 (he was born in Plymouth, England, on July 23, 1913) he left the Liberals, with whom his family had strong links, to express his revulsion against the mass unemployment of the mid-1930s. From 1945, apart from a break between 1955 and 1960, he was a member of Parliament. In 1974 he established himself as a leading member of Prime Minister Harold Wilson's Cabinet team, first as secretary of state for employment in charge of complex and controversial trade union legislation and then, from 1976 to 1979, as leader of the House of Commons, a role that required him to hold the parliamentary party together. It was this experience that led him to the party leadership.

Meanwhile, in his first 40 years in the party Foot had won a reputation as a wild and wayward rebel of the left. This image did less than justice to his place in the rich tradition of dissent in British politics. As a writer and journalist, Foot was in the line of political pamphleteers reaching back to William Cobbett, John Wilkes, and Jonathan Swift. He was the author of a two-volume biography of Aneurin Bevan, his close friend and mentor, and was involved in the left-wing Labour weekly *Tribune* from the time of its founding in the 1930s until he joined the Cabinet.

Foot was a gifted speaker, whether in Parliament, on the platform, or in front of the television camera, one of the very few orators in contemporary British politics who could rouse an audience by the passion, conviction, and wit of his argument. Upon his election as party leader, he promised to launch "a hurricane of national protest" against unemployment and to bring the arms race back into the centre of political debate.

Fox, Terry

On the eve of the operation that removed his right leg because of bone cancer, Terry Fox read an article about a U.S marathon runner who had only one leg. Then and there, he was determined to run across Canada to help people who suffered from cancer. In October 1977 Fox asked the Canadian Cancer Society to sponsor what he called his "Marathon of Hope." His objective was to raise $1 million for cancer research. He did not wish to do this for fame or for financial gain, but instead to set a good example. As he told the Society, "The people in cancer clinics all over the world need people who believe in miracles. . . . I believe in miracles. I have to."

Terrence Stanley Fox of Port Coquitlam, B.C., was born in Winnipeg, Man., on July 28, 1958. At the time that he had his operation for removal of his right leg, he was a student at Simon Fraser University in British Columbia. After 14 months of training to learn how to use his artificial limb, he proclaimed himself ready for his marathon.

On April 12, 1980, Fox dipped his artificial limb into the Atlantic Ocean at St. John's, Newfoundland, and then began his cross-Canada run. Accompanying him was his friend Doug Alward, who drove a van supplied by Ford Canada. The War Amputees Association kept Fox's three artificial limbs in repair during his run and paid to have two new legs made. Jogging an average of 42 km (26 mi) a day, he received an enthusiastic welcome in every community through which he passed. Donations and pledges poured in from as far away as Cape Town, South Africa. Early in September, however, Fox was forced to stop his marathon at Thunder Bay, Ont., after running 5,375 km (3,339 mi), because it was discovered that cancer had spread to his lungs.

Fox had run slightly more than halfway to his goal and had collected nearly $2 million in donations. Although he was no longer running, his marathon continued. On Sept. 9, 1980, the CTV television network in Canada organized a four-hour telethon. This program sent the total donations skyrocketing to $12 million.

Fox became a Canadian folk hero. The government of British Columbia presented him with the province's highest honour, the Order of the Dogwood. Canadian Press named him Canadian of the Year, the first nonpolitician in 15 years to receive the award, and on September 19 he became the youngest Companion of the Order of Canada.

Gandhi, Indira Priyadarshini

In January 1980 Indira Gandhi marched back to power and took office for the fourth time as prime minister of India. But even in the 33 months that she had been out of power, the country's politics had revolved around her. The collapse of the Janata Party government was as much due to her strategy as to the contradictions and feuds among its components. The incapacity of the caretaker government of Charan Singh and his Lok Dal Party made people long for a "government that works," and in the January general elections the country entrusted itself to the hand that would govern. In her victory statement Mrs. Gandhi called for an end to "mutual recrimination and vindictiveness." Unlike the Janata government, she did not set up inquiry commissions against her opponents, but she got the president to dissolve assemblies in states that had Janata or Lok Dal governments. In subsequent elections her Congress (Indira) Party won handsomely.

The popular impression was that the mandate was not only for Indira Gandhi but also for her younger son and political protégé Sanjay Gandhi. At least half the new legislators were of the youth wing of the Congress Party. This created problems in running the party as well as in forming the Cabinet. Many of Indira Gandhi's old colleagues in government had cast their lot with the opposition. Some came back during and after the elections, but there was a reluctance to reward them with office in preference to those who had stood by her in her ordeals.

Sanjay Gandhi's death in a plane crash in June introduced new uncertainties in the party. Indira Gandhi chose to tread warily. Persistent economic trouble, the unresolved crisis in Assam, and the eruption of religious and caste riots gave an opportunity to the opposition to accuse her of indecisiveness and nonperformance. But public opinion polls and the result of 15 by-elections to various state assemblies held in November, of which Congress won 10, showed that her popular support was solid.

Indira Gandhi was born in Allahabad on Nov. 19, 1917, the only child of Jawaharlal Nehru, India's first prime minister. Educated mainly in Europe, in 1942 she married a lawyer, Feroze Gandhi (d. 1960), by whom she had two sons. Elected president of the Congress Party in 1959, she was minister for information and broadcasting from 1964 until 1966, when she became prime minister.

García, Matías William

The United States is a nation of immigrants, people who came to escape persecution or to find opportunity. Many of these new citizens follow a typical pattern. They arrive poor and uneducated. They encounter discrimination and often must take the worst jobs. After a few years they learn English and may begin to prosper. Their children become Americans.

Communist Cuba provided the U.S. with large numbers of immigrants in 1980. Some of these people were permitted to fly out. Others fled in boats, sailing 145 km (90 mi) to the coast of Florida. So many came that they overwhelmed the U.S. Immigration and Naturalization Service. They were housed in military camps while officials struggled to settle them permanently. It soon became apparent that Cuba had deliberately sent a number of undesirables along with the other refugees. Some new arrivals had psychiatric problems, while others had criminal records. There were riots in refugee camps and even a murder.

Matías William García, who was appointed commissioner of the Immigration and Naturalization Service in July 1980, stated that the service needs "a new policy and a new direction." He planned a reorganization to cope with the backlog of work resulting from the Cuban refugees, to improve administrative procedures, and to raise employee morale.

Thoroughly familiar with the problems of Spanish-speaking Americans, García was born on Nov. 7, 1927, in San Antonio, Texas, of Mexican descent. In 1951 he received a law degree from St. Mary's University in San Antonio. Until the late 1960s he practiced as a trial lawyer. At that time he became politically active as an advocate of the Mexican-American minority in Texas by challenging the validity of equal employment practices at a U.S. Air Force base near San Antonio. From 1972 to 1980 he was a Texas state representative, aggressively speaking in the legislature on behalf of Hispanics.

Griffith, Darrell

Darrell Griffith could leap four feet, toes to floor, on a single bound, but he did not seem to be able to keep his University of Louisville team from landing in a heap. As a freshman Griffith had promised to lead his college team to a national basketball championship. As a junior he watched from the bench as his team was upset in the national tournament for the third consecutive year. It was there that he decided that in building his playing style around fancy dunk shots he had made the frosting but forgotten the cake.

"I knew I was going to have to be able to do more than just jump if I wanted to be a complete player," Griffith said. So before his senior season he dribbled basketballs through an obstacle course of 12 chairs for three hours a night. As the only senior starter on Louisville's team, Griffith was better than ever in 1979–80, averaging 22.9 points, 4.8 rebounds, and 3.8 assists per game. He won two player of the year awards and made virtually every All-America team. He also led Louisville to the 1980 national championship on March 24.

In the championship game Louisville trailed the University of California at Los Angeles (UCLA) 50–45 with less than six and a half minutes to play. Within slightly more than four minutes, Griffith was responsible for a total of 11 points, giving Louisville a 56–54 lead it never lost in winning 59–54. UCLA coach Larry Brown called him "the greatest player in the country."

UCLA had tried guarding Griffith with three different people. The University of Iowa had tried four in the semifinal game, when Griffith scored 34 points. "I've guarded other guys who could leap high before," said Bob Hansen of Iowa, "but all of them could come down." After the season the Utah Jazz made Griffith the second choice in the professional National Basketball Association's draft of college players.

Griffith was born in Louisville, Ky., June 16, 1958, and began practicing dunk shots ten years later. He ran toward a netless basket in the alley behind his home and scaled a garage door to stuff the ball through the hoop. He was eight when he started shooting balls at that basket and throwing wadded-up socks at the light fixture in his room when he could not go outdoors.

Hagman, Larry

Question: What combines Texas oil, Hollywood soap, Byzantine intrigue, a $700,000-a-week price tag, 300 million addicts worldwide, and the seven deadly sins? Answer: "Dallas," a television serial that triumphed over everything but the Super Bowl in the U.S. TV ratings game and attracted more than half of Great Britain's population for one episode alone.

This slick multigenerational family saga features more skullduggery than the Old Testament as it strobes the sexual and corporate misdoings of more than 30 characters—all of them variously related by blood, marriage, venery, venality, vanity, vengeance, vendetta, and other vices. In the eye of this maelstrom oil baron J. R. Ewing, Jr., boozes, bribes, and debauches his way through some of the fastest paced scripts ever to haul prime time's winged chariot across the purple stage.

J. R. is played by Larry Hagman, whom critics say fits the part "like an iron whip in a velvet glove." He's "an overstuffed Iago in a Stetson hat" and has "a barracuda smile." Born in Weatherford, Texas, in 1931 to musical-comedy star Mary Martin and a Texas lawyer-politician, Hagman turned misfit after his parents' divorce. After a year of college he dropped out and joined his mother in *South Pacific* during its London run. After managing USO tours for the Air Force, he acted in New York City both on and off Broadway. He then moved to California, where he appeared in many movies and television shows. They included "I Dream of Jeannie," which featured him as an Air Force officer whose private and professional lives were alternately sandbagged and saved by the gorgeous genie he found in a bottle while marooned on a desert island. It ran on television for years.

According to Hagman, his character of J. R. Ewing in "Dallas" resembles some of the live oilmen, cattlemen, and politicians he met while chauffeuring his father, then a state senate candidate, around Texas. "My character is milk toast compared with some of those people," Hagman says. "Fratricide, patricide, brothers and sisters shooting each other. It was unbelievable." In the 1980 season's final episode he got shot, lying at death's door all summer while millions of fans waited—longer than expected because of an actors' strike—to find out whodunit.

Hawley, Sandy

When Sandy Hawley was a child, he liked to ride the hobbyhorse in the local five-and-dime store. Thus began a lifetime career of riding horses. On Sept. 1, 1980, Hawley won his 4,000th race, the 11th jockey in Thoroughbred racing history to reach that mark and the first to do so in only 12 seasons of racing. Hawley, whose mounts have earned over $2 million each year since 1973, has been considered a top jockey in Canada—and, in fact, in all North America—almost since his career began.

It was Hawley's uncle who suggested that Sandy would make a good jockey because of his small size, 5 ft 2 in tall and 110 lb. Sandford Desmond Hawley, who was born in Oshawa, Ont., on April 16, 1949, was always a good athlete in school. When he was 15, his uncle got him a job with Duke Campbell, a Canadian horse trainer who boarded his horses at E. P. Taylor's National Stud Farm (now Windfields Farm) in Oshawa. The first Thoroughbred that Hawley petted bit him; the first he rode bolted. Undeterred, he quickly established a rapport with horses. In his first full season of riding (1969) he was Canada's leading jockey. In 1973 Hawley set a record of 515 victories in one season and was acknowledged to be the top jockey in Canada and North America. In that same year, and again in 1976, Hawley won the Lou Marsh Trophy as Canada's best athlete. He was the second jockey to be made a Companion of the Order of Canada (1976); the first to be so honoured was Ron Turcotte.

In 1976 Hawley became the youngest jockey to achieve 3,000 victories. He also received in that year the Eclipse Award, North America's highest honour for a jockey, and the George Woolf Memorial Jockey Award for the rider who reflects credit on racing, his profession, and himself.

Although he resided in Ontario until 1979, Hawley began riding at the large California racetracks in 1974. Because he spent so much of the racing season there, Hawley moved to Arcadia, Calif., in 1979. He was injured in a race at the Santa Anita track in Arcadia in January 1980 and missed much of the racing season before scoring his 4,000th win.

Heiden, Eric Arthur

In the 1980 Winter Olympic Games, Eric Arthur Heiden took a sport that involves going in circles to a level of dizzying heights. By his performance he aroused interest in speed skating, a demanding exercise that previously had stirred fewer hearts in the U.S. than mud wrestling and tug-o'-war. The pride of Madison, Wis., was on the covers of three national magazines in the same week as he became the first skater in Olympic history to win gold medals in every one of the five events.

Heiden was not an overnight phenomenon. He and his younger sister, Beth, had been the darlings of U.S. speed skating since 1977. Eric was just 18 then and became the first world champion since 1891 from the United States, which had only one speed-skating rink (at West Allis, Wis.) until another was built at Lake Placid, N.Y., for the Olympics. Subsequently, he won three world championships and four world sprint championships. "And nobody knew. Nobody cared," Heiden said. Most U.S. sports fans prefer their competition man-against-man, and Heiden competed man-against-clock, circling an oval in a monotonous rhythm that an untrained eye found no more entertaining than watching a second hand sweep.

To make those eyes pop, Heiden had to make time stand still. He won the 1,000-m Olympic race by more time than separated the second- and ninth-place finishers. His winning margin in the 1,500 m was the same as the margin between number two and number seven. In his fifth victory on February 23, Heiden set a world record in the 10,000 m and won by the equivalent of 100 m. His closest call was in the 5,000 m, when he turned a 4.47-sec deficit after 1,400 m into a 1-sec lead at 4,200.

"There is no excitement to skating now," said Frode Rønning of Norway. "The medals can be delivered before the race. He is the greatest speed skater there has ever been, without a doubt. A lot of us are going to keep on skating next year because Eric is giving up."

All along, Heiden called the publicity surrounding his quest "the Great Whoopee," refusing to capitalize commercially on his Olympic success. He tried for a fourth world championship in Heerenveen, Neth., but, probably affected by a post-Olympic letdown, he won only one of the four races to finish second overall. Plans for his future included returning to college and possibly a career in medicine. For most of 1980, however, he was engaged in competitive bicycle racing and in promoting the sport of cycling.

Hunt, (Nelson) Bunker

Bunker Hunt lost money in 1980—something he rarely does. He lost so much and in such an extraordinary way that his failure caused a brief finan-

cial panic late in March. Hunt and his brother W. Herbert had been speculating in silver bullion and silver futures contracts (those that promise delivery of a commodity at a specified price and time). They started this in 1973 after concluding that they needed investments that were safer than foreign oil. Because silver consumption substantially exceeded production each year, the brothers foresaw a long-term silver price rise and began to purchase large quantities of the metal at $2 and $3 per troy ounce.

By January 1980 the Hunts, in association with Arab investors, were reputed to own more than 120 million oz of silver bullion and futures contracts, a substantial fraction of the world's annual production. By that time silver had risen to $52.50 per troy ounce. The brothers acquired their holdings by buying on margin (paying only a small fraction of the cost of the future in cash and borrowing the balance) and by reinvesting their profits from a steadily rising market in further purchases which drove the price still higher.

Silver prices collapsed when the Commodity Futures Trading Commission, a U.S. government agency, forced the Chicago Board of Trade and the New York Commodity Exchange to raise margin requirements (the fraction of a commodity future's cost payable in cash) for silver and to limit the number of futures contracts that any individual could hold. In so doing, the commission was attempting to lessen the rate of inflation. Its actions depressed the price of silver, causing the Hunts's brokers to withdraw credit and require cash. When the brothers were unable to meet these demands, their paper empire collapsed. In May the Hunts obtained a $1.1 billion loan from a consortium of 13 banks to help put their affairs in order.

Bunker Hunt would suffer few privations in spite of his 1980 losses. Born on Feb. 22, 1926, in El Dorado, Ark., he was the second of 14 children that H. L. Hunt sired by three wives. The elder Hunt, a legendary oilman, started with a $5,000 inheritance and built a fortune of more than $2 billion by the time of his death in 1974.

Kania, Stanislaw

Quite unexpectedly, on Sept. 6, 1980, Poland learned that Edward Gierek, leader of the Polish United Workers' (Communist) Party (PUWP) since Dec. 20, 1970, had been hospitalized following a heart attack. The party's Central Committee had released him from his post of first secretary and had unanimously called Stanislaw Kania to replace him in that position. Kania had been a full member of the Politburo since December 1975, but he was barely known to the Polish public. He immediately received a congratulatory telegram from Soviet Pres. Leonid Brezhnev, who described him as "standing firmly on the position of proletarian internationalism."

Kania told the Central Committee that the wave of strikes rolling across Poland was directed not

CAMERA PRESS

against the role of the party and its foreign policy but against the party's serious mistakes in economic matters and against "distortions in public life." He developed his policies in detail in his report presented to the Central Committee on October 6. Repeating his attachment to "democratic centralism" (*i.e.*, Communist Party predominance), he avoided mentioning "proletarian internationalism" (*i.e.*, undisputed Soviet leadership of the "socialist camp"). On October 21 Kania met the Polish primate, Stefan Cardinal Wyszynski, in Warsaw to discuss problems of internal peace and development. On October 30 he visited Moscow, and on November 14 he received strike leader Lech Walesa (*q.v.*). Kania appeared to wish to cooperate with the new independent trade union, and in this he was supported by the "liberal" wing of the party.

Son of a smallholder, Kania was born on March 8, 1927, at Wrocanka, a village near Krosno. He joined the anti-Nazi resistance movement in 1944 and the Communist Party in April 1945. After helping its Rzeszow provincial organization create a party youth movement, he was sent to the party school, graduating in 1952. He was made an alternate member of the Central Committee in 1964, a full member of that body in 1968, and a full member of the Politburo in 1975.

King, Stephen

"I like to scare people, I really do," says the young author who has terrified 22 million of them—assuming at least one reader finished each printed copy of his six published novels. Stephen King, in person a "tall, pudgy, bearlike," and basically amiable man, has been riding a wave of popularity since *Carrie* was published in 1974. According to the *New York Times Magazine*, he is a gentle nonconformist who lives quietly in a tiny Maine town and interrupts work to pick up his kids from nursery school. According to horror cultists, he is King of the Bizarre.

"I write about ordinary people caught up in extraordinary circumstances," he says, but this ordinariness is tinged with the psychic and the supernatural. *Carrie* concerns a high school girl who ignites her classmates at the senior prom by pyrokinesis. In *The Shining*, a boy sees murders in the past while his father, caretaker of a snowbound resort hotel in the Rockies, goes homicidally mad. *The Stand* constructs a thermonuclear Armageddon between the normally human and satanic survivors of a chemical warfare plague that accidentally sweeps the world. *Firestarter*, a best-seller in 1980, focuses on an eight-year-old girl who incinerates objects just by looking at them.

In his own view, King is the beneficiary of a popular craving for catharsis—an inevitable phenomenon in hard times. During the depression of the '30s, "people went to the movies for the same reason they go to the movies now—either to laugh or to get scared out of their minds." (Two of his novels have lit up box offices from coast to coast, *Carrie* and *The Shining*, which Stanley Kubrick made with Jack Nicholson and Shelley Duvall in 1980.) King goes on to describe a theory of "luridical" positivism. Horror fans, he believes, seek a kind of humane affirmation in scary fictions that present an outsider who threatens normal people, then is vanquished in the end. (By contrast, he says, science fiction celebrates the alien, the outsider, as heroic.)

The novelist was born in Portland, Me., on Sept. 21, 1947, and was raised in small towns by his mother after her husband deserted the family. He graduated from the University of Maine and taught English locally for $6,000 a year before writing *Carrie*, which earned a $2,500 advance. Published in paperback, it sold four million copies before becoming the film that made Sissy Spacek (*q.v.*) a star.

Lansing, Sherry Lee

Hollywood has known powerful women—and not only the "box-office bombshells," from Jean Harlow to Bo Derek. Performers like Gloria Swanson and Marilyn Monroe consorted with statesmen. Barbra Streisand and Goldie Hawn became sometime producers and directors. "Superagent" Sue Mengers was said to have at least as much influence as any executive in putting film "packages" together. But none ever quite held the title that bespoke her power. When Sherry Lansing took over as president of 20th Century-Fox in January 1980, she became the first to have the actual clout and the executive accoutrements.

She was the daughter of a lucky and aggressive woman who fled Europe with the Nazis at her heels before World War II, settled in Chicago, and supported herself as a realtor. Sherry Lee Lansing, born July 31, 1944, attended a school for gifted children and was graduated summa cum laude from Northwestern University's speech school in 1966. Her first job was teaching math in the riot-torn Watts section of Los Angeles. Burned out emotionally after three years, she turned to modeling, appeared in TV ad campaigns for Max Factor and Alberto-Culver, and then tried her hand at acting. She was featured in two films. "I wasn't interested in being an actress at first," she recalls, "but when I walked onto that set I started to become obsessed with film."

After taking courses at UCLA and USC, she started reading scripts at $5 an hour, became a story analyst at Universal, and then accepted Daniel Melnick's offer to be story editor at MGM. Promoted to the vice-presidency for creative affairs, she left MGM to take a similar job at Columbia when Melnick moved there. Before her ultimate promotion, she had had "total control" of only two films, but both were critical and commercial successes: *Kramer vs. Kramer* and *The China Syndrome*.

Known as hard working, efficient, and personable, she evidently meant to be a no-frills executive. At Fox, she was the fifth president in a decade, succeeding Richard Zanuck and Alan Ladd, Jr. Some insiders predicted she would be kept under the

TONY KORODY–SYGMA

thumbs of the parent corporation's officers, but no one quibbled about her reported $300,000 salary and possible bonuses totaling $1 million. One wag suggested that "Hollywood has a new story line: Girl meets Boy, Girl works for Boy, Girl replaces Boy at the top."

Lieberman, Nancy

Nancy Lieberman has taken the stereotype of a female basketball player to the baseline and destroyed it. In the 1980 New York Pro Summer League, the 5-ft 10-in, 146-lb guard was the only woman in a league dominated by professional stars, but former National Basketball Association scoring leader Nate Archibald said, "She's not a woman out there. She's a player."

Lieberman came along at just the right time for an aggressive player to yank women's basketball out of the sewing room and into the showroom. When she entered high school, girls' teams had just recently begun playing basketball with boys' rules instead of using a half-court version. College teams had not recruited women heavily until Lieberman started touring campuses. She chose Old Dominion University in Norfolk, Va. Her school won national championships in 1979 and 1980, with Lieberman averaging more than 20 points a game in her junior and senior years.

The Women's Professional Basketball League hoped she would do the same for its box offices when Dallas made her the first choice in its draft of college players. The league was struggling financial-

ly—several of its franchises had drowned in red ink —and it needed a star with the name recognition of Lieberman.

The national attention began in 1975 when, shortly before her 17th birthday on July 1, Lieberman became the youngest player ever to make the U.S. Olympic women's basketball team, which finished second in the 1976 Games. People began to notice then how much Lieberman played like the best men in the game, dribbling with her head up and the ball protected, passing behind her back to unguarded teammates, lifting her elbows to wedge into place for a rebound.

She had learned by playing against boys on the playgrounds, first in her Far Rockaway, N.Y., hometown and later in nearby New York City's Harlem ghetto. Her mother was not entirely sure that basketball was a properly dainty hobby for her daughter to be pursuing, and she once punctured the ball with a screwdriver. But she knew there was no stopping her daughter the day she flat out told her that basketball was for boys. Nancy stuck out her chin, assuming the posture of a guard about to make a charge, and told her mother, "Yeah? Then I'll make history."

Marriner, Neville

Only with the birth in London in 1959 of the Academy of St. Martin in the Fields (ASM) chamber ensemble under the direction of a dashing young violinist-conductor, Neville Marriner, did works such as Bach's *Brandenburg Concertos* and Vivaldi's *The Four Seasons* take on for the first time in more than a century the kind of sparkle and polish their composers surely intended. Gone, under Marriner's inspired stewardship, was the opaque, unornamented turgidity of 19th-century baroque performing style. Instead, everything was light and shade, the crisp virtuosity of ASM members yielding a fresh sophistication captivating in its transparency.

Such was the great success, critical and public, enjoyed by the ASM that Marriner's name within a short time became a watchword among the cognoscenti. Then, encouraged by Pierre Monteux to study conducting, Marriner turned to the larger symphonic forms. He subsequently conducted major symphony orchestras throughout the world, and for the 1979–80 season took up the music directorship of the Minnesota Symphony in succession to Stanislav Skrowaczewski.

Marriner was born in Lincoln, England, on April 15, 1924, into a family in which "music was . . . what television is for most people today." He studied at London's Royal College of Music (RCM)— with an interval of military service during 1941–43 —and later at the Paris Conservatory. His early career was as a violinist; he played with a number of small ensembles before gaining his first orchestral experience with the London Philharmonia and then joining the London Symphony Orchestra (LSO) to lead its second violin section. Meanwhile, he taught

Neville Marriner
MIKE EVANS–PHONOGRAM
INTERNATIONAL

briefly at Eton College and in 1950 became a professor at the RCM. It was during this time with the LSO that he turned to conducting, and subsequently his violin playing was reserved for private occasions.

In 1969 Marriner became music director and conductor of the Los Angeles Chamber Orchestra, with which he made a highly successful tour of Europe in 1974. In the summer of 1979 the ASM was resident orchestra at the Aix-en-Provence Festival in France, where Marriner directed it in concerts and in a new production of *The Marriage of Figaro*. In addition to his Minnesota directorship, he served as music director of the Detroit Symphony's Meadow Brook Festival.

Mondale, Walter

Walter Mondale's principal role during much of 1980 was to act as chief surrogate for Pres. Jimmy Carter in his campaign for reelection. In January he traveled to Iowa several times in advance of the state's Democratic caucus January 21. On January 10, during a three-day campaign swing through the state, Mondale accused Sen. Edward Kennedy of playing politics with the national interest in criticizing the Carter administration's grain embargo against the Soviet Union. On the same day, he suggested that the upcoming Summer Olympics should be moved out of Moscow because of the Soviet invasion of Afghanistan. On January 12 Mondale faced Carter's Democratic challengers in Iowa, Senator Kennedy and California Gov. Edmund G. (Jerry) Brown, in a minidebate. On January 16 he returned to the state for a final three-day campaign trip, again defending the administration's grain embargo to Iowa farmers.

Early in February the vice-president was in Maine, defending President Carter's decision not to campaign personally. At a luncheon meeting in Saco on February 5, he said, "The American people need their president down there in Washington working for them in these perilous times more than they need one more political speech." In March Mondale campaigned in Illinois, where Carter was the victor in the primary March 18.

On April 12 the vice-president attended the meeting of the House of Delegates of the U.S. Olympic Committee, held in Colorado Springs, Colo. He spoke to the delegates in support of the administration proposal to have U.S. athletes boycott the Moscow Summer Olympics. Afterward the delegates voted 1,604 to 797 in favour of a resolution to boycott the Games. The decision was seen as a major victory for the Carter administration.

On May 8 the vice-president arrived in Belgrade at the head of the American delegation attending the funeral of Yugoslav President Tito, who had died May 4 after a prolonged illness. The absence of President Carter from the U.S. delegation was criticized by many commentators.

On July 7 Mondale arrived in Detroit leading an administration team preparing for Carter's visit there the following day to discuss a package of proposals to help the auto industry recover from its severe economic slump.

At a meeting at the vice-president's home July 15 attended by Cabinet officers and White House and Carter campaign officials, it was decided that the Democratic strategy in the campaign would be "to set the record straight about Ronald Reagan," according to Democratic National Chairman John White.

Mondale was in Africa July 17–23, visiting Senegal, Niger, Cape Verde, and Nigeria, where July 23 he and Nigerian Vice-Pres. Alex Ekwueme signed economic accords aimed at strengthening trade and investment between the two countries. The administration hoped that the agreements would help reduce a projected $13 billion trade deficit in 1980 with Nigeria, the second-largest (after Saudi Arabia) exporter of oil to the U.S.

At the 38th Democratic national convention in New York City August 11–14, Mondale was renominated as President Carter's running mate. In his acceptance speech he delivered a sharp attack on Reagan and the Republicans.

Mondale's travels as the president's chief surrogate increased during the postconvention period. He sought to build party unity and to evoke traditional Democratic support, making many appearances before labour groups. Kicking off his fall campaigning with a home-state visit August 28 to the Minnesota State Fair, he addressed Labor Day gatherings in western Pennsylvania and in Cleveland, Ohio, on September 1.

In his campaign speeches the vice-president followed the campaign strategy established at the July 15 meeting, attacking Reagan's record on domestic issues and criticizing his statements on foreign policy. At a St. Louis press conference September 18 Mondale said that "in all the great civil rights fights, Mr. Reagan has opposed progress," while "virtually every significant black and Hispanic leader in the country supports President Carter." In a speech given in Rochester, N.Y., September 23 Mondale charged that Reagan had abandoned hope of arms control, and in another speech delivered the following day in Rhode Island, the vice-president maintained that Reagan would be too prone to dispatch troops to foreign trouble spots.

Mondale completed a coast-to-coast campaign trip on October 26, predicting a close win for President Carter. When the president abandoned campaigning during the final days before the election, Mondale filled in for him once again, completing Carter's scheduled itinerary to Chicago, Detroit, and Philadelphia on November 2–3, before joining the president for an appearance in Akron, Ohio, their only joint appearance of the fall campaign.

Mugabe, Robert

Robert Mugabe became prime minister of the new republic of Zimbabwe in April 1980 after his Zimbabwe African National Union (ZANU) won a clear majority in elections held to determine the future of the country formerly known as Rhodesia. Although he had been widely portrayed as a revolutionary Marxist and a tough guerrilla leader, Mugabe surprised his critics by displaying a spirit of forgiveness and tolerance toward his black and white opponents after gaining power. He included a number of his defeated black opponents in his government, as well as two white ministers, one of whom had been a Rhodesian Front leader in Ian Smith's former white supremacist regime. While Mugabe took his country into the nonaligned camp, he made it clear that he would look largely to the Western community for economic and technical aid. His tolerance and calm approach to the bristling problems inherited after a long and bitter war were decisive in preventing the chaos that many had predicted would be the fate of Rhodesia if the guerrillas of the Patriotic Front ever came to power.

Born in Kutama on Feb. 21, 1924, Mugabe was the son of a labourer. Educated by Roman Catholics, he became a teacher but soon showed his militant temperament when he threatened to "box the ears" of the then prime minister, R. S. Garfield Todd, when the government made deductions from the meagre wages of teachers. (He nominated Todd as a senator in his new Parliament.) He continued his education in South Africa at the University for Fort Hare, a nursery for black nationalism. From 1956 to 1960 he taught in Ghana.

Returning home, Mugabe joined Joshua Nkomo in the African nationalist movement. In 1963, however, he helped the Rev. Ndabaningi Sithole form ZANU, a breakaway from Nkomo's Zimbabwe African People's Union (ZAPU). Arrested in 1964, Mugabe was held in detention until 1974. He used this time to study law by correspondence and gained degrees from the University of London. After being released, he went into exile and established himself as an effective political leader of ZANU's military forces based in Mozambique. Mugabe cooperated with his old political rival, Nkomo, within the Patriotic Front uniting ZANU and ZAPU during the Lancaster House negotiations in London which ended the war in Rhodesia. After the agreement, however, his party decided to end its alliance with ZAPU in order to fight the elections on its own.

Muskie, Edmund Sixtus

When Cyrus Vance suddenly resigned as U.S. secretary of state in April 1980 to protest the ill-fated attempt to rescue the U.S. hostages in Iran, Pres. Jimmy Carter surprised Washington by giving the job to Sen. Edmund S. Muskie of Maine. It was seen as a masterful political stroke that removed from contention one of the few Democrats who might be a compromise presidential candidate should the Democratic convention become deadlocked between Carter and Ted Kennedy. The appointment also generated some badly needed support from the party's mainstream which viewed Muskie as the type of experienced leader who should have been on the Carter team from the beginning.

Knowing Muskie's pride and famous temper, Washington insiders also saw it as a setback for Zbigniew Brzezinski, the president's national security adviser, who frequently had outmaneuvered Vance in the ongoing rivalry between the National Security Council and the State Department. But five months later there were rumours that a frus-

Noguchi, Isamu

"His great strength is that he does not belong." Thus Calvin Tomkins summed up a *New Yorker* profile on Isamu Noguchi at a time when three major galleries, including the Whitney Museum of American Art, simultaneously were celebrating his work. Genetically Occidental and Oriental, artistically surrealistic, naturalistic, and traditional, Noguchi has been described as the "preeminent American sculptor." Yet other critics regard him as Japanese like his father, a poet and professor of English, or as pan-national like his mother, a woman of Scots-Irish and U.S. Indian descent.

Born in Los Angeles on Nov. 17, 1904, Noguchi was reared in Japan. Returning to the United States, he was apprenticed to sculptor Gutzon Borglum, who told him to quit sculpting. Noguchi was then taken in by Romanian sculptor Constantin Brancusi, from whom he learned the art by example because neither spoke the other's language. Noguchi later designed dance sets for Martha Graham, New York City playgrounds for parks commissioner Robert Moses, and gardens for UNESCO headquarters in Paris and for the *Reader's Digest* building in Tokyo.

The materials and forms of Noguchi's work are as varied as his credits: huge steel fountains; featherweight lamps made of mulberry paper; table-sized stone "landscapes" like "The Wave," which looks like a crystal bubble of Swedish granite; such structures as the 12-story aluminum "Detroit Pylon"; interior furniture.

Art critics despair at fitting his works into conventional cubbyholes, just as museum directors despair at finding floors strong enough to support his largest polished stones. "There is, in any case, no reason to feel frustrated because we cannot find a skeleton key to Noguchi's oeuvre," an *Art in America* critic mused. "He spreads himself willfully, not to say in spite of himself, all over the place, and in so doing produces an art whose frequent appearance of simplicity is only the mask for a diversity of motives issuing from a highly convoluted expressive temperament."

Obote, Milton

In December 1980 Apollo Milton Obote became the first African leader to regain his presidency through an electoral process after having been deposed by a military coup. He had been overthrown as president of Uganda by Gen. Idi Amin in January 1971. Obote spent the next eight years in exile in neighbouring Tanzania as the guest of his friend Pres. Julius Nyerere. He used the time to establish a new core for his former ruling Uganda People's Congress (UPC) and to sustain his army in exile, numbering about 700 men. These two elements played a leading role in helping the Tanzanian Army to overthrow Amin in early 1979 and provided the foundation on which Obote was able to build the electoral organization that enabled him

trated and angry Muskie was ready to quit because of his inability to control the State Department bureaucracy and Brzezinski's continuing influence over foreign policy. Both Carter and Muskie denied the reports.

But it all became academic when Carter lost the election to Ronald Reagan. With a dozen leading Democratic senators going down to defeat as well, the party was left desperately short of leaders with Muskie's experience and stature. Born March 28, 1914, in Rumford, Maine, he had served six years in the Maine House of Representatives before being elected governor in 1954 and U.S. senator four years later. In 1968 he became nationally known as Hubert Humphrey's vice-presidential running mate. His excellent performance in that losing cause made him a favourite for the 1972 Democratic presidential nomination, but a combination of poor organization, fatigue, and the famous Muskie temper lost it in the early primaries.

In his fourth term and 22nd year in the Senate, Muskie was a powerful and respected figure when Carter named him to the Cabinet. As the first and only chairman of the Budget Committee, he had forced the committees to work within their budget and spending targets. It was uncertain what Muskie would do after a lifetime in office, but Republicans as well as Democrats agreed that the Senate would miss him.

to defeat his Democratic Party opponents.

Milton Obote (he does not use the name Apollo) was born Dec. 28, 1925, in the village of Akokoro in the Lango district in central Uganda, the third of nine children of a peasant family. After completing secondary school, he entered the East African university college of Makerere but was expelled for his political activities before he could graduate. When the colonial government prevented the militant young nationalist student from accepting scholarships offered to him in the U.S. and West Germany, he crossed the border into Kenya in 1950 to work as a labourer on the sugar plantations and to acquire experience in trade unionism. He joined the party of Kenyan leader Jomo Kenyatta, the Kenya African Union, and became involved in the independence struggle of that country.

Obote returned to Uganda in 1957 and was at once nominated by his district to represent it in the colonial Legislative Council. A year later he was elected to the new legislature as a member of the Uganda National Congress, which he soon left to form the UPC. In 1962 he led his party to victory in the elections immediately prior to Uganda's independence.

A conflict between Obote's ruling party and the ruling Kabaka of Buganda, which led to the defeat and exile of the Kabaka, left deep tensions between it and the people of Buganda (a large district of Uganda). Obote narrowly escaped two attempts to assassinate him. However, by 1967 he felt sufficiently strong to present a new constitution, based on a multiparty parliamentary system, and proposed to campaign for election. He was overthrown by Amin before the new elections could take place.

Raja'i, Mohammad Ali
Mohammad Ali Raja'i, a former teacher of mathematics and a leading member of the clergy-dominated Islamic Republican Party (IRP), was elected by the Majlis (parliament) on Aug. 11, 1980, to be the second prime minister of the Islamic Republic of Iran. For more than nine months following the resignation of Mehdi Bazargan, Iran had had no prime minister. Three candidates for the post proposed by Pres. Abolhassan Bani-Sadr (*q.v.*) were rejected by the IRP, and Raja'i became prime minister against the advice of the president. He soon came in conflict with Bani-Sadr over his choice of ministers; only two-thirds of those originally put forward by Raja'i were included in the Cabinet approved by the Majlis on September 10.

Born in 1933 in Kazvin, about 160 km (100 mi) northwest of Teheran, Raja'i enlisted in the Iranian Air Force at the age of 16. In 1960 he obtained his teacher's diploma. He joined the Iranian Liberation Movement in 1960 and was imprisoned three times for his political activities. He became a member of the Central Committee of the Association of Islamic Teachers and headed the Ministry of Education in the first post-revolutionary Cabinet.

WIDE WORLD

Six weeks after Raja'i became prime minister, Iraq launched its attack against Iran. According to Teheran radio, he replied to an offer of Soviet military assistance by telling the Soviet ambassador that "Iran is not ready to exchange its independence for Soviet aid." In New York City in October to address the UN Security Council, Raja'i declared that "a fair settlement can be found only if the aggressor is conquered and punished; this is our final position." While in New York City, he told reporters that a decision on the U.S. hostages was "not far away" but alluded to some "obstacles to a solution" and declined to meet any U.S. officials before returning to Teheran.

Rather, Dan
After becoming television's first "anchorman" at the 1952 political conventions, Walter Cronkite covered every major news event and countless minor ones for three decades. As on-camera managing editor of the "CBS Evening News," he rose to unrivaled esteem; one pollster found him to be the most respected man in America. But he moaned, "I'm not a newsman anymore, I'm just a personality." Having covered every presidential inauguration from Harry Truman's to Jimmy Carter's, he decided to step down after one more. CBS executives piously said nobody would ever "replace" him, but the question remained: "Who would succeed Cronkite?"

After months of secret negotiations, Dan Rather answered that he would. But this was not just a matter of being chosen for the job. Rather had already turned down offers for the top newsman job at ABC and NBC in order to remain at CBS with a contract that would earn him at least $1 million a year for five years.

Born in Wharton, Texas, on Oct. 31, 1931, the son of a waitress and an oil pipeline labourer, Rather studied at Sam Houston State Teachers College in Huntsville, Texas. After graduation he went to work for the *Houston Chronicle* but soon left print journalism for radio station KTRH, the Houston affiliate of CBS. There he climbed the ladder from writer to reporter to news director before switching to the network's local television outlet as director of news and public affairs.

He first gained national attention when happenstance put him in the right place at the right time—marooned with a TV crew on Galveston Island during a killer hurricane in 1961. His unruffled performance won him a job covering civil rights for CBS, and two years later he happened to be in Dallas when Pres. John F. Kennedy was assassinated. He not only covered that shattering story and its aftershocks but also skillfully coordinated nonstop coverage for days. He became CBS's White House correspondent in 1964 and then was sent abroad to assignments in London and Vietnam. In 1966 he returned to his White House post, where his aggressive questioning often incurred the ire of Richard Nixon's administration. In 1975 Rather was named a co-anchorman of CBS's popular television news show "60 Minutes."

Reagan, Ronald Wilson

On Nov. 4, 1980, Ronald W. Reagan was elected the 40th president of the United States, in a landslide that produced a nationwide Republican victory. The former governor of California received 51% of the popular vote to 41% for Pres. Jimmy Carter, 7% for independent John Anderson, and 1% for minor candidates. Reagan carried 44 of the 50 states, overwhelming Carter 489 to 49 in electoral votes.

At the age of 69, Reagan was the oldest man to become president, though his age never became an issue in the campaign. Born in Tampico, Ill., on Feb. 6, 1911, he was graduated from Eureka College in Illinois. After graduation he became a radio sports announcer, first in Davenport and then in Des Moines, Iowa. In 1937 he began a long career as a motion-picture actor. Among his most notable films were *Knute Rockne—All American* (1940), *Kings Row* (1942), and *The Hasty Heart* (1950). From 1947 to 1952 and from 1959 to 1960 he served as president of the Screen Actors Guild.

When his movie career declined, Reagan became a traveling spokesman for General Electric Co. as well as host of "General Electric Theater" on television. During that time he changed from a Democrat to a conservative Republican and campaigned for Barry Goldwater for president in 1964.

Reagan's success as a political speaker led to his decision to run for governor of California as a Republican in 1966. He won and was reelected in 1970, serving in that office until 1974. He made a halfhearted bid for the Republican presidential nomination in 1968 and seriously attempted to take it away from Pres. Gerald Ford in 1976.

The 1980 Reagan campaign got off to a shaky start when he was upset by George Bush (*q.v.*) in the Iowa precinct caucuses. But Reagan quickly came back to win the New Hampshire primary and never again was seriously threatened for the nomination. At the July convention in Detroit he chose Bush to balance the ticket over objections from his conservative supporters, who felt that Bush was a "moderate."

But that was exactly what Reagan wanted, and throughout the campaign he moderated his own

Ronald Reagan
STEVE MELTZER–AUTHENTICATED NEWS INTERNATIONAL

conservative positions on many issues in order to attract the independent and Democratic voters he needed to win. In his acceptance speech and during the televised debates, Reagan quoted Franklin D. Roosevelt and made a special effort to convince Democrats that he was not a right-wing ideologue.

While Reagan attacked the Carter administration's record, Carter painted Reagan as a simplistic and dangerous right-winger whose policies might lead the country into war or a depression. This strategy was partly successful until the Carter-Reagan televised debate on October 28 in Cleveland, during which Reagan skillfully refuted the charges.

Rogers, Kenny

The recipient of the 1980 Grammy for best male country vocalist (awarded by the National Academy of Recording Arts and Sciences) is not only a survivor in a business dependent on fickle fans and changing styles but a good subject for nostalgia buffs. Kenny Rogers began his career with the Bobby Doyle Jazz Trio and later was a member of The New Christy Minstrels folk singers and The First Edition pop/rock group.

Rogers's ability to adapt and assimilate various musical genres is a key factor in his continuing success, but the common denominator in his style is the influence of country music. His soft, yet grainy voice has always reflected the country sound of his Texas childhood. Equally important is that he recognizes what he does best, the country story-ballad. One of the biggest hits for The First Edition was "Ruby Don't Take Your Love to Town," written by country singer Mel Tillis.

After The First Edition broke up in 1975, Rogers enjoyed steady but modest success as a solo country artist. Then in 1977 his career skyrocketed. His recording of "Lucille" hit number one early in the year and won him a Grammy, four Academy of Country Music (ACM) awards, and the Country Music Association's award for male vocalist of the year. Between 1977 and mid-1979 he had sold more than five million records, collected two platinum and five gold solo albums, and recorded two gold duet albums with Dottie West. As well as receiving more awards, including the 1979 ACM entertainer of the year, he has been host on the Johnny Carson "Tonight" show, emceed two television specials of his own, and starred in a made-for-TV movie based on his recording of "The Gambler."

Born in 1938, Rogers grew up with six other children in what he refers to as a Houston tenement. His father's family enjoyed playing musical instruments and, after briefly attending college in Houston, he decided to try to make his living with music. By 1980 he was performing in more than 200 sold-out concerts a year.

Salnikov, Vladimir

The young man had put Soviet swimming on the world map in the late 1970s. Before him, said Sergey Vaitsekhovsky, senior coach of the Soviet national swimming team, "not a single Soviet swimmer won at major contests, to say nothing about approaching world records." But he surpassed himself at the 1980 Moscow Olympic Games. On July 22 Vladimir Salnikov won the 1,500-m freestyle in a world record time of 14 min 58.27 sec, more than 4 sec faster than Brian Goodell's previous record of 15 min 2.40 sec set at the Montreal Olympic Games in 1976. On July 24 Salnikov won his second Olympic gold medal in the 400-m freestyle in 3 min 51.31 sec. Of Salnikov's 1,500-m performance, John Hennessy, *The Times* of London correspondent who witnessed it, wrote, "He was well ahead at the finish and no doubt could have clipped a few more seconds off his time had he been extended."

Leading up to his 1980 Olympic triumphs, Salnikov was European 1,500-m champion in 1977, world champion in the 400-m and 1,500-m freestyle in 1978, and winner of all his races in a brilliant 1979 season, setting new world records for the 400-m (3 min 51.40 sec, later surpassed) and 800-m (7 min 56.49 sec) freestyle.

Salnikov was born in Leningrad on May 21, 1960, the son of a sea captain. He began swimming at the age of six and quickly drew the attention of coaches from the Ekran Juvenile Sport School in Leningrad, one of the leading swimming centres of the U.S.S.R. Salnikov then devoted almost all his spare time to training sessions in the school's swimming pool. However, regular training and frequent trips to contests did not affect his studies. He finished secondary school with good marks and was admitted into the Leningrad Lesgaft Institute of Physical Culture, where he was a second-year student in 1980.

Sauvé, Jeanne

The first order of business when the 32nd Canadian Parliament convened on April 14, 1980, was the election of the first woman speaker of the House, the Hon. Jeanne Sauvé. Competent, conscientious, and pragmatic, Sauvé studied her House of Commons catechism for an hour a day to prepare herself for the job.

This was the fourth time in her eight years in Parliament that Sauvé had had to acclimatize herself to a new position. After she was elected in 1972 to represent the riding of Ahuntsic (Montreal), she was made the minister of state for science and technology, becoming the first Quebec woman to serve in the federal Cabinet. She also served in the Cabinet as minister of the environment (1974) and as minister of communications (1975–79). On Nov. 29, 1978, she assumed the position of adviser to the secretary of state for external affairs. In this role she was responsible for advising on relations with the French-speaking world. Sauvé was reelected as the member of Parliament for the riding of Laval-des-Rapides in 1979.

Born on April 26, 1922, in Prud'Homme, Sask.,

the former Jeanne Mathilde Benoit grew up in Ottawa. From 1942 to 1947 she served as the national president of Jeunesse Étudiante Catholique Internationale, a Roman Catholic students' organization. She studied economics in London (1948–50) and was granted a diploma in French civilization by the University of Paris in 1951.

After a year working for UNESCO in Paris, she returned to Canada and began a career as a journalist and broadcaster. From 1952 to 1972 she worked for the Canadian Broadcasting Corporation and La Société Radio Canada. In 1972 she was one of the founders of the Institute of Political Research, a government-sponsored agency formed to advise the federal Cabinet.

It was but one step from adviser to the Cabinet to elected member of the Cabinet. She had married the Hon. Maurice Sauvé, who was himself a member of Parliament from 1962 to 1968 and forestry minister in the Cabinet of Lester Pearson from 1964 to 1968. During her years in the House of Commons, Jeanne Sauvé was both popular and powerful. When Prime Minister Pierre Trudeau (*q.v.*) proposed her for the office of speaker of the House, she believed that she had been chosen partly because of her sex.

Seaga, Edward Philip George
Edward Seaga, who took office as Jamaica's prime minister on Nov. 1, 1980, was both by personality and by politics almost the exact opposite of his predecessor, Michael Manley. While Manley had the charisma and oratorical skills that kept audiences spellbound, Seaga, though certainly capable of holding his own at public meetings, was much more of a private person. This had the effect on both Jamaicans and outsiders of making him appear calculating, uncompromising, and lacking in warmth. But in reality he was a caring man of ideas, with a strong resolve to carry through what he believed to be right. Though unsmiling in public and a disciplinarian within the Jamaica Labour Party (JLP), he was more relaxed in private.

Seaga was pro-Western, pro-free enterprise, and generally to the right of centre in terms of Caribbean politics. His support of big business, Western models of development, and International Monetary Fund (IMF) assistance for Jamaica earned him the largely unwarranted reputation of not being concerned about the poor. Both his personal and public life belied this; unlike many JLP parliamentarians, he had a clear understanding of the poor, having spent several months living and working in rural communities while undertaking research. His constituency incorporated an area that, as minister of development, he had transformed from a slum into a model of rehabilitation.

The son of a Lebanese immigrant to Jamaica, Seaga was born in Boston, Mass., in 1930. He was educated at Wolmer's Boys School (Kingston), Harvard University, and the University of the West Indies, where he studied child development, revival cults, and faith healing. In 1959, while working as a financial consultant and university lecturer, he entered the upper house of the Jamaican Legislative Council as its youngest member ever. He was elected to Parliament and was appointed minister of development and welfare. In 1967 he became minister of finance and planning and developed a reputation as something of a financial wizard. When the People's National Party won the 1972 election, the then JLP leader, Hugh Shearer, stepped down. Seaga was appointed to succeed him and, despite criticism, remained party leader when the JLP suffered its second consecutive defeat in 1976.

Shaffer, Peter
British playwright Peter Shaffer won his greatest theatrical triumph in 1980. His drama *Amadeus*, premiered at London's National Theatre in the autumn of 1979, won several top honours in 1980: the Best Play Award given by the London daily newspaper *The Evening Standard* and *Plays and Players* magazine's Best New Play of the Year Award. Also, for the best performance of the year, the Variety Club of Great Britain Award was given to Paul Scofield in the leading role of Salieri, the Austrian composer and contemporary of Mozart whose rivalry with the younger man of genius provided the framework for the most controversial drama of the season.

Amadeus was highly praised as one of the finest plays of its day by every critic except one. The exception was James Fenton of *The Sunday Times*, who vilified it but provided the National Theatre with a useful quote in its advertisements: "the play James Fenton loves to hate."

Most of Shaffer's plays were performed by the National Theatre. His psychological drama *Equus* (1973), about the mutilation of a stableful of horses by a deranged stable lad, also won accolades in its time, was widely staged throughout the world, and made an absorbing film.

Born in Liverpool on May 15, 1926, and educated at St. Paul's School in London and Trinity College, Cambridge, Shaffer—after completing his national service in the coal mines—worked in the New York City Public Library and for a London music publisher. He was also music critic of a London weekly for a year, but after the success of his first acclaimed play, *Five Finger Exercise* (1958), he devoted all his time to writing dramas and comedies, television plays, film scripts, and thrillers, the last in collaboration with his twin brother, Anthony. The epic *The Royal Hunt of the Sun* (1964) dealt with the search of the Spanish conquistador Francisco Pizarro for the Inca god Atahuallpa. He wrote *The Battle of Shrivings* (1970) for John Gielgud, who had made Shaffer's name by directing *Five Finger Exercise*. *Amadeus*, directed by Peter Hall, opened at New York City's Broadhurst Theatre in December 1980.

Spacek, Sissy

If Monday's child is fair of face and Tuesday's tot is full of grace, perhaps a Christmas baby comes with gifts to personify everything in Santa's stocking from lumps of coal to sugarplums. Sissy Spacek, born in a small Texas town on Dec. 25, 1949, was variously a squirrel hunter, frog gigger, rodeo rider, drum majorette, Spanish Club officer, and homecoming queen. Starting out with a mail-order guitar, she studied with a local preacher and then gave lessons herself at 50 cents an hour. But before she could even get a part in her high-school play, her brother was stricken with leukemia and she was packed off to visit cousins Rip Torn and Geraldine Page in New York City.

They introduced her to show business, and she aimed at wowing the world as a rock singer before enrolling in Lee Strasberg's Theatrical Studio—and discovering that she knew everything the "Method" master had to teach. Between modeling stints, bubble-gum commercials, and nightclub singing jobs, she auditioned for movies and won a featured role in *Prime Cut*, a morbid white-slavery saga that the public ignored. In one critic's view it bombed because Spacek's sensitive performance "made too many people feel guilty."

Next she appeared as the passive-romantic-sadistic tagalong to Martin Sheen's teenage psychopathic murderer in *Badlands* and then as a waif in the homespun television serial "The Waltons." Her first major recognition came in the title role in *Carrie*, a terrifying film adaptation of a horror novel by Stephen King (*q.v.*). She played a miserable teenager who repays various tormentors by destroying them via telekinesis. In this as in previous performances, she won favourable reviews and the attention of her peers.

In 1980 Spacek won her second motion picture Academy Award nomination for portraying country music star Loretta Lynn in *Coal Miner's Daughter*. Aging 22 years in the film, she grows from barefoot urchin to the epitome of Nashville chic. Roger Angell applauded in *The New Yorker* "her ability to convince us so easily that she is a young-looking 14-year-old at the beginning, and a bewigged, decked-out, 40ish celebrity-star, and a mother of six, at its end."

Stirling, James Frazer

An unusual honour for an architect still in his prime is to receive the Gold Medal for Architecture of the Royal Institute of British Architects, but this award was bestowed upon James Stirling in 1980. Best known for his three "red" buildings of the 1960s, major monuments of a style later termed "brutalist," he was a powerful spokesman for the generation of architects who entered practice after World War II. Typically, his work emphasized the importance of materials, especially in his use of hard technological surfaces of brilliant red brick, glass, tiles, metal, and plastic. His buildings stand in sculptural

COURTESY, THE ROYAL INSTITUTE OF BRITISH ARCHITECTS

isolation from their landscapes in their uncompromising geometrical organization, their different parts clearly articulated as form and texture contrast and curves and angles collide, defined by bright strident colours and hard shiny surfaces.

Stirling was born in Glasgow on April 22, 1926, and educated in Liverpool, receiving his architectural training at the University of Liverpool's School of Architecture (1945–50). He began practice in the early 1950s in London and from 1956 to 1963 was in partnership with James Gowan. His early projects consisted of housing. His work always showed a concern for social usage and a sense of community, and he was one of the first to advocate the type of low-rise mass housing that found favour in Britain after the failure of high-rises as a solution to low-cost housing problems. His first major "red" building was the Engineering Department building for Leicester University (1959–63). Two variations on this theme followed: the History Faculty Library for Cambridge University (1964–67) and the Florey Building at Queen's College, Oxford (1966–71). In these three works Stirling integrated the industrial ethic with architectural form in a new way. The Leicester building arguably had the greatest impact on architects of any postwar building. With its hard red brick and tile and its glass and industrial framing, it was a radical departure.

Stirling's Olivetti Training School at Haslemere, Surrey (1969–72), exhibited a change of emphasis toward a greater manipulation of space and the use of newer materials. Later works were less "hard" and technological, revealing an increasing interplay of shapes, spaces, and symbols.

Suzuki, Zenko

Zenko Suzuki was virtually unknown at home and abroad when he was elected prime minister of Japan on July 17, 1980. Masayoshi Ohira, his predecessor, had been forced in mid-May to call new elections when factious members of his own Liberal-Democratic Party (LDP) withheld their support in a crucial parliamentary vote of no confidence. Ohira died unexpectedly ten days before the election, which the LDP won overwhelmingly. Then a three-week battle for succession was on. When supporters of the three main candidates refused to compromise, party leaders Takeo Fukuda and Kakuei Tanaka, both former prime ministers, swung their support to dark horse Suzuki. Though he had never served as party secretary-general or held any of the key portfolios, Suzuki, a loyal and longtime party workhorse, was elected party president, assuring him the prime ministership.

Suzuki was born on Jan. 11, 1911, in Yamada Town, Iwate Prefecture. Because his fisherman father could afford nothing better, Suzuki attended Imperial Fisheries Institute (now Tokyo University of Fisheries), then joined the Japan Fisheries Association. In 1947, "burning with humanitarianism,"

KEYSTONE

he won a seat in the lower house of the Diet (parliament) as a Socialist. Realizing he had little hope of getting government funds to aid constituents recovering from two devastating 1948 typhoons, he switched to the conservative Liberal Party (forerunner of the LDP) and won reelection 12 times. His gifts as a mediator in Japan's complex political world also brought him the chairmanship of the LDP executive council a record ten times.

It comes as no surprise, therefore, that Prime Minister Suzuki has adopted the slogan "politics of harmony." He is continuing Ohira's foreign policy of moderate internationalism and is working closely with the U.S., other Western nations, and China. In matters of finance, trade, and defense he has been cautious. If recent polls are to be trusted, excessive caution may contain the seeds of Suzuki's eventual downfall. Numerous voters apparently feel he has not been aggressive enough in facing controversial issues, such as debating a revision of the postwar constitution and solving the dilemma of visiting Yasukuni Shrine, which honours Japan's war dead. An official visit would be an implicit endorsement of Shinto as a state religion, a status it no longer enjoys. One newspaper editorial urged Suzuki to speak out more clearly on his political beliefs. The prime minister doubtless heard the message; time will tell if he feels he must also heed it.

Taylor, Kenneth

A man who enjoyed reading cloak-and-dagger novels, Ambassador Kenneth Taylor masterminded his own "Canadian Caper" in Iran. After the U.S. embassy was seized by militants on Nov. 4, 1979, Taylor, the Canadian ambassador to Iran, found himself host to six members of the U.S. embassy staff who had escaped capture. After hiding them for more than three months, Taylor helped engineer their escape from the country. While Iranians were preoccupied with their presidential election, the Canadian embassy was closed and the Americans, supplied with Canadian passports, were spirited out of the country as part of the Canadian entourage.

Although he insisted that his was not an individual effort and that he had had the advice of others in engineering the escape, Taylor became a hero for the U.S. The U.S. Congress awarded him a specially struck gold medal. For six months Taylor and his wife crisscrossed the United States, making speeches, shaking hands, and receiving awards. The American Academy of Achievement presented him with its Gold Plate Award; the state of California with its Medal of Merit; and the Detroit-Windsor Border Area with the International Freedom Festival Award.

Born in Calgary, Alta., on Oct. 5, 1934, Taylor received a B.A. degree from the University of Toronto in 1957 and an M.A. degree in business administration from the University of California at Berkeley in 1959. After graduation in 1959 Taylor joined the Canadian Foreign Service's Trade Com-

missioner Service, for which he served in several posts, both in Canada and abroad, until 1977. His first posting with the Canadian Department of External Affairs took place in 1977, when he was made ambassador to Iran. He was chosen for this post because he had the skills and experience to promote sales of Canadian-made pulp and paper equipment and thermal power plant parts.

Canadians were also proud of Taylor's Iranian success. The Canadian government made him an Officer of the Order of Canada, and Laurentian University in Sudbury, Ont., gave him an honorary degree. The citizens of New York City, who had given Taylor the key to their city in 1980, were delighted when in July 1980 he was appointed the Canadian consul general in New York and the commissioner to Bermuda.

Thatcher, Margaret Hilda

In her second year as Britain's first woman prime minister, Margaret Thatcher reinforced her claim to the nickname "the iron lady." There were to be no reversals of policy, none of the so-called U-turns which had characterized the governments of the 1970s. Committed to a monetarist policy of squeezing inflation out of the economy by cutting government expenditure and holding down the money supply by high interest rates, she had said in 1979 that things would get worse before they got better.

Get worse they did, with unemployment over two million, inflation rising from 10 to 20% in the government's first year and falling only slowly in the later months of 1980, sky-high interest rates, and a surge of bankruptcies. But Thatcher did not flinch from the consequences of the monetarist remedy. She resisted pressures from business to lower interest rates, and she persisted with a crusade against government and public-sector expenditure regardless of mounting protests from within her own Conservative Party. In one sector she could claim some success—there was a decline in the level of wage increases as trade unions came to see that there was a limit to the employers' capacity to pay.

Thatcher's abrasive, hawkish style was also seen in her conduct of foreign affairs. She secured a substantial refund of British contributions to the European Economic Community, though at the cost of some ill feeling among her fellow heads of state. She echoed the hard-line attitudes of the U.S. toward the Soviet Union, and she brought the U.K. into the nuclear arms race with decisions to provide bases in Britain for cruise missiles and to spend £5 billion on a new generation of nuclear submarines. She was coldly unsympathetic to the Brandt Commission's proposals to move ahead with aid for the third world.

Margaret Thatcher was born on Oct. 13, 1925, the daughter of a successful grocer who became the mayor of the small market town of Grantham, Lincolnshire. After studying science at the University of Oxford, she worked for a time as a research chemist. But politics was her first interest, and in 1959 she was elected to Parliament. A member of the Cabinet (as minister of education and science) in

Edward Heath's government of 1970–74, she was elected leader of the Conservative Party after the defeat of the Heath government in the 1974 general election.

Thompson, Daley Francis

The 1980 Olympic Games decathlon champion, Daley Thompson, was never reluctant to come forward. Before the Moscow Games he said: "I don't even think about the possibility of not winning—it never occurs to me. I really am that confident." An engaging, articulate young man who was given much television and press coverage, Thompson earned the tag of the "Muhammad Ali of track."

The brash 22-year-old justified his confidence with a briefly held world record score (8,622 points) for the tough ten-event test at Götzis, Austria, in May 1980. In Moscow Thompson ran, jumped, hurdled, and threw his way to the Olympic decathlon title, running up 8,495 points; his chief rival, Guido Kratschmer (West Germany), the current world record holder (8,649), did not compete because of West Germany's Olympic boycott.

Born in London on July 30, 1958, the son of a Nigerian father and a Scottish mother, Thompson completed his first decathlon at 16 in Cwmbran, Wales, in 1975 and won it with 6,685 points, a record total for his age. He then trained under coach Bruce Longden at Crawley, West Sussex, for the 1976 Olympic Games where he finished 18th. Later, Thompson raised the U.K. record to 7,905 and then ran up 7,921 in May 1977 at Götzis. In 1977 he amassed 8,190 in Madrid and won the European junior title at Donetsk, Ukraine. Thompson boosted the U.K. record to 8,238 points in 1978 and gained world acclaim when he took the Commonwealth title at Edmonton, Alta., in 1978 with 8,467 points (later invalidated because of wind assistance). In the 1978 European championships at Prague he lost to A. Grebenyuk of the U.S.S.R., though his 8,289 was a U.K. record till May 1980.

In the 1980 Olympic decathlon Thompson's marks for the ten events were: 100 m, 10.62 sec; 400 m, 48.01 sec; 1,500 m, 4 min 39.90 sec; 110-m hurdles, 14.47 sec; high jump, 2.08 m; pole vault, 4.70 m; long jump, 8.00 m; shot put, 15.18 m; discus, 42.24 m; and javelin, 64.16 m.

Thorn, Gaston

After a long and varied career both as a politician in his native Luxembourg and as an international statesman, Gaston Thorn in June 1980 was designated next president of the Commission of the European Community. He would take office in January 1981, succeeding Roy Jenkins of the U.K. Meanwhile, he resigned as Luxembourg's foreign minister and as president of the European Community's Council of Ministers.

Born in Luxembourg on Sept. 3, 1928, Thorn was educated there (where as a schoolboy during World War II he took part in anti-Nazi activities) and also in France and in Switzerland. He qualified as a doctor of law and was appointed to the Luxembourg bar. During the 1950s he took an active part in local politics, becoming a Luxembourg City municipal councillor and then mayor of Luxembourg (1961–63). Meanwhile, he had joined the liberal Democratic Party and in 1959 became a member of Parliament and, soon afterward, of the European Parliament. In 1961 he was named the Democratic Party's chairman.

Thorn had extensive ministerial experience. Following the 1968 general election he became foreign minister and minister for trade in the Christian Social-Democratic coalition. His personal popularity—he was as much at ease among soccer fans as with fellow statesmen—contributed to his party's success in the 1974 election, which ended 50 years of Christian Socialist domination in Luxembourg politics. He then served as prime minister in a coalition with the Workers' Socialist Party. He also took responsibility for the portfolios of foreign affairs and foreign trade, economy, and the middle classes, retaining these responsibilities after the 1979 election in a new Christian Socialist-Liberal coalition headed by Pierre Werner.

In September 1975 Thorn was elected president of the 30th UN General Assembly, and the following year he was chosen to head the newly formed Federation of Liberal and Democratic Parties within the European Community. Multilingual, living at the crossroads of the Germanic and Latin civilizations of Europe, he was a firm believer in the need for European unity. However, his appointment as president of the Commission had been preceded by some disagreement, and it was known that he had not been the favoured candidate of France's Pres. Valéry Giscard d'Estaing.

Tikhonov, Nikolay Aleksandrovich

Nobody was surprised when on Oct. 23, 1980, Pres. Leonid Brezhnev informed the Supreme Soviet of the U.S.S.R. that Aleksey Kosygin had written to announce his resignation from the premiership because of ill health. Nor was there surprise when Brezhnev proposed the election of Nikolay Tikhonov in his place; the Supreme Soviet unanimously accepted the proposal. For in November 1979 Tikhonov, first deputy premier of the Soviet government, had been elected a full member of the party's ruling Politburo, a move paving his way to still higher promotion.

On Nov. 6, 1980, shortly after his appointment as premier, Tikhonov delivered a traditional speech celebrating the 63rd anniversary of the October Revolution. He pointed out that the national income for only five days was now equal to the national income total for the whole of 1928, on the eve of the first five-year plan period.

Tikhonov was born on May 14, 1905, in Kharkov, Ukraine, the son of a Russian, not Ukrainian, worker. He began his career as an engine driver's assistant on the railways but subsequently graduated from the Dnepropetrovsk Metallurgical Institute and obtained a doctorate in engineering science. From 1930 he worked as an engineer, as head of a production shop, and then as director of a plant at Dnepropetrovsk. At that time Brezhnev served in that city as secretary of the Communist Party's regional committee. As the two men became friends, Brezhnev advised Tikhonov to join the party, which he did in 1940.

During World War II and afterward, Tikhonov held many leading posts in the Soviet Ministry of Ferrous Metallurgy. From 1957 to 1960, at the peak of Pres. Nikita Khrushchev's reforming zeal, he was chairman of the short-lived Dnepropetrovsk Economic Council. In 1963 he became a vice-chairman of the State Planning Committee (Gosplan), a post carrying the rank of minister. In 1965, one year after Brezhnev became the party's leader, Tikhonov was appointed a deputy premier of the Soviet Council of Ministers. Observers ruled out Tikhonov as a contender for the party leadership in the event of Brezhnev's resignation or death.

Trudeau, Pierre Elliott

The political career of 60-year-old Pierre Elliott Trudeau was unexpectedly extended and his power restored in 1980. After 11 consecutive years in office, Prime Minister Trudeau's Liberal government had been defeated in the May 1979 general election, and in November he had announced his resignation as his party's leader. But three weeks later Parliament rejected the first budget of the Progressive Conservative government, forcing Prime Minister Joe Clark to call an election for Feb. 18, 1980. Trudeau withdrew his resignation and returned to lead the Liberals through a victorious campaign culminating in a majority victory, with 146 of the 281 seats contested on election night. The Liberals added a 147th seat in a later by-election.

The election result was attributed in large measure to massive energy price increases proposed in the budget, together with the lacklustre public image of Clark. At the same time, the public's anger at Trudeau appeared to have been spent in dealing him an electoral punishment in 1979. The Liberals made a comeback in populous Ontario and won all but one of Quebec's 75 seats, gaining the majority despite their being almost shut out in the western Canadian provinces.

After the election Trudeau turned his attention to the great preoccupation of his previous years in office: national unity and the preservation of the French-speaking province of Quebec in confederation. He plunged into the campaign that preceded Quebec's May 20 referendum on "sovereignty-association," a proposal of the province's Parti Québécois government for political separation from the rest of Canada but with a form of continuing economic union. Trudeau, his Cabinet ministers, and premiers of English-speaking provinces intervened at strategic points in the referendum debate, pledging action to meet Quebec's grievances. Their speeches may have been the decisive factor in the final overwhelming rejection of the separatist alternative.

The referendum campaign and its result served to generate a tide of enthusiasm for action to reform Canada's constitution. Taking advantage of this momentum, Trudeau directed his minister of justice, Jean Chrétien, to convene a grueling, summer-long series of meetings aimed at narrowing federal and provincial differences over changes to the constitution in 12 major subject areas.

With agreement apparently possible, Trudeau himself chaired a marathon six-day constitutional conference with the premiers in September. The conference was unable to put together even a limited package of constitutional amendments, however, and dissolved in bitterness between Trudeau and most premiers.

The prime minister quickly moved to carry out a threat to ignore the provinces and take unilateral action. In October he proposed to Parliament a major reform package that would request Great Britain to "patriate" the constitution, that is, to return the document as well as the power to amend it to Canada. The resolution also asked the British Par-

RON DESMARAIS—KEYSTONE

liament to include two key amendments, one establishing a charter of rights and freedoms binding on both the federal and provincial governments and the other requiring the continuation of the current system of equalization payments from rich provinces to poorer ones in order to achieve parity in public services. At the end of the year, Trudeau's unilateral move was being challenged in the courts by several provinces and making its way slowly through the Canadian Parliament, with its presentation to the British Parliament still to come.

The other burning postelection issue facing Trudeau was energy, one that had been fatal to the Clark government and that had merged with power-sharing discussions related to the constitution. The key energy questions were the rate of price increases in Canada for domestic and imported oil and the sharing of the revenues from domestic production among the federal government, the producing provinces of Alberta and Saskatchewan, and the petroleum industry.

In their turn, the Trudeau Liberals presented a budget October 28 that sought to resolve these issues. While no more popular than that of the Conservatives, it was not in danger of defeat because of Trudeau's commanding majority. But it was nevertheless challenged by Premier Peter Lougheed of Alberta, who set a 90-day deadline for resolution of pricing and revenue-sharing differences between the two governments, failing which Alberta would begin cutting back on oil production.

Having won a place for Canada at summit meetings of Western leaders during his earlier years of office, Trudeau relished his return to the table in 1980. He participated in the Vienna summit in June, following which he and his nine-year-old son, Justin, met Pope John Paul II in Rome and then visited a number of European capitals. Trudeau also visited the Middle East late in the year.

Walesa, Lech

After mid-August 1980, Lech Walesa was recognized at home and abroad as a charismatic leader of millions of Polish workers organized in the independent, self-governing trade union federation Solidarity.

Listening on August 14 to protests at the huge Gdansk shipyard caused by an increase in food prices and the dismissal of another union activist, Walesa—then unemployed—climbed over the wall and appealed to 17,000 workers to strike. A strike committee headed by Walesa was elected to negotiate with management. Three days later the strikers' demands were conceded, but when strikers in other Gdansk enterprises asked Walesa to continue his strike out of solidarity, he immediately agreed. An Interfactory Strike Committee uniting the enterprises of the Gdansk-Sopot-Gdynia area was formed, and a general strike was proclaimed.

The workers of the Baltic seaboard had learned a lesson from December 1970, when their street

ALAIN NOGUES—SYGMA

demonstrations were fired upon leaving some 20 dead. In 1980 they occupied the plants and closed the gates. On August 31 Walesa and Mieczyslaw Jagielski, Poland's first deputy premier, signed an agreement conceding the right of workers to organize freely and independently. On December 16, at Gdansk, the creator and leader of Solidarity lit the flame at a monument erected to the memory of the workers killed by the militiamen ten years earlier. In the presence of dignitaries of state and church and 200,000 people, Walesa pleaded forcefully for national reconciliation: "No one should undertake action which might threaten Poland's freedom and sovereignty."

Lech Walesa, son of a carpenter, was born on Sept. 29, 1943, at Popowo near Wloclawek. He received only primary and technical education and in 1967 began work as an electrician at the Gdansk shipyard. Having witnessed the 1970 tragedy, he decided to struggle for really free trade unions. In 1976 Walesa, then delegate to the official trade union at the shipyard, drew up a list of workers' grievances, but the management dismissed him. In January 1979 he was fired from an electrical engineering plant for taking part in a demonstration.

A short man with a splendid mustache and a round face alive with nervous energy, Walesa showed himself to be a skilled negotiator. Asked by a French reporter about the source of his moral strength, he replied, "I am a Christian. . . . Without (God) I would be a nobody."

Warren, Robert Penn

With the publication at age 75 of his 13th volume of poetry, *Being Here*, Robert Penn Warren added another work to a literary output that has earned him the title of "the most distinguished man of letters still at work in the U.S. today." Though best known for the 1946 novel that won him the Pulitzer Prize, *All the King's Men*, based on the life of Louisiana demagogue Huey Long, Warren also made important contributions as a poet, essayist, and teacher.

Warren was born on April 24, 1905, in Kentucky, in a tobacco-farming region that forms the background for many of his novels. He grew seriously interested in literature while attending Vanderbilt University in Tennessee, where he fell in with the leading members of the Fugitives, a group of poets who emerged as one of the driving forces behind the Southern literary renaissance. In 1935 he helped to found the *Southern Review*, one of the leading literary journals of the U.S. during its seven years of existence. He collaborated with Cleanth Brooks to write *Understanding Poetry* (1938), the first of several widely used textbooks in which he introduced the methods of the New Criticism into U.S. colleges and universities.

Warren's own creative potential began to emerge with the publication of his first book of poems, *Thirty-Six Poems*, in 1935 and his first novel, *Night Rider*, in 1939, after which the stream never stopped. His finest novels are all firmly based on real historical incidents and personages, out of which Warren invents the painful moral dilemmas

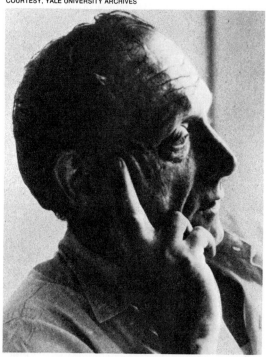

that confront his characters. Using a rich and powerful style, he describes in tones of tragic irony the individual's attempt to define himself and find a line of acceptable conduct in the face of a hostile and degrading environment. The search is often unsuccessful and may end in violence and death rather than ennoblement. Warren's preoccupation with the full range of human character and his emphasis on moral seeking mark him as one of the last remaining giants of the literary tradition that produced an older figure to whom he is sometimes compared, William Faulkner.

Wenzel, Hanni and Andreas

"The mouse that roared" aptly described how the tiny principality of Liechtenstein produced in 1980 both the men's and women's skiing World Cup winners—brother and sister Andreas and Hanni Wenzel from Planken, a village with 200 residents on a plateau overlooking the Rhine River. Furthermore, in the 1980 Winter Olympics at Lake Placid, N.Y., Hanni won two gold medals, for the slalom and giant slalom, and a silver in the downhill. Her brother completed a unique family record by adding a silver in the men's giant slalom. In the Olympic events collectively, Hanni won the women's overall title and Andy was the men's runner-up; these were also the concurrently decided world championship combined rankings recognized by the International Ski Federation.

Each thus proved to be a consistent and versatile three-event skier. Andreas finished respectably high in all three types of race in the 1980 World Cup competition, while Hanni did exceptionally well. En route to winning the overall award, she won five giant slaloms, two slaloms, and two combined events. She ended victor in the giant slalom, runner-up in the slalom, and third in the downhill. During the season's 24 World Cup races she failed to finish only once and was placed 19 times among the top five. Her lowest place in the seven downhill races was seventh. Her giant slalom victory at Mégève, France, by 5.02 sec was the second biggest winning race margin in the history of the World Cup, bettered only by Marie-Theres Nadig's 5.5 sec at Furano, Japan, in 1979.

Hanni, who first raced internationally in 1973, also won the World Cup in 1978, was runner-up in 1975 and 1979, and finished third in 1974. Her career total of World Cup race victories was 22 at the end of the 1979–80 season. She was named 1980 "skier of the year" by *Ski Racing* magazine.

Hanni was born on Dec. 14, 1956, and her brother, Andreas, on March 18, 1958. A younger sister, Petra, born on Nov. 20, 1961, also became an international ski racer.

Williams, John

Arthur Fiedler, commercially America's most successful orchestral conductor and arguably the greatest popularizer of ensemble music since Sousa, personified the Boston Pops Orchestra for half a century. His death in 1979 left the Boston Symphony (the Pops' parent organization) bereft and seriously concerned about the future, since Fiedler's concerts had provided a third of its earnings. Choosing a successor, in *Newsweek*'s view, was tantamount to electing a new pope. A six-month search found a fitting maestro in John Williams, a Hollywood conductor and composer with almost as many film scores to his credit as Fiedler had encores in his repertoire.

Born Feb. 8, 1932, in Queens, N.Y., Williams moved to California as an adolescent when his father, a jazz drummer and orchestra percussionist, began working for movie companies. He studied music briefly at UCLA, then joined the Air Force and arranged pieces for service bands. After a year at the Juilliard School in New York, he returned to California, where he continued his private studies and began working in the film studios.

Williams seemed to have no short suits when it came to contriving cinematic scores. By the time he had written more than 50 of them, his oeuvre included such varied vehicles as *Dracula*, *Gidget Goes to Rome*, and *Towering Inferno*. He won his first Oscar for adapting the stage musical *Fiddler on the Roof* for the screen. His second was for *Jaws*, which owed much of its suspense to the score. (Once the shark's theme was established, Williams would reintroduce it before the shark, one of its victims, or some red herring appeared.) In 1977 he was nominated twice for Academy Awards; his *Star Wars* beat out *Close Encounters of the Third Kind*. For *Superman* he contrived a planet Krypton theme that according to *High Fidelity* magazine was a "single tonic-dominant brass motif—an apparent inversion" of the benevolent aliens' theme in *Close Encounters*.

His film work aside, Williams enjoyed a substantial reputation as a conductor and composer—notably of two symphonies and a violin concerto. At the Pops, he said, he would hire more young soloists, experiment with electronic and mixed-media pieces, and offer more film music. As a guest conductor, he once had *Star Wars* android C3PO share the podium.

Yourcenar, Marguerite

On March 6, 1980, by 20 votes to 12, the French Academy elected Marguerite Yourcenar as its first woman member since it was founded in 1635. While most felt that the revolution was long overdue, conservative academicians fought hard to prevent it, making a last stand on the issue of the candidate's nationality. Belgian by birth, she acquired U.S. citizenship in 1947 and lived in Maine. But Alain Peyrefitte, justice minister and himself an academician, granted her dual nationality on the grounds of her "evident cultural links" with France.

After that, even the most fervent male chauvinist must have found Yourcenar's claim hard to deny.

UPI

Marguerite de Crayencour, born June 8, 1903, in Brussels of a French father and Belgian mother, had created a body of work that, despite its cosmopolitan outlook, manifestly belonged to the French cultural tradition and was remarkable for its qualities of style and intellect. To such writers, immortality may come more easily than popular acclaim, but in 1951 *Mémoires d'Hadrien* (*Memoirs of Hadrian*, 1954), her brilliant excursion into the world of imperial Rome, achieved immediate success. It was an imaginative tour de force, a historical novel that convincingly penetrated the mind of its 2nd-century hero, revealing him as a man haunted by the impermanence of human culture and thus oddly close to the sensibility of our own time.

The personality of Hadrian had fascinated her long before the novel appeared, and the book's concerns were central to all her work. In 1968, with *L'Oeuvre au noir*, she set in northern Europe during the 16th century an imaginary figure who, like Hadrian, ultimately transcended the age to which he belonged.

In 1973, with *Souvenirs pieux*, she began a unique "family autobiography," which won over some earlier critics of her work. In recent years she gained many awards, among them the Grand Prix national des Lettres and the Grand Prix de la Litterature de l'Académie française. Austere, dedicated to her craft, she was likened to the 19th-century novelist Gustave Flaubert, who also adopted the viewpoint

469

of someone of the opposite sex for his masterpiece *Madame Bovary*. In one thing, however, she succeeded where Flaubert failed: inconceivable though it would have been in his day, she was elected to the French Academy.

Zhao Ziyang

Zhao Ziyang (Chao Tzu-yang) became premier of China in September 1980, succeeding Hua Guofeng (Hua Kuo-feng), who remained chairman of China's Communist Party. Zhao's elevation followed his election to full membership in the Politburo in 1979 and his appointment as vice-premier earlier in 1980. It was his years as governor of Sichuan (Szechwan) Province and party first secretary (1975–80) that brought Zhao to the forefront. During that time he was remarkably successful in reviving the province's economy, which had been badly damaged by the disasters of the Cultural Revolution. As China's chief administrator, Zhao now has the formidable task of implementing the Four Modernizations: agriculture, industry, national defense, and science and technology.

Born into a landlord family in Henan (Honan) Province in 1919, Zhao joined the Young Communist League in 1932 and became a member of the Chinese Communist Party in 1938. During World War II he served in local party organizations in northern China. After the establishment of the People's Republic in 1949, he was moved to Guangdong (Kwangtung) Province, where he became provincial first party secretary in 1965. Purged in 1967 during the Cultural Revolution, he was later rehabilitated and sent in 1975 to Sichuan, China's most populous province, where through bold and flexible programs he increased industrial output and raised agricultural production. These results were achieved through such innovative policies as rewarding workers on the basis of work rather than need and providing incentives based on free enterprise and market forces rather than on rigid quotas established by central authorities. In addition, factory managers were given much greater autonomy and peasants were allowed to benefit from individual initiative. For such achievements as raising Sich-

RICHARD MELLOUL–SYGMA

uan's industrial output by 81% in three years, Zhao was made a Politburo alternate in 1977 and a full member in 1979.

An economic experimenter, Zhao has advocated "any structure, system, policy, or measure" that might stimulate the forces of production. He has also redefined Communism as "state ownership of the means of production and paying workers according to their work." All these changes are in harmony with the pragmatism of Vice-Chairman Deng Xiaoping (Teng Hsiao-p'ing) and have become guiding principles for China's future economic development. Zhao is perhaps the most important member of a new team of energetic, fairly young leaders entrusted to carry out the transformation of China into a stable and prosperous superpower during the coming decades.

OUR FAMILY RECORD

1981

THIS SPACE FOR FAMILY GROUP PHOTO

WHAT WE DID
AND
HOW WE LOOKED

*Each year important events highlight the life of every
family. Year after year these events may be noted
in the Family Record pages of your Compton Yearbooks.
You will then have a permanent record of your family's
significant achievements, celebrations, and activities.*

OUR FAMILY TREE

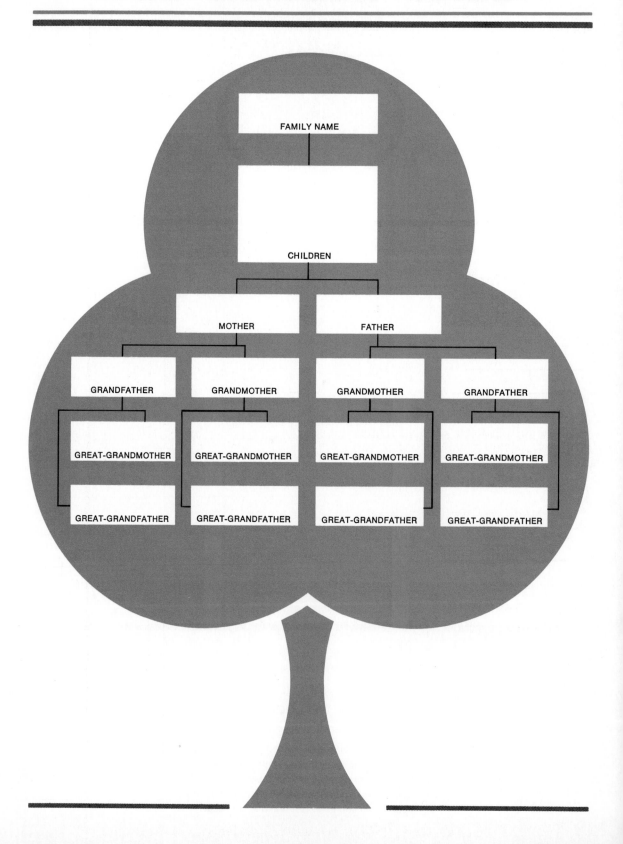

DATES TO REMEMBER

JANUARY

FEBRUARY

MARCH

APRIL

MAY

JUNE

JULY

AUGUST

SEPTEMBER

OCTOBER

NOVEMBER

DECEMBER

Birthdays, weddings, anniversaries, graduations, gifts sent

FAMILY CELEBRATIONS

BIRTHDAYS

NAME

DATE

NAME

DATE

NAME

DATE

NAME

DATE

NAME

DATE

ANNIVERSARIES

NAMES

DATE

NAMES

DATE

NAMES

DATE

WEDDINGS

NAMES

DATE

NAMES

DATE

NAMES

DATE

NAMES

DATE

NAMES

DATE

BIRTHS

NAME

DATE

PARENTS

NAME

DATE

PARENTS

NAME

DATE

PARENTS

PROMOTIONS

NAME

FIRM

TITLE

DATE

NAME

FIRM

TITLE

DATE

HOLIDAYS

OCCASION

OCCASION

OCCASION

SPIRITUAL MILESTONES

NAME _____

MILESTONE _____

_____

_____

NAME _____

MILESTONE _____

_____

_____

NAME _____

MILESTONE _____

_____

_____

NAME _____

MILESTONE _____

_____

_____

NAME _____

MILESTONE _____

_____

_____

OTHER EVENTS

_____

_____

_____

_____

_____

_____

_____

_____

_____

_____

PASTE PHOTO HERE

PASTE PHOTO HERE

PASTE PHOTO HERE

VACATION 1981

WHEN AND WHERE WE WENT

_____
_____
_____
_____
_____
_____
_____

FAVORITE SIGHTS

_____
_____
_____
_____
_____
_____

WHAT WE DID

_____
_____
_____
_____
_____
_____
_____
_____
_____
_____
_____
_____
_____
_____

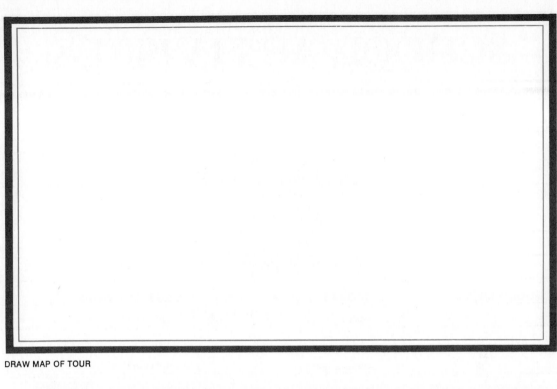

DRAW MAP OF TOUR

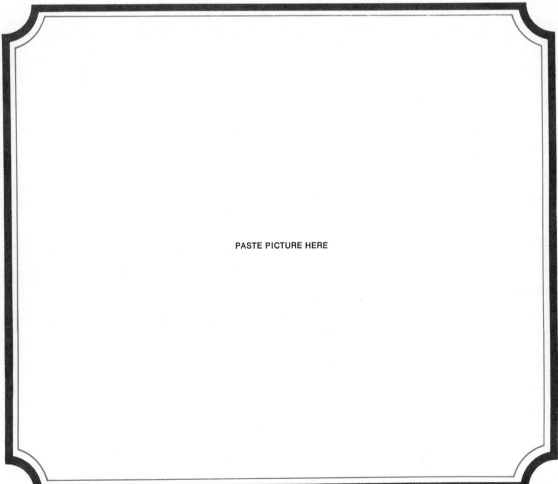

PASTE PICTURE HERE

SCHOOL ACTIVITIES

NAME _____

SCHOOL _____

GRADE _____

NAME _____

SCHOOL _____

GRADE _____

NAME _____

SCHOOL _____

GRADE _____

NAME _____

SCHOOL _____

GRADE _____

SCHOOL PARTIES

DATE _____

OCCASION _____

_____

DATE _____

OCCASION _____

_____

DATE _____

OCCASION _____

_____

DATE _____

OCCASION _____

_____

DATE _____

OCCASION _____

_____

DATE _____

OCCASION _____

_____

DATE _____

OCCASION _____

_____

DATE _____

OCCASION _____

_____

SPORTS

NAME _____

SPORT _____

ACHIEVEMENT _____

NAME _____

SPORT _____

ACHIEVEMENT _____

NAME _____

SPORT _____

ACHIEVEMENT _____

NAME _____

SPORT _____

ACHIEVEMENT _____

NAME _____

SPORT _____

ACHIEVEMENT _____

NAME _____

SPORT _____

ACHIEVEMENT _____

NAME _____

SPORT _____

ACHIEVEMENT _____

NAME _____

SPORT _____

ACHIEVEMENT _____

CLUB ACTIVITIES

NAME _____

CLUB _____

ACHIEVEMENT _____

NAME _____

CLUB _____

ACHIEVEMENT _____

NAME _____

CLUB _____

ACHIEVEMENT _____

NAME _____

CLUB _____

ACHIEVEMENT _____

NAME _____

CLUB _____

ACHIEVEMENT _____

NAME _____

CLUB _____

ACHIEVEMENT _____

NAME _____

CLUB _____

ACHIEVEMENT _____

NAME _____

CLUB _____

ACHIEVEMENT _____

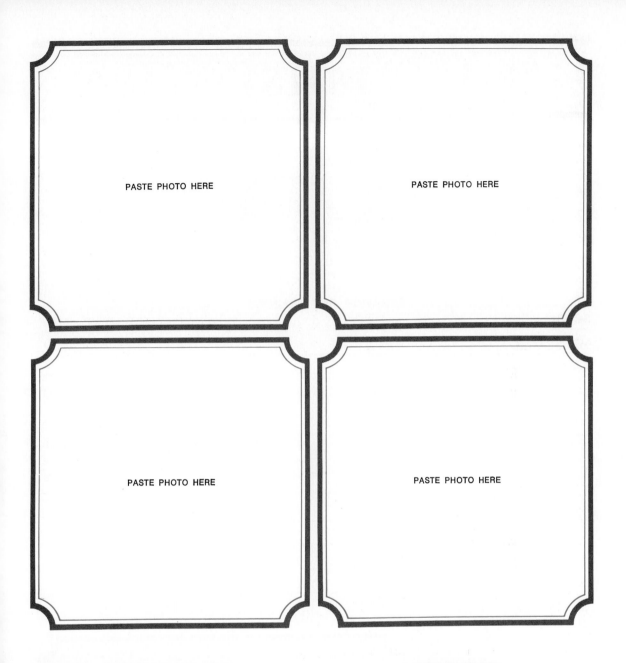

AWARDS, HONORS, AND PRIZES

NAME _____

GRADE _____

HONOR _____

NAME _____

GRADE _____

HONOR _____

NAME _____

GRADE _____

HONOR _____

NAME _____

GRADE _____

HONOR _____

NAME _____

GRADE _____

HONOR _____

NAME _____

GRADE _____

HONOR _____

GRADUATIONS

NAME _____

SCHOOL _____

NAME _____

SCHOOL _____

NAME _____

SCHOOL _____

NAME _____

SCHOOL _____

PETS

NAME AND BREED

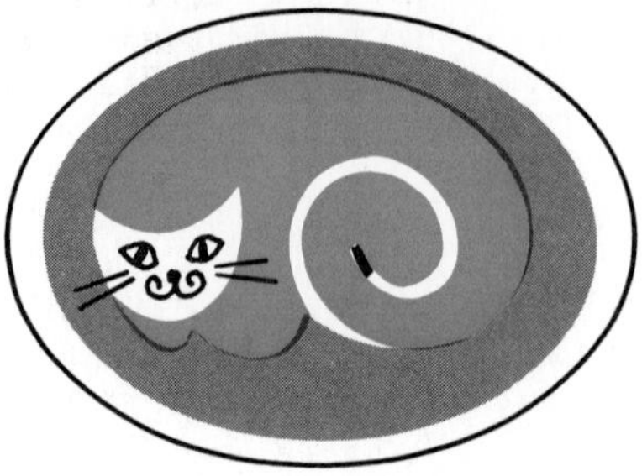

VET'S RECORD

BEHAVIOR AND TRAINING

PASTE PHOTO HERE

LEISURE HOURS

FAVORITE MOVIES

_____
_____
_____
_____
_____
_____
_____
_____
_____
_____
_____
_____

FAVORITE BOOKS

_____
_____
_____
_____
_____
_____
_____
_____
_____

FAVORITE
TELEVISION PROGRAMS

_____
_____
_____
_____
_____
_____

FAVORITE RECORDS

_____
_____
_____
_____
_____
_____
_____
_____
_____
_____
_____
_____

_____
_____
_____
_____
_____
_____
_____
_____
_____
_____
_____

HOBBIES

_____
_____
_____
_____
_____
_____
_____
_____
_____
_____
_____
_____

OUR HEALTH RECORD

RECORD OF HEIGHT

FEET   DATE   NAME

6
5
4
3
2
1

Check Height on
This Scale.
Write Name and
Date Opposite It.

RECORD OF WEIGHT

POUNDS DATE   NAME

225
200
175
150
125
100
75
50
25

Check Weight on
This Scale.
Write Name and
Date Opposite It.

DOCTORS' NAMES

NAME

ADDRESS

TELEPHONE NUMBER

NAME

ADDRESS

TELEPHONE NUMBER

DENTISTS' NAMES

NAME

ADDRESS

TELEPHONE NUMBER

NAME

ADDRESS

TELEPHONE NUMBER

VISITS

NAME

DATE

ILLNESS

NAME

DATE

ILLNESS

NAME

DATE

ILLNESS

NAME

DATE

ILLNESS

NAME

DATE

ILLNESS

INOCULATIONS

NAME

DATE

TYPE

NAME

DATE

TYPE

OPERATIONS

NAME

DATE

TYPE

NAME

DATE

TYPE

calendar for 1981

JAN

Thurs.	1	New Year's Day. Japanese New Year 2641. Earth at perihelion. Circumcision of Christ. Mummers Day and Tournament of Roses parades. International Year of Disabled Persons begins.
Sun.	4	Mother Elizabeth Seton's Feast Day.
Mon.	5	Twelfth Night.
Tues.	6	Epiphany, or Twelfth Day. Count of electoral votes.
Tues.	13	Stephen Foster Memorial Day.
Wed.	14	Julian New Year 6694. Roman New Year 2734.
Thurs.	15	Martin Luther King, Jr.'s birthday, 1929.
Sat.	17	Benjamin Franklin's birthday, 1706.
Sun.	18	Prophet Muhammad's birthday, 570.
Mon.	19	Robert E. Lee's birthday, 1807.
Tues.	20	Aquarius begins. Penumbral eclipse of Moon. U.S. presidential inauguration.
Sun.	25	Superbowl XV.
Mon.	26	Australia Day.
Tues.	27	Vietnam war cease-fire anniversary, 1973.
Sat.	31	American space exploration anniversary, 1958.

FEB

Sun.	1	National Freedom Day. Afro-American History, American Heart, American History, American Music, International Friendship, National Cherry, and Potato Lover's months begin.
Mon.	2	Candlemas Day. Groundhog Day. National Pay Your Bills Week begins.
Wed.	4	Annular eclipse of Sun.
Thurs.	5	Chinese New Year 4679, Year of the Cock.
Fri.	6	Ronald Reagan's birthday, 1911.
Sun.	8	Boy Scouts of America birthday, 1910.
Thurs.	12	Abraham Lincoln's birthday, 1809.
Sat.	14	St. Valentine's Day.
Sun.	15	Septuagesima Sunday. Susan B. Anthony's birthday, 1820. Brotherhood Week begins. Daytona 500. Remember the Maine Day.
Mon.	16	George Washington's birthday (Feb. 22, 1732) celebrated.
Thurs.	19	Pisces begins.
Sun.	22	International Friendship Week begins.
Tues.	24	Gregorian Calendar Day.

MARCH

Sun.	1	Shrove Sunday. Mental Retardation, National Nutrition, National Peanut, and Red Cross months begin.
Tues.	3	Shrove Tuesday. Mardi Gras.
Wed.	4	Ash Wednesday—Lent begins.
Fri.	6	World Day of Prayer.
Sun.	8	Girl Scout and Women's History weeks begin. International (Working) Women's Day.
Tues.	10	Harriet Tubman Day.
Sun.	15	Ides of March. Buzzards return to Hinckley, Ohio. National Wildlife Week begins.
Tues.	17	St. Patrick's Day.
Thurs.	19	American Agriculture Day. Swallows return to Capistrano, Calif.
Fri.	20	Spring begins. Earth Day. Purim.
Sat.	21	Aries begins.
Sun.	22	Indian New Year 1903.
Mon.	23	World Meteorological Day.
Wed.	25	Annunciation.
Mon.	30	Doctors' Day. National Cherry Blossom Festival begins.

APRIL

Wed.	1	April Fools' Day. Cancer Control and National Home Improvement months begin.
Thurs.	2	International Children's Book Day.
Sun.	5	Passion Sunday. National Dance and National Library weeks begin.
Tues.	7	World Health Day.
Sat.	11	Barbershop Quartet Day.
Sun.	12	Palm Sunday. Pan American Week begins.
Tues.	14	Pan American Day.
Fri.	17	Good Friday.
Sun.	19	Easter. Passover begins at sunset. National Boys' Club and National YWCA weeks begin.
Mon.	20	Taurus begins. White House Easter egg roll.
Tues.	21	Queen Elizabeth II's birthday, 1926.
Wed.	22	Secretaries Day.
Fri.	24	Arbor Day.
Sun.	26	Low Sunday. Daylight Saving Time begins. Canada-U.S. Goodwill Week begins.
Wed.	29	World YWCA Day.
Thurs.	30	Walpurgis Night.

MAY

Fri.	1	May Day. Save the Children Day. American Bike, National Humor, National Mental Health, and Senior Citizens months begin.
Sat.	2	Kentucky Derby.
Sun.	3	Jewish Heritage, National Family, and National Music weeks begin.
Mon.	4	National Pet Week begins.
Wed.	6	Nurses' Day.
Fri.	8	V-E Day. World Red Cross Day.
Sat.	9	Native American Day.
Sun.	10	Mother's Day. Girls Club and National Historic Preservation weeks begin.
Sat.	16	Armed Forces Day.
Sun.	17	World Trade Week begins.
Mon.	18	Mt. St. Helens eruption anniversary, 1980. Pope John Paul II's birthday, 1920. Victoria Day, Canada.
Thurs.	21	Gemini begins. Teachers Day.
Sat.	23	Gathering of the Clans, Scotland.
Sun.	24	Rogation Sunday.
Mon.	25	Memorial Day. Prayer for Peace.
Thurs.	28	Ascension Day.

JUNE

Mon.	1	Fight the Filthy Fly, June Dairy, National Adopt-a-Cat, and National Rose months begin. National Safe Boating Week begins.
Thurs.	4	America the Beautiful Week begins.
Fri.	5	World Environment Day.
Sun.	7	Whitsunday, or Pentecost.
Mon.	8	National Little League Baseball Week begins. Stratford Festival, Canada. Shavuot begins.
Sun.	14	Trinity Sunday. Children's Sunday. Flag Day. U.S. Army birthday, 1775.
Mon.	15	Magna Carta Day.
Wed.	17	Watergate Day.
Thurs.	18	Corpus Christi.
Sun.	21	Summer begins. Father's Day.
Mon.	22	Cancer begins. Lawn Tennis Championships, Wimbledon, England.
Tues.	23	Midsummer Eve.
Thurs.	25	Korean War anniversary, 1950.
Sun.	28	Freedom Week begins. Anniversary of World War I's beginning (1914) and end (1919).
Mon.	29	Peter and Paul Day.

JULY

Wed.	1	Dominion Day, Canada. National Baked Bean and Hot Dog months begin.
Fri.	3	Earth at aphelion. Dog Days begin. Ramadan begins.
Sat.	4	Independence Day. National Safe Boating Week begins.
Mon.	6	Caricom Day.
Sun.	12	Captive Nations and National Ice Cream weeks begin.
Tues.	14	Bastille Day.
Wed.	15	Edmonton Klondike Days, Canada. St. Swithin's Day.
Thurs.	16	Atomic Bomb Day. Partial eclipse of Moon.
Fri.	17	"Wrong Way" Corrigan Day.
Mon.	20	Moon Day, anniversary of first landing on moon, 1969.
Wed.	22	Spooner's Day.
Thurs.	23	Leo begins.
Sat.	25	National Farm Safety Week begins.
Mon.	27	Korean War Armistice, 1953.
Wed.	29	Boy Scouts of America National Scout Jamboree begins.
Thurs.	30	Total eclipse of the Sun.

AUG

Sat.	1	Good Nutrition and International Air Travel months begin. National Clown Week begins.
Sun.	2	American Family Day. Ramadan ends.
Mon.	3	Canada Civic Holiday. National Smile Week begins.
Tues.	4	Coast Guard Day.
Wed.	5	Anniversary of federal income tax, 1862.
Thurs.	6	Hiroshima Day. Transfiguration.
Sun.	9	Family Day.
Mon.	10	American Indian Exposition begins.
Thurs.	13	Berlin Wall anniversary, 1961.
Fri.	14	Atlantic Charter Day. Victory, or V-J, Day.
Sun.	16	Edinburgh Festival begins.
Mon.	17	Anniversary of first balloon crossing of Atlantic Ocean, 1978.
Wed.	19	National Aviation Day. Canadian National Exhibition begins.
Sun.	23	Virgo begins.
Mon.	24	St. Bartholomew's Day Massacre. Vesuvius Day.
Wed.	26	Women's Equality Day.
Fri.	28	World Sauntering Day.

SEPT

Tues.	1	Emergency Care, National Sight-Saving, and Wood Energy months begin. Boy Scouts of America Fall Roundup begins.
Fri.	4	Newspaper Carrier Day.
Mon.	7	Labor Day. Grandma Moses Day. Full Employment Week begins.
Tues.	8	International Literacy Day.
Sun.	13	National Hispanic Heritage and National Rehabilitation weeks begin. National Grandparents Day. Harvest Moon.
Mon.	14	National Anthem Day.
Wed.	16	Mayflower Day.
Thurs.	17	Citizenship Day. Constitution Week begins.
Fri.	18	U.S. Air Force birthday, 1947.
Tues.	22	Autumn begins. Hobbit Day.
Wed.	23	Libra begins. Checkers Day.
Fri.	21	Native American Day.
Sat.	26	National Hunting and Fishing Day.
Sun.	27	Gold Star Mother's Day.
Mon.	28	Confucius's birthday, 551 BC. National Chimney Sweeps Week begins.
Tues.	29	Michaelmas. Rosh Hashanah, or Jewish New Year 5742, begins at sunset.

OCT

Thurs.	1	World Vegetarian Day. National Employ the Handicapped Week begins. National Apple Month begins.
Sun.	4	Fire Prevention and National 4-H weeks begin.
Tues.	6	Universal Children's Day.
Thurs.	8	Yom Kippur begins at sunset.
Sat.	10	National Jogging Day.
Sun.	11	National Handicapped Awareness and National Y-Teen weeks begin.
Mon.	12	Columbus Day. Thanksgiving Day, Canada.
Tues.	13	U.S. Navy birthday, 1775.
Fri.	16	World Food Day.
Sat.	17	Sweetest Day.
Sun.	18	Pierre Trudeau's birthday, 1919.
Fri.	23	Scorpio begins. Swallows depart from Capistrano, Calif.
Sat.	24	United Nations Day. Disarmament Week begins.
Sun.	25	Mothers-in-Law Day. Return to Standard Time.
Fri.	30	Islamic New Year 1402 begins at sunset.
Sat.	31	Halloween. National UNICEF Day.

NOV

Sun.	1	All Saints' Day. National Epilepsy and National Stamp Collecting months begin.
Mon.	2	All Souls' Day.
Tues.	3	General Election Day.
Wed.	4	Anniversary of seizure of U.S. embassy in Teheran, Iran, 1979.
Thurs.	5	Guy Fawkes Day.
Sat.	7	Sadie Hawkins Day. World Community Day.
Sun.	8	Dunce Day.
Tues.	10	U.S. Marine Corps birthday, 1775.
Wed.	11	Veterans, or Armistice, Day.
Sun.	15	American Education Week begins. Centennial anniversary of founding of American Federation of Labor.
Mon.	16	National Children's Book Week begins.
Tues.	17	Opening of Suez Canal anniversary, 1869.
Thurs.	19	Lincoln's Gettysburg Address anniversary, 1863.
Sun.	22	Sagittarius begins. Latin America Week begins.
Thurs.	26	Thanksgiving Day. Sojourner Truth Day.
Sun.	29	First Sunday in Advent.

DEC

Wed.	2	Pan American Health Day. Monroe Doctrine anniversary, 1823.
Sun.	6	St. Nicholas's Day.
Mon.	7	Pearl Harbor Day.
Tues.	8	Feast of the Immaculate Conception.
Thurs.	10	Human Rights Day.
Fri.	11	UNICEF anniversary, 1946.
Sun.	13	St. Lucia's Day, Sweden.
Mon.	14	Halcyon Days begin.
Wed.	16	Boston Tea Party anniversary, 1773.
Thurs.	17	Pan American Aviation Day. Wright Brothers Day.
Sun.	20	Louisiana Purchase Day.
Mon.	21	Winter begins. Hanukkah begins at sunset.
Tues.	22	Capricorn begins. International Arbor Day.
Wed.	23	Feast of the Radishes, Mexico.
Thurs.	24	Christmas Eve.
Fri.	25	Christmas Day.
Sat.	26	Boxing Day, Canada.
Mon.	28	Childermas, or Holy Innocents Day.
Tues.	29	Anniversary of Wounded Knee Massacre, 1890.
Thurs.	31	New Year's Eve.

Contributors and Consultants

These authorities either wrote the articles listed or supplied information and data that were used in writing them:

Stener Aarsdal, Economic and Political Journalist, *Børsen,* Copenhagen, *Denmark*

Joseph C. Agrella, Former Turf Editor, *Chicago Sun-Times,* correspondent, *Blood-Horse* magazine, *Horse Racing* (in part)

Leslie C. Aiello, Lecturer, Department of Anthropology, University College, London, *Anthropology*

J. A. Allan, Lecturer in Geography, School of Oriental and African Studies, University of London, *Libya*

Peter J. Anderson, Assistant Director, Institute of Polar Studies, Ohio State University, Columbus, *Arctic and Antarctic* (in part)

John J. Archibald, Feature Writer and TV Columnist, *St. Louis Post-Dispatch, Bowling* (in part)

Mavis Arnold, Free-lance Journalist, Dublin, *Ireland*

Raphael BarOn, Director of Research and Statistics, Israel Tourism Administration, *Tourism*

Howard Bass, Journalist and Broadcaster, *Biographies* (in part); *Ice Skating; Olympic Games* (in part); *Skiing*

David Bayliss, Chief Planner (Transportation), Greater London Council, *Transportation* (in part)

John V. Beall, Sales Manager, Davy McKee Corp., *Mines and Mining*

David C. Beckwith, Editor, *Legal Times of Washington,* Washington, D.C., *Consumer Affairs SPECIAL REPORT: Where Does the Buck Stop?; State Governments*

Stuart Bentley, Principal Lecturer in Sociology, Sheffield City Polytechnic, England, *Refugees and Migrants* (in part)

William C. Boddy, Editor, *Motor Sport,* Full Member, Guild of Motoring Writers, *Auto Racing* (in part)

Dick Boonstra, Assistant Professor, Department of Political Science, Free University, Amsterdam, *Biographies* (in part); *Caribbean States* (in part); *The Netherlands*

John B. H. Box, Free-lance Writer and Researcher, *Cuba*

Arnold C. Brackman, Asian Affairs Specialist, *Indonesia*

Henry S. Bradsher, Diplomatic Correspondent, *Washington Star, Philippines*

Robert J. Braidwood, Professor Emeritus of Old World Prehistory, the Oriental Institute, University of Chicago, *Archaeology* (in part)

Chris Brasher, Sports Correspondent, *The Observer;* Reporter and Producer, BBC Television, *Olympic Games* (in part)

Rutlage J. Brazee, Program Manager for Seismological Research, U.S. Nuclear Regulatory Commission, Washington, D.C., *Earth Sciences* (in part)

Kenneth Brecher, Associate Professor of Astronomy, Boston University, *Astronomy*

Hal Bruno, Director of Political Coverage, ABC News, Washington, D.C., *Biographies* (in part)

Steve Bufkin, Special Services Editor, Public Relations Service, Boy Scouts of America, *Youth Organizations* (in part)

Joel L. Burdin, Professor of Educational Administration, The American University, *Education* (in part)

Ardath W. Burks, Professor of Asian Studies, Rutgers University, New Brunswick, N.J., *Japan*

Robin Buss, Lecturer in French, Woolwich College of Further Education, *Biographies* (in part)

Frank Butler, Sports Editor, *News of the World,* London, *Boxing*

Eugena E. Callwood, Public Information Assistant, Future Homemakers of America, *Youth Organizations* (in part)

Sarah Cameron, Economist, Lloyds Bank International Ltd., London, *Dominican Republic; Ecuador; Peru; Venezuela*

Roger Caras, Lecturer, Animal Biology, School of Veterinary Medicine, University of Pennsylvania, *Pets*

Marybeth Carlson, Environmental Writer and Editor, *Animals and Wildlife; Environment*

Victor M. Cassidy, Writer and Editor, currently at work on a biography of Wyndham Lewis, *Biographies* (in part)

Peter B. Cawley, Business Writer, Contributing Editor, *New England Business, Business and Industry; Housing; Insurance; World Trade*

Charles Cegielski, Associate Editor, Encyclopædia Britannica, Yearbooks, *Biology* (in part), *Toys and Games: Sidebar*

Kenneth F. Chapman, Editor, *Philatelic Magazine,* Philatelic Correspondent, *The Times,* London, *Stamps and Coins* (in part)

Robin Chapman, Senior Economist, Lloyds Bank International Ltd., London, *Caribbean States* (in part); *Latin-American Affairs*

Duncan Chappell, Professor, Department of Criminology, Simon Fraser University, Vancouver, British Columbia, *Crime and Law Enforcement*

Hung-Ti Chu, Expert in Far Eastern Affairs, former International Civil Servant and University Professor, *China; Taiwan*

Stanley W. Cloud, Assistant Managing Editor, *Washington Star, Biographies* (in part)

Richard L. Clutterbuck, Senior Lecturer in Politics, University of Exeter, *Law SPECIAL REPORT: Diplomats Under Siege*

David Cocksedge, Features Writer, *Athletics Monthly, Biographies* (in part)

Stanley H. Costin, British Correspondent, *Herrenjournal International* and *Men's Wear, Australasia* magazine, *Fashion* (in part)

Rufus W. Crater, Chief Correspondent, *Broadcasting,* New York City, *Television and Radio* (in part)

Norman Crossland, Bonn Correspondent, *The Economist,* London, *Germany*

K. F. Cviic, Leader Writer and East European Specialist, *The Economist,* London, *Yugoslavia*

Hiroshi Daifuku, Chief, Section for Operations and Training, Cultural Heritage Division, UNESCO, Paris, *Landmarks and Monuments*

Daphne Daume, Editor, Encyclopædia Britannica, Yearbooks, *Prisons: Sidebar*

Tudor David, Managing Editor, *Education,* London, *Education* (in part)

Raul d'Eça, Retired from foreign service with U.S. Information Service, *Brazil*

Philippe Decraene, Member of editorial staff, *Le Monde,* Paris, *Tunisia*

Marta Bekerman de Fainboim, Economist, Lloyds Bank International Ltd., London, *Paraguay*

Kenneth de la Barre, Staff Scientist, Arctic Institute of North America, Montreal, *Arctic and Antarctic* (in part)

Robin Denselow, Rock Music Critic, *The Guardian, Music* (in part)

Elfriede Dirnbacher, Austrian Civil Servant, *Austria*

Chris Drake, Managing Editor, *The Cyprus Weekly,* Nicosia, Cyprus, *Cyprus*

Jan R. Engels, Editor, *Vooruitgang,* (Quarterly of the Belgian Party for Freedom and Progress), Brussels, *Belgium*

Basco Eszeki, Managing Editor, *Chicago Faces, Biographies* (in part)

W. D. Ewart, Editor and Director, *Fairplay International Shipping Weekly,* London, *Shipping*

D. M. L. Farr, Professor of History, Carleton University, Ottawa, *Canada*

Robert J. Fendell, Auto Editor, *Science & Mechanics,* Auto Contributor, *Gentlemen's Quarterly* magazine, *Auto Racing* (in part)

Donald Fields, Helsinki Correspondent, BBC, *The Guardian,* and *The Sunday Times,* London, *Finland*

David Fisher, Civil Engineer, Freeman Fox & Partners, London, formerly Executive Editor, *Engineering,* London, *Engineering Projects* (in part)

Marilyn Francis, Editor, *YWCA Interchange, Youth Organizations* (in part)

Peter W. Gaddum, Chairman, H. T. Gaddum and Company Ltd., Silk Merchants, Macclesfield, Cheshire, England, Honorary President, International Silk Association, Lyons, *Textiles* (in part)

Mary Jo Gallo, Girls Clubs of America, Inc., *Youth Organizations* (in part)

T. J. S. George, Editor, *Asiaweek,* Hong Kong, *Biographies* (in part); *Cambodia; Korea; Laos; Southeast Asian Affairs; Thailand; Vietnam*

Hugh M. Gillespie, Director of Communications, International Road Federation, Washington, D.C., *Engineering Projects* (in part)

Fay Gjester, Oslo Correspondent, *The Financial Times,* London, *Norway*

Arthur Goldsmith, Editorial Director, *Popular Photography* and *Camera Arts,* New York City, *Photography*

Harry Golombek, British Chess Champion, 1947, 1949, and 1955, Chess Correspondent, *The Times,* London, *Chess*

R. M. Goodwin, Free-lance Writer, London, *Biographies* (in part)

Martin Gottfried, Drama Critic, *Saturday Review,* New York City, *Theatre* (in part)

Donald W. Gould, Medical Writer and Broadcaster, *Medicine* (in part); *Mental Health*

A. R. G. Griffiths, Senior Lecturer in History, Flinders University of South Australia, *Australia*

Joel W. Grossman, Director, Archaeological Survey Office, Rutgers University, New Brunswick, N.J., *Archaeology* (in part)

David A. Harries, Director, Tarmac International Ltd., London, *Engineering Projects* (in part)

H. B. Hawley, Specialist, Human Nutrition and Food Science, Switzerland, *Food*

Myrl C. Hendershott, Professor of Oceanography, Scripps Institution of Oceanography, La Jolla, Calif., *Oceanography*

Robin Cathy Herman, Sports Reporter, *New York Times, Ice Hockey*

G. Fitzgerald Higgins, Editor, High School Language Arts Dept., Scott Foresman & Co., *Biographies* (in part); *Safety*

June Hill, Home Furnishings Editor, *Chicago Tribune, In-*

terior Design

Harvey J. Hindin, Communications Editor, *Electronics* magazine, New York City, *Communications*

Louis Hotz, Former Editorial Writer, Johannesburg (S.Af.) *Star, South Africa*

John Howkins, Editor, *InterMedia,* International Institute of Communications, London, *Television and Radio* (in part)

Kyle D. Husfloen, Editor, *The Antique Trader Weekly,* United States SPECIAL REPORT: *Emptying the Attic*

Kenneth Ingham, Professor of History, University of Bristol, England, *Angola; Kenya; Mozambique; Tanzania; Uganda; Zaire; Zambia; Zimbabwe*

Adrian Jardine, Company Director and Public Relations Consultant, Member, Guild of Yachting Writers, *Boating* (in part)

Peter Jenkins, Policy Editor and Political Columnist, *The Guardian,* London, *Great Britain*

David A. Jessop, Editor, *Caribbean Chronicle* and *Insight,* Consultant on Caribbean Affairs, *Biographies* (in part); *Caribbean States* (in part)

George Joffé, Journalist and Writer on North African Affairs, *Algeria; Morocco*

D. A. N. Jones, Assistant Editor, *The Listener,* London, *Literature* (in part)

Lou Joseph, Manager of Media Relations, Bureau of Communications, American Dental Association, *Dentistry*

William A. Katz, Professor, School of Library Science, State University of New York, Albany, *Magazines*

John A. Kelleher, Editorial Consultant, *The Dominion,* Wellington, N.Z., *New Zealand*

Jerold L. Kellman, Editor in Chief, Publications International Ltd., *Computers*

Richard M. Kennedy, Agricultural Economist, International Economics Division, Economics, Statistics, and Cooperatives Service, U.S. Department of Agriculture, *Agriculture*

John V. Killheffer, Associate Editor, Encyclopædia Britannica, Chicago, *Nobel Prizes* (in part)

Jon Kimche, Editor, *Afro-Asian Affairs,* London, *Israel*

Joshua B. Kind, Associate Professor of Art History, Northern Illinois University, DeKalb, *Museums* (in part)

Hugh J. Klare, Chairman, Gloucestershire Probation Training Committee, England, Secretary, Howard League for Penal Reform 1950–71, *Prisons*

Jean Knecht, Former Assistant Foreign Editor, *Le Monde,* Paris, former Permanent Correspondent in Washington and Vice-President of the Association de la Presse Diplomatique Française, *France*

Philip Kopper, Free-lance Writer, Washington, D.C., *Biographies* (in part); *Nobel Prizes* (in part)

Gene H. Koretz, Associate Economics Editor, *Business Week,* New York City, *Financial Institutions; Labour and Employment* (in part)

Julie A. Kunkler, Picture Editor, Encyclopædia Britannica, *Yearbook of Science and the Future, Biographies* (in part)

Kevin M. Lamb, Sportswriter, *Chicago Sun-Times, Biographies* (in part); *Football* (in part)

Timothy J. Larkin, Director, TL Communications, *Drugs*

Roy Larson, Religion Editor, *Chicago Sun-Times, Religion*

Colin Legum, Associate Editor, *The Observer,* Editor, *Middle East Contemporary Survey* and *Africa Contemporary Record,* London, *African Affairs; Biographies* (in part)

Michael Leifer, Reader in International Relations, London School of Economics and Political Science, *Malaysia*

Peter Lennox-Kerr, Editor, *High Performance Textiles,* European Editor, *Textile World,* Publisher of *OE-Report,* New Mills, England, *Textiles* (in part)

Diane S. Liebman, Manager, Special Services, Office of In-

formation and Public Affairs, Association of American Railroads, Washington, D.C., *Transportation* (in part)
Robert G. Logan, Sportswriter, *Chicago Tribune, Basketball* (in part)
John H. Love, Executive Director, American Power Boat Association, *Boating* (in part)
Anders S. Lunde, Consultant, Adjunct Professor, Department of Biostatistics, University of North Carolina, *Population*
Martin McCauley, Lecturer in Russian and Soviet Institutions, School of Slavonic and East European Studies, University of London, *Union of Soviet Socialist Republics*
Keith S. McLachlan, Senior Lecturer, School of Oriental and African Studies, University of London, *Iran*
H. M. F. Mallett, Editor, *Wool Record Weekly Market Report,* Bradford, England, *Textiles* (in part)
Andrew Mango, Orientalist and Broadcaster, *Turkey*
J. G. Scott Marshall, Horticultural Consultant, *Flowers and Gardens* (in part)
Martin E. Marty, Fairfax M. Cone Distinguished Service Professor, University of Chicago, Associate Editor, *The Christian Century, Religion SPECIAL REPORT: The New Christian Right*
James L. Mateja, Auto Editor and Financial Reporter, *Chicago Tribune, Automobiles*
Björn Matthíasson, Economist, European Free Trade Association, Geneva, *Iceland*
David M. Mazie, Associate of Carl T. Rowan, Syndicated Columnist, Free-lance Writer, *Social Services*
Edward Mark Mazze, Dean and Professor of Marketing, School of Business Administration, Temple University, Philadelphia, Pa., *Advertising; Consumer Affairs* (in part)
Christine Mellor, Economist, Lloyds Bank International Ltd., London, *Argentina; Chile; Colombia; Costa Rica; El Salvador; Guatemala; Honduras; Nicaragua*
Paul Mendelson, Assistant Copy Editor, Encyclopædia Britannica, *Biographies* (in part)
Sandra Millikin, Architectural Historian, *Architecture; Art and Art Exhibitions; Biographies* (in part); *Museums* (in part)
Denise Mitchell, Girl Scouts of the U.S.A., New York City, *Youth Organizations* (in part)
K. K. Mitchell, Lecturer, Department of Physical Education, University of Leeds, England, *Basketball* (in part)
Mario Modiano, Athens Correspondent, *The Times,* London, *Greece*
Shirley Montague, Public Relations Director, Camp Fire, Inc., Kansas City, Mo., *Youth Organizations* (in part)
John E. Moore, Hydrologist, Water Resources Division, U.S. Geological Survey, *Earth Sciences* (in part)
Donald Morrison, Senior Editor, *Time* magazine, *Newspapers*
Molly Mortimer, Commonwealth Correspondent, *The Spectator,* London, *Nigeria*
Chris Mosey, Associate Editor, *Sweden Now, Sweden*
Mozelle A. Moshansky, Music Journalist, Writer, *The Guardian, International Music Guide, Classical Music,* and BBC Radio, *Biographies* (in part); *Music* (in part)
Bert Nelson, Editor, *Track and Field News, Track and Field*
Bruce C. Netschert, Vice-President, National Economic Research Associates, Washington, D.C., *Fuel and Energy*
H. S. Noel, Free-lance Journalist, former Managing Editor, *World Fishing,* London, *Fish and Fisheries*
Ronald R. Novales, Professor of Biological Sciences, Northwestern University, Evanston, Ill., *Biology* (in part)
K. Elliot Nowels, Director of Information, Future Farmers of America, Alexandria, Va., *Youth Organizations* (in part)

Michelle O'Leary, Executive Assistant, Big Brothers/Big Sisters of America, *Youth Organizations* (in part)
P. J. S. Olney, Curator of Birds, Zoological Society of London, *Zoos*
John Palmer, European Editor, *The Guardian,* London, *Biographies* (in part); *European Affairs*
S. B. Palmer, Senior Lecturer, Department of Applied Physics, University of Hull, England, *Physics*
Charles Robert Paul, Jr., Director of Communications, U.S. Olympic Committee, Colorado Springs, Colo., *Gymnastics*
Irving Pfeffer, Attorney, Chairman, Pacific & General Insurance Co., Ltd., *Stocks and Bonds*
Geoffrey M. Pinfold, Associate, NCL Consulting Engineers, London, *Engineering Projects* (in part)
Frederick S. Plotkin, Professor of English Literature and Chairman, Division of Humanities, Stern College, Yeshiva University, New York City, *Literature* (in part)
Arthur Plotnik, Editor, *American Libraries,* American Library Association, *Libraries* (in part)
Carl A. Posey, Public Affairs Officer, National Oceanic and Atmospheric Administration, Boulder, Colo., *Weather*
H. Y. Sharada Prasad, Information Adviser to the Prime Minister, New Delhi, India, *Biographies* (in part); *India*
Jane Bryant Quinn, Contributing Editor, *Newsweek,* Personal Finance Columnist, *Washington Post, Financial Institutions SPECIAL REPORT: The 1980 Credit Crunch* (in part)
Margaret H. Quinn, Reporter, *Sun-Gazette,* Williamsport, Pa., *Baseball* (in part)
Robin J. Ranger, Associate Professor, Department of Political Science, St. Francis Xavier University, Antigonish, Nova Scotia, *Defense and Arms Control*
Robert Reinhold, Reporter, *New York Times,* Washington, D.C., *Cities and Urban Affairs*
David Robinson, Film Critic, *The Times,* London, *Motion Pictures*
Yrjö Sarahete, General Secretary, Fédération Internationale des Quilleurs, Helsinki, *Bowling* (in part)
Albert Schoenfield, Co-publisher, *Swimming World* magazine, Vice-Chairman, U.S. Olympic Swimming Committee, *Swimming*
George Schöpflin, Lecturer in East European Political Institutions, London School of Economics and School of Slavonic and East European Studies, University of London, *Czechoslovakia*
Mitchell R. Sharpe, Science Writer, Historian, Alabama Space and Rocket Center, Huntsville, *Space Exploration*
Noel Simpson, Managing Director, Sydney Bloodstock Proprietary Ltd., Sydney, Australia, *Horse Racing* (in part)
Glenn B. Smedley, Public Relations Director, American Numismatic Association, *Stamps and Coins* (in part)
K. M. Smogorzewski, Writer on contemporary history, Founder and Editor, *Free Europe,* London, *Albania; Biographies* (in part); *Bulgaria; Hungary; Poland; Romania*
Arthur J. Snider, Medical Columnist, *Chicago Sun-Times, Medicine* (in part)
Melanie Staerk, Member, Swiss Press Association, former Member, Swiss National Commission for UNESCO, *Switzerland*
Tom Stevenson, Garden Columnist, *Washington Post,* Washington Post-Los Angeles Times News Service, *Flowers and Gardens* (in part)
Zena Sutherland, Editor, Children's Books, *Chicago Tribune,* Editor, *Bulletin of the Center for Children's Books,* and Associate Professor, The University of Chicago, *Literature for Children*
Thelma Sweetinburgh, Paris Fashion Correspondent for the British Wool Textile Industry, *Fashion* (in part)

Index

This index is arranged in alphabetical order. Words beginning with "Mc" are alphabetized as "Mac," and "St." is alphabetized as "Saint."

The figures shown in brackets [77, 78] indicate earlier editions of **The Compton Yearbook** in which the topic has appeared since 1977.

Entry headings in boldface type indicate articles in the text.

Cross-references refer to index entries in this volume.

b

f

g

o

p

Radar 311 [77–80]
Radiation 46, 222 [77–80]
Radio: *see* Television and radio
Radner, Gilda 263
Rafsanjani, Hashemi 181
Raft, George 270
Rahman, Ziaur 39 [80]
Railroads 349, *picture* 351 [77–80]
deregulation 83
disasters 109
stocks 320
United States 366
Raja'i, Mohammad Ali 181, 458
Rallis, Georgios 163
Rand (South African currency) 178 [80]
Rarick, John 283
Ras al-Khaimah 273
Rashchupkin, Viktor 346
Rather, Dan 458
Rationing, gasoline 82, 154 [80]
Raven, Simon 210
Read, Ken 302
Reagan, Ronald P. 263
Reagan, Ronald Wilson 361, 459 [77, 78, 80]
busing views 84
education 115
election 120, 296, 332
Middle Eastern affairs 226
political parties 281
social services policy 303
Southeast Asian policies 307
U.S.S.R. relations 357
U.S. defense policy 100
urban tensions 76
world trade policies 375
Real estate 88
Recession 55 [77–80]
credit controls 140
economic cooperation 404
European affairs 135, 159, 253
financial institutions 138
housing industry 167
international finance 180
Japan 189
labour and employment 196
transportation 348
United States 282, 365, 382, *picture* 133
world trade 374
Record industry 244 [80]
Red Brigades 187 [77, 79, 80]
Redford, Robert 235
Redgrave, Vanessa 331, picture 332 [79]
Red Sea 391
Reed, Stanley Forman 270
Refugees and migrants 289 [77–80]
Afghan exodus 6, 227, *picture* 5
African affairs 8, 132, 381, *picture* 133
boat people 156, 175
Cuban refugees 91, 95
danger signals from the Middle East 398
education 116
Haitians 68, 69
Iran-Iraq war 181, 194
Pakistan 260
Qatar 273
Southeast Asia 60, 337, *picture* 308
U.S.S.R. 356
United States 231, 366
West German immigration policy 155
Regan, Donald 361
Regoczy, Krisztina 172
Reindustrialization 56
Reinisch, Rica 325
Religion 290 [77–80]
Bahrain 273
Bangladesh dispute 39
discrimination 116
Egyptian unrest 119
Iranian Muslims 181
law 204
"New Christian Right, The" (special report) 296
Pope's visits 150, 156
prayer legislation 84
Romero's assassination 92
Switzerland 326
U.S. 121, 323
Renaldo, Duncan 270

Renault 37 [80]
Representatives, House of: *see* Congress, U.S.
Republican Party, U.S. 281, 365 [77–80]
defense policy 100
elections 80, 120
governorships 315
Rescue mission, U.S. hostages 363
Research Libraries Information Network 208
Reserpine 221
Resnais, Alain 236
Reutemann, Carlos 38
Reuters 418
Rhine, J(oseph) B(anks) 270
Rhinoceros 13 [80]
Rhode Island 316 [77–80]
governor, *list* 317
Rhodesia: *see* Zimbabwe
Rhoodie, Eschel Mostert 307 [80]
Ribonucleic acid: *see* RNA
Rice: *see* Grains
Richard Meier & Associates 21, *picture* 22
Richler, Mordecai 213
Richmond, Va. 239 [78]
Richmond Newspapers *v.* Virginia 248
Righter, Rosemary
"Media and the Third World: A Fair Shake?" (feature article) 417
Right to Life Party 284 [79]
Riha, Bohumil 217
Riots [77–80]
Afghanistan 4
Algerian Berbers 11
danger signals in the Middle East 398
Dominican Republic 110
India 174
insurance claims 176
Korea 193
law 204
Netherlands 245
United States 76, 95, 231, 288, *picture* 77
Zaire 381
Ritter, John 262 [78]
Ritter, Louise 347 [79]
Rive, Louis 305
RNA (ribonucleic acid) 70
Roads and highways 126, 350 [77–80]
Robinson, Larry 170 [78]
Robison, James 292, 296
Robots 428, *picture* 431 [78]
Rodnina, Irina 172, 256 [77–79]
Rodney, Walter 68
Rodriguez, Andrés 261
Rogers, Bernard 163
Rogers, George 148
Rogers, Kenny 245, 460
Roldós Aguilera, Jaime 114 [79, 80]
Roller skates 344 [80]
Roman Catholicism 246, 281, 291 [77–80]
Romania 297 [77–80]
Bulgarian relations 55
gymnastics 165
Zaire 381
Romanishin, Oleg 72
Rome, Italy 18, 126 [80]
tennis tournament 334
tourism 343
Romero y Goldames, Oscar Arnulfo 123, 270, 416
Roosevelt, Franklin D. 413
Rosa, Lita de la 50, *picture* 51 [80]
Rosenberg, Stuart 234
Roses (plants) 144 [80]
Rossley, Karin 347
Rossner, Judith 211, *picture* 210 [78]
Rosso, Franco 236
Roth, Lillian 270
Roth, Mark 51 [78, 80]
Roth, William 282
Roukema, Marge 120
Royal Academy (London) 29
Royal Albert Hall, London 336
Royal Canadian Mounted Police 94 [78]
Royal Court (theatre, London) 341
Royal Danish Ballet 99
Royal Shakespeare Company (RSC) 340 [78]
Royo, Aristides 261 [79, 80]
Rudman, Warren 121
Rukavishnikova, Olga 347

Rukeyser, Muriel 270
Runcie, Robert 293, *picture* 291 [80]
Russell, Willy 341
Rutherford, Johnny 38 [77]
Ruttman, Joe 39
Ruzic, Neil P.
"American Ingenuity—Does It Still Thrive?" (feature article) 424
Ruzici, Virginia 335 [79]
Ryumin, Valery V. 309, *picture* 310 [79, 80]

S

Sabotage 13
Sá Carneiro, Francisco 270, 286 [80]
Saccharin 221 [78–80]
Sachs, Marilyn 216
Sadat, Anwar El- 118, 184 [77–80]
"Global Views of President Sadat, The" (feature article) 386
Sadat, Jihan El-, *picture* 104
Safety 297 [77–80]
American ingenuity 429
automobiles 298
consumerism 90
Ford Pinto lawsuit 89, 93
Swiss seat belt law 326
traffic accidents 109
Safire, William 213 [78, 79]
Sagan, Carl 332
Saharan Arab Democratic Republic 6 [78, 79]
Sail-freighter 424
Sailing: *see* Boating
St. Helens, Mt. 112, 366, 373
disasters 108
insurance claims 176
St. Joe Lead Co. 230
Saint-Laurent, Yves, *picture* 137 [77, 80]
St. Louis, Mo. 76, 384 [77, 79, 80]
Saint Lucia 69 [80]
Saint Vincent and the Grenadines 69 [80]
United Nations 361
Saito, Kunikichi 189
Sakharov, Andrey 356, *picture* 358 [77, 78, 80]
Sakurauchi, Yoshio 189
Salaries: *see* Wages and salaries
Salazar, Alberto, *picture* 347
"Salem" (ship) 93
Sallay, Andras 172
Salnikov, Vladimir 460 [80]
swimming 259, 324, *picture* 326
SALT (Strategic Arms Limitation Treaty) [77–80]
opposition from Christian right 292
U.S.S.R. policy 357
U.S. 100, 283, 366
Salt Lake City, Utah 92 [77]
Salto Grande, Uruguay 369
Saltwater ponds 426
Salvemini, Matteo 53
Salyut (spacecraft) 309 [77–80]
Sampson, Ralph 43
Samuelsson, Bengt I. 70
San'a': *see* Yemen Arab Republic
Sánchez, Salvador 53
Sanders, "Colonel" Harland 270
San Diego, Calif. 146, 147, 384 [80]
Sandinista National Liberation Front 249, *picture* 415 [80]
San Francisco, Cal. 99, 351 [77–80]
symphony hall, *picture* 243
Sa-ngad Chaloryu 337
Sanger, Frederick 70, 218, 252, *picture* 71
Santa Cruz Islands 111
Sante Fe, N.M. 287, 288 [77]
Santos, José Eduard dos 12
Sargent, Sarah 215
Sarkis, Elias 207 [77–80]
Sartre, Jean-Paul 271
Saskatchewan, prov., Can. 66 [77, 79]
SAT: *see* Scholastic Aptitude Test
Satellites, natural 311 [80]
Satellites and space probes 311, 372 [77–80]
American ingenuity 428

u

To extend the tradition of excellence of your Compton educational program, you may also avail yourself of other aids for your home reference center that have been created for "the Britannica family."

Described on the next page is a companion product–the Britannica 3 bookcase–that is designed to help you and your family. It will add attractiveness and value to your home library, as it keeps it well organized.

Should you wish to order it, or to obtain further information, please write to us at

Compton Home Library Service
Attn: Year Book Department
P. O. Box 4928
Chicago, Illinois 60680

Britannica 3
custom-designed
BOOKCASE

- requires less than 1 x 3-ft. floor space

- laminated pecan finish resists burns, stains, scratches

- Early American styling enriches any setting

- case size: 35$\frac{3}{4}$″ wide, 9$\frac{3}{4}$″ deep, 27$\frac{5}{8}$″ high